Beginning HTML5 and CSS3

Richard Clark, Oli Studholme,
Christopher Murphy and Divya Manian

Beginning HTML5 and CSS 3

ISBN 978-1-4302-2874-5

ISBN 978-1-4302-2875-2 (eBook)

Distributed to the book trade worldwide by Springer Science+Business Media New York, 233 Spring Street, 6th Floor, New York, NY 10013. Phone 1-800-SPRINGER, fax (201) 348-4505, e-mail orders-ny@springer-sbm.com, or visit www.springeronline.com.

For information on translations, please e-mail rights@apress.com or visit www.apress.com.

Apress and friends of ED books may be purchased in bulk for academic, corporate, or promotional use. eBook versions and licenses are also available for most titles. For more information, reference our Special Bulk Sales–eBook Licensing web page at www.apress.com/bulk-sales.

Any source code or other supplementary materials referenced by the author in this text is available to readers at www.apress.com. For detailed information about how to locate your book's source code, go to www.apress.com/source-code/.

Credits

President and Publisher:
Paul Manning

Copy Editor:
Mary Behr

Lead Editor:
Ben Renow-Clarke

Compositor:
Bytheway Publishing Services

Technical Reviewers:
Andrew Zack and Chris Mills

Indexer:
SPi Global

Editorial Board:
Steve Anglin, Mark Beckner, Ewan Buckingham, Gary Cornell, Morgan Ertel, Jonathan Gennick, Jonathan Hassell, Robert Hutchinson, Michelle Lowman, James Markham, Matthew Moodie, Jeff Olson, Jeffrey Pepper, Douglas Pundick, Ben Renow-Clarke, Dominic Shakeshaft, Gwenan Spearing, Matt Wade, Tom Welsh

Artist:
SPi Global

Cover Designer:
Anna Ishchenko

Coordinating Editor:
Christine Ricketts and Jennifer Blackwell

For K & J.

—Richard

For C, R & C

—C

Contents at a Glance

Contents

Forewords

HTML5. It's the most significant web spec today, and the first upgrade of the Web's ubiquitous language in a decade. Together with its cousin CSS 3, it's very powerful,very exciting and ludicrously over-hyped. Some "experts" will tell you that you can only use HTML5/ CSS 3 in the bleeding-edge nightly build of their favourite browser. Other pundits will tell you that you can't use them because "the specs aren't finished", or there is no support in Internet Explorer, or other such blahblahblah.

When you're trying to learn you need trustworthy teachers who are neither pedantic zealots or flatulent marketeers. You need people like Rich, Oli, Chris and Divya.

Richard Clark is a fellow HTML5 Doctor, curator of HTML5 gallery and, crucially, is a man who builds things. Oli Studholme is also a fellow HTML5 Doctor and developer working in the trenches, only these trenches are in his adopted homeland of Japan. Chris is Subject Director of Interactive Multimedia Design, at the University of ulster - one of the few universities in the world that teaches modern web design that employers actually need graduates to know. Divya is one of the team behind HTML5 Boilerplate and an Adobe representative on the CSS Working Group.

Bruce Lawson
Co-author *Introducing HTML5* (New Riders), Open Web Evangelist, Opera Software

It's hard to believe it, but there was a time when CSS was considered a dying technology. Riven by incomplete and (worse) incompatible implementations, mired by a legacy not of its own making, it seemed destined to join the towering scrap-heap of interesting-yet-failed technologies-and now, thanks to some lucky breaks and hard work, here it is, a fundamental aspect of the web. Indeed, it has spread far beyond the web, showing up as the display mechanism in software as diverse chat clients and operating systems. If it is less critical to our modern networks than HTML, it cannot be by much.

Even more exciting, after a relatively quiet period, CSS is being rapidly expanded and enriched on multiple fronts. Ideas from frameworks and libraries are being merged into the official specifications. Long-standing proposals are gaining monentum. Ancient omissions are being addressed. All in all, there's so much happening that it could be an expert's full-time job keeping track of it all.

Fortunately, what you have here in your hands is the product of several experts' combined knowledge, skills, and insight. Chris, Divya, Oli, and Rich are all veterans at navigating the sometimes dense language of W3C specifications to extract the shining jewels found within. Furthermore, they excel at taking those rough diamonds and polishing them to brilliant examples of how and why a feature should be used. If I were starting out, I could hardly wish for better guides to understanding what's important and interesting in CSS today-and as the old, grizzled codger I actully am, I look to them forclues regarding where I should or shouldn't be looking, in order to stay abreast of everything that's happening.

CSS is experiencing nothing short of a Renaissance. Enjoy learning from these four masters of its art.

Eric A. Meyer
Author, 'CSS: The Definitive Guide' (O'Reilly); Co-founder, An Event Apart

About the Authors

Richard Clark is Head of Interactive at KMP Digitata, a digital agency based in Manchester, UK. With over 10 years industry experience he oversees the user experience, design and front-end work at KMP and is a regular contributor to industry leading publication, .net magazine. He's the founder and curator of HTML5 Gallery (www.html5gallery.com), co-founder, editor and author for HTML5 Doctor (www.html5doctor.com). You'll also occasionally find him organising Speak the Web a series of gig like web conferences.

Christopher Murphy (www.christophermurphy.org) is a writer, designer and educator based in Belfast. Creative Review described him as, "a William Morris for the digital age," an epithet that he aspires to fulfill daily.

Informing his role as an educator, Murphy is a practicing designer whose work spans a variety of media. His work has featured in numerous magazines and books including Eye Magazine, widely acknowledged as one of the world's leading design journals, and Influences: A Lexicon of Contemporary Graphic Design Practice.

A writer on the 8 Faces team, he has also written for The Manual, 24 Ways, and .net magazine. As an internationally respected speaker he is invited to speak regularly on web standards and the importance of improving design education, and has spoken at conferences worldwide, including: Build, New Adventures and The Future of Web Design.

Oli Studholme is a New Zealander living in the bright lights of Tokyo, Japan. His love of the web bega in with his first website in 1995, and sharing this love has involved helping organize Web Directions East and becoming an HTML5 Doctor. He's currently a developer for internationally renowned design agency Information Architects, Inc.

Divya Manian A Computer Engineer by training, Divya made the the jump from developing device drivers for Motorola phones to designing websites and has not looked back since. Divya Manian is part of the Adobe Web Platform Team in San Francisco and a member of the CSS Working Group. She takes her duties as an Open Web vigilante seriously which has resulted in collaborative projects such as HTML5 Please and HTML5 Boilerplate.

About the Technical Reviewers

Chris Mills is a web technologist, open standards evangelist, and education agitator working at Opera Software. He writes about open standards for dev.opera.com, .net magazine, A List Apart, and more, and speaks at universities and industry conferences worldwide. Chris is the creator of the Opera Web Standards Curriculum and co-chair of the W3C Web Education Community Group. Outside work he is a heavy metal drummer, beer lover, and proud father of three.

Andrew Zack is the CEO of ZTMC, Inc. (ztmc.com) specializing in Search Engine Optimization (SEO and Internet marketing strategies. His project background includes almost twenty years of site development and project management experience and over fifteen years as a SEO and Internet Marketing expert.

Mr. Zack has also been very active in the publishing industry having co-authored Flash 5 studio and served as a technical reviewer on over ten books and industry publications.

Having started working on the Internet close to its inception Mr. Zack has continually focuses on the cutting edge and beyond focusing on new platforms and technology to continually stay in the forefront of the industry.

Finally, for HTML examples that contain repeating data, rather than writing out every line, the ellipsis character (. . .) is used to denote code continuation:

```
<ul>
  <li>Red</li>
  <li>Yellow</li>
  <li>Pink</li>
  <li>Green</li>
    ...
</ul>
```

With the formalities out of the way, let's get started.

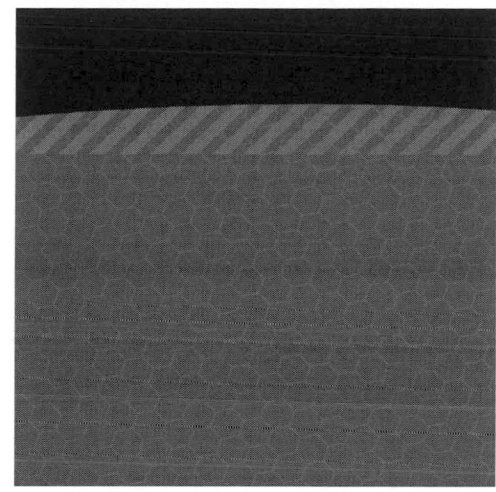

Chapter 1

HTML5: Now, Not 2022

Congratulations, you've reached Chapter 1! Your journey through the evolution of the Web is about to begin. This chapter establishes the basic principles. Its focus, along with the rest of the first half of this book, is mostly HTML5. We'll cover how HTML5 came about, what problems it aims to solve, what design principles have guided Its development, and what new features it brings to the table. We'll also debunk some HTML5 myths. We'll start off, however, by looking at the basic tenets we follow in our web development work, why standards are so important, and why we should strive to make our markup universally accessible and well crafted.

It's a roller coaster ride of ups and downs, but it's an exciting journey. Without further ado, let's get started…

Basic tenets

The information in this book is built on a number of strongly held principles: the importance of open web standards, the craft of well-structured semantic markup, and a firm belief that well-written HTML is a part of the design process. Our solid HTML structure should be styled with CSS (an approach we'll cover when we look at separation of layers later in this chapter).

A web standards approach

The movement towards a standards-driven Web has been thanks in no small part to the Web Standards Project, or WaSP (http://j.mp/webstandardsproject[1]). In the late '90s, Internet Explorer and Netscape were fighting to gain supremacy of the Web in a period known as "the browser wars." This was a horrible time, as these rivals were trying to win users over by introducing countless new features that were incompatible across browsers. The result was sites that either only worked in one browser or had two different versions to support both the major players. This was a nightmare for web developers, and it hurt the users.

Founded in 1998, WaSP campaigned for standard implementations across the different browsers and a standards-based approach to web design. The aims were to reduce the cost and complexity of web development and to increase the accessibility of web pages by making web content more consistent and more compatible across devices and assistive technologies. They lobbied browser and tool vendors to improve support for web standards recommended by the World Wide Web Consortium (W3C), such as HTML and CSS.

> Note: The World Wide Web Consortium, or W3C, is an international community that develops standards to ensure the long-term growth of the Web. In its own words, "the W3C mission is to lead the World Wide Web to its full potential by developing protocols and guidelines that ensure the long-term growth of the Web."

And they had a lot of success. Skip forward to the modern day, and web standards are consistently implemented across all major browsers. Although you do still get the occasional weird bit of browser behavior, it is miles better than it was. Let's now take a brief look at what web standards actually are.

What are web standards?

We use standards on a daily basis, often without realizing it. When we buy a light bulb, for example, we know that if we buy a screw-in or bayonet bulb, it will fit our light fittings when we get it home. Standards ensure that the bulb we buy isn't just a little too large or just a little too wide to fit our light fixture. Standards are all around us: look at the plugs in your home, the power rating of your appliances, and the time, distance, and temperature measurements used by everything in our society.

Web standards pick up from the same principle. As browser manufacturers and web developers have moved toward embracing standards, the need to write browser-specific markup has diminished. By using well-structured HTML to mark up content and CSS to control presentation, we should now be able to design one web site that will display consistently across standards-compliant browsers regardless of operating system (although the occasional quirk still exists). Equally importantly, when the same markup is rendered by less-capable, non-standards-compliant browsers—in older text-based or mobile browsers— the content should still remain accessible. Web standards save us time as designers and allow us to sleep

---

[1] www.webstandards.org

at night, safe in the knowledge that our carefully crafted masterpiece is accessible regardless of who's viewing it on which browser and which platform.

> Note: What we call standards are officially termed "Recommendations" by the W3C. They are the recommended way that web technologies should work. There is nothing in law forcing browsers and tool vendors to adopt them; rather, adoption is agreed upon for the good of the Web and the mutual benefit of everyone.

Why use web standards?

Perhaps a better question to ask is, "Why ignore web standards?" The benefits of adopting a web standards approach are so compelling, why wouldn't you use them?

The benefits of using web standards include the following:

- *Cuts down on development time*: You can build a single site that will work across all platforms, browsers, devices, etc. Without standards, you'd probably have to develop a different site for each browser, etc.

- *Creates sites that are easy to update and maintain*: With web standards and best practices, you can, for example, update a single CSS file to change styling for a whole site of many HTML pages. Before this was the norm, we used to put the styling information inside the HTML, which meant changing the information on every page. This was really repetitious and inconvenient.

- *Improves search engine rankings*: The content inside HTML is text-based and therefore readable by search engines. In addition, writing good copy and using semantic HTML (like headings) appropriately can give more weight to appropriate keywords and send your pages shooting up the Google charts.

- *Improves accessibility*: Well-written HTML and CSS makes web sites more accessible to diverse user groups such as people with disabilities, people using mobile devices, people on low bandwidth connections, etc.

Now that we've got a clear insight into the main benefits of a web standards approach, let's take a look at two principles we'll be looking at in depth in this book: the importance of semantic markup and the infamous web trifle.

Semantic markup

We believe in the importance of semantic markup (sometimes called POSH for Plain Old Semantic HTML). We believe that HTML is a *design element* and that, before adding a presentational layer (which enhances the underlying markup), it's important to focus on building a solid foundation of well-structured content.

Semantic markup is self-describing and uses the correct HTML elements for the correct job. For example, you could mark up a heading like this:

```
<div id="heading" style="font-size:300%; padding: 10px;">My heading</div>
```

It would look like a heading, sure, but it would not function as a heading in terms of meaning or purpose. Therefore, it would have a negative effect on search engine optimization (keywords in headings have more weight), accessibility (screen readers use heading elements as navigational signposts), development (it is a lot trickier to target elements with styles and scripts when you don't use proper semantic elements), and more.

It's much better to use the proper element, like so:

```
<h1>My heading</h1>
```

Semantic markup should also be as lightweight as possible, which means removing all those nested `<divs>` and other spaghetti code. This makes file sizes smaller and coding easier.

Now that we understand the importance of crafting a solid HTML foundation, it's time to meet the Web trifle.

The web trifle: separating those layers

Everyone loves a trifle, especially at Christmas.

Andy Clarke, writing in Stuff &Nonsense (`http://j.mp/stuffandnonsense`[2]) in 2005, took the metaphor of the humble trifle to new heights when he used it to describe the "Web Standards Trifle," a heady mixture of sponge, fruity jelly, custard, cream, and the all-important topping. You can read his original post at `http://j.mp/standardstrifle`[3]. Most of it still hold true today.

The essence of what he is saying is that you should separate your data structure, styling information, and scripting/behavior into separate layers.

- Semantic HTML provides the data structure, a clean, easy-to-access set of content. HTML5 provides this nicely. You should make this data as accessible and usable as possible, without any styling of scripting enhancements.

- CSS provides the styling information, which takes our data and gives it the visual presentation we desire. CSS3 provides more powerful tools than its predecessor, CSS2.

- JavaScript (including the base language and scripting APIs defined inside HTML5 and elsewhere) provides the scripting/behavior layer, which adds usability enhancements and richer functionality to our sites.

The Dao of web design: embracing uncertainty

The browser landscape is rapidly evolving. However, unlike the Wild West days of the browser wars, today's landscape is evolving and converging towards standards. Firefox, Safari, Opera, Chrome and, of course, our old friend IE are all—admittedly at different rates—moving forward towards supporting all the

---

[2] `www.stuffandnonsense.co.uk/blog`
[3] `www.stuffandnonsense.co.uk/archives/web_standards_trifle.html`

new standard features inside HTML5, CSS3, etc. Many web developers are also moving towards web standards and their associated best practices, although many are being left behind.

But we've now got a new type of uncertainty to worry about: we no longer just have desktop browsers to support. There's a rapid growth of people accessing the Web on the go via mobile devices, tablets, TVs, games consoles, and more. The explosion of devices like Apple's iPhone and iPad, Google Android devices, Blackberrys, the Wii, DS, and Philips and Sony web-enabled TVs has given way to a significant rise in the number of people accessing the Web while on the move, in the living room, and away from their desks.

Opera, creators of Opera Mini (one of the world's most popular mobile browsing platforms), reports significant growth year-on-year (and month-on-month) in users browsing the Web while on the go. This looks set to grow exponentially with the inexorable rise of smartphones.

With so many different devices upon which to consume web content, it is becoming harder and harder to predict exactly what your site will look like across all your user's devices. Rather than obsessing about having pixel-perfect control, we need to embrace the uncertainly and design flexible sites that adapt to different browsing contexts.

This is by no means a new idea. John Allsopp's "The Dao of Web Design," published on A List Apart way back in 2000, stressed the importance of web designers learning to let go, learning to live with the complexity—and uncontrollability—of the Web, and embracing the lack of control that is an inherent part of the complex world of web delivery we design for. Underlining the variables that come into play when designing for the Web (screen size, resolution differences, monitor depth, installed fonts, etc.), Allsopp encouraged web designers at the turn of the millennium to embrace the inherent unpredictability of web design and to design for a Web that lacked the precise control of print media.

Encouraging web designers to look through "the other end of the microscope," he reframed the "control" of print design as a "limitation," stating "the fact we can control a paper page is really a limitation of that medium." Read that again; it's a subtle but important point.

Fast forward to today and this view isn't quite so unusual. The fluidity of the Web is celebrated by many more people these days. You will still meet many designers and clients who obsess about print-design pixel perfection on the Web, but it is easier to convince them that the fluid way is right, especially now that browsing devices are more varied than ever before.

Dan Cederholm's 2007 site, Do Web Sites Need to Look the Same In Every Browser (Figure 1-1), answers the question clearly with a resolute "No!"

Figure 1-1. Do web sites need to look the same in every browser? No!

As Allsopp puts it, web designers aren't controllers and the Web is not print. This is a fundamental shift. For designers used to the fixed frame of reference that is typical of the world of print, this can take a great deal of getting used to. Allsopp reiterates, "as designers we need to rethink this role, to abandon control, and seek a new relationship with the page."

Rethink the lack of control; stop seeing it as a weakness, and see it as a strength. This is the key point of Allsopp's piece. As he puts it, "make pages which are adaptable." Why? Because adaptable is accessible. As Allsopp puts it, think about "designing the universal page."

This next quote reinforces what we said earlier about semantic HTML: "Where HTML provides an appropriate element, use it. Where it doesn't, use classes." Simple. HTML is, despite the tendency of many lazy designers to over-rely on needless class attributes, a rich and comprehensive semantic language, so we should use it to our full advantage.

And, as we'll see when we look at HTML5 in upcoming chapters, there are richer semantic elements at our disposal and thus need to rely even less on classes in the future. If anything, our task looks to get easier. Good times!

Accessibility

Accessibility, sometimes shortened to a11y (a numeronym, or number-based word: "a, then 11 letters, then y"), should be a fundamental of our approach. Embracing the Dao of web design brings with it a number of benefits including wider accessibility to a broader, more diverse audience.

Key to this is considering how different users use the Web. Some people use it just like you do. Some people use different devices or have slower web connections. Some people only use the keyboard. Some people user screen readers to read web pages out to them. Some people can't hear audio content. Whatever you do, familiarize yourself with a diverse population of web users. Don't just assume everyone else uses the Web exactly like you.

We think that accessibility is AGoodThing™ so don't be surprised to see us highlighting some of the benefits (and potential pitfalls) that HTML5 brings to the accessibility party.

Crafting your markup

We're firm believers in the emphasis on craft in web design and web development. Paying attention to details is important, as is taking pride in one's work, even when writing markup.

In his excellent book *The Craftsman*, Richard Sennett writes about the craftsmen involved in the creation of Linux, stressing their focus "on achieving quality [and] on doing good work." Closer to the world of web design, Dan Cederholm in *Handcrafted CSS* states

> The details are not always obvious. With a well-made piece of furniture, you might not notice how well made it is until you start using it. Pull out the drawer and notice the dovetail joints, for instance.
>
> All of this can be related to web design. Seemingly non obvious details can often separate good web design from great web design. You might not appreciate the quality of a well-designed web site until you start using it, looking under the hood, putting it through tests.

We completely agree with Mr Cederholm. The difference between good web content and great web content is craft, taking the extra time to dot the i's and cross the t's—paying attention to the details.

As the world of web design evolves, we increasingly find ourselves collaborating with others and working within teams. A solid, well crafted approach to markup—based on agreed rules and standards—can considerably enhance collaboration, streamlining the process and (we'd even go so far as to say) making it more enjoyable.

We feel craft is important, and we're sure you do, too.

How was HTML5 created?

You may ask yourself, well, how did I get here?

-- Talking Heads, "Once in a Lifetime"

HTML5 is just one point in a long line in the development of HTML that has seen a variety of flavors with different specifications. Though they might have differed in their details, every flavour of HTML had one fundamental aspect in common: HTML is a markup language.

Yes, HTML 4.01 and XHTML 1.0 might differ in coding style, but they share this common goal. With the differing, and often strongly voiced opinions from the two—at times opposing—camps that support them, it's often been easy to lose sight of the common ground.

HTML5 in many ways represents the best of all worlds, with a great deal of new potential thrown in for good measure, as you'll see later. Before we introduce HTML5 and its different facets, let's do a very brief recap of how we found ourselves where we are now.

Beyond HTML 4...

HTML4 had nothing wrong with it, really. It was a perfectly good spec, and the technology was perfectly fine for doing the job it was originally intended for: marking up static documents with links in between them. But things never sit still. Web developers weren't happy to just carry on making static documents for the rest of their lives. They wanted to make dynamic web sites that behaved more like applications than pages and were starting to do that using technologies like PHP, JavaScript, and Flash.

Hence the need for evolution.

> *Note: Flash originally became popular because cross-browser web standards support was really bad in the late '90s and the Flash plug-in offered a way to make content behave consistently across browsers. Also, Flash allowed web developers to do things like animation and video on the Web. Web standards, at the time, had no facilities to support this.*

XHTML 1.0

It was actually all the way back in 1998, around the time when the HTML4 spec was nearing completion, when the decision was made by the W3C to move the Web towards XHTML and not HTML (see http://j.mp/futuremarkup[4]). They then drew a line under HTML4 (the last version was actually 4.01, which included some bug fixes and the like) and instead concentrated on the XHTML1.0 spec.

In August 2002, the W3C commented that

> *The XHTML family is the next step in the evolution of the Internet. By migrating to XHTML today, content developers can enter the XML world with all of its attendant benefits, while still remaining confident in their content's backward and future compatibility.*

With this rallying call, it was no surprise that when considering how best to evolve HTML, the W3C initially threw its weight behind XHTML (note the word "initially"). XHTML1.0 seemed like a sensible move. It was basically just HTML4 reformulated as an XML vocabulary, which brought with it the stricter syntax rules of XML (for example, attribute values must have quotes around them, elements need to be closed). The goal was better quality, more efficient markup.

XHTML 2.0 and the backlash

However, the next move the W3C made didn't go down so well. The next version of XHTML, XHTML 2.0 was created with a somewhat utopian approach. it contained some great ideas and was a well-written spec, but it simply didn't reflect what web developers were actually doing on the Web. It was more of what the W3C would like them to do ideally.

Also, it was not backward compatible with the content already on the Web. A lot of the features worked differently; for example, the XHTML mimetype (application/xhtml+xml) did not work at all on IE, and the developer tools available weren't ready for working with XML

The community was dismayed at this and a backlash occurred. Most notably, in 2004 a group of like-minded developers and implementers (including representatives from Opera, Mozilla, and slightly later, Apple) banded together to form a renegade spec group called the WHATWG (www.whatwg.org) that aimed to write a better markup spec with a more effective set of features for authoring the new breed of web applications and without—crucially—breaking backwards compatibility.

The WHATWG created the Web Applications 1.0 specification (http://j.mp/webappliactions1[5]), which documented existing interoperable browser behaviors and features as well as new features for the Open Web stack such as APIs and new DOM parsing rules. After many discussions between W3C Members, on March 7, 2007 the work on HTML was restarted with a new HTML Working Group in an open participation process. One of the first decisions of the HTML WG was to adopt the Web Applications 1.0 spec and call it HTML5.

The WHATWG and the W3C now develop the HTML5 spec in tandem with two different specs.

---

[4] www.w3.org/Markup/future/
[5] www.whatwg.org/specs/web-apps/2005-09-01/

- The WHATWG HTML spec (`http://j.mp/html5-current`[6]) is a place for contributors to rapidly create and work on innovative new features, way before they might make it into an official recommendation. Note that the version number has been dropped; this is a living standard that will continue to evolve as a single entity, free of versioning.

- The W3C HTML5 spec (`http://j.mp/w3c-html5`[7]) is where the most stable, agreed-upon features are documented. This version paints a truer picture of where we are in terms of what features are most complete and most likely to be supported in browsers.

Google's Ian Hickson was until recently the editor of both specs. He is somewhat of a "benevolent dictator" and not everyone agrees with the way he works. But he does an admirable job of dealing with all the feedback he receives about the specs and generally keeping things sane—no easy task indeed for documentation of such magnitude.

> *Note: The beauty of open standards is that anyone can have a say in their development, and provide feedback. If you want to get involved, pop along to the W3C HTML working group (`www.w3.org/html/wg`) and/or the WHATWG (`www.whatwg.org`) and join in the discussion on the mailing list, IRC channel, etc.*

HTML5 moving forward!

HTML5 has succeeded where XHTML2.0 failed because it has been developed with current and future browser development and past, present, and future web development work in mind. As a result, it's gained significant momentum. Driven by pragmatism, it has emerged as the W3C's choice for Accelerated Development. John Allsopp summarised it best:

> *One of the lessons the Web continues to teach us is that it values pragmatic development over theoretical perfection.*

HTML5 is backwards compatible. It contains all the features of the HTML4 spec, albeit with a few changes and improvements. But it also contains much more extra stuff for building dynamic web applications and creating higher quality markup, such as:

- New semantic elements to allow us to define more parts of our markup unambiguously and semantically rather than using lots of classes and IDs.

- New elements and APIs for adding video, audio, scriptable graphics, and other rich application type content to our sites.

---

[6] www.whatwg.org/specs/web-apps/current-work/
[7] www.w3.org/TR/html5/

- New features for standardising functionality that we already built in bespoke, hacky ways. Server-sent updates and form validation spring to mind immediately.

- New features to plug gaps in the functionality we traditionally had available in open standards, such as defining how browsers should handle markup errors, allowing web apps to work offline, allowing us to use always-open socket connections for app data transfer, and again, audio, video and scriptable images (canvas).

HTML5 has been deliberately built to compete with proprietary plug-ins such as Flash and Silverlight. It looks like such technologies are increasingly taking a back seat. And as you'll see as you move through this book, a lot of HTML5 has good support across all modern browsers and therefore is usable right now in your production projects. It can even be made to work in older browsers with a bit of JavaScript coaxing.

HTML5 is so cool that it's even got its own logo; see `http://j.mp/html5-logo`[8]. This W3C publicity campaign was one of many (with Apple, Microsoft, and others providing similar outreach) designed to get developers interested in adopting the new language and popularizing HTML5 as a buzzword as well as a set of technologies.

The trouble with most of these initiatives is that they were confusing in terms of defining HTML5. If you look at the W3C page just mentioned, you'll see that it lists many different technologies as being part of HTML5, including many that really aren't (CSS3 and SVG being the most glowing examples). CSS and SVG are completely different technologies from HTML with completely different purposes! We would like to advise you to take care not to confuse the different technologies in conversation, as it makes communication more difficult, especially when you are talking to less technical members of a web team (such as project managers and marketers).

So, now we know that the browser support is there, and we've covered some of the history leading up to the emergence of HTML5. Let's take a look at some of the principles that have guided the development of the specification. We mentioned some of those already, but now let's go into a bit more detail.

HTML5 design principles

HTML5 is guided by a number of design principles designed to support existing content while paving the way for the new approaches to markup. Among others, the W3C defines these principles as follows:

- Ensuring support for existing content.

- Degrading new features gracefully in older browsers.

- Not reinventing the wheel.

- Paving the cow paths.

- Evolution, not revolution.

---

[8] www.w3.org/html/logo/

- Enabling universal access.

Unlike XHTML 2.0, HTML5 takes a pragmatic approach to markup, favoring a "real world" approach over the utopian approach adopted by those developing XHTML 2.0 (the approach that ultimately led to its demise). This pragmatic approach allows us to use HTML5 now, safe in the knowledge that it's been designed with moving forward in mind.

Let's take a look at some of the principles outlined by the W3C in "HTML Design Principles" (http://j.mp/html-design-principles[9]) and explain what they mean in practice.

Supporting existing content

The Web celebrated its 21st birthday in 2011. Its phenomenal growth is unparalleled in history and has resulted in billions of web pages in existence already. At the heart of the development of HTML5 lies the importance of supporting all of this existing content.

HTML5 isn't about sweeping out the old and replacing it lock, stock, and barrel with something new. It's about keeping what we already have and adding enhancements on top. With this in mind, the W3C states that

> *It should be possible to process existing HTML documents as HTML5 and get results that are compatible with the existing expectations of users and authors, based on the behavior of existing browsers.*

In short, as HTML5 takes hold, consideration will be given to how existing content designed and developed using older versions of HTML will be handled.

Degrading gracefully

In line with supporting existing content, as HTML5 evolves, the W3C HTML design principles ensure that thought is given to how older browsers handle new elements. With this in mind, the W3C states that

> *HTML5 ... should be designed so that web content can degrade gracefully in older or less capable user agents, even when making use of new elements, attributes, APIs and content models.*

A key part of this principle lies in giving consideration to "user agents designed to meet specific needs or address specialized markets, such as assistive technologies," thereby aiding and improving accessibility. No bad thing.

---

[9] www.w3.org/TR/html-design-principles

Don't reinvent the wheel

As you'll see in Chapter 3 when you learn how the new elements HTML5 introduced came to be named, the design of HTML5 gives consideration to what has gone before. The W3C places a heavy emphasis on not reinventing the wheel, or to put it less formally, "If it ain't broke, don't fix it."

The W3C states that

> If there is already a widely used and implemented technology covering particular use cases, consider specifying that technology in preference to inventing something new for the same purpose.

If you've been working on the Web for some time and embracing web standards, this means that—by design—most of what you're accustomed to informs the development of HTML5 and you shouldn't need to relearn everything.

Paving the cowpaths

Paving? Cowpaths?

Essentially this phrase means that if a path or a way of working has evolved naturally and is in widespread use among developers, it's better to work with it than to replace it. Embrace and adopt the de facto standards in the official specs. Again, we'll see how this design principle has been put into practice in Chapter 3 when we look at the origin of the new element names introduced in HTML5.

Evolution, not revolution

As the W3C put it,

> Revolutions sometimes change the world to the better. Most often, however, it is better to evolve an existing design rather than throwing it away. This way, authors don't have to learn new models and content will live longer.

In practice, this should mean less of a requirement for existing designers and developers to relearn everything. Again, a good thing.

So now we know who is driving forward the development of HTML5 and the guiding principles. It's time to wrap up this chapter with a spot of myth-busting.

A dozen myths about HTML5

Now that you've had a brief history of HTML and we've introduced the context surrounding the development of HTML5, it's time to dispel a few myths and refute a few untruths. HTML5 is plagued with rumour but a lot of this is flatly untrue. Let's bust some myths.

1. Browsers don't support HTML5.

One misconception about HTML5 is that browser support for HTML5 is too unpredictable to start using the specification now. As we said earlier, this isn't the case. The proliferation of books on HTML5 since 2010— by a cross-section of respected authors—clearly indicate that browser support exists and that the time for HTML5 is now, not 2022.

When mainstream sites like Newsweek (`http://newsweek.com`) and YouTube (`http://youtube.com`) are beginning to wholeheartedly embrace HTML5, clearly you can, too. (That's why you're reading this book, after all!)

2. OK, most browsers support HTML5, but IE surely doesn't.

Given our good friend IE's historical idiosyncrasies when it comes to all things standards related, you might be forgiven for thinking this was the case. This time, however, it's not true. Reviewing IE9 in June 2010, The Web Standards Project stated

> *We've been really impressed so far. IE9 really puts the oft-maligned browser on par with the remainder of the browser landscape and even gives them the edge in certain cases. Hats off to the IE team, this is great work.*

When IE is singled out for praise, you know the times they are a-changin'. IE9 and IE10 have introduced support for many HTML5 features, such as `<video>`, `<audio>`, `<canvas>`, HTML5 semantic elements, and more.

3. HTML5 won't be finished until 2022.

Again, not true. The mythical date of 2022, taken from an Ian Hickson interview (`http://j.mp/hixie-interview`[10]) is for a final Proposed Recommendation status.

Given that this is something we still don't have for CSS 2.1, a technology that we're all using every day, it's clear that the 2022 date resolves around a semantic issue (specifically how one defines the term "finished").

---

[10] `www.techrepublic.com/blog/programming-and-development/html-5-editor-ian-hickson-discusses-features-pain-points-adoption-rate-and-more/718`

4. Now I have to relearn everything!

Not at all. As you've already seen in this chapter, at the heart of HTML5 development lie the twin concepts of embracing evolution, not revolution (*evolving* existing standards rather than *replacing* them) and paving the cowpaths (using established tried-and-tested practices to build on).

Most of what you've learned to date simply integrates into HTML5.

5. HTML5 uses presentational elements.

At first glance, you might be forgiven for thinking this, but look a little closer and you'll see this isn't the case. Yes, the HTML5 specification lists elements like <small>, previously admonished for being presentational. Taking this element as an example, it's been redefined. <small> is no longer presentational (meaning "display this at a small size"). It's now semantic, meaning "this is the small print."

6. HTML5 is a return to tag soup.

No, certainly not. HTML5 includes new semantic elements that will allow us to streamline our markup further, not bloat it.

7. HTML5 kills accessibility kittens.

There are huge efforts to ensure that new HTML5 features are accessible moving forward (and to protect kittens). No need to worry. And HTML5 allows us to write accessible markup in just the same way that HTML4 always did.

8. Flash is dead.

Not really, no. It is true that proprietary technologies are taking more of a back seat these days in many contexts, due to open standards now providing a lot of the same functionality, and that a lot of Flash developers are moving over to open standards, but it will still have its uses for a few years to come.

9. HTML5 will break the Web!

Absolutely not. As discussed already, HTML5 is backwards compatible, and we're already seeing well-known commercial sites being kitted out with HTML5 features.

10. HTML5's development is controlled by browser vendors.

Again, not true. Although the WHATWG was established by browser vendors, the process of agreeing the development of HTML5 is open to all. Yes, the browser vendors are innovating rapidly, but everyone can have a say, you included.

11. HTML5 includes CSS3, Geolocation, SVG, and every other modern technology under the sun.

No! There is still a great deal of confusion about what HTML5 is and isn't. As Bruce Lawson of Opera puts it, "Like 'Ajax,' HTML5 has become a bit of an umbrella term [with] people lumping all kinds of unrelated technology like SVG, CSS3, JavaScript, Geolocation, even webfonts in with it." It's true. Many designers confusingly refer to CSS3 as being "a part of HTML5." It isn't. This is another thing we aim to clear up in this book. If you are unsure whether a feature is part of HTML5 or not, look it up in the spec.

Bruce created the following diagram to help us out with defining the Web ecosystem: `http://j.mp/lawson-html5-sketch`[11].

12. So when can I start using HTML5?

Right now!

Summary

So ends our introduction to HTML5. We hope this has set the scene nicely on where front-end web development is going and given you a thirst to learn more and update your skillset! In this chapter, we covered the web standards approach; the most important web design principles; the importance of semantic markup and separation of layers; the modern web browser landscape; accepting uncertainty; and embracing accessibility. We also looked at the history and origins of HTML5, the design principles guiding its development, and what problems it aims to solve. And we rounded our tour off by debunking some HTML5 myths.

---

[11] `www.flickr.com/photos/24374884@N08/4603715307`

Homework

One of the principles of this book is that we use homework to ensure the reader understands the principles of each chapter. At the end of each chapter we'll set you some tasks to complete that are mapped to the content covered in that Chapter.

For some of the Chapters we have provided example content that can be downloaded from the accompanying website `http://thewebevolved.com`. If you get stuck at any point or require further advice please do not hesitate to contact us authors via the website. Good luck!

Chapter 1 homework

For Chapter 1, it's simple: We've provided you with some content about Gordo (a monkey who proved to be a pioneer in the space race), that some of you may have met from *HTML and CSS Web Standards Solutions: A Web Standardistas' Approach* further adventures (download it from `http://thewebevolved.com`).

We've structured it to look like typical content with a mix of headings, paragraphs, a blockquote or two, and some lists. In short, it's the kind of thing you encounter every day.

Your first task is to mark up the content provided using your current flavor of choice (XHTML 1 or HTML 4.01). You'll use the results of this homework in Chapter 2 to compare and contrast how your current flavour of HTML relates to HTML5.

Directed reading

It's a testament to the rapid rise of HTML5 that not only are there a number of vanguard books being published on it, but a number of freely accessible web sites exist with reference material and tutorials.

We recommend the following resources:

- `http://html5doctor.com`: It should come as no surprise to see HTML5 Doctor on the list. In addition to two of the authors of this book, HTML5 Doctor plays host to a number of extremely talented authors including Bruce Lawson and Remy Sharp, the authors of *Introducing HTML5* (New Riders).

- `http://dev.opera.com`: As a founding member of the HTML5 WHATWG, Opera has been at the forefront of promoting standards-based development focusing largely on the promotion of HTML5. It's no surprise to see Opera promoting standards through the Opera Developer Community. Regular contributors to the community include Patrick Lauke and Chris Mills (the technical reviewer for this book). It's well worth bookmarking and checking into regularly.

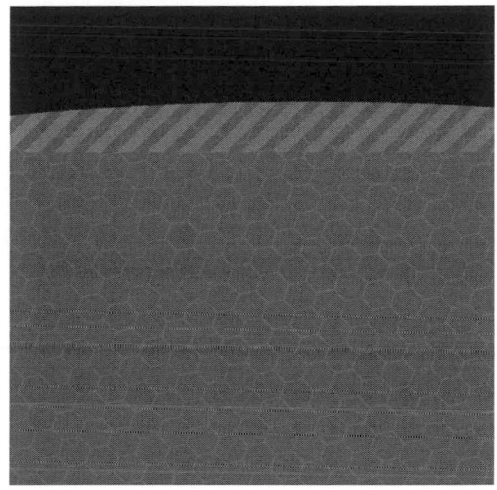

Chapter 2

Your First Plunge into HTML5

In our first chapter we covered the background of HTML5, why we should start using it now, and some modern web standards development principles. In this chapter, we'll get started with creating some actual HTML5 web pages.

We'll begin this chapter with a look at how we marked up Chapter 1's homework page. We'll use it as the basis for an exploration of how some well-known elements have changed, especially the DOCTYPE, which is now considerably simpler and easier to remember.

Once we've covered that we undertake a time-honored tradition by embarking on a "Hello World!" journey, culminating in the creation of our first HTML5 page. Next, we introduce some workarounds that will help you deliver finely crafted HTML5 pages so that they work in current browsers (no prizes for guessing that our old friend IE gets a mention here). Finally, we'll look at the pros and cons of HTML5 vs. XHTML5 and how validators and lint checkers handle HTML5.

That's a lot of ground to cover, so, without further ado, let's get started...

Homework review

At the end of Chapter 1, we asked you to mark up a typical web page using your current preferred flavour of markup, either XHTML1 or HTML4. As we embark on this chapter and the following chapter, we'll show you how that very same web page might be marked up using HTML5. The aim here is to show you the relationship between the markup you're currently using and HTML5 markup—and in the process highlight the new features of HTML5 and the advantages they offer.

Working with real content as opposed to latin or other filler text gives you an insight into how real content affects real markup. In short, the content drives the markup. This is why we're not supplying meaningless lorem ipsum.

So, how did we mark up our web page?

We chose XHTML 1 and, as you'll see in the example below, we looked at the content provided and marked it up using the most appropriate elements possible. To save paper (and trees) we've replaced some of the content with ellipses, but you should recognize the content (if you did the homework in Chapter 1). In addition to using good old semantic markup, we've also chosen id and class names to provide additional meaning.

Our page

The resulting page is as follows:

```
<!DOCTYPE html PUBLIC "-//W3C//DTD XHTML 1.0 Strict//EN"
        "http://www.w3.org/TR/xhtml1/DTD/xhtml1-strict.dtd">
<html xmlns="http://www.w3.org/1999/xhtml">
<head>
    <meta http-equiv="content-type" content="text/html; charset=UTF-8" />
    <title>Miss Baker | Space Pioneers | The Web Evolved, Chapter 2 Example File</title>
</head>
<body>
<div id="container">
    <div id="header">
        <h1>The Original Space Pioneers</h1>
        <h4>America's Unsung Heroes</h4>
    </div>
    <div id="article">
        <h2>Miss Baker</h2>
        <h4>First Lady of Space</h4>
        <div id="introduction">
            <p>Before humans were launched into space, many animals were propelled↪
heavenwards…</p>
            …
        </div>
        <div class="section">
            <h3>Miss Baker's Historic Flight</h3>
            <p>Miss Baker and fellow female pioneer Able's historic flight…</p>
            …
        </div>
        <div class="section">
            <h3>The Mission</h3>

            <p>Miss Baker's flight was another milestone in the history of space flight…</p>
            …
        </div>
        <div class="aside">
            <h3>The US Space Programme</h3>
```

```
        <p>A technological and ideological competition between the United States and➡
the Soviet Union…</p>
            …
        </div>
        <div class="section">
            <h3>Life in Retirement</h3>

            <p>Miss Baker spent the latter part of her life at the US Space and Rocket➡
Centre…</p>
            …
        </div>
        <p class="smallprint">Copyright 2010 &middot; Christopher Murphy</p>
    </div>
    <div id="footer">
        <p>The Space Pioneers web site is an example site, designed to accompany The Web➡
Evolved, published by Apress. Text: The Web Evolved; Design: Jonny Campbell.</p>
        <p>HTML + CSS released under a Creative Commons Attribution 3.0 license.</p>
        <p>Photography &copy; iStockphoto</p>
    </div>
</div>
</body>
</html>
```

This should be familiar territory for you. Your choice of markup might differ—you might have chosen HTML4 and you might have chosen different elements—but the bottom line is that you should have used semantic markup in an effort to craft the most meaningful page possible.

For the remainder of this chapter we'll be making the transition to HTML5 so we can begin to embrace the opportunities it offers. Though some aspects of this will be new to you, have no fear—a lot of the ground we cover will be familiar, as you'll soon see. On that note, we have some good news.

84.8% of your markup remains

While we can't 100% guarantee that the figure of 84.8% is scientifically accurate (truth be told, we made that figure up), it's accurate in spirit. As mentioned in Chapter 1, the guiding principles behind HTML5 include an emphasis on not reinventing the wheel, paving the cowpaths, and embracing a pragmatic spirit of evolution not revolution.

In short, the emphasis is on building upon what has gone before. As we progress through this chapter and throughout this book you'll see these principles in action. So rest assured: as we embark on our journey toward HTML5 development, you won't need to relearn everything. Yes, all that semantic goodness we've learned to use is still there. There are some new elements at our disposal (as we'll see in the next chapter), but a great deal of what we've learned remains.

AN ASIDE ON CODING STYLE

As you'll see when we run through a number of different markup styles—HTML 4.01, XHTML 1.1, and HTML5—there certainly are differences. The author team of this book prefers to write markup in XHTML style but using HTML5's new elements; you may prefer to write your HTML using a more relaxed HTML style instead. HTML permits both, allowing you to stick with what you prefer.

Coding styles have changed a great deal since HTML was first implemented by Tim Berners-Lee in 1990. When Berners-Lee first published "Tags Used in HTML" (`http://j.mp/tags-in-html`[1]), the style he used was to write elements in uppercase, opening and closing some tags while leaving others opened and unclosed. Berners-Lee stated, "The names of tags and attributes are not case sensitive: they may be in lower, upper, or mixed case with exactly the same meaning. (In this document they are generally represented in upper case.)"

It's all in the head

Before we get started on creating some good, old-fashioned "Hello World!" web pages (a tradition when embarking on any new programming venture), let's take a look at some of the changes we'll encounter, specifically changes we'll be making in the <head> as we move toward HTML5. It's a good idea to understand these fundamentals before getting into the practical details of the <body> markup.

In this section, we'll introduce the new HTML5 DOCTYPE, explain how to declare languages in HTML5, and introduce a new, simpler meta charset attribute.

Before we embark on this journey, let's take a look at what we have now. (Remember that we chose XHTML 1 for our Miss Baker page; your <head> might be different.) At present, the <head> on our Miss Baker page is as follows:

```
<!DOCTYPE html PUBLIC "-//W3C//DTD XHTML 1.0 Strict//EN"
        "http://www.w3.org/TR/xhtml1/DTD/xhtml1-strict.dtd">
<html xmlns="http://www.w3.org/1999/xhtml">
<head>
    <meta http-equiv="content-type" content="text/html; charset=UTF-8" />
    <title>Miss Baker | Space Pioneers | The Web Evolved, Chapter 2 Example File</title>
</head>
```

Now let's take a look at it in HTML5.

```
<!DOCTYPE html>
<html lang="en">
    <head>
        <meta charset="UTF-8" />
        <title>Miss Baker | Space Pioneers | The Web Evolved, Chapter 2 Example File</title>
```

---

[1] www.w3.org/History/19921103-hypertext/hypertext/WWW/MarkUp/Tags.html

```
</head>
```

As you can see, this is considerably simpler, which is no bad thing. Now let's get started. We'll begin with some welcome changes to the always-impossible-to-remember DOCTYPE.

A more perfect DOCTYPE

The dreaded DOCTYPE. Few—those with photographic memory excluded—can remember it. Until now, whether your flavor of choice has been XHTML 1 Strict or HTML 4 Strict (or any other of the multitude available), the DOCTYPE has been an all-but-unintelligible string of characters. If you've been writing markup using XHTML 1 Strict, you're used to seeing the following DOCTYPE:

```
<!DOCTYPE html PUBLIC "-//W3C//DTD XHTML 1.0 Strict//EN"
    "http://www.w3.org/TR/xhtml1/DTD/xhtml1-strict.dtd">
```

If your markup flavor of choice has been HTML 4 Strict, then you're more familiar with this DOCTYPE:

```
<!DOCTYPE HTML PUBLIC "-//W3C//DTD HTML 4.01//EN"
    "http://www.w3.org/TR/html4/strict.dtd">
```

There is no need for the DOCTYPE to be this complicated and unmemorable. The W3C probably had grand designs concerning purposes it might serve when they first created the markup specs, but in reality all it has ever done for us is tell the browser to render our pages in standards mode rather than quirks mode (http://j.mp/quirks-mode[2]). When writing the HTML5 spec, the WHATWG recognized this and changed the DOCTYPE to the shortest possible sequence of characters that constitute a valid DOCTYPE.

```
<!DOCTYPE html>
```

That's it. Simpler and, dare we say it, even memorable.

Even if you do nothing else, you can start using the new HTML5 DOCTYPE now, safe in the knowledge that these 15 characters are all it takes to trigger standards mode. Try it now by changing the DOCTYPE on your Chapter 1 homework and revalidating your page. It will work just fine. Given that Google is already using the HTML5 DOCTYPE on its search pages, there's no reason not to change your DOCTYPE.

Declaring languages in HTML5

Now let's look at how to declare languages in HTML5. But why declare languages at all? The W3C answers this question as follows:

> *Specifying the language of content is useful for a wide number of applications, from linguistically-sensitive searching to applying language-specific display properties. In some cases the potential applications for language information are still waiting for implementations to catch up, whereas in others, such as detection of language by voice browsers, it is a necessity today.*

---

[2] http://en.wikipedia.org/wiki/Quirks_mode

Adding markup for language information to content is something that can and should be done today. Without it, it will not be possible to take advantage of any future developments.

Declaring a default language is already important for applications such as accessibility and search engines, but other possible applications may emerge over time.

The easiest way to specify the language of an HTML document is to add a `lang` attribute to the root element of our HTML page. The root element of an HTML page is always `<html>`, so to specify a language, we do the following:

```
<html lang="en">
```

In this example, the value of the `lang` attribute is en, which specifies that the document is written in English. But what if your document contains elements written in a language other than the specified `lang`? No problem. The language attribute can also be used inline. The following example includes an inline `<span>` element containing a `lang` attribute with a value of `fr`, indicating that the content contained within is written in French:

```
<p>Miss Baker, on entering the capsule, declared to her fellow astronaut Able: <span>➥
lang="fr">"Bon chance!"</span></p>
```

Trés bon.

And as you'd expect, two-letter primary codes exist for other languages—for example de (German), `it` (Italian), `nl` (Dutch), `es` (Spanish), `ar` (Arabic), `ru` (Russian), and `zh` (Chinese). If that's not enough, there are over 8,000 language attribute values available; these are listed in full at the IANA Language Subtag Registry (`http://j.mp/lang-subtag`[3]).

It's also possible to specify dialects within a language. These are generally represented with the base language code, for example en, followed by a hyphen and the dialect in question. The following examples show UK English and US English respectively:

```
en-US: US English
en-GB: UK English
```

Should you wish to embrace a more avant garde language, the inclusion of a primary tag x indicates an experimental language, as follows:

```
<p lang="x-klingon">nuqDaq 'oH puchpa''e'</p>
```

For the uninitiated, the Klingon phrase "nuqDaq 'oH puchpa"e'" translates as "Where is the bathroom?"You can hear it pronounced at the wonderfully old school web site for The Klingon Language Institute (`http://j.mp/klingon-language`[4]).

---

[3] `www.iana.org/assignments/language-subtag-registry`
[4] `www.kli.org/tlh/phrases.html`

Finally—and we only include this for the sake of completeness—should you wish to create your own language code, it's entirely possible (though not recommended). Geoffrey Snedders, the author of the HTML5 Outliner (discussed in the next chapter), uses the following language code for his personal site:

```
<html lang="en-gb-x-sneddy">
```

If you've followed along, it should be clear that Mr Snedders' `lang` attribute translates as follows:

```
English - Great British - Experimental - Sneddy
```

(Though why you might want to specify your own particular language is questionable.) Enough said.

THE XMLNS ATTRIBUTE

If you're accustomed to writing markup using XHTML, you might be wondering what happened to the `xmlns` attribute that we had on our Miss Baker page.

```
<html xmlns="http://www.w3.org/1999/xhtml">
```

The answer is that it's no longer needed. The `xmlns` attribute informs the browser that all the elements on this page are in the XHTML namespace; however, in HTML5, elements are always in this namespace so this no longer needs to be declared explicitly. You can remove the `xmlns` attribute, safe in the knowledge that your page will work fine in all browsers.

Character encoding

Let's take a look at our Miss Baker page as it stood at the beginning of this chapter. We specified the character encoding as follows:

```
<meta http-equiv="content-type" content="text/html; charset=UTF-8" />
```

In HTML5, specifying your page's character encoding is considerably simpler. Let's take a look at the HTML5 version:

```
<meta charset="UTF-8" />
```

You don't really need to know what character encoding is in detail, but basically, it defines the set of valid human language characters that can be used in the document. It is safest to stick to UTF-8, a universal character set that allows all characters from all languages, just about.

Mr. Memory

So there we have it: taking all of the above together, it's easy to see how you might now astound your friends with memory feats. No more complicated boilerplates; the following should be easy enough for anyone to remember:

```
<!DOCTYPE html>
<html lang="en">
    <head>
```

```
    <meta charset="UTF-8" />
    <title>Miss Baker | Space Pioneers | The Web Evolved, Chapter 2 Example File</title>
</head>
```

So let's see everything working together on some actual pages. It's time for a spot of "Hello World!" action.

A "Hello World!" journey

Tradition dictates that we introduce you to your first HTML5 page using the time-honored "Hello World!" page. As the wonderful Wikipedia puts it,

> *It is often considered to be a tradition among programmers for people attempting to learn a new programming language to write a "Hello World!" program as one of the first steps of learning that particular language.*

Who are we to break with tradition?

To show you how markup differs depending upon the flavor of HTML you've been using, and to show you how the transition into HTML5 reflects previous practice (as in evolution, not revolution), we're going to quickly run through a series of "Hello World!" web pages to demonstrate, among other things, that HTML5 offers a variety of markup style preferences. We'll conclude by looking at the markup style we feel is best: merging the best aspects of XHTML (a stricter, easier-to-learn syntax) and HTML5 (a forward-looking, richer semantic palette).

Let's get started.

"Hello World!" in XHTML1.0 style

Our first example is a very simple "Hello World!" web page, marked up using an XHTML 1 Strict DOCTYPE. It's perfectly valid and, if you've been using XHTML for your markup, it should come as no surprise.

```
<!DOCTYPE html PUBLIC "-//W3C//DTD XHTML 1.0 Strict//EN"
        "http://www.w3.org/TR/xhtml1/DTD/xhtml1-strict.dtd">
<html xmlns="http://www.w3.org/1999/xhtml">
<head>
    <meta http-equiv="content-type" content="text/html; charset=UTF-8" />
    <title>Hello World! XHTML 1 Strict</title>
</head>
<body>
    <p>Hello World!</p>
</body>
</html>
```

No surprises here. This is a typical page, well-formed and perfectly valid, but what if your preference is HTML 4? Let's take a look in the next example.

"Hello World!" in HTML4 style

The example that follows is identical to the previous example but marked up using HTML 4 Strict DOCTYPE and with a considerably simpler opening `<html>` tag (minus the XML namespace declaration in our XHTML 1 version).

Like the preceding example, it's perfectly valid. Again, this should come as no surprise.

```
<!DOCTYPE HTML PUBLIC "-//W3C//DTD HTML 4.01//EN"
        "http://www.w3.org/TR/html4/strict.dtd">
<html>
<head>
    <meta http-equiv=content-type content="text/html; charset=UTF-8">
    <title>Hello World! HTML 4 Strict</title>
</head>
<body>
    <p>Hello World!</p>
</body>
</html>
```

So far, so…familiar. It's time to take a look at an HTML5 example.

"Hello World!" in HTML5 "loose" style

The XHTML 1 and HTML 4 pages we've demonstrated previously should come as no surprise. Now let's take a look at an HTML5 page in its simplest, most minimal form. The following page, though just a few lines long, is a 100% valid HTML5 "Hello World!" page:

```
<!DOCTYPE html>
    <meta charset=UTF-8>
    <title>Hello World!</title>
    <p>Hello World!
```

If you've been using XHTML syntax to date, this might come as a little bit of a shock. No opening and closing `<html>` tags? No `<head>` or `<body>` elements? Unquoted attributes? This is because HTML5 inherits many of the characteristics of HTML 4, which has a much less restrictive syntax than XHTML 1.

As we outlined in the previous chapter, HTML5's development has been characterized by a pragmatic approach with the WHATWG allowing all general syntax variations, including the strict syntax of XHTML and the loose syntax of HTML 4. To underline this point and to see how HTML5 has evolved from what has gone before, let's take a look at a slightly more minimal—but still perfectly valid—HTML 4 page.

```
<!DOCTYPE HTML PUBLIC "-//W3C//DTD HTML 4.01//EN"
        "http://www.w3.org/TR/html4/strict.dtd">
    <meta http-equiv=content-type content="text/html; charset=UTF-8">
    <title>Hello World! HTML 4.01 Strict</title>
    <p>Hello World!
```

Other than the more verbose HTML 4 DOCTYPE and the lengthier meta charset attribute, the two examples are identical. Neither has opening or closing `<html>` tags, or `<head>` or `<body>` elements.

The reason for this is simple and we touched on it in Chapter 1 when we looked at the HTML design principle of supporting existing content. For backward compatibility, HTML5 allows web pages to be marked up using either HTML 4 or XHTML 1 syntax. Regardless of your syntax preference, HTML5 embraces what's gone before.

If you've been working with XHTML, you've been using lowercase for tag and attribute names, closing elements, quoting elements, and giving all attributes a value. Some find these rules restrictive; others appreciate the consistency they give to markup.

In summary, it's possible to write your HTML5 pages using the syntax of your choice and you're entirely free to do so; however, we recommend retaining the stricter syntax of XHTML.

Why? Rules are useful. They enable collaborative working, allowing everyone to conform to a standardized syntax. Rules also make it easier to learn markup. There are some other reasons why you should stick to XHTML; for example, accessibility best practices demand that you specify a language for the document using a `lang` attribute on the `<html>` tag. This isn't possible if you don't include it in the page!

With that in mind, let's take a look at a final HTML5 page that embraces the rules and syntax of XHTML.

"Hello World!" in HTML5 "strict" style

If you've been writing your markup using the strict syntax and rules of XHTML, you're used to lowercase elements, quoting attributes, and closing empty elements. As you saw from the last example, with HTML5, anything goes. Uppercase elements? No problem. Unquoted attributes? A-OK.

But what if you'd like to make the jump to HTML5 but you want to bring along all your XHTML habits? Have no fear; we can choose to markup our pages using XHTML syntax and get the best of both worlds. Let's take a look at an example.

```
<!DOCTYPE html>
<html lang="en">
    <head>
        <meta charset="UTF-8" />
        <title>Hello World!</title>
    </head>
    <body>
        <p>Hello World!</p>
    </body>
</html>
```

It's 100% valid. This page combines the benefits of HTML5 with the strictness of syntax of XHTML 1. In short: it's the best of both worlds.

Supporting HTML5 cross-browser

Let's continue by looking at techniques we can employ to get the new HTML5 semantic elements working across browsers, even older browsers like IE6. Then we'll take the last, well-styled HTML5 "Hello World!" example page and add to it, providing you with a boilerplate you can use to get started using HTML5 now.

We'll start by looking at how browsers deal with unknown elements.

How do browsers deal with unknown elements?

HTML is a forgiving language. For quite some time, most browsers have gracefully handled the inclusion of elements and attributes they didn't recognize by treating them as anonymous inline elements and allowing us to style them.

Every browser has a list of elements it supports. For example, Firefox's list is stored in a file called nsElementTable.cpp. This file tells the browser how to handle the elements it encounters, informing the browser how to style them and how they should be treated in the Document Object Model (DOM).

The best way to demonstrate this is to run through an example. The following, very basic page uses the new <time> element (which we'll meet properly In Chapter 4). We've included a very simple style sheet with a rule targeting the new element. The question is, how will browsers style the <time> element?

```
<!DOCTYPE html>
<html lang="en">
  <head>
    <meta charset="UTF-8" />
    <title>Styling Unknown Elements - 1</title>
    <style>
      time
      {
      font-style: italic;
      }
    </style>
  </head>
  <body>
    <p>Miss Baker made her historic journey on <time datetime="1959-05-28">May 28, ↪
1959</time>.</p>
  </body>
</html>
```

First, the good news: Most modern browsers will see the <time> element fine and style the date "May 28, 1959" in italics. Our old friend IE, however, has different ideas. IE (up to and including version 8) doesn't even see the <time> element and as a consequence this text is not styled.

Needless to say, this is something we need to resolve if we're to make any further progress. The good news is that there is a solution to the problem: we can use a little JavaScript to explicitly declare the element for the benefit of IE. (Think of it as giving IE a mild slap in the face.)

The technique, credited to Sjoerd Visscher, involves creating a new DOM element (of the same name as the one being targeted) to trick IE into "seeing" the new element and, ta-da!, the style is applied (see `http://j.mp/trick-ie`[5]).

Let's take a look. Here is a line of JavaScript using `document.createElement` to explicitly create an instance of the `<time>` element in the DOM:

```
<!DOCTYPE html>
<html lang="en">
  <head>
    <meta charset="UTF-8" />
    <title>Styling Unknown Elements - 2</title>
    <script>document.createElement('time');</script>
    <style>
      time
      {
      font-style: italic;
      }
    </style>
  </head>
  <body>
    <p>Miss Baker made her historic journey on <time datetime="1959-05-28">May 28,➥
1959</time>.</p>
  </body>
</html>
```

With this simple piece of JavaScript, IE is tricked into seeing the `<time>` element, allowing the italic style to bite. Clearly this only solves the problem for a single element (in this case the `<time>` element). The next example demonstrates how to solve the problem for all the new elements introduced in HTML5. Here we include all the elements we'd like to force IE to recognize:

```
<!DOCTYPE html>
<html lang="en">
  <head>
    <meta charset="UTF-8" />
    <title>Styling Unknown Elements - 3</title>
    <script>
      (function(){if(!/*@cc_on!@*/0)return;var e = "abbr,article,aside,audio,canvas,➥
datalist,details,eventsource,figure,footer,header,hgroup,mark,menu,meter,nav,output,➥
progress,section,time,video".split(','),i=e.length;while(i--)➥
{document.createElement(e[i])}})()
    </script>
    <style>
      time
      {
      font-style: italic;
      }
    </style>
```

---

[5] http://intertwingly.net/blog/2008/01/22/Best-Standards-Support#c1201006277

```
    </head>
    <body>
      <p>Miss Baker made her historic journey on <time datetime="1959-05-28">May 28,↵
  1959</time>.</p>
    </body>
  </html>
```

Obviously, that's quite lot of JavaScript to include on every page. What if, heaven forbid, any new HTML5 elements are added to the list of new elements? While it might be possible to work a little regular expression magic to do a spot of find-and-replace on any HTML5 pages you might have created, a far simpler option is at hand.

The solution is the shiv, which we meet next.

Meet the shiv

We promised an easier solution to the thorny problem of styling unknown elements in IE and, true to our word, here it is. Courtesy of Remy Sharp and christened the "HTML5 Enabling Script" (or more colloquially, "the shiv"), here it is:

```
<!DOCTYPE html>
<html lang="en">
  <head>
    <meta charset="UTF-8" />
    <title>Styling Unknown Elements - 4</title>
    <!--[if lt IE 9]>
      <script src="http://html5shiv.googlecode.com/svn/trunk/html5.js"></script>
    <![endif]-->
    <style>
      time
      {
      font-style: italic;
      }
    </style>
  </head>
  <body>
    <p>Miss Baker made her historic journey on <time datetime="1959-05-28">May 28,↵
  1959</time>.</p>
  </body>
</html>
```

Include this script in your page and it will take care of all the things we discussed previously and more. Remy has hosted it at Google Code, so you just need to link to it; you don't need to worry about what's inside the JavaScript or think about whether you've got the latest version.

By nesting the script in conditional comments, we can target it at versions of IE older than IE 9 (which has considerably better support for HTML5). This allows the browsers that don't need it to treat it as a straightforward HTML comment and skip right past it. The result? Browsers that don't need the script don't download it, saving an HTTP request.

In closing, there a couple of points to stress. Firstly, the shiv needs to be placed in the `<head>` element so that IE knows about the new HTML5 elements before it comes to render them. Secondly, the shiv relies on JavaScript being enabled. If the majority of your audience is browsing the Web with JavaScript disabled, you need to consider an alternative, such as using semantic HTML5 `class` names in your markup. (We'll revisit this idea in Chapter 3 when we introduce our very own specification, HTML4.5.)

IE print protector

As Columbo would say,"Just one more thing...."We promised that linking to the shiv at Google Code had the added benefit of offering you the latest version of the shiv. We weren't lying.

Remy Sharp's html5shiv now also includes Jonathan Neal's IE Print Protector (`http://j.mp/ie-print`[6]), which solves a problem IE has when trying to print HTML5 pages (it doesn't render the `element` properly on the printed page, either). IE Print Protector works by temporarily replacing HTML5 elements with supported fallback elements (like `<div>` and `<span>`) when you print, creating a special style sheet for these elements based on your existing styles.

This solves the problem with IE, but we also need to add a fragment of CSS for any browsers that don't know how to render HTML5's new semantic elements.

Declaring block-level elements

As mentioned, when it comes to styling, browsers treat unknown elements as anonymous inline elements. HTML5 introduces a number of new block level elements: if these elements aren't included in the browser's lookup table of known elements, they will be treated as inline. We therefore need to add a CSS rule declaring them as block-level elements.

```
<style>
article, aside, details, figcaption, figure, footer, header, hgroup, menu, nav, section {
  display: block;
}
</style>
```

This simple rule instructs browsers to treat the new HTML5 `<article>`, `<aside>`, `<details>`, `<figcaption>`, `<figure>`, `<footer>`, `<header>`, `<hgroup>`, `<menu>`, `<nav>` and `<section>` elements as block-level elements and display them accordingly.

> Note: As the HTML5 spec changes and more features are added, you should update these Shiv techniques periodically to make sure they stay current.

---

[6] `www.iecss.com/print-protector/#about`

Also, for those of you who use CSS resets in your styling work, note that many of these will have been updated to include the HTML5 display: block declarations in them. Examples include Normalize and Eric Meyer's Reset. CSS resets will be discussed in more detail in Chapter 7.

An HTML5 boilerplate page

So, we've discussed the importance of the shiv and of declaring HTML5 elements as block level so that browsers will know how to handle them. We've also introduced the new HTML5 DOCTYPE, looked at how to declare languages, and character encoding works with the simplified meta charset attribute. Let's put everything together to create a simple HTML5 boilerplate page. The following HTML5 boilerplate includes everything covered in this chapter:

```
<!DOCTYPE html>
<html lang="en">
<head>
    <meta charset="UTF-8" />
    <title>Insert Your Title Here</title>
    <!--[if lt IE 9]>
      <script src="http://html5shiv.googlecode.com/svn/trunk/html5.js"></script>
    <![endif]-->
    <style>
      article, aside, details, figcaption, figure, footer, header, hgroup, menu, nav, section
      {
      display: block;
      }
    </style>
</head>
<body>
    <p>Insert your content here.</p>
</body>
</html>
```

We'll provide a more advanced version of this boilerplate when we introduce CSS resets in the second half of this book. For now, you might want to experiment with this file as you prepare for the next chapter. You can download the HTML5 boilerplate from http://thewebevolved.com[7].

The astute amongst you might notice one small thing missing from the previous example.

No more type attribute

We no longer need to include a type attribute when declaring JavaScript or CSS. In the past, we would have included a type attribute as follows:

---

[7] http://thewebevolved.com/02/boilerplate.html

```
<!--[if lt IE 9]>
  <script type="text/javascript" ➡
          src="http://html5shiv.googlecode.com/svn/trunk/html5.js"></script>
<![endif]-->
<style type="text/css">
  article, aside, details, figcaption, figure, footer, header, hgroup, menu, nav, section
  {
  display: block;
  }
</style>
```

The type attributes, `type="text/javascript"` and `type="text/css"`, are no longer needed. You can now save a few bytes and drop them, as follows:

```
<!--[if lt IE 9]>
  <script  src="http://html5shiv.googlecode.com/svn/trunk/html5.js"></script>
<![endif]-->
<style>
  article, aside, details, figcaption, figure, footer, header, hgroup, menu, nav, section
  {
  display: block;
  }
</style>
```

This is because there aren't any other styling and scripting languages that you want to use and therefore differentiate between—only CSS and JavaScript. (In the past, we used to use VBScript for scripting on some occasions, but VBScript has gone the way of the dodo.)

So that's one less thing to remember. Good times!

Polyfills and alternatives

The HTML5 boilerplate we just showed you—and the wealth of support for HTML5 and CSS3 across modern browsers—has taken us a long way toward being all set for creating awesome modern web experiences, but in many situations they are not enough. You'll often be called on to support older browsers (like IE 6-8) that don't support the new features found in HTML5 and CSS3, and sometimes you'll want to use cutting edge features that don't have support across all modern browsers.

There are ways to handle these situations, and we'll see many different techniques to do so throughout the book, but generally these techniques fall into one of three camps.

- *Graceful degradation*: We have already talked about the idea that many web features can be built so that they look great in modern browsers, and then in older browsers they degrade so that although they don't look as nice, they are still accessible and usable.

- *Progressive enhancement/alternatives*: As we have already discussed, progressive enhancement is the opposite of graceful degradation. Here, we build up a base level of functionality that works across all browsers, and then we build stylistic and usability enhancements on top for browsers that support advanced features. Sometimes this can be done as a matter of course when you build up your markup and styles, and sometimes we need a little extra help.

> *Note: In Chapter 7, you'll come across a feature detection library called Modernizr. It detects whether a browser supports various features of CSS3, HTML5, etc., and then allows you to serve different styles and script to suit. For example, if you have a web site that uses CSS animations for an interface feature, you could detect support for it using Modernizr and then serve a simpler set of styling to non-supporting browsers that still renders the content accessible and usable, albeit perhaps not in quite as exciting a way.*

- *Polyfills*: You'll meet many polyfills throughout the book. These are programs usually built in JavaScript that add support for a web technology into a browser that doesn't already support it natively. A good example is CSSPie, which adds support for CSS gradients, rounded corners, and other CSS3 features into older versions of IE.

Validation

We've covered a lot in this chapter; by the end of it you'll be able to update your Miss Baker page to HTML5. In Chapter 3 we'll introduce a number of the new semantic elements added in HTML5 that you can use to further improve your Miss Baker page.

One thing that we haven't covered, which we'll remedy right now, is the topic of validating our shiny, new HTML5 pages.

Why validate? Validating your pages is often the first stage in picking up problems. Using a validator can help you to pick up simple, easy-to-overlook mistakes and learn more about how the markup works. Validation is a useful habit to get into, especially when learning, and one we hope you're aware of, if not actively using. With that in mind, let's take a look at validating our HTML5 pages.

HTML5 validator

The WHATWG maintains a list of currently known HTML5 validators, and other tools, at `http://j.mp/whatwg-validator`[8].

There are several HTML5 validators available but we'll focus on one created by Henri Sivonen: `http://j.mp/nu-validator`[9]

Let's check the boilerplate to see if it's valid HTML5 (Figure 2-1).

---

[8] `http://validator.whatwg.org`
[9] `http://html5.validator.nu/`

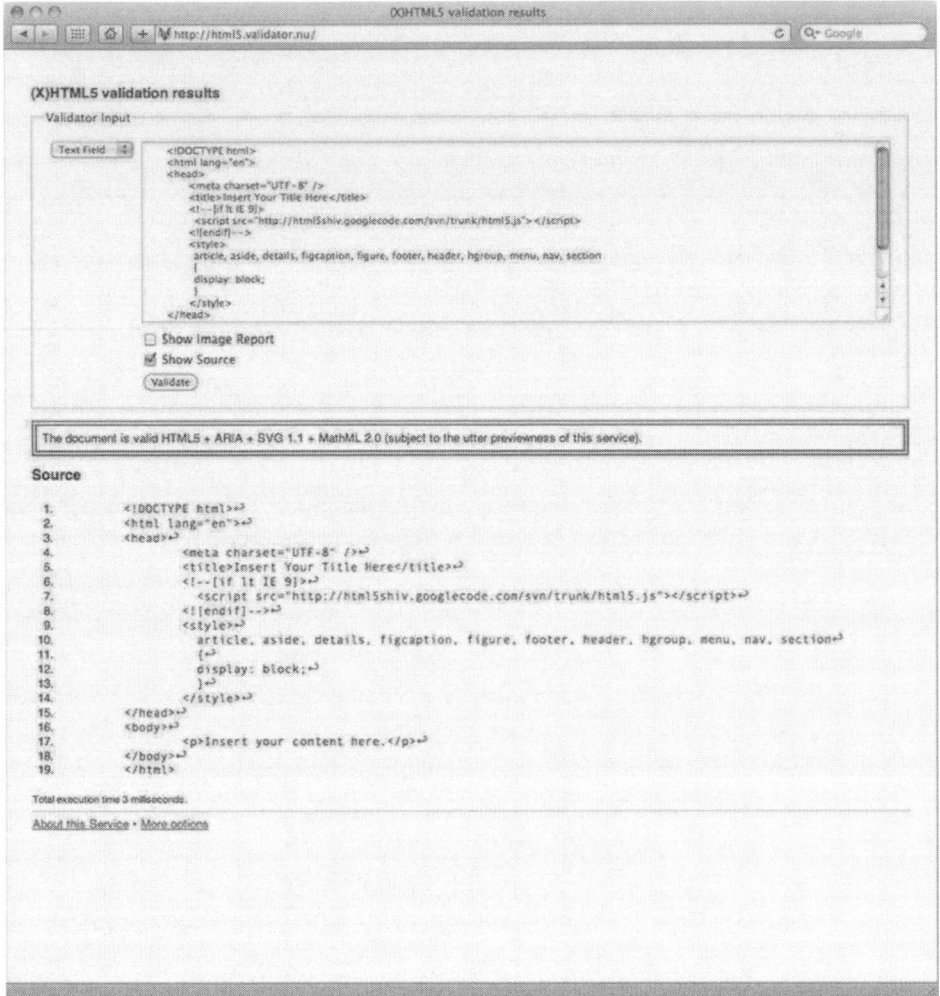

Figure 2-1. Good news! The boilerplate HTML5 page is valid… subject to the utter previewness of the service.

The result? The validator returns the following: The document is valid HTML5 + ARIA + SVG 1.1 + MathML 2.0 (subject to the utter previewness of this service)."

What Henri Sivonen's HTML5 Validator does not do is check against specific syntax settings (such as checking XHTML style syntax). Dan Cederholm remarked on the topic:

> It's important for the validator to simply and easily add an option for checking syntax that would help to foster good coding habits, avoid head-scratching rendering issues, etc. That's why I choose to code XHTML today — it's a

> *personal preference that helps me maintain, optimize and troubleshoot code,*
> *and I'll continue with that convention no matter the doctype.*

That said, the absence of an option for checking syntax at the HTML5 Validator doesn't mean we can't check syntax elsewhere; it's just a little less convenient. The next section covers HTML Lint, a tool you can use to ensure your markup is well-formed and perfectly crafted.

HTML Lint

In the absence of a validator that allows us to check against a preferred syntax, we recommend HTML Lint at `http://j.mp/htmllint`[10].

Developed by MMM to "make sure your code looks good," HTML Lint (see Figure 2-2) is a lint checker that enables you to specify options to check against. (The term *lint* was derived from the name of the undesirable bits of fiber and fluff found in sheep's wool.)

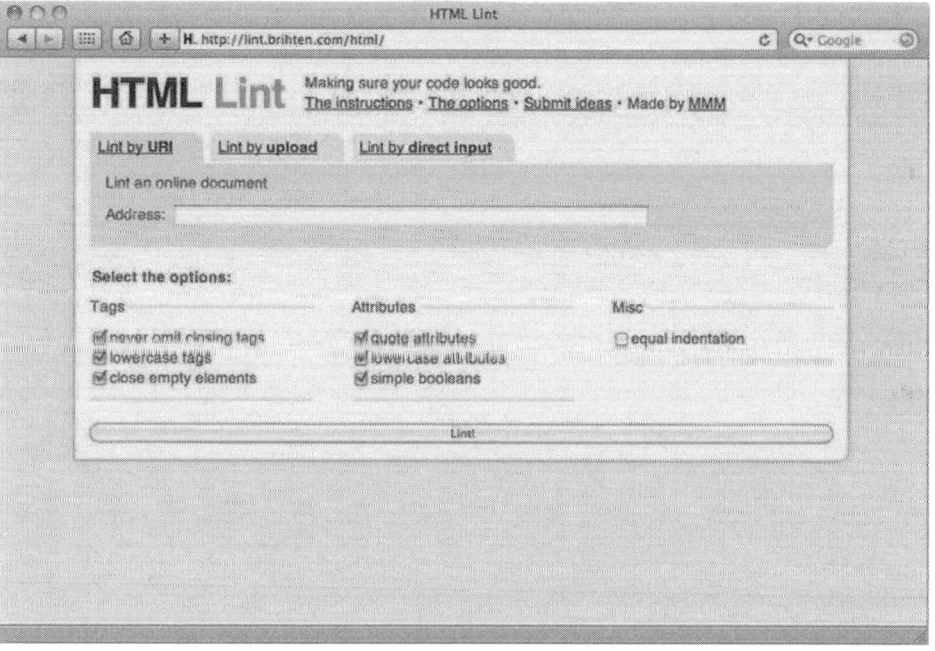

Figure 2-2. MMM's HTML Lint enables you to ensure your markup is well formed by checking against a series of user-electable options.

---

[10] `http://lint.brihten.com`

As MMM states,

> *While XHTML was very strict with syntax, HTML5 is more lenient…which means keeping consistent code styles becomes more difficult.*

Anyone who prefers the strict syntax of XHTML will appreciate the options HTML Lint offers, which include the ability to check for closing tags, closed empty elements, quoted attributes, and lowercase elements and attributes.

Until a validator is created that allows for both validation and syntax checking (and we hope one is created soon), you can use the HTML5 Validator and HTML Lint for validation and neat markup, respectively.

Revisiting Miss Baker

So now we've seen a few HTML5 pages in action. Our last exercise—to show you how simple the transition to HTML5 can be—is to revisit the Miss Baker page we introduced at the start of this chapter to give it a new DOCTYPE and make the changes to the <head> we introduced earlier.

```
<!DOCTYPE html>
<html lang="en">
<head>
    <meta charset="UTF-8" />
    <title>Miss Baker | Space Pioneers | The Web Evolved, Chapter 2 Example File</title>
    <!--[if lt IE 9]>
      <script  src="http://html5shiv.googlecode.com/svn/trunk/html5.js"></script>
    <![endif]-->
    <style>
      article, aside, details, figcaption, figure, footer, header, hgroup, menu, nav, section
      {
      display: block;
      }
    </style>
</head>
<body>
<div id="container">
    <div id="header">
        <h1>The Original Space Pioneers</h1>
        <h4>America's Unsung Heroes</h4>
    </div>

    <div id="article">
    …
    </div>

    <div id="footer">
        <p>The Space Pioneers web site is an example site, designed to accompany The Web↪
Evolved, published by Apress. Text: The Web Evolved; Design: Jonny Campbell.</p>
        <p>HTML + CSS released under a Creative Commons Attribution 3.0 license.</p>
```

```
        <p>Photography &copy; iStockphoto</p>
    </div>
</div>
</body>
</html>
```

http://thewebevolved.com/02/miss_baker_html_4.5.html

Testing this page in the HTML5 Validator results in Figure 2-3.

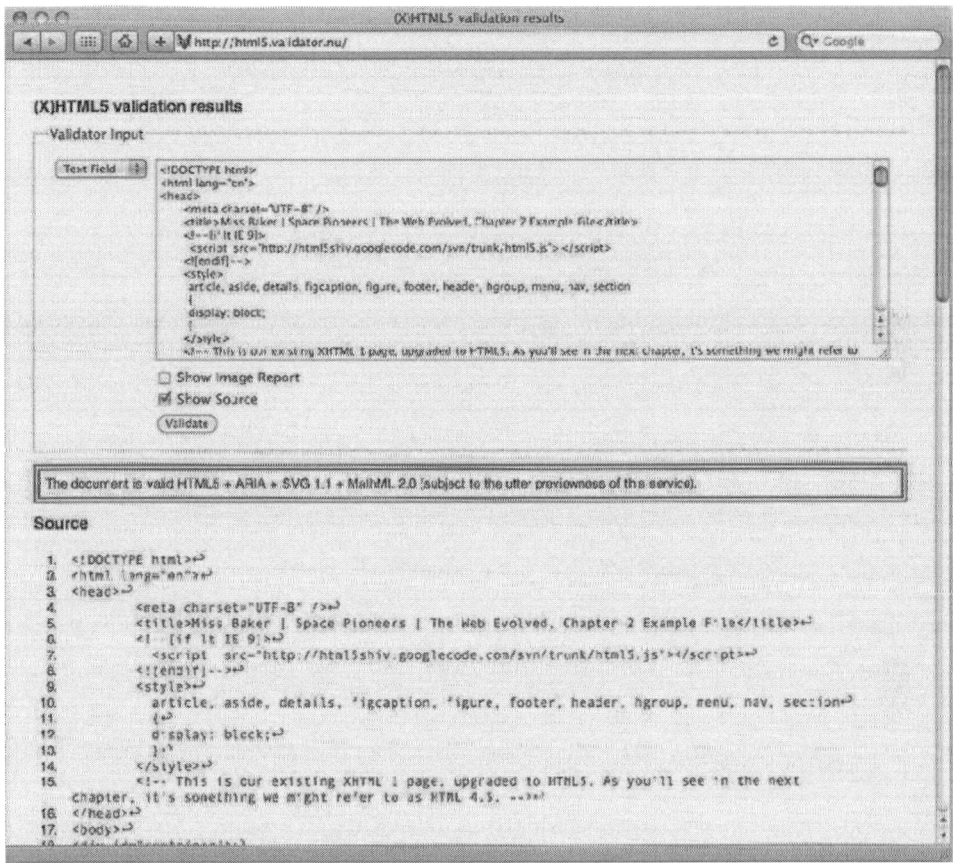

Figure 2-3. The updated Miss Baker page validates perfectly.

Testing it for syntax using HTML Lint results in Figure 2-4.

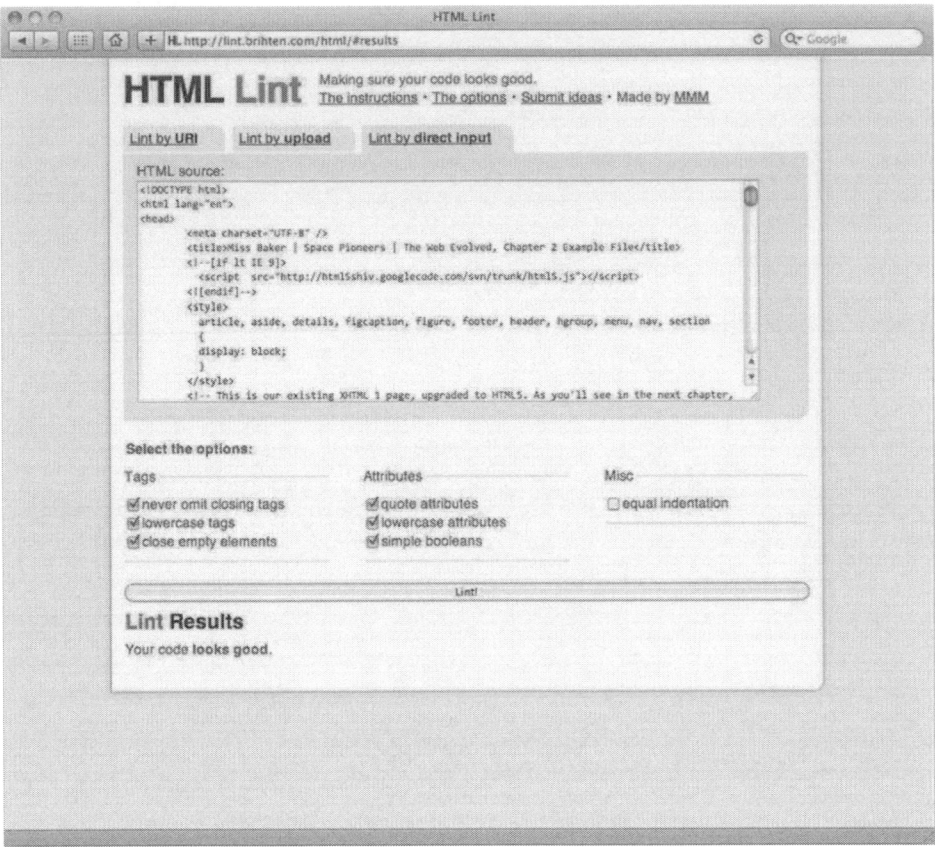

Figure 2-4. The updated Miss Baker page validates perfectly.

Simply changing the Miss Baker page's <head> element, without altering the markup in the body, results in a valid HTML5 page. It's that simple.

Summary

At this point we've gotten our hands dirty with HTML5 and learned the syntax differences between XHTML1, HTML4, "loose" HTML5 style, and stricter HTML5 with XHTML syntax (the latter is the one we recommend you use). We've also shown the new HTML5 DOCTYPE, the changes you need to make to the <head> of your documents to upgrade them to HTML5, and how to get HTML5 content working across all browsers, even older versions of IE. To round off, we presented an HTML5 boilerplate you can use as the starting point of all your HTML5 documents, and showed how best to validate your HTML5 markup. Easy, wasn't it?!

Homework

1. Create a "Hello World!" web page by referring to our examples in this chapter.

2. Validate it.

3. Revisiting your Gordo page, change it to HTML5 by following the examples in this chapter.

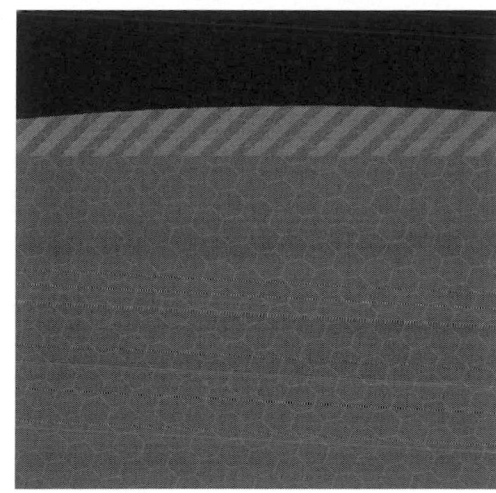

Chapter 3

New Structural Elements

As we saw in the exercises at the end of Chapter 1, *it's all about the semantics*. The mistaken idea of choosing our markup solely for its presentation, as epitomized by <table>-based layouts and spacer.gifs, has been thoroughly shown the door by the "standardista" movement. Instead, our rallying cry is

> *"Use the most semantically appropriate element."*

Happily, most of the time the default browser presentation of each element closely maps to its semantic meaning. This gives us accessibility benefits, as semantic markup provides a foundation of meaning regardless of presentation. It also has the benefit of future-proofing our content, allowing it to generally "just work" on new and alternative devices. Given the bright future of the so-called Open Web Stack as a ubiquitous platform, this is a pretty big plus.

In this chapter we'll look at HTML5's new elements for indicating structure, which are perhaps some of the most noticeable (and potentially confusing) additions to our toolkit. We'll also look at how they are used with related elements from earlier versions of HTML, the outlining algorithm that HTML5 introduces, and HTML5-style heading element levels. We'll then take what we've learned and apply it, comparing it to pre-HTML5 coding patterns. Finally, we'll look at other ways of adding the semantic meaning of these new elements for older browsers and address accessibility changes in HTML5.

But first, let's digress with a brief look at workflow…

Workflow practices, evolving?

Traditionally, web designers created beautiful pixel-perfect mockups using flowing lorem ipsum, then painstakingly tried to fit the *real* content in after the design was approved. Sadly, presenting flat mockups to clients is doomed to failure—if "pixel-perfect" was ever possible, with the current multitude of mobile devices, that age is long gone. Another thing that dooms this process is the *interactivity* of web sites. Without being able to even test link rollovers, these mockups are waxworks, uncannily lifelike but most certainly dead.

Instead, we prefer a workflow generally referred to as "designing in the browser." As the name implies, this involves creating mockups based on HTML and CSS, starting with content semantics and layout, and then moving on to details like color. For commercial work, this occurs after establishing the project's scope and goals with the client and deciding on a general design via sketches and mood boards. The mockups are then shared with the client during the process for feedback, rather than only the finished version. Naz Hamid succinctly sums up the benefits of this approach in this tweet:

You can prototype and *fail* faster than you would in a static environment. You get the *feel* quickly (http://j.mp/fail-faster[1]).

The standard of our preferred workflow is waved aloft most prominently by Andy Clarke, whose "Walls Come Tumbling Down" presentation (http://j.mp/in-the-browser[2]) helped bring this workflow revolution to prominence. While critics have argued that HTML and CSS can fundamentally limit your potential creativity, we think the same argument applies to any tool. Recent advances in CSS3 are starting to make Photoshop look fairly (dare we say it?) ordinary as a web design tool, and we trust that you begin your designs *the right way* with paper and pencil, before moving to the computer.

Some of you may be working in large organizations and are thus unable to influence your workflow. We encourage you to try this method for a personal project and see how it compares. You may find that your enthusiasm plus the mention of cost and time savings interests your manager. Others among you may have no knowledge of HTML and CSS, producing designs for others to implement. We hope that, having made it this far into a book on HTML and CSS, you are encouraged to continue learning. The more

---

[1] www.twitter.com/weightshift/statuses/161915550052786178

[2] www.stuffandnonsense.co.uk/blog/about/

walls_come_tumbling_down_presentation_slides_and_transcript/

knowledge you have of how your designs are implemented, the better your work will be. By the end of this book you will know enough HTML and CSS to make web sites.

While designing in HTML can initially be scary, discussing your progress (even when very rough) with your client helps both to include them in the process and to prevent any disastrous surprises upon reveal. Adding progressively more detail naturally focuses the client's feedback, avoiding comments like "I don't like that color" when you're discussing the layout (we find designing in shades of gray during the layout stage helps, too). Of course, you can also demonstrate interactivity and show the mockups working, including how different browsers display things differently, giving the client a much better idea of how the finished product feels. This is a big help in countering the "must look the same in every browser" fallacy and explaining the joys of progressive enhancement. Finally, you won't be constrained to a fixed-width layout because your client signed off on an inflexible mockup.

> Note: This is our preferred workflow for the moment; however, we also look forward to the day when someone creates an application that really is better than hand-coding. We are not alone, as indicated by the mass of comments following Jason Santa Maria's "A Real Web Design Application" article (http://j.mp/webdesign-app[3]).

Once your research, planning, sketching, and iterating are done, the next step—as in the Chapter 1 exercise —is to start *identifying and marking up the content*. In doing so, the onus is on us to know and understand the full range of markup at our disposal—a fundamental toolset of our craft. Let's start with the new structural elements of HTML5.

A brave new semantic dawn

In HTML 4 and XHTML 1, our markup choices were somewhat limited. While <div> is far more appropriate than <table> for layout, it's still just a generic container for flow content. We can add CSS styles using classes and IDs, and if we use names that describe the element's content (rather than its presentation), we can also use them to add additional, ad hoc semantics. However, while <ul class="nav"> and <div class="sidebar"> work just fine, the extra semantics we've added aren't accessible for users, and they're not even recognized by browsers (except for styling). We might just as well use <ul class="naomi"> and <div class="mike">.

---

[3] www.jasonsantamaria.com/articles/a-real-web-design-application/

> *Note: HTML 4 referred to* block *elements and* inline *elements. This becomes rather confusing when CSS is added to the mix, so in HTML5 these are referred to as* flow *elements and* phrasing *elements, respectively.*

So what's changed in HTML5? Well, one of the first things you'll notice once you start using HTML5 are the new elements for sections of a page (http://j.mp/html5-structural[4]), which we'll refer to as *structural elements*. These elements are replacements for the common ad hoc semantics for parts of the page that we applied using class and id attributes before, only this time with standardized *media-independent* semantics. These new structural elements are

<section>

<article>

<header>

<footer>

<hgroup>

<nav>

<aside>

> *Note:* Media-independent *just means it should work across different platforms, devices, and media. For more information, refer to the "Accessibility and HTML5" section later in this chapter.*

This chapter covers several other elements, including our old friends <div> and <h1>–<h6>, plus newcomers <figure> and its child <figcaption>, to aid us in comparing and contrasting the structural elements.

---

[4] www.whatwg.org/specs/web-apps/current-work/multipage/sections.html

FORGING NEW ELEMENTS

You might be wondering where the names of these new elements came from. In December 2005, Ian Hickson, the HTML5 specification editor, organized the Web Authoring Statistics study. This study analyzed the real-world use of class names, elements, attributes, and related metadata of about a billion documents. The findings on popular class names (http://j.mp/class-names[5]) revealed some common semantic patterns used by authors. While *not* using the class attribute was by far the most common practice, the most popular class names were as follows:

1. footer
2. menu
3. title
4. small
5. text
6. content
7. header
8. nav
9. copyright
10. button
11. main
12. search
13. msonormal
14. date
15. smalltext
16. body
17. style1
18. top
19. white
20. link

In this list, we can see several semantic indicators that map closely to new HTML5 elements, as outlined in Table 3-1.

---

[5] code.google.com/webstats/2005-12/classes.html

Table 3-1. Popular Class Names and Their Approximate HTML5 Element Equivalents

Class Name	HTML 5 Element
Footer	<footer>
Menu	<menu>
Title, header, possibly top	<header>
Small, copyright, smalltext	<small>
Text, content, main, body	<article>
Nav	<nav>
Search	<input type="search">
Date	<time>

So if you've been a good standardista and used meaning-based class names, *you* have helped choose these new HTML5 element names. Bravo! There are some that are a little more abstract, such as <aside> (which we'll meet soon) over class="sidebar", but in these cases the popular class name would have been *too* specific, limiting the element's possible use.

Structural building blocks: <div>, <section>, and <article>

Let's start by comparing three easily confused elements used to structure a page.

- <div>: The generic container we all know and love. It's a flow content element with no additional semantic meaning (http://j.mp/html5-div[6]).

- <section>: A generic document or application section, almost always with a heading (maybe in a <header>) and sometimes a <footer>, too. It's a chunk of *related content*, like a subsection of a long article, a major part of the page (like the news section on the home page), or a page in a web application's tabbed interface (http://j.mp/html5-section[7]).

- <article>: An *independent* section of a document or site. This means it should be able to stand alone and still make sense if you encounter it somewhere else (e.g., in an RSS feed). Examples include a weblog article (duh), a forum post, or a comment. Like <section>, these should have a heading and may have a header and/or footer (http://j.mp/html5-article[8]).

The difference between <div>, <section>, and <article>

Those definitions initially sound pretty similar, so let's compare and contrast them, starting with <div>.

The <div> element

In writing POSH (plain old semantic HTML), we should use the most suitable or semantically accurate element. While <div> has the semantics of a general flow container element, it doesn't have any semantic meaning beyond this, and it's used when there are no elements that are more appropriate (i.e., *all the time* in HTML 4). There is no requirement for the contents of a <div> to be related to each other.

---

[6] www.whatwg.org/specs/web-apps/current-work/multipage/grouping-content.html#the-div-element

[7] www.whatwg.org/specs/web-apps/current-work/multipage/sections.html#the-section-element

[8] www.whatwg.org/specs/web-apps/current-work/multipage/sections.html#the-article-element

The <section> element

The new HTML5 <section> element is similar to <div> as a general container element, but it *does* have some additional semantic meaning—the things it contains are *a logical group of related content*.

> Note: The *<section>* element represents a generic section of a document or application. A section, in this context, is a thematic grouping of content, typically with a heading.

<section> is also a *sectioning content element*. Along with <article>, <nav>, and <aside>, it indicates a new section in the document. Imagine making your page into a nested list of related parts, or using a word processor's outline view: the heading of each sectioning content element is a new item and indentation reflects nesting.

1. Example list item
2. Another item
    1. A nested item
        i. You get the idea

We'll cover how sectioning content elements creates HTML5 document outlines in "The HTML5 outlining algorithm" section later in this chapter, but the important thing to note is that <div> isn't a sectioning content element.

The <article> element

The new HTML5 <article> element is like a specialized kind of <section>; it has the more specific semantic meaning that it is *an independent, self-contained part* of the page. We *could* use <section>, but using <article> gives more semantic meaning.

Which one to choose?

To think about HTML 4, we can compare this choice to the choice between <p> and <pre>. Both are flow content elements for text, but <pre> is like a specialized kind of <p> with a more specific meaning ("this is a block of *preformatted* text"). The same is true with <section> and <article>; <section> means "related content," whereas <article> means "one piece of related content that *makes sense on its own*," even outside the context of the page (the page's header and footer, etc.).

The potentially confusing part of this is that <section> can be used for parts of a page and can contain <article>s (like the "Recent Articles" section of a home page) and can also be used for sections of a long <article> (*inside* an <article>).

So, to decide whether <article>, <section>, or <div> is appropriate, choose the first suitable option.

1. Would the enclosed content make sense on its own in a feed reader? If so, use <article>.

2. Is the enclosed content related? If so, use <section>.

3. If there's no semantic relationship, use <div>.

Except for occasional use to provide a hook for styles where there isn't already one, we expect the humble <div> will often be superseded by <section>, <article>, and the other new structural elements—where appropriate—in semantic HTML5. However, don't be afraid to use <div> where appropriate; it is still valid HTML5.

<section> and <article> are used like <div> is used in HTML 4; for example, these elements can't be used inside <blockquote> or <address>. Also, in general, avoid nesting an <article> inside another <article>. Use <section>s for indicating logical parts of an <article> instead. A notable exception to this is comments on a weblog article. Finally, the cases where <section> and <article> don't need a heading are in web applications (think of an e-mail application's main list view), but *it's better to add a heading,* even if you then hide it via CSS.

Basic structures using these elements

Here are a couple of examples showing the use of <section> and <article>.

A weblog article

Here's the structure we are working with:

- Weblog article
    - Heading
    - Content…

In HTML 4, we'd probably wrap the article in <div class="article">, etc. Obviously, we should use <article> instead in HTML5.

```
<article>

  <h1>Heading</h1>

  <p>Content…</p>

</article>
```

A long article with subsections (like a thesis)

Here is the article structure we are working with:

- Article
  - Heading
    - Section
      - Section heading
      - Content
    - Section
      - Section heading
      - Content
    - Section
      - Section heading
      - Content

Again, the article would generally be wrapped in a <div> in HTML 4, and the subsections would only be suggested by <h1>–<h6> elements. In HTML5, the article should be wrapped in <article>, and the subsections of the <article> should be explicitly indicated by wrapping them in <section> elements, perhaps in ordered list items if you'd like section numbering.

```
<article>

  <h1>Heading</h1>

  <section>

    <h2>Section heading</h2>

    <p>Content</p>

  </section>

  <section>

    <h2>Section heading</h2>

    <p>Content</p>

  </section>

  <section>

    <h2>Section heading</h2>

    <p>Content</p>
```

```
</section>
```

```
</article>
```

These are somewhat simplistic examples, so toward the end of the chapter we'll look at the structure of a basic weblog home page.

Headings: <header>, <hgroup>, and <h1>–<h6>, plus <footer>

Next, let's look at the new <header>, <footer>, and <hgroup> elements in detail.

> Note: Sectioning elements include <section>, <article>, <aside>, and <nav>, and also <blockquote>, <body>, <details>, <fieldset>, <figure>, and <td>. We'll cover this concept in "The HTML5 outlining algorithm" section later in this chapter.

- <header>: Used for *introductory and navigational content* of a *sectioning element*. This typically includes the heading (an <h1>–<h6> element or an <hgroup> element), but can also contain other content, such as a <nav> element or navigational links, a table of contents, a search form, or any relevant logos. It can't contain <footer> or another <header> (see http://j.mp/html5-header).

- <footer>: Used for *additional information* about the content, such as who wrote it, links to related documents, copyright data, a link to the top of the page, etc., and usually appears at the end of the content. Like <header>, it can't contain <header> or <footer> elements (see http://j.mp/html5-footer).

- <hgroup>: A specialized form of <header> that can contain only <h1>–<h6> elements. It is for grouping a heading with subheading(s) (see http://j.mp/html5-hgroup[9]).

- <h1>–<h6>: The heading elements from HTML 4 are back and basically unchanged, except for HTML5's stronger guidance on using them correctly (generally, don't skip levels), and the interesting addition of HTML5-style heading levels, which we cover later in this chapter. (http://j.mp/html5-h1-h6).

---

[9] www.whatwg.org/specs/web-apps/current-work/multipage/sections.html#the-hgroup-element

<header>'s defining purpose is to contain *introductory or navigational aids*, rather than define their placement (headers are usually at the top of a section, but not necessarily).

<footer> is for *related links, copyright, and author information*. A <footer> is usually at the end of a section but can appear at the top and more than once (for example, a "Top of page" link). For some content, there is some crossover in which of these elements to use—author information would be fine in either.

<header> and <footer> seem to suggest the page header and footer familiar to designers. Don't let first impressions fool you, however, as these elements apply to the current sectioning element. If that element is <body>, then the <header> or <footer> does apply to the whole page. But if it's another sectioning element, then <header> or <footer> only applies to that element. Think Russian nested dolls…in cute little angle brackets.

> Note: The *<address>* element has changed from supplying contact information for the page (only one per page) to being "scoped" by context. In HTML5, *<address>* contact information is for the nearest *<article>* or *<body>* element ancestor. As in HTML 4, it's not for literal addresses, unless the address is also contact information—a rare occurrence (for marking up normal postal addresses, refer to "Microformats" in Chapter 4). A list of recent articles on a home page could use *<address>* for each article's author name and bio link (or other contact information), assuming each post was an *<article>*.

A <header> or <footer> can itself contain sectioning content elements—for example, in a <footer>, this could be an appendix, index, long colophon, or license agreement. However, don't get too carried away because they *can't* contain <header> or <footer>. For a complex page header or footer that requires nested sectioning content elements with their own <header>s and <footer>s, use a <section> instead.

While <header> and <hgroup> are initially easy to confuse, remember that <hgroup> can only contain a *heading group* of <h1>–<h6> elements and is for subtitles, alternative titles, or taglines. <header> can contain an <h1>–<h6> element or <hgroup> *in addition to* other elements that introduce the section. If there's no other <header> content, only one heading (so no need for <hgroup>), and no need for a style hook, just use the relevant <h1>–<h6> element.

Let's look at some examples.

An article with one heading

This has a heading <h1> only. No <hgroup> or <header> is needed.

```
<article>

  <h1>Article heading</h1>

  <p>Content…</p>
```

```
</article>
```

An article <header> with heading and metadata

Now we wrap a heading and metadata in <header>.

```
<article>

  <header>

    <h1>Article heading</h1>

    <p>(<time datetime="2009-07-13" pubdate>13th July, 2009</time>)</p>

  </header>

  <p>Content…</p>

</article>
```

An article with an <hgroup>-enclosed subheading

This example has a heading <h1> and subheading <h2> in <hgroup>.

```
<article>

  <hgroup>

    <h1>Article heading</h1>

    <h2>Article subheading</h2>

  </hgroup>

  <p>Content…</p>

</article>
```

An article with heading, subheading, and metadata

Finally, here's an example of a heading that uses <header> and <hgroup>.

```
<article>

  <header>
```

```
    <hgroup>

        <h1>Article heading</h1>

        <h2>Article subheading</h2>

    </hgroup>

    <p>(<time datetime="2009-07-13" pubdate>13th July, 2009</time>)</p>

  </header>

  <p>Content…</p>

</article>
```

Some examples of <hgroup> use

In this section, you can visualize the effect of using <hgroup>. Here is an article heading with an alternative heading.

Here is a site name with a tagline (branding phrase).

Here is a long article heading split into a heading and a subheading.

Now, you may be wondering why you need to have both <header> and <hgroup>—they both appear to be a wrapper for <h1>–<h6> elements. Well, <hgroup> actually performs another function: hiding subheadings from the outlining algorithm. Let's take an exciting dive into the world of HTML5 outlines to work out what that actually means.

The HTML5 outlining algorithm

Being able to make a page outline automatically is a useful trick for browsers and robots alike. It could, for example, be used to generate a table of contents for a blind user, enabling them to quickly skim the page. To make a page outline from an HTML 4 or XHTML 1 document, we could find all the <h1>–<h6> elements and use each heading's number to indicate the level of nesting. However, subtitles would increase nesting, and many less-semantic pages skip levels for the sake of presentation, both of which would give an inaccurate outline. Also, an outlining tool would not be able to tell which titles are part of the main content and which are in the sidebar, for example, as both sets of headings are generally inside generic <div> elements.

HTML5 addresses this via a new outlining algorithm (http://j.mp/html5-outline[10]), which we touched on when mentioning sectioning content elements (a "plain old nested list"). While this may not sound exciting, it's a boon in making our content more accessible and usable. In addition, understanding the creation of outlines will explain a couple of otherwise confusing things. These outlines are formed from headings in *sectioning content elements*, such as <section> and <article>, which we've met, plus <nav> and <aside>, which define the major chunks of related content on a page.

The first <h1>–<h6> in each sectioning content element is used as the heading of that section in the outline, and any subsequent headings create an *implicit* enclosing section in the outline (http://j.mp/headings-sections[11]); that is, it's not in your code or the DOM, but the outlining algorithm pretends it is. Heading elements of a lower level make a nested implicit section, whereas the same or higher levels make a new implicit section after the current one and at the same level.

> *Note:* Implicit enclosing sections are how HTML5's outlining copes with errors and pro HTML5 content.

The exception to this is the <hgroup> element, which hides all but the first child <h1>–<h6> from the outlining algorithm and which we'll meet soon. Note that <header> is not a heading content element (spec-speak for <h1>–<h6> and <hgroup>) or sectioning content element, and it does not affect the outline algorithm.

---

[10] www.whatwg.org/specs/web-apps/current-work/multipage/sections.html#outline

[11] www.whatwg.org/specs/web-apps/current-work/multipage/sections.html#headings-and-sections

Outlining in action

That's all very well in theory, but what does it all mean? Well, let's have a look at some outlining in action to get a feel for what's going on. You can play along at home with an outliner such as h5o (http://j.mp/html5-outliner[12]) or (http://j.mp/gsnedders-outliner[13]).

The following is a basic HTML 4 example and its outline:

```
<body>

  <h1>Article heading</h1>

  <h3>Article subheading</h3>

  <p>Some text</p>

  <h2>Section heading</h2>

  <p>More text</p>

  <h2>Another section heading</h2>

  <p>A little more text</p>

</body>
```

Note that the article subheading shows up in the outline as the equivalent of a section heading because its heading is lower. However, its heading level (<h3>) doesn't affect the outline—it's only indented one level, not two.

1. Article heading (implicit section)
    1. Article subheading (implicit section)
    2. Section heading (implicit section)
    3. Another section heading (implicit section)

---

[12] http://code.google.com/p/h5o/

[13] http://gsnedders.html5.org/outliner/

Here is the same example in HTML5, using explicit sectioning elements and <hgroup>.

```
<body>

  <article>

    <hgroup>

      <h1>Article heading</h1>

      <h2>Article subheading</h2>

    </hgroup>

    <p>Some text</p>

    <section>

      <h2>Section heading</h2>

      <p>More text</p>

    </section>

    <section>

      <h2>Another section heading</h2>

      <p>A little more text</p>

    </section>

  </article>

</body>
```

No more article subheading, but a mystery "Untitled section" appears. Read on to find out why.

2. Untitled section
    1. Article heading
        1. Section heading
        2. Another section heading

Sectioning root elements

In addition to sectioning content elements, there's another group of elements that can have their own outlines.

- <blockquote>

- <body>

- <details>

- <fieldset>

- <figure>

- <td>

These *sectioning root elements* don't contribute to the outlines of their ancestors. In general, this means they hide things from the outlining algorithm that wouldn't be useful to include. While <body> is also on this list, it's the base element of the document outline. Like sectioning content elements, sectioning root elements define the scope of contained <header> and <footer> elements, and they're never children of implicit sections.

The scourge of the untitled section

So what happens when we have a *sectioning element* without a heading? As you may have guessed, we get a section in the outline called "untitled section." We saw this in the previous outline example—in that case, the untitled section came from <body>. Of course, "untitled section" isn't particularly helpful, so in general <section>, <article>, and <body> should *always* have a heading. For other sectioning elements such as <aside>, check the page with CSS disabled and see if the content still makes sense. If you don't want a heading to appear in the finished design, you can add one and hide it via CSS. This makes sure the heading is still available to screen readers and robots, and is sometimes done for accessibility in HTML 4 and XHTML 1 with <div class="nav">, for example. When in doubt, we recommend you add one—blind users (including Google) will thank you for it.

> *Note:* Sectioning element *is our shorthand for "sectioning content and sectioning root elements," because that's quite a mouthful.*

Here's another outline example showing how the outlines of sectioning root elements (<blockquote>, <body>, <details>, <fieldset>, <figure>, and <td>) are excluded from the outlines of their ancestors.

```
<body>

  <h1>Exciting simian adventures</h1>

  <article>

    <h1>Article heading</h1>

    <p>Some text</p>

    <!-- woops! we forgot the section -->

    <h2>Section heading</h2>

    <p>More text</p>

    <blockquote>

      <h3>Quote heading</h3>

      ...

    </blockquote>

    <h3>Subsection heading</h3>

    ...

    <section>

      <!-- woops! we forgot the heading -->

      <p>A little more text</p>

    </section>

  </article>

</body>
```

Here is the outline, showing sectioning root elements, implicit sections, and untitled sections in action.

3. Exciting simian adventures

    1.   Article heading

        1.   Section heading (note there's no <blockquote> heading)

1. Subsection heading (implicit section based on heading level)

2. Untitled section (<section> without heading)

In addition we can see that the implicit section creates a nested section due to its relatively lower header—<h2>Subsection heading</h2> would have made it the same level as "Section heading," but an <h4> header wouldn't have further indented the heading in the outline. Finally, the explicit "Untitled section" closes the previous implicit sections.

This outlining algorithm, and the creation of implicit sections for it, explains why we should always use a heading content element for at least <section> and <article>, why subheadings should be wrapped in <hgroup>, and why every heading element should be in its own sectioning element. However, it also has an interesting side effect: decoupling heading levels from the document outline.

HTML5-style heading element levels

In HTML authors are encouraged to use the heading elements <h1>–<h6> *rationally*—using the levels to indicate nesting, and not skipping levels—but this can be a problem in long or complex documents. There are some documents that actually need more than six levels of headings! (Actually, we always wondered what became of poor <h7>–<h9>.) Due to the outlining algorithm, there are now two ways we can use headings in HTML5.

- As in HTML 4, where the heading element (<h1>–<h6>) dictates the level of the content's importance (think of making an outline). <h1> is used for the page or article title, and subsequent headings increase rationally as required to indicate the outline.

- A new way introduced in HTML5, where the nesting of explicit sectioning content elements dictates the document outline. This means the highest-ranking heading element (<h1>–<h6> or <hgroup>) inside a sectioning content element (<section>, <article>, <nav>, or <aside>) becomes that section's header, regardless of whether this skips levels.

This new way is potentially much easier because heading levels in the document's outline become separate from the heading element used (and how the heading is styled using CSS). As most sections will only need one heading element, you could just use <h1> (almost) everywhere, styling based on number of <section> parents. However, current browsers won't interpret this correctly (e.g., when CSS is disabled), and this requires advanced CSS selector support to style, so for now we recommend that you don't do this.

Alternatively, because the use of explicit sectioning elements allows us to skip heading levels, you can use whatever headings you want (e.g., based on CSS styles) without worrying about using <h1>–<h6> rationally. Stylistic exceptions such as subtitles can be addressed via styles for <hgroup> or classes when needed.

Example of nesting heading element levels

This is a standard nesting of heading elements (uses <h1> to <h4>).

```
<article>

  <hgroup>

    <h1>Article heading</h1>

    <h2>Article subheading</h2>

  </hgroup>

  <section>

    <h3>Section heading</h3>

    <p>Content...</p>

      <section>

        <h4>Subsection heading</h4>

        <p>Content...</p>

      </section>

  </section>

</article>
```

Example of the new style for heading element levels

This example uses HTML5-style heading levels—new section resets (<h3> is skipped intentionally so that the subsection's heading uses <h4> styles).

```
<article>

  <hgroup>

    <h1>Article heading</h1>

    <h2>Article subheading</h2>

  </hgroup>
```

```
<section>

  <h2>Section heading</h2>

  <p>Content...</p>

    <section>

      <h4>Subsection heading</h4>

      <p>Content...</p>

    </section>

  </section>

</article>
```

Both of these will produce the same HTML5 outline.

4. Article title

   1. Section title

      1. Subsection title

As mentioned, in HTML5 all but the first heading element in a sectioning content element generate an implied section in the document outline. Because of this, it's recommended to *add explicit sectioning wrappers*. If you don't, make sure you don't skip heading levels.

Even more structural elements: <nav>, <aside>, <figure> (and <figcaption>)

Now we'll look at the other two sectioning content elements, <nav> and <aside>. We'll also touch on <figure> and its child <figcaption>, and compare them with <aside>.

- <nav>: A section of navigational links, either to other pages (generally site navigation) or to sections on the same page (such as a table of contents for long articles). This is for *major navigation blocks*, not just for any group of links. A rule of thumb is that you would add a "skip navigation" link for it (http://j.mp/html5-nav[14]).

- <aside>: A section of a page that consists of content that is *tangentially related* to—but separate from—the surrounding content. In print, this would be a sidebar, pull quote, or footnote. In a weblog article, this could be related information about the article, extra information in the margin, or the comments section (http://j.mp/html5-aside[15]).

- <figure>: For content that is essential to understanding but can be removed from the document's flow (moved to a different place) without affecting the document's meaning. This can be used for images or video, but it can also be used for any other content including a graph, code sample, or other media. Use the optional (and delicious) child <figcaption> to provide a label (http://j.mp/html5-figure[16]).

You're probably already using a <ul class="nav"> or something similar for site navigation. The <nav> element allows us to explicitly mark up groups of navigational links. This has accessibility benefits; for example, it allows users of assistive technology like screen readers to skip the navigation and go straight to the content, or skip *to* the navigation. We can use this as another way to decide if something is a major navigation block—would a blind user be helped by having that navigation accessible via a hotkey? While site and in-page navigation are obviously essential, content highlights in the page's footer probably aren't. The search box? Well, it depends...would the site's users think so? Note you'll still need the <ul> or <ol> element if you are using a list for your navigation (and you should be—it's the most appropriate element), but you can also include a heading or other relevant content. Here is an example of <nav> in use, with a heading (most probably hidden via CSS).

```
<nav>

  <h2 class="a11y">Main navigation</h2>

  <ul>
```

---

[14] www.whatwg.org/specs/web-apps/current-work/multipage/sections.html#the-nav-element

[15] www.whatwg.org/specs/web-apps/current-work/multipage/sections.html#the-aside-element

[16] www.whatwg.org/specs/web-apps/current-work/multipage/grouping-content.html#the-figure-element

```
    <li><a href="/">Home</a></li>

    <li><a href="/blog/">Weblog</a></li>

    <li><a href="/about/">About</a></li>

    <li><a href="/contact/">Contact</a></li>

  </ul>

</nav>
```

<aside> content should be additional to (but not essential to the understanding of) the main content; that is, *any* related content. While print design can provide inspiration, don't stop at pull quotes. For example, a footnote provides extra but unessential information, and a pull quote (while essential content) is a quoted copy of text from the main content. However, keep in mind the <aside> *must be related.* Having your site's sidebar in an <aside> as a child of <body> is fine, but site-wide information shouldn't appear in an <aside> that is the child of an <article>, for example. Also, <aside> would be appropriate for advertising, as long as it was related to the parent sectioning element. Here is an example <aside> providing extra information in the margin of an article.

```
<aside class="sidenote">

  <p><em>Sectioning root</em> elements are <code>&lt;blockquote&gt;</code>,
<code>&lt;body&gt;</code>, <code>&lt;details&gt;</code>, <code>&lt;fieldset&gt;</code>,
<code>&lt;figure&gt;</code>, and <code>&lt;td&gt;</code></p>

</aside>

<p><code>&lt;header&gt;</code> and <code>&lt;footer&gt;</code> apply to the current sectioning
content or 'sectioning root' element…</p>
```

<figure> content *is* essential, but its placement is not. Any part of a section that you'd currently use CSS positioning for would be a good candidate. Generally this would be referred to from the text, as shown next, but this is not required.

```
<p>… Here is an example of using <code>hgroup</code> for a subtitle.</p>

<figure>

  <img src="img/hgroup-subtitle.png" width="500" height="136" alt="hgroup example usage; an
article heading with an alternative heading" />

</figure>
```

You can also provide an optional caption for the <figure> using <figcaption>, as shown next, as either the first or the last child element.

```
<figure>

  <figcaption>An article heading with an alternative heading</figcaption>

  <img src="img/hgroup-subtitle.png" width="500" height="136" alt="hgroup example usage; an
article heading with an alternative heading" />

</figure>
```

Finally, <figure> can contain more than one piece of content, as shown next.

```
<figure>

  <pre><code>&lt;ruby&gt;&lt;strong&gt;cromulent&lt;/strong&gt;
&lt;rp&gt;(&lt;/rp&gt;&lt;rt&gt;crôm-yü-
lənt&lt;/rt&gt;&lt;rp&gt;)&lt;/rp&gt;&lt;/ruby&gt;</code></pre>

  <img src="img/cromulent.png" width="570" height="80" alt="Displaying ruby text after the
base text for an English dictionary">

  <figcaption>Using ruby text for a dictionary definition by displaying the ruby text inline
after the base text</figcaption>

</figure>
```

Choose between <aside> or <figure> by asking yourself if the content is essential to the section's understanding. If the content is just related and not essential, use <aside>. If the content is essential but its position in the flow of content isn't important (could it be moved to an appendix?), use <figure>. Of course, if its position relates to previous and subsequent content, use something else more appropriate! Remember too that <nav> and <aside> are sectioning content elements, so their headings will be added to the document outline. <figure> is a sectioning root element, so any child headings will be hidden from the outline.

Putting it all together

We've covered a lot of ground. To recap, HTML5 has several new elements for chunks of related content—basically a logical section of the document. Using these elements instead of <div> is more semantically meaningful and gives us added benefits (such as improved accessibility) for free. Let's review what we've covered so far and see how we can use these new elements in practice by converting a simple page to HTML5. We'll also look at a couple of alternatives to help you think about the new semantics without committing to using the new semantic elements.

New sectioning content elements in a nutshell

Here is a summary of the new elements we have discussed.

- <section>: A chunk of related content.

- <article>: An independent, self-contained chunk of related content that still *makes sense on its own* (e.g., in an RSS feed).

- <aside>: A chunk of content that is tangentially related to the content that surrounds it but isn't essential for understanding that content.

- (cf. <figure>: A chunk of content that is essential for understanding surrounding content but which could be moved (e.g., to an appendix).

- <nav>: A major navigation block (generally site or page navigation).

- <div>: A chunk of content *with no additional semantics* (e.g., for CSS styling hooks).

With very few exceptions (generally in web applications), <section> and <article> *elements should have a heading*, possibly in a <header> element with any other introductory information. We can use the following comment posted on the HTML5 Doctor website (following the article "The section element") (http://j.mp/section-heading[17]) as a rule of thumb for deciding between <section> and <div>:

> [C]onsciously add a title for each *<section>*, even if you then hide the title with CSS (as is generally the case with *<nav>* for accessibility). If it seems like content that shouldn't have a title when CSS is disabled, then it's most probably not a *<section>*.

> Oli Studholme

Remember, a heading with one or more subheadings should be in an <hgroup>. In addition to <header>, sectioning elements can also contain one or more <footer> elements with additional information, such as author (<address>) or copyright (<small>) content, related links, etc. It's important to note that <header> and <footer> apply to the sectioning element they're in (this is <body> for a page header or footer). Also, remember <header> and <footer> can't contain <header> or <footer> themselves.

---

[17] http://html5doctor.com/the-section-element/#comment-940

> Note: Sectioning elements include the sectioning content elements <section>, <article>, <aside>, and <nav> as well as the sectioning root elements <blockquote>, <body>, <details>, <fieldset>, <figure>, and <td>.

Finally, while the words "header," "footer," and "aside" all come with preconceptions, *their semantic meaning comes from the types of content they contain*, not from their presentation or relative placement. For example, <aside> could contain a footnote, and a <footer> containing a "Top of Page" link could appear at both the top and bottom of a section.

Now let's look at example structures for an idealized article page, using the standard layout of a page header (with logo, etc.), site navigation, a main column, a side column, and a page footer.

Converting a simple page to HTML5

Here's the outline of the parts of our page.

- Page header (site name, logo, search, etc.)
- Main navigation
- Main content (wrapper)
  - Article (main column)
    - Article title
    - Article metadata
    - Article content
    - Article footer
  - Sidebar
    - Sidebar title
    - Sidebar content
- Page footer

Figure 3-1 illustrates the page.

Figure 3-1. Article page layout

So let's write it in standard POSH (XHTML 1.0 style).

```
<!DOCTYPE html PUBLIC "-//W3C//DTD XHTML 1.0 Strict//EN"

   "http://www.w3.org/TR/xhtml1/DTD/xhtml1-strict.dtd">

<html lang="en" xml:lang="en">

  <head>

    <title>Article (XHTML 1)</title>

    <meta http-equiv="Content-Type" content="text/html; charset=utf-8" />

  </head>

  <body>

    <div id="branding">

      <h1>Site name</h1>

      <!-- other page heading content -->

    </div>

    <ul id="nav"><li>Site navigation</li></ul>
```

```
    <div id="content">

      <div id="main"> <!-- main content (the article) -->

        <h1>Article title</h1>

        <p class="meta">Article metadata</p>

        <p>Article content…</p>

        <p class="article-footer">Article footer</p>

      </div>

      <div id="sidebar"> <!-- secondary content -->

        <h2>Sidebar title</h2>

        <p>Sidebar content…</p>

      </div>

    </div>

    <div id="footer">Footer</div>

  </body>

</html>
```

Now let's convert that to HTML5 using the new structural elements.

> Note: We'll leave out the CSS and JavaScript for browser support covered in Chapter 2
> for brevity. Remember to add them if you're coding along at home.

```
<!-- 'HTML-style' HTML5 -->

<!DOCTYPE html>

<html lang="en">

  <head>

    <meta charset="utf-8">

    <title>Article (HTML5)</title>
```

```
</head>

<body>

  <header id="branding"><!-- page header (not in section etc) -->

    <h1>Site name</h1>

    <!-- other page heading content -->

  </header>

  <nav>

    <ul><li>Main navigation</li></ul>

  </nav>

  <div id="content"> <!-- wrapper for CSS styling and no title so not section -->

    <article> <!-- main content (the article) -->

      <header>

        <h1>Article title</h1>

        <p>Article metadata</p>

      </header>

      <p>Article content…</p>

      <footer>Article footer</footer>

    </article>

    <aside id="sidebar"> <!-- secondary content for page (not related to article) -->

      <h3>Sidebar title</h3> <!-- ref: HTML5-style heading element levels -->

      <p>Sidebar content</p>

    </aside>

  </div>

  <footer id="footer">Footer</footer> <!-- page footer -->
```

```
    </body>

</html>

<!-- 'XHTML-style' HTML5 -->

<!DOCTYPE html>

<html lang="en">

  <head>

    <meta charset="utf-8" />

    <title>Article (HTML5)</title>

  </head>

  <body>

    <header id="branding"> <!-- page header (not in section etc) -->

      <h1>Site name</h1>

      <!-- other page heading content -->

    </header>

    <nav>

      <ul><li>Main navigation</li></ul>

    </nav>

    <div id="content"> <!-- wrapper for CSS styling and no title so not section -->

      <article> <!-- main content (the article) -->

        <header>

          <h1>Article title</h1>

          <p>Article metadata</p>

        </header>

        <p>Article content…</p>
```

```
        <footer>Article footer</footer>

    </article>

    <aside id="sidebar"> <!-- secondary content for page (not related to article) -->

        <h3>Sidebar title</h3> <!-- ref: HTML5-style heading element levels -->

        <p>Sidebar content</p>

    </aside>

    </div>

    <footer id="footer">Footer</footer> <!-- page footer -->

  </body>

</html>
```

The changes we've made almost seem like a code spring cleaning. We've changed to the simple HTML5 DOCTYPE and charset introduced in Chapter 2 and swapped the <div>s being used for semantic parts of the page for the new HTML5 structural elements. Our code is different, but the "evolution, not revolution" aspect of HTML5 is obvious.

Note here we assume that the sidebar contains content that's not related to the article (such as recent articles, etc.), so it's a descendent of <body> (a *page* sidebar) not <article>. If it contained only content tangentially related to the article, we could make <aside> a child of <article>. Also, we assume that the page header and footer don't contain nested <header> or <footer> elements, as in that case we'd have to use <section> instead (remember that <header> and <footer> can't themselves contain <header> or <footer>).

So what about web sites where you're concerned about Internet Explorer users with JavaScript turned off, or your boss is the cautious type? Does this mean the exciting HTML5 elements we've covered are but a pipe dream? Fear not, gentle reader.

Introducing "HTML4.5": Adding HTML5's semantics via <div class="">

One aspect of HTML5 we keep coming back to is that it's a sliding scale, not all or nothing. In this spirit, we've invented a whole new meta-specification for you and we call it "HTML4.5". Rather than a W3C-style specification, this is more of an idea—we can use the parts of HTML5 we want without needing to go all out. In this case, we want the semantic goodness of HTML5's new elements, but without the fear of

Internet Explorer breaking everything. We can do this by using HTML5's new element names (and implied semantics) as <div> class names.

Of course, we don't get any of the benefit of built-in semantics. However, just *thinking about* HTML5's structural elements will make our code more logical and semantic. If you think you might convert to HTML5 in the future, the HTML5-elements-as-class-names approach should remove a lot of the pain of converting, especially with a little regexp magic.

Here's the XHTML 1 version using HTML5 element class names.

```
<!DOCTYPE html PUBLIC "-//W3C//DTD XHTML 1.0 Strict//EN"

  "http://www.w3.org/TR/xhtml1/DTD/xhtml1-strict.dtd">

<html lang="en" xml:lang="en">

  <head>

    <title>Article (XHTML 1), with HTML5 class names</title>

    <meta http-equiv="Content-Type" content="text/html; charset=utf-8" />

  </head>

  <body>

    <div id="page-header" class="header"> <!-- page header -->

      <h1>Site name</h1>

      <!-- other page heading content -->

    </div>

      <ul id="main-nav" class="nav">

        <li>Site navigation</li>

      </ul>

    <div id="content">

      <div id="main" class="article"> <!-- main content -->

        <div class="header">

          <h1>Article title</h1>
```

```
        <p>Article metadata</p>

      </div>

      <p>Article content…</p>

      <p class="footer">Article footer</p>

    </div>

    <div id="sidebar" class="aside"> <!-- secondary content -->

      <h2>Sidebar title</h2>

      <p>Sidebar content…</p>

    </div>

  </div>

  <div id="page-footer" class="footer">Footer</div>

  </body>

</html>
```

Here it is in HTML5, again using <div> with HTML5 element class names rather than the new HTML5 elements.

```
<!-- 'HTML-style' HTML5 -->

<!DOCTYPE html>

<html lang="en">

  <head>

    <title>Article (HTML5), with HTML5 class names</title>

    <meta charset="utf-8">

  </head>

  <body>

    <div id="page-header" class="header"> <!-- page header -->

      <h1>Site name</h1>
```

```
      <!-- other page heading content -->

    </div>

      <ul id="main-nav" class="nav">

        <li>Site navigation</li>

      </ul>

    <div id="content">

      <div id="main" class="article"> <!-- main content -->

        <div class="header">

          <h1>Article title</h1>

          <p>Article metadata</p>

        </div>

        <p>Article content…</p>

        <p class="footer">Article footer</p>

      </div>

      <div id="sidebar" class="aside"> <!-- secondary content -->

        <h2>Sidebar title</h2>

        <p>Sidebar content…</p>

      </div>

    </div>

    <div id="page-footer" class="footer">Footer</div>

  </body>

</html>


<!-- 'XHTML-style' HTML5 -->
```

```
<!DOCTYPE html>

<html lang="en">

  <head>

    <title>Article (HTML5), with HTML5 class names</title>

    <meta charset="utf-8" />

  </head>

  <body>

    <div id="page-header" class="header"> <!-- page header -->

      <h1>Site name</h1>

      <!-- other page heading content -->

    </div>

      <ul id="main-nav" class="nav">

        <li>Site navigation</li>

      </ul>

    <div id="content">

      <div id="main" class="article"> <!-- main content -->

        <div class="header">

          <h1>Article title</h1>

          <p>Article metadata</p>

        </div>

        <p>Article content…</p>

        <p class="footer">Article footer</p>

      </div>

      <div id="sidebar" class="aside"> <!-- secondary content -->
```

```
    <h2>Sidebar title</h2>

    <p>Sidebar content…</p>

  </div>

 </div>

 <div id="page-footer" class-"footer">Footer</div>

</body>

</html>
```

You may be wondering why these two examples are so similar—after all, only the DOCTYPE and charset differ! The answer is that one of HTML5's core principles is *compatibility* (http://j.mp/html-design[18], and <div> is still a perfectly cromulent HTML5 element.

Adding semantics to "HTML4.5" and HTML5 via ARIA landmark roles

Having just said that browsers won't get any semantic benefits if we use <div class="">, there is a way that we can bolt on semantics—via ARIA landmark roles (http://j.mp/landmark-roles[19]). The Web Accessibility Initiative-Accessible Rich Internet Applications specification (WAI-ARIA) is a W3C accessibility specification that provides a framework for adding attributes to identify features for user interaction, how they relate to each other, and their current state. For example, if you styled a link to act as a button, you could use role="button" to apply button semantics to the link. This makes a big difference to screen readers, for example, allowing users to more easily navigate and interact with our content.

The good news is that as long as we don't try to change the strong native semantics of HTML5 elements, it's fine to use ARIA in HTML5 (http://j.mp/html5-semantics[20]). Using the appropriate roles will convey our semantics, making those elements *navigational landmarks* for supporting screen readers. As screen

---

[18] dev.w3.org/html5/html-design-principles/#compatibility

[19] www.w3.org/WAI/PF/aria/roles#landmark_roles

[20] www.whatwg.org/specs/web-apps/current-work/multipage/elements.html#wai-aria

readers have been slow to implement HTML5 support, for now this applies just as much to the new HTML5 elements that *already* have these semantics (the belt-and-suspenders approach) as to our <div class=""> style. An added bonus is that we can validate our code when using ARIA with HTML5, something that wasn't possible in HTML 4 with the W3C Validator. Table 3-2 shows the default implied ARIA roles for HTML5 structural elements.

Table 3-2. Mapping HTML5 Structural Elements to Appropriate ARIA Landmark Roles

HTML5 Element	ARIA Landmark Role	Notes on Using the ARIA Landmark Role
<article>	role="main" for the main content	role="main" is for the main content of a document. There should be only one per page. The default semantics of <article> is role="article".
<aside>	role="complementary"	
<footer>	role="contentinfo"	Should be only one instance of role="contentinfo" per page.
<header>	role="banner" for the page header	This is for a page header only (not for an <article> header, for example), containing the logo, site name, search, etc. There should be only one per page.
<nav>	role="navigation"	

Reality rains on our accessible parade

But now for the bad news—at least one popular screen reader (Window-Eyes v7.5 in Internet Explorer) has significant problems when using ARIA roles on new HTML5 elements (http://j.mp/aria-support[21]).

---

[21] www.accessibleculture.org/articles/2011/04/html5-aria-2011

Despite this, we still think it's worthwhile to include landmark roles where appropriate, as there are other popular screen readers that *do* support this, while not yet supporting HTML5's native semantics.

Thankfully, most people using screen readers use more than one, and at worst the semantics will be the same as a standard HTML 4 page. Until the happy day when HTML5's native semantics are recognized, support the noble cause of increasing accessibility by adding these roles to your code when possible. After that day, a well-coded HTML5 page (using the new structural elements) will in general not need ARIA roles, thanks to HTML5's native semantics.

Accessibility and HTML5

Since we've mentioned that it's possible to use WAI-ARIA in HTML5, it's a good time to briefly touch on HTML5 accessibility in general. Unfortunately, accessibility is a topic of poor support, worse application, and passionate politics (otherwise known as flame wars), but at least the fireworks are pretty.

Luckily, the W3C HTML Design Principles are both accessibility-friendly and pragmatic. The "universal access" principles mention *media independence* and *access by everyone regardless of ability* (http://j.mp/html-design[22]). Media independence means that HTML5 features should work on a variety of platforms, not just in visual browsers. We'll see examples of this in the realigning of HTML 4's presentational elements in Chapter 4.

However, access by everyone hints at a more fundamental change in how HTML5 approaches accessibility. Traditionally, making content accessible has depended heavily on using accessibility-specific features, such as <img alt=""> and <table summary="">. Unfortunately, in the real world, such hidden metadata is hardly ever added, and poorly or incorrectly done when it *is* added. Because it's hidden, it also often becomes out of sync when the main content is updated. HTML5's underlying philosophy has been to expose this information by moving it into the main content, as it's often beneficial to all users. This has led to detailed guidance in the HTML5 specification about how we should ensure images, tables, etc. are sufficiently described, and that this should be done in preference to hiding the information inside attributes. This philosophy could be summarized as follows:

---

[22] http://dev.w3.org/html5/html-design-principles/#universal-access

> *"Where possible, trick authors into writing accessible content without realizing it." (http://j.mp/trick-authors[23])*

While this is somewhat sardonic, the new elements in this chapter (which all have "built-in" semantics) are obvious examples of how HTML5 sneakily encourages us to create accessible content by default. While great accessibility will always require extra work, we welcome this new approach, which should significantly increase baseline accessibility.

Accessibility techniques, evolving

It's important to note that not everyone is enthusiastic about the "pragmatic" stance HTML5 currently takes on accessibility staples like longdesc on <img> ("obsolete"!), and summary on <table> ("authors should use a different technique instead"!). However, as long as we stick to HTML5's design principles and focus on access by everyone regardless of ability, we can ignore the fracas.

The changes affect some of our standard techniques for making our content accessible, so let's cover the basics.

The alt attribute on <img>

HTML5 more clearly defines alt as "the <img> element's *fallback content*" (emphasis added), rather than just alternate text. The specification also states that (except in a few specific cases) alt *text is required*, and *must be an appropriate replacement for the image*. However, what is appropriate depends on the image's purpose.

- *Provides useful information*: The alt text should convey the same information.

- *Performs a function*: The alt text should convey the functionality.

- *Enhances aesthetics (e.g., a decorative image that doesn't add any information)*: While this depends on the case, most decorative images should have blank alt text (alt="").

Figure 3-2 shows an image with descriptive alt text, providing an appropriate textural replacement for the image.

---

[23] www.krijnhoetmer.nl/irc-logs/whatwg/20100604#l-479

```
<img src="/img/albert.jpg" alt="A close-up in profile of the rhesus monkey Albert I, looking
intently to the right. The background is out of focus and the photo is in black and white.">
```

Figure 3-2. An image with alt text that describes the image's content

Figure 3-3 is an image where the alt text contains the button's content—"Log in"—to convey its functionality.

```
<button><img src="/img/log-in-button.png" width="91" height-"43" alt="Log in"></button>
```

Figure 3-3. A functional Image with alt text describing the image's function

The image In Figure 3-4 is only for decoration, and because it doesn't convey any information, an empty alt="" is appropriate.

```
<img src="/img/swash-separator.png" width="64" height-"24" alt="">
```

Figure 3-4. A decorative image with empty alt text

In some specific cases, the HTML5 specification states we should use blank alt text (alt="").

- When the image is already described in the surrounding content, such as a `<figcaption>` (to avoid repetition).

- When the image is a part of a larger image, where another image contains appropriate alt text for all the images.

And in the following situations, as demonstrated in Figure 3-4, HTML5 says we *must* use alt="":

- When an image is solely for decoration (it isn't content; it provides no function or information beyond aesthetics).

- When an image isn't visible; for example, a stats counter (width and height must be set to 0).

- When an icon or logo appears beside text with the same meaning.

This means that the same image can have completely different alt text (or even alt="") depending on where it's used and what it's intended to convey.

> *"The intent is that replacing every image with the text of its alt attribute not change the meaning of the page." (http://j.mp/alt-guidelines[24])*

We can use the ARIA attribute aria-describedby="" to make an explicit semantic connection between the image and its description in content, but in general context makes this unnecessary. Remember that alt text is fallback content and not an image caption or title. Use <figure> with <figcaption> (which have the same native semantics as aria-labelledby), or the title attribute, for an image's caption or other extra information.

Here is an example of an image with fallback content provided in alt and a caption in <figcaption>. We could add aria-labelledby="albert" to <img> to explicitly associate it with <figcaption> (via id="albert") until user agents understand the native semantics of <figcaption>, but given the context, this probably isn't necessary.

```
<figure>

  <img src="http://famousprimates.com/images/albert.jpg" alt="A close-up in profile of↪

the rhesus monkey Albert I, looking intently to the right. The background is out of↪

focus and the photo is in black and white.">

  <figcaption id="albert">Albert I before his historic trip to space on 14th
```

---

[24] www.whatwg.org/specs/web-apps/current-work/multipage/embedded-content-1.html#general-guidelines

```
June, 1949.</figcaption>

</figure>
```

When writing alt text, imagine describing the page to someone over the phone. Refer to the HTML5 specification for more detailed advice (http://j.mp/html5-alt[25]).

The obsolete longdesc attribute on <img>

The longdesc attribute was intended to provide a link to a separate page with more information about the image. Because this was basically hidden content that was almost never used, and was almost always used incorrectly, it's now obsolete in HTML5. That means if it's already in your content, there's no change in (the lack of) browser support, but the HTML5 specification is encouraging you not to use longdesc, and you'll get an error from an HTML5 validator.

The recommended HTML5 alternative is to add this content to the current page, perhaps explicitly connected using aria-describedby="", which we just met and which allows us to move the description away from the image. If the content can't be included in the current page (for example, because it describes a very detailed chart and is too long), we can make a link to a descriptive page using <a>, which is basically the function of longdesc anyway. This makes the content accessible to all users, not just those with assistive technology browsers.

The obsolete but conforming summary attribute on <table>

First off, what does that even mean? Well, obsolete features give an error in validation, whereas obsolete but conforming features only give a warning. So it's a less severe way of saying "don't use this," but the message is unchanged.

The summary attribute was meant to allow a detailed description of a <table> specifically for users of assistive technology. Real-world use closely mirrors that of longdesc. HTML5 advocates moving this explanatory text into the main content and recommends that we should introduce any table that might be difficult to understand. This can be done in a variety of ways, such as in surrounding content, in <caption>, in <details> inside <caption>, via <figure>, etc. The ideal solution is to adjust the <table> layout and headings to make it easy to understand, so that an explanation isn't needed.

The following is an example of Table 3-2 ("HTML5 Element and ARIA Landmark role Comparison" table), which uses <caption>, <thead>, and scope, and is clear enough to not need additional explanation:

---

[25] www.whatwg.org/specs/web-apps/current-work/multipage/embedded-content-1.html#alt

```
<table id="mapping-html5-to-aria-landmark">

  <caption>Mapping HTML5 Structural Elements to Appropriate <abbr>ARIA</abbr>➥

 Landmark Roles</caption>

  <thead>

    <tr>

      <th scope="col">HTML5 Element</th>

      <th scope="col"><abbr>ARIA</abbr> Landmark <code>role</code></th>

      <th scope="col">Notes</th>

    </tr>

  </thead>

  <tbody>

    …
```

The obsolete axis attribute on <th> and <td>

The axis attribute allowed authors to place cells into conceptual categories that could be considered to form axes in an n-dimensional space. If that makes sense to you, well…

Moving right along, it was basically intended to be used by some future browser with a "table query language," presumably in a similar way to SQL accessing database information by allowing users to filter a table. It works by applying categories to header cells…at least in theory. More than ten years after HTML 4 was finalized, the axis attribute still has zero browser support and almost as little tool support. Luckily, in practice the scope attribute combined with a clear, well-coded <table> is generally enough to duplicate this functionality. You can see scope in use in the previous code example.

Other HTML5 accessibility issues

Several other areas of HTML5 accessibility are still being actively worked on, most notably the new elements <video>, <audio> (now with <track>), and <canvas>. We'll cover these in more detail in Chapter 5.

HTML5 accessibility: A new hope

Despite the challenges of accessibility issues, as the W3C HTML Design Principles state "access by everyone regardless of ability is essential" (http://j.mp/html-design[26]). For us as much as HTML5's creators, the important part is achieving this aim, rather than the specific techniques we use. With the greatly enhanced built-in semantics of the new elements, and media independence as a basic principle, HTML5 is already more accessible than its predecessors by default. And although it should generally be unnecessary in well-coded HTML5, having the ability to use WAI-ARIA as well lets us supplement accessibility when required—as long as we don't try to override HTML5's built-in semantics. Now all we need is for user agent support to catch up!

Summary

We've met a bunch of new, more semantic replacements for HTML 4's <div>, such as the sectioning content elements (<section>, <article>, <aside>, and <nav>). We've also discovered the algorithmic fun of outlines, which are based on sectioning content elements and headings (<h1>–<h6>). We've seen how outlines are affected by <hgroup>, implicit sections, and sectioning root elements (<blockquote>, <body>, <details>, <fieldset>, <figure>, and <td>). We've also covered how <header> and <footer> are used in (and scoped by) sectioning elements, had a look at HTML5-style headings, and learned about <figure> and <figcaption>. Putting all of this together, we've seen how to make HTML5 *and* "HTML4.5" pages, plus we've had a brief overview of accessibility in HTML5. All in all, that's quite some progress.

While HTML5 is evolutionary, these new semantics require us to rethink past habits while providing a new perspective. You can start using HTML5 just by changing the DOCTYPE, as covered in Chapter 2, and probably should make the transition a little at a time as you learn more. However, to really benefit from HTML5's new mindset, we recommend rethinking any current site from an HTML5 perspective. It's also a great chance to reevaluate your techniques and workflow and to replace now outdated ideas.

---

[26] http://dev.w3.org/html5/html-design-principles/#accessibility

Homework

We've been working on pages for Gordo and Miss Baker, so choose one and add HTML5's semantic elements *where appropriate*. As you do this, try forgetting your HTML 4- and XHTML 1-based assumptions of what elements to use, and more importantly any assumptions of what elements should look like. Focus on semantics when applying what you've learned in this chapter. If you feel yourself starting to slip down a semantic rabbit hole, take a deep breath and remember that semantic hair-splitting is not required. Sometimes there is more than one way to mark things up, and that's fine. If in doubt, remember that <div> is still perfectly fine to use.

Check your homework by doing the following:

1. Validate your pages.

2. Install and use the HTML5 Outliner (h5o) bookmarklet. Are the results as you expected?

3. View the page in a browser. While our page might look a little chunky, there should still be a clear visual hierarchy even with browser default styles, and everything should still make sense.

For extra credit, try doing this with another page you've made and see if your new semantic goggles have you seeing things differently.

Further Reading

There are articles on HTML5 Doctor for each of the elements covered in this chapter, which you can find links to at http://html5doctor.com/article-archive. If you found the outline algorithm section confusing, the HTML5 Doctor article on Document Outlines by Mike Robinson will help (http://html5doctor.com/outlines). Make sure to read the comments on each article!

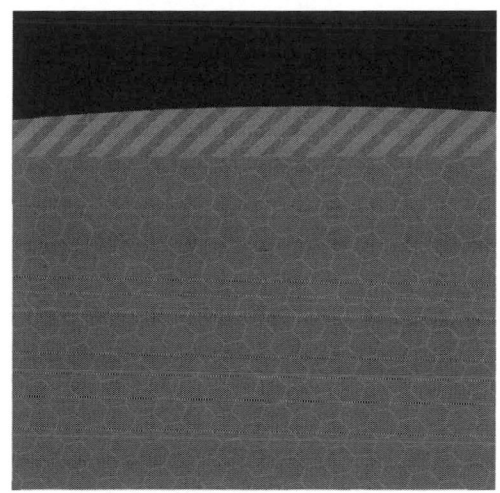

Chapter 4

A Richer Approach to Marking Up Content

Baking the best cake we possibly can

As we stressed in Chapter 1, creating a high quality website involves craftsmanship, and a big part of our craft is knowing how to use the tools involved. As HTML is the base of the "web trifle," being intimately familiar with it is essential. While the new semantic elements in Chapter 3—and stars like <video> and <canvas> that we'll cover in Chapter 5—get a lot of the attention, HTML5 also offers many small additions and changes. They may not be as exciting, but they'll help smooth your workflow. These additions and changes include elements you'll use all the time and new elements that are just right for certain kinds of content.

In keeping with "HTML5 as an evolution," changed HTML 4 elements have generally been realigned to better fit the evolving Web. There's also the underlying drive for *media independence*—ensuring each element will convey the same *semantics* regardless of the medium used, be it visual, aural, or tactile. While this can make definitions seem a little general or vague, it's of vital importance in increasing the web's inclusivity. This will only become more important in time, as more people use the Internet and do so on more varied devices.

This chapter covers HTML 4 elements that have been modified, redefined, or even made obsolete; tackles block-level links; looks at some new text-level elements; and ends with ways to extend HTML5, including using microformats and microdata. Let's begin with the realignments to some of our most well-used markup tools.

Ex-presentational elements and friends

While many HTML 4 elements have been brought into HTML5 essentially unchanged, HTML 4's *presentational elements* have either been made obsolete (replaced by CSS) or have been given new semantic meanings. This has been done because the presentational definitions they had were based around how they looked on screen, which doesn't help users of assistive technology such as people with visual impairments. HTML5 fixes this.

First let's look at the old font styling elements <i> and <b>, and compare them to semantic stalwarts <em> and <strong>.

- <i> was italic and is now for text in an *"alternate voice,"* such as foreign words, technical terms, and taxonomic designations.

- <b> was bold and is now for *"stylistically offset"* text, such as keywords, product names in a review, or an article lede.

- <em> was emphasis and is now for *stress emphasis*, such as something you'd pronounce differently.

- <strong> was for stronger emphasis and is now for *strong importance* (it's basically the same).

We'll also look at four more elements in HTML5 that have undergone the transmogrification to media-independent semantics.

- <small> was for smaller text and is now used for *side comments* such as small print.

- <hr> was a horizontal rule and is now used for *a paragraph-level thematic break.*

- <s> was for strike-through and is now for content *that is no longer relevant or accurate* (we'll briefly touch on <del> and <ins> for comparison).

- <u> was for underlined text and is now used for *a span of text with an unarticulated, though explicitly rendered, non-textural annotation*; read on to find out what that actually means!

Giving the <i> and <b> elements new semantic meanings

In HTML 4, <i> and <b> were font style elements (http://j.mp/html4-fse[1]). However, they now have semantic meaning and of course their default style can be changed via CSS (for example <b> doesn't have to be bold). Because of this **we recommend adding meaningful CSS class names** to make it easy to change the style later.

The <i> element

> The *<i>* element represents a span of text in an alternate voice or mood, or otherwise offset from the normal prose in a manner indicating a different quality of text.
>
> HTML Living Standard, WHATWG (http://j.mp/html5-i[2])

Things that are typically italicized include foreign words (using the attribute lang=""), taxonomic and technical terms, ship names, inline stage directions in a script, some musical notation, and when representing thoughts or hand-written text inline. Figures 4-1, 4-2, and 4-3 show examples.

DECKARD: Move! Get out of the way!

Deckard fires. Kills Zhora in dramatic slow motion scene.

DECKARD: *The report would be routine retirement of a replicant which didn't make me feel any better about shooting a woman in the back. There it was again. Feeling, in myself. For her, for Rachael.*

DECKARD: Deckard. B-263-54.

Figure 4-1. Using <i class="voiceover"> to indicate a voiceover (alternate mood)

---

[1] www.w3.org/TR/html401/present/graphics.html#h-15.2.1

[2] www.whatwg.org/specs/web-apps/current-work/multipage/text-level-semantics.html#the-i-element

> We ate *unagi*, *aburi-zake*, and *tako* sushi last night, but the *toro* sushi was all fished out.

Figure 4-2. Using <i lang="ja-latn"> to indicate transliterated prose from a foreign language (with lang="ja-latn" being transliterated Japanese).

> *Nanotyrannus* ("dwarf tyrant") is a genus of tyrannosaurid dinosaur, and is possibly a juvenile specimen of *Tyrannosaurus*. It is based on CMN 7541, a skull collected in 1942 and described by Charles W. Gilmore described in 1946, who gave it the new species *Gorgosaurus lancensis*.

Figure 4-3. Using <i class="taxonomy"> for taxonomic names

To check character sets for lang="" values you can use the excellent Language Subtag Lookup tool (http://j.mp/subtags[3]) by Richard Ishida, W3C.

Only use <i> when nothing more suitable is available, such as <em> for text with stress emphasis; <strong> for text with semantic importance; <cite> for titles in a citation or bibliography; <dfn> for the defining instance of a word; and <var> for mathematical variables. Use CSS instead for italicizing blocks of text, such as asides, verse, figure captions, or block quotations. Remember to use the class attribute to identify why the element is being used, making it easy to restyle a particular use. You can target lang in CSS using the attribute selector (eg [lang="ja-latn"]), which we covered in Chapter 8. Full sentences of foreign prose should generally be set in quotes in their own paragraph (or <blockquote>) and should *not* use <i>. Add the lang attribute to the containing element instead.

The <b> element

> *The <b> element represents a span of text to which attention is being drawn for utilitarian purposes without conveying any extra importance and with no implication of an alternate voice or mood.*

> HTML Living Standard, WHATWG (http://j.mp/html5-b[4])

---

[3] http://rishida.net/utils/subtags

[4] www.whatwg.org/specs/web-apps/current-work/multipage/text-level-semantics.html#the-b-element

For <b> text that should merely look different, there is no requirement to use font-style: bold;. Other styling could include a round-cornered background, larger font size, different color, or formatting such as small caps. The script in Figure 4-1 contains an example of this, as <b class="character"> is used to indicate who's speaking or narrating.

You could use <b> for product names in a review, key words in a document abstract, and the initial text on a complex or traditionally designed page, as in Figures 4-4 and 4-5.

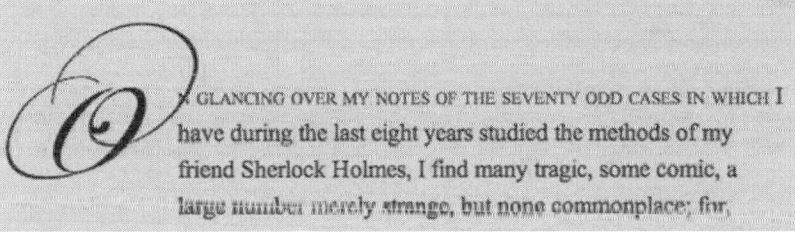

Figure 4-4. Connecting the versal (drop cap) with the text using <b class="opening-phrase">

The pseudo-element selector :first-letter is used to create the versal. In this case, the opening phrase is bold only for stylistic reasons. If it was semantically important, <strong> or some other element would be more appropriate.

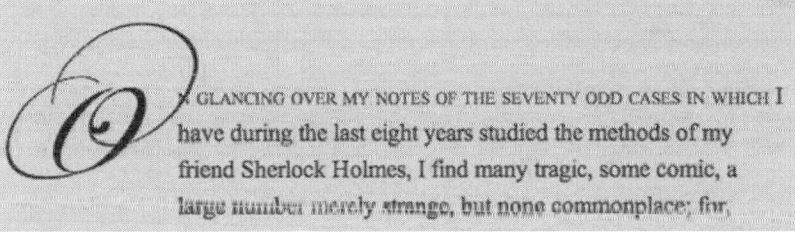

Figure 4-5. The CSS pseudo-element selector :first-line is more appropriate in this case

While we can use <b> to apply a traditional typographic style like small caps to the first word, phrase or sentence, the CSS pseudo-element selector :first-line is more appropriate in cases like Figure 4-5 (see Chapter 8 for more details).

Only use <b> when there are no other more suitable elements, such as <strong> for text with semantic importance; <em> for emphasized text (text with "stress emphasis"); <h1>-<h6> for titles; and <mark> for highlighted or marked text. Use classes on list items for a tag cloud. To recreate traditional typographic effects use CSS pseudo-element selectors like :first-line and :first-letter instead where appropriate (refer to Chapter 8). Again, remember to use the class attribute to identify why the element is being used, making it easy to restyle a particular use.

The <em> and <strong> elements

While <em> and <strong> remain pretty much the same, there has been a slight realignment in their meanings. In HTML 4, they meant *emphasis* and *strong emphasis*. Now their meanings have been differentiated into <em> representing *stress emphasis* (such as something you'd pronounce differently) and <strong> representing *importance*.

The <em> element

> *The em element represents stress emphasis of its contents.*
>
> HTML Living Standard, WHATWG (http://j.mp/html5-em[5])

The "stress" being referred to is linguistic; if spoken it would be emphasized pronunciation on a word that can change the nuance of a sentence. For example "Call a *doctor* now!" stresses doctor, perhaps in reply to someone asking "She looks thirsty, should I call a homeopath?" In comparison, "Call a doctor *now*!" changes the emphasis to doing so quickly.

Use <strong> instead to indicate importance and <i> when you want italics without implying emphasis. If an <em> element occurs in text that is already emphasized with <em>, the level of nesting represents the relative level of emphasis.

The <strong> element

> *The strong element represents strong importance for its contents.*
>
> HTML Living Standard, WHATWG (http://j.mp/html5-strong[6])

There's not much more to say, really—it's the <strong> we all know so well. Indicate relative importance by nesting <strong> elements and use <em> instead for text with stress emphasis, <b> for text that is "stylistically offset" or bold without being more important, or <mark> for highlighting relevant text.

---

[5] www.whatwg.org/specs/web-apps/current-work/multipage/text-level-semantics.html#the-em-element

[6] www.whatwg.org/specs/web-apps/current-work/multipage/text-level-semantics.html#the-strong-element

The <small> element

The <small> element represents side comments such as small print.

HTML Living Standard, WHATWG (http://j.mp/html5-small[7])

<small> is now for side comments, which are the inline equivalent of <aside>—content that is not the main focus of the page. A common example is inline legalese, such as a copyright statement in a page footer, a disclaimer, or (as in Figure 4-6) for licensing information. It can also be used for attribution. **Don't use it for block-level content** (paragraphs, lists, etc.), as this would be considered main content.

Figure 4-6. Using <small class="font-license"> to fulfil the requirements of a font license agreement

Another example is around an attribution, like so:

```
<small><a rel="license" href="http://creativecommons.org/licenses/by-sa/3.0/">Creative Commons
Attribution Share-alike license</a></small>
```

<small> text does not need to be smaller than surrounding text. If you just want smaller text, use CSS instead. Use <small> only on inline content. Finally, <small> doesn't affect the semantics of <em> or <strong>.

The <hr> element

The hr element represents a paragraph-level thematic break.

HTML Living Standard, WHATWG (http://j.mp/html5-hr[8])

---

[7] www.whatwg.org/specs/web-apps/current-work/multipage/text-level-semantics.html#the-small-element

[8] www.whatwg.org/specs/web-apps/current-work/multipage/grouping-content.html#the-hr-element

The "paragraph-level" bit means a block of text, such as <p> or <ul>, but not, for example, inline content or a heading. A thematic break is a change in topic, such as between scenes in a novel. <hr> is semantically the same as </section><section>, so it's better to use CSS instead of <hr> before or after sectioning elements and headings. However, you can use it anywhere you can use a <p>. While not widely used these days (given the dull default browser renderings), it can be replaced via CSS with an image, as demonstrated in Figure 4-7.

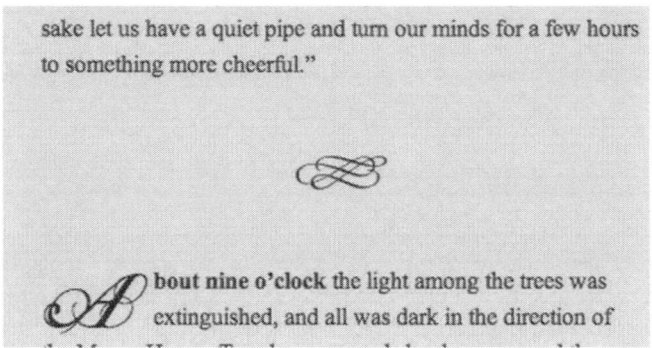

Figure 4-7. Styling <hr> by removing borders and adding margins and a background image using CSS: hr {height: 24px; background: url('flourish.png') no-repeat 50% 50%; margin: 3em 0; border: 0;}

IE7 and below live up to reputation by adding a border around the image regardless, but this can often be worked around (http://j.mp/hr-ir[9]). Alternatively, you can just hide it via an IE7-and-lower stylesheet. Finally, as demonstrated in Figure 4-8, <hr> isn't appropriate if the thematic break is obvious (for example, between weblog comments) or the intended use is solely presentational. Add a CSS border or background image (possibly using :before or :after, which we covered in Chapter 8) to another element instead.

Figure 4-8. Cork'd.com uses a decorative CSS background image on titles. This would **not** be a good place to use <hr>.

---

[9] http://blog.neatlysliced.com/2008/03/hr-image-replacement

The <s> element, together with <del> and <ins>

The <s> element was initially obsolete in HTML5, but has made a comparatively recent return to the spec as semantic use cases have come forward. The definition for <s> is succinct.

> *The s element represents contents that are no longer accurate or no longer relevant.*
>
> HTML Living Standard, WHATWG (http://j.mp/html5-s[10])

Initially this role was to be covered by the <del> element, which is defined as

> *The del element represents a removal from the document. del elements should not cross implied paragraph boundaries.*
>
> HTML Living Standard, WHATWG (http://j.mp/html5-del[11])

However, the semantics are slightly different. <s> is for content that *was* accurate or relevant, but is not anymore, and is being left to provide context. <del> is for content that (for whatever reason) has been marked as deleted from the document as part of a document edit, is not required to provide context, and may not even be displayed or communicated to the reader. Examples of <s> include an obsolete price or sold out event listing.

```
<ol> <!-- between April 7th and May 1st -->

  <li><s>Early bird (ends Apr 6): $799<s></li>

  <li>Middle bird (Apr 7~May 1): $899</li>

  <li>Late bird (May 2~May 23): $999</li>

</ol>
```

Since we're discussing <del>, let's also briefly look at its twin, <ins>.

---

[10] www.whatwg.org/specs/web-apps/current-work/multipage/ text-level-semantics.html#the-s-element

[11] www.whatwg.org/specs/web-apps/current-work/multipage/ edits.html#the-del-element

The ins element represents an addition to the document. ins elements should not cross implied paragraph boundaries.

HTML Living Standard, WHATWG (http://j.mp/html5-ins[12])

<del> and <ins> are unusual elements in that they can be used as phrasing or flow elements, so they can go inside a <p> element or contain a <p> element. The "should not cross implied paragraph boundaries" admonition tells us to not use them as both at once, or, literally, not from inside one <p> element to inside a different <p> element.

```
<!-- don't do this -->

<p>Be careful using ins and del.<del> They shouldn't cross a paragraph boundary.</p>

<!-- del's opening tag is in one block-level element, but the closing tag is in another -->

<p>You have two options.</del> Use an ins or del element inside each containing element, or
one ins or del element outside.</p>
```

```
<!-- instead, use two ins or del elements inside the containing elements -->

<p>Be careful using ins and del.<del> They shouldn't cross a paragraph boundary.</del></p>

<p><del>You have two options.</del> Use an ins or del element inside each containing element,
or one ins or del element outside.</p>
```

```
<!-- or one ins or del element outside the containing elements -->

<del>

  <p> Be careful using ins and del They shouldn't cross a paragraph boundary.</p>

  <p>You have two options. Use an ins or del element inside each containing element, or one
ins or del element outside.</p>
```

---

[12] www.whatwg.org/specs/web-apps/current-work/multipage/ edits.html#the-ins-element

```
</del>
```

```
<ins>
```

```
   <p>Be careful using ins and del. Use an ins or del element inside each containing element,
or one ins or del element outside.</p>
```

```
</ins>
```

We also have to be careful using them inside lists and tables, where they should wrap the content in, for example, an <li> element and *not* the <li> element itself.

<del> and <ins> can both have two optional attributes. The cite attribute is for adding the URL of a page that gives more information (such as explaining the reason behind the edit).

```
<del cite="/edits/r102.html">
```

The datetime attribute is for recording the date and time of the edit. The format is:

```
year-month-date then T then hour:minute:second then a timezone
```

Consider the following examples (these datetimes are the same time, but in different timezones):

```
<ins datetime="2012-03-05T23:16:00Z">
```

```
<ins datetime="2012-03-06T08:16:00+09:00">
```

We'll meet the datetime attribute again soon when we cover the <time> element.

The <u> element

As with <s>, the <u> element has recently returned from the obsolete section, with the following definition:

> *The u element represents a span of text with an unarticulated, though explicitly rendered, non-textual annotation.*

HTML Living Standard, WHATWG (http://j.mp/html5-u[13])

---

[13] www.whatwg.org/specs/web-apps/current-work/multipage/ text-level-semantics.html#the-u-element

Some examples of text with these "non-textural" annotations include Chinese proper name marks, indicating spell-checking feedback, and indicating the family name of a romanized non-western name. Outside of these three uses there's almost certainly a more appropriate element to use, but it's one more tool in our toolbox. Remember that *any semantic meaning should be present in the HTML layer*. While these use cases may seem diverse, the important part is the text is flagged for the reader's attention—they'll make sense of it in context.

Finally, as with all elements that have default browser styling, there's nothing to stop you changing the default underline styling to something more appropriate using CSS. For example, spell checkers often indicate misspellings with a red dotted underline, and a romanized Japanese family name may be indicated using upper case. These are easy to apply with `<u class="spelling-error">` or `<u class="family-name">` and a little CSS, as we'll find out in Chapter 7.

Presentational elements: relics of a bygone era

As we've seen, the HTML 4 presentational elements <b>, <hr>, <i>, <s>, <small>, and <u> have been redefined to be *non*-presentational in HTML5, with useful media-independent semantics that relate to their typical use. The other presentational elements that HTML 4 depreciated or discouraged—<basefont>, <big>, <font>, <tt>, and <strike>—have been made obsolete in HTML5. Use CSS instead.

Block-level links with the <a> element

Hyperlinks are the original "killer app" of HTML. However, historically linking more than some text or other inline content in an <a> element wasn't officially possible. This has also been something of an accessibility problem, as a large clickable area is a big help for those that have trouble using a mouse or anyone browsing on a touch-sensitive phone. The problem was also exacerbated by Internet Explorer 6's inability to style :hover on anything except the <a> element.

Our workarounds included making the link display:block; and stuffing it full of padding, or adding individual links to several elements to give the impression of one large clickable area (breaking DRY). Then there was just wrapping everything in a link, although this was incorrect according to the spec (and validation).

However, in general, it actually works. So in keeping with HTML5's practical bent, this gray-zone technique has become part of the spec. You can now officially wrap flow content in an <a> element, providing it does not contain any interactive content, including form elements and especially other links. This is easy to do and causes issues with Internet Explorer <8, so be careful not to nest one link inside another.

> *The a element may be wrapped around entire paragraphs, lists, tables, and so forth, even entire sections, so long as there is no interactive content within (e.g. buttons or other links).*

> HTML Living Standard, WHATWG (http://j.mp/html5-a[14])

Writing a Block Link

Now if we want to make several things in a heading into a block link, it's easy. Traditionally, making a block link involves lots of links plus CSS gymnastics.

```
<!-- faking a block-level link: don't do this -->

<header>

  <hgroup>

    <h1><a href="/">Space monkeys</a></h1>

    <h2><a href="/">Going were no primate has dared to go</a></h2>

  </hgroup>

  <a href="/"><img src="monkey-helmet.jpg" alt="A brave money all suited up"></a>

</header>
```

In HTML5, you can add a link pretty much anywhere—much easier.

```
<!-- HTML5 block-level link -->

<a href="/" class="block-link">

  <header>

    <hgroup>

      <h1>Space monkeys</h1>
```

---

[14] www.whatwg.org/specs/web-apps/current-work/multipage/text-level-semantics.html#the-a-element

```
    <h2>Going were no primate has dared to go</h2>

  </hgroup>

  <img src="monkey-helmet.jpg" alt="A brave money all suited up">

 </header>

</a>
```

By default, links are treated as {display:inline;}, so you may need to set {display:block;} or {display:inline-block;} for some styles to apply. Block-level elements like <h1> inside a block-level link will not inherit some link styles, so you may need to explicitly declare them using inherit, such as h1 {background-color:inherit;}. You can do this using a class name like <a class="block-link">.

Browser caveats with Firefox <4

This all sounds great, but as per usual there's one or two little wrinkles to catch us out. In Firefox versions before Firefox 4 (which is sporting a sexy new HTML5-based DOM model), if the block-level link's first child is one of the new HTML5 elements we met in Chapter 3, the block-level link will be closed, and individual inline links will be added for each block-level element. While the contained content is still linked and usable, this also generally means that the block level link's :hover etc styles won't look quite right.

One solution is to **add a <div> wrapper** (or another HTML 4 element) just inside the block-level link.

```
<div>

  <a href="/">

    <div><!-- wrapper div for Firefox 3.x and below -->

      <hgroup>

        <h1>Title</h1>

        <h2>Subtitle</h2>

      </hgroup>

    </div>

  </a>

</div>
```

Firefox 3.x handles tag mismatch errors in block-level links … poorly. When in doubt, validate.

Unfortunately, using a <div> wrapper isn't a magic bullet. There is still the small potential for this problem due to Firefox's mysterious "packet boundary" bug, again fixed in Firefox 4. This only shows up occasionally, and not on every block-level link (making it mighty difficult to test for), but again the links will still work. Luckily, given Firefox's fast upgrade cycle, the packet boundary issue is probably too minor (both in affected users and bug severity) to bother worrying about—unless your site has a large number of pre-Firefox 4 users.

Other elements with minor changes from HTML 4

A few other elements have seen their usage slightly changed in HTML5 or have new attributes. Let's look at these elements and attributes, including <ol> and the associated attributes type, start, value and reverse, <dl>, and <cite>.

The <ol> element and related new (and old) attributes

While <ol> is the same ordered list containing list items wrapped in <li> elements from HTML 4, in HTML5 it now has the new reversed attribute. There are also some *ex-presentational* attributes dropped from HTML 4 that have returned—type and start for <ol>, and value for <li>. As with the ex-presentational elements, covered earlier, these attributes actually have semantic meaning, and semantics belongs in HTML. Let's look at how we can use each of these attributes in turn.

The type attribute

Generally an ordered list's counter style is presentational and should be handled in CSS. But in some documents it can be part of the document's *meaning*, such as legal or technical documents that refer to non-decimal list items in prose. In these cases, we can specify the list's style in HTML using the type attribute, as seen in Table 4-1.

Table 4-1. Type Attribute Values and the Corresponding List Counter Types

<ol type=""> values	Equivalent list-style type
type-"1"	decimal (1, 2, 3, 4... the default style)
type="a"	lower-alpha (a, b, c, d...)
type="A"	upper-alpha (A, B, C, D...)
type="i"	lower-roman (i, ii, iii, iv...)
type="I"	upper-roman (I, II, III, IV...)

The start and value attributes

The start attribute lets us set the ordered list's first counter, handy for splitting a list over several <ol> elements, but continuing the second list's numbering from where the previous list left off. The related value attribute lets us set an <li>'s value, allowing us to manually number one or more list items. The following code shows how to use start or value to continue a list and also demonstrates type:

```
<!-- Continuing a previous list with value="" -->

<ol type="I">

  <li value="7">seventh item</li>

  <li>eighth item</li>

  <li>ninth item</li>

</ol>


<!-- Continuing a previous list with start="" -->

<ol type="I" start="7">

  <li>seventh item</li>

  <li>eighth item</li>

  <li>ninth item</li>

</ol>
```

While these are handy additions to our HTML toolbox, adding or removing list items can make the numbering appear broken. For this reason, you will probably want to investigate CSS-generated content counters instead; read "Automatic numbering with CSS Counters" by David Storey (http://j.mp/css-counters[15]). You'll also need them for nested list counters like "1.2.1".

---

[15] http://dev.opera.com/articles/view/automatic-numbering-with-css-counters

The reversed attribute

<ol reversed> is completely new and allows us to create *descending* lists, which are very handy for top ten lists and rocket launches. While browser support for reversed is nascent at the time of writing, we can always fake it using value, which, like the other HTML 3.2 attributes, is still supported by all browsers. This is handy as we can use Modernizr together with a JavaScript polyfill to easily add support (for the definition of polyfill, see Chapter 2). For more information on this (and on all of these attributes), refer to our more detailed article "The ol Element and Related Attributes: type, start, value, and reversed" (http://j.mp/ol-attrib[16]).

The <dl> element

In HTML 4, <dl> was for definition lists and was the topic of some heated debate amongst standardistas. Depending on whom you talked to, it was either solely for dictionary-style definitions or potentially a container suitable for all sorts of content: conversations, addresses, you name it. HTML 4's somewhat loose description and unusual examples didn't help.

In HTML5, things have become a lot clearer. The biggest change is it's now a *description list* for *name-value pairs*.

> The dl element represents an association list consisting of zero or more name-value groups (a description list). ... Name-value groups may be terms and definitions, metadata topics and values, questions and answers, or any other groups of name-value data.

> HTML Living Standard, WHATWG (http://j.mp/html5-dl[17])

Our new description list still uses good old <dt> for names and <dd> for values, and we can still have multiples of each (hence "groups"). One new caveat is that a <dt> name may only be used once per <dl>, requiring us to list all relevant <dd> values together under the relevant <dt> (or group of <dt>s), rather than repeat names.

While the HTML5 specification is a lot more specific about what <dl> now is, it actually has fairly wide-ranging uses.

---

[16] http://html5doctor.com/ol-element-attributes

[17] www.whatwg.org/specs/web-apps/current-work/multipage/grouping-content.html#the-dl-element

Defining words in a dictionary or glossary

This is still a perfect use of <dl>, as long as we denote the word being defined with the semantically appropriate "defining instance" <dfn> element.

```
<dl>

  <dt lang="en"><dfn>rocket</dfn></dt>

  <dt lang="ja"><dfn>ロケット</dfn></dt>

  <dd lang="en">A vehicle that is propelled by the high-speed expulsion of exhaust gases, from propellants the vehicle carries.</dd>

</dl>
```

Metadata

Metadata often consists of names and values. For example, the EXIF data of a photo could be displayed using <dl>.

```
<dl>

  <dt>Camera</dt>

  <dd>Canon EOS 5D Mark II</dd>

  <dt>Exposure</dt>

  <dd>0.01 sec (1/100)</dd>

  <dt>Aperture</dt>

  <dd>f/1.2</dd>

</dl>
```

While the HTML 4 specification showed an example using <dl> for a dialog, this is no longer a valid use. Use <p> or perhaps <ol> with <li> as the container; if necessary, use <b> for marking up speaker names.

While we've shown some good uses, and one inappropriate one, some content may be harder to decide. If you're not sure a <dl> would be appropriate, consider if a <table> (for more semantic structure) or just <h1>-<h6> with paragraphs (for values with a lot of content) would be better suited to the content instead.

The <cite> element

This element has also been the subject of much debate, again due to a wooly HTML 4 specification. Despite some use of <cite> to cite people (most notably by Mark Pilgrim and Jeremy Keith), the HTML5 specification now says

> *The cite element represents the title of a work. [...] A person's name is not the title of a work—even if people call that person a piece of work—and the element must therefore not be used to mark up people's names.*

> HTML Living Standard, WHATWG (http://j.mp/html5-cite[18])

The spec lists these examples of "a piece of work:"

- Book

- Paper

- Essay

- Poem

- Score

- Song

- Script

- Film

- TV show

- Game

- Sculpture

- Painting

---

[18] www.whatwg.org/specs/web-apps/current-work/multipage/text-level-semantics.html#the-cite-element

- Theatre production

- Play

- Opera

- Musical

- Exhibition

- Legal case report, etc.

Using <cite>

Here are examples of citing a book, with and without a link.

```
<p>While Remy and Bruce did a masterful job on <cite>Introducing HTML5</cite>, I'm not sure
about that shade of brown.</p>
```

```
<p>While Remy and Bruce did a masterful job on <cite><a
href="http://introducinghtml5.com/">Introducing HTML5</a></cite>, I'm not sure about that
shade of brown.</p>
```

When not to use <cite>

The HTML5 specification does not explicitly list web pages as an example of a "piece of work" and adding a link with <a> is enough, unless you're specifically after a more academic-style citation. This is just as well, as otherwise we'd be wrapping every link to an external site in <cite>. Here is an academic-style citation for a quote in <blockquote>:

```
<blockquote>

    <p>A person's name is not the title of a work – even if people call that person a piece of
work</p>

</blockquote>
```

```
<p><cite><a href="http://www.whatwg.org/specs/web-apps/current-work/multipage/text-level-
semantics.html#the-cite-element">HTML Living Standard</a></cite>, WHATWG, retrieved 25 March
2012</p>
```

Assuming you have *not* decided to cling to the HTML 4 definition of <cite> that included people, any names could be marked up using <b>. We recommend you consider using microdata or microformats to semantically indicate people (we'll cover both soon). Also, beware of using <cite> when you want to quote some text, as an inline quotation should use <q> (or even just the appropriate apostrophes, such as "").

New semantic elements

Now let's meet some new elements that plug semantic gaps in HTML: <mark>, <time>, and the threesome of <ruby>, <rt>, and <rp>. These will help us semantically expose some specific kinds of data that we just haven't had the tools for up until now.

The <mark> element

This new element is for indicating text that you are specifically trying to highlight or draw attention to, *without* changing its importance or emphasis. The spec description sounds rather unspecific.

> *The mark element represents a run of text in one document marked or highlighted for reference purposes, due to its relevance in another context.*
>
> HTML Living Standard, WHATWG (http://j.mp/html5-mark[19])

However, for a certain kind of content, it's just what you always wanted. To make things clearer, there are several concrete use cases.

- Indicating a searched-for word or phrase in a search results page.

- Indicating specific code of interest in a code sample such as a change that's discussed in the surrounding text

- Highlighting part of a quotation that wasn't emphasized in the original.

Highlighting search terms is something we can all imagine, but not something we'll do often, so let's look at some code examples instead. To achieve the same formatting, we could use the following HTML:

<p>While Remy and Bruce did a masterful job on <mark><cite></mark>Introducing

HTML5<mark></cite></mark>, I'm not sure about that shade of brown.</p>

While Remy and Bruce did a masterful job on **<cite>**Introducing HTML5**</cite>**, I'm not sure about that shade of brown.

---

[19] www.whatwg.org/specs/web-apps/current-work/multipage/text-level-semantics.html#the-mark-element

Note that in indicating relevance, <mark> is different from <em> and <strong>. This is very handy in a quote where the original text already contains <em> or <strong>, but where you want to draw attention to an especially relevant part (the result is shown in Figure 4-9).

```
<blockquote>

  <p><strong>Dogs are the best!</strong> They are <em>obviously</em> much cooler than monkeys,
even if <mark>the first animal in space was a monkey</mark>.</p>

</blockquote>
```

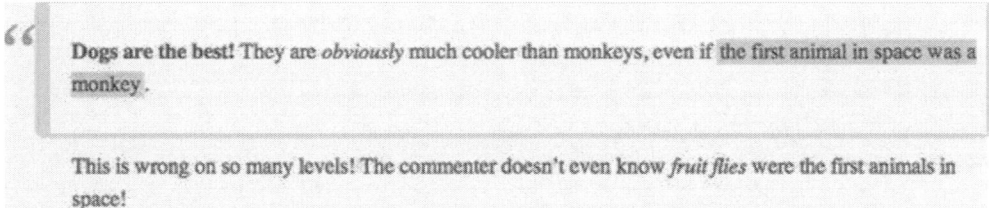

Figure 4-9. An example rendering of quoted text that contains <em>, <strong>, and <mark>

As usual, consider if there isn't a more semantically appropriate element. In addition to <strong>, <em>, <b>, and <i>, use <a> with no href attribute for indicating the current page (active tab) in navigation and a class on <a> instead for permalinks. <mark> isn't something you'll need every day, but now you know how to use it.

Ruby annotations with <ruby>, <rt>, and <rp>

Ruby text is a short annotation of some base text. It's typically used to give pronunciation guidance in a phonetic script for hanzi or kanji in Chinese, Japanese, and Korean (CJK) languages. It's named after an old printers' term for the very small size of 5.5 points.

> *The ruby element allows one or more spans of phrasing content to be marked with ruby annotations.*
>
> HTML Living Standard, WHATWG (http://j.mp/html5-ruby[20])

---

[20] www.whatwg.org/specs/web-apps/current-work/multipage/text-level-semantics.html#the-ruby-element

As the name implies, ruby text is small, displayed by default above the base text in horizontal text and to the right in vertical text. Browsers without <ruby> support put the ruby text inline after the base text.

These are the elements used in creating ruby text in HTML5:

- <ruby> is an inline element that contains base text with ruby annotations and optional ruby parentheses.

- <rt> is for ruby text, coming after the base text it defines.

- <rp> is for ruby parentheses, an element used to wrap opening and closing parentheses around <rt> (ruby text). These are for user agents that don't support ruby text, so that it makes sense when displayed inline. Browsers that support <ruby> hide <rp> via {display:none;}.

If you've never seen ruby in action, you're probably wondering what I'm talking about, so Figure 4-10 shows an example from a Japanese comic. The tiny characters are ruby annotations for the kanji to their left, showing readers the correct pronunciation.

Figure 4-10. Ruby text (called *furigana* in Japanese) in the *manga* Vagabond by Inoue Takehiko

As is often the way with internationalization features, browser support is, well, sparse. In a break from your expectations, Internet Explorer has supported <ruby> since IE5—three years before the actual 2001 W3C

Ruby Annotation specification! While this specification was incorporated into XHTML 1.1, no browser ever implemented it.

<ruby> in HTML5 is based on a reverse-engineering of IE's implementation and is simpler than the old Ruby Annotation specification. WebKit browsers added HTML5 <ruby> support at the start of 2010, but Firefox and Opera have yet to implement <ruby> natively. There are also CSS3 properties for ruby support in CSS Text Layout Module Level 3, but again these have poor implementation. Luckily, there is a CSS 2.1-based polyfill and a community add-on for detecting support via Modernizr. First, we'll look at how to use it for English, before showing the polyfill.

Using <ruby> for English

Not everyone is using East Asian languages, but any short annotation is (theoretically) applicable and no polyfill is required. While English doesn't typically have pronunciation guidance, phonetic annotations are used in dictionaries. The following code uses ruby text for a dictionary definition by displaying the ruby text inline after the base text. We've used the <dfn> element to indicate this is the *defining instance* of the term (see the results in Figure 4-11).

```
<style> /* display rt and rp elements inline */

  rt, rp {display: inline; font-size: 100%;}

  dfn {font-weight: bold; font-style: normal;}

</style>

<ruby><dfn>cromulent</dfn> <rp>(</rp><rt>crôm-yü-lənt</rt><rp>)</rp></ruby>
```

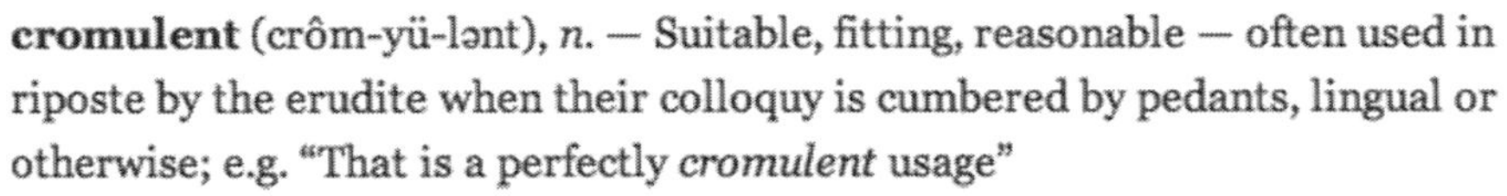

> **cromulent** (crôm-yü-lənt), *n.* — Suitable, fitting, reasonable — often used in riposte by the erudite when their colloquy is cumbered by pedants, lingual or otherwise; e.g. "That is a perfectly *cromulent* usage"

Figure 4-11. Using ruby text for a dictionary definition by displaying the ruby text inline after the base text.

We definitely see <ruby> as semantic (and valuable) for *phonetic annotation* in the same way that the <abbr> element's title attribute provides extra information on potentially confusing content. Outside of this usage, however, <ruby> could be seen as a presentational hack. Much like <q>, the extra code of using <ruby> may not be justified when the default presentation is the same as plain text.

The <ruby>, <rt>, and <rp> elements are valid HTML5, and even if they're not widely supported, they will by default display *as if they were* <span>s in non-supporting browsers. Combined with the ability to polyfill support, we say use them *if* you actually need the semantics of <ruby>, such as for CJK phonetic annotations (see the next section). For non-phonetic annotation, consider using <abbr title=""> to give an expanded reading via mouse-over for an abbreviation or acronym, unless displaying the reading by default is important. Consider <small> for *phrasing content*-level side comments like legalese.

Polyfilling <ruby> support for East Asian languages

As <ruby>'s polyfill only requires Modernizr and CSS, let's look at how to implement it for East Asian text as an example of polyfilling (which will give you an idea of how to use it in other situations where you genuinely need its annotations). First, we'll need a custom build of the Modernizr script that includes the "elem-ruby" add-on to detect <ruby> support. You can get this by going to www.modernizr.com and choosing "Production: configure your build." In the configuration window, make sure you've selected at least

- Extra ➤ Modernizr.load

- Extensibility ➤ Modernizr.addTest

- Community add-ons ➤ elem-ruby

Add this script to your page's <head> after your stylesheet references:

```
<!DOCTYPE html>

<html lang="en">

  <head>

    <meta charset="utf-8">

    <title>Ruby test</title>

    <link rel="stylesheet" href="main.css">

    <script src="modernizr.js"></script><!-- for ruby -->

  </head>

  ...
```

After successfully adding the script, inspecting the page using your browser's developer tools will show that the <html> starting tag has been updated by Modernizr to <html lang="en" **class="js ruby"**> for supporting browsers or <html lang="en" **class="js no-ruby"**> for non-supporting browsers (assuming

113

JavaScript is not disabled). We can now use the `no-ruby` class in our stylesheet to add our CSS polyfill. The CSS we'll use is based on "Cross Browser HTML5 Ruby Annotations Using CSS" by Zoltan "Du Lac" Hawryluk (http://j.mp/ruby-polyfill[21]).

```css
ruby {ruby-align: center;}

.no-ruby ruby {

  display: inline-table;

  text-align: center;

  border-collapse: collapse;

  border: none;

  vertical-align: middle;

}

.no-ruby rp {display: none;}

.no-ruby rt {

  display: table-header-group;

  font-size: 0.5em;

  line-height: 1.2em;

  white-space: nowrap;

}

.no-ruby rt + rt {

  display: table-row;

  border-bottom: hidden;

}
```

---

[21] www.useragentman.com/blog/2010/10/29/cross-browser-html5-ruby-annotations-using-css

For examples of how this would display, both with the polyfill (or with native support) and without, see Figures 4-12 (without `<rp>`) and 4-13 (using `<rp>`). Don't worry about what the Japanese means; just keep in mind that the simple characters wrapped in `<rt>` are the ruby readings for the complex characters that precede them.

Figure 4-12 shows a series in *furigana*, with the code sample, a supporting or polyfilled browser rendering, and an non-supporting browser rendering (for example, in Opera with no polyfill or with the polyfill but with JavaScript disabled). The lack of parentheses around the ruby annotations when they're "inline" makes the last example difficult to read.

```
<ruby>攻殻<rt>こうかく</rt>機動隊<rt>きどうたい</rt></ruby>
```

こうかくきどうたい
攻殻 機動隊
攻殻こうかく 機動隊きどうたい

Figure 4-12. Using <ruby> to indicate the pronunciation of the Japanese name of the Ghost in the Shell anime

Figure 4-13 adds `<rp>` elements, an HTML-level fallback for the ruby text in non-supporting browsers, which degrades gracefully even on non-supporting browsers without the polyfill.

```
<ruby>攻殻<rp>（</rp><rt>こうかく</rt><rp>）</rp>機動隊<rp>（</rp><rt>きどうたい</rt><rp>）</rp></ruby>
```

こうかくきどうたい
攻殻 機動隊
攻殻 （こうかく） 機動隊 （きどうたい）

Figure 4-13. The same example but with <rt> text surrounded by parentheses in <rp> elements

The <time> element

Another new element is <time>, which finally gives us an official machine-readable way of representing time, date, and time duration data.

> *The time element represents its contents, along with a machine-readable form of those contents in the datetime attribute. The kind of content is limited to various kinds of dates, times, time-zone offsets, and durations.*

> HTML Living Standard, WHATWG (http://j.mp/html5-time[22])

The date or time information can be the content of the element, but often you'll want to use a more natural expression (for example "three days ago"). <time> uses the attribute datetime for this. Table 4-2 illustrates the types of dates and times (which are subsets of ISO8601) that are allowed.

Table 4-2. Permitted HTML5 Datetime Attribute or <time> Element Content Values (http://j.mp/html5-datetime[23])

Type	Description
Date	Year-month-day, separated by dashes, such as 2012-03-23
Month	2012-03
Year	2012
Yearless date	03-23 or --03-23

---

[22] www.whatwg.org/specs/web-apps/current-work/multipage/text-level-semantics.html#the-time-element

[23] www.whatwg.org/specs/web-apps/current-work/multipage/common-microsyntaxes.html#dates-and-times

Type	Description
Week	2012-W12 (the 12th week of 2012)
Time	The hour and minute in 24 hour time, plus optional seconds, such as 08:03, or 08:03:55, or 08:03:55.001
Local date and time (no timezone)	A valid date and time, separated by "T" or a space, such as 2012-03-23T08:03:55, or 2012-03-23 08:03:55
Time-zone offset	+09:00, or -0800, or Z (which is equivalent to +0000 or +00:00)
Global date and time (with timezone)	A valid date and time, separated by "T" or a space, with a timezone, such as 2012-03-26T02:03Z, or 2012-03-25 18:03-08:00
Duration (represented internally as a number of seconds)	"P" plus days (D), hours (H), minutes (M), and/or seconds (S), with time preceded by "T", such as P10D, or PT4H18M3S, or P10D14H18M3S Or, weeks (W,w), days (D,d), hours (H,h), minutes (M,m), and/or seconds (S,s), in any order, with optional spaces, such as 4h 18m 3s

A local datetime is local relative to the author. For a global datetime timezone, Z represents coordinated universal time, or UTC; it's sometimes known as Zulu time (hence the "Z"), is equivalent to the timezone of +00:00, and is more commonly known as GMT.

When not to use <time>

<time> uses Gregorian calendar-based dates, which only go back to 0000, so it's not possible to use <time> for dates before this (consider microdata or RDFa instead). Also, history buffs will need to convert Julian dates to Gregorian for the datetime value, like so:

```
Gaius Julius Caesar Augustus was born 23 September 63 BC<!-- we can't use <time> for this date
-->, and died <time datetime="0014-07-17">19 August AD 14</time> (Julian calendar).
```

The <time> element can't be used for date ranges, durations that can't be converted into seconds (excluding months and years), or for approximate times like "a few weeks before launch" or "Laika was born around 1954."

Changes to <time>

<time> has undergone some changes since its initial addition to the specification. One positive change is the element can now represent yearless dates, weeks, time-zone offsets, and durations, which weren't covered previously. This enables it to represent the <input> element's new date-related types (covered in Chapter 6).

Another change is the removal of the pubdate attribute, a Boolean attribute for indicating this datetime value is the publishing date of the nearest ancestor <article> element, or if there isn't one, of the entire document. At the time of writing, this attribute has been removed from the HTML5 specification and the suggested replacement is to use the <time> element together with the hAtom microformat vocabulary or the Schema.org Article microdata vocabulary. Microformats and microdata are covered later this chapter.

Extending HTML5

While HTML5 has a bunch of great new semantic elements like `<article>` and `<time>`, sometimes there just isn't an element with the right semantic meaning. What we want are ways to extend what we've been given—to add *machine-readable data* that a browser, script, or robot can use. This can range from adding metadata to use with JavaScript to adding extra semantics to HTML5 elements to adding completely new semantic data that's not in your content.

There were five fundamental ways in which HTML 4 could be extended.

- The <meta> element

- The class, rel, rev, and profile attributes

While rev and profile have fallen by the wayside (due to hardly anyone using rev correctly, and hardly anyone actually using profile), <meta>, class, and rel have remained in HTML5. In fact, <meta> now has spec-defined names (http://j.mp/html5-meta-name[24]) plus a way to submit new name values, and rel has

---

[24] www.whatwg.org/specs/web-apps/current-work/multipage/semantics.html#standard-metadata-names

several new link types defined in the HTML5 specification (http://j.mp/html5-rel-type[25]) plus a way to submit more, too. Even better, ARIA's role and aria-* attributes (which we met at the end of Chapter 3 and which were not part of HTML 4) can be used for adding accessibility-related roles ("bolt-on" accessibility) in HTML5, and HTML5 validators can check HTML5+ARIA.

In addition to these, there are several new methods of extending HTML5, including:

- The <data> element and its val attribute

- Custom data attributes (data-*)

- Microdata

- RDFa

While we won't cover RDFa, we will have a quick look at microformats, which are a way to add semantic meaning using agreed-on class attribute values and a precursor to the creation of HTML5's microdata. Let's begin with a look at the newly minted <data> element, which is basically a generalized version of the <time> element we just met.

The <data> element

The <time> element gives us an easy way to represent dates, times, and time durations in a machine-readable way, but there are many other types of data we may also want to make machine readable while displaying human-readable content. The <data> element with its value attribute has been introduced for this purpose.

> *The data element represents its contents, along with a machine-readable form of those contents in the value attribute.*
>
> HTML Living Standard, WHATWG (http://j.mp/html5-data[26])

---

[25] www.whatwg.org/specs/web-apps/current-work/multipage/links.html#linkTypes

[26] www.whatwg.org/specs/web-apps/current-work/multipage/text-level-semantics.html#the-data-element

It's great for using with microdata and (potentially) microformats, and allows us to associate data for scripts with a human-readable equivalent. The only restriction is that <data> *must* have the value attribute, which must be a representation of the element's content. The following code shows how this works:

```
The Kármán Line is <data value="100km">62 miles</data> above the Earth's sea level, and
defines the boundry between the atmosphere and outer space.
```

The custom data attribute (data-*)

You may need to store values in HTML for use by JavaScript, for example. It's best to avoid hidden metadata and instead use elements like <time> and <data> to tie machine-readable data to the page's content. However, sometimes having a way to append data for scripts to *any* element is really handy. Rather than abuse other global attributes like class, HTML5 has introduced the custom data attribute ("data-*") for this use. The "data-*" name comes from this global attribute being "data-" plus the name you want to use.

> *Custom data attributes are intended to store custom data private to the page or application, for which there are no more appropriate attributes or elements.*
>
> HTML Living Standard, WHATWG (http://j.mp/html5-data-[27])

An example use (that we'll cover in more detail in Chapter 9) is for *responsive* images, where you show small images by default, then use JavaScript to swap in a large image on large-screened devices. We can store the large image using data-* directly in the <img> element.

<img src="picture.small.jpg" **data-fullsrc="picture.large.jpg"**>

A script could then update this to

<img **src="picture.large.jpg"** data-smlsrc="picture.small.jpg">

on a suitable device. Just remember that data-* is for your own scripts and is not suitable for any data you want external scripts to use. For more information, including how to access, create, and change data-*

---

[27] www.whatwg.org/specs/web-apps/current-work/multipage/elements.html#embedding-custom-non-visible-data-with-the-data-*-attributes

values in JavaScript, read "HTML5 Custom Data Attributes (data-*)" by Chris Bewick (http://j.mp/html5-data2[28]).

Microformats

Microformats are a simple way of extending HTML with additional *machine-readable* semantics and are designed for humans first and machines second. They were developed from Plain Old Semantic HTML (POSH) coding patterns for use with HTML 4 and XHTML 1 and work via agreed class, rel, rev, and profile syntax, coding patterns, and nesting. The machine-readable part means a robot or script that understands the microformat vocabulary being used can understand the extra semantics added by the microformat to the marked-up data. Each microformat is for a specific type of data and is usually based on existing data formats, like vcard (address book data; RFC2426) and icalendar (calendar data; RFC2445), or common coding patterns ("paving the cowpaths" of the web). Microformats are easy to implement, so many services offer, for example, profile information in hCard format; thus you may already have a microformatted profile even if you've never used microformats before. You can find out more about the many microformats and the process for creating a new one on the Microformats wiki (http://microformats.org/wiki).

A lightning introduction to microformats

Just in case you've never used them before, I'll briefly introduce some simple microformats—hopefully so simple you'll be encouraged to try them right away.

Using rel-license for licensing information

Adding license information is quite a common activity, and while we can add a link to Creative Commons or another license easily enough, someone would have to read it to understand the content's license.

```
<small>This article is licensed under a <a href="http://creativecommons.org/licenses/by-nc-sa/2.0/">Creative Commons Attribution Non commercial Share-alike (By-<abbr>NC</abbr>-<abbr>SA</abbr>) license</a>.</small>
```

If this information was machine-readable, it would help consumers searching for content with a specific license. By using the rel-license microformat to add rel="license" to the link (indicating it's the license for the page's main content), we can do just that.

---

[28] http://html5doctor.com/html5-custom-data-attributes

```
<small>This article is licensed under a <a rel="license"
href="http://creativecommons.org/licenses/by-nc-sa/2.0/">Creative Commons Attribution Non-
commercial Share-alike (By-<abbr>NC</abbr>-<abbr>SA</abbr>) license</a>.</small>
```

This may be so easy you don't even realize you've just microformatted the link. Google uses this data to allow searches by license, as shown in Figure 4-14 (look in advanced search, in the extra options).

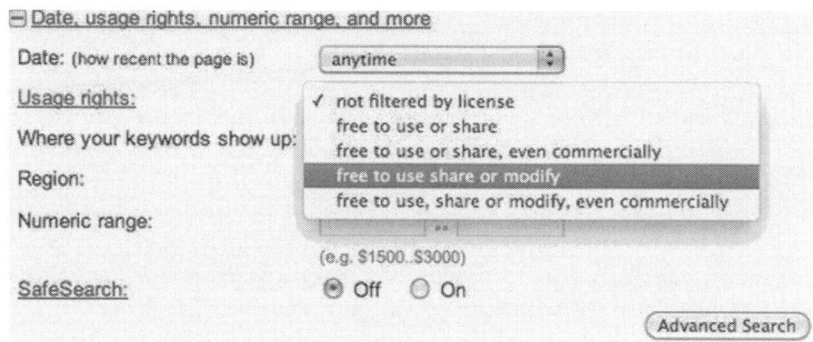

Figure 4-14. The Usage Rights pulldown in Google's advanced search options

This basic microformat has become part of HTML5 as one of the link types, added as a `rel=""` value to an `<a>`, `<link>`, or `<area>` element (http://j.mp/html5-rel-type[29]).

Using XHTML Friends Network (XFN)

Maybe we should term this one eXtensible Friends Network instead :-) This is a way of specifying your relationship with people—everything from "met" to "sweetheart"—using the rel attribute on a link to their homepage. However, there are three main values.

- rel="contact": Someone you know how to get in touch with.

- rel="me": Allows you to claim your various websites, including your accounts on social networks.

- rel="author": A link to the current article's author, such as to their website or profile page (and the only one of these three link types that's in the HTML5 spec).

We can use the last two to prove our identity online using only links. For example, if I have a website or profile page, I could add a link to my Twitter account.

---

[29] www.whatwg.org/specs/web-apps/current-work/multipage/links.html#linkTypes

```
<p>Oli Studholme — <a href="https://twitter.com/boblet">follow me on Twitter (@boblet)</a></p>
```

While a person can infer that @boblet is my Twitter username, by adding rel="me" we can state this relationship in a *machine-readable* way.

```
<p>Oli Studholme — <a rel="me" href="https://twitter.com/boblet">follow me on Twitter (@boblet)</a></p>
```

This would need to be on my own profile page, with the same profile page URL added to my Twitter profile, to actually work. But by doing this, a social web app that understands XFN can confirm @boblet is me, check my friends on Twitter, check if those people are already registered, and then allow me to follow them all with one click—much easier.

Google will also allow you to prove authorship of articles (as long as you have a Google+ profile or Google profile) by using rel="me" in conjunction with rel="author". There are several ways to do this, so we'll refer you to Google's documentation on proving authorship (http://j.mp/google-author[30]), and, if you use WordPress, see Joost de Valk's article "rel="author" and rel="me" in WP and other platforms" (http://j.mp/wp-rel-me[31]). Doing this can change how search results are displayed, such as by including your profile picture next to articles you've authored in search results.

Rel-license and XFN are simple rel-based microformats, but even with their simplicity you can see the potential power in this machine-readable stuff. Now let's look at using microformats for contact information.

Using hCard for contact information

Almost every website has an About page with some contact information.

```
<p>By Oli Studholme — <a href="http://oli.jp/">http://oli.jp</a>, or <a href="http://twitter.com/boblet">follow me on Twitter (@boblet)</a>.</p>
```

Unfortunately, adding someone's contact information to your phone or address book generally involves a lot of copying and pasting. If the data was machine-readable, we could use a tool to import it. Let's add the hCard microformat to the following code:

```
<p class="vcard">By <span class="fn">Oli Studholme</span> — <a class="url" href="http://oli.jp/">http://oli.jp</a>, or <a class="url"
```

---

[30] http://support.google.com/webmasters/bin/answer.py?hl=en&answer=1229920

[31] http://yoast.com/wordpress-rel-author-rel-me

```
href="http://twitter.com/boblet">follow me on Twitter (@<span
class="nickname">boblet</span>)</a>.</p>
```

The classes we added are the following:

- vcard on the containing <p> element, which establishes that there is microformatted hCard data here .

- fn, which stands for full name.

- url for an associated homepage.

- nickname for, well, a nickname.

Because we're only adding classes (and the occasional <span> element to add a class to), unless we also start adding CSS styles there's no change to how our content looks or behaves. And if we *did* need to style this information we've just added some classes we can use. Now this is a pretty easy example, but hCard has depth. We can mark up all kinds of contact-related data, such as addresses, company information, even a profile photo. For example, by default hCard maps the two words in fn to be given name and family name (as is typical in English). But for a language with a different order, or middle names and titles etc, we can (well, must) explicitly state that data. The following code shows updates the previous hCard code, only this time with the name in Japanese, and explicit family-name and given-name hCard classes:

```
<span class="vcard"><span class="fn n" lang="ja"><span class="family-
name">スタッドホルム</span>・<span class="given-name">オリ</span></span></span>
```

So what's the benefit of this? Well, there are several tools that will convert this hCard-microformatted data into a vcard file we can download and automatically add to our address book, such as the Operator plugin for Firefox shown in Figure 4-15.

Figure 4-15. The Firefox plugin Operator can save hCard-formatted content as a vcard, a format most address book and email programs can import

It's also recognized by Google's Rich Snippets (a predecessor to shcema.org, which we covered in the Microdata section later this chapter), as seen in Figure 4-16, and Yahoo's SearchMonkey, which would be very useful for the contact information on any company website.

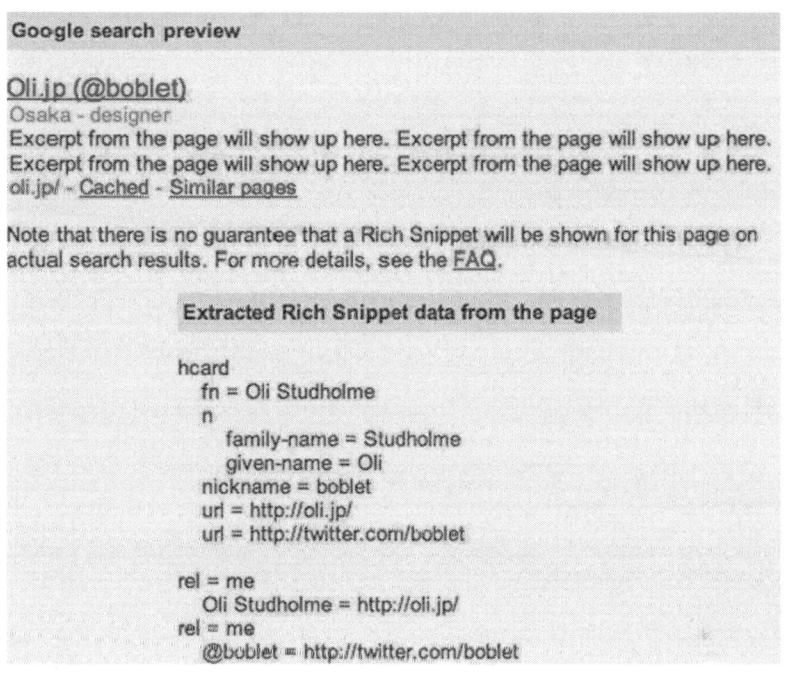

Figure 4-16. Google's Rich Snippet testing tool

Using microformats in HTML5

Microformats were developed before HTML5, and a few use attributes (rev and profile) that have been dropped. However, most microformats use only class and/or rel, so they're completely fine in HTML5. But because microformats were developed before HTML5, they don't (yet) take advantage of things like the new <time> and <data> elements. Some of the tools that process or produce microformats are also not yet HTML5-ready. While microformats remain perhaps the easiest way of extending HTML5 with predefined semantics, let's compare and contrast them with the new "native" HTML5 extension method, microdata.

Microdata: HTML5's semantic sprinkles

Microdata is a new lightweight semantic meta-syntax, using nested name-value pairs of data, generally based on the page's content. This is a whole new way to add extra semantic information and extend HTML5.

> *Sometimes, it is desirable to annotate content with specific machine-readable labels, e.g. to allow generic scripts to provide services that are customised to the page, or to enable content from a variety of cooperating authors to be processed by a single script in a consistent manner. [...] Microdata allows*

> *nested groups of name-value pairs to be added to documents, in parallel with the existing content.*

(http://j.mp/html5-microdata[32])

> *Note: Microdata has been somewhat controversial, so it is a separate specification at W3C, but still part of the WHATWG HTML5 specification. Keep calm and carry on.*

The main differences between microdata and microformats are

- Microdata uses new global attributes, rather than "overloading" the `class` attribute.

- Microdata is machine-parseable without knowledge of the vocabulary used.

- While we recommend marking up values that are part of the page's content, there's no intrinsic connection between the page's content and any microdata items present.

Microdata syntax

Microdata introduces five new global attributes.

- Itemscope: Defines a group of name-value pair(s), called an *item*.

- itemprop="property-name": Adds a *property* to a microdata item. The name of the property can be a word or URL, and the value is the "content" of the element with this attribute:

- For most elements, the value is the element's text content (not including any HTML tags).

- For elements with a URL attribute, the value is the URL (<img src="">, <a href="">, <object data=""> etc).

- For the <time> element, the value is the datetime="" attribute.

- For the <data> element, the value is the value="" attribute.

- For <meta itemprop="" content="">, the value is the content="" attribute.

---

[32] www.whatwg.org/specs/web-apps/current-work/multipage/microdata.html

- itemref="": Allows a microdata item to include *non-descendent properties* by referring to their id attributes.

- itemtype="": Defines the item's *type* by using itemtype="" on the same element as itemscope (contains a URL that acts as a unique vocabulary name).

- itemid="": Allows a microdata item to be associated with a *unique identifier* specified by the vocabulary, for example an ISBN number for a book. Use itemid on the same element as the item's itemscope and itemtype.

Let's go through these new attributes and see how to use microdata in practice.

itemscope and *itemprop*

The presence of itemscope makes the <p> element into a microdata item. The attribute itemprop on a descendent element defines a property of this item called name, and associates it with the value Salter Cane (the <span>'s content). An item must have at least one itemprop to be valid.

```
<p itemscope>I'm going to the <span itemprop="name">Salter Cane</span> gig next week.
Excited!</p>
```

itemprop names can be words or URL strings. Using URLs makes the name *globally unique*. If words are used it's best to use defined words via a vocabulary, which also makes the name unique. We'll cover this in more detail in the section "Typed items and globally unique names" soon.

itemprop value from an attribute

For some elements an itemprop's value comes from an attribute of the element.

```
<p itemscope>I'm going to the <a itemprop="url" href="http://www.saltercane.com/">Salter
Cane</a> gig <time itemprop="date" datetime="2012-08-18">next week </time>. Excited!</p>
```

This defines an item with the properties url and date, with the values http://www.saltercane.com/ and 2012-08-18, respectively.

Note that the link's itemprop="url" value is http://www.saltercane.com/ and not the element's "Salter Cane" text content. In microdata, the following elements contribute their URLs as values:

- <a href="">

- <area href="">

- <audio src="">

- <embed src="">

- <iframe src="">
- <img src="">
- <link href="">
- <object data="">
- <source src="">
- <track src="">
- <video src="">

> *Note: HTML5 elements with URL-containing attributes that are not used are*
>
> *<base href="">*
> *<script src="">*
> *<input src="">*

To use the text of <a href=""> as a property's value, we need to add an additional itemprop.

```
<p itemscope>I'm going to the <a itemprop="url" href="http://www.saltercane.com/"><span
itemprop="name">Salter Cane</span></a> gig <time itemprop="date" datetime="2012-08-18">next
week</time>. They're gonna rawk!</p>
```

This defines an item with three properties: the url is http://www.saltercane.com/, the name is Salter Cane, and the date is 2012-08-18.

Nested items

Add itemscope to an element with itemprop to make a property into a nested item.

```
<p itemscope>The <span itemprop="name">Salter Cane</span> drummer is <span itemprop="members"
itemscope><span itemprop="name">Jamie Freeman</span>.</span></p>
```

This defines an item with two properties: name and members. The name is Salter Cane and members is a nested item containing the property name with the value Jamie Freeman. Note that members doesn't have a text value.

Items that aren't part of other items (i.e. anything with itemscope but not itemprop) are called top-level microdata items. The microdata API only returns top-level microdata items and their properties (which includes nested items).

Multiple properties

Items can have multiple properties with the same name and different values.

```
<span itemprop="members" itemscope>The band members are <span itemprop="name">Chris
Askew</span>, <span itemprop="name">Jeremy Keith</span>, <span itemprop="name">Jessica
Spengler</span> and <span itemprop="name">Jamie Freeman</span>.</span>
```

This defines the property name with four values: Chris Askew, Jeremy Keith, Jessica Spengler, and Jamie Freeman.

One element can also have multiple properties (multiple itemprop="" names separated by spaces) with the same value.

```
<p itemscope><span itemprop="guitar vocals">Chris Askew</span> is so dreamy.</p>
```

This defines the properties guitar and vocals, both of which have the value Chris Askew.

In-page references

Items can use non-descendant properties (name-value pairs that aren't children of the itemscope element) via the attribute itemref="". Use this to list IDs of properties or nested items elsewhere on the page.

```
<p itemscope itemref="salter-cane-members">I'm going to the <a itemprop="url"
href="http://www.saltercane.com/"><span itemprop="name">Salter Cane</span></a> gig <time
itemprop="date" datetime="2012-08-18">next week</time>. Excited!</p>

...

<p>Salter Cane are <span id="salter-cane-members" itemprop="members" itemscope><span
itemprop="name">Chris Askew</span>, <itemprop="name">Jeremy Keith</span>, <span
itemprop="name">Jessica Spengler</span> and <span itemprop="name">Jamie
Freeman</span>.</span></p>
```

This defines the properties url, name, and date, and references the ID salter-cane-members, which contains the item members with four name properties, which each have a different value. We can also use this to keep our code DRY (don't repeat yourself) and, for example, have several events at the same place in one page include the location by using itemref, saving us repeating it for each event.

Using <meta> to add content via attributes

If the text you want to add *isn't* already part of the page's content, you can use the content attribute (<meta itemprop="" content="">) to add it inside an item.

```
<p itemscope><span itemprop="name" itemscope>Jessica Spengler<meta itemprop="likes"
content="Mameshiba"></span>'s fans are always really raucous.</p>
```

Unfortunately some non-supporting browsers move <meta> into <head>. The elegant workaround is to use an in-page reference via itemref.

```
<p itemscope><span itemprop="name" itemscope itemref="meta-likes">Jessica Spengler<meta
id="meta-likes" itemprop="likes" content="Mameshiba"></span>'s fans are always really
raucous.</p>
```

Both of these code snippets define the property name with the value Jessica Spengler and the nested property likes with the value Mameshiba.

> Note: There's no relationship between microdata and the page's content. Adding all microdata via <meta> is equivalent to adding metadata using the page's content—just not recommended.

While microdata is best suited to annotate your existing content, by using <meta>-based or hidden values, microdata doesn't have to be tied to a page's content. However, in general, adding hidden content to a page is a bad idea because it's easy to forget about it and not keep it current. If the information is useful to some users, add it to the page's content. If it's inconvenient to add the content inside an item, consider putting it in a <footer> and including an in-page reference.

Global identifiers with itemid

Sometimes an item may be identified by a unique identifier, such as a book by its ISBN number. This can be done in microdata using a *global identifier* via the attribute itemid="". Add this attribute to an element with both itemscope and itemtype="".

```
<p itemscope itemtype="http://vocab.example.com/book" itemid="isbn:1-59059-533-5">

  <!-- book info… -->

</p>
```

This would define an item that contains information about a book identified by the ISBN number 1-59059-533-5, *as long as* the http://vocab.example.com/book vocabulary defines this global identifier.

Typed items (itemtype) and globally unique names

We can tie an item to a microdata vocabulary by giving it a *type* using the attribute itemtype="" on an element with itemscope. The itemtype="" value is a URL representing the microdata vocabulary. Note that this URL is only a text string that acts as a unique vocabulary identifier; it doesn't actually need to have any content. After doing this we can use names in the vocabulary as itemprop names to apply vocabulary-defined semantics.

```
<p itemscope itemtype="http://schema.org/MusicGroup">I went to hear <a itemprop="url"
href="http://saltercane.com/"><span itemprop="name">Salter Cane</span></a> last night. They
were great!</p>
```

This example defines the property URL with the value of http://saltercane.com/ and the property name with the value of Salter Cane, according to the http://schema.org/MusicGroup vocabulary (MusicGroup is a specialized kind of Organization vocabulary on schema.org).

Alternatively, if you use URLs for itemprop names, there's no need to use itemtype because the vocabulary information is already contained in the name. These are referred to as *globally unique names*. While vocabulary-based names must be used inside a typed item to have the vocabulary-defined meaning, you can use a URL itemprop name anywhere. Let's rewrite the previous example using URL-based names.

```
<p itemscope>I went to hear <a itemprop="http://schema.org/MusicGroup/url"
href="http://saltercane.com/"><span itemprop="http://schema.org/MusicGroup/name">Salter
Cane</span></a> last night. They were great!</p>
```

This allows you to use multiple vocabularies in the same code snippet, even if they use the same property names.

Microdata in action

So now we know *how*, but *why* would we want to use microdata? One use is to add extra semantics or data that we can manipulate via JavaScript in a similar way to custom data attributes (data-*), etc. However, if we use a vocabulary via itemtype or URL-based itemprop names, microdata becomes considerably more powerful. While microdata is *machine-readable* without needing to know the vocabulary, once we use a vocabulary, others can know what our properties mean. This allows the data to take on a life of its own. Say what? Well, in effect using a vocabulary makes microdata a lightweight API for your content.

Now we could start making up our own itemprop names on an ad-hoc basis, but this pretty much limits anyone else from using our data. By using a vocabulary and following its rules, others can also use our data. It's a good idea to use a vocabulary, so where do we find one?

Using schema.org vocabularies

Bing, Google, and Yahoo have collaborated on a set of microdata vocabularies under the name schema.org (http://schema.org). By using these vocabularies we can convey semantic information in our content in a way these search engines can understand. While adding semantics using these vocabularies won't affect your search ranking, the included data may be shown in search results. The main vocabularies schema.org offers are

- Creative works: CreativeWork, Book, Movie, MusicRecording, Recipe, TVSeries…

- Embedded non-text objects: AudioObject, ImageObject, VideoObject

- Event

- Organization

- Person

- Place, LocalBusiness, Restaurant…

- Product, Offer, AggregateOffer

- Review, AggregateRating

They're the cross-search engine successors to Google's earlier Rich Snippets vocabularies. Unlike Rich Snippets, which also came in microformats and RDFa versions, schema.org vocabularies controversially only support microdata at the moment.

Here is a basic HTML snippet.

```
<section>

  <h3><a href="http://code12melb.webdirections.org/">Designing in the browser</a> by <a
href="http://nimbupani.com/">Divya Manian</a></h3>

  <p><time datetime="2012-05-23T16:20:00+10:00">May 23rd 4:20pm</time>-<time datetime="2012-
05-23T17:15:00+10:00">5:15pm</time> at the <abbr title="Royal Automobile Club of
Victoria">RACV</abbr> City Club, 501 Bourke St, Melbourne, Australia</p>

  <p>The new technologies available in HTML5 already allow you to create prototypes quickly in
the browser. Learn how to create a prototype from start to finish using these new technologies
while taking advantage of quick prototyping tools.</p>

</section>
```

Let's add some microdata pixie dust to it. Adding microdata attributes (plus the occasional <span> to add them to) for the event, speaker, and location, with no change to how the HTML is displayed.

```
<section itemscope itemtype="http://schema.org/Event">

  <h3><a itemprop="url" href="http://code12melb.webdirections.org/"><span
itemprop="name">Designing in the browser</span></a> by <span itemprop="performers" itemscope
itemtype="http://schema.org/Person"><a itemprop="url" href="http://nimbupani.com/"><span
itemprop="name">Divya Manian</span></a></span></h3>

  <p><time itemprop="startDate" datetime="2012-05-23T16:20:00+10:00">May 23rd 4:20pm</time>-
<time itemprop="endDate" datetime="2012-05-23T17:15:00+10:00">5:15pm</time> at the <span
itemprop="location" itemscope itemtype="http://schema.org/Organization"><a itemprop="url"
href="http://j.mp/HdvMwM"><span itemprop="name"><abbr title="Royal Automobile Club of
Victoria">RACV</abbr> City Club</span></a></span></p>

  <p itemprop="description">The new technologies available in HTML5 already allow you to
create prototypes quickly in the browser. Learn how to create a prototype from start to finish
using these new technologies while taking advantage of quick prototyping tools.</p>

</section>
```

While nothing has changed in how this content is displayed, with these microdata items the following information is now machine readable (the vocabulary treats this one speech as an event, or more precisely a sub-event of a conference, although we'll leave that out for simplicity):

- Speech name (name)

- Speech URL (url on <a>)

- Speaker (performers), which is represented by

  - Speaker's name (name)

  - Speaker's associated URL (url)

- Speech start and end time (startDate and endDate)

- Speech location (location), which is represented by

  - Place name (name)

  - Place URL (url on <a>)

- Speech description (description)

133

> Note: While these *itemprops* are probably be self-explanatory, you can see descriptions of what each *itemprop* means on the event, person, and place vocabulary pages.

This would give the following machine-readable output:

```
:type: http://schema.org/Event

:properties:

  url:

  - http://code12melb.webdirections.org/

  name:

  - Designing in the browser

  performers:

  - :type: http://schema.org/Person

    :properties:

      url:

      - http://nimbupani.com/

      name:

      - Divya Manian

  startDate:

  - Wed, 23 May 2012 16:20:00 +1000

  endDate:

  - Wed, 23 May 2012 17:15:00 +1000

  location:

  - :type: http://schema.org/Place

    :properties:

      url:
```

```
- http://j.mp/HdvMwM

name:

- RACV City Club
```

description:

```
- The new technologies available in HTML5 already allow you to create prototypes quickly in
the browser. Learn how to create a prototype from start to finish using these new technologies
while taking advantage of quick prototyping tools.
```

Google provides a Rich Snippet testing tool that shows what data it can extract from the microdata (plus any recognized microformats and RDFa) on a page (see Figure 4-17).

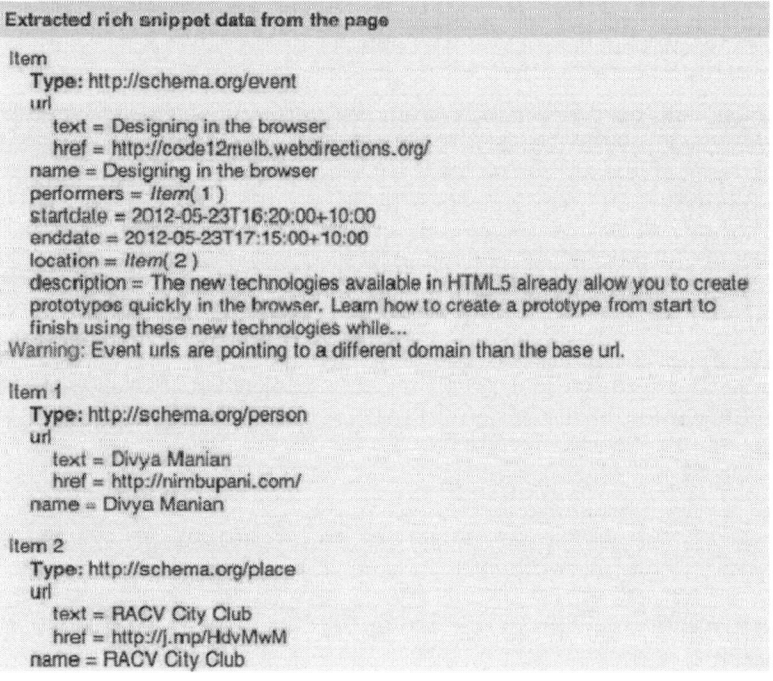

Figure 4-17. Lalala

A search engine could then use this additional data when displaying search results, for example adding the date and location to the result, all without needing one of those pesky natural language interpreters (otherwise known as humans).

Anyone who has used microformats before will notice these vocabularies look very similar to hCard and hCalendar, although there are a couple of name changes (for example, Calendar's class="dtstart" becomes itemprop="startDate").

While the schema.org vocabularies are all the search engines are promising to support, you can extend these vocabularies yourself. The safest ways to do this would be via

- The Product Types Ontology (www.productontology.org) for products or services, based on Wikipedia.

- The GoodRelations vocabulary terms for e-commerce (http://j.mp/goodrel[33]).

- Making your own schema.org vocabulary extension collaboratively, using the schema.org e-mail list (http://j.mp/public-vocabs[34]). Be sure to read the "Making your own vocabulary" section first.

Tools and browser support

With the right tools we can use this data, complete with its explicit semantics, for example, to add this event directly into a calendar—very handy if you were planning to go! With the release of schema.org, tools for microdata are starting to appear, but are still somewhat thin on the ground. However, the following libraries are available:

- Live Microdata and the associated microdatajs by Philip Jägenstedt (http://j.mp/live-md[35])

- The PHP Microdata Parser by Alex Holt (http://j.mp/php-md[36])

- Mida, a Microdata parser/extractor library for Ruby and command line tool by Lawrence Woodman (http://j.mp/ruby-mida[37])

- Microdata-JS by Termi (http://j.mp/md-js[38])

---

[33] www.heppnetz.de/projects/goodrelations

[34] http://lists.w3.org/Archives/Public/public-vocabs

[35] http://foolip.org/microdatajs/live

[36] http://soyrex.com/projects/php-microdata

[37] http://lawrencewoodman.github.com/mida

Live Microdata converts microdata into JSON. The PHP Microdata library allows you to parse microdata in an HTML file, returning JSON or a PHP array. Mida allows you to extract microdata as JSON and then search for or inspect items. It supports defining vocabularies and includes schema.org vocabularies. You can even use it from the command line. Microdata-JS is a polyfill for microdata. Validator.nu (http://validator.nu) will also validate your use of microdata, but not whether it conforms to a vocabulary. And, as we already saw, the Google Rich Snippets testing tool validates microdata and *should* display how that data could be incorporated into search results if you're using the schema.org vocabularies.

The microdata specification describes the microdata DOM API, which allows us to access top-level items and their properties. API browser support is still nascent, with only an Opera 12 preview release at the time of writing, although Firefox and WebKit are working on it. Luckily, that's OK because this data is still useful for search engine robots and third party tools, and until there is native API support we can use microdatajs.

Making your own vocabulary

If you don't see a suitable vocabulary at schema.org, you could consider making your own. Here are the steps.

1. Work out your vocabulary's rules. This is a little like setting up a database. Work out names for each type of data, then think what kind of data each name's value should/must contain (URL, datetime, free text, text with restrictions...), and whether something needs to be the child of something else.

2. Make up a URL on a domain you control, and ideally put your vocabulary specification there.

3. Use the URL In Itemtype="" to reference your vocabulary.

There are also very good reasons *not* to make your own vocabulary. They can be quite hard to create, as evidenced by the work that goes into making microformats vocabularies. For truly site-specific data, you're fine with HTML5 custom data-* attributes or using microdata the same way. But to really get the quasi-API benefits of microdata, you need to use a vocabulary that's on more than just your site. To make a vocabulary like that, you need to cover not just your own needs, but 80% of the needs of everyone else in the same subject area.

First, check out microformats.org to see if there's anything in roughly the same area you can just microdata-ify. After that, try RDFa vocabularies. If you still have no luck, try collaborating on a vocabulary with other people in your subject domain. If you're going to write your own microdata vocabulary from

---

[38] https://github.com/termi/Microdata-JS

scratch, we recommend trying to write a microformat first (http://j.mp/uf-process[39]), as you'll get a lot of good feedback and they have good information on how to write one. It's easy to then convert the resulting microformat vocabulary into a microdata vocabulary.

It's also possible to use RDFa vocabularies directly by specifying **both** the itemtype and using URLs for itemprop names. Refer to the RDF vocabulary clearing-house ("namespace lookup") at http://prefix.cc to find them.

Final thoughts on microdata

We went through the building blocks of microdata, a simple five-attribute combo of itemscope, itemprop, itemref, itemtype, and itemid on any element, plus using content on <meta>. We looked at how to combine these attributes to add complex semantic annotations and relationships to your content. We also looked at using a common vocabulary to allow the annotated data to be reused widely (including by search engines), which makes creating a meta-API for your website easy.

There are other ways to extend HTML5 with semantic data. Although we covered microformats briefly, we will not touch on RDFa, the heavyweight method by which data.gov.uk, data.gov, and hardcore data geeks annotate their data—and the basis of the "web of linked data" that Tim Berners-Lee has so eloquently promoted in a TED talk. While more powerful than microdata, RDFa is also more complex and (for your humble authors at least) somewhat of a challenge to understand and implement. However, if you dig triples or always wanted to SPARQL, then RDFa could be just your thing.

Here are some stand-out points on microdata and how it compares to microformats and RDFa:

- Microdata can be used for any data. There's no need for a pre-defined vocabulary (as there is in microformats), although using one will make your data far more useful.

- Microdata has a little more rigor than microformats. You can parse microdata without knowing the vocabulary

- Microdata, like microformats, is comparatively easy to hand-author. RDFa can be complex for non-computer science people (well, for us anyway).

- Microdata doesn't have equivalents for RDFa's XML literals (code in values) or datatypes. In other words, you can't specify "this is a date" explicitly, although a vocabulary can specify this information.

---

[39] http://microformats.org/wiki/process

Or, to summarize each technology:

- Microformats are easy, somewhat limited by HTML 4, work in HTML5 (with some caveats), and will most likely eventually transition to using new HTML5 elements and attributes.

- Microdata is new (few tools) but shows promise as a lightweight way to add extra semantics to page content for all common use cases.

- RDFa is more powerful, with a corresponding increase in difficulty, and has entrenched supporters.

While microdata and RDFa could be seen to be competing technologies (politics!), we personally see them as complementary. We could probably represent the relationship between microformats, microdata, and RDFa as a sliding scale from easy/limited to difficult/powerful. As they all use different techniques to add annotations, you could even use them together on the same page (semantic overload!). Our opinion: for designers, microdata falls into the sweet spot in the middle, but each method of adding extra semantics has its benefits and weaknesses.

Summary

In this chapter we covered a grab-bag of tools for making our code really shine. We looked at how old favorites have evolved to keep up with the needs of an evolving Web. We also showed you several new elements and attributes that expand the types of content we can semantically represent. Finally, we looked at ways to extend HTML5 even further, including using microdata.

For homework, try to use as many of this chapter's elements as you can, while thinking about their semantic meanings. Practice will also help you cement the HTML5 definitions of changed elements if you're used to the HTML 4 ones. Finally, mark up something with microformats or microdata, then use a tool to do something with the extra semantics you've added. So much power! Use it wisely to prepare a rich, semantic cake—a solid base for all the awesome we have to come in the second half of the book.

Further reading and related links

- HTML5 Element Index — HTML5 Doctor (http://html5doctor.com/element-index)

- *Towards a Unified Ruby Model* by Fantasai (http://fantasai.inkedblade.net/weblog/2011/ruby)

- *Microformats: Empowering Your Markup for Web 2.0* by John Allsopp [book] (http://microformatique.com/book)

- Dive into HTML5 — "Distributed," "Extensibility," & Other Fancy Words by Mark Pilgrim (http://diveintohtml5.net/extensibility.html)

- Linked data tutorial (introduction to RDFa) (http://ld2sd.deri.org/lod-ng-tutorial)

- Microformats vs RDFa vs Microdata by Philip Jägenstedt (http://blog.foolip.org /2009/08/23/microformats-vs-rdfa-vs-microdata)

- Google Help — Rich Snippets; contains a great introduction to microdata, microformats and RDFa, with code samples in each language (www.google.com/support/webmasters/bin/topic.py?topic=21997)

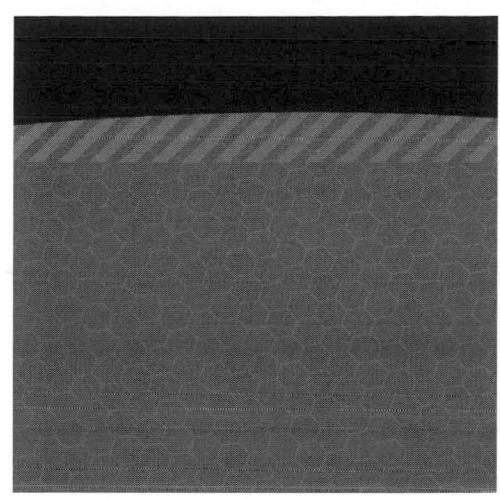

Chapter 5

Rich Media

Remember the days when the Web was just a series of interlinking documents containing text and images? No? Well, don't worry. We're going to give you a short history lesson. In the mid-nineties most websites contained lots of text and a few images. Then something came along that was destined to change the playing field: the FutureSplash plug-in. Because it was a proprietary plug-in as opposed to a ratified *open* specification, the debate remains over whether it should have formed such a fundamental part of the Web's architecture. FutureSplash wasn't the only one, though; Real Player and QuickTime were among those wanting to join the proprietary plug-in party.

You may be aware of how the story continues. FutureSplash was bought by Macromedia, who renamed it Flash, and it became ubiquitous on the desktop. Its success was based on the fact that it provided a lot of functionality that open standards were missing, such as video and animation. Plug-ins, such as Flash, solved the problem of cross-browser compatibility. But how will the story end? What does the future hold for Flash and other proprietary formats? Will the rise of HTML5 and the Open Web spell the end for proprietary formats? In this chapter, we'll discuss the direction we're heading and introduce you to native video and audio along with a brief look at canvas and SVG (Scalable Vector Graphics), which may well hold the answer.

The case for Flash

Let us be clear: we're not against Flash. In fact, very much the opposite is true. The rich authoring tool for the plug-in allows developers who are accustomed to writing HTML 4.01 to bring their sites to life with movement, audio, video, animation, and, crucially, out-of-the-box cross-browser compatibility. It enhances browser functionality far more than our basic web trifle ever could—until now, perhaps. Flash has also become the universally accepted method for adding video and audio to sites. It's very much a front-runner when it comes to pushing the boundaries of what's possible online.

While there was a time when you couldn't visit a site and not be struck with a ghastly intro screen created in Flash, it has evolved into a sophisticated software package capable of creating highly complex applications. This holds especially true when built using Flash's native authoring language, ActionScript, which, along with Adobe Flex and Adobe AIR, has encouraged skilled developers to flex their creative muscles and break new ground on the Web.

The problem with the Flash plug-in has been the barrier to entry caused by the fact that it's a closed, proprietary format. Flash files can, in the main, be created only by using an expensive software package that remains in the hands of a single vendor—Adobe. The alternative to proprietary formats? Open standards.

Proprietary formats vs. open standards

Before we discuss how HTML5 is aiming to change the playing field, let's take a brief detour into the differences between proprietary formats and open standards. Wikipedia describes proprietary formats as being

> *typically controlled by a private person or organization for the benefit of its applications, protected with patents or as trade secrets, and intended to give the license holder exclusive control of the technology to the (current or future) exclusion of others.*

> http://en.wikipedia.org/wiki/Proprietary_format

Openformats.org describes open standards as being

> *standards fixed by public authorities or international institutions whose aim is to establish norms for software interoperability.*

> www.openformats.org/en1

Proprietary formats, including Flash, offer a challenge for accessibility, device independence, and data portability out of the box. In addition, they don't always play nicely with open standards or native browser functionality. On the flip side of the coin, open standards promote interoperability across platforms and devices. Open standards provide a low barrier to entry; all you need to get started is a text editor coupled with a browser and you're on your way to creating a website.

As you'll see, even HTML5 isn't quite free of proprietary formats (although they aren't explicitly identified in the specification), but in the long run, open standards tend to win out due to their device and platform independence.

When it comes to the crunch, what would happen if Adobe or Apple were to go bankrupt tomorrow, next week, or next year? Flash wouldn't suddenly disappear but, arguably, developers would have to think of another solution to deliver their project. In contrast, open standards can't go bankrupt. The Web is all encompassing and shouldn't—no, mustn't—be held captive by several large companies touting their proprietary formats.

Enter HTML5 and friends

The Open Web is moving—fast. HTML5 is beginning to show us what can be achieved using only open standards. As you'll see in this chapter, HTML5 provides video and audio native to the browser. It also provides us with `canvas` and the ability to directly embed SVG files into our pages. These technologies allow us to draw and manipulate dynamic pixel-based (`canvas`) and vector-based (SVG) images using simple scripting techniques.

These rich media elements combined with powerful APIs go a long way to providing interoperable, accessible, rich, compelling experiences using only Open Web standards. The question is, are proprietary plug-ins such as Flash willing to lie down and be overtaken by open standards?

Does HTML5 signal the end of Flash?

In a fantastic article on A List Apart, Dan Mall likens the HTML5 vs. Flash debate to the Cold War of the Web. He goes on to say that

> *Technologies aren't inherently bad or good. They're only appropriate or inappropriate for certain circumstances. They're a means to an end, not solutions within themselves.*

> `www.alistapart.com/articles/flashstandards/`

Dan's approach is akin to our own, in that we believe developers should use the most appropriate technology in their armory. In fact, if you're a Flash developer, you've got most of the skills you already need to create great things with `canvas`; just take a look at Seb Lee-Delisle's 3D particles (`http://j.mp/3dparticles`[1]) to see how easy it is to convert from ActionScript to JavaScript. This is because both scripts are based on the ECMAScript language, meaning switching between one and the other is a relative breeze!

Flash will certainly continue to push the boundaries of what's possible online in the coming years, the likelihood being that gaming will be at the forefront of that push (although its stranglehold is waning). However, even Adobe is running scared of HTML5, stating "HTML5 poses a threat to Adobe Flash" in a report carried out by Gartner on Adobe's behalf. The decision by Apple to not support Flash on the iPhone or iPad certainly hasn't helped either. Even Ricardo Cabello (who some of you will know as Mr. Doob) has removed all Flash projects from his portfolio because he has "no interest on doing Flash projects any more" (`http://j.mp/doobnoflash`[2]).

---

[1] `http://sebleedelisle.com/2010/03/html5-canvas-3d-particle/`
[2] `http://ricardocabello.com/blog/post/715`

In short, Flash isn't going anywhere anytime soon, but the contents of this chapter will, hopefully, make you think about which technology you *actually* need to use on the next site you build.

Video the HTML5 way

Not a day passes without us being told that video (and we're not just talking about YouTube) is the future of the Web. If that is to be the case, particularly for the average user, we surely need an easy, reliable way of including video content without having to invest in expensive proprietary software. HTML5 provides just that, directly in the browser with (at its minimum) a single line of markup.

Let's take a look at how we've been adding video to our sites using the object tag in recent years. We're sure you'll all recognize YouTube's embed code.

```
<object width="640" height="385">
  <param name="movie" value="http://www.youtube.com/v/24FNE60FRzw&hl=en_GB&fs=1&">
  </param>
  <param name="allowFullScreen" value="true"></param>
  <param name="allowscriptaccess" value="always"></param>
  <embed src="http://www.youtube.com/v/24FNE60FRzw&hl=en_GB&fs=1&"
      type="application/x-shockwave-flash" allowscriptaccess="always"
      allowfullscreen="true" width="640" height="385">
  </embed>
</object>
```

Pretty ugly, huh? Well, as you've probably already guessed, HTML5 not only helps us to be a little more semantic, but also makes adding video to our sites as easy as ABC (OK, almost as easy). The basic markup you need is

```
<video src="gordoinspace.webm"></video>
```

By default, the browser doesn't show any play controls; the user needs to open a context menu (right click or cmd+click) to play the video using this markup, which is not very intuitive. You'll also see a small glitch when loading the page if you don't explicitly set the width and height of the video while the browser calculates the dimensions. Also, the user doesn't get a sneak peek of what they're going to be watching. To remedy the situation, we'll add the poster and controls attributes along with the dimensions (we'll explain these attributes in more detail in a bit).

```
<video src="gordoinspace.webm" width="720" height="405" poster="poster.jpg" controls>
</video>
```

In Chrome you should see something like Figure 5-1.

Figure 5-1. Basic video element in Chrome

The standard global attributes, along with poster and controls, aren't the only attributes available, though.

The standard global attributes defined in HTML5 are:

accesskey   dropzone
class   hidden
contenteditable   id
contextmenu   itemid
dir   itemprop
draggable

Let's take a look at each one in a little more detail.

- autoplay: Tells the browser to start playing the video as soon as it is downloaded.

- controls: Displays built-in controls that are native to the browser. Basic controls tend to include a play/pause button, time counter, volume control, and time scrubber.

- crossorigin: Either allows or prohibits the sharing of a video across other domains using CORS (Cross-Origin Resource Sharing).

- height: Identifies the height of the video (if your height/width aren't in the correct ratio, you will see black banding above and below the video; it will not distort).

- loop: Tells the browser to loop the video after playback has been completed.

- mediagroup: Allows multiple media elements to be linked together by creating a media controller. Therefore you can synchronize multiple videos or a video with audio.

- muted: Allows the author to specify if the video should be muted when it begins to play.

- poster: Identifies the location of a still image to use as a holding frame.

- `preload`: Allows the author to inform the browser to start (or not start) downloading the video as soon as the page is loaded. `preload` has replaced the `autobuffer` attribute. The `autoplay` attribute can override the `preload` attribute if present. The available states are

- `none`: Tells the browser not to preload the file. The file will begin to load when the user clicks Play.

- `metadata`: Tells the browser to only preload the metadata (dimensions, first frame, duration, etc.). The rest of the file will begin to load when the user clicks Play.

- `auto`: Tells the browser to choose whether to download the entire file, nothing, or only the metadata. This is the default state if `preload` isn't specified.

- `src`: Identifies the location of the video file (note that this is not required if a child `source` element is present, which we'll cover later).

- `width`: Identifies the width of the video (if your height/width aren't in the correct ratio, you will see black banding above and below the video; it will not distort).

`loop`, `autoplay`, `preload`, and `controls` are Boolean attributes, meaning that if the keyword exists in the code, the value is `true`. If you are writing XHTML, you should write `controls` as `controls="controls"`.

> Note: The *mediagroup* and *crossorigin* attributes have only been added to the specification recently and as such aren't implemented in any browser.

As we'll see, some browsers don't yet support the `video` element (or specific codecs—more on those shortly). Using graceful degradation, though, we can cater to those browsers by providing fallback content in the form of a link to download the video. This works because browsers always display the content inside of HTML5 elements they don't recognize.

```
<video src="gordoinspace.webm" width="720" height="405" poster="poster.jpg" controls>
Download <a href="gordoinspace.webm>Gordo in Space</a> the movie.
</video>
```

> Note: We don't believe that autoplaying videos is ever a good idea, predominantly from an accessibility (a11y) standpoint. The same goes for always including controls. In fact, Disney had a lawsuit brought against them for having video and audio that could not be turned off by blind users (*http://j.mp/noaccessdisney*[3]) and you don't want to find yourself in that situation.

Easy so far, right? Unfortunately, nothing's ever quite that simple, is it? Let's talk about the elephant in the room.

---

[3] `www.iheni.com/dickensian-disney`

Video formats

The elephant—no, elephants—hiding at the rear are video formats and codecs. An early version of the HTML5 spec specified the Theora codec (see the following section) but Apple refused to implement it. The Theora codec was then removed from the spec because browser vendors couldn't agree on a common codec. This means that a preferred codec is no longer documented.

Before we dive any deeper into which browsers support which codecs, let's veer off the beaten track and briefly describe the difference between video containers and codecs.

Video containers and codecs

The file extensions .mp4, .avi, and .flv that we associate with video aren't codecs themselves, but rather a container format. Think about how ZIP or RAR files can contain several types of files within them; video container formats do just the same thing. The container format should be thought of as the "how to store data" and the codec as the "how to understand and play the data."

These containers tend to include multiple tracks, generally at least one for the video and one for the audio. The tracks are synchronized by markers contained in the audio track. There can be multiple audio tracks for different languages or tracks for subtitles (more on that later). Containers can also have associated metadata that might include the title of the video or chapter points.

You're probably thinking, "But what has this got to do with HTML5 video?" The answer is that in order to implement HTML5 video cross browser, we need to be aware of three container formats.

- *WebM*: The newest container format to join the HTML5 party (http://j.mp/webmproject[4]). It was announced at the Google I/O conference in 2010, following Google's acquisition of On2 Technologies (http://j.mp/googleon2[5]). Based on the Matroska container format, it is designed to be used with the open source VP8 video codec and Vorbis audio codec. YouTube supports the WebM format, provided that you have opted into its HTML5 experiment (http://j.mp/youtubehtml5[6]) and are using a compatible browser.

- *Ogg*: An open standard container format without any patent restrictions, it is maintained by the Xiph.Org Foundation (http://j.mp/oggtheora[7]). Ogg's video codec is called Theora and the audio equivalent is Vorbis.

---

[4] www.webmproject.org/
[5] http://investor.google.com/releases/2010/0219.html
[6] www.youtube.com/html5
[7] http://en.wikipedia.org/wiki/Ogg

147

- *MPEG-4*: Based on Apple's QuickTime container format MOV (`http://j.mp/mpeg4container`[8]). It is associated with the file extensions `.mp4` and `.m4v`. The downside to MPEG 4 is that it is patent encumbered, which may mean the user will have to pay royalties starting in 2016. MPEG 4 uses the H.264 video codec.

We've introduced the container formats that we're interested in, but what about the specific codecs? Although the number of codecs is wide ranging (even for these three container formats), we're only interested in the following three:

- *VP8*: An open video codec that isn't encumbered by any known patents. It's owned by Google, having been created by On2 Technologies, which Google acquired. Its quality is similar to H.264 and it is expected to be developed further in coming years.

- *Theora*: Also originally created by On2 Technology (a clever bunch, don't you think?) but is now developed by the Xiph.Org Foundation. Like VP8, it is royalty free and not encumbered by any known patents. Theora is equivalent to VP3 and is generally used with the Ogg container, but its quality is far lower than that of VP8 or H.264

- *H.264*: Developed by the MPEG group and designed to create high-quality video at lower bit rates than previous standards. H.264 can be split into different profiles that cater to different devices, so a desktop device may require a higher profile than a mobile device, for example. It can be used with most container formats (usually MPEG-4) but has the downside that it is patent encumbered by MPEG-LA.

As we touched on earlier, because browser vendors couldn't agree on a codec, there isn't one detailed in the specification. You're now aware that there are three to choose from, but which browsers support which?

Browser support

All five of the main browsers support (or will in upcoming releases) HTML5 `video`. Table 5-1 shows the current state of browser support for different codecs.

Table 5-1. HTML5 Video Format Compatibility

	Internet Explorer				Mozilla		WebKit					Opera	
	IE 6	IE 7	IE 8	IE 9+	FF3.6	FF4+	SAF4	SAF5	CHR4	CHR5	CHR6+	O10.5	O10.6+
H.264 (MP4)	.	.	.	✓^	.	.	✓^	✓^	✓	✓	✓	.	.
Ogg Theora (ogg)	.	.	.	.	✓	✓	.	.	✓	✓	✓	✓	✓
VP8 (WebM)	.	.	.	✓*^	.	✓	.	.	.	.	✓	.	✓

---

[8] `http://en.wikipedia.org/wiki/MPEG-4_Part_14`

* Supported if the user has the codec installed.
^ User must have the QuickTime plug-in installed to run native multimedia.

Google did announce in January 2011 that they were going to drop support for H.264 (`http://j.mp/chromeh264`[9]) but at the time of writing this hasn't happened and the browser still supports all three codecs. For the current state of HTML5 video, LongTail has produced a comprehensive report titled "*The State of HTML5 Video*" that is a must-read for anyone wanting to use native video (http://j.mp/h5longtail[10]).

To quote Mark Pilgrim on Dive Into HTML5,

> *There is no single combination of containers and codecs that works in all HTML5 browsers. This is not likely to change in the near future. To make your video watchable across all of these devices and platforms, you're going to need to encode your video more than once.*

> `http://diveintohtml5.info/video.html#what-works`

With VP8 support being announced for Flash Player (`http://j.mp/adobevp8`[11]), there is a workaround whereby you can use a Flash fallback for browsers that don't support the VP8 codec but do support other HTML5 video formats (Safari).

The other option for achieving cross-browser compatibility is to encode your video more than once. There are a number of tools available to achieve this, one of which is Miro Video Converter (`http://j.mp/miroconverter`[12]), shown in Figure 5-2, which is available for PC and Mac. Converting videos with Miro is as easy as dragging a file, choosing the output format you require, and clicking Convert!

---

[9] `http://blog.chromium.org/2011/01/html-video-codec-support-in-chrome.html`
[10] `www.longtailvideo.com/html5`
[11] `http://blogs.adobe.com/flashplatform/2010/05/adobe_support_for_vp8.html`
[12] `www.mirovideoconverter.com/`

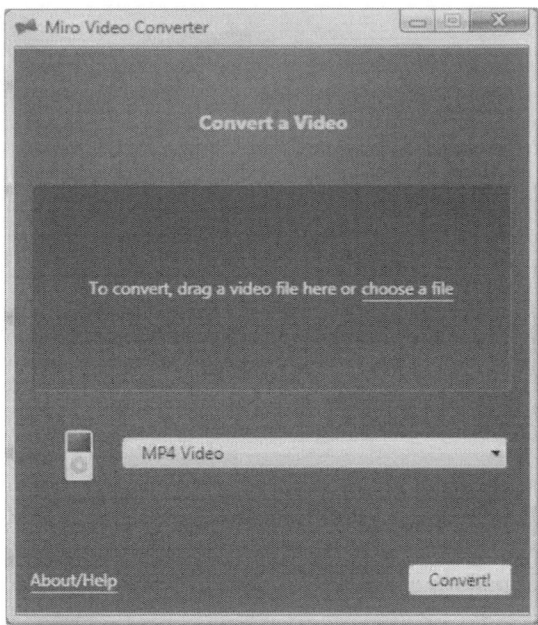

Figure 5-2. Miro Video Converter

For further encoding options, Mark Pilgrim offers a great tutorial on Dive Into HTML5 (http://j.mp/videopilgrim[13]).

Adding video source

We now have our video encoded three times, but so far we can only add one src attribute to our video element—Houston, we have a problem. We could detect support using JavaScript and serve the appropriate file to each browser. However, a more bulletproof way would be to use the source element.

source allows us to specify multiple alternative videos (or audio when using audio, which we'll cover later) for our media elements, as shown next. It is an invisible element, which means that nothing is rendered by the browser to indicate its presence visually in the document.

```
<video poster="poster.jpg" controls width="720" height="405">
  <source src="gordoinspace.mp4" type="video/mp4">
  <source src="gordoinspace.webm" type="video/vp8">
  <source src="gordoinspace.ogv" type="video/ogg">
  Download <a href="gordoinspace.webm>Gordo in Space</a> the movie.
</video>
```

Notice how we've added three source elements with their appropriate type attributes to cater for all browsers (OK, not quite *all*, as you may have spotted earlier, but we'll get to that).

---

[13] http://diveinto.html5doctor.com/video.html

> Note: Don't confuse the *source* element with the *src* attribute.

We've now removed the src attribute from the video element because we're using the child element source. Note that the link to download the video remains—primarily for those users who may be viewing in text-only browsers or alternative devices.

If you don't add the type attribute to the source element, the browser will download a small part of each file before realizing the codec is unsupported. Therefore, you should ensure that the type attribute is always included for each video source.

> Caution: When using the *type* attribute with Ogg Theora–encoded videos, you must specify it as *video/ogg*, not *video/ogv* (last letter g, not v). This has caught us out a few times, the source of confusion being that the file type has an *.ogv* extension.

The browser will play the first video that is in a format it understands. For example, in the case of Chrome 6, which is able to play all formats, it will play the MP4 file. If a browser doesn't understand the type of video, it will simply skip to the next source element until it finds one it does understand.

The order of the source elements is equally important: MP4 must come first because on older iPads it only looks at the first source element (now resolved). WebM is placed second due to that fact that its quality is higher than that of Ogg, thus ensuring Opera 10.6+ and Firefox 4+ will play the WebM file rather than the Ogg; Ogg is placed third to support Opera 10.5 and Firefox 3.5/3.6. As time passes (or perhaps even now if you're so inclined), it's likely we won't have to encode our videos with Ogg, as newer versions of browsers that currently use it will also support the higher-quality WebM. Triple encoding our video and adding three source elements covers us for a number of browsers and platforms, but what about IE6, 7, and 8?

> Note: Depending on your server configuration, the video may not play. If this is the case on Apache servers, you may need to specify the way your video is served. You can do this by adding the following lines to your *.htaccess* file:
>
> AddType video/webm .webm
> AddType video/ogg .ogg
> AddType video/mp4 .mp4
>
> Also note that you might need to do the same for *audio*.
>
> AddType audio/webm .webm
> AddType audio/ogg .oga
> AddType audio/mp3 .mp3

Enter our old friend Flash

That's right, folks: although we've discussed the benefits of open standards replacing proprietary technologies like Flash, in this instance our trusty old friend Mr. Flash helps us to support older versions of Internet Explorer. There are a number of Flash video players available, so which one you use is up to you. This example uses the non-commercial version of JW Player (http://j.mp/jwplayer[14]). The default code that it provides after linking the script follows:

```
<object id="player" classid="clsid:D27CDB6E-AE6D-11cf-96B8-444553540000" name="player"
width="720" height="429">
        <param name="movie" value="player.swf" />
        <param name="allowfullscreen" value="true" />
        <param name="allowscriptaccess" value="always" />
        <param name="flashvars" value="file=gordoinspace.mp4&image=poster.jpg" />
        <embed  type="application/x-shockwave-flash"  id="player2" name="player2"
src="player.swf"         width="720"  height="429"  allowscriptaccess="always"
allowfullscreen="true" flashvars="file=file= gordoinspace.mp4&image= poster.jpg" />
</object>
```

By combining the Flash object with our earlier example, we end up with an accessible, cross-browser, *native* solution. You'll note that inside the object is an img element for users who don't have the Flash plug-in installed, as you can see in this complete document example:

```
<!DOCTYPE HTML>
<html lang="en-UK">
<head>
        <meta charset="UTF-8">
        <title>Gordo in Space</title>
        <script src="js/jwplayer.js"></script>
        <script src="js/swfobject.js"></script>
</head>
<body>
<h1>Gordo in Space</h1>

<video poster=" poster.jpg" controls width="720" height="405">
  <source src="gordoinspace.webm" type="video/vp8" />
  <source src="gordoinspace.mp4" type="video/mp4" />
  <source src="gordoinspace.ogv" type="video/ogg" />
  <object id="player" classid="clsid:D27CDB6E-AE6D-11cf-96B8-444553540000" name="player"
width="720" height="429">
        <param name="movie" value="player.swf" />
        <param name="allowfullscreen" value="true" />
        <param name="allowscriptaccess" value="always" />
        <param name="flashvars" value="file=gordoinspace.mp4&image=poster.jpg" />
        <embed
        type="application/x-shockwave-flash"
        id="player2"
        name="player2"
```

---

[14] www.longtailvideo.com/players/jw-flv-player

```
        src="player.swf"
        width="720"
        height="429"
        allowscriptaccess="always"
        allowfullscreen="true"
        flashvars="file=file= gordoinspace.mp4&image= poster.jpg"
        />
        <img src="poster.jpg" title="No video playback capabilities, please download the video
below">
        <p>Your browser doesn't support video, please <a href="gordoinspace.webm">download
it</a>.</p>
        </object>
</video>

</body>
</html>
```

The preceding technique is based on a solution by Kroc Camen of Camen Design. We recommend you read Kroc's "Video for Everybody!" (http://j.mp/videoforeverybody[15]) article for updates on the latest browser support and gotchas. There is also a "Video for Everybody" generator available for automating the process a little (http://j.mp/vfegenerator[16]).

The track element

source isn't the only element we can use with native video, though. A relative latecomer to the HTML5 spec, the track element (and its associated API, the Text Track API) is designed to allow authors to specify an external timed track or data for both video and audio. track is only to be used as a child of a video or audio media element. Its use is as follows (we've removed the source elements for simplicity):

```
<video src="gordoinspace.webm" width="720" height="405" poster="poster.jpg" controls>
  <track kind="subtitles" src="gordo_subtitles.vtt" />
</video>
```

track can take the following attributes:

- default: Sets the track element in which it is used as the default unless a user's preferences indicate an alternative track would be more appropriate.

- kind: Describes what type of information this track element provides. It can take the following values (if no value is specified, subtitles is used by default):

    - subtitles: A transcript or translation of the dialogue. The text will be displayed as an overlay on the video.

    - captions: Similar to subtitles but can also include sound effects or other relevant audio information. Suitable when audio is unavailable. The text will be displayed as an overlay on the video.

---

[15] http://camendesign.com/code/video_for_everybody
[16] http://sandbox.thewikies.com/vfe-generator

153

- **descriptions:** Provides a textual description of the media element for when the video is unavailable (e.g., when a user is using a screen reader).

- **chapters:** Defines chapter titles to navigate the contents of a media element.

- **metadata:** Includes information and content about the media element, which isn't intended to be displayed to the user by default. You can, if you wish, expose this information using JavaScript.

- **label:** Defines a user-readable title for the text track. The label must be unique for every track element with the same kind attribute within the same media element.

- **src:** The URL of the text track data.

- **srclang:** The language of the text track data

Let's now look at an example with subtitles in multiple languages (English, French, and German).

```
<video src="gordoinspace.webm" width="720" height="405" poster="poster.jpg" controls>
    <track kind="subtitles" src="gordo_subtitles_en.vtt" srclang="en" label="English"  />
    <track kind="subtitles" src="gordo_subtitles_de.vtt" srclang="de" label="Deutsch"  />
    <track kind="subtitles" src="gordo_subtitles_fr.vtt" srclang="fr" label=" Français"  />
</video>
```

track enables us to have built-in, interoperable accessibility for our videos, but because it's so new, it isn't yet supported by any browser (but they're currently working on it). Until then, the best workaround is to use a JavaScript polyfill to provide support (we'll look at these further later in the chapter, including some with track support).

WebVTT

The astute will have noticed the file extension ".vtt" in our previous two examples. This is a WebVTT (Web Video Text Tracks) (http://j.mp/w3cwebvtt[17]) file format that is used for marking up external text tracks. The format was previously called WebSRT (Web Subtitle Resource Tracks) (http://j.mp/videowebsrt[18]), about which there was been some debate (http://j.mp/annevkwebsrt[19]) due to the fact that it competes with more than 50 other timed text formats. All major browsers plan to support WebVTT, with Microsoft announcing that it will also support TTML (Timed Text Markup Language).

WebVTT is currently only specified in the WHATWG HTML specification, but a W3C Web Media Text Tracks Community Group has been formed to help smooth its passage into the W3C specification.

A WebVTT file is a very simple text file that contains a number of "cues." These cues distinguish when text should appear and what text should be shown. Each cue has a unique ID and must be on its own line. A simple WebVTT file is as follows (note the first WEBVTT line is required for the file to be valid):

[17] http://dev.w3.org/html5/webvtt
[18] www.whatwg.org/specs/web-apps/current-work/multipage/video.html#websrt
[19] http://annevankesteren.nl/2010/05/websrt

```
WEBVTT

1
00:00:01.000 --> 00:00:10.000
The first lot of subtitles displays from 1 to 10 seconds

2
00:00:15.000 --> 00:00:20.000
The next line displays from 15 to 20 seconds
and can run onto two lines
```

You'll notice that the time format used for each cue is hh:mm:ss:msmsms. You can also wrap timers inline around the text to make it appear sequentially in a karaoke style, as shown in here:

```
WEBVTT

1
00:00:01.000 --> 00:00:10.000
The first lot of subtitles <00:00:03.000> displays from <00:00:07.000>1 to 10 seconds
```

You can also optionally style your subtitles (well, *style* might be a bit of a strong word). Going against everything you learned in Chapter 4, you can use <b> for bold text, <i> for italic, <u> for underline, and <ruby> and <rt> for err, ruby text. You can also use <c.className> to define a class with which you can style the text. Finally, using <v> you can define a voice with which to associate the text. This uses the following format <v Speaker Name> and will render the speaker name as well as the caption on the subtitles. Let's look at an example incorporating some of these tags.

```
WEBVTT

1
00:00:01.000 --> 00:00:05.000
<v James Misson Control>Gordo are you ready for takeoff?

2
00:00:05.000 --> 00:00:08.000
<v Gordo><i>Laughs uncontrollably</i>

3
00:00:08.000 --> 00:00:16.000
<v James Mission Control>Good, we're ready for launch
in 3, 2, … 1 …
We are <c.launch>go</c>!

4
00:00:16.000 --> 00:00:20.000
<v James Mission Control>Good, we're ready for launch
in 3, 2, … 1

5
00:00:20.000 --> 00:00:30.000
<v Gordo><b>Arrrghhhhhhhhhhh</b>
```

Finally, with WebVTT we can specify the position where we want the captions to appear by adding some cue settings after the timestamps. Table 5-2 shows which settings are available.

Table 5-2. WebVTT Cue Settings

Meaning	Format	Values	Effect
Text direction	D:value	vertical	Vertical from right to left
		vertical-lr	Vertical from left to right
Line position	L:value	0-100%	Percent position of the cue relative to the frame
		[x]number	Line number to be displayed on
Text alignment	A:value	start	Text is aligned to the start of the line.
		middle	Text is aligned to the middle of the line
		end	Text is aligned to the end of the line.
Text position	T:value	0-100%	Percent position of the cue text relative to the frame
Text size	S:value	0-100%	The size of the cue text

Let's look at an example.

```
WEBVTT

1
00:00:01.000 --> 00:00:05.000 A:start T:0
<v James Misson Control>Gordo are you ready for takeoff?

2
00:00:05.000 --> 00:00:08.000 A:end L:10% D:vertical
<v Gordo><i>Laughs uncontrollably</i>
```

The first cue in the example places the text far left in the frame with the text aligned to the start of the line. The second cue is 10 percent from the top, vertical, and with the text aligned to the end. You can see this more clearly in Figure 5-3.

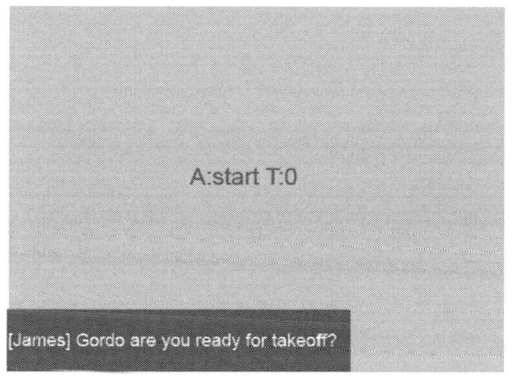
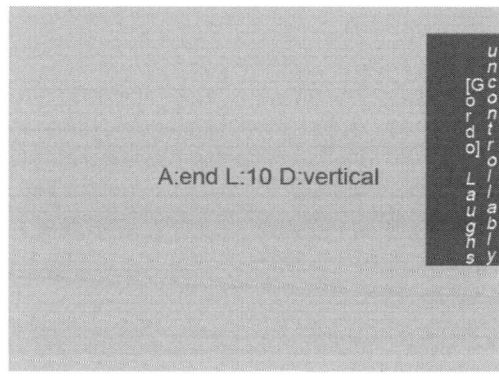

Figure 5-3. Example of where captions would appear on a video using WebVTT cue settings

That has been a gentle introduction to WebVTT. There is much more to research, explain, and learn as the specification and browser support develops, so be sure to keep your finger on the pulse.

Do more with video

There'll come a time when you'll need to do more with your video, whether it's creating custom controls that are on brand or adding fast forward and rewind buttons. Some of these actions can be achieved using the HTML5 DOM media elements API (http://j.mp/dommediaelements[20]). Because complex JavaScript is outside the scope of this book, we'll briefly introduce some of the methods and properties available to us, leaving you free to experiment some more. *HTML5 Multimedia* by Ian Devlin (http://j.mp/devlinbook[21]) and The *Definitive Guide to HTML5 Video* by Silvia Pfeiffer (http://j.mp/pfeifferbook[22]) explain this in greater detail.

> *Note: The DOM (Document Object Model) media elements API that we're discussing here in relation to video also largely applies to audio, which we'll cover later.*

We'll start by adding custom play and pause buttons to our video. In the example, we've removed the controls attribute from the video element, but we would suggest that in a production environment you remove these in your script to ensure that users without JavaScript can still see the native controls. Here is the simplified video code:

```
<video src="gordoinspace.webm">
  Download <a href="gordoinspace.webm>Gordo in Space</a> the movie.
</video>
```

Next we'll assign a variable for the video.

---

[20] www.w3.org/TR/html5/video.html#media-elements
[21] http://html5multimedia.com
[22] http://html5multimedia.com

```
<video src="gordoinspace.webm">
  Download <a href="gordoinspace.webm>Gordo in Space</a> the movie.
</video>
<script>
  var gordovid = document.getElementsByTagName('video')[0];
</script>
```

Finally, we'll add two buttons to play and pause our video.

```
<video src="gordoinspace.webm">
  Download <a href="gordoinspace.webm>Gordo in Space</a> the movie.
</video>
<script>
  var gordovid = document.getElementsByTagName('video')[0];
</script>
<input type="button" value="Play" onclick="gordovid.play()">
<input type="button" value="Pause" onclick="gordovid.pause()">
```

The controls can then be styled using CSS and positioned over the video. If required, you can style them to only show on hover, focus, or whatever else you want. That's the beauty of native video in the browser working in tandem with other open standards. If you wanted to go one step further, you could use the following DOM events to create fully customizable controls:

- volume: Used to change the volume of the audio; ranges from 0.0 to 1.0

- muted: Mutes the video regardless of the volume's value

- currentTime: Returns the current playback position, in seconds

Combine the preceding events with event listeners for loadeddata, play, pause, timeupdate, and ended and you have everything you need to build your own set of controls.

You can see the possibilities that begin to open up. Since video is now a block-level element in the DOM, we can use CSS to style it or we can add hover or focus effects. We'll see some more exciting things that you can do with HTML5 video later in the chapter when we introduce canvas.

Extra homework?

For you eager beavers who want to do that little bit more, go ahead and create a set of your own custom-controlled subtitled videos. Let Google be your friend.

Take out the heavy lifting

If writing and remembering all that code for implementing cross-browser video seems like too much hard work, there are a number of tools available to help automate the process. These polyfills cover all the detection required and serve the appropriate file to each browser. The following are our top five tools, in no particular order. However, there are many more available with VideoSWS (Video, See What Sucks) maintaining a comparative list of HTML5 Video Players (http://j.mp/html5videochart[23]).

JW Player

JW Player, which we met earlier, is a fully configurable, skinnable player from LongTail Video, available to download from www.longtailvideo.com/players. It uses jQuery and provides a fallback to the standard JW player for Flash (see Figure 5-4). For the current state of HTML5 video, LongTail is also the producer of the State of HTML5 Video report mentioned earlier (http://j.mp/h5longtail[24]).

Figure 5-4. JW Player for HTML5

Playr

Playr is an extremely simple, stripped down video player (Figure 5-5) created by Julien 'delphiki' Villetorte. It doesn't include a Flash fallback but does include fantastic support for the track element so it therefore offers captions. In addition, it is keyboard accessible. The code and documentation are available at www.delphiki.com/html5/playr.

---

[23] http://praegnanz.de/html5video/index.php
[24] www.longtailvideo.com/html5

Figure 5-5. Playr with captions in action

MediaElement.js

MediaElement.js is a powerful script created by John Dyer that works cross browser (Figure 5-6). There are a series of plug-ins available to add a loop button, translations (using `track`), and backlight the video—and more are coming soon. You can download it from `http://mediaelementjs.com`.

Figure 5-6. MediaElement.js by John Dyer

VideoJS

VideoJS (Figure 5-7) is a small, open source JavaScript library that works cross browser. Like the other players, it falls back to Flash for browsers that don't support `video`. There is also a full-window mode. It's available at `http://videojs.com`.

Figure 5-7. VideoJS by Steve Heffernan and Zencoder Inc

SublimeVideo

SublimeVideo Player (Figure 5-8) from Jilion is built using a stand-alone JavaScript library with Flash fallback for less advanced browsers. It has a full-window mode and a full-screen mode, playlist support, and more. You can download a trial from `http://sublimevideo.net`.

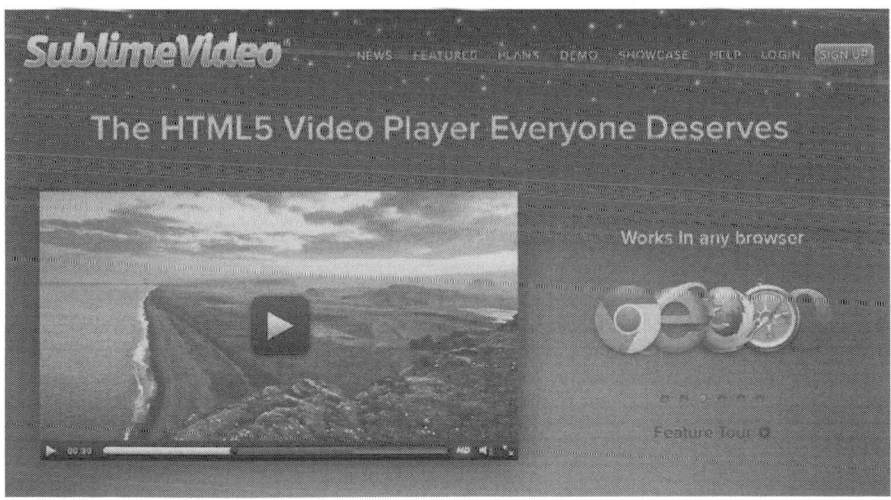

Figure 5-8. SublimeVideo from Jilion

Audio

We've already seen what's possible with native video in the browser, so now it's time to have a look at `video`'s younger sister, audio. While `video` might be the slightly sexier sibling, `audio` has more than its fair share of use cases, not least of which are online radio and services such as Last.fm and Spotify. Here's the markup for adding `audio` to your page:

```
<audio src="gordo_interview.ogg" controls></audio>
```

As you can see, it works in much the same way as `video` and shares some of the same attributes and APIs. The attributes common to `audio` and `video` are

- src
- controls
- autoplay
- preload
- loop
- muted
- crossorigin
- mediagroup

> Note: There's no need to specify the width and height of the `audio` element in the HTML.

Like `video`, the controls are styled differently cross browser (see Opera's styling in Figure 5-9), but you can create your own using JavaScript. The media API for `audio` is the same as that of `video` and uses the same methods.

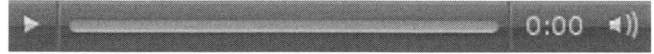

Figure 5-9. Opera's audio controls

There's nothing complicated in what we've seen so far, but we need to talk about those elephants again—audio codecs.

Audio codecs

In the same vein as `video`, no audio codecs are specified in the HTML5 spec because browser vendors support different codecs. In essence, the audio codec decodes the stream into a format that it can play back through your speakers. There are dozens of audio codecs available, but we're only interested in the following five:

- *Vorbis*: An open codec without any patent restrictions. It tends to be wrapped in an Ogg container, but it can also be wrapped in WebM or others.

- *MP3*: A patent-encumbered codec that was standardized in 1991.

- *AAC*: Short for Advanced Audio Coding, it is used in Apple's iTunes Store. It is patent encumbered and differs from MP3 by defining multiple profiles.

- *WAV*: Short for Waveform Audio File Format, it is the standard for storing audio on a PC. WAV files are generally large in size, so they are not suited for streaming audio; we mention them here because there is browser support available.

- *MP4*: Mainly used for video but it can also be used for audio.

With these five codecs to choose from, we're sure you've got an idea of which browsers support the different formats, but let's clarify it in the next section.

Browser support

Support is spread cross browser between codecs, but most browsers (with the exception of IE8 and below) support more than one codec, as shown in Table 5-3.

Table 5-3. HTML5 Audio Format Compatibility

	Internet Explorer				Mozilla		WebKit				Opera	
	IE 6	IE 7	IE 8	IE 9+	FF3.6	FF4+	SAF4	SAF5+	CHR5+	CHR8+	O10.5	O10.6+
AAC	.	.	.	.	.	.	✓	✓	✓	✓	.	.
MP3	.	.	.	✓	.	.	✓	✓	✓	✓	.	.
Ogg Vorbis	.	.	.	.	✓	✓	.	.	✓	✓	✓	✓
WAV	.	.	.	.	✓	✓	✓	✓	.	✓	✓	✓
MP4	.	.	.	✓	.	.	✓	✓	✓	.	.	.

As with video, there isn't a single codec that works cross browser, which means you'll have to encode your audio more than once. Thankfully, as we'll see, we can again use the source element to support multiple browsers.

Adding audio source

Using the source element in the same way as we did with video, we can specify multiple audio files and allow the browser to play the first file it understands. To cater to those browsers that don't support the audio element, we'll add a link to download the audio file.

```
<audio controls>
  <source src="gordo_interview.mp3" type="audio/mp3">
  <source src="gordo_interview.aac" type="audio/aac">
  <source src="gordo_interview.ogg" type="audio/ogg">
```

```
  Download <a href="gordo_interview.ogg>Gordo interview</a>.
</audio>
```

You can use the same technique described earlier in the chapter for video to provide a Flash fallback for cross-browser compatibility. If you don't want to do all that yourself, you can use a plug-in or library to help you out. Also, be sure to refer to the earlier sections on the track element and the DOM media elements API ("Do more with video"), which are both applicable to audio as well as video.

Using jPlayer

Developed by Happyworm, jPlayer (Figure 5-10) is a jQuery plug-in that provides HTML5 audio and video support for compatible browsers and falls back to Flash for those that don't. You can download it from www.jplayer.org.

Figure 5-10. jPlayer demo by Happyworm

Video and audio summary

That wraps up our introduction to native audio and video in HTML5. With 24 hours' worth of video being uploaded to YouTube every minute (http://j.mp/youtube24[25]), it's probably time you started experimenting with it. In the second half of this chapter, we're going to add some dynamic graphics elements to our arsenal and show some examples of how they can be combined with video and audio to stunning effect.

Canvas

If you're a Mac user, you've likely come into contact with canvas without even knowing it. It was created by Apple to form part of its Dashboard widgets and Safari. This work continued with WebKit browsers, closely followed by Mozilla and Opera. canvas then became part of the WHATWG's version of HTML5. Whereas Microsoft Internet Explorer up until version 8 supported only VML (a deprecated markup language for producing vector graphics), IE9 supports canvas. However, fear not if you think you can't use it now; by using the ExplorerCanvas library (http://j.mp/excanvaslib[26]), we can get canvas to work on IE7 upward. That's all very well, but what does it do?

---

[25] http://youtube-global.blogspot.com/2010/03/oops-pow-surprise24-hours-of-video-all.html
[26] http://code.google.com/p/explorercanvas/

Pixel-based freedom

Put simply, canvas and its associated APIs offer the ability to write scripts for producing dynamic images and interactions on the fly. Unlike SVG, which we'll see shortly, canvas is pixel (raster) based, allowing for quick rendering but poor scaling. It also means that changes require the whole canvas to be redrawn. canvas can be used to create games, diagrams, graphs, interactive graphics, and, in some cases, full applications; whether it's the correct tool for the job is another matter entirely. You can even combine it with video and audio to create some really interesting experiments, as we'll see later.

canvas includes both a 2D and 3D context for drawing and manipulating dynamic images. We'll be concentrating on the 2D context here due to its range of browser implementation; however, experimental builds of Firefox and Opera include support for the 3D context.

> While the canvas element remains in the HTML5 specification, the context APIs (methods for using canvas) have been broken off into their own independent specifications.

Adding/implementing canvas

In order to implement a canvas and start drawing in our document, we need to do two basic things.

1. Add a canvas element to the document.

2. Get the context using JavaScript.

Adding canvas to your document is just like adding any other element.

```
<!DOCTYPE HTML>
<html lang="en_UK">
  <head>
    <meta charset="UTF-8">
    <title>Canvas</title>
  </head>
<body>
  <canvas width="640" height="480" id="outerspace"></canvas>
</body>
</html>
```

The width and height need to be explicitly set for the canvas within the HTML in order to define the available drawing area. If you don't set the dimensions, the canvas defaults to 300 × 150 pixels. Giving it an id allows us to easily target that element in the script.

canvas works in exactly the same way as video and audio do and allows fallback content within the element for browsers that don't support it. IE9 has added support for exposing the fallback content to assistive technologies even when canvas is supported. Steve Faulkner has written about this on the

Paciello Group Blog (`http://j.mp/canvasie9`[27]). This is an issue that is now being addressed by the working group. Here's an example of a `canvas` with some fallback content:

```
<canvas width="640" height="480" id="outerspace">
  Sorry, your browser doesn't support canvas.
</canvas>
```

That's it; we've added `canvas` to our markup. If you view the example in a browser, you'll see, um, nothing—the reason being that `canvas` is transparent by default. We need to use JavaScript to really show off our drawing skills.

> Note: When drawing or animating with `canvas`, nothing appears in the DOM, meaning that it isn't very accessible—a black box, if you will. Thankfully, a task force has been set up by the W3C to address this issue.

The 2D context

Before we can draw, though, we need something to draw on: that's the context. Think of it as a sketchpad or, more specifically, a page in a sketchpad. We can get the context like so:

```
<script>
var canvas = document.getElementById('outerspace');
var ctx = canvas.getContext('2d');
</script>
```

First, we declare a variable for our `canvas` and use the `getElementById` method to select our `canvas` (outerspace). We then declare a second variable (`ctx`) and use the `getContext` method to select the context (in this case, 2D).

We can take this a stage further in the interests of accessibility and use unobtrusive JavaScript (`http://j.mp/gracefuljs`[28]) to prevent errors across unsupported browsers. This is achieved by adding a simple `if` statement.

```
<script>
var canvas = document.getElementById('outerspace');
if (canvas.getContext){
        var ctx = canvas.getContext('2d');
} else {
        // canvas not supported do something
}
</script>
```

OK, boring stuff over, we promise. Now we'll start drawing. To ease you in gently, we'll start with a simple rectangle. For that we use the `fillRect` method and declare properties for the x axis start position, y axis

---

[27] www.paciellogroup.com/blog/?p=670
[28] http://en.wikipedia.org/wiki/Unobtrusive_JavaScript

start position, width, and height. When declaring coordinates, the grid (or coordinate) space for canvas starts in the top-left corner and increases to the right for the x axis and down for the y axis.

```
<script>
var canvas = document.getElementById('outerspace');
if (canvas.getContext){
  var ctx = canvas.getContext('2d');
  //set the size and shape (x, y, width, height)
  ctx.fillRect(180, 180, 240, 120);
}
</script>
```

Finally, we add an onload function and add the script to a document. The results are shown in Figure 5-11.

```
<!DOCTYPE HTML>
<html lang="en_UK">
<head>
<meta charset="UTF-8">
<title>Canvas</title>
<script>
window.onload = function() {
var canvas = document.getElementById("outerspace"),
    ctx = canvas.getContext("2d");
// x = 10, y = 20, width = 200, height = 100
ctx.fillRect(180, 180, 240, 120);
};
</script>
</head>

<body>
<canvas width="640" height="480" id="outerspace">
    Sorry, your browser doesn't support canvas.
</canvas>
</body>
</html>
```

Figure 5-11. Simple rectangle drawn using canvas

We can change the rectangle's color by using the fillStyle method. Note that it appears *before* fillRect. As Remy Sharp points out, "if you're going to paint, you need to dip your brush in to the paint pot first" (http://j.mp/sharpcanvas[29]). fillStyle can use values provided by keyword (blue), hex code (#002654), or rgba (see Chapter 11), as shown in the following example:

```
<script>
window.onload = function() {
var canvas = document.getElementById('outerspace');
if (canvas.getContext){
  var ctx = canvas.getContext('2d');
  ctx.fillStyle="rgba(0,149,197,0.8)";
  ctx.fillRect(180, 180, 240, 120);
};
</script>
```

If we prefer that the rectangle has an outline instead of being filled, we can use the strokeRect method, shown next (see Figure 5-12 for the results). You can also use the clearRect method to make an area transparent.

```
<script>
window.onload = function() {
var canvas = document.getElementById('outerspace');
if (canvas.getContext){
  var ctx = canvas.getContext('2d');
  ctx.fillStyle="rgba(0,149,197,0.8)";
  ctx.strokeRect(180, 180, 240, 120);
};
</script>
```

Figure 5-12. Stroked rectangle drawn with canvas

Thankfully, we're not stuck with rectangles; we can also draw lines, paths (for complex curves), gradients, and text. We can also work with images, transparencies, and transformations, all of which allow us to flex our creative muscles.

The next example shows a simple circle (see Figure 5-13). Hopefully you remember your math from school, as you're going to need it.

---

[29] http://html5doctor.com/an-introduction-to-the-canvas-2d-api

Figure 5-13. Circle drawn with canvas

> *Tip: In the Canvas API, angles are measured in radians, not degrees. Use the following JavaScript expression to convert from degrees to radians:*
>
> var radians = (Math.PI/180)*degrees.

To create the circle, we follow these steps:

1. Start the path (beginPath).

2. Draw an arc (ctx.arc), with a center position of 320, 240 and a radius of 200.

3. Rotate it from an angle of 0 to 2*PI radians (360 degrees).

4. Close the path using the closePath method and apply the predefined fill.

This code example shows how to do it:

```
<script>
window.onload = function() {
var canvas = document.getElementById('outerspace');
if (canvas.getContext){
  var ctx = canvas.getContext('2d');
  ctx.fillStyle = "rgba(0,149,197,0.8)";
  ctx.beginPath();
  // begin the path
  ctx.arc(320,240,200,0,Math.PI*2,true);
  // draw an arc - (x, y, radius, startAngle, endAngle, anticlockwise)
  ctx.closePath();
  // close path
  ctx.fill();
};
</script>
```

If you're having trouble following along, revisit the preceding steps until you understand them. We'll now take our circle a step further and add a gradient. To do that, we first define a variable for the gradient (mygrad) and then apply the createLinearGradient method and specify the start (x1, y1) and end points (x2, y2) of the gradient, as follows:

```
var mygrad = ctx.createLinearGradient(300,100,640,480);
// varmygrad = ctx.createLinearGradient(x1,y1,x2,y2);
```

Now that we have an object in which to house our gradient, we will assign colors to it using the addColorStop method. The method takes two arguments: position and color. The position is a value between 0 (min) and 1 (max), which defines the position of the color relative to the size of its shape. For example, setting the position to 0.25 would place the color a quarter of the way along the gradient. The color argument is a CSS-based string and can use a keyword, hex value, or rgba.

```
mygrad.addColorStop(0, '#6c88ba');
// mygrad.addColorStop(position, color);
```

To ensure the gradient is smooth and doesn't take over the whole circle, add three color stops positioned at 0 (min), 0.9, and 1 (max) in the linear gradient example (see Figure 5-14 for the results).

```
<script>
window.onload = function() {
var canvas = document.getElementById('outerspace');
if (canvas.getContext){
var ctx = canvas.getContext('2d');

// Define the gradient
var mygrad = ctx.createLinearGradient(300,100,640,480);
mygrad.addColorStop(0, '#6c88ba');
mygrad.addColorStop(0.9, 'rgba(0,0,0,0.5)');
mygrad.addColorStop(1, 'rgba(0,0,0,1)');

// Draw the circle
ctx.fillStyle = mygrad;
ctx.beginPath();
ctx.arc(320,240,200,0,Math.PI*2,true);
ctx.closePath();
ctx.fill();
};
</script>
```

Figure 5-14. Circle with a linear gradient drawn with canvas

Note that we haven't used a radial gradient to achieve this effect. Using a radial gradient is a little more complicated, so let's go through it.

Start by using the `createRadialGradient` method, which works like the `createLinearGradient` method with two additional arguments for the radius.

```
var radgrad = ctx.createRadialGradient(305,215,150,320,240,200);
// var radgrad = ctx.createRadialGradient(x0, y0, radius1, x1, y1, radius2)
```

We then define our color stops in the same way as we did in the linear example (this time we're using four color stops).

```
radgrad.addColorStop(0, '#6c88ba');
radgrad.addColorStop(0.8, 'rgba(61,71,89,0.7)');
radgrad.addColorStop(0.9, 'rgba(61,71,89,0.8)');
radgrad.addColorStop(1, 'rgba(255,255,255,1)');
```

Finally, we draw a rectangle to house the radial gradient.

```
ctx.fillStyle = radgrad;
ctx.fillRect(0,0,640,480);
//rectangle that fills the whole canvas
```

Let's combine the previous pieces of code to arrive at the complete example.

```
<script>
window.onload = function() {
var canvas = document.getElementById('outerspace');
if (canvas.getContext){
var ctx = canvas.getContext('2d');

// Create gradient and color stops
var radgrad = ctx.createRadialGradient(305,215,150,320,240,200);
radgrad.addColorStop(0, '#6c88ba');
radgrad.addColorStop(0.8, 'rgba(61,71,89,0.7)');
radgrad.addColorStop(0.9, 'rgba(61,71,89,0.8)');
radgrad.addColorStop(1, 'rgba(255,255,255,1)');

// draw shapes
ctx.fillStyle = radgrad;
ctx.fillRect(0,0,640,480); };
</script>
```

You should be able to see the difference between the two examples in Figures 5-14 and 5-15.

Figure 5-15. Circle with a radial gradient drawn with canvas

Reverting to the linear gradient example, we can add a shadow to the circle using the following four properties. They are inserted after defining the gradient but before drawing the circle.

```
// Create a drop shadow
ctx.shadowOffsetX = 5;
ctx.shadowOffsetY = 10;
ctx.shadowBlur = 20;
ctx.shadowColor = rgba(0,0,0,0.9);
```

It's all very straightforward. Note that the offsets can be set to negative numbers, meaning that the shadow won't always appear down and to the right of your shape. Combining this with our linear gradient from earlier, we end up with the following script:

```
<script>
window.onload = function() {
var canvas = document.getElementById('outerspace');
if (canvas.getContext){
var ctx = canvas.getContext('2d');

// Define the gradient
var mygrad = ctx.createLinearGradient(300,100,640,480);
mygrad.addColorStop(0, '#6c88ba');
mygrad.addColorStop(0.9, 'rgba(0,0,0,0.5)');
mygrad.addColorStop(1, 'rgba(0,0,0,1)');

//Create a drop shadow
ctx.shadowOffsetX = 5;
ctx.shadowOffsetY = 10;
ctx.shadowBlur = 20;
ctx.shadowColor = "black";

// Draw the circle
ctx.fillStyle = mygrad;
ctx.beginPath();
ctx.arc(320,240,200,0,Math.PI*2,true);
ctx.closePath();
ctx.fill();
};
</script>
```

If you add the script to your HTML document complete with a canvas element and open it in a browser that supports canvas, you should end up with something like that shown in Figure 5-16.

Figure 5-16. Circle with gradient and shadow drawn with canvas

Looks nice, huh? We think so. We've been through some of the basic drawing methods for canvas, but there's much more you can get from the API, such as incorporating images using createPattern and drawing lines, Bezier curves, and text. You can also use transformations, translations, and animation. If you really want to push the boat out, you can save your canvas as an image by calling the toDataURL method. We don't have enough room to cover it all here, but there are books available that concentrate solely on canvas.

Canvas in IE

We'll get to some amazing examples of demos people have created using canvas soon enough, but first we're going to address that question you're probably asking, "What about canvas in IE?"

When we first introduced canvas, we mentioned that you can support IE by using a JavaScript library called ExplorerCanvas (excanvas.js) (http://j.mp/excanvaslib[30]). It works by converting your script into Microsoft's proprietary VML technology, which is not dissimilar to the canvas API we've been describing. It's as simple as downloading the file and adding a link to it in the head of your page, as follows:

```
<!DOCTYPE html>
<html>
 <head>
  <meta charset="utf-8">
  <title>Gordo's Space Adventures</title>
  <!--[if lt IE 9]>
    <script src="excanvas.js"></script>
  <![endif]-->
  <script>
    // your canvas script
  </script>
 </head>
<body>
  <canvas id="outerspace" width="640" height="480"></canvas>
</body>
```

---

[30] http://code.google.com/p/explorercanvas

```
</html>
```

You should be aware when using excanvas.js that it can be slow to execute and render depending on the complexity you're trying to achieve. The following are a few more gotchas:

- Radial gradients aren't supported.

- Patterns must repeat in the x axis and y axis.

- Clipping regions aren't supported.

- Shadows aren't implemented.

With IE9 including `canvas` support, we hope that excanvas.js will become a thing of the past.

The power and potential of canvas

We've talked about the potential of `canvas`, so now we'll briefly look at a few examples of demos that people have created using `canvas` and its API.

Games

First up, we'll look at a couple of game examples.

Cut the Rope

Cut the Rope (Figure 5-17) is an iPhone gamers favorite, and it's been ported to HTML5 by Microsoft, ZeptoLab, and Pixel Lab. They've ported the game from Objective-C to JavaScript, specifically making use of `canvas` for the graphics. They even found that in some areas `canvas` offered more functionality than OpenGL that they had been using on the iPhone version. Find it at www.cuttherope.ie.

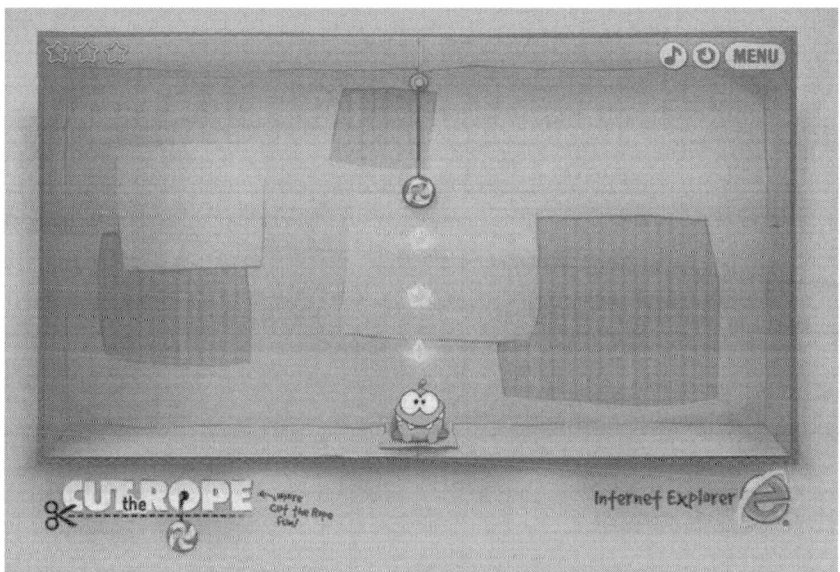

Figure 5-17. Cut the Rope was created using canvas.

Canvas Rider

Canvas Rider (Figure 5-18) allows users to control a rider along a course without falling off. The game allows users to submit their own levels, created using canvas. Visit http://canvasrider.com to play.

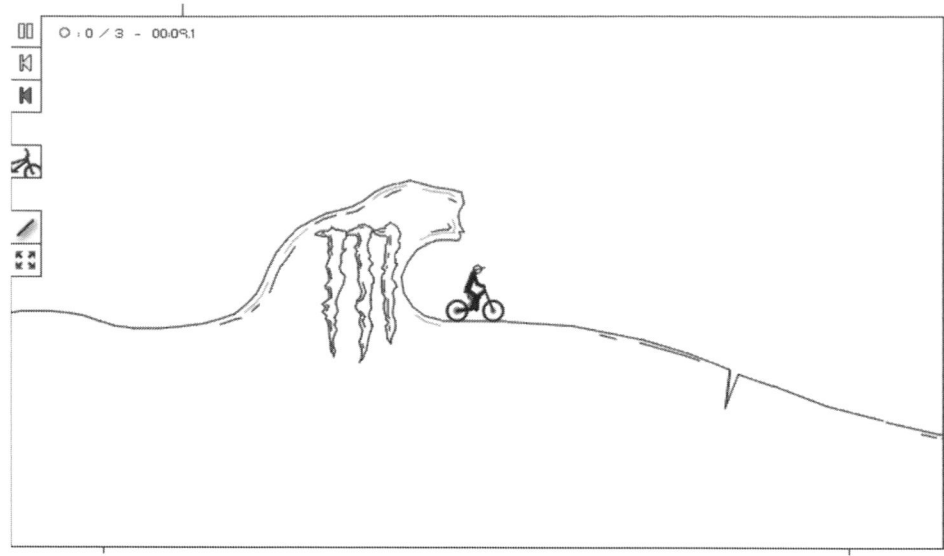

Figure 5-18. Canvas Rider, a game created with canvas

3D Tetris

Another gaming classic re-created in 3D using canvas, 3D Tetris (Figure 5-19) was created by Ben Joffe. Be sure to look at Ben's site (www.benjoffe.com) for more examples of canvas games.

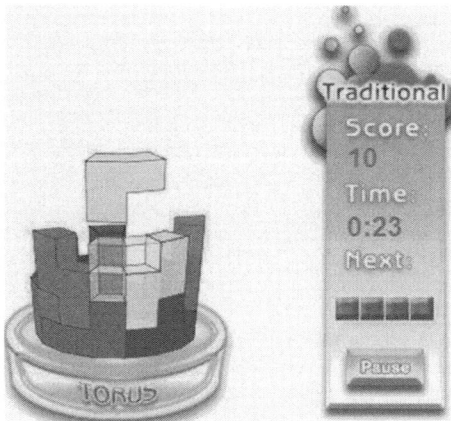

Figure 5-19. Pseudo 3D Tetris created with canvas

Applications

Now we'll look at some application examples.

Darkroom

Created by MugTug, Darkroom (http://mugtug.com/darkroom) is an all-in-one image processing package built using canvas (see Figure 5-20). Darkroom has a wide-ranging feature set that allows designers to crop, mirror, and rotate images on the fly. As with Photoshop, users can change the levels of an image, up the brightness or contrast, or apply one of the default filters such as "black and white." Once you've edited your image, you can save it to your desktop.

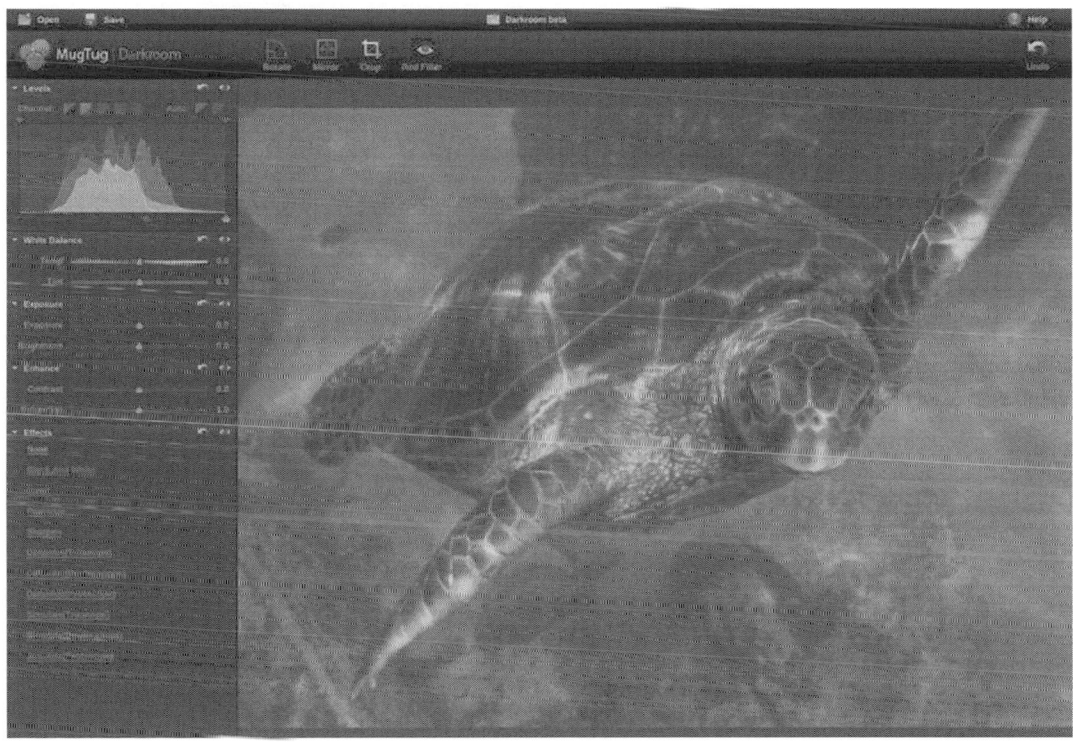

Figure 5-20. Darkroom from MugTug

Sketchpad

MugTug has also released another online tool, Sketchpad (http://mugtug.com/sketchpad). It's a fully featured drawing package that runs in the browser and is built with canvas (see Figure 5-21).

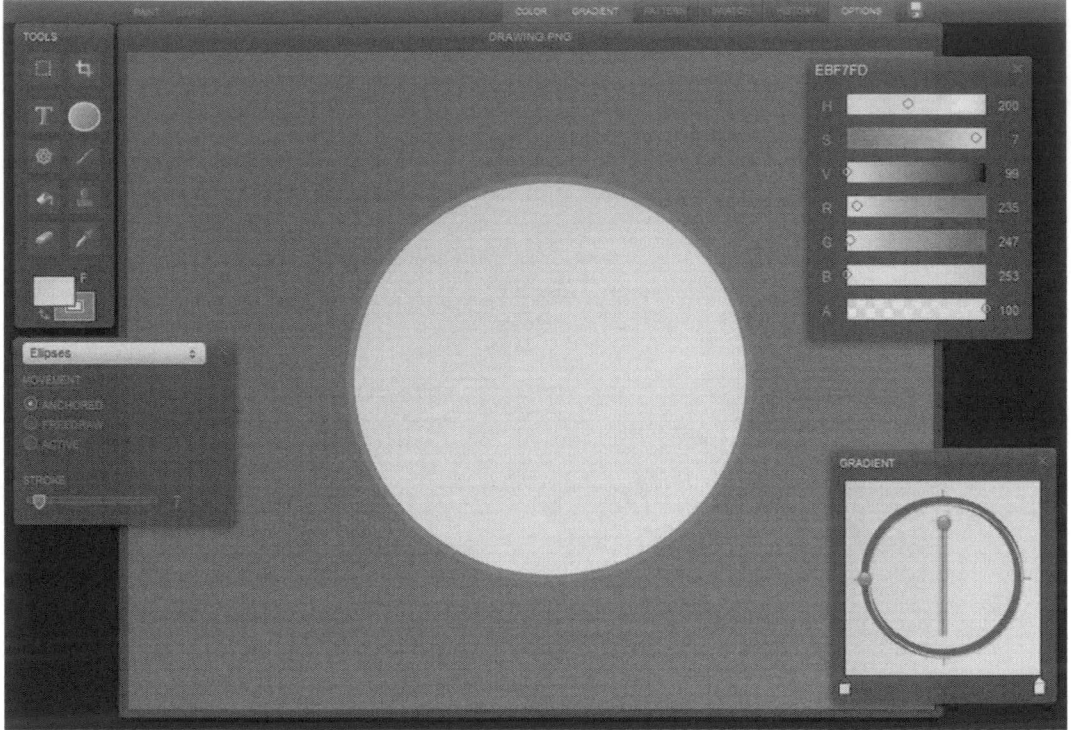

Figure 5-21. Sketchpad by MugTug

Picozu Editor

Picozu Editor (Figure 5-22) is a drawing and photo re-touching application built with JavaScript, HTML5, and CSS3. The app uses canvas for applying image filters and the Drag and Drop API to allow users to add images from their desktop. You can have a play at www.picozu.com/editor.

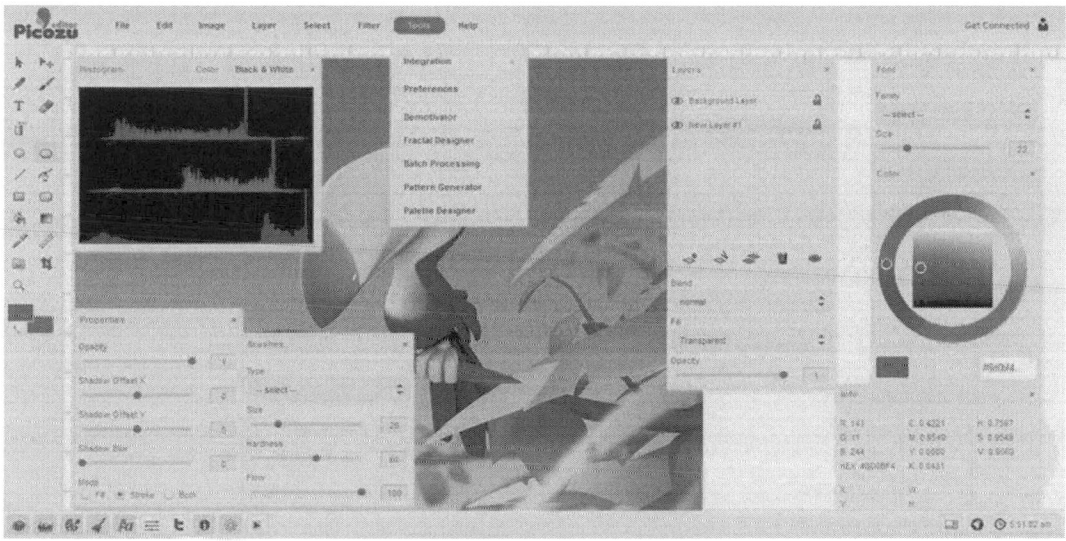

Figure 5-22. Some of the options available In Picozu Editor

Combining video and audio with canvas

We talked earlier in the chapter about how the new native media elements (audio and video) are designed to work together with canvas to create rich, compelling experiences online. Here are some examples of that in action, giving you some ideas of how to truly add some sprinkles to your site.

9elements HTML canvas experiment

The guys at 9elements began to experiment with new HTML5 features, specifically audio and canvas. They combined this with the Twitter API (searching for the term "HTML5") and Processing.js (http://processingjs.org) for particle rendering to create a beautiful animated visualization of tweets and particles that syncs to an audio track (see Figure 5-23). A write-up of the experiment is available on the 9 elements blog (http://j.mp/9elementsblog[31]).

---

[31] http://9elements.com/io/?p=153

Figure 5-23. 9elements canvas experiment

Ambilight

If you've seen the Philips Ambilight TVs (http://j.mp/ambilighttv[32]) and were impressed, then this demo is for you. Created by Sergey Chikuyonok, Ambilight works by gathering pixel color data from each frame of the video and reflecting the ambient light onto two canvas elements on either side of the video. The effect, shown in Figure 5-24, is nothing short of sublime: http://j.mp/ambilightcanvas[33] .

---

[32] www.philips.co.uk/c/televisions/33092/cat/#/cp_tab2
[33] http://media.chikuyonok.ru/ambilight

Figure 5-24. Ambilight by Sergey Chikuyonok

Video destruction

Sean Christmann of Crafty Mind created a demo that combines the video and canvas elements. The basic premise of the demonstration is to show how canvas can be used in conjunction with other elements (video) to create stunning effects. Clicking the video causes it to "explode," as shown in Figure 5-25; the accompanying article (http://j.mp/blowupvideoarticle[34]) explains how it was achieved.

It also gives a sneak preview of some transforms and translations that can be carried out on these elements using CSS. Rest assured you'll be learning all about those in Chapter 12.

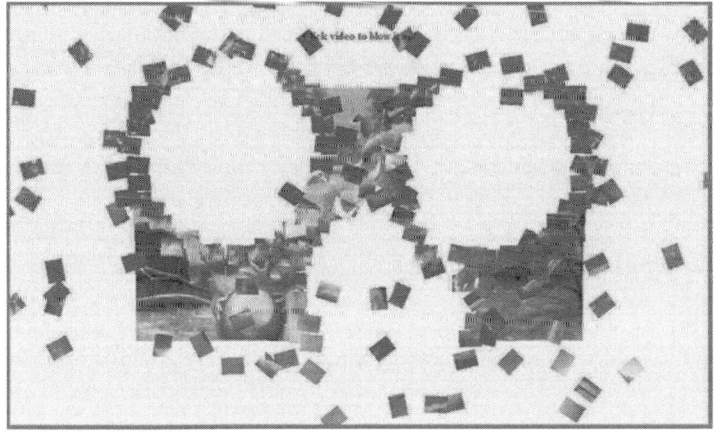

Figure 5-25. Video destruction

---

[34] www.craftymind.com/2010/04/20/blowing-up-html5-video-and-mapping-it-into-3d-space

Further canvas resources

We've taken a whistle-stop tour through the power canvas has to offer. To cover it in more detail would require a book of its own, so for now we'll introduce you to some further canvas resources and leave you to experiment:

- *Dev.Opera*: "HTML5 canvas — the basics" by Mihai Sucan (http://dev.opera.com/articles/view/html-5-canvas-the-basics)

- *Mozilla Developer Center*: Canvas tutorial (https://developer.mozilla.org/En/Canvas_tutorial)

- *HTML5 Doctor*: "An introduction to the canvas 2D API" by Remy Sharp (http://html5doctor.com/an-introduction-to-the-canvas-2d-api)

- *HTML5 Doctor*: "video + canvas = magic" by Tab Atkins Jr. (http://html5doctor.com/video-canvas-magic)

- *Canvas Demos*: Applications, games, tools, and tutorials that use the HTML 5 <canvas> element (www.canvasdemos.com)

- *.net magazine*: "Learning the basics of HTML5 canvas" by Rob Hawkes (www.netmagazine.com/tutorials/learning-basics-html5-canvas)

SVG

Scalable Vector Graphics is a technology for creating vector graphics in the browser based on the XML file format. It is an open standard that has been actively developed by the W3C since 1999 (www.w3.org/TR/SVG). We must point out that SVG *is not* part of HTML5. Repeat after us—"SVG **is not** part of HTML5." HTML5 does, however, allow the embedding of inline SVG, which is why we're looking at it here.

Vector power

As you've no doubt gathered by the name, SVG files are vector based, meaning they can be scaled up or down without the loss of quality. This is in direct contrast to canvas, which is pixel (raster) based and doesn't scale gracefully. Basic SVG is supported by all major browsers (with the exception IE8 and below). SVG embedded in HTML5, also known as "inline SVG" (which we'll be concentrating on), is supported by Chrome 7+, Internet Explorer 9+, Firefox 4+, Opera 11.5+ and Safari 5.1+. It can achieve many of the same effects as canvas. A major difference is that every SVG element becomes part of the DOM (remember we said that canvas is always empty), allowing each object to be indexed and providing a more accessible solution. We're now left with a dilemma of which to choose, canvas or SVG?

Choosing between canvas and SVG

We've already touched upon the fact that both canvas and SVG are scriptable images and both can create shapes, lines, arcs, curves, gradients, and much, much more, but how do you decide between the two?

SVG content can be static, animated, or interactive. You can style it with CSS or add behavior with the SVG DOM. Because each element becomes part of the DOM, this means that SVG is relatively accessible. It is also resolution independent and can scale to any screen size. It can, however, be slow to render with more complex shapes.

canvas, in contrast, uses a JavaScript API that allows us to draw programmatically. It has two context objects, 2D or 3D. There is no specific file format, and you can only draw using script. Because there are no DOM nodes (unlike SVG), you can concentrate on drawing (scripting) without taking a performance hit as the image complexity increases. You can also save the resulting images as a PNG or JPG.

Before deciding which technology is best suited for your project, consider some use case: SVG is good for data charts and resolution-independent graphics, interactive animated user interfaces, or vector image editing. canvas is suited for games, bitmap image manipulation (like the Darkroom example we saw earlier), generating raster graphics (data visualizations, fractals, etc.), and image analysis (histograms, etc.).

To summarize, use both—appropriately. On some occasions, the two will even complement each other (if you're creating an image editor that can render both raster and vector images, for example).

If you're still not clear about which to use, read these excellent articles on the pros and cons of both technologies:

- Dev.Opera: (http://j.mp/canvasorsvg1[35])
- SitePoint (http://j.mp/canvasorsvg2[36])
- The IE blog (http://j.mp/iecanvassvg[37])

Vectors unleashed with SVG

To produce SVG graphics, you can go down either of two routes: use a graphics package such as Adobe Illustrator or Inkscape (an open source SVG graphics editor) or write it yourself. Guess which one we're going to show you.

Implementing basic SVG

The syntax for writing inline SVG is relatively straightforward; you start by adding an svg element into the body of your HTML. You then add an SVG XML namespace to the element along with dimensions. Remember, though, that because it's XML, you have to ensure that you always quote your attributes and include those trailing slashes. First, we create the svg element in our page.

---

[35] http://dev.opera.com/articles/view/svg-or-canvas-choosing-between-the-two
[36] www.sitepoint.com/blogs/2010/07/06/canvas-vs-svg-how-to-choose/
[37] http://blogs.msdn.com/b/ie/archive/2011/04/22/thoughts-on-when-to-use-canvas-and-svg.aspx

```
<!doctype html>
<html lang="en_UK">
<head>
  <meta charset="UTF-8">
  <title>SVG</title>
</head>
<body>

<svg xmlns="http://www.w3.org/2000/svg" width="400px" height="400px">
  <!-SVG content will go here -->
</svg>

</body>
</html>
```

Next, we add the basic SVG shape element(s) inside the parent SVG element. There are several basic shapes available: rect, circle, ellipse, line, polyline, and polygon. We'll start by creating a simple rectangle with a stroke. These examples will work in all the browsers mentioned previously.

```
<!doctype html>
<html lang="en_UK">
<head>
  <meta charset="UTF-8">
  <title>SVG</title>
</head>
<body>

<svg xmlns="http://www.w3.org/2000/svg" width="400px" height="400px">
  <rect fill="black" stroke="red" x="150" y="150" width="100" height="50"/>
</svg>

</body>
</html>
```

You should see something similar to Figure 5-26. The attributes are self-explanatory. The x and y values represent the starting coordinates (from the top left of SVG the element) for drawing. This means the rectangle will be drawn 150 pixels from the left edge of the SVG element and 150 pixels from the top. The stroke and fill values can be specified as hex codes, keywords, rgba, or rgba values.

Figure 5-26. Rectangle created with SVG

We'll now create the same example as we did with canvas to allow you to compare the two. First, create a circle using the basic circle shape.

```
<circle fill="#6c88ba" stroke="red" cx="150" cy="150" r="150"/>
```

The cx and cy values represent the center point of the circle and r represents the radius. Replacing the rectangle from our earlier example with the circle shape should render as shown in Figure 5-27.

Figure 5-27. Circle created with SVG

We'll now continue on and add a gradient. This is achieved by creating a set of definitions (defs) and specifying parameters such as the type of gradient (linearGradient), an id (id="MyGradient"), the angle (gradientTransform="rotate(45)"), and a series of color stops (<stop ... />).

```
<defs>
  <linearGradient id="MyGradient" gradientTransform="rotate(45)">
    <stop offset="0%" stop-color="#6c88ba" />
    <stop offset="90%" stop-color="#677794" />
    <stop offset="100%" stop-color="#6e747f" />
  </linearGradient>
</defs>
```

Now that we've defined the gradient, we need to apply it to the circle shape. This is achieved by referencing the gradient id value (MyGradient) of the fill property on the circle with the url delimiter. This creates the same effect we achieved earlier using canvas (see Figure 5-28).

```
<!DOCTYPE HTML>
<html lang="en_UK">
<head>
  <meta charset="UTF-8">
  <title>SVG</title>
</head>
<body>

<svg xmlns="http://www.w3.org/2000/svg" width="400px" height="400px">
  <defs>
    <linearGradient id="MyGradient" gradientTransform="rotate(45)">
      <stop offset="0%" stop-color="#6c88ba" />
      <stop offset="90%" stop-color="#677794" />
      <stop offset="100%" stop-color="#6e747f" />
```

```
    </linearGradient>
  </defs>

  <circle fill="url(#MyGradient)" cx="150" cy="150" r="150"/>
</svg>

</body>
</html>
```

Figure 5-28. Circle with gradient created with SVG

You can also create radial gradients with SVG, as well as much, much more. We've only scratched the surface of what's possible with this powerful language when embedded in HTML5. We hope we've whetted your appetite and convinced you to investigate further as to what can be achieved with SVG.

SVG-related reading

If you're interested in learning more about SVG, we highly recommend the following resources:

- *Dev.Opera*: SVG articles (`http://dev.opera.com/articles/svg`)

- *Mozilla Developer Center*: "SVG in HTML Introduction" (`https://developer.mozilla.org/en/svg_in_html_introduction`)

- *Carto:net*: Examples and papers on SVG (`www.carto.net/papers/svg`)

- *Raphaël*: A library for supporting SVG in IE (`http://raphaeljs.com`)

- *A List Apart*: "SVG with a little help from Raphaël," by Brian Suda (`www.alistapart.com/articles/svg-with-a-little-help-from-raphael`)

Summary

As you've seen throughout this chapter, the possibilities for using rich media in browsers are endless. By combining one or more of the technologies we've described, stunning effects can be created, the likes of which have only been achievable using Flash or other proprietary plug-ins up until now. The benefits of having this native multimedia content in our browsers means that plug-ins are no longer required; the browser provides native controls in which keyboard accessibility is built in. Finally, site performance will be improved because the plug-ins aren't required.

By covering how to implement video, audio, canvas, and SVG into your HTML5 documents, we hope we've opened your eyes to a new wave of opportunity for using rich media online. It's now up to you to break with convention and create truly compelling, open, and accessible interactive experiences.

As for Flash and those other plug-ins, the jury is still out on whether they're dead, but one thing's for sure—the competition is catching up.

Homework

We've split your homework into two parts. Start by encoding the files provided on the book website into enough formats to ensure cross-browser compatibility, and then display them on your sample site using video and audio elements. If you're feeling keen, you can complete the extra homework we mentioned earlier and create your own custom play controls.

Secondly, choose either canvas or SVG to produce a simple diagram showing the earth, moon, and sun in orbit and add it to your site. Continue by animating the diagram, after carrying out some further research based on the links provided.

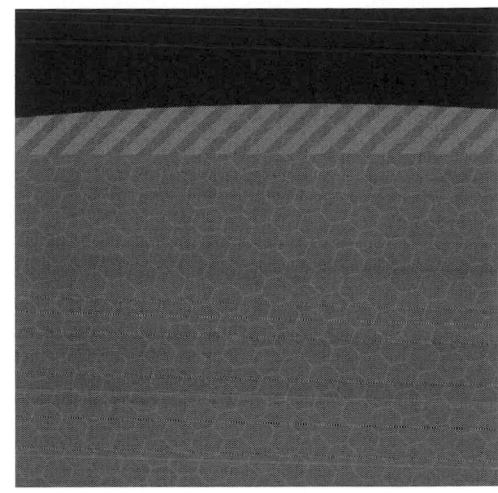

Chapter 6

Paving the Way for Web Applications

To ensure we're all singing from the same hymn sheet, let's start by defining a web application. Broadly speaking, a *web application* is an application that is accessed over a network, generally the Internet or an intranet. Web applications typically are built with a server-side technology (like .NET, PHP, Python, or Rails) and use HTML, CSS, and JavaScript to render the application in a browser.

The quantity of web applications (web apps) has risen sharply over the past few years. Undoubtedly, this is in part attributable to the introduction of Ajax. We already had JavaScript and XML, as well as Microsoft's XMLHttpRequest (now officially part of HTML5), when Jesse James Garrett coined the phrase *Ajax* back in 2005. This seemed to create a tipping point with an inexorable rise in the number of web apps on the scene. Ajax isn't restricted to applications, of course; the technology is also used in websites to make them look, feel, and act like applications.

In this chapter we'll take you through some of the web app–related developments and APIs within and related to the HTML5 specification. We'll start by looking at HTML5 forms and the new features they offer. This will be followed by a brief look at some of the web application–specific elements such as menu and command introduced in HTML5. We'll finish by introducing HTML5's APIs, plus some additional APIs that are associated with the umbrella term "HTML5."

HTML5 forms

No doubt you interact with at least one form on the Web every day. Whether you're searching for content or logging in to your e-mail account or Facebook page, using online forms is one of the most common tasks performed on the Web. As designers and developers, creating forms has a certain monotony about it, particularly writing validation scripts for them. HTML5 introduces a number of new attributes, input types, and other elements to our markup toolkit.

As you'll see, these new features will go a long way toward making our lives easier while delivering a delightful user experience. The best thing about all this? You can start using them *now*.

A history of HTML5 forms

The forms section of HTML5 was originally a specification titled Web Forms 2.0 (`http://j.mp/web-forms`[1]) that added new types of controls for forms. Started by Opera and edited by then-Opera employee Ian Hickson, it was submitted to the W3C in early 2005 (`http://j.mp/opera-forms`[2]). The work was initially carried out under the W3C. It was then combined with the Web Applications 1.0 specification to create the basis of the breakaway Web Hypertext Application Technology Working Group (WHATWG) HTML5 specification.

Using HTML5 design principles

One of the best things about HTML5 forms is that you can use almost all of these new input types and attributes right now. They don't even need any shivs, hacks, or workarounds. That isn't to say they're all "supported" right now, but they do cool things in modern browsers that do support them—and degrade gracefully in browsers that don't understand them.

For that we have to thank HTML5's design principles (`http://j.mp/designprinciples`[3]) that you learned about in Chapter 1. In this instance we're specifically referring to the principle of graceful degradation. In essence, this means that there's no excuse for not using these features right now. In fact, it means you're ahead of the curve.

HTML5 forms attributes

This section covers several of the new attributes that we can add to our forms and start using today. Not only will they improve your users' experience, but they'll save you from having to write a lot of JavaScript. Ready? Then let's get cracking.

placeholder

First up is the `placeholder` attribute, which allows us to set placeholder text as we would currently do in HTML4 with the `value` attribute. It should only be used for short descriptions. For anything longer, use the `title` attribute. The difference from HTML4 is that the text is only displayed when the field is empty and hasn't received focus. Once the field receives focus (e.g., you click or tab to the field), and you begin to type, the text simply disappears. It's very similar to the search box you see in Safari (see Figure 6-1).

---

[1] www.whatwg.org/specs/web-forms/current-work
[2] www.w3.org/Submission/2005/SUBM-web-forms2-20050411
[3] www.w3.org/TR/html-design-principles/

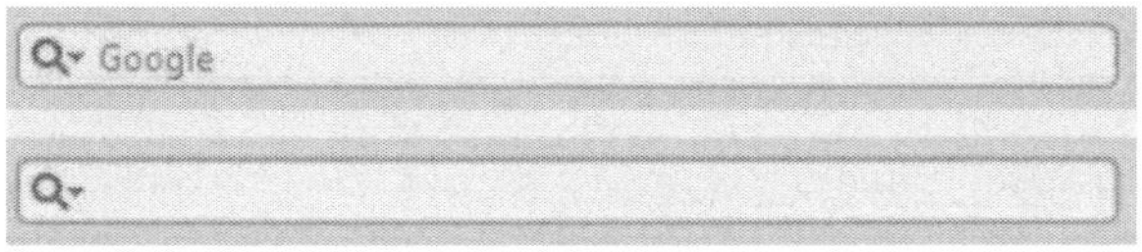

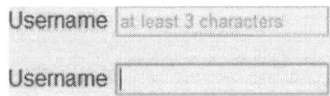

Figure 6-1. Browser search box in Safari without and with focus

Let's have a look at how to implement the placeholder attribute.

```
<input type="text" name="user-name" id="user-name" placeholder="at least 3 characters">
```

That's it! We can hear you thinking, "What's so great about that? I've been doing it with JavaScript for years." Yes, that's true. However, with HTML5, it's part of the browser, meaning less scripting is required for a more accessible, cross-browser solution (even when JavaScript is disabled). Figure 6-2 shows the placeholder attribute working in Chrome.

Figure 6-2. Placeholder attribute support in Chrome, unfocused and focused

Browsers that don't support the placeholder attribute ignore it, so it won't render. By including it, though, you're providing an enhanced user experience for those users who have browser support and you're "future proofing" your site (we talk about checking for support a little later in the chapter). All modern browsers support placeholder and it will also be supported in Internet Explorer 10.

> Note: There is no official pseudo-class for styling placeholder text but both Mozilla (makers of Firefox) and WebKit offer vendor prefixed properties for styling (-moz-placeholder and -webkit-input-placeholder). This makes it safe to assume that a pseudo-class will become standard for styling placeholder text. For further detail there is a thread on the WHATWG mailing list about this topic at http://j.mppseudoplaceholder[4]).

autofocus

autofocus does exactly what it says on the tin. Adding it to an input automatically focuses that field when the page is rendered. As with placeholder, autofocus is something that we used JavaScript for in the past.

Traditional JavaScript methods do, though, have some serious usability problems. For example, if a user begins completing the form before the script loads, they will (jarringly) be returned to the first form field when the script is loaded. The autofocus attribute in HTML5 gets around this issue by focusing as soon

---

[4] http://lists.w3.org/Archives/Public/www-style/2011Apr/0240.html

as the document loads, without having to wait for the JavaScript to be loaded. However, we only recommend using it for pages whose sole purpose is the form (like Google) to prevent the usability issues.

It is a Boolean attribute (except if you are writing XHTML5; see the note) and is implemented as follows:

```
<input type="text" name="first-name" id="first-name" autofocus>
```

All modern browsers support the attribute and, like `placeholder`, browsers that don't support the `autofocus` attribute simply ignore it.

> *Note: Several new HTML5 form attributes are Boolean attributes. This just means they're set if they're present and not set if they're absent. They can be written several ways in HTML5.*
>
> *autofocus*
> *autofocus=""*
> *autofocus="autofocus"*
>
> *However, if you are writing XHTML5, you have to use the autofocus="autofocus" style.*

autocomplete

The `autocomplete` attribute helps users complete forms based on earlier input. The attribute has been around since IE5.5 but has finally been standardized as part of HTML5. The default state is set to on. This means that generally we won't have to use it. However, if you want to insist that a form field be entered each time a form is completed (as opposed to the browser autofilling the field), you would implement it like so:

```
<input type="text" name="tracking-code" id="tracking-code" autocomplete="off">
```

The `autocomplete` state on a field overrides any `autocomplete` state set on the containing `form` element.

required

The `required` attribute doesn't need much introduction; like `autofocus`, it does exactly what you'd expect. By adding it to a form field, the browser requires the user to enter data into that field before submitting the form. This replaces the basic form validation currently implemented with JavaScript, making things a little more usable and saving us a little more development time. `required` is a Boolean attribute, like `autofocus`. Let's see it in action.

```
<input type="text" id="given-name" name="given-name" required>
```

`required` is currently implemented only in Opera 9.5+, Firefox 4+, Safari 5+, and Chrome 5+, so for the time being you need to continue writing a script to check that fields are completed on the client side in other browsers (*cough* IE!). Internet Explorer 10 will support `required`. Opera, Chrome, and Firefox show the user an error message (see Figure 6-3) upon form submission. In most browsers, the errors are then localized based on the declared language. Safari doesn't show an error message on submit, but instead places focus on that field.

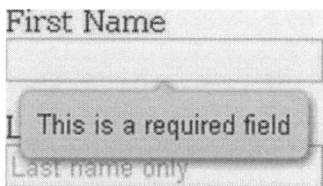

Figure 6-3. Form field with required attribute displaying a browser-generated error message in Opera

The default rendering of "required" error messages depends on the individual browser; at present the error message bubble can't be styled with CSS in all browsers. Chrome, however, does have a proprietary property that you can use to style the error bubble. Peter Gasston has written an article about the syntax (http://j.mp/stylingformerrors[5]). You can also style the input using the :required pseudo-class (http://j.mp/pseudoforms[6]) (see Chapter 7 for more on pseudo-classes). An alternative is to override the wording and styling using the setCustomValidity() method in JavaScript. Importantly, don't forget that this browser validation is no substitute for validating on the server as well.

pattern

The pattern attribute is likely to get a lot of developers very excited (well, as excited as you can get about form attributes). It specifies a JavaScript regular expression for the field's value to be checked against. pattern makes it easy for us to implement specific validation for product codes, invoice numbers, and so on. The possibilities for pattern are wide-ranging, and this is just one simple example using a product number.

```
<label> Product Number:
<input pattern="[0-9][A-Z]{3}" name="product" type="text" title="Single digit followed by
three uppercase letters."/>
</label>
```

This pattern prescribes that the product number should be a single digit [0-9] followed by three uppercase letters [A-Z]{3}. For more examples, the HTML5 Pattern website (http://j.mp/html5p[7]) lists common regex style patterns to help get you started.

As with required, Opera 9.5+, Firefox 4+, Safari 5+, and Chrome 5+ are the only browsers with support for pattern at present. Internet Explorer 10 will support pattern. However, with the browser market moving at a fast pace, the others will soon catch up.

---

[5] www.broken-links.com/2011/06/16/styling-html5-form-validation-errors
[6] http://html5doctor.com/css3-pseudo-classes-and-html5-forms/
[7] http://html5pattern.com

> *A regular expression (regex or regexp) provides a way to match entered strings of text to particular patterns. A regex might be used to check a particular format for a product or ZIP code. They can be used with a number of programming languages, some of which (Perl, Ruby) have them built into their syntax. Regex is where the* pattern *attribute originates.*

list and the datalist element

The list attribute enables the user to associate a list of options with a particular field. The value of the list attribute must be the same as the ID of a datalist element that resides in the same document. The datalist element is new in HTML5 and represents a predefined list of options for form controls. It works in a similar way to the in-browser search boxes that autocomplete as you type (see Figure 6-4).

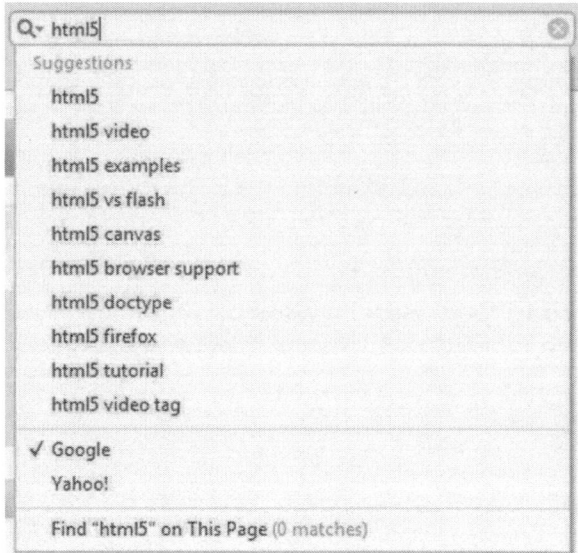

Figure 6-4. Google search autosuggestions in Safari

The following example shows how list and datalist are combined (see Figure 6-5):

```
<label>Your favorite fruit:
<datalist id="fruits">
    <option value="Blackberry">Blackberry</option>
    <option value="Blackcurrant">Blackcurrant</option>
    <option value="Blueberry">Blueberry</option>
    <!-- … -->
  </datalist>
If other, please specify:
<input type="text" name="fruit" list="fruits">
</label>
```

By adding a select element inside the datalist you can provide superior graceful degradation than by simply using an option element. This is an elegant markup pattern designed by Jeremy Keith (http://j.mp/datalistpattern[8]) that adheres perfectly with HTML5's principle of degrading gracefully.

```
<label>Your favorite fruit:
<datalist id="fruits">
  <select name="fruits">
    <option value="Blackberry">Blackberry</option>
    <option value="Blackcurrant">Blackcurrant</option>
    <option value="Blueberry">Blueberry</option>
    <!-- … -->
  </select>
If other, please specify:
</datalist>
<input type="text" name="fruit" list="fruits">
</label>
```

Browser support for list and datalist is currently limited to Opera 9.5+ (see Figure 6-5) and Firefox 5+. Internet Explorer 10 will support the list attribute and datalist.

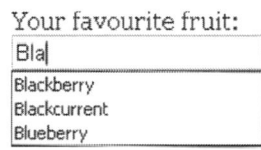

Figure 6-5. The datalist element rendered in Opera

multiple

We can take our lists and datalists one step further by applying the Boolean attribute multiple to allow more than one value to be entered from the datalist. Here is an example.

```
<label>Your favorite fruit:
<datalist id="fruits">
  <select name="fruits">
  <option value="Blackberry">Blackberry</option>
  <option value="Blackcurrant">Blackcurrant</option>
  <option value="Blueberry">Blueberry</option>
  <!-- … -->
  </select>
If other, please specify:
</datalist>
<input type="text" name="fruit" list="fruits" multiple>
</label>
```

multiple isn't exclusively for use with datalists, though. A further example for multiple might be for e-mail addresses when sending items to friend or the attachment of files, as shown here:

---

[8] http://adactio.com/journal/4272

```
<label>Upload files:
<input type="file" multiple name="upload"></label>
```

`multiple` is supported in Firefox 3.6+, Safari 4+, Opera 11.5+, and Chrome 4+. It will also be supported in Internet Explorer 10.

novalidate and formnovalidate

The `novalidate` and `formnovalidate` attributes indicate that the form shouldn't be validated when submitted. They are both Boolean attributes. `formnovalidate` can be applied to `submit` or `image` input types. The `novalidate` attribute can be set only on the `form` element.

An example use case for the `formnovalidate` attribute could be on a "save draft" button, where the form has fields that are required for submitting the draft but aren't required for saving the draft. `novalidate` would be used in cases where you don't want to validate the form but do want to take advantage of the more useful user interface enhancements that the new input types offer, which we'll see later in the chapter.

The following example shows how to use `formnovalidate`:

```
<form action="process.php">
  <label for="email">Email:</label>
  <input type="text" name="email" value="gordo@example.com">
  <input type="submit" formnovalidate value="Submit">
</form>
```

And this example shows how to use `novalidate`:

```
<form action="process.php" novalidate>
<label for="email">Email:</label>
  <input type="text" name="email" value="gordo@example.com">
  <input type="submit" value="Submit">
</form>
```

form

The `form` attribute is used to associate an `input`, `select`, or `textarea` element with a form (known as its *form owner*). Using `form` means that the element doesn't need to be a child of the associated form and can be moved away from it in the source. The primary use case for this is that input buttons that are placed within tables can now be associated with a form.

```
<input type="button" name="sort-l-h" form="sort">
```

formaction, formenctype, formmethod, and formtarget

The `formaction`, `formenctype`, `formmethod`, and `formtarget` attributes each have a corresponding attribute on the `form` element, which you'll be familiar with from HTML4, so let's run through each of them briefly. These new attributes have been introduced primarily because you may require alternative actions for different submit buttons, as opposed to having several forms in a document.

formaction

formaction specifies the file or application that will submit the form. It has the same effect as the action attribute on the form element and can only be used with a submit or image button (type="submit" or type="image"). When the form is submitted, the browser first checks for a formaction attribute; if that isn't present, it proceeds to look for an action attribute on the form.

```
<input type="submit" value="Submit" formaction="process.php">
```

formenctype

formenctype details how the form data is encoded with the POST method type. It has the same effect as the enctype attribute on the form element and can only be used with a submit or image button (type="submit" or type="image"). The default value if not included is application/x-www-form-urlencoded.

```
<input type="submit" value="Submit" formenctype="application/x-www-form-urlencoded">
```

formmethod

formmethod specifies which HTTP method (GET, POST, PUT, DELETE) will be used to submit the form data. It has the same effect as the method attribute on the form element and can only be used with a submit or image button (type="submit" or type="image").

```
<input type="submit" value="Submit" formmethod="POST">
```

formtarget

formtarget specifies the target window for the form results. It has the same effect as the target attribute on the form element and can only be used with a submit or image button (type="submit" or type="image").

```
<input type="submit" value="Submit" formtarget="_self">
```

Form attributes summary

We've looked at several new form attributes that help improve user experience and save you development time. There are some more new attributes to discuss, but we'll introduce them together with HTML5's new input types in the next section.

New input types

HTML5 introduces no less than a baker's dozen (yes, that's 13!) new input types for forms. We're going to take a brief look at each of them and explain why you should be using them *right now*. These new input types have dual benefits: using them means less development time and an improved user experience. The new input types we'll be looking at are

- search
- email
- url
- tel

- number
- range
- date

- month
- week
- time

- datetime
- datetime-local
- color

search

Search seems like an appropriate place to start our foray into HTML5 input types. When we talk about search, we're not just talking about Google, Bing, or Yahoo. We're talking about the search field on that e-commerce site you just made a purchase from, on Wikipedia, and even on your personal blog. It's probably the most common action performed on the Web every day, yet it's not marked up very semantically, is it? We all tend to write something like this:

```
<input type="text" name="search">
```

Well, what if we could write something like...

```
<input type="search" name="search">
```

With HTML5 we can. Feels much better, doesn't it? Desktop browsers will render this in a similar way to a standard text field—until you start typing, that is. At this point, a small cross appears on the right side of the field. Notice the x in Figure 6-6. This lets us quickly clear the field, just like Safari's built-in search field.

Figure 6-6. type="search" as displayed in Safari for Windows

On a mobile device, however, things start to get interesting. Take the example shown on an iPhone in Figure 6-7; when you focus on an input using type="search", notice the keyboard, specifically the action button on the keyboard (bottom right). Did you spot that it says "Search" rather than the regular "Go"? It's a subtle difference that most users won't even notice, but those who do will afford themselves a wry smile.

Figure 6-7. type="search" on the iPhone

As we've seen with the new attributes, browsers that don't understand them will simply degrade gracefully. The same applies to all of the new input types discussed here. If a browser doesn't understand type="search", it will default to type="text". This means you're not losing anything. In fact, you're using progressive enhancement and helping users to have an enhanced experience. Let's face it: filling out web forms isn't very fun, so anything we can add to ensure a smoother experience, the better.

email

In rendering terms, the email input type is no different from a standard text input type and allows for one or more e-mail addresses to be entered. Combined with the required attribute, the browser is then able to look for patterns to ensure a valid e-mail address has been entered. Naturally, this checking is rudimentary, perhaps looking for an @ character or a period (.) and not allowing spaces. Opera 9.5+, Firefox 4+, and Chrome 5+ have already implemented this basic validation, with support coming in IE 10. The browser goes as far as presenting the user with an error message (see Opera in Figure 6-8) if the e-mail address entered isn't valid. You can style the field for when an value is entered using the :valid, :invalid, or :required pseudo class (assuming you have the required attribute on the input).

```
<input type="email" name="email" required>
```

Note: For more on styling forms using pseudo-classes the "CSS Ninja", Ryan Seddon, has put together a great demonstration on A List Apart[9] at *http://j.mp/alaninja*.

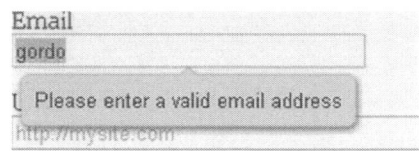

Figure 6-8. Opera e-mail address error messaging

Note: The specification details that one or more e-mail addresses are allowed. This means that the *multiple* attribute could be used with *type="email"* too.

Pretty cool, huh? Again, this highlights how HTML5 forms help to cut down the amount of JavaScript that we have to write when carrying out form validation. There's always a catch, though, right? At the time of writing, there is an internationalization issue with type="email". When using it with double-byte internationalized domain names, the browsers invalidate them; so this example

```
<input type="email" name="email" value="gordo@日本.jp">
```

isn't valid in Firefox, Safari, or Chrome (there is no issue in Opera). However, a workaround has been created by Kyle Barrow (http://j.mp/emaili18n[10]) that uses type="text" with the pattern attribute we met earlier, as shown here:

```
<input type="text" name="email" value="gordo@日本.jp" pattern="[^ @]*@[^ @]*">
```

An alternative solution is to continue using type="email" with the formnovalidate attribute on the submit button, as follows. This ensures that no validation will be carried out on form submission, which may or may not be suitable for your needs.

```
<form action="process.php">
<label for="email">Email:</label>
<input type="email" name="email" value="gordo@日本.jp">
<input type="submit" formnovalidate value="Submit">
```

Or you could use the novalidate attribute on your form, like so:

```
<form action="process.php" novalidate> <label for="email">Email:</label>
<input type="email" name="email" value="gordo@日本.jp">
<input type="submit" value="Submit">
```

[9] www.alistapart.com/articles/forward-thinking-form-validation
[10] http://barrow.io/posts/email-validation-of-double-byte-domains/

Internationalization issues aside, remember how we said there are dual benefits to HTML5's input types—less development time and better user experience? Let's go back and look at the iPhone once more, as shown in Figure 6-9.

Figure 6-9. The iPhone displays a custom keyboard when using type="email".

Did you notice it this time? No? Look at the keyboard again. That's right, the keyboard is different. There are dedicated keys for the @ and . characters to help you complete the field more efficiently. As we discussed with type="search", there is no downside to using type="email" right now. If a browser doesn't support it, it will degrade to type="text". And in some browsers, users will get a helping hand.

url

The url input type, as you might expect, is for web addresses. You can use the multiple attribute to enter more than one URL. Like type="email", a browser will carry out simple validation on these fields and present an error message on form submission. This is likely to include looking for forward slashes, periods, and spaces, and possibly detecting a valid top-level domain (such as .com or .co.uk). Use the url input type like so:

```
<input type="url" name="url" required>
```

> *There is currently some debate about whether the user has to enter* http:// *into a field using* input="url"*. Browser vendors are discussing the possibility of pre-pending* http:// *to a URL following a check upon form submission. For up-to-date information, refer to the HTML5 specification.*

Again, we'll take a look at how the iPhone renders type="url". As you can see in Figure 6-10, it has again updated the onscreen keyboard to ensure that completing the field is as simple as possible for the user by swapping the default space key for period, forward slash, and .com keys. (To access more endings like .org and .net, tap and hold the .com key.)

Figure 6-10. type="url" activates a URL-specific keyboard on the iPhone.

tel

tel differs from email and url in that no particular syntax is enforced. Phone numbers differ around the world, making it difficult to guarantee any type of specific notation except for allowing only numbers and perhaps a + symbol to be entered. It's possible that you can validate specific phone numbers (if you can guarantee the format) using client-side validation. type="tel" is marked up as follows:

```
<input type="tel" name="tel" id="tel" required>
```

Once more, the iPhone recognizes type="tel", only this time it goes one step further and completely changes the keyboard to the standard phone keyboard, as shown on the left in Figure 6-11. In addition to the iPhone, some Android devices (such as HTC Desire, shown on the right in Figure 6-11) also display a numeric keyboard for type="tel". That's pretty handy, don't you think? Nice, big keys for entering a phone number help you to get that big, nasty form completed quickly.

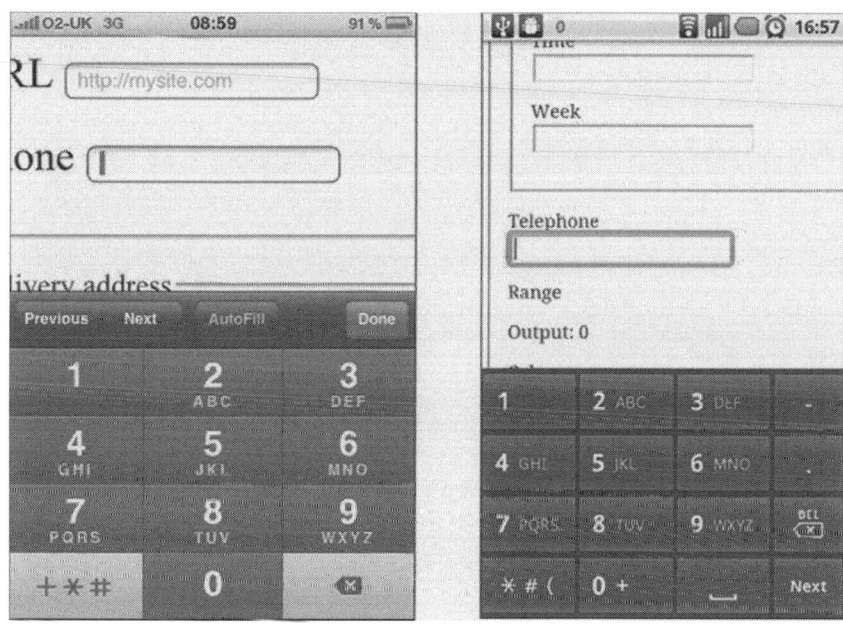

Figure 6-11. type="tel" on the iPhone and some Android devices dynamically changes the keyboard to a numeric keypad. (Android screenshot provided by Stuart Langridge)

number

number, as you might expect, is used for specifying a numerical value. As with the majority of these new input types, Opera was the first to implement type="number". It, Safari, and Chrome render the input as a spinbox control (see Figure 6-12) whereby you can click the arrows to move up or down. Or if you prefer, you can type directly into the field. Firefox, on the other hand, renders the field like a standard text box. Support for type="number" will be in IE 10 also.

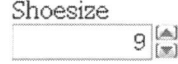

Figure 6-12. type="number" in Opera

With the additional attributes `min`, `max`, and `step`, we can change the default step value of this spinbox control as well as set minimum, maximum, and starting values (using the standard HTML `value` attribute). This example shows how these attributes work:

```
<input type="number" min="5" max="18" step="0.5" value="9" name="shoe-size" >
```

In this example , `min` represents the minimum value the field will accept, and `max` represents the maximum value. If we reach the maximum or minimum value, the appropriate arrow on the spinbox control will be greyed out so you can no longer interact with it. `step` is the increment that the value should adjust up or down, with the default step value being 1. This means we can include negative values or step up in increments of 0.5 or 5. `value` is that attribute you're used to from previous versions of HTML. Each of the attributes are optional, with defaults being set if they aren't used.

In contrast to Opera's implementation, the iPhone (shown on the left in Figure 6-13) and some Android devices (such as HTC Desire, shown on the right in Figure 6-13) simply render the field as a standard text box but optimize the keyboard for easy input.

Figure 6-13. type=number on iPhone and Android HTC Desire (Android screenshot provided by Stuart Langridge)

To make the iPhone render with the standard telephone keypad as we saw for `type="tel"` Chris Coyier, of CSS Tricks devised a little hoax you can use. Rather than using `type="number"`, use a standard `type="text"` input and add a pattern attribute that accepts only numbers, as shown below. This solution isn't ideal but if you think it could be useful, Chris has put a short video together showing it in action (http://j.mp/numbertrick[11]).

```
<input type="text" pattern="[0-9]*" name="shoe-size">
```

Chris' technique may soon become absolute though with the introduction of the inputmode attribute. The attribute, recently added to the specification will allow users to specify the type of input mechanism that is most useful for users. When implemented, you will be able to choose between numeric, latin, email, or kana input modes.

range

The range input type is similar to number but more specific. It represents a numerical value within a given range. Why the difference, I hear you cry? Because when you're using range, the exact value isn't important. It also allows browsers to offer a simpler control than for number. In Opera, Safari, and Chrome, type="range" renders as a slider (see Figure 6-14). Additionally, in Opera, if the CSS defines the height greater than the width, the slider control will be rendered vertically as opposed to the standard horizontal rendering.

> Note: For browsers that don't support type="range", Remy Sharp has created a JavaScript polyfill to plug the gaps. You can find out more about it on his blog (http://j.mp/rangepolyfill[12]).

The following code shows how we might mark up our skill level on a scale of 1 to 100 by setting the min and max attributes (see Figure 6-14). We can also set the starting point for range using the value attribute.

```
<input id="skill" type="range" min="1" max="100" value="0">
```

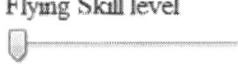

Figure 6-14. type=range in Chrome

Dates and times

If you've ever booked tickets online, you will have come across date pickers to help you quickly and easily choose the date you require. Perhaps you've even implemented a date picker on your own website. Generally, this is done using a JavaScript library such as jQuery, Dojo, or YUI. It can be a pain when you need to load a whole library and associated plug-ins just to implement a simple date picker. Well, with HTML5 we get that functionality baked into the browser. Not only that, but we don't have to stop at just

---

[11] www.youtube.com/watch?v=NmikW6QqaDo
[12] http://remysharp.com/2011/07/18/input-range-polyfill

selecting a single date; we can select a week, month, time, date and time, and even date and time with a time zone using the different input types. The markup is pretty straightforward.

```
<input id="dob" name="dob" type="date">
```

You can go a step further by using the min and max attributes to ensure the user can only choose from a specified date range.

```
<input id="startdate" name="startdate" min="2012-01-01" max="2013-01-01" type="date">
```

As with many of the other form implementations, Opera leads the way. Let's take a look next at how browsers render these input types.

> You may have noticed that there isn't a *type="year"* input type defined in HTML5. The reason for this is a lack of relevant use cases. All the use cases for a year input type that have been proposed can be achieved using *type="number"*.

date

Figure 6-15 shows Opera 10.5's rendering of type="date".

Figure 6-15. type=date in Opera 10.5

These date pickers aren't restricted to desktop devices; some Blackberry devices and Chrome for Android render its internal date picker when used with type="date" (see Figure 6-16).

Figure 6-16. type=date on Blackberry (screenshot provided by Terence Eden)

month

Next up, Figure 6-17 shows type="month", which might, for example, be used for a credit card expiry date.

```
<input id="expiry" name="expiry" type="month" required>
```

Figure 6-17. type=month in Opera 10.5

week

You can also drill down to type="week". Notice how Opera highlights a specific week using the same date picker control, as shown in Figure 6-18.

```
<input id="vacation" name="vacation" type="week">
```

207

Figure 6-18. type=week in Opera 10.5

time

You can see in Figure 6-19 that `type="time"` renders a spinbox similar to that used earlier for selecting the precise time.

```
<input id="exit-time" name="exit-time" type="time">
```

Time:

Figure 6-19. type=time in Opera 10.5

datetime

We can combine the date and time by using `type="datetime"` for specifying a precise time on a given day, as shown in Figure 6-20.

```
<input id="entry-day-time" name="entry-day-time" type="datetime">
```

Figure 6-20. type=datetime in Opera 10.5

datetime-local

Finally, Figure 6-21 shows that we can achieve slightly more granular control by selecting a precise time on a given day with a local time zone variation using type="datetime-local".

```
<input id="arrival-time" name="arrival-time " type="datetime-local">
```

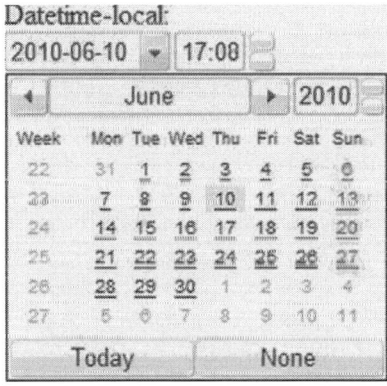

Figure 6-21. type=datetime-local in Opera 10.5

DATE AND TIME CAVEATS

There are two caveats with these implementations. First, with the current implementation, it isn't possible to type a date into the field (in all browsers). The date picker is keyboard accessible, though. However, we can foresee a potential issue; if implemented on a form that a data entry clerk regularly completes, they are likely to be quicker at typing the date than tabbing through with the keyboard or selecting from a date picker. Second, it isn't possible to style the look of the date picker. We tend to think that this is a good thing, as users will receive a common experience across all websites they visit (provided they use the same browser all the time). Undoubtedly, though, corporations will require a branded date picker. Safari 5 and Chrome 5 have implemented these input types, but, unfortunately, they aren't very user friendly. Dates have to be entered in the same format as the time element that we met in Chapter 4. So for dates, the format would be YYYY-MM-DD, and for dates with time, a user would have to enter YYYY-MM-DDT00:00Z, which is not very friendly at all.

As with the other new input types, if a browser doesn't recognize them, it will simply default back to type="text" and let the user continue to use your JavaScript date picker.

color

The color input type is pretty self-explanatory: it allows the user to select a color and returns the hex value for that color. It is anticipated that users will either be able to type the value or select from a color picker, which will either be native to the operating system or a browser's own implementation. Opera 11 has implemented type="color" with a simple color picker that offers a number of standard color choices or the option to select Other, which brings up the operating system color picker (shown on the right in Figure 6-22).

<input id="color" name="color" type="color">

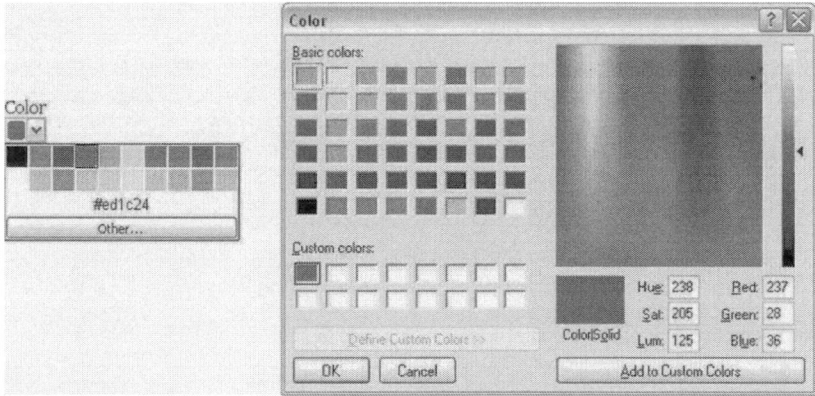

Figure 6-22. type="color" in Opera on the left and the result of clicking Other shown on the right

In contrast, certain Blackberry devices have implemented the color input type that renders a color picker, as shown in Figure 6-23.

Figure 6-23. type=color on Blackberry (screenshot provided by Terence Eden)

Input types summary

By using HTML5's new form input types *right now*, we can enhance the user's experience, future-proof our site, and make our life as developers easier. Obviously, we can't just leave the browsers that don't support all these new features hanging, so in the next section we'll take a look at how we can detect support for these form features using JavaScript.

Validation and how to provide fallbacks

Throughout the chapter, we've introduced new attributes and input types, but we haven't discussed validation or how to provide suitable fallbacks for these additions. That's what we'll be concentrating on in this section.

The difference between client-side and server-side validation

Before we proceed, we need to take a quick detour to define the difference between client-side and server-side validation. These two technologies should complement each other to provide a seamless experience for the user while helping you, the developer, get high-quality form submissions that are rich with the accurate data you so desire.

Validating form fields on the client side using JavaScript can save you time and bandwidth. It also helps show the user where they may have entered a field incorrectly or in the wrong format. It's run on form submission (or sometimes during form completion, a method known as inline validation) in the browser and allows you to guide the user through the errors made. Naturally, this makes the process quicker for the user, as it negates the need for a round trip to the server if invalid data has been entered.

Server-side validation, on the other hand, is more secure and checks the submitted data to ensure it's correct. This helps to protect against malicious users who might bypass your client-side validation and submit potentially dangerous data to the server (for example, a custom-written script designed to hack your site). Validating on the server side also aids compatibility to ensure form errors can still be displayed to users who may not have JavaScript enabled.

To answer the question of "which type of validation should I use?" the answer is nearly always "both." The advantage of using the HTML5 form attributes and input types in this situation is that a large portion of the client-side JavaScript that we have to write now will be native to the browser and not bypassable by turning off JavaScript. You'll still need server-side validation, but the time you save on the front end will leave you time to concentrate on other exciting additions to your sites and applications.

Browser error handling and processing

As we've seen with the `required` attribute as well as the `email` and `url` input types, one of the major advantages of using HTML5 forms is that the browser can carry out some of the heavy lifting for us. This means the browser can carry out basic error handling and processing negating the need for lots of additional JavaScript or regular expressions to perform straightforward tasks.

We've also seen that some of these features won't work in all browsers (more on support in the next section), but instead will either be skipped without impacting user experience or default back to `type="text"` if they're not understood. So how can we check if a feature is supported and how do we detect that support? For that we'll need to use JavaScript detection.

Feature detection with JavaScript

Using Mark Pilgrim's detection techniques (`http://j.mp/pilgrimdetect`[13]) as a basis, we can use JavaScript to detect "support" for a particular feature in a few different ways.

1. Check whether a property exists on a global object like `window`.

2. Create an element and test to see if a property exists on it.

3. Create an element, test to see if a method exists on that element, and then call the method to test the value it returns.

4. Create an element, set a property to a value, and check the retained value.

As we're particularly interested in which input types are supported, we would use detection technique #4 to test whether `input type="email"` is supported.

```
var input = document.createElement('input');
input.setAttribute('type','email');
return input.type !== 'text';
```

This piece of JavaScript tells the browser to create an `input` element and set the `type` attribute to the one you are detecting support for (in this case email). For browsers that support the input type, this value is retained. For those that don't, the value we set will be ignored and the `type` property will default to "text".

You could go ahead and write out the preceding function 13 times to detect each of the new HTML5 forms `input` types. However, to make your life easier, we suggest that you investigate a handy tool called Modernizr (`http://j.mp/modernizr`[14]), which we briefly introduced in Chapter 2 and which you'll learn about in more detail in the next chapter. Modernizr detects support for all 13 input types and gives back a

---

[13] `http://diveinto.html5doctor.com/detect.html`
[14] `http://modernizr.com`

value of true or false for each. You can then use another method to provide a suitable fallback for the effect you want to achieve.

```
// if placeholder isn't supported:
if (!Modernizr.input.placeholder){
  // provide a fallback with a hint script
  setInputHint(document.getElementById('user-name'),at least 3 characters');
}
```

To detect support for some of the new attributes that we've discussed, we'll use detection technique #2. Here's how it works for the placeholder attribute:

```
function support_placeholder () {
var input = document.createElement('input');
return 'placeholder' in input;
```

If your browser doesn't support the placeholder attribute, you can use JavaScript to write in a value that can be cleared on focus instead.

As you can see, the checks we have to run to detect support for HTML5 forms features cross browser are very straightforward. If you build these functions into your development toolkit, you're all set to start using these new features today.

Forms polyfills

Modernizr doesn't automatically add support for those missing features, so you need to use another technique. For browsers that don't support certain attributes or input types (see the next section), there are a number of polyfills available to help plug those gaps. If you look in the "Web Forms" section of the HTML5 Cross Browser Polyfills page (http://j.mp/h5fills[15]) you'll find a number of scripts that can help you mimic native support in non-supporting browsers.

Current browser support

We've hinted throughout the chapter at which browsers have support for HTML5 forms. Table 6-1 and Table 6-2 show the current state of play for the new attributes and input types, respectively. As you can see, Opera and Chrome lead the way in terms of support. In fact, Opera has an almost complete implementation of HTML5 forms since version 9.5.

With new versions of browsers being released at an ever-increasing rate, it can be difficult to keep up with what is or isn't supported. If you want to keep an eye on the current progress, we suggest visiting When can I use... (http://j.mp/caniuse[16]) or FindMeByIP (http://j.mp/findmebyip[17]) or Wufoo's HTML5 forms research (http://j.mp/wufooh5[18]).

---

[15] https://github.com/Modernizr/Modernizr/wiki/HTML5-Cross-Browser-Polyfills
[16] http://caniuse.com
[17] http://findmebyip.com/litmus/#target-selector
[18] http://wufoo.com/html5

213

In addition to those sites, king of compatibility tables, Peter-Paul Koch (PPK) has written an excellent article on his findings from tests carried out the new input types and attributes (http://j.mp/ppkinput[19]). Some of the information is now slightly out of date (because browser UIs have improved) but to see where we've come from to where we are will do you no harm at all.

Table 6-1. HTML5 Form Attribute Implementation

	Trident					Gecko		WebKit				Presto	
	IE 6	IE 7	IE 8	IE 9	IE 10	Firefox 4	Firefox 6	Safari 4	Safari 5	Chrome 4	Chrome 5-13	Opera 9.5+	Opera 11 beta
autocomplete	.	.	.	.	.	✓	✓	.	.	.	.	✓	✓
autofocus	.	.	.	.	✓	✓	✓	✓	✓	✓	✓	✓	✓
list	.	.	.	.	✓	✓^	✓	.	.	.	.	✓	✓
max	.	.	.	.	✓		.	.	✓	✓	✓	✓	✓
min	.	.	.	.	✓		.	.	✓	✓	✓	✓	✓
multiple	.	.	.	.	✓	✓^^	✓	✓	✓	✓	✓	.	✓*
pattern	.	.	.	.	✓	✓	✓	.	.	✓	✓	✓	✓
placeholder	.	.	.	.	✓	✓	✓	✓	✓	✓	✓	.	✓
required	.	.	.	.	✓	✓	✓	.	✓	✓	✓	✓**	✓**
step	.	.	.	.	✓		.	.	✓	.	✓	✓	✓

^ *Partial implementation, list renders permanently*

^^ *Currently not implemented for type="email"*

* *For <input type="file">*

** *No support for select elements*

---

[19] www.quirksmode.org/blog/archives/2011/03/the_new_input_t.html

Table 6-2. HTML5 Input Type Implementation

	Trident					Gecko		WebKit				Presto	
	IE 6	IE 7	IE 8	IE 9	IE 10	Firefox 4	Firefox 6	Safari 4	Safari 5	Chrome 4	Chrome 5-13	Opera 9.5+	Opera 11 (beta)
color	.	.	.	.	.	.	.	.	✓	.	.	.	✓
date	.	.	.	.	.	.	.	.	✓	.	✓	✓	✓
datetime	.	.	.	.	.	.	.	.	✓	.	✓	✓	✓
datetime-local	.	.	.	.	.	.	.	.	✓	.	✓	✓	✓
email	.	.	.	.	✓	✓	✓	✓*	✓	.	✓	✓	✓
month	.	.	.	.	.	.	.	.	✓	.	✓	✓	✓
number	.	.	.	.	✓	.	.	✓*	✓	✓	✓	✓	✓
range	.	.	.	.	.	.	.	✓*	✓	✓	✓	✓	✓
search	.	.	.	.	✓	✓	✓	✓	✓	✓	✓	✓	✓
tel	.	.	.	.	✓	✓	✓	✓*	✓	.	✓	.	✓
time	.	.	.	.	.	.	.	.	✓	.	✓	✓	✓
url	.	.	.	.	✓	✓	✓	✓*	✓	.	✓	✓	✓
week	.	.	.	.	.	.	.	.	✓	.	✓	✓	✓

* Works in mobile Safari

Note that Chrome and Safari offer no enhanced user interface for the following input types: datetime, date, month, week, time, and datetime-local.

Forms in action

Now that we've seen the power of HTML5 forms, let's put what we've learned to good use by marking up a couple of forms that are commonly found online. We'll start by looking at a login form and then work through a blog's comment form.

Figure 6-24 shows a login form. Take a look at the image and the following HTML 4 markup, and then see if you can mark up the form in HTML5 based on what you've learned.

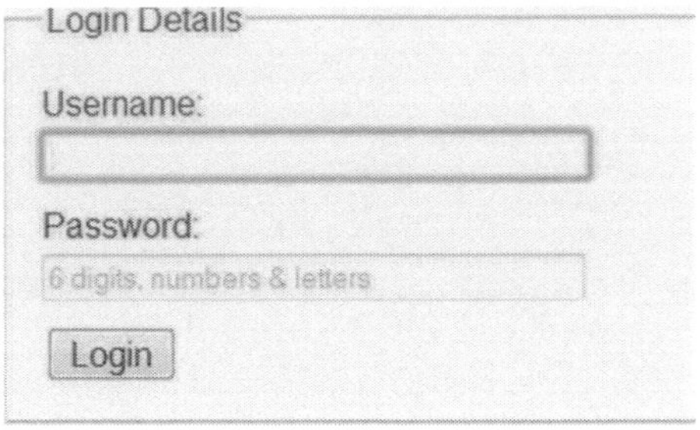

Figure 6-24. Common login form in Safari

```
<form id="app-login" action="process.php">
<fieldset>
<legend>Login Details</legend>
<div>
  <label>Username:
  <input name="user-name" type="text" value="Your username is your email address" onfocus=➥
"if (!this.reset) { this.value = ''; this.reset = true }">
  </label>
</div>
<div>
  <label>Password:
  <input name="password" type="password" value="Your username is your email address"➥
 onfocus="if (!this.reset) { this.value = ''; this.reset = true }">
  </label>
</div>
<div>
  <input name="login" type="submit" value="Login">
</label>
</div>
</fieldset>
</form>
```

How did you do? Here's how we've marked it up in HTML5, making use of the email input type as well as the placeholder, required, and autofocus attributes:

```
<form id="app-login" action="process.php">
<fieldset>
<legend>Login Details</legend>
<div>
  <label>Username:
  <input name="user-name" type="email" placeholder="Your username is your email address"➥
 required autofocus>
  </label>
</div>
<div>
  <label>Password:
  <input name="password" type="password" placeholder="6 digits, numbers & letters" required>
  </label>
</div>
<div>
```

```
    <input name="login" type="submit" value="Login">
  </label>
  </div>
  </fieldset>
</form>
```

We're now going to look at a blog's comment form, shown in Figure 6-25. Take a look at the image and the following HTML 4 markup, and see if you can mark up the form in HTML5 based on what you read earlier in the chapter.

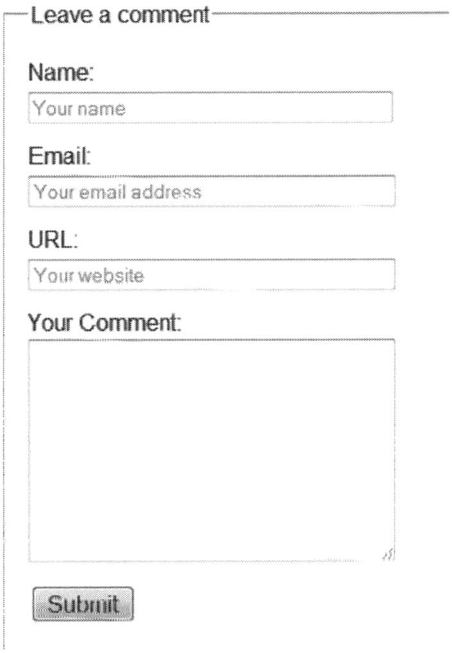

Figure 6-25. Basic comment form in Safari

```
<form id="respond" action="process.php">
<fieldset>
<legend>Leave a comment</legend>
<div>
  <label>Name:
  <input name="name" type="text" value="Your name" onfocus="if (!this.reset) { this.value =➥
  ''; this.reset = true }">
  </label>
</div>
<div>
  <label>Email:
  <input name="email" type="text" value="Your email address" onfocus="if (!this.reset)➥
  { this.value = ''; this.reset = true }">
  </label>
</div>
```

```
<div>
  <label>URL:
  <input name="url" type="text" value="Your website" onfocus="if (!this.reset)➥
 { this.value = ''; this.reset = true }">
  </label>
</div>
<div>
  <label>Your Comment:
  <textarea name="comment"></textarea>
  </label>
</div>
<div>
  <input name="submit" type="submit" value="Submit" formaction="comments.php">
</label>
</div>
</fieldset>
</form>
```

How did you do? Here's how we've marked it up in HTML5, making use of the email and url input types as well as the placeholder, required, autofocus, and formaction attributes:

```
<form id="respond" action="process.php">
<fieldset>
<legend>Leave a comment</legend>
<div>
  <label>Name:
  <input name="name" type="text" placeholder="Your name" required autofocus>
  </label>
</div>
<div>
  <label>Email:
  <input name="email" type="email" placeholder="Your email address" required>
  </label>
</div>
<div>
  <label>URL:
  <input name="url" type="url" placeholder="Your website">
  </label>
</div>
<div>
  <label>Your Comment:
  <textarea name="comment"></textarea>
  </label>
</div>
<div>
  <input name="submit" type="submit" value="Submit" formaction="comments.php">
</label>
</div>
</fieldset></form>
```

HTML5 forms APIs

To complement these new input types and attributes, there are many new objects, methods, events, and functions that gel together to create a number of APIs for HTML5 forms. We can't cover them all in this book but they include functions such as stepUp and stepDown to work with the step attribute, the valueAsNumber function that converts text to a number (see the output element later in the chapter) and the ValidtyState object. For more information about these APIs, Chapter 7 of *Pro HTML5 Programming* (http://j.mp/prohtml5[20]), by Peter Lubbers, Brian Albers, and Frank Salim, is worth checking out.

HTML5 forms summary

We've shown you a number of new form attributes and input types and briefly discussed the related APIs. In summary, the three main benefits of using them are an improved user interface and therefore experience; restricted user input on certain fields; and automatic, in-browser validation of form fields with no additional scripting required. If that's not enough to convince you to go and start using them, we don't know what is.

---

[20] www.prohtml5.com

Web applications

As Internet connection speeds increase and we hurtle toward universal, ubiquitous connectivity to the Web, it's plain to see that the Internet is no longer made up of static documents that link to one another. We now are regularly engaged in listening to music or watching video online. Services like Facebook and Twitter have sprung up, bringing with them powerful APIs that allow developers to build their own custom web applications.

Moreover, in the past few years we've seen increasingly rich Internet applications ("web apps") become commonplace online. Examples such as Gmail, Google Docs, and Basecamp have enabled us to move from the desktop to carry out more and more of our work online.

As we saw in Chapter 1, Opera, Mozilla, and Apple began to document a specification termed *Web Applications 1.0* in 2004. They'd foreseen this rise in web applications and introduced a number of new elements and APIs to help deal with this seismic shift from documents to applications online.

Unfortunately, covering all of the APIs in detail is not within the scope of this book. Instead, we're going to take a brief look at some of these new application elements in HTML5 and related APIs, and show you where you can investigate further.

Introduction to elements for web applications

There are nine elements that we'll be looking at in this section, including one that has been redefined. They are categorized in the HTML5 specification as either *form* elements or *interactive* elements.

Form elements

We'll start with the form elements.

datalist

As we saw earlier in the chapter, the datalist element represents a predefined list of options for form controls. A code example is shown here:

```
<label>Your favorite fruit:
<datalist id="fruits">
    <select name="fruits">
    <option value="Blackberry">Blackberry</option>
    <option value="Blackcurrant">Blackcurrant</option>
    <option value="Blueberry">Blueberry</option>
    <!-- … -->
  </select>
If other, please specify:
</datalist>
<input type="text" name="fruit" list="fruits">
</label>
```

datalist has been implemented in Opera 9.5+ (as shown in Figure 6-26), Firefox 4+, and Internet Explorer 10.

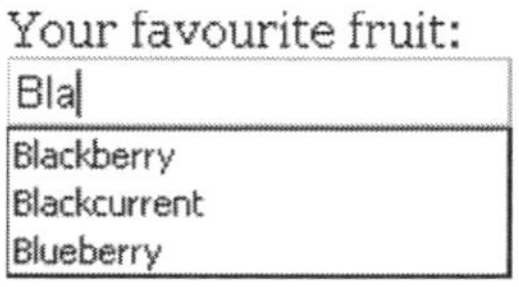

Figure 6-26. The datalist element rendered in Opera

New input types aren't the only items that have user experience enhancements on mobile devices; datalist functionality has also been implemented on some Blackberry devices, allowing the user to choose from a drop-down list of selectable items.

keygen

Invented by Netscape and re-engineered by other browser vendors (Microsoft excepted), the keygen element represents a control for generating a public-private key pair and for submitting the public key from that key pair. When a form is submitted, a public key and a private key are generated. A private key is stored on the client side and the public key is sent to the server. The public key can then be used with secure servers to generate certificates, making it more secure and preventing your site from being hacked. Here is an example of keygen in action.

```
<form action="process.php" method="post" enctype="multipart/form-data">
<keygen name="key">
<input type=submit value="Submit">
</form>
```

output

The output element is rather simple; it represents the result of a calculation or user action. Using the for attribute, a relationship is created between the result of the calculation and the value(s) that went into the calculation. The output element is supported in Opera 9.5+, Firefox 4+, Chrome, Safari 5+, and Internet Explorer 10. The following example (depicted in Figure 6-27) adds the values of two inputs together to create the output. This is triggered by the oninput event placed on the output element and handled by the browser using the new valueAsNumber function—no complex scripting required! For more information, see a detailed write up on output by author Richard Clark (http://j.mp/outputelement[21]).

```
<form onsubmit="return false" oninput="o.value = a.valueAsNumber + b.valueAsNumber">
  <input name="a" id="a" type="number" step="any"> +
  <input name="b" id="b" type="number" step="any"> =
  <output name="o" for="a b"></output>
</form>
```

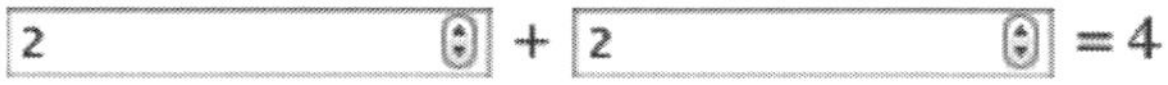

Figure 6-27. The output element with input type="range" in Opera 10.5

---

[21] http://html5doctor.com/the-output-element

progress

The progress element is fairly self-explanatory. It represents the completion progress of a given task. The progress can be shown as indeterminate (if no value attribute is specified) or a number ranging from zero to maximum, based on the percentage of work that has so far been completed. Using JavaScript to update the current value, a visual representation of the progress made is shown to the user (see Figure 6-28). The progress element is supported in Opera 11+, Firefox 6+, and Chrome 7+.

Figure 6-28. The progress element at 60% complete in Chrome 7

```
<p>Percent Downloaded:
<progress id="p" max="100" value="0"><span id="completed">0</span>%</progress>
</p>
<script>
var progress  = document.getElementById('p');
function updateProg(newValue) {
progress.value = newValue;
progress.getElementById('completed')[0].textContent = newValue;
}
</script>
```

Mounir Lamouri, a developer for Mozilla, has written a detailed article on how to use pseudo-classes (some with a vendor prefix) to style the progress element. It's an interesting and informative article (http://j.mp/stylingprogress[22]).

meter

Not to be confused with progress, the meter element represents a scalar measurement within a known range, or a fractional value. Examples of this are the percentage completion of a social networking profile (see Figure 6-29) or the relevance of a particular search result. The meter element should not be used for arbitrary values such as height or weight unless there is a maximum known value. Using the high, low, max, and min attributes, the color of the element will change depending on the current value. Typically the value will be written server side prior to page load, but it may also be the case that the value is updated using JavaScript. The meter element is supported in Opera 11+ and Chrome 7+.

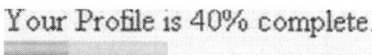

Figure 6-29. The meter element at 40% complete in Chrome

```
<p>Your profile is <span id="completed">40</span>% complete.</p>
```

---

[22] http://blog.oldworld.fr/index.php?post/2011/07/The-HTML5-progress-element-in-Firefox

```
<meter min="0" max="100" value="40"></meter>
```

Interactive elements

Now let's look at the interactive elements. Browser support for these elements is sparse, so we suggest that you run your own tests when you're implementing them.

details

The `details` element represents a control from which the user can obtain additional information or controls on demand if required. The information inside `details` is hidden by default and the user can request to "open" the control. It should be noted that the `details` element isn't appropriate for footnotes. `details` is currently implemented in Chrome and will soon be supported in Opera.

Because `details` is generally paired with `summary`, the code example is shown in the next section.

summary

The `summary` element represents a summary, caption, or legend for the contents of the `summary` element's parent `details` element, if any. `summary` must always be the first child of `details`, but more than one `summary` element can be used per `details` element.

```
<details>
<summary>Name & Extension:</summary>
<p><input type="text" name="fn" value="Space Cadet Handbook.pdf">
<p><label><input type="checkbox" name="ext" checked> Hide extension</label>
</details>
```

command

The `command` element represents a command that the user can invoke. `command` is shown only when used as a child of `menu`, and it can be used with a choice of three `type` attributes: `radio`, `checkbox`, or `command`. If no `type` attribute is set, the default behavior is that of `type="command"`. `command` is likely to be used in web applications in place of buttons to complete specific actions (save, publish, etc.) and is generally invoked using a JavaScript `onClick` event. See it in the code example in the `menu` section.

menu

Although `menu` isn't new to HTML5, it has been redefined. It represents a list of interactive options or commands. It is to be used for web applications only. For documents, authors should use `nav`, which we met in Chapter 3.

```
<menu type="toolbar">
<command type="command" disabled label="Save" icon="icons/save.png" onclick="save()">
<command type="command" disabled label="Publish" icon="icons/pub.png" onclick="publish()">
</menu>
```

Introduction to HTML5-related APIs

So far in this book we've covered the new markup that HTML5 brings us. We've also seen some new rich media elements in the form of audio, video, and canvas. If you think that seems like a lot, there's a whole lot more found under the HTML5 umbrella in the shape of APIs.

As you know, there are two versions of the HTML5 specification, one published by the W3C and another by the WHATWG. The living HTML specification maintained by the WHATWG contains additional APIs to those in the W3C HTML5 spec (although generally they are also maintained by the W3C but in separate specifications).

Alongside those in the specification are a number of related APIs that form part of the standards stack and are often grouped under the "HTML5" umbrella term. In some cases, the APIs have been around and implemented for a while, but they've never been documented (something that HTML5 has set out to change). Figure 6-30 gives an indication of how each of the APIs relates to HTML5 but is by no means comprehensive.

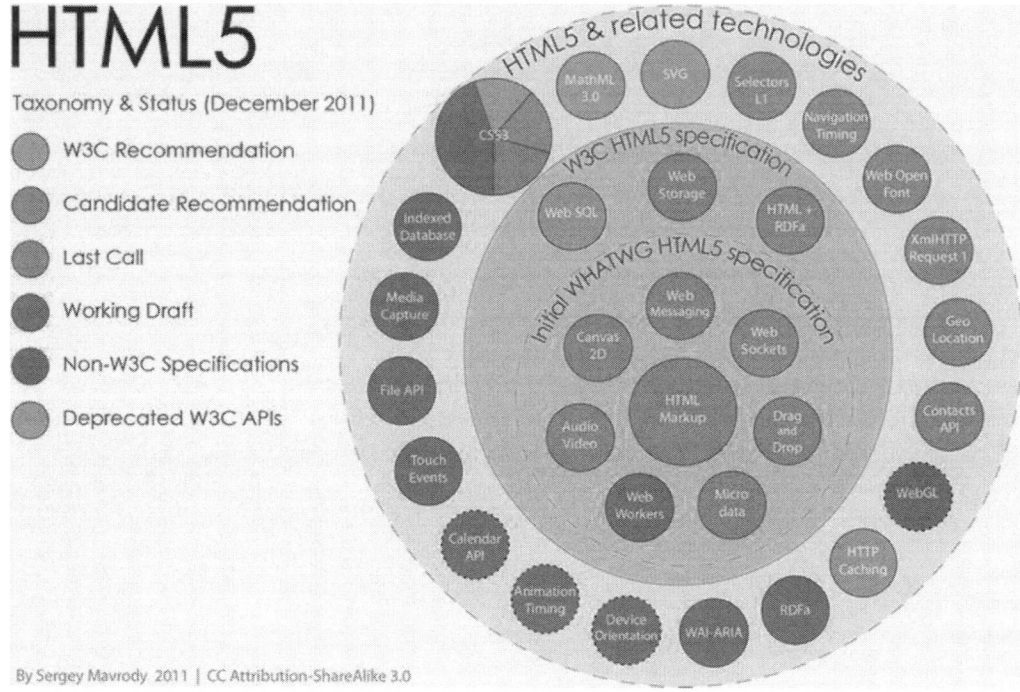

Figure 6-30. HTML5 Taxonomy and Status by Sergey Mavrody

We like to think that each of the APIs helps to form the basis of the web's architecture and thus is important in its own right. In this section, we're not going to look at code but instead we'll focus on describing the APIs, their purpose, and progress. If you wish to investigate further, this book's sister publication, *Pro HTML5 Programming* (http://j.mp/prohtml5[23]), by Peter Lubbers, Brian Albers, and Frank Salim, is a great place to start.

APIs in the HTML5 specification

We'll start by looking at the APIs in the W3C HTML5 spec (the Media and Text Track APIs introduced in Chapter 5 are also in the HTML5 specification).

Drag and Drop API

The Drag and Drop API has been the topic of much debate. Originally created by Microsoft in version 5 of Internet Explorer, it is now supported by Firefox, Safari, and Chrome. So what does it do?

Well, as the name suggests, it brings native drag-and-drop support to the browser. By adding a draggable attribute set to true, the user has the ability to move any element. You then add some event handlers on a target drop zone to tell the browser where the element can be dropped.

The API's real muscles are flexed when you start to think outside of the browser. Using drag and drop, a user could drag an image from the desktop into the browser or you could create an icon that gets loaded with content when dragged out of the browser by the user to a new application target.

Drag and Drop is covered in depth in the following articles/specs:

- Drag and Drop API, W3C (http://dev.w3.org/html5/spec/dnd.html#dnd)
- Native Drag and Drop, HTML5 Doctor, Remy Sharp (http://html5doctor.com/native-drag-and-drop)
- Drag and Drop, MDN (https://developer.mozilla.org/en/DragDrop/Drag_and_Drop)
- The drag and drop API, HTML5 Laboratory, Ian Devlin (www.html5laboratory.com/drag-and-drop.php)

Offline web applications/application cache

With the blurring of native apps (mobile and desktop) and web apps comes the inevitable task of wanting to take applications offline. The Offline Web Applications specification details how to do just that using application caching.

Application caching is carried out by creating a simple manifest file that lists the files required for the application to work offline. Authors can then ensure their sites function offline. The manifest causes the user's browser to keep a copy of the files for use offline later. When a user views the document/application without network access, the browser switches to use the local copies instead. So in theory, you should be able to finish writing that important e-mail or playing the web version of Angry Birds while you're on the underground/subway.

---

[23] www.prohtml5.com

With relatively strong browser support, particularly in the mobile arena (Firefox, Safari, Chrome, Opera, iPhone, and Android), it's something you can start using right now. For further reading, we suggest

- Offline Web Applications, W3C (`http://dev.w3.org/html5/spec/offline.html#offline`)

- Let's Take This Offline, Dive into HTML5, Mark Pilgrim
  (`http://diveinto.html5doctor.com/offline.html`)

- Running your web applications offline with HTML5 AppCache, dev.opera, Shwetank Dixit
  (`http://dev.opera.com/articles/view/offline-applications-html5-appcache`)

- Go offline with application cache, HTML5 Doctor, Mike Robinson
  (`http://html5doctor.com/go-offline-with-application-cache`)

- Offline Browsing in HTML5 with ApplicationCache, Sitepoint, Malcolm Sheridan
  (`www.sitepoint.com/offline-browsing-in-html5-with-applicationcache`)

- Get off(line), Web Directions, John Allsopp (`www.webdirections.org/blog/get-offline`)

User interaction

Like offline, user interaction is part of the primary HTML5 specification. It's worth mentioning here because some of its features, such as the `contenteditable` attribute, are extremely useful when you're creating web applications. `contenteditable` has been around in internet Explorer since version 5.5 and works in all five major browsers. Setting the attribute to `true` indicates that the element is editable. Authors could then, for example, combine this with local storage to track changes to documents.

For more, look at the current spec (`http://dev.w3.org/html5/spec/Overview.html#editing`) but note that there are some sections that have been moved to the HTML Editing APIs (`http://dvcs.w3.org/hg/editing/raw-file/tip/editing.html`) work in progress.

History API

A browser's back button is the most heavily used piece of its chrome. Ajax-y web applications break it at their peril. Using HTML5's History API, developers have a lot more control over the history state of a user's browser session.

The pre-HTML5 History API allowed us to send users forward or back, and check the length of the history. What HTML5 brings to the party are ways to add and remove entries in the user's history, hold data to restore a page state, and update the URL without refreshing the page. The scripting is fairly straightforward and will help us build complex applications that don't refresh the page from which we can continue to share URLs as we've always done.

For more detail on the History API, see

- History API, W3C (`http://dev.w3.org/html5/spec/history.html#history`)

- Manipulating History for Fun & Profit, Dive into HTML5, Mark Pilgrim
  (`http://diveinto.html5doctor.com/history.html`)

- Introducing the HTML5 History API, dev.opera, Mike Taylor & Chris Mills
  (`http://dev.opera.com/articles/view/introducing-the-html5-history-api`)

- Manipulating the browser history, MDN
  (https://developer.mozilla.org/en/DOM/Manipulating_the_browser_history)

- Pushing and Popping with the History API, HTML5 Doctor, Mike Robinson
  (http://html5doctor.com/history-api)

MIME type and protocol handler registration

This API allows sites to register themselves as handlers for certain schemes. By using the registerProtocolHandler method, an example use case could be an online telephone messaging service registers itself as a handler of the sms: scheme so that if the user clicks on such a link, he is given the opportunity to use that website.

Certain schemes are whitelisted (such as sms, tel, and irc). In addition, there is a registerContentHandler method that allows sites to register as handlers for content with a certain mime type. The spec (http://dev.w3.org/html5/spec/timers.html#custom-handlers) is the best place to get started when learning about MIME type and protocol handler registration.

APIs in the WHATWG specification

So far we've looked at specs that exist in both the W3C and WHATWG versions of HTML5. We'll now very briefly introduce a few more APIs that are documented within WHATWG's living standard HTML spec but have been broken out into smaller, more manageable specifications by the W3C. The purpose and the majority of the content is the same in both versions. You've already seen one in Chapter 5, the canvas 2D context, so we'll ignore that.

- **Cross document and channel messaging**: Cross document messaging defines a way for documents to communicate with each other regardless of their source domain and without enabling cross-site attacks. In a similar vein, channel messaging uses independent pieces of code to communicate directly.

- **Microdata**: Adds an additional layer of semantics to your documents from which search engines, browsers, and more can extract information and provide an enhanced browsing experience.

- **Web Workers**: An API for running JavaScript in the background, independent of any user scripts. Allows for long running tasks to be completed without preventing the page from becoming unresponsive.

- **Web Storage**: A spec for storing client-side data (key value pairs), similar to cookies.

- **Web Sockets**: Allows pages to use the WebSocket protocol to send two-way messages between a browser and server.

- **Server sent events**: Allows for push notifications to be sent from a server to a browser in the form of DOM events.

The "HTML5" buzzword APIs

If I were to list all the other APIs that are closely related to HTML5, I'd be here for a while. Another time, perhaps. A few of those often incorrectly described as HTML5 are Geolocation, Indexed DB, Selectors, the Filesystem API, and even CSS3!

Mike Smith from the W3C has compiled a comprehensive list of all aspects of the web platform and browser technologies and it's well worth bookmarking (`http://j.mp/h5platform`[24]).

We've merely scratched the surface of each of these detailed, useful, powerful APIs. In order to find out more and get under the skin of each, go and throw yourself knee deep in code. You'll be surprised at what you'll find while researching and experimenting. As for those APIs that aren't quite fully baked yet, hopefully we've whetted your appetite for what will be coming to a browser near you soon.

The glorious dawn of the age of the standards-based Web, accessible to all, in a world of compliant browsers, on a variety of devices

Before you crack on through to the presentational beauty that is CSS3, let us take you on a journey.

The year is 2022 and HTML5 has just been ratified by the W3C. It is now an official, fully-fledged specification. Web designers and developers around the world rejoice in the knowledge that they can now go out and build standards-based sites and applications that are accessible to all on a range of devices.

Universally expected behavior across browsers is drawing ever closer. Web applications can cater to touch-, voice-, and gesture-driven devices. The public has learned that an application may behave differently depending on whether it's used on a television, a computer, or a handheld device, or even depending on the user's location. *Context* is king online.

The Web has exploded into a tangled maze of ubiquitous, ever-present networks. Your car is driven by Google Maps, and your personalized news is delivered instantly by citizen journalists the world over. Oh, and Great Grandma is on Twitter.

We are approaching the tipping point for a Web built on solid, fundamental, open standards. The Web is larger than any one vendor, group, corporation, government, or individual. The Web *is* open, and that's the way it should stay.

If you have read the first six chapters of this book, you realize that the scenario we've just described is not 2022, but is in fact the state of the Web today.

---

[24] `http://platform.html5.org`

Homework: Mark up the "Join Gordo's Space Cadets" form using the new markup covered

Now that you are armed with the knowledge of how to build standards-compliant HTML5 forms, it's time to put it into practice. Don't forget to use your knowledge of HTML 4 when writing the markup, as not all of the data will require HTML5. Here's the data you need to capture:

- First name
- Last name
- Date of birth
- E-mail address
- URL
- Telephone number
- Shoe size
- Flying skill level
- Address (including ZIP/post code) and country
- Why they want to join the space cadets
- Register button

Chapter 7

CSS3, Here and Now

Congratulations! You've reached the second part of the book. The first half focused on the importance of building a solid, structural foundation in HTML, creating a semantic layer upon which to build. We've introduced you to HTML5, the next generation of markup for the Web, and we've highlighted the benefits HTML5 has to offer, including some of the great new APIs and a large number of new, semantic elements that will ensure your web pages are just that extra bit future-friendly.

It's been a roller coaster ride and we've covered a great deal. If you've been following along with the homework, you've built a solid HTML5 site built that's now ready for the addition of a little—some may say, long overdue—style. The second half of this book is where we add that style by introducing CSS3, the next evolution of the Cascading Style Sheets specification. Along the way, we'll show you a number of methods you can use to create beautifully designed web sites that, amongst other things, deliver beautiful experiences to contemporary browsers, degrade gracefully for less capable browsers, and are easy to maintain, accessible, and as future-proofed as possible.

This chapter provides a little contextual awareness on the current state of CSS. We'll outline some of the history and development of CSS, and we'll provide an indication of where CSS3 is heading. That might sound a little like a history lesson and you may be tempted to skip this chapter, but we urge you not to. We'll be covering some basic tenets—principles we urge you to adhere to—and we'll also look at how CSS has evolved, highlighting the fact that we can do a lot with CSS 2.1 already and that CSS3 builds upon what is already a powerful, if under-used, specification.

We'll revisit some CSS basics such as the definition of a declaration, how you calculate specificity, and the cascade. We'll also look at some best practices such as progressive enhancement—ways of writing code to ensure your style sheets are easy to maintain and play nice in a team context where more than one person might be involved in maintaining a style sheet.

So, without further ado, let's get started.

A Refresher on the importance of web standards

By now you should be well aware of the benefits of web standards. We made the case for web standards throughout the first half of the book. You should now be equipped with a comprehensive toolbox to create HTML5 markup that allows you to easily handle any semantic situation. You should also be proudly POSH (writing Plain Old Semantic HTML) with a solid semantic foundation of structured markup on which to build beautifully crafted web sites.

So now it's time to create a presentational layer of valid, standards-compliant CSS with all the tastiness that brings. This is what we'll cover in the second half of the book.

One important way to ensure our CSS layer is easy to maintain is to ensure our style sheets are DRY. What do we mean by DRY? Simple: Don't Repeat Yourself (`http://j.mp/drywiki`[1]). The "cascade," as we'll see later, allows us to set styles at the top level and have these styles cascade down the elements we establish subsequently, enabling us to set generic styles at a global level and only override them when we need to.

Before we get down to business, let's take a look at a little history by recapping the CSS timeline. The Cascading Style Sheets specification has evolved incrementally to address new challenges as the web has evolved. We'll briefly recap on a little of that history in the next section.

CSS 1, CSS 2.1, CSS3 ...

The W3C's Cascading Style Sheets (CSS) specification has evolved over the last decade and a half, moving from the CSS 1 specification, which became a W3C Recommendation on December 17, 1996, to the CSS 2 specification, which finally became a recommendation on June 7, 2011 (although the creation of CSS3 began long before). A lot has changed in that evolution, though—let's not forget—a lot remains the same. That's how standards evolve, after all.

> Note: In passing, and lest you think we've been clumsy with our writing, it's worth noting how the naming of the different CSS specifications has changed. Note how CSS3, unlike its predecessors CSS 1 and CSS 2 (and CSS 2.1) isn't "CSS 3" but "CSS3" (no space). Most people miss these nuances, but you (we hope) won't. (Don't ask us who decided to abandon the all-important space, but be aware that it's gone.)

---

[1] `http://en.wikipedia.org/wiki/Don%27t_repeat_yourself`

Though the evolution of the CSS specification has been slow, browser vendors have increasingly driven the pace in recent years. The age-old chicken and egg problem of which comes first, specifications or implementations, has moved on. Specifications (established and outlined by standards-setting bodies like the W3C) and implementations (proposals by browser vendors, innovating around specifications) have come slowly together. It's a good thing, as you'll see shortly.

We might not have solved the chicken and egg conundrum, but the separation that used to exist between specifications, established by standards-setting bodies often accused of being slow to innovate, and implementations proposed by browser vendors, often accused of innovating too quickly and thus breaking specifications, is less pronounced than it once was. More importantly, there's a growing sense that neither the chicken nor the egg comes first; in fact, both are equally important.

But enough of this metaphorical meandering around chickens and eggs. The burning question is simple: Is CSS3 ready?

Good news! We answer that question in the next section.

Is CSS3 ready?

It's worth noting as we embark on the second half of this book that CSS3 has been a W3C Working Draft since May 23, 2001. That's—unbelievably—more than a decade, at the time of writing! So, for everyone that claims to be waiting for CSS3 to be "finished" before they embrace it, it might at first glance appear that there's a lot to still be waiting for…

Thankfully, the W3C maintains "a rough schedule of what the CSS WG is working on," so if you want to follow the development of CSS3, this allegedly is the place to start. To get an overview of "CSS current work and how to participate," see the schedule at http://j.mp/currentcss[2].

So, where are we now? Well, CSS Level 2 Revision 1 (that's the CSS 2.1 you're probably more familiar with) is finally complete. (Happy news, since you've no doubt been using it in your everyday work for years.) But what of CSS3?

CSS3 is evolving at an equally rapid rate and, as we'll see shortly, is ready to be embraced right here, right now. Just as you've already embraced CSS 2.1 and use it as a part of your web designer workflow, we and many others encourage you to take the plunge with CSS3. The specification is evolving, yes, but there's no better time to dip your toe in the water and avail yourself of the opportunities it offers.

Context

Let's put the CSS adventure in context. As Håkon Wium Lie and Bert Bos said in their book *Cascading Style Sheets: Designing for the Web* (published way back in 1997), the saga of CSS began in 1994 and it's been a roller-coaster ride ever since.

---

[2] www.w3.org/Style/CSS/current-work

If you don't believe us that as far back as 1994, CSS was a proposal, we urge you to read Håkon Wium Lie's proposal (published on October 10, 1994). Back then Lie referred to Cascading Style Sheets (CSS) as "Cascading HTML Style Sheets," but if you take a few moments for historical curiosity's sake to read the short proposal, you'll be surprised at how it forms a fundamental building block for what we know today (`http://j.mp/csshtml`[3]).

So, we started with CSS 1, which evolved into CSS 2, which subsequently evolved into CSS 2.1, and this is evolving into CSS3.

It's worth noting that CSS 2.1 offers a lot of often-overlooked potential. A huge amount of loveliness has been added to the CSS specification over the years that many, mistakenly, think was only first added as a part of the CSS3 specification. This includes `@font-face`, attribute selectors, generated content, and text shadows.

As we move towards increasingly widespread support for CSS3 amongst a landscape of ever-evolving browsers, many mistake the current style sheet landscape as something new. It isn't.

In much the same way that we embraced CSS 2.1 before it became a W3C recommendation, as a part of your presentation layer *here and now*, we encourage you to embrace CSS3 *right here, right now*. The benefits are many; moreover, as browser support continues to roll out, the impact upon your workflow will pay itself back over and over.

CSS3 modularity

One major change to the evolution of CSS is the W3C's decision to split CSS3 into a series of modules. As the CSS Working Group put it,

> *As the popularity of CSS grows, so does interest in making additions to the specification. Rather than attempting to shove dozens of updates into a single monolithic specification, it will be much easier and more efficient to be able to update individual pieces of the specification. Modules will enable CSS to be updated in a more timely and precise fashion, thus allowing for a more flexible and timely evolution of the specification as a whole.*

> `www.w3.org/TR/2001/WD-css3-roadmap-20010119`

This is good news for us craftsmen of the Web. As the CSS specification has evolved and grown in order to respond to the needs and demands of designers, the need to modularize the specification has become pressing. With so many new developments in CSS, the idea of an enormous, all-encompassing CSS3 specification had become increasingly unrealistic, resulting in the W3C's decision to adopt a modular approach.

---

[3] `www.w3.org/People/howcome/p/cascade.html`

The benefits of this are many: browser vendors are innovating rapidly within the CSS space, so by embracing a modular approach, elements of the CSS3 specification can move forward at different rates as different browser vendors implement support for given features. Of course, there is a downside to this: having different features supported at different times by different browsers can make cross browser development complicated, but there are strategies to work around this.

So how does the move towards modularity affect the development of the CSS3 specification? One important point is to note that modules run through a series of *maturity levels*, enabling us to see what is moving towards Recommendation status (and, therefore, reliable use).

Maturity levels

The W3C assigns each of their specifications a maturity level, which gives an indication of its current state within the development process. Modules move up a series of levels from Working Draft through Last Call to Candidate Recommendation and, finally, to Proposed Recommendation.

The process might at first appear a little unwieldy, but it allows you to see what's supported and, equally importantly, what is likely to be supported in the near future. The W3C define the maturity levels in typically opaque language on the web site (`http://j.mp/reclevels`[4]).

Although the maturity levels aren't necessarily indicative of browser support, generally there is a level of parity between the two (in some areas more than others). We'll discuss browser support in greater detail later in the chapter but first let's take a look at some of the modules in question.

The benefits of CSS3

Let's take a little detour into the benefits of CSS3 and why embracing the next evolution of CSS now can make your life as a web designer a little easier. With browsers vendors working together to shape these new standards, major differences in the rendering of sites is slowly becoming a thing of the past. New properties (with or without vendor prefixes) defined in CSS3 arrive in browsers in flurries through silent background updates, ensuring that standards support increases at a growing rate. This means we can craft richer web experiences for our clients and users than ever before.

> Note: Bear in mind that some older versions of IE—namely 6-8—still have a significant user base, which does upset the apple cart somewhat. Again, there are strategies to ensure content is still accessible and usable in non-supporting browsers, which we'll look at later on in the book.

As CSS3 evolves, our job as designers is becoming easier and we can begin to see a number of appealing benefits. Design is streamlined, our workflows are improved, and, as we offload presentational

---

[4] www.w3.org/2005/10/Process-20051014/tr#RecsWD

aspects to the browser, we can benefit from less time spent in Photoshop and more writing markup or CSS.

Streamlining design

Traditionally, the web design process (from a visual perspective) began by creating a new design in Photoshop and then attempting to re-create it in HTML and CSS. This is starting to change. With a plethora of devices, browsers, and therefore contexts to be catered for, more and more designers are beginning to design "in the browser." A technique long trumpeted by Andy Clarke, the concept is that by working within the medium for which we are designing, we embrace its flaws and unpredictability much like John Allsopp described in *The Dao of Web Design* all those years before.

It would be unrealistic to suggest that we will never open Photoshop (or another image editor) again, but increasingly and with the help of CSS3, that need is dissipating. We can offload a great deal of the visual heavy lifting to the browser and create effects directly in the browser that previously would have required an image editor.

This not only improves our workflow and reduces the length of a project, but it makes maintenance and change requests easier to handle as well. The client asks to make a change? No problem; change the CSS. No more painstaking (and painful) round trips to the image editor.

As we'll see in the next section, CSS3 provides a number of new ways to create effects for which we would previously had to work around or (whisper it quietly) hack.

Reduced workarounds and hacks

There are a whole host of workarounds that can be avoided with CSS3, including

- *Specifying rich web fonts*: No more creating type in an image editor and serving it via image replacement or using a tool like sIFR.

- *Creating round corners automatically*: No more reliance on images for creating boxes with rounded corners. It can all be handled automatically with `border-radius`.

- *Opacity and alpha channels*: Create transparency without images using `opacity` or `rgba`.

- *Creating gradients on the fly*: No more creating repeating images for gradients or patterns. Simply use CSS gradients (radial or linear).

- *Reducing heavy scripting for simple animations*: No need to use JavaScript to create simple transitions or transforms. It can now be handled in CSS.

- *Cutting additional markup*: No need to write additional markup to create columns.

- *Less classitis*: No need to add additional extraneous classes when elements can be targeted using new CSS3 selectors.

These changes should save you time and allow you to concentrate on other aspects of the project without having to hack around as much. We'll come back to this idea of progressive enhancement but now let's briefly go through CSS basics to ensure we're speaking the same language. In the next section, we'll look at the language and terms of CSS as well as some best practices.

CSS basics refresher

This section is all about CSS fundamentals. It's really a refresher and most of it should be common knowledge, but we feel it's important to run through. Don't skip it! Though this returns to the basics of CSS, we feel it's important to understanding the vocabulary used when writing style sheets. The second half of the book focuses on CSS3, so a poor understanding of CSS vocabulary will get in the way of developing your style sheet chops.

To help us run through the fundamentals in a timely manner, one of our authors (Divya Manian) has created an extremely helpful checklist for you that we've reorganized and summarized to provide a short, at-a-glance CSS reference (http://j.mp/cssvocab[5]).

Anatomy of a rule (or rule set)

As you're hopefully aware, a simple CSS rule is written as follows:

```
selector {
        property: value;
}
```

Let's break down a simple CSS rule to take a look at properties, values, declarations, and declaration blocks. Once we've covered these, we'll dive a little deeper.

A property

In the following example the border is the property:

```
h1 {
        border: 1px;
}
```

A *property* is a style that you apply to a selector. Looking at the generic example in the previous section, a selector can be any of a number of elements, such as an h1, p, or img element.

So the border, in this case, is a property, let's take a look at its value. It shouldn't surprise you to discover that the value in this case is 1px.

A value

The *value* of the border is set at 1px.

---

[5] http://nimbupani.com/css-vocabulary.html

```
h1 {
        border: 1px;
}
```

As we'll see in the next section we can set multiple values in a single declaration.

A declaration

A *property: value pair* is called a *declaration*. Continuing with the same example, the declaration is border: 1px;, as follows:

```
h1 {
        border: 1px;
}
```

Looking at a slightly more complex declaration, again using the border property, you can set multiple values in a declaration, as follows:

```
h1 {
        border: 1px dotted red;
}
```

In the previous example we've established multiple values - 1px, dotted, and red - to create a more complex declaration. We've written this using shorthand notation, but we could also write this across multiple declarations to create a series of declarations, or a declaration block.

Declaration block

A rule can have more than one declaration—and frequently does. Expanding the previous example from a single-line shorthand declaration to a multi-line *declaration block*, we get the following:

```
h1 {
        border: 1px;
        border-style: dotted;
        border-color: red;
}
```

Clearly, the shorthand version in the previous example is more efficient but the long-hand version can be easier to maintain. Hold that thought for now; we'll return to it later when we look at CSS shorthand.

Keywords

In our previous example, we set the width of the border using a length unit, in this case px. The CSS specification also defines a number of *keywords* that can be used to define values. Our previous example showed two additional keywords in action: the border-style, set to dotted and the border-color, set to red.

You're probably already familiar with many CSS keywords, such as different color names (red, green, blue, etc) and different border styles (dashed, dotted, solid). There are many more and you'll pick them up as we go through the book.

CSS units

Returning to the example again,

```
h1 {
        border: 1px;
}
```

In this case, the value of the border property has been set to 1px. CSS defines a number of *units* that we can use to declare values. These include relative length units, absolute length units, CSS units, and color units. Mozilla provide a useful overview of these at http://j.mp/css-units[6].

Looking at CSS units further, let's explore color units. We're used to seeing colors defined using hexadecimal, such as #FF0000 (or red as a keyword). As we'll see in the next section, we can also express these units using what's known as *functional notation*.

Functional notation

As the W3C helpfully put it, "functional notation is used to denote colors, attributes, and URIs in CSS3." Should you wish to dig a little deeper than this small quoted fragment, feel free to do so at the following location, where numerous examples are outlined: http://j.mp/css-values[7].

Rest assured, though, we're on hand to provide a little translation. (Would we leave you at the mercy of the W3C's somewhat dry, and often confusing, descriptions?)

Let's take a look at the previous example using color where we considered the two equivalents, #FF0000 (written in hexadecimal) and red (written as a keyword). We can write the same color using functional notation. All three of the following examples (written in *hexadecimal*, using a *keyword*, and using *functional notation*) display identically.

First, using *hexadecimal*:

```
blockquote {
        background: #FF0000;
}
```

Second, using a *keyword*:

```
blockquote {
        background: red;
}
```

---

[6] https://developer.mozilla.org/en/CSS-2_Quick_Reference/Units
[7] www.w3.org/TR/css3-values/#functional

Third, using *functional notation*:

```
blockquote {
        background: rgb(255,0,0);
}
```

In the functional notation example, we establish that the background value is set using the "function" rgb (red, green. blue) and define this function with an "argument" set in parenthesis (that's brackets to you and us). This is akin to functions in JavaScript.

Written in pseudo-code, this looks like so:

```
blockquote {
        background: function(argument);
}
```

Though this might be a little confusing now, as we run through some examples over the coming chapters everything should fall into place. Other examples of functional notation include the url function, which you're used to seeing as follows:

```
blockquote {
        background: url(http://www.example.com/background.png);
}
```

In this case, the function is the url with the argument (in brackets) being the location of the background image in question (in this case http://www.example.com/background.png).

An understanding of functional notation can offer a number of very powerful opportunities and it's worth reading the full W3C specification (yes, all of it!) to really explore the opportunities offered. One promising aspect of functional notation is the use of the calc function, which the W3C outlines at http://j.mp/csscalc[8].

As the W3C put it, "The calc(<expression>) function can be used wherever length values are allowed. The expression within the parenthesis is computed at the same time as em lengths are computed...." That might be a little confusing, but an example will hopefully cast a little light.

```
section {
        float: left;
        margin: 1em;
        border: solid 1px;
        width: calc(100%/3 - 2*1em - 2*1px);
}
```

Without getting into too much detail (as it's covered in greater depth in Chapter 12), the calc() function allows the user of mathematical expressions as values. It can be used in place of length, frequency, angle, time, or number values. It is certainly a feature to watch as it gains more browser support in the future.

---

[8] www.w3.org/TR/css3-values/#calc

Selectors

Selectors are the way to declare which elements the styles should apply to and h1, blockquote, .callout, and #lovelyweather are all selectors. There are many types of selectors and we'll be delving deeper in the next chapter.

Combinators

The selection of an element based on its occurrence in relation to another element (chosen by the choice of combinator: whitespace, >, +, or ~). As with selectors, we'll be focusing on the various types of combinators in Chapter 8.

At-rules

At-rules begin with the @ character, such as @import, @page, @media, and @font-face. We'll look at some of these at-rules and how they work in Chapters 9 and 10.

Vendor-specific extensions

Vendor-specific extensions are exactly what they seem. They provide functionality specific to that particular vendor (i.e. the browser). They do not always necessarily represent a feature declared in a standard. We'll touch on vendor prefixes later in this chapter.

We'll be using this language frequently throughout the second half of this book, so for now let's look at time-saving with some CSS shorthand

CSS shorthand

One way to bloat your style sheet (although sometimes it can be useful) is to use multiple declarations when one will do. There are a number of properties that can be turned into CSS shorthand, saving both time and file size. We'll look at margin and padding but similar rules apply to the various background, border, font, list-style, and outline properties. For more detail on those, read *Efficient CSS with Shorthand Properties* by Roger Johansson (http://j.mp/456css[9]) and *CSS Shorthand Guide* by Dustin Diaz (http://j.mp/diazcss[10]).

You can specify padding and margin in several ways. There are individual values for -top, -right, -bottom, and -left, and also a shorthand version. Here's an example:

```
p {padding-top: 1.5em;}
p {padding-right: .5em;}
p {padding-bottom: 1.5em;}
p {padding-left: 3em;}
```

---

[9] http://www.456bereastreet.com/archive/200502/efficient_css_with_shorthand_properties/
[10] http://www.dustindiaz.com/css-shorthand/

These four CSS rules specify the individual properties for `<p>`. However, you can write the same thing in just one line by using shorthand.

```
p {padding: 1.5em .5em 1.5em 3em;}
```

The four values in the shorthand property are top, right, bottom, and left, respectively. Remember it like an analog clock: starting at 12 o'clock will keep you out of TRouBLe.

It's common to have several values be the same, such as the top/bottom or left/right, so there are three more forms of shorthand. If there are only three values, they represent the top, left *and* right, and bottom values, respectively.

```
p {margin-top: .75em;}
p {margin-right: .5em;}
p {margin-bottom: 1.5em;}
p {margin-left: .5em;}
```

```
p {margin: .75em .5em 1.5em;}
```

The next form of shorthand has only two values, which stand for top/bottom and right/left, respectively.

```
blockquote {margin-top: .75em;}
blockquote {margin-right: 3em;}
blockquote {margin-bottom: .75em;}
blockquote {margin-left: 3em;}
```

```
blockquote {margin: .75em 3em;}
```

Finally, the last form of shorthand only has one value, making all four sides the same.

```
div {margin-top: 1.5em;}
div {margin-right: 1.5em;}
div {margin-bottom: 1.5em;}
div {margin-left: 1.5em;}
```

```
div {margin: 1.5em;}
```

In general, it's best to set good default `margin` and `padding` values for elements, using the shorthand property to assign all four values. If you need to override this style, the individual properties are handy if you only want to change one or two of the values. This helps prevent problems if you later change your default values, as the new default values will still cascade down to the other properties you didn't change.

```
/* Recommended example - only override what you need to */
ul {margin: .75em 1.5em;}
li ul {margin-top: 0; margin-bottom: 0;}
```

```
/* We don't recommend setting the same value in two places where possible */
ul {margin: .75em 1.5em;}
li ul {margin: 0 1.5em;}
```

As you go through the next five chapters, you'll see that some of the new properties introduced in CSS3 can also use shorthand notation. We'll introduce those as they arise. Let's now look at another some fundamental aspects of CSS; the cascade, specificity, and inheritance.

The cascade, specificity, and inheritance

When dealing with large CSS files, we often veer blindly down a path—only to find ourselves writing incredibly long and complex rules in order to override another rule found earlier in the document. In the majority of cases, writing long rules such as these can be avoided with a clear understanding of CSS cascade, specificity, and inheritance.

CSS cascade

The cascade is very much the backbone of CSS. It works by assigning a level of importance to each rule and determining which rules and properties affect a given element. Its aim is to find the "top trump."

Now seems an appropriate time to remind ourselves that style sheets can come from different sources, not only from us designers and developers. They can come from browsers (user agents), from a user's styles, or from us, the authors.

The use of the !important flag becomes evident when describing the cascade. !important was created as a method to allow users with specific accessibility needs to override author styles. For example, it can be used to increase the font size or increase the contrast. Because of this, the !important flag should never be found in author style sheets, although this is rarely the case.

In ascending order (where 5 is most important), the cascade works as follows.

1. User agent styles
2. User styles
3. Author styles
4. Author styles flagged as !important
5. User styles flagged as !important

Following the cascade, rules are ordered by their specificity, and that's what we'll look at next.

Calculating specificity

Specificity comes into play when two or more style rules apply to the same element and set the same property, with the same importance, in the same position in the cascade. In this case, the rule with the highest specificity is the top trump.

Specificity is calculated by assigning a numerical value to each type of selector. A total is then worked out for a specific rule. Four levels are stated for numbering types of selectors, each of which has its own weight in the calculation. These break down into a, b, c, and d, where a = inline style

b = the total number of ID selectors

c = the number of class and attribute selectors and pseudo-classes in the selector

d = the number of type selectors and pseudo-elements in the selector

Selectors using the negation pseudo-class (:not) are treated like any other; however, the negation itself isn't a pseudo-class. The universal * {...} selector is ignored in the calculations.

To ensure your calculations remain simple, we'll use base 10 to see a clear difference in results. Therefore, we'll add 1000 for each inline style; 100 for each ID; 10 for each class, attribute, and pseudo-class; and 1 for each element and pseudo-element. Clear? Probably not, so let's look at some examples.

Let's say you wanted to style paragraphs, so in your style sheet you would write:

p {...}

Referencing the definitions from earlier in the chapter, we can see that p {...} is a type selector, which falls under d in the specificity levels. This means the specificity for a paragraph on its own is a=0, b=0, c=0, d=1, giving a total of 1.

If we add a class to that paragraph, p.author {...}, the scores are as follows: a=0, b=0, c=1, d=1. Using base 10 as a multiplier, we can calculate a total of 11 (10 for the class selector). Therefore, the class selector trumps the type selector and would win out in a specificity celebrity death match. Table 7-1 shows further examples of specificity totals.

Table 7-1. Specificity Examples and Calculations

Selector	Specificity (a,b,c,d)	Specificity Total (Base 10)
style="color:red;"	1,0,0,0	1000
#comments #respond {...}	0,2,0,0	200
#respond input[type="checkbox"] {...}	0,1,1,1	111
body#blog article.hentry p:first-child {...}	0,1,2,3	123
body#blog article[role="main"] p:first-child {...}	0,1,2,3	123
#comments {...}	0,1,0,0	100
p.author .fn {...}	0,0,2,1	21
p.author {...}	0,0,1,1	11
article p {...}	0,0,0,2	2
p {...}	0,0,0,1	1

Notice that two of the selectors (rows four and five) in Table 7-1 have the same specificity. When two selectors have the same specificity, the selector that appears later in the source order takes precedence.

> *Note: If you want to see or think about CSS specificity in a more visual way, Andy Clarke wrote about it way back in 2005 using a Star Wars analogy (http://j.mp/ starwarsspecificity) to illustrate the point. Alternatively, if poker is more your thing, Carl Camera compared specificity to poker hands in an article in 2007 (http://j.mp/pokerspecificity).*

CSS specificity can be a tricky skill to master but, once you understand it, it is a powerful tool that allows you to target elements with the minimum of bother and saves you from having to go back and alter your perfectly crafted semantic markup.

CSS inheritance

The notion of inheritance in CSS is relatively straightforward but can be the cause of some confusion. In its simplest form, inheritance allows authors to only declare a property and value once, thus avoiding the need to set the same property on a number of elements. For example, we could write the following to change the site's typeface to Georgia:

`article, section, h1, h2, h3, p, ol, ul, dl {font-family:georgia, serif;}`

However, it's much easier (not to mention more maintainable) to write.

`body {font-family:georgia, serif;}`

The `font-family` property is then inherited by the body's child elements until another style rule overrides it. When used intelligently, inheritance combined with the cascade and specificity can save you development time and keep your style sheet's file size small and easy to maintain. And this leads us nicely on to the subject of maintenance and organization.

> *Note: Although not all CSS properties are automatically inherited, you can force them to be by using the `inherit` value. This is a good thing. Imagine if `margin` and `padding` were inherited and you then had to override these inherited styles on each declaration. A word of warning: `inherit` doesn't work in versions of IE less than 8 except on the `direction` and `visibility` properties.*

CSS organization and maintenance

When it comes to writing CSS, everyone has their own unique preferences, be it single line vs. multi-line, indentation with tabs or spaces, or the order in which rule sets or properties appear. In isolation, many of these points become moot, but when we factor in that many team members may work on any given style sheet or that you haven't worked on that site for a year and now need to make some updates, it's generally best to have some conventions in place to ease these issues. We'll start by looking at some CSS conventions and commenting best practices before detouring into a look at CSS resets and frameworks.

CSS conventions

CSS conventions can be broadly broken down into two key areas: coding style and naming conventions. These two areas can then be sub-divided into individual debates (the kind of which designers have been arguing over for years). We'll explain the pros and cons of each argument, but generally we'll leave you to pick the approach that's right for you.

Single line vs. multi-line CSS

The biggest debate usually revolves around whether a rule should be written on a single line, like:

```
h1 {font-family:Georgia; color: green; line-height:1.3; }
```

or multi-line, like:

```
h1 {
        font-family:Georgia;
        color: green;
        line-height:1.3;
}
```

Arguments for single line formatting are few and far between. The number of lines and whitespace is reduced and thus the file size is smaller, but you could always just minify your code before putting it on your live production server if you are concerned about this (a *minifier* is a program that removes all possible whitespace from a code file). It is also easier to scan through large numbers of selectors if you use single line rules, but it is then harder to scan individual properties and attributes.

The pros for using multi-line CSS are easier to see. First, it is a heck of a lot easier to decipher the code. When using source control, it's easy to track which properties have been edited within a rule set (because they are on an individual line). You can also simply use Cmd+F (or Ctrl+F) to find the selector, eliminating the need to visually scan the file. The same applies when passing the file through a validator: when using multi-line, it's easy to see which property is causing the issue but with single line, it isn't. It is also argued that it's easier to place comments next to individual declarations in the multi-line approach.

There is an added nuance to the multi-line approach that revolves around the placement of the closing curly bracket. Should it reside on its own line (as shown previously) or on the same line as the final declaration, as follows?

```
h1 {
        font-family:Georgia;
        color: green;
        line-height:1.3;}
```

It doesn't make a lot of difference, to be honest. Either way works well.

A side argument in the single line vs. multi-line debate revolves around the use of tabs or spaces for indentation of declarations in the multi-line approach. This debate predates CSS and isn't resolved easily.

Some people prefer a single tab, others two spaces, others four. We recommend using tabs for indentation but feel free to arm wrestle over it.

The style you choose is up to you. Each of us authors has our preferred approach that works for us individually but by and large we're multi-liners. Try both approaches and decide which you and any other team members prefer.

Ordering declarations

Another area that stirs debate in CSS circles is people's preferences for the ordering of declarations within individual rule sets. Some prefer to alphabetize their declarations, others group them by type or relevance, and some have no order at all (pro tip: don't choose this option). Here is the alphabetical approach, ordered by the first letter of the property name:

```css
header {
        background:#f8f8f8 url(img/bg.png);
        border-bottom:1px solid #ccc;
        color:#333;
        font-family:Georgia;
        font-size:16px;
        font-weight:normal;
        height:60px;
        left:0;
        line-height:1.5;
        margin:0 auto;
        padding:5px 20px;
        position:fixed;
        top:0;
        z-index:2;
}
```

The next example shows the declarations grouped by type (in the following order):

1. Position

2. Display and box model

3. Font and typography

4. Color

5. Background and borders

```css
header {
        position:fixed;
        top:0;
        left:0;
        z-index:2;
        height:60px;
        margin:0 auto;
        padding:5px 20px;
        font-family:Georgia;
        font-size:16px;
```

```
        font-weight:normal;
        line-height:1.5;
        color:#333;
        background:#f8f8f8 url(img/bg.png);
        border-bottom:1px solid #ccc;
}
```

As with all these debates, choose the solution that best suits you. One could argue that the alphabetical approach is easier to learn and that properties are easier to scan. However, with the grouped approach it is easier to see which how the declarations (in the case of this example) form a fixed light grey bar that is 60 pixels high without resorting to looking at the result in a browser. This also makes it easier to see how the different properties affect and interact with one another.

We shan't open the hornets' nest of whether or not the final semi-colon on the last declaration should be included; suffice to say it's our belief that it always should.

Ordering rule sets

In the last section we discussed the ordering of declarations within an individual rule set, but what about the order of those rule sets within the style sheets? Take the following markup:

```
<aside>
  <section class="history">
    <a href="history.html">
    <h2>History</h2>
    <img src="img/history.png" alt="The first space shuttle" height="75" width="100%" />
    <p>Before humans were launched into space, many animals were propelled heavenwards to pave
the way for mankind's pioneering endeavors. These original pioneers, including numerous
monkeys, served their nations in order to investigate the biological effects of space travel.
Find out more about these pioneers that changed the face of space forever.</p>
    </a>
  </section>
<aside>
```

Now let's assume we want to have distinct styles for the section, anchor, heading, image, and paragraph within that section. It would make sense to structure our CSS as follows (note we've used single line notation here to highlight the selectors):

```
.history {...}
.history a {...)
.history h2 {...}
.history img {...}
.history p {...}
```

This approach follows the layout of our markup (and coincidentally is in alphabetically order). For some this makes sense; others group all the heading styles (within a sheet) together like so:

```
h2 {...}
.history h2 {...)
.mission h2 {...}
```

It's difficult to provide general guidance here (we'll touch on it some more in the commenting best practice section) but in general the first approach, possibly with some slight re-ordering depending on your preference, makes it easier to manage specificity and inheritance.

Naming conventions

Now let's look at naming conventions in CSS, which refers to class or ID names as opposed to the name of a file (although that can be important, too). Class names should be descriptive and semantic; they should describe your content and not the presentation. Take the following two examples and see which you think is more descriptive of the content:

```
.bigLeftCol {...}
.littleRightCol {...}

.primary-content {...}
.secondary-content {...}
```

Hopefully you can see that the second example more accurately describes the content as opposed to the presentation. Although the first example might not seem bad at first, what if you were to change your design and switch the columns around? In order to do so you would then have to edit your underlying markup, which is inefficient.

> *Note: The first example also highlights another naming convention bug bear of ours: CamelCase. CamelCase is used in multiple programming languages and as such is ingrained in some developers' DNA. But here's the thing: CSS isn't a programming language, it's a presentation language. So while there are some helpful conventions we can borrow from programming, CamelCase isn't one of them. We use hyphens within our property names, so why not in our class names? After all .primary-content is much easier to read and work with than .primaryContent. If you don't believe us, read Harry Roberts' write up on why CamelCase Seriously Sucks at http://j.mp/camelcasesucks[11] and you'll be converted.*

Remember that names should be semantic and descriptive, not structural and presentational. In the future, rather than class names such as `.bigRedbox`, try `.warning-block`.

Commenting best practices

Commenting your CSS can only be beneficial for your project. There are several reasons for this, such as reminding you why you wrote certain rules or what calculation you used for font sizing. Comments are also extremely useful to other team members working on the project. While basic comments like this are par for the course, adding metadata and a table of contents can dramatically improve the readability and maintenance of a file. Consider the following:

---

[11] http://csswizardry.com/2010/12/css-camel-case-seriously-sucks/

```
/*-----------------------------------------------
[Master sheet]

Project:       Animals in Space
URL:           http://thewebevolved.com
Version:       1.1
Creator:       Rich Clark
Last changed:  01/02/12
Last Updated:  Oli Studholme
Primary use:   Demo site for book
-----------------------------------------------*/
```

By incorporating this information, everyone working on a specific project can see at a glance what the style sheet is for, who created it, and when it was last updated. The benefits of this approach become more apparent on larger projects when multiple style sheets are required with multiple team members working on the project. It isn't complicated and is good practice to get into.

Creating a table of contents

Following the metadata, it's also a good idea to include a table of contents for your file, which may look like the following:

```
/*-----------------------------------------------
Table of contents

1. Reset
2. Typography
3. Basic layout
4. Widgets
5. Media items
6. Forms
7. Media queries
8. IE specific styles
-----------------------------------------------*/
```

This table of contents can be as brief or as detailed as your project requires. Using this approach and splitting your file into sections like this makes it easy to maintain and add other styles to logical areas within your file. You should clearly break up each section with comments and add an additional character that isn't likely to appear in any of your actual code (such as | or £) to use as a flag when searching through your document. The additional character acts as a differentiator from a class or ID selector that may have the same name.

```
/*-----------------------------------------------
£Widgets
-----------------------------------------------*/
```

This sets out a basic framework for the beginning of a file, but we can take it a step further by also including a reference sheet for information such as color and typography.

Color and typography reference sheet

In languages such as JavaScript we can declare variables to be reused throughout the script. This functionality doesn't yet exist in CSS (although it can be added using a library like `less.js`). To combat this it, makes sense to include a brief reference sheet (or glossary) in our style sheet for things like color and typography. An example is shown below.

```
/*------------------------------------------------
Color reference sheet

Background:    #f8f8f8 (off white)
Body text:     #444444 (dark grey)
Headings:      #888888 (light grey)
:link          #0090D2 (blue)
:hover,
:active,
:focus         #0063A6 (dark blue)
-------------------------------------------------*/


/*------------------------------------------------
Typography reference sheet

Body copy:          1.2em/1.6em Georgia, serif;
Headers:            2.7em/1.3em Helvetica, Arial, "Lucida Sans Unicode", Verdana, sans-
serif;
Input, textarea:    1.1em Helvetica, Verdana, Geneva, Arial, sans-serif;
Buttons:            1.2em Georgia, serif;

Notes: reduce heading by 0.4cm with every lower heading level
-------------------------------------------------*/
```

This provides an introduction on how to structure your style sheets and create a style guide for starting projects, ensuring that files remain well structured and are easy to maintain. To truly create a level playing field, many like to use a CSS reset.

CSS resets and normalize.css

A reset style sheet resets everything to zero across all browsers, enabling us to start building again from zero. Essentially we're neutering all of the rules in the browser's default style sheet. Think about this for a moment.

- Goodbye to h1-h6 visual hierarchy.
- Lists no longer have bullets.
- Default padding and margin is removed.

On the one hand, this is useful (it's like clearing the ground before rebuilding), but you've removed everything so you need to put it all back again (or at least consider what you choose not to put back).

Consider this as a part of your process in the same as commenting your code. A reset style sheet coupled with a solid rebuild of style equals the beginnings of a framework. You can build your own framework or use one created elsewhere such as the HTML5 Boilerplate (http://j.mp/h5boiler[12]) created by a team including Paul Irish and co-author Divya Manian. If you decide to use a framework created by others, be sure to understand its inner workings before getting part way through a project and getting stuck.

Using resets

Returning to resets, the most basic of resets uses the * selector to reset properties for all elements.

```
* {
  margin:0;
  padding:0;
}
```

While this method is effective, it's not recommended because it slows your site and there are elements whose style you don't want to remove (inputs for example).

A more common approach, popularized by Eric Meyer, is to use a custom reset style sheet, many of which are now available. With the advent of HTML5, most of these style sheets now also include a rule for setting the new elements to display:block;, as described in Chapter 2.

A search for "CSS resets" will return thousands of results but some of the more popular reset style sheets are

- Meyer's reset reloaded (http://meyerweb.com/eric/tools/css/reset)

- HTML5 Doctor reset stylesheet (by author Richard Clark) (http://html5doctor.com/html-5-reset-stylesheet/)

- YUI Reset CSS (http://developer.yahoo.com/yui/reset/)

A copy of Meyer's reset reloaded (for use with HTML5) is shown next so you can see how it differs significantly from the * approach shown previously.

```
/* http://meyerweb.com/eric/tools/css/reset/
   v2.0 | 20110126
   License: none (public domain)
*/

html, body, div, span, applet, object, iframe,
h1, h2, h3, h4, h5, h6, p, blockquote, pre,
a, abbr, acronym, address, big, cite, code,
del, dfn, em, img, ins, kbd, q, s, samp,
small, strike, strong, sub, sup, tt, var,
b, u, i, center,
dl, dt, dd, ol, ul, li,
fieldset, form, label, legend,
table, caption, tbody, tfoot, thead, tr, th, td,
article, aside, canvas, details, embed,
figure, figcaption, footer, header, hgroup,
```

---

[12] www.html5boilerplate.com

```
menu, nav, output, ruby, section, summary,
time, mark, audio, video {
        margin: 0;
        padding: 0;
        border: 0;
        font-size: 100%;
        font: inherit;
        vertical-align: baseline;
}
/* HTML5 display-role reset for older browsers */
article, aside, details, figcaption, figure,
footer, header, hgroup, menu, nav, section {
        display: block;
}
body {
        line-height: 1;
}
ol, ul {
        list-style: none;
}
blockquote, q {
        quotes: none;
}
blockquote:before, blockquote:after,
q:before, q:after {
        content: '';
        content: none;
}
table {
        border-collapse: collapse;
        border-spacing: 0;
}
```

> Note: Think about using resets carefully—they can often be overkill for many projects, as
> you really do need to redefine everything yourself. In simpler projects, it's often good
> enough to set *margin: 0* and *padding: 0* on *<html>*, *<body>* and a few more.

Using normalize.css

An alternative approach is normalize.css, developed by Nicholas Gallagher and Jonathan Neal (http://j.mp/normalizecss[13]). In contrast to the reset stylesheets, normalize.css aims to make browsers render elements more consistently inline with modern standards. Unlike resets, the ground isn't completely cleared. normalize.css preserves useful defaults and goes further by correcting bugs and adds subtle usability improvements. normalize.css is also packaged with the HTML5 Boilerplate project.

---

[13] http://necolas.github.com/normalize.css/

As with the coding styles discussed earlier, which option you choose (if indeed any) is entirely dependent on the projects requirements and personal preference. It is important to note that none of these files should be taken as gospel (a common problem with Meyer's original reset). You should go through the file line by line and edit, add, or remove rules on a project by project basis.

CSS frameworks and toolkits

CSS frameworks take your starting point a step further than CSS resets by providing styles for things such as a pre-defined grid system, typography, colors, print styles, and more. Some go even further to include HTML and JavaScript on top of the CSS.

They can be extremely useful for rapid prototyping and taking care of the heavy lifting carried out in most projects. The downside is that they add bloat to your projects by including rules you won't need. They can also hamper the craftsmanship of the design process, making your designs look very similar and using non-semantic class names.

Our preference is to veer away from frameworks where possible, but you may find that some clients insist that you use a particular framework because it's used throughout the organization. For this reason it's worth familiarizing yourself with a few of the more popular frameworks.

- Blueprint, one of the early CSS frameworks (`http://blueprintcss.org/`).

- 960.js, a system to aid rapid prototyping that can also be used in a production environment (`http://960.gs/`).

- Bootstrap, a toolkit from Twitter designed to kickstart development of web apps and sites (`http://twitter.github.com/bootstrap/`).

- Foundation, built by Zurb as an easy-to-use, powerful, and flexible framework for building prototypes and production code on any kind of device (`http://foundation.zurb.com/`).

- Skeleton, a boilerplate for responsive, mobile-friendly development (`http://www.getskeleton.com/`).

One thing you can learn from CSS frameworks is their flexibility and way they abstract styles for reuse on multiple elements. This leads us nicely into how to make projects easier to maintain.

Maintainable CSS

As front-end craftsmen, we occupy a crucial role in the design process. We are the glue that binds great research, user experience, information architecture, and design with server side code. Whether the starting point is from wireframes or from Photoshop comps, one thing's for sure: we need to be superb communicators. Allied to this communication, we should create and follow a three-fold process.

1. *Discovery*: Interrogate user experience architects to frame their vision, to understand how the system of wireframes fit together, and to get to know the system we'll be developing.

2. *Implementation*: Write semantic markup and flexible, maintainable CSS.

3. *Delivery*: Communicate with server-side developers and content editors to explain how our beautifully crafted markup and CSS should be used, and which classes should be applied in which scenario in order to for our work to remain well structured for launch and beyond.

Herein lie the main principles behind maintainable CSS.

In his book *Bulletproof Web Design* (http://j.mp/bulletproofcss[14]), Dan Cederholm explains how we should always plan for the worst case scenario with both our markup and CSS. Creating a bulletproof site is more than simply testing your design with images or stylesheets turned off. It's about asking, "What if?"

Next time you receive wireframes or Photoshop comps, before you dive head first into HTML, ask the designer some questions.

- Is this site fixed-width or responsive?

- What happens if there's no image in that container?

- What if more text is entered there?

- What if this headline wraps?

The earlier you can find the answers to these questions, the earlier you can plan around them. Once you've received the answers, it pays to spend some time reviewing the designs. Print them all out, draw all over them, and look for common components used throughout. Take time to understand the underlying grid structure, look for common colors, and see how typography is treated. This may seem a time-consuming and unnecessary step in the process, but it avoids any repetition (remember DRY from earlier in the chapter) and prevents problems from arising down the line.

Creating a pattern primer or components library

Rather than diving straight into building templates when you begin a project, let us introduce you to the concept of a pattern primer (http://j.mp/patternprimer[15]) or components library (Figure 7-1). A pattern primer is an excellent starting point for your CSS (and markup).

Creating a pattern primer is simple: you build and style each component (identified in your earlier review) individually, thereby creating reusable chunks of code with semantic classes.

Essentially, you're building a templating toolkit. By creating each component or module independently, you can ensure that each will fit together snugly when you come to create templates—without specificity, cascade, or inheritance-based CSS headaches being induced. You can then test the pattern primer equally independently and fix any issues knowing that your fix for one issue won't create another. This highlights where your earlier review really pays off.

---

[14] http://simplebits.com/publications/bulletproof/
[15] http://adactio.com/journal/5028/

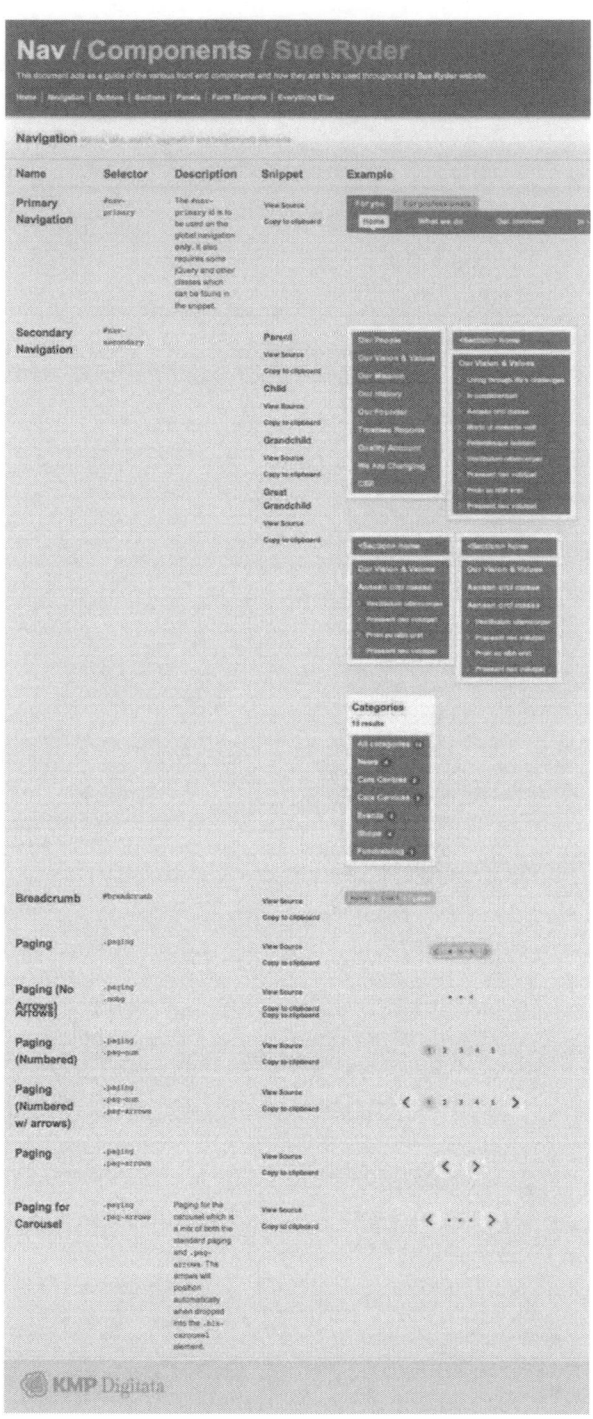

Figure 7-1. Components library for the sueryder.org website created by Tim Brook.

Naming components and including notes on where each should be used is also a must. The pattern primer is then extremely useful when passed to server-side developers who, no matter how many templates are designed, will always have to implement some unforeseen eventuality for which there is no template. They will have a site-specific vocabulary from which to work. The developer then simply copies the appropriate code snippet and voilà, it's styled to perfection.

Practical, maintainable CSS

Now that you've planned out your project and started creating components, what are the core coding styles you should be sticking to in order to ensure you're writing maintainable CSS?

In two excellent presentations (CSS Systems (`http://j.mp/css-systems`[16]) and Practical, Maintainable CSS (`http://j.mp/practical-css`[17])) Natalie Downe (go and find them now in your favourite search engine and have a read—we'll wait) lists eight rules of thumb to remember when crafting your stylesheets, and these tie nicely into the practices we've described throughout the chapter:

- Think in terms of components, not pages.
- Think about types of things, not individual things.
- Prefer classes to IDs.
- Create composable classes.
- Use descendent selectors to avoid redundant classes.
- Keep your selectors as short as possible.
- Order your CSS rules loosely by specificity.
- Prefer percentages for internal layout dimensions.

A little time spent learning the fundamentals of CSS, as covered earlier in this chapter, followed by time spent putting in place systems such as these can ensure your CSS is more efficient, easier to maintain, and plays better within a team context. Generous to a fault, Natalie has provided links to both presentations as PDFs, which include speaking notes for context.

If the above principles have got you thinking about creating maintainable, sustainable, and flexible CSS, why not go that step further and learn about another method in the same vein? It's Object Oriented CSS, devised by Nicole Sullivan.

---

[16] `http://natbat.net/2008/Sep/28/css-systems/`
[17] `http://natbat.net/2009/Mar/10/practical-maintainable-css/`

Object Oriented CSS (OOCSS)

Nicole Sullivan presented a talk on Object Oriented CSS (`http://j.mp/oo-cs`[18]) at Web Directions North in 2009 and she has very kindly written up some thoughts on the principles (`http://j.mp/oocss-principles`[19]) at her site. Answering the question, "How do you scale CSS for millions of visitors or thousands of pages?" she outlines the concept of Object Oriented CSS as

> *an approach for writing CSS that's fast, maintainable, and standards-based. It adds much needed predictability to CSS so that even beginners can participate in writing beautiful websites.*

Nicole Sullivan, OOCSS Github Wiki

What Nicole proposes is interesting—though you'll need to fetch a pot of tea and set aside some serious reading time—and her ideas, especially those around drawing on traditional software engineering concepts, make for rewarding reading. (Anyone that uses Lego as a metaphor for CSS component libraries gets a thumbs up.)

There are two overriding principles of OOCSS: separating structure and skin, and separating container and content. The first involves defining common visual features such as border styles as "skins" that you can apply to components without the need for a large amount of additional code. It also leans towards adding classes to elements within your markup rather than relying solely on type selectors. The second assumes that an "an object should look the same no matter where you put it." By applying a `class` to an element you can ensure that it's not dependent on its location (within a `section class="history"` for example).

Many disagree with the principles of OOCSS, highlighting that a large number of classes causes code bloat and style sheets become unmanageable. When writing CSS, we tend to pick certain aspects of OOCSS and combine them with a healthy dose of our own knowledge and working practices, thereby creating our own system and workflow perfectly suited to our and our clients' needs. We urge you to do the same.

In summary, by planning ahead and creating independently styled components devoid of any layout restrictions you can ensure that your CSS is flexible and maintainable, not only by you but also others on your team. Over the last few pages, we've shown you several approaches for structuring, ordering, and maintaining your CSS. Ultimately, the route you take is your call and down to individual (or company) preference. If you're working on a team, be sure to validate the approach with your colleagues while teaching and documenting the practices for the benefit of all involved. While we're on the subject of validation, let's sidestep to a look at CSS validation.

---

[18] `https://github.com/stubbornella/oocss`
[19] `http://www.stubbornella.org/content/2009/02/28/object-oriented-css-grids-on-github/`

CSS validation

You learned about the importance of validating your HTML in Chapter 2, and now it's time to look at CSS validation. In our experience, the validation of CSS occurs less frequently than HTML and generally speaking, that's a good thing.

The important thing to note about any form of validation is that it's a tool, not a goal. Validators should be used to check your work, but don't be precious about receiving that seal of approval. Just be sure you know why your CSS isn't validating.

The W3C have a validator for CSS (`http://j.mp/css-validator`[20]), just as they do for HTML. Note that, by default, it does not check against CSS3 properties, so you must select "CSS level 3" in the options under the Profile drop-down, as shown in Figure 7-2.

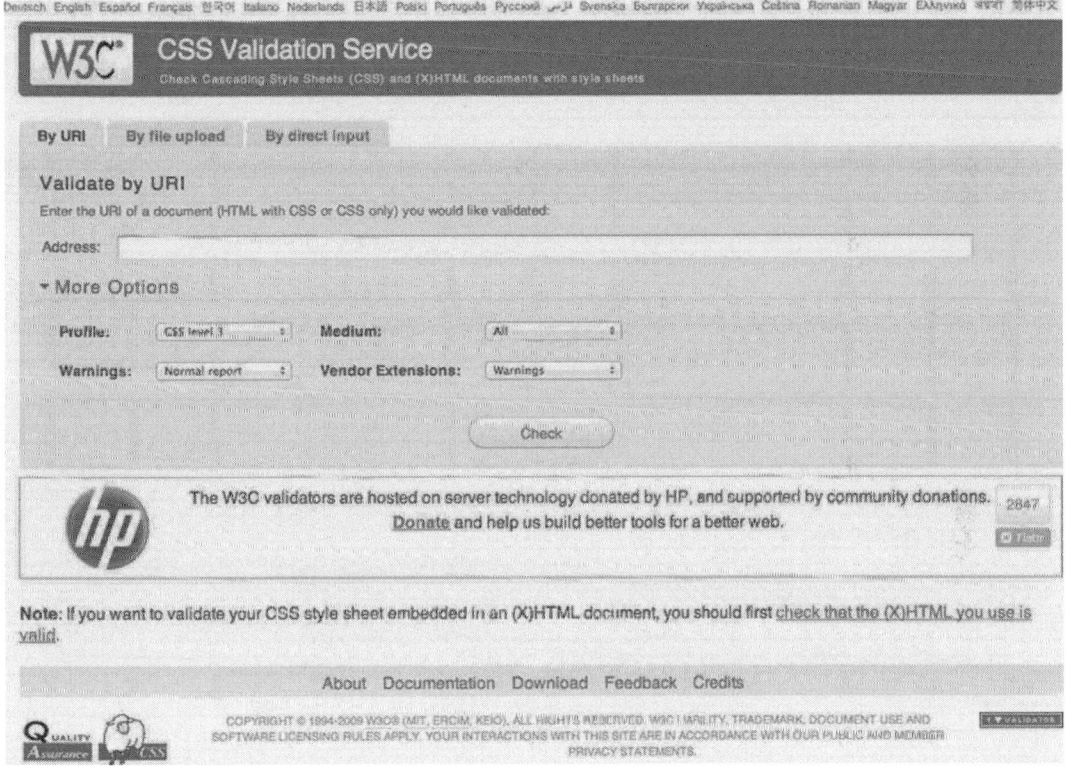

Figure 7-2. W3C CSS Validator

Because the specs aren't finalized and are regularly changing, so is the validator. So if a property is added or changed in a spec, it won't automatically make its way to the validator. Someone has to update it, which

---

[20] `http://jigsaw.w3.org/css-validator`

takes time. We'll look at the thorny issue of vendor prefixes later in the chapter but another useful option within the validator is to change the Vendor Extensions drop-down from "default" to "warnings" (again, bear in mind all these extensions may not be up to date).

If the W3C isn't your cup of tea, you can try one of the many browser extension validators or one of the other online tools for CSS validation. A quick Google search will help you on your way.

Outside of validation, how can you check that you're writing well-formed CSS? Well, just like for HTML, you can use a tool to help you out.

CSS lint

Launched in June 2011, CSS Lint (`http://j.mp/css-lint`[21]) caused some controversy when it arrived on the scene. Developed by Nicholas Zakas and Nicole Sullivan (of OOCSS, mentioned earlier in the chapter), it is intended to spot problems with your CSS. It was initially based on a number of rules (some wise, some perhaps foolish) that many disagreed with. Now the project is hosted on Github and as such can be customized to suit your needs (Figure 7-3).

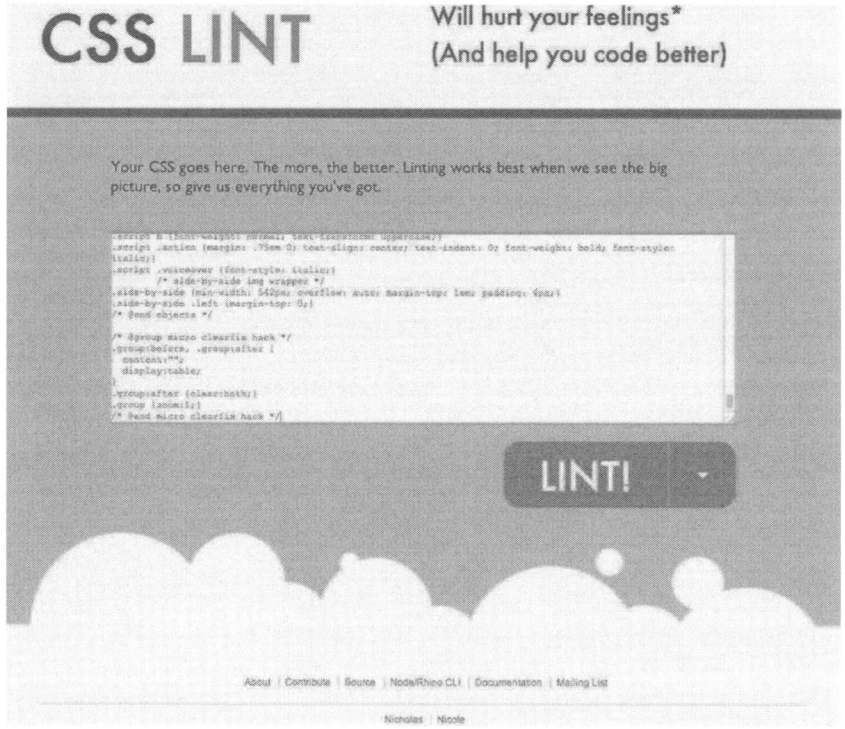

Figure 7-3. CSS Lint

---

[21] http://www.nczonline.net/blog/2011/06/15/introducing-css-lint-2/

Our advice is to treat CSS Lint just as you do the CSS Validator: as a tool, not a goal. If errors or warnings are flagged, understand why they were flagged.

We've highlighted how validation should be used as a tool rather than a goal but all this is meaningless without the most important aspect of our craft: users and their browsers. In the next section, we'll look at browser support, vendor prefixes, polyfills, and that oft-used term, *progressive enhancement*.

Browser support, vendor prefixes, polyfills, and progressive enhancement

As we move into this brave new world of CSS3 and rapidly evolving design opportunities, it's worth pausing for a moment to talk about the importance and definition of browser support allied with its relationship to progressive enhancement and graceful degradation.

It's time we celebrated the diversity of opportunities we have at our disposal and consider a world of progressive enhancement. A world where not every web site looks or behaves exactly the same across browsers and where we accept that browser-based experiences are, as a natural by-product of our multi-platform medium, different. With that thought in mind, ask yourself the following questions:

- What is browser support?

- Do web sites need to look or behave the same in every browser?

The latter is easy to answer: when we think of the range of devices available to us, from phones to tablets to TVs and e-book readers, it's impossible to think they could.

The former is harder for us to answer. Support could be classed as being usable or indeed support could be classed as looking, reacting. and functioning the same in every browser.

Our view is that sites should be usable, accessible, and inclusive to all no matter their browser or device. In order to achieve this, and before we look at browser support in more depth, we need to take a deeper look at progressive enhancement and graceful degradation.

Progressive enhancement

Embracing a forward-looking approach, as touched on in Chapter 1 when we discussed John Allsopp's seminal article *The Dao of Web Design*, is key to the concept of progressive enhancement. The term was invented by Steve Champeon, co-founder of the Web Standards Project, in 2003. In essence, the term describes the technique of catering for the lowest common denominator and building on that to provide enhanced experiences for more capable browsers and devices. The basic principles of progressive enhancement remain very much the same today as in 2003.

- Content should be inclusive and accessible to all.

- The HTML markup should describe the content. It should be clean, semantic, and free from presentational naming or order.

- CSS should be used to cater for all aspects of presentation.

261

- JavaScript should be used to add behavior where required.

Dan Cederholm took this concept and modified it, describing it as "progressive enrichment" in his book *Handcrafted CSS*. Andy Clarke in his book *Hardboiled Web Design* takes the visual aspect of progressive enhancement and reverses it. He says

> *Instead of starting from the lowest performing browsers, hardboiled means working from the top down and designing for the best browsers first. This way we can make the most of everything that more capable browsers and emerging technologies like HTML5 and CSS3 have to offer.*

Progressive enhancement in action

In the following example we've taken an element from your homework site. It's a background box with some `border-radius` to give it rounded corners and the `box-shadow` property to give it some subtle shading. Looking at this markup rendered in a contemporary browser (in this case Safari) the box has rounded corners and a subtle shadow (Figure 7-4).

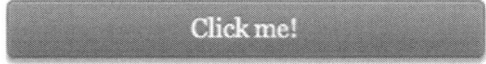

Figure 7-4. Button rendered in Safari with CSS rounded corners and shadow

Taking a look at the same example in a less capable browser, in this case IE8, the box has lost its rounded corners and no longer has a shadow (Figure 7-5).

Figure 7-5. Button rendered in IE8 without CSS rounded corners and shadow

The question you need to ask yourself when looking at these two versions is this: Did any cats die in the second experience? No. The rounded corners and shadow are enhancements aimed at contemporary browsers. They improve and enhance the experience, but they aren't mission critical. Before embarking on a project, it's worth considering what is and isn't critical. Ask yourself (and your clients) if it's worth the extra time, money, and effort to add rounded corners in older browsers whose market share will only drop. We tend to find the answer is nearly always a resolute no.

CSS3 browser support

If you're embarking on your web design journey today, you are in many ways spared a great deal of the less-than-stellar browser support that marked the beginning of our journey towards web standards, the time of the browser wars. The browser landscape today is markedly different to the past, with browser vendors now iterating rapidly, innovating, and pressing forward in the support of the new and emerging standards that we'll be describing in the following five chapters.

CSS3 support across browsers is, generally speaking, in a good state. With many browsers carrying out silent auto updates, there's no reason for users not to be using the most current technology. This means that more of the HTML5 and CSS3 goodness you're learning about can be used in the wild, *today*.

Even our old friend IE is getting in on the game and, dare we say it, leading the way with numerous innovations. Sites such as Lost World's Fairs (http://lostworldsfairs.com/), curated by Jason Santa Maria, showcased IE 9's support of the emerging WOFF (Web Open Font Format), allowing designers like Frank Chimero, Trent Walton, and Naz Hamid (not to mention Santa Maria himself) to explore the typographic possibilities the web now offers. Within each chapter we'll take you through browser support in detail and we'll return to the intricacies of web fonts in Chapter 10, so hold that thought.

For a current and wider overview of support, we recommend you check the following sites because they can be updated far more regularly than this publication.

- When can I use…, a huge resource created by Alexis Deveria that not only shows what is currently supported but also what is soon to be supported along with global browser market shares (http://caniuse.com/).

- HTML5 Please, created by one of the authors of the book (Divya Manian), Paul Irish, and a team of contributors. HTML5 Please lists HTML5 and CSS3 features and indicates whether they are ready for prime time use (with or without fallbacks), should be used with caution, or should be avoided (http://html5please.us/).

- HTML5 Readiness, another collaboration between Divya Manian and Paul Irish. HTML5 Readiness allows you to see which HTML5 and CSS3 features are ready for use today. Unlike HTML5 Please, you can also view the differences over time (http://html5readiness.com/).

- HTML5 & CSS3 Support, a very detailed list compiled and maintained by Deep Blue Sky. It lists a number of CSS3 properties against a range of browsers (http://findmebyip.com/litmus/).

Wider support for certain properties exists if you use vendor prefixes (or extensions). In addition, it is possible to recreate some of the CSS3 effects in browsers without support by using a combination of feature detection and polyfills. That's what we'll look at in the next two sections.

Vendor prefixes

If you're not familiar with the term, a *vendor prefix* allows browser vendors to add a prefix to a CSS property for experimentation or debugging purposes. Consider it a way of marking them "in progress."

By embracing an approach based on vendor prefixes, browser vendors can implement support for different CSS modules, effectively sandboxing them from other browser vendors' implementations so they can test them safe in the knowledge that they won't affect the way the prefixes are handled in other browsers.

Be warned that using CSS with vendor prefixes can be risky. They or their underlying specifications and notation can change regularly, so use with caution. However, when those implementations become stable, vendors will stop using the prefixed version, leaving only the final implementation.

By using vendor-prefixes to test new CSS properties as the standards process iterates (remember the chicken-and-egg problem where browsers innovate incrementally, moving towards a standard that all (hopefully) adopt, which is then implemented as a standard), we can embrace evolving CSS properties, tailoring them to different browsers' current implementations. But how do we do this? The best way is to run through an example, which we do in the next section.

Vendor prefixes have been the cause of some debate: some people are in favor of them, and some think they are harmful. They are here to stay for now, but who knows about the future? Although the topic is far too involved for us to enter here, we offer some articles for review that present a balanced view.

- Vendor Prefixes are Hurting The Web by Henri Sivonen (`http://hsivonen.iki.fi/vendor-prefixes/`)

- *Prefix or Posthack* by Eric Meyer on A List Apart (`http://alistapart.com/articles/prefix-or-posthack/`)

- CSS Vendor Prefixes Considered Harmful by Peter-Paul Koch (PPK) (`http://quirksmode.org/blog/archives/2010/03/css_vendor_pref.html`)

- Vendor Prefixes Have Failed. What's Next? by Lea Verou (`http://lea.verou.me/2011/11/vendor-prefixes-have-failed-whats-next/`)

- An Argument In Favor Of Vendor Prefixes by Peter Gasston (`http://www.broken-links.com/2011/11/15/an-argument-in-favour-of-vendor-prefixes/`)

- Google + Discussion on Vendor Prefixes discussion started by Simurai plus (`https://plus.google.com/110156363849628236019/posts/UGQhEgxmJx5`)

Vendor prefixes in action

We now understand that different browser vendors use vendor prefixes to target their specific implementation of a CSS property, so let's take a look at this in action. We're going to use a made-up property so as not to hurt any browser's feelings if they haven't implemented a feature just yet.

Assume that the makers of the Firefox browser (Mozilla) wish to develop a proprietary property called dancing-monkeys that covers your background in, you guessed it, dancing monkeys. Because this property isn't in a CSS specification and isn't fully tested or implemented, Firefox would *prefix* the property with their unique identifier (-moz-), placed before the property name like so:

```
body{
        -moz-dancing-monkeys: loop;
}
```

If that property was then added to a specification and a Firefox build shipped without needing the prefix, you could simply update your CSS to:

```
body{
        dancing-monkeys: loop;
}
```

Now let's assume that Microsoft decides to implement this feature, so for the time being it also requires a prefix. We would add that in before the unprefixed version.

```
body{
        -ms-dancing-monkeys: loop;
        dancing-monkeys: loop;
}
```

Starting with vendor-specific prefixes such as -ms-dancing-monkeys and -moz-dancing-monkeys and leaving the generic property of dancing-monkeys until last means the generic property overrides declarations that have gone before. This means that as support for implementations is standardized, the generic property will trump all, and one day in the future when all is good in the world of CSS3 and no one uses outdated browsers, you'll be able to remove your vendor-specific prefixes and all will be good in the world. Until then, you can rest assured that the last declaration (dancing-monkeys: loop;) overrides those that have gone before.

As we close this section, our role here wouldn't be complete without providing you with a table of common browser vendor-prefixes for reference, so without further ado and thereby fulfilling our promise, Table 7-2 provides the most widely used vendor prefixes and their associated browsers.

Table 7-2. Prefixes for the Main Browser Vendors

Prefix	Browser/Company
-khtml-	Konqueror browser
-ms-	Microsoft
-moz-	Mozilla (Gecko browsers)
o-	Opera
-webkit-	Safari and Chrome (plus other WebKit browsers)

The Opera Effect

What do we mean by "The Opera Effect?" When it comes to adding vendor-specific CSS declarations to rules, many web designers and developers opt for the lazy option: including only -webkit- to take care of Safari and Chrome. You, however, know better than to cut such a corner. What of the other browsers?

Referring back to Table 7-2, we can see that by including all vendor prefixes we could end up with a rather large amount of code for something simple as simple as a dancing monkey background.

```
body{
        -khtml-dancing-monkeys: loop;
        -moz-dancing-monkeys: loop;
        -ms-dancing-monkeys: loop;
        -o-dancing-monkeys: loop;
        -webkit-dancing-monkeys: loop;
        dancing-monkeys: loop;
}
```

The problem with only selectively including vendor prefixes, and not considering *all* vendor prefixes, is the pressure it puts on, amongst others, Opera, who (as we saw in the last chapter) trailblazed support for

HTML5 forms. Spare some thought for *all* of your potential users. Many access the web via browsers other than those catered to by -webkit- (and the generic property you're using).

The bottom line? Build your rules to include declarations for *all* browsers and remember to include the generic, prefixless versions for the day (coming soon, we hope) when vendor prefixes will be A Thing of the Past™. With that thought fresh in our heads, we shall introduce to you the Good CSS Developers Pledge™.

The Good CSS Developers Pledge™

If you thought the previous example was a lot of code for one rule set, you're right. Creating and working with style sheets using vendor prefixes can be a painful job, which is why we implore you to sign up to the Good CSS Developers Pledge™. Repeat after us:

> *I do solemnly swear to only use prefixed properties on the condition I include all relevant browser prefixes, and keep them up to date!*

In essence this means

- You will include a separate prefixed line for all browsers that support each prefix.

- When (not if) another browser adds prefixed support, you'll add it.

- If (and, more likely, when) the spec changes, you will update your code.

- You will remove prefixed declarations when they're no longer needed

Now that you've signed up, remember to keep to your pledge because we'll be checking.

-prefix-free

If you feel daunted by the thought of writing out declarations multiple times and can't promise to keep to your pledge, there are tools out there to help. The best of which is –prefix-free by Lea Verou (http://j.mp/prefixfree/[22]), which is a small JavaScript file you can include in your site. According to the site, it

> *lets you use only unprefixed CSS properties everywhere. It works behind the scenes, adding the current browser's prefix to any CSS code, only when it's needed.*

> http://leaverou.github.com/prefixfree

---

[22] http://leaverou.github.com/prefixfree/

-prefix-free comes with comprehensive documentation and more detail can be found on *Smashing Magazine* (http://j.mp/smashing-prefix-free[23]).

To summarize our look at vendor prefixes, personal choice is again at the front of the queue when considering whether or not to use them. So, looking at the rule that showed vendor-prefixes in action, you might be forgiven for wondering, "What about our old friends, IE pre-IE9, that have little, if any CSS3 support?" Good question! Let's take a look at some solutions for handling IE.

IE Filters, standards, and performance

A long time ago, in a galaxy far, far away, before we'd ever heard of vendor prefixes, our old friend Microsoft introduced filters and transitions to, as they put it, "apply various multimedia-style visual effects to web pages." Supported in IE 4 and above, Microsoft's filters and transitions are a proprietary set of CSS extensions that offer effects similar to those that can be achieved using CSS3. It's worth noting that IE's filters and transitions are extensions, not standards (but hold that thought because we'll return to it).

The easiest way to get a feel for how Microsoft's IE filters work is to show an example. Let's say we'd like to give an element on our page a box-shadow. For everyone but IE, we'd write the following:

```
.boxshadow {
        -webkit-box-shadow: 2px 2px 5px #333;
        -moz-box-shadow: 2px 2px 5px #333;
        box-shadow: 2px 2px 5px #333;
}
```

Note that we don't need to add the oft forgotten -o- prefix mentioned earlier because Opera supports the box-shadow property without the use of a prefix.

The good news: IE9, thanks to its native support of box-shadow, will handle this just fine (via the generic declaration box-shadow: 2px 2px #333;). The bad news: IE8 and older won't. The following example shows two added declarations, one for IE8 and one for versions of IE older than version 8:

```
.boxshadow {
        -webkit-box-shadow: 2px 2px #333;
        -moz-box-shadow: 2px 2px #333;
        -ms-filter:"progid:DXImageTransform.Microsoft.dropShadow(color=#333,offX=2,offY=2)";
        filter:progid:DXImageTransform.Microsoft.dropShadow(color=#333,offX=2,offY=2);
        box-shadow: 2px 2px #333;
}
```

In case you're wondering why you need two declarations here, in essence IE<8 looks at the filter declaration and IE>=8 uses the -ms- prefixed version. If you're so inclined, you might like to take a sojourn and read a detailed article on IE filters at http://j.mp/msfilters[24].

In the code example we hope you see the heart of the problem and why IE filters differ, quite substantially, from vendor prefixes. Though IE has supported a number of CSS3-like properties for some time, this

---

[23] http://coding.smashingmagazine.com/2011/10/12/prefixfree-break-free-from-css-prefix-hell/
[24] www.javascriptkit.com/filters/filterschecklist.shtml

support is proprietary and non-conforming to standards. Looking at this example, the generic box-shadow declaration and the WebKit/Mozilla versions with their vendor prefixes are essentially the same. All the vendor prefixes do is sandbox WebKit and Mozilla's particular implementations of how to handle box-shadow until the specification is reached. Both—it's important to stress—are paving the way towards a standard. The IE filters, on the other hand, are a proprietary approach to the problem and, thankfully, will soon be a thing of the past thanks to IE9's forward-looking nature.

Finally, it's worth noting that IE filters can have a negative impact upon performance. See where we're heading with this? We don't recommend you use them or, if you absolutely must, use them as a measure of last resort.

So, if IE filters and transitions aren't the way to go, what else is out there to plug the gaps for IE and help move things forward?

Feature detection and polyfills

In the past, it was common practice for developers to use JavaScript to detect which browser a user was using. It's an evil technique that should be buried along with IE6. Developers should be encouraged to use feature detection instead. In essence, we should ask the question (in whatever browser) "Do you support feature X?" That means we only end up with two possible answers from which we can act accordingly; yes or no. Compare this with asking "Which browser are you?" and there are hundreds if not thousands of possible answers.

You might think it a little laborious to write countless feature tests, and it is. But that's where libraries come in—specifically Modernizr by Faruk Ateş, Paul Irish, and Alex Sexton. Modernizr is a small JavaScript library that detects the availability of native implementations for next-generation web technologies (i.e. features that stem from the HTML5 and CSS3 specifications). Modernizr (www.modernizr.com/docs/) is a breeze to use; simply link to the script in the head of your document

```
<script src="js/modernizr-1.0.min.js"></script>
```

and add a fallback class of no-js to the html element

```
<html class="no-js">
```

and you're good to go. When the script runs, it adds a whole host of classes to the html element based on the feature support (or lack thereof) of the browser it's running in. You can then use these classes to offer fallbacks for browsers that don't support certain features. Consider the following: you want to apply a shadow to a box (with a class of box). You can do this using CSS3s box-shadow property (see Chapter 11) but you want to have the shadow appear in all browsers—even those without box-shadow support.

For browsers with box-shadow support you can write your CSS as normal.

```
.box {
        box-shadow: 3px 3px 5px #ccc;
}
```

For browsers without box-shadow support, Modernizr adds a class of no-boxshadow to the html element. You can then add a rule to your stylesheet to use an image that will create a similar effect to the in-browser shadow.

```
.no-boxshadow .box {
        background:url(img/shadow.png) repeat-x 100% 100%;
}
```

Modernizr tests for over 40 HTML5 and CSS3 features, making it extremely useful to today's conscientious developers. There are some features that quite simply can't be feature detected—the undetectables (http://j.mp/undetectables[25]). For those cases, you'll have to resort to evil, underhand tactics such as browser detection. The Modernizr web site (www.modernizr.com/) has links to further documentation and tutorials.

> Note: Modernizr also includes the HTML5 Shiv referred to in Chapter 2. If you decide to use Modernizr, you don't need to include the Shiv as well.

Polyfills

So Modernizr handles the feature detection but what if you want to fill the gaps for those less capable browsers? What if you want as many browsers as possible to have the same experience? Enter stage right, polyfills.

Polyfill is a term coined by Remy Sharp (http://j.mp/polyfillwtf[26]); it's been taken on board in the web community and can largely be described as a shim or shiv that mimics functionality that you would expect to find natively in your browser.

Broadly speaking, polyfills are scripts used to plug gaps in HTML5, CSS3, and other specifications until native browser implementations catch up. We'll introduce a range of polyfills throughout the book for different eventualities. The Modernizr team maintains a list of useful cross-browser polyfills on Github (http://j.mp/h5fills[27]).

A word of caution regarding polyfills: before you use them or build them into your toolkit, consider the benefits vs. the drawbacks. Do you really need to load that extra script or can you handle it using graceful degradation instead? How reliable is this script? Can I rely on someone else's work for my client projects?

If you've truly bought into the progressive enhancement mindset, this is the approach we recommend: build for the future. However much you polyfill, the past will never quite catch up.

---

[25] https://github.com/Modemizr/Modernizr/wiki/Undectectables
[26] http://remysharp.com/2010/10/08/what-is-a-polyfill/
[27] https://github.com/Modernizr/Modernizr/wiki/HTML5-Cross-Browser-Polyfills

IE-specific polyfills

Earlier we promised some solutions for kicking our old friend IE into a CSS3 shape. Here are two possible solutions.

Selectivizr

One JavaScript solution to CSS3 support in IE is Selectivizr (`http://j.mp/selectivizr`[28]), written by Keith Clark. While it doesn't add support for all the goodness CSS3 has to offer, it does provide support for CSS selectors (a powerful aspect of CSS that we'll explore in full in the next chapter).

Selectivizr requires a JavaScript framework to run and it supports numerous options including jQuery, Prototype, MooTools, and more. Formerly known (in beta) as iecss3.js, Selectivizr uses JavaScript to enable IE6 through 8 to identify CSS3 pseudo-class selectors and, as a result, apply any style rules defined by them. As Andy Clarke puts it, "Selectivizr works automatically so you don't need any JavaScript knowledge to use it – you won't even have to modify your style sheets. Just start writing CSS3 selectors and they will work in IE."

As we'll see in the next chapter, CSS3 pseudo-classes and attribute selectors, when used well, can be hugely effective. Selectivizr is one way to use their power in older versions of IE.

CSS3 PIE

What is CSS3 PIE? (`http://j.mp/css3pie`[29]) Well, the acronym PIE stands for Progressive Internet Explorer. As Jason Johnston, CSS3 PIE's creator, puts it, "PIE makes Internet Explorer 6-8 capable of rendering several of the most useful CSS3 decoration features." These features include `border-radius`, `box-shadow`, and `border-image` plus gradients and multiple background images. Other features are currently under development.

Let's take a look at an example. Here's a class used to define an element with a defined `border-radius`:

```
.roundcorners {
        -webkit-border-radius: 5px;
        -moz-border-radius: 5px;
        border-radius: 5px;
}
```

This, in a contemporary browser, results in a box with nicely rounded corners. In IE 6, 7 or 8, however, the result is a square box—no rounded corners. Add the following declaration (`behavior: url(PIE.htc);`) to the CSS as follows and we solve the problem for IE:

```
.roundcorners {
        -webkit-border-radius: 5px;
        -moz-border-radius: 5px;
        behavior: url(PIE.htc);
```

---

[28] `http://selectivizr.com`
[29] `http://css3pie.com/`

```
    border-radius: 5px;
}
```

How does this work? In the declaration we added CSS3 PIE references an HTML Component (HTC), a throwback to the good (read bad) old days of DHTML. We won't bore you with the details but feel free to explore more at your leisure at `http://j.mp/dhtml-behaviors`[30].

The downside of this is that the .htc behavior file that CSS3 PIE relies on is 30K (uncompressed). Even with compression, that's still an extra hit, so ask yourself if it's worth adding this extra weight (albeit just for IE) to your site. There are upsides and downsides to cajoling IE into submission. Let's consider these now.

One clear upside is support for a number of lovely new CSS3 techniques in our old friend IE. One clear downside is yet more material to learn and support as the web evolves. It's also worth remembering that all of these extra requests can add a hit to your site's speed through the need for additional HTTP requests (this is worth considering before adding support through multiple behaviors and libraries).

So ask yourself if you need to include all of these extras to cajole IE or is it time, as we highlighted earlier, to stop worrying about trying to make every web site look the same in every browser. The answer to this question, of course, depends upon your circumstances (and the needs of your clients). As we've seen, a considered approach embraces a progressive enhancement philosophy—where design aspects like rounded corners are considered non-mission-critical and there is some flexibility about how pages display across browsers. So you might choose intentionally *not* to support these aspects among non-capable browsers.

To end this section on a positive note, IE9's support for CSS3 is very good and IE10 looks even better. We might just make it to the Nirvana where workarounds are a thing of the past. Here's hoping!

Summary

In this chapter we gave you a recap in CSS fundamentals—some of which you no doubt already knew, some of which you probably didn't—including a look at the cascade, inheritance, and specificity. We looked at the development of CSS and the modularity of CSS3. We showed how using CSS3 along with standard ways of working, such as progressive enhancement, will benefit and streamline your process. The same applies to creating maintainable, flexible, easy-to-understand CSS. Finally, we talked about browser support, vendor prefixes and feature detection.

All of this will stand you in good stead for what you'll find in the next six chapters. We will take you through the crazy maze of CSS3 where you'll dig deep with selectors, create various layouts using new techniques, do more with amazing typography, implement a whole host of new properties, and learn to make animations using CSS. Let's go exploring!

---

[30] `http://msdn.microsoft.com/en-us/library/ms531079(v=vs.85).aspx`

Homework

For your homework, you need to do some reading. Start by reading the articles and presentations referred to throughout the chapter. Follow this up by going through some of your current or older projects and re-work your CSS to make it more maintainable and future-friendly. Then you'll be all set up to tackle the next chapter.

Appendix: CSS3 Module Status

The current state of CSS3 modules (taken from CSS3.info/modules)

Module	Last Update	Upcoming
Recommendation		
CSS Color (Complete)	June 7, 2011	REC
CSS Namespaces (Complete)	September 29, 2011	REC
Selectors (Complete)	September 29, 2011	REC
Candidate Recommendation		
Media Queries (Stable)	July 27, 2010	PR
CSS Style Attributes (Stable)	October 12, 2010	PR
CSS Backgrounds and Borders (Testing)	February 15, 2011	CR
CSS Marquee (Testing)	December 5, 2008	PR
CSS Multi-column Layout (Testing)	April 12, 2012	CR
CSS Basic User Interface (Revising)	May 11, 2004	LC
Last Call		
CSS Speech (Refining)	August 18, 2011	CR
CSS Paged Media (Revising) (Inactive)	October 10, 2006	LC
Working Draft		
CSS 2D Transformations (Refining)	December 15, 2011	WD
CSS Transitions (Refining)	December 1, 2009	WD
CSS Animations (Revising) (Outdated)	March 20, 2009	WD
CSS Flexible Box Layout (Revising)	November 29, 2011	WD
CSS Fonts Level 3 (Revising)	October 4, 2011	LC
CSS Image Values & Replaced Content (Revising)	December 6, 2011	WD
CSS Text (Revising)	September 1, 2011	WD
CSS 3D Transformations (Revising)	March 20, 2009	WD
CSS Values and Units (Revising)	September 6, 2011	WD
CSS Writing Modes (Revising)	September 1, 2011	WD
CSSOM View (Revising)	August 2011	WD
CSS Cascading and Inheritance (Exploring) (Inactive)	December 15, 2005	WD

Module	Last Update	Upcoming
CSS Conditional Rules (Exploring)	September 1, 2011	WD
CSS Device Adaptation (Exploring)	September 15, 2011	WD
CSS Exclusions and Shapes (Exploring)	December 15, 2011	WD
CSS Generated Content for Paged Media (Exploring)	November 19, 2011	WD
CSS Grid Layout (Exploring)	April 7, 2011	WD
CSS Lists (Exploring)	May 24, 2011	WD
CSS Presentation Levels (Exploring) *(Inactive)*	August 13, 2003	WD
CSS Regions (Exploring)	November 29, 2011	WD
CSS Template Layout (Exploring)	November 29, 2011	WD
CSS Object Model (Exploring)	July 12, 2011	WD
CSS Basic Box Model (Rewriting) *(Dangerously outdated)*	August 9, 2007	WD
CSS Generated Content (Rewriting) *(Severely outdated)*	May 14, 2003	WD
CSS Line Layout (Rewriting) *(Severely outdated)*	May 15, 2002	WD
CSS Ruby (Rewriting) *(Outdated and majorly underdefined)*	June 30, 2011	WD
CSS Syntax (Rewriting) *(Severely outdated)*	August 13, 2003	WD
Announced		
CSS Positioning (Exploring)	-	WD
CSS Tables (Exploring) *(Inactive)*	-	WD
CSS Line Grid (Rewriting) *(Being redesigned)*	-	WD

Chapter 8

Keeping Your Markup Slim Using CSS Selectors

In order to style an element with CSS, we need to be able to target it. Enter CSS selectors, which allow us to target specific elements in the DOM.

Using CSS3 selectors, we can target elements at an even more granular level than we've been able to previously. This means that your markup can be super slim, semantic, and flexible. What's more, the new element states pseudo-classes allow for additional highlighting of dynamic state changes.

You had a refresher on the cascade, Inheritance, and CSS specificity in the previous chapter. In this chapter, we're going to remind ourselves of selector basics. We'll then look at CSS3 attribute selectors, followed by the structural element states, :target, and negation pseudo-classes. We'll then take a brief detour into CSS 2.1's generated-content pseudo-elements :before and :after to see how they play nicely with parts of HTML5 and we'll introduce the new double-colon syntax in CSS3. We'll also look at current browser support for CSS selectors and what's around the corner for CSS selectors. Finally, we'll discuss briefly the Selectivzr polyfill described in Chapter 7 that allows you to use these new selectors across all browsers.

Selectors rundown

The W3C Selectors Level 3 (http://j.mp/w3cselectors[1]) module became a recommendation in September 2011. It lists *all* selectors (in total just fewer than 40), not only those in CSS3. This is because, as you've already learned, CSS3 isn't a totally new specification but instead builds on CSS1 and CSS 2.1. If you think 40 selectors is a lot to learn, don't worry—you probably know quite a few already.

The following selectors were introduced in CSS1:

- Type (e.g., p {...}, blockquote {...})

- Descendant combinator (e.g., blockquote p {...})

- ID (e.g., #content {...} on <article id="content">)

- Class (e.g., .hentry {...} on < article class="hentry">)

- Link pseudo-class (e.g., a:link {...} or a:visited {...})

- User action pseudo-class (e.g., a:active {...})

- :first-line pseudo-element (e.g., p:first-line {...})

- :first-letter pseudo-element (e.g., p:first-letter {...})

If any of those don't look familiar to you (we'll excuse the last two), then we suggest you look them up. The SitePoint CSS Reference is as good a place as any to start, http://j.mp/sitepointref.[2]

Another 11 selectors were added in CSS 2.1.

- Universal (e.g., * {...})

- User action pseudo-class (e.g., a:hover {...} and a:focus {...})

- The :lang() pseudo-class (e.g., article:lang(fr) {...})

- Structural pseudo-class (e.g., p:first-child {...})

- The :before and :after pseudo-elements (e.g., blockquote:before {...} or a:after {...})

- Child combinator (e.g., h2 > p {...})

- Adjacent sibling combinator (e.g., h2 + p {...})

- Attribute selectors (e.g., input [required] {...})

- Attribute selectors; exactly equal (e.g., input [type="checkbox"] {...})

- Substring attribute selectors; one equal to string (e.g., input [class~="long-field"] {...})

---

[1] www.w3.org/TR/selectors
[2] http://reference.sitepoint.com/css

- Substring attribute selectors; hyphen separated beginning with string (e.g., input [lang|="en"] {...})

Some of these you probably know. But don't worry if you haven't seen them all before because the CSS3 Selectors Level 3 module builds on these and adds functionality.

The selectors added in CSS3 that we'll be looking at in this chapter are as follows:

- General sibling combinator (e.g., h1 ~ pre {...})

- Substring attribute selectors; string starts with (e.g., a[href^="http://"] {...})

- Substring attribute selectors; string ends with (e.g., a[href$=".pdf"] {...})

- Substring attribute selectors; string contains (e.g., a[href*="twitter"] {...})

- The :target() pseudo-class (e.g., section:target {...})

- Structural pseudo-classes; :nth-child (e.g., tr:nth-child(even) td {...})

- Structural pseudo-classes; :nth-last-child (e.g., tr:nth-last-child(-n+5) td {...})

- Structural pseudo-classes; :last-child (e.g., ul li:last-child {...})

- Structural pseudo-classes; :only-child (e.g., ul li:only-child {...})

- Structural pseudo-classes; :first-of-type (e.g., p:first-of-type {...})

- Structural pseudo-classes; :last-of-type (e.g., p:last-of-type {...})

- Structural pseudo-classes; :nth-of-type (e.g., li:nth-of-type(3n) {...})

- Structural pseudo-classes; :nth-last-of-type (e.g., li:nth-last-of-type(1) {...})

- Structural pseudo-classes; :only-of-type (e.g., article img:only-of-type {...})

- Structural pseudo-classes; :empty (e.g., aside:empty {...})

- Structural pseudo-classes; :root (e.g., :root {...})

- UI element states pseudo-classes; :disabled and :enabled (e.g., input:disabled {...})

- UI element states pseudo-classes; :checked (e.g., input[type="checkbox"]:checked {...})

- Negation pseudo-classes; :not (e.g., abbr:not([title]) {...})

We can conclude from looking at these three lists that the same number of CSS selectors has been introduced in CSS3 as were introduced in CSS 1 and CSS 2.1 combined. That's a lot for us to get through, so let's dive straight in.

CSS3 selectors

We've reached the juicy part—CSS3 selectors. With a range of different selectors available to us, it can be difficult to determine which type of selector to use. As the new CSS3 selectors are introduced, we'll provide real-world use cases for them, which you can use in your projects starting today. First up are the combinators.

Combinators

Assuming you've worked with CSS before, you've almost certainly come across combinators. You're no doubt aware of descendant selectors, so called because they target children, grandchildren, or later of a given element in the document tree. At their simplest, descendant combinators allow you to target all instances of a single element type that lie within another, such as `article p {...}`.

Child combinators, in contrast, target only those elements that are immediate children of the parent. They use the greater than (>) operator. Therefore, `article > p {...}` targets those paragraphs that are children of the `article`, but *not* the paragraphs nested in `sections` beneath the article, as highlighted in the following code example:

```
article > p {
font-size:125%;
}
```

The next combinator, adjacent sibling, targets elements that are next to each other in the document tree and have the same parent. Using the preceding example again, we could style just the opening paragraph in each `section` (assuming they all use a h2 heading) using the + operator by writing `h2 + p {...}`:

```
h2 + p {
font-weight:bold;
}
```

The following code shows which selector targets which paragraph:

```
<article>
  <h1>Article Title</h1>
  <p>...</p><!-- Child combinator targets this paragraph -->
  <section>
    <h2>Section Title</h2>
    <p>...</p><!-- Adjacent sibling combinator targets this paragraph -->
    <p>...</p>
  </section>
  <p>...</p><!-- Child combinator targets this paragraph -->
</article>
```

The examples we've seen so far are combinators included in CSS 2.1, so what about CSS3?

CSS3 adds the general sibling combinator, which uses the tilde (~) operator. When using the general sibling combinator, the second selector *doesn't* have to immediately follow the first; however, both parts of the selector must still share the same parent. Extending the example, we can target the `ul` within the deeply nested section using the general sibling combinatory like so:

```
h3 ~ ul {
list-style-type:binary;
}

<article>
  <h1>Article Title</h1>
  <p>...</p><!-- Child combinator targets this paragraph -->
<section>
  <h2>Section Title</h2>
  <p>...</p><!-- Adjacent sibling combinator targets this paragraph -->
  <p>...</p>
  <ul>
      <li>...</li>
      <li>...</li>
      <li>...</li>
  </ul>
  <section>
    <h3>Section Title</h3>
    <p>...</p>
    <p>...</p>
    <ul><!-- General sibling combinator targets this list -->
      <li>...</li>
      <li>...</li>
      <li>...</li>
    </ul>
  </section>
</section>
  <p>...</p><!-- Child combinator targets this paragraph -->
</article>
```

This shows the power of combinators in CSS and specifically how CSS3 gives us more control over the element(s) we're targeting.

Attribute and substring selectors

In the introduction to this chapter you learned that CSS 2.1 introduced attribute selectors. CSS3 has extended the list of attribute selectors we can use by increasing the number of substring selectors in our toolkit. This means we can now target a rule and apply CSS styling to an element based on part of an attribute's value. Shortly, we'll see how these can be put to use for styling document download links or e-mail addresses, but first let's briefly recap CSS 2.1's attribute and substring selectors.

The most basic of attribute selectors allows you to style an element if a given attribute exists. For example, we can style any abbreviation elements that have a `title` attribute by using the following:

```
abbr[title] {
  border-bottom:1px dotted #000;
}
```

Or we can indicate those fields that are required by using the `required` attribute you met in Chapter 6.

```
input[required] {
  background:url(img/mandatory-icon.png) 100% 50% no-repeat;
```

```
  padding-right:20px;
}
```

Using the equals (=) operator, our attribute selector can match specific values for a given attribute, such as a check box.

```
input[type="checkbox"] {
  width:20px;
  height:20px;
}
```

Nothing too crazy so far. Next we can use the tilde (~) operator to target a specific attribute value from a list of whitespace-separated values. This is often useful for content marked up with microformats or microdata, which often use multiple attribute values.

```
<a ... rel="external license">...</a>
```

The CSS to target the license value of the rel attribute would be:

```
a[rel~="license"] {
  background:url(img/copyright.png) 100% 50% no-repeat;
  padding-right:20px;
}
```

The final CSS 2.1 attribute selector isn't used very often but can be useful if you're working on sites with multiple languages. The vertical bar (|) operator allows you to target elements that are contained in a hyphenated list, starting with specific values. Let's say you want to target anchors with an English language specified, regardless of whether it is British (en-GB) or American (en-US) English (because they both contain "en").

```
a[hreflang|="en"] {
        border-bottom:3px double #000;
}
```

The last two examples introduced two operators that we can use for substring matching parts of an attribute's value. CSS3 goes a step further and provides three additional substring selectors using the ^, $, and * operators. They are extremely useful and can be used to ensure that your markup remains super clean, with no unnecessary classes, while enhancing a user's experience at the same time.

"Starts with" substring attribute selector

The caret (^) operator, when related to the substring selector, means "starts with." We can use this, for example, to target all external links in our content and to add a small icon indicating that they are external links. The following code adds a background image and padding to all links that start with http:// by using the ^ attribute substring selector:

```
a[href^="http://"] {
        background:url(img/external.png) 100% 50% no-repeat;
        padding-right:15px;
}
```

In Figure 8-1 you can see that the external link is styled with a small icon at the end of the anchor. The icon, a box with an arrow pointing out of it, has become a widely recognized symbol for external links.

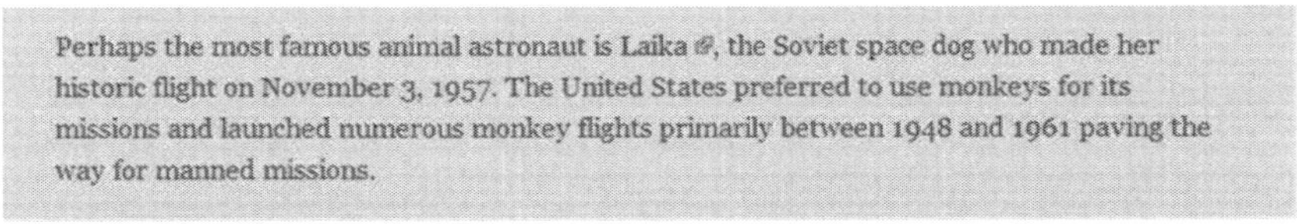

Perhaps the most famous animal astronaut is Laika ⌀, the Soviet space dog who made her historic flight on November 3, 1957. The United States preferred to use monkeys for its missions and launched numerous monkey flights primarily between 1948 and 1961 paving the way for manned missions.

Figure 8-1. External link styled using the ^ attribute substring selector

This is a great way to quickly add an icon to your external links, but you may have some links that begin with http:// that aren't external links, such as those to your own website. In this case you don't want the icon to appear. We can work around this exception by adding another rule beneath our initial one (because they have the same specificity) to nullify the properties set for external links for our domain. The ^ operator is retained because the link(s) may be going to various pages within the site.

```
a[href^="http://"] {
        background:url(img/external.png) 100% 50% no-repeat;
        padding-right:15px;
}

a[href^="http://thewebevolved.com"] {
        background:none;
        padding-right:0;
}
```

Figure 8-2 shows this in action. There are two external links indicated with icons and one internal link ("numerous monkeys") where the icon is removed.

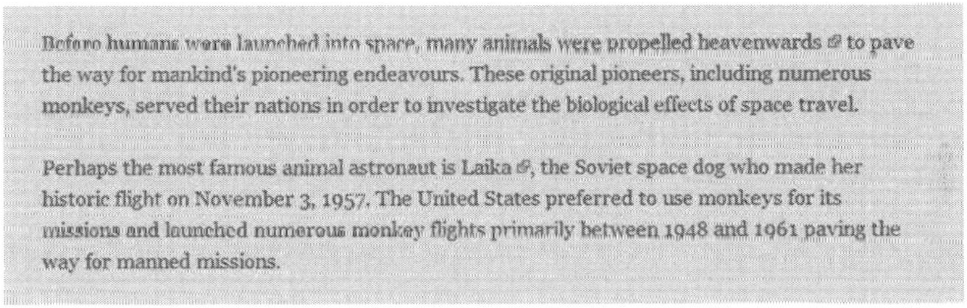

Before humans were launched into space, many animals were propelled heavenwards ⌀ to pave the way for mankind's pioneering endeavours. These original pioneers, including numerous monkeys, served their nations in order to investigate the biological effects of space travel.

Perhaps the most famous animal astronaut is Laika ⌀, the Soviet space dog who made her historic flight on November 3, 1957. The United States preferred to use monkeys for its missions and launched numerous monkey flights primarily between 1948 and 1961 paving the way for manned missions.

Figure 8-2. External links styled using the ^ attribute substring selector and an internal link beginning with http:// without the styling

Another use for the ^ operator might be to target e-mail links starting with the mailto: string and add an icon and padding.

```
a[href^="mailto:"] {
        background:url(img/email.png) 100% 50% no-repeat;
        padding-right:15px;
}
```

"Ends with" substring attribute selector

We've dealt with "starts with," so now let's look at "ends with." The operator for this is the dollar symbol, $, and the syntax is exactly the same as the ^ syntax. Common uses include adding icons to represent different files types for document downloads or to indicate different feed types.

To indicate that a link goes to a PDF document, you can use

```
a[href$=".pdf"] {
        background:url(img/pdf.png) 100% 50% no-repeat;
        padding-right:18px;
}
```

In Figure 8-3, the text "Life magazine" links to a PDF document. Using the preceding code, we've added a small PDF icon to the link to indicate this.

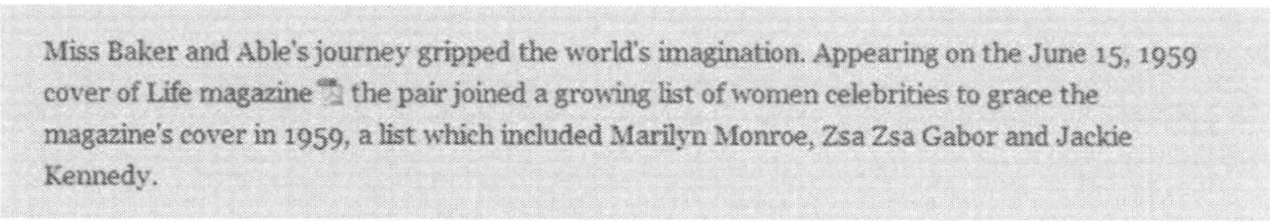

> Miss Baker and Able's journey gripped the world's imagination. Appearing on the June 15, 1959 cover of Life magazine 🔳 the pair joined a growing list of women celebrities to grace the magazine's cover in 1959, a list which included Marilyn Monroe, Zsa Zsa Gabor and Jackie Kennedy.

Figure 8-3. PDF link styled using the $ attribute substring selector

You can use this method to target any file type, such as .doc, .jpg, or .xml.

"Contains" substring attribute selector

The final substring selector for us to look at uses the star or asterisk (*) operator, which stands for "contains." It allows you to target elements that have more than one class applied. It can also be used to target specific domains within an anchor. It's used it in the following example to highlight those anchors that are linking to a person's Twitter account (see Figure 8-4 for the results):

```
a[href*="twitter"] {
        background:url(img/twitter.png) 100% 50% no-repeat;
        padding-right:20px;
}
```

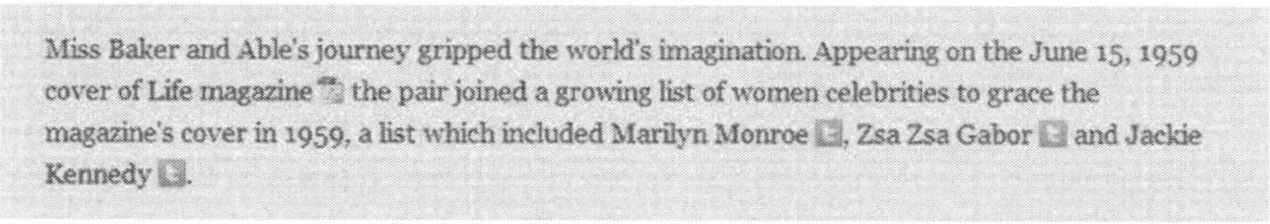

> Miss Baker and Able's journey gripped the world's imagination. Appearing on the June 15, 1959 cover of Life magazine 🔳 the pair joined a growing list of women celebrities to grace the magazine's cover in 1959, a list which included Marilyn Monroe 🔳, Zsa Zsa Gabor 🔳 and Jackie Kennedy 🔳.

Figure 8-4. Twitter account links styled using the * attribute substring selector

The same effect could have been achieved using the ^ operator and the value `http://twitter.com`, but using the * operator helps us save a few bytes. The real power of the * substring selector comes when we want to style one of the Twitter links differently based on the Twitter handle (e.g., `http://twitter.com/ZsaZsa`). To clarify, all the links contain "twitter," as in the preceding example, but only one contains "ZsaZsa."

```
a[href*="ZsaZsa"] {
        background:url(img/twitter.png) 100% 50% no-repeat;
        padding-right:20px;
        color:#ff0;
}
```

We could also use the * operator to indicate our relationship status with friends, families, and others by using XFN microformats, as introduced in Chapter 4. For example, if we wanted to indicate that Marilyn Monroe is our sweetheart, our markup might look something like this:

```
<a href="http://twitter.com/marilynmonroe" rel="met sweetheart friend">Marilyn Monroe</a>
```

Because there are three values for the `rel` attribute, it becomes difficult to target using the ^ or $ operator, so * (contains) becomes an option, as does the CSS 2.1 tilde (~), which could also be used in this instance as the values are whitespace separated. For this example, we'll use the new CSS3 substring selector *:

```
a[rel*="sweetheart"] {
        background:url(img/sweetheart.png) 100% 50% no-repeat;
        padding-right:20px;
}
```

There you have it! Marilyn Monroe is our sweetheart (see Figure 8-5).

Figure 8-5. Sweetheart relationship styled using the * attribute substring selector

You may have spotted a problem, though: the Twitter icon for Marilyn has disappeared. This is because both style rules have the same specificity and the `a[rel*="sweetheart"] {...}` rule appears further down the style sheet. We can get around this by adding some additional padding to our sweetheart rule and using multiple background images (for more detail, see Chapter 11) to add both icons placed in different positions.

```
a[rel*="sweetheart"] {
        background:
          url(img/sweetheart.png) 100% 50% no-repeat,
          url(img/twitter.png) 85% 50% no-repeat;
        padding-right:40px;
}
```

UI element states pseudo-classes

Most form elements have the potential to be enabled, disabled, or checked. By using UI element states pseudo-classes, we can target these elements when they are in a specific state, such as a check box being checked. Let's look at a basic login form and see how we can implement these element states pseudo-classes. Figure 8-6 shows the form as it would look normally.

Figure 8-6. A login form with normal styling

Now imagine that the username and password fields and the login button have been disabled. The HTML for this is shown next, with the disabled attribute applied where required.

```
<form action="">
<fieldset>
<legend>Login</legend>

<label for="uname">Username
<input type="text" id="uname" placeholder="e.g. hello@webevolved.com" disabled />
</label>

<label for="password">Password
<input type="password" id="password" disabled />
</label>

<input type="checkbox" id="rememberme" checked disabled />
<label for="rememberme">Remember me</label>

<input type="submit" value="Login" id="login" disabled />

</fieldset>
</form>
```

We now need to style the fields appropriately to show that they are disabled. We can style these states using the :disabled pseudo-class on those elements that require it (in this case all inputs).

```
input:disabled {
        background:#999;
        border:1px solid #666;
}
```

We've made the background color of the disabled fields and button gray so that they don't look "active" or clickable. This is shown on the right of Figure 8-7.

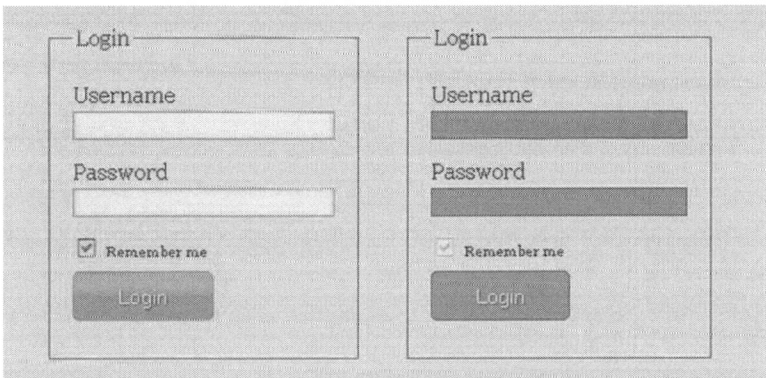

Figure 8-7. Two instances of a login form using the :disabled, :enabled, and :checked UI element states

The :checked and :enabled pseudo-classes work in exactly the same way. As you can see in the form on the left of Figure 8-7, we've highlighted the "Remember me" label (using an adjacent sibling combinator) next to the checked check box. We've also highlighted the enabled fields with a different border color (the attribute selector is used to ensure a higher specificity).

```
input[type="checkbox"]:checked + label {
        display:inline;
        background: #F9FDA2;
}
```

```
input[type="text"]:enabled, input[type="password"]:enabled {
        border:1px solid #75aadb;
}
```

These UI element state pseudo-classes are toggled (checked/unchecked) and applied when the state is active. Using them provides users with helpful visual feedback and improves the experience of your sites without much effort on your part.

THE CSS BASIC USER INTERFACE MODULE LEVEL 3

Outside of the selectors module lies another module containing pseudo-classes, the CSS Basic User Interface Module Level 3 (`http://j.mp/css3uimodule`[3]). Within this module you'll find some additional UI state pseudo-classes similar to those discussed above. They are:

default	required
valid	optional
invalid	read-only
in-range	read/write
out-of-range	

These pseudo-classes are extremely useful when considered in conjunction with HTML5 forms that we met in Chapter 6. Browser support is similar to that of CSS3 selectors. Some require a vendor prefix but rest assured they'll be coming to a browser near you soon. For more detail and polyfill support, read Ryan Seddons' "Forward Thinking Form Validation" article on A List Apart (http://j.mp/forwardforms[4]).

Target pseudo-class

CSS3 introduces a new `:target` pseudo-class. `:target` is designed to work when the selected element becomes the active target of a link (a fragment identifier in the URL that points to it). Although you may not have come across the term *fragment identifier* before, you will have used them. Fragment identifiers are named anchors or IDs on a specific element (e.g., `#flight`) within a page. When you click a link that ends with a fragment identifier, the element to which the link refers becomes the `:target`.

We can style `:target` in just the same way as `:hover` or `:focus`. The use cases are wide ranging, from a simple list of FAQs to directory pages, in-page navigation, and footnotes.

Here's an example that highlights the section of the page you've linked to from the in-page navigation. This is the page's basic markup:

```
<article>
<hgroup>
<h1>Miss Baker</h1>
<h2>First Lady of Space</h2>
</hgroup>

<nav>
<ol>
  <li><a href="#introduction">Introduction</a></li>
  <li><a href="#flight">Flight</a></li>
```

---

[3] www.w3.org/TR/css3-ui
[4] www.alistapart.com/articles/forward-thinking-form-validation

```
    <li><a href="#mission">Mission</a></li>
    <li><a href="#retirement">Retirement</a></li>
  </ol>
</nav>

<div id="introduction">
  <p>...</p>
</div>

<section id="flight">
  <h1>Miss Baker's Historic Flight</h1>
  ...
</section>

<section id="mission">
  <h1>The Mission</h1>
  ...
</section>

<aside>
  <h1>The US Space Program</h1>
  ...
</aside>

<section id="retirement">
  <h1>Life in Retirement</h1>
  ...
</section>

<footer>
  ...
</footer>
</article>
```

Notice how each section and div has been given its own ID. We've then added corresponding anchors to those IDs in the nav. This provides us the fragment identifiers (IDs) we need to work with :target.

We'll add a rule to highlight the appropriate section when it's clicked from the navigation. The :target pseudo-class is added to the element with the ID (fragment identifier), *not* the anchor. Because we've got two types of elements with fragment identifiers, we'll add the rule to both the section and div elements by grouping the selectors.

```
section:target, div:target {
background: #F9FDA2;
}
```

Figure 8-8 shows the highlighted section after the anchor has been clicked. To take this a step further, you could animate the change in background color using CSS animations, which are introduced in Chapter 12.

Figure 8-8. A highlighted section is achieved by using the `:target` pseudo-class.

Of course, applying `:target` for all types of elements could get rather messy, but we can get around that by using the universal selector (*), as shown in the following code. However, using the * selector can have a negative impact on site performance, so use it with care.

```
*:target {
background: #F9FDA2;
}
```

Lovely! A simple rule you can add to your CSS to help users easily see where they are within a document when navigating via in-page links.

As an additional example, we're now going to create a basic CSS-only tabbed interface similar to the ones you're used to creating with JavaScript using `:target`. Here's our simplified markup for the tabbed panels and associated navigation:

```
<article>
<h1>Features</h1>
<a href="#s-one">One</a> | <a href="#s-two">Two</a> | <a href="#s-three">Three</a> | <a
href="#s-four">Four</a>

<div>
<section id="s-one">
  <h1>Section One</h1>
  <p>Lorem ipsum dolor set amet.</p>
</section>
<section id="s-two">
  <h1>Section Two</h1>
  <p>Lorem ipsum dolor set amet.</p>
</section>
<section id="s-three">
  <h1>Section Three</h1>
  <p>Lorem ipsum dolor set amet.</p>
</section>
<section id="s-four">
  <h1>Section Four</h1>
  <p>Lorem ipsum dolor set amet.</p>
</section>
</div>

</article>
```

We've wrapped our tabbed area in an `<article>` and then included the navigation links. This is followed by a `<div>` (for styling) and several `<section>`s, each with a unique ID that each of the anchors will link to. Note that we've not used the `<nav>` tag or placed our navigation items in a list, for reasons that will be explained shortly.

We'll now apply some basic styles to the article, div, and sections to position them absolutely and act as tabbed content areas.

```
article, div {
        position:relative;
}

section {
        display:block;
        position:absolute;
        top:10px;
        left:0;
        background:#333;
        color:#fff;
        width:100%;
        min-height:400px;
}
```

The next step is to activate the :target pseudo-class. We want to apply it to each section, and we'll change the z-index property to make that section appear above the others. Remember, we apply

:target to the element(s) with the fragment identifier, not the anchor. Because of the simplicity of the example, we can create a rule that targets all sections in the document.

```
section:target {
        z-index:2;
}
```

To ensure that the first tab is visible on initial page load, we'll use the :first-of-type selector (more on that later in the chapter) to change its z-index, too.

```
section:target,
section:first-of-type {
        z-index:2;
}
```

That gives us a basic CSS-only tab switcher. The next step is to get the active tab to highlight in some way. To do this we need to be able to target the anchors that are above the sections in our markup. In our example, the sections are children of the surrounding div, which is in turn a sibling of the anchors. This presents you with a problem; using only CSS, you are unable to target parent elements (CSS by nature is "cascading," after all), which *is* required to highlight the active tab. To get around the issue, we need to add an ID to each of the anchors, like so:

```
<a href="#one" id="one">One</a> | <a href="#two" id="two">Two</a> | <a href="#three" id="three">Three</a> | <a href="#four" id="four">Four</a>
```

We then apply the :target to our anchors to set the active state.

```
a:target {
        background:#f5f5f5;
        font-weight:bold;
}
```

This solves the active tab problem but breaks the tabbed panels, which no longer switch. To get around this issue, use the child and adjacent sibling combinators (introduced earlier in the chapter) to target each section.

```
#one:target ~ div > section#s-one,
#two:target ~ div > section#s-two,
#three:target ~ div > section#s-three,
#four:target ~ div > section#s-four,
section:first-of-type {
        z-index:2;
}
```

The rule is set to target each section element that is a child (using the > operator) of the div that is adjacent (~ operator) to an anchor in the markup. Also included is the default section:first-of-type rule to ensure that the first section is highlighted on page load. Because, as mentioned earlier, you can't select a parent element using CSS, this is the reason for not placing your anchors within a ul or nav element. If we had written our markup in that way, it would mean that the preceding rule couldn't be implemented. So there we have it: a simple tabbed interface built using CSS3's :target pseudo-class (see Figure 8-9).

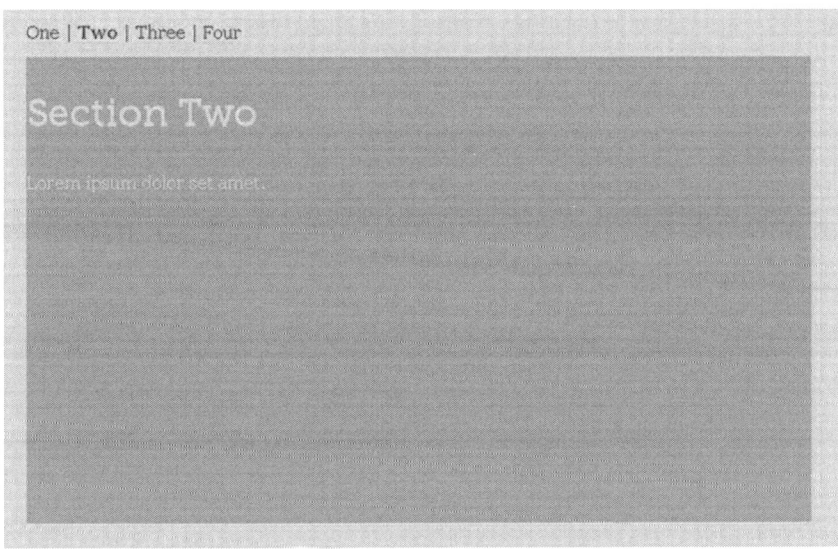

Figure 8-9. Tabbed interface built using CSS3's :target pseudo-class

While this technique isn't completely foolproof, there are other techniques for creating CSS tabs that you can investigate further, as described by Corey Mwamba on Dev.Opera (http://j.mp/operatargettabs[5]) and Chris Coyier on CSS-Tricks (http://j.mp/targettabs[6]).

If you're feeling even more adventurous, you can reduce the need for JavaScript in your page by using :target to create image galleries (http://j.mp/targetgallery[7]), slideshows, and accordions (http://j.mp/targetaccordion[8]). To push the boundaries even further, you can combine :target with CSS transitions or transformations, which you'll be learning about in Chapter 12, to add those subtle sprinkles to improve a user's experience.

Structural pseudo-classes

We've already seen several pseudo-classes: :target and the UI element state pseudo-classes. Now it's time to look at the super-powerful structural pseudo-classes. These selectors allow us to style elements or parts of elements that are in the DOM but can't be targeted via the use of other selectors without adding IDs or classes. They are starting to be used to minimize the addition of extraneous classes in your markup, either those in the source code or those added dynamically using a JavaScript library such as jQuery.

---

[5] http://dev.opera.com/articles/view/css3-target-based-interfaces/
[6] http://css-tricks.com/css3-tabs/
[7] http://rem.im/css-gallery/
[8] http://webdesignernotebook.com/css/the-css3-target-pseudo-class-and-css-animations/

All but one of the structural pseudo-classes have been introduced in CSS3, but because we're good to you, we'll even give you a little bonus and explain :first-child, which was introduced in CSS 2.1. Plus, it seems as good a place as any to start our foray into structural pseudo-classes.

:first-child

Hands up if you've ever added a class of first to the first item in a list or to the first paragraph in a post. Guilty? Rest assured our hands are up, too. Don't worry—we won't tell anyone, but we will show you how to avoid it. As the name suggests, :first-child allows you to target the first child of a given element in the document tree.

Taking the sample page from earlier in the chapter, let's say we want to increase the font size and weight of the first paragraph in the introduction. We can do this by using the :first-child pseudo-class on paragraph in a div with an ID of "introduction."

```
div#introduction p:first-child {
        font-size:18px;
        font-weight:bold;
}
```

Figure 8-10 shows this in action.

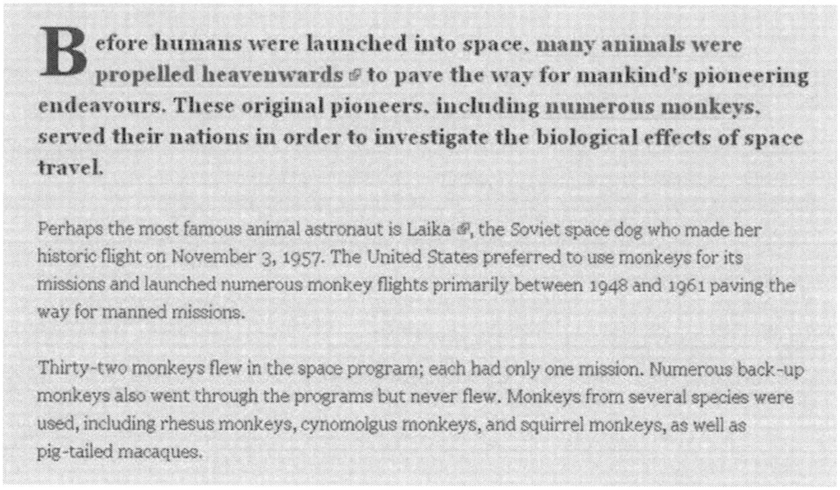

Figure 8-10. First paragraph font size increased using the :first-child pseudo-class

As you can see, this is a simple but effective method to help you avoid getting a nasty bout of classitis.

> Note: There is a very strange bug in Internet Explorer 7 with :first-child, discovered by Robert Nyman. If you place a comment before the first element (that you are trying to target), IE 7 will treat the comment as the first child and therefore not apply the rule to the element you're attempting to target. The solution? Move your comment if you can. Robert has written this up on his blog (http://j.mp/ie7firstchild[9]).

:last-child

No prizes for guessing what this selector might help you target. It's also the first of the CSS3 pseudo-selectors. Figure 8-11 shows an example navigation menu in which each item has a right border.

Figure 8-11. Navigation menu with each item with a right border

We can use :last-child to remove the border from the last list item, like so:

```
nav li:last-child {
        border-right:0;
}
```

You can see in Figure 8-12 that the border has been removed from the last list item. Brilliantly simple, don't you think?

Figure 8-12. Navigation menu using :last-child to remove the right border from the last menu item

:nth-child

The :nth-child pseudo-class is where things start to get a little tricky because we need to start using math. We're sure you're all thrilled at that prospect, but trust us, it's not *that* hard.

---

[9] http://robertnyman.com/2009/02/04/how-to-solve-first-child-css-bug-in-ie-7

:nth-child allows you to target one or more specific children of a given parent element. It can take the form of a number (integer), keywords (odd or even), or a calculation (expression). It can really come in handy when you want to style data tables like the one shown in Figure 8-13.

Year	Shuttle	Type of Animal	Name
1947	V2 Rocket	Fruit Flies	N/A
1949	V2 Flight	Rhesus Monkey	Albert II
1950	V5 Flight	Mouse	N/A
1951	R1 IIIA-1	Dogs	Tsygan & Dezik
1957	Sputnik	Dog	Laika
1958	Jupiter IRBM AM-13	Monkey	Gordo
1959	Jupiter IRBM AM-18	Monkies	Able & Miss Baker
1960	Sputnik 5	Dogs	Belka & Strelka
1961	Mercury Atlas-5	Chimpanzee	Enos
1963	Unknown	Cat	Felix

Figure 8-13. HTML data table with simple styling

We'll start by using the keyword value even and adding a background color to create a zebra-striping effect on alternate table rows to improve readability.

```
tr:nth-child(even) td {
        background-color:#eee;
}
```

Figure 8-14 shows our table complete with zebra stripes.

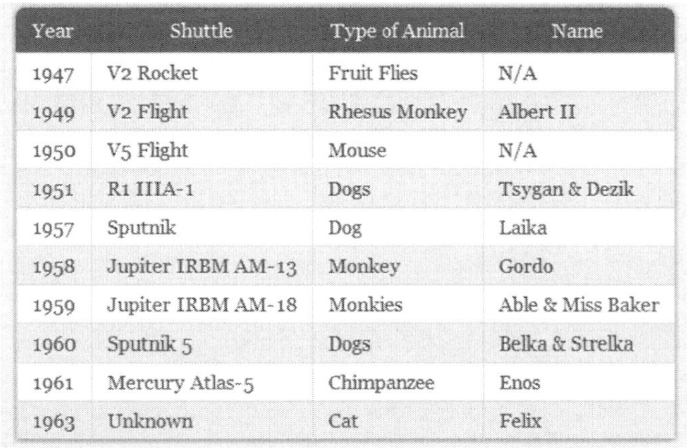

Year	Shuttle	Type of Animal	Name
1947	V2 Rocket	Fruit Flies	N/A
1949	V2 Flight	Rhesus Monkey	Albert II
1950	V5 Flight	Mouse	N/A
1951	R1 IIIA-1	Dogs	Tsygan & Dezik
1957	Sputnik	Dog	Laika
1958	Jupiter IRBM AM-13	Monkey	Gordo
1959	Jupiter IRBM AM-18	Monkies	Able & Miss Baker
1960	Sputnik 5	Dogs	Belka & Strelka
1961	Mercury Atlas-5	Chimpanzee	Enos
1963	Unknown	Cat	Felix

Figure 8-14. HTML data table with zebra-striped table using :nth-child

Now, as the saying goes, "there's more than one way to skin a cat." For the previous example we could achieve the same effect using the expression 2n or 2n+0, which means "style every second row."

```
tr:nth-child(2n) td {
        background-color:#eee;
}
```

If we wanted to reverse the rows and have the background color applied to the odd rows, we could use either the odd keyword or the expression 2n+1, which means "every second row starting from the first." The following examples have exactly the same effect:

```
tr:nth-child(odd) td {
        background-color:#eee;
}
```

```
tr:nth-child(2n+1) td {
        background-color:#eee;
}
```

Following along OK so far? Good, because we're going to increase the complexity ever so slightly. Using expressions similar to those we've seen before, let's assume we want to target every fourth line of the table. We would simply use

```
tr:nth-child(4n) td {
        background-color:#eee;
}
```

How about every fourth item starting from the second row?

```
tr:nth-child(4n+2) td {
        background-color:#eee;
}
```

You can see a pattern emerging here. Now let's deal with that smart kid in class who wants to count backward. Imagine you want to style the first five rows in your table. You can do this by using a negative value for n.

```
tr:nth-child(-n+5) td {
        background-color:#eee;
}
```

:nth-last-child

Another option available to us in our quest for ultimate styling with minimal markup is the :nth-last-child pseudo-class, which is essentially the same as :nth-child but starts counting from the *last* element. Using the same expression as the previous example highlights the last five (note the difference from the *first* five rows in the previous example) rows in the table.

```
tr:nth-last-child(-n+5) td {
        background-color:#eee;
}
```

Also, just like :nth-child, :nth-last-child accepts the odd and even arguments and doesn't have to use a negative value for n.

:only-child

There's one more "child" pseudo-class to look at before we move on, and that is :only-child. It works like you'd expect, by targeting any element that is the only child of its parent. This might come in handy should you have a dynamically generated list that contains only one item, in which case you might wish to decrease the margins.

```
ul li:only-child {
        margin-bottom:2em;
}
```

:first-of-type

The "type" pseudo-classes tend to work in the same way as the "child" selectors, the key difference being that the "type" pseudo-classes only target those elements that are the same as the element to which the selector is applied. They are most useful when you can't guarantee that there won't be any different child elements in place. For example, if an hr was placed between each paragraph, by using :first-of-type, we can ensure that we target only the paragraphs.

Taking our :first-child example from earlier, we can use the <div id="introduction"> as a styling hook. Using :first-of-type, we would write

```
div#introduction p:first-of-type {
      font-size:18px;
      font-weight:bold;
}
```

For added fun, we can combine :first-of-type with the ::first-letter pseudo-element from CSS1 (yes, 1) to style the first letter of the first paragraph in the introduction (shown in Figure 8-15). CSS3 introduced a new double-colon (::) syntax for pseudo-elements to distinguish between them and pseudo-classes such as :hover. Here's the double-colon syntax in an example:

```
div#introduction p:first-of-type::first-letter {
      font-size:60px;
      float:left;
      width:auto;
      height:50px;
      line-height:1;
      margin-right:5px;
}
```

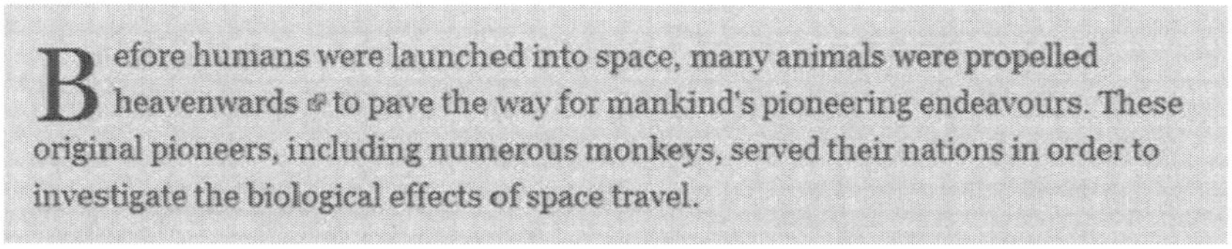

Before humans were launched into space, many animals were propelled heavenwards ☞ to pave the way for mankind's pioneering endeavours. These original pioneers, including numerous monkeys, served their nations in order to investigate the biological effects of space travel.

Figure 8-15. The first letter of the first paragraph styled using CSS pseudo-selectors

:last-of-type

As with :first-of-type, you can achieve the same effects as :last-child using :last-of-type. To remove the right border from the last menu item, you can use

```
nav li:last-of-type {
        border-right:0;
}
```

:nth-of-type

:nth-of-type works in the same way as :nth-child and uses the same syntax. However, it can be more useful than :nth-child should there be elements between those you are targeting. Let's take a look at the following example, a section with a heading followed by a list of animals in space pictures:

```
<section id="animals">
<h1>Animals in Space</h1>
<ul>
  <li><img src="img/fly.png" alt="Fruit Flies" /></li>
  <li><img src="img/albert.png" alt="Albert II" /></li>
  <li><img src="img/mouse.png" alt="Mouse" /></li>
  <li><img src="img/tsygan.png" alt="Tsygan" /></li>
  <li><img src="img/laika.png" alt="Laika" /></li>
  <li><img src="img/gordo.png" alt="Gordo" /></li>
  <li><img src="img/baker.png" alt="Miss Baker" /></li>
  <li><img src="img/belka.png" alt="Belka & Strelka" /></li>
  <li><img src="img/enos.png" alt="Enos" /></li>
  <li><img src="img/felix.png" alt="Felix" /></li>
</ul>
</section>
```

Now, remove the bullet points created by the list, float each of the lis, and add some margins.

```
#animals ul {
        list-style-type:none;
}

#animals li {
        float:left;
        width:200px;
        text-align:center;
        margin-right:2em;
        margin-bottom:2em;
}
```

Figure 8-16 shows what you have so far; you can see that the margins have caused the third list item to drop onto a new row. The trouble is that your design dictates that there should be three images per row.

Figure 8-16. A list of animals in space

Now use :nth-of-type to target every third list item (3n) and remove the right margin to ensure they don't drop onto a new line.

```
#animals li:nth-of-type(3n) {
        margin-right:0;
}
```

The results are shown in Figure 8-17.

Figure 8-17. A list of animals in space with three items on each row

As with :nth-child, you can also use expressions (2n+1) or keywords (odd or even) to target specific elements.

You can also use :nth-of-type to target the first item in a group using the expression li:nth-of-type(1) {...}, which has the same effect as using :first-of-type.

:nth-last-of-type

Using :nth-last-of-type(1) {...} is the same as using :last-of-type but, combined with expressions, allows you to count backwards starting from the last item, just like :nth-last-child. Using the nth-of-type example, move the last lonely animal to the center by adding a large left margin (see Figure 8-18).

```
#animals li:nth-last-of-type(1) {
        margin-left:232px;
}
```

Figure 8-18. A list of animals in space with the last item centered

:only-of-type

`:only-of-type` targets elements whose parent elements have no other children of the same type. Imagine you have an article that might contain several images; however, if there is only one image, you want to treat it differently, such as making it full width, for instance. This is where `:only-of-type` comes into its own.

```
article img:only-of-type {
  width:100%;
}
```

:empty

`:empty` can be an extremely useful pseudo-class. It represents an element with no content. Imagine we've got a dynamically generated `aside` in our page that has no contents; we can hide it using `:empty`.

```
aside:empty {
        display:none;
}
```

Before you start jumping for joy, a word of warning: If a browser finds a single character, or even whitespace, the element will be rendered because it no longer correctly matches the `:empty` selector. Rubbish. You're safe to add HTML comments to the markup, but ensure there's no whitespace.

:root

One structural pseudo-class that we can't ignore is the `:root` class. The root of the document in HTML is generally always the `html` element and that's precisely what `:root` targets. Should you manage to think up a use case for this selector (we're sure someone must have), be sure to let us know. For completeness, it works like so:

```
:root {
        background-color:red;
}
```

Pseudo-elements

We briefly discussed the `::first-letter` pseudo-element earlier in the chapter and how CSS3 introduced a new double-colon (`::`) syntax for pseudo-elements to distinguish between them and pseudo-classes. This new syntax applies to the following pseudo-elements found in CSS1 and CSS2:

- `::first-letter`
- `::first-line`
- `::before`
- `::after`

Although these pseudo-elements can be found in previous versions of CSS, they haven't had wide-ranging browser support until recently. Because of this, we're going to take a brief look at how to use the `::before` and `::after` pseudo-elements.

::before and ::after

The `::before` and `::after` pseudo-elements are used to generate content either before or after an element's content (or another pseudo-element). The "after an element's content" phrase is important here. This means that you can't use `::before` and `::after` on elements that have an empty content model such as `<img>` or `<input>`. This is unfortunate, as there are several possible use cases for `::before` and `::after`, such as with `input type="range"` to show the minimum and maximum values. A change in the spec is required to allow this. Opera currently allows this but goes against the spec by doing so.

While generating content that doesn't exist in your markup can be frowned upon, there are a number of legitimate use cases, as we'll see. The generated content for these pseudo-elements is provided by the content property, which can take one or more of the following values:

- *A string*: Text content

- *A URI*: The URI of an external resource such as an image

- *A counter*: For generating automatic numbering of elements

- *An attribute value*: A string with the value of the specified attribute

- *Opening or closing quotes*: Values are replaced by a string specified in the quotes property.

- *No opening or closing quotes*: No content is introduced but increments are added to the level of nesting.

First, we'll look at adding a string. To insert the word "Figure" before every `<figcaption>` element, we would write

```
figcaption::before {
    content:"Figure:";
}
```

The string must be surrounded by quotes. You can also include unicode characters, which need to be escaped with a backslash (\). Consider the following example, in which we want to append an up-arrow symbol (Unicode 2191) to the end of links that go to the top of the page. The HTML snippet is as follows:

```
<p><a href="#top">Back to top</a></p>
```

The CSS rule using the `::after` pseudo-element to add the arrow is next (see Figure 8-19). It uses an attribute selector to only target anchors with the #top `href`.

```
a[href="#top"]::after {
        content:" \2191";
}
```

Back to top ↑

Figure 8-19. An anchor using generated content to add an arrow symbol after the element's content

Let's now look at appending an attributes value using the content property. This example shows the URL of a link when an anchor has focus (or hover). We only want this to occur for links that are external, so we'll use the "starts with" (^) substring selector described earlier in the chapter.

```
a[href^="http://"]:hover::after, a[href^="http://"]:focus::after {
        content:attr(href);
        position:absolute;
        width:auto;
        bottom:-22px;
```

```
        left:0;
        padding:0 5px;
        color:#fff;
}
```

You used the content property with the attr value accompanied by the href argument. You then positioned the content to appear under the link.

Finally, to show how to combine several values, we've added a string ("External link") followed by the href attribute.

```
a[hrcf^="http://"]:hover::after, a[href^="http://"]:focus::after {
        content:"External Link " attr(href);
        position:absolute;
        width:auto;
        bottom:-22px;
        left:0;
        padding:0 5px;
        color:#fff;
}
```

Exploring pseudo-elements further

The potential for pseudo-elements is far and wide ranging, from page curls to autonumbering for sections or chapters. You can even include URLs in print style sheets. Now that browser support for pseudo-elements is improving (even though it's been around since CSS 2.1), it's helping to remove unnecessary divs that have been used for styling purposes as well.

If you wish to investigate further and see how to implement counters, quotes, and more, we suggest reading the appropriate parts of both the CSS 2.1 (http://j.mp/css2gencontent[10]) and CSS3 specifications (http://j.mp/css3content[11]).

For a number of other uses that utilize some of the properties you'll meet in Chapter 11, take a look at Nicolas Gallagher's personal website (http://j.mp/necolas[12]) where he details several experiments using pseudo-elements. Finally, Jon Hicks wrote a detailed article for 24ways on how to combine HTML5 data-* attributes, @font-face (see Chapter 10), and generated content to display icons without using images (http://j.mp/hicksfonts[13]). It's an extremely innovative and intelligent technique indeed.

Negation pseudo-class

The final selector that we'll be looking at is the negation pseudo-class, :not(). In many ways, it works in reverse to other selectors because it allows you to target elements that *do not match* the selector's

---

[10] www.w3.org/TR/2009/CR-CSS2-20090908/generate.html

[11] www.w3.org/TR/css3-content/

[12] http://nicolasgallagher.com/

[13] http://24ways.org/2011/displaying-icons-with-fonts-and-data-attributes

argument. Strange, we know, but it's very practical all the same—and something that you'll find yourself using more and more.

A prime example is styling all form inputs that *are not* Submit buttons.

```
input:not([type="submit"]) {
        width:250px;
        border:1px solid #333;
}
```

This saves you from having to add an extraneous class to a Submit button simply for styling purposes. Or looking from the other way, it saves you from having to add a class to every other `input`. That markup is looking leaner already, right?

You can also use the negation pseudo-class during testing to catch those things that validation won't. For example, if you want to see all abbreviations that don't have a `title` attribute specified, just use

```
abbr:not([title]) {
        outline:2px dotted red;
}
```

Figure 8-20 shows the dotted outline that has shown up through the use of the `:not()` pseudo-class.

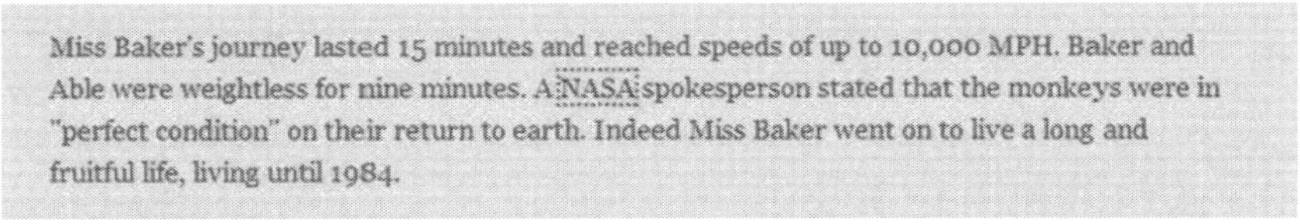

> Miss Baker's journey lasted 15 minutes and reached speeds of up to 10,000 MPH. Baker and
> Able were weightless for nine minutes. A NASA spokesperson stated that the monkeys were in
> "perfect condition" on their return to earth. Indeed Miss Baker went on to live a long and
> fruitful life, living until 1984.

Figure 8-20. An `abbr` with no `title` attribute gets styled using the negation pseudo-class.

You could use the same technique to highlight images that don't have an `alt` attribute specified.

```
img:not([alt]) {
        outline:2px dotted red;
}
```

This is a technique Eric Meyer uses in his diagnostic style sheet (`http://j.mp/diagnosticss`[14]). You can add the diagnostic CSS when testing to catch all these errors and fix them. Simply remove the file when you're ready to deploy to the site.

Browser support

CSS3 selectors are fully supported in IE9+, Firefox 3.5+, Chrome 4+, Safari 4+, and Opera 10+ (albeit with three minor exceptions).

---

[14] `http://meyerweb.com/eric/tools/css/diagnostics`

Support in IE6, IE7, and IE8 is virtually non-existent (IE7 and IE8 support the general sibling combinatory, `:first-child`, and all the attribute selectors), but you can get around this by polyfilling with native JavaScript or a jQuery library.

One additional caveat with Internet Explorer is that if you are grouping selectors and IE comes across a selector it doesn't understand, it will ignore the whole rule. For example, if you have

```
ul li:nth-child(3n), ul li.last {
  margin-right: 0;
}
```

IE will not recognize the rule, so you need to split them into their own rules, like so:

```
ul li:nth-child(3n) {
  margin-right: 0;
}

ul li.last {
  margin-right: 0;
}
```

One useful polyfill you can use is Selectivzr (`http://j.mp/selectivzr`[15]), introduced in the last chapter. The library simulates the pseudo-class selectors in versions of IE from 5.5 through 8. Unfortunately, at present, it doesn't simulate all the attribute selectors or combinators covered in this chapter when used with certain JavaScript libraries.

Alternatively, you could decide that if some of these sprinkles are only added as enhancements and aren't crucial for the site's functionality, then it's fine for them not to show in less-capable browsers. The choice is yours.

Selectors of the future

Although this book focuses on CSS3, we'd like to let you in on a little secret. CSS4 is around the corner. Well, it is in terms of selectors. The Selectors Level 4 Module is currently in "working draft" and being updated regularly. Although in its early stages (and expect significant revisions), some selectors have been moved out of the selectors spec and some have been added. Those out include the pseudo-elements, due to be re-housed elsewhere. In contrast, the UI state pseudo-classes currently in the Basic User Interface spec have been incorporated into the Selectors Level 4 Module. There are many other changes currently ongoing, such as the widening scope for the negation (`:not`) pseudo-class.

In terms of new selectors, there are currently many, including those to match similar selector strings (`:matches`), a linguistic pseudo-class (`:dir`), time dimensional pseudo-classes (`:current`, `:past` and `:future`), grid structure selectors (`:column`, `:nth-column`, `:nth-last-column`) and finally, with much excitement, a parent selector (syntax to be defined). For more detail than we can provide here you can, of

---

[15] `http://selectivizr.com`

course, read the spec (http://j.mp/css4selectors[16]). Alternatively, David Storey has written an excellent summary on his blog (http://j.mp/storeycss4[17]) but bear in mind this may be out of date by the time you read it.

Summary

In this chapter you learned that by using powerful CSS3 selectors, we don't need to add unnecessary classes and IDs to our markup, ensuring that we can truly separate our content and presentation from one another. You saw how to target the first, last, odd, or even item in a group. We've also shown how to target groups of elements using expressions and elements on their own.

You saw how to use negative pseudo-classes to help with your testing and diagnostics. We introduced the idea of adding generated content where appropriate. We also showed you how to improve a user's experience by giving better feedback using :target and the UI element states pseudo-classes. Finally, we gave you a glimpse into the future with a brief look at CSS4 Selectors and (as Mr Storey describes) that magic unicorn parent selector.

Now that you're armed with a means of targeting the various elements in your pages, the next chapter will show you how to use your new-found selector powers to create beautiful CSS-based layouts that work seamlessly across devices.

---

[16] http://dev.w3.org/csswg/selectors4
[17] http://generatedcontent.org/post/10865123182/selectors4

Homework

For your homework, start by creating your own diagnostic style sheet and then testing it against your site to pick up any empty attributes or missing values.

Continue by looking at the site you're developing and deciding where you can make use of these new powerful selectors to save you from having to add classes or IDs to your markup. You should be able to include a number of the selectors that we've used throughout this chapter. Follow this by integrating some generated content using the `::before` and `::after` pseudo-elements.

Finally, build a CSS-only image gallery using only the `:target` selector.

Appendix

Table 8-1 is a table of CSS selectors, their meaning, the part of the spec they're described in, and in which version of CSS they were added. This table is based on the W3C table at www.w3.org/TR/css3-selectors/#selectors.

Table 8-1. CSS Selectors

Pattern	Meaning	Described in section	Version of CSS
*	Any element	Universal selector	2
E	An element of type E	Type selector	1
E F	An F element descendant of an E element	Descendant combinator	1
E > F	An F element child of an E element	Child combinator	2
E + F	An F element immediately preceded by an E element	Adjacent sibling combinator	2
E ~ F	An F element preceded by an E element	General sibling combinator	3
E.warning	An E element whose class is "warning" (the document language specifies how class is determined)	Class selectors	1
E#myid	An E element with ID equal to "myid"	ID selectors	1
E[foo]	An E element with a "foo" attribute	Attribute selectors	2
E[foo="bar"]	An E element whose "foo" attribute value is exactly equal to "bar"	Attribute selectors	2
E[foo~="bar"]	An E element whose "foo" attribute value is a list of whitespace-separated values, one of which is exactly equal to "bar"	Attribute selectors	2
E[foo^="bar"]	An E element whose "foo" attribute value begins exactly with the string "bar"	Attribute selectors	3
E[foo$="bar"]	An E element whose "foo" attribute value ends exactly with the string "bar"	Attribute selectors	3
E[foo*="bar"]	An E element whose "foo" attribute value contains the substring "bar"	Attribute selectors	3
E[foo|="en"]	An E element whose "foo" attribute has a hyphen-separated list of values beginning (from the left) with "en"	Attribute selectors	2
E:lang(fr)	An element of type E in language "fr" (the document language specifies how language is determined)	The :lang() pseudo-class	2

Pattern	Meaning	Described in section	Version of CSS
E:link E:visited	An E element being the source anchor of a hyperlink of which the target is not yet visited (:link) or already visited (:visited)	The link pseudo-classes	1
E:active E:hover E:focus	An E element during certain user actions	The user action pseudo-classes	1 and 2
E:target	An E element being the target of the referring URI	The target pseudo-class	3
E::first-line	The first formatted line of an E element	The ::first-line pseudo-element	1
E::first-letter	The first formatted letter of an E element	The ::first-letter pseudo-element	1
E::before	Generated content before an E element	The ::before pseudo-element	2
E::after	Generated content after an E element	The ::after pseudo element	2
E:nth-child(n)	An E element, the n-th child of its parent	Structural pseudo-classes	3
E:nth-last-child(n)	An E element, the n-th child of its parent, counting from the last one	Structural pseudo-classes	3
E:nth-of-type(n)	An E element, the n-th sibling of its type	Structural pseudo-classes	3
E:nth-last-of-type(n)	An E element, the n-th sibling of its type, counting from the last one	Structural pseudo-classes	3
E:first-child	An E element, first child of its parent	Structural pseudo-classes	2
E:last-child	An E element, last child of its parent	Structural pseudo-classes	3
E:first-of-type	An E element, first sibling of its type	Structural pseudo-classes	3
E:last-of-type	An E element, last sibling of its type	Structural pseudo-classes	3
E:only-child	An E element, only child of its parent	Structural pseudo-classes	3
E:only-of-type	An E element, only sibling of its type	Structural pseudo-classes	3
E:empty	An E element that has no children (including text nodes)	Structural pseudo-classes	3
E:root	An E element, root of the document	Structural pseudo-classes	3
E:enabled E:disabled	A user interface element E that is enabled or disabled	The UI element states pseudo-classes	3

Pattern	Meaning	Described in section	Version of CSS
E:checked	A user interface element E that is checked (for instance a radio-button or checkbox)	The UI element states pseudo-classes	3
E:not(s)	An E element that does not match simple selector s	Negation pseudo-class	3

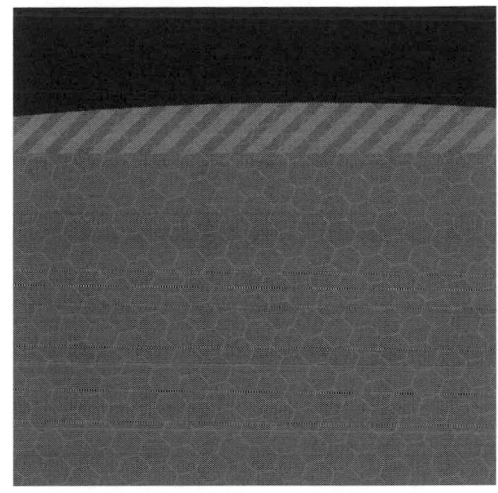

Chapter 9

A Layout for Every Occasion

In this chapter you'll learn how to use CSS to position elements, and create CSS layouts. This is something that CSS has historically been weak at—CSS 2.1-based layout techniques use properties not originally intended for page layout, and unsuited for today's web applications. We'll start by revisiting the basics: the CSS box model, floats, positioning and friends, and how to use them to create flexible and fixed layouts. We'll then take a look at the hidden power of @media media queries and see how you can adapt your CSS to present a customized experience to devices based on their capabilities, under the banner of Responsive Web Design. Then we'll end with a peek into the future of CSS3 layout specifications. But first let's visit the past to examine some trends that have influenced CSS layouts and set the stage for why media queries have become so important recently.

The web of many devices

When writing the original proposal for the WWW in March 1989, Tim Berners-Lee mentioned "heterogeneity" as one of the requirements.

> *Access is required to the same data from different types of system*
>
> *-Information Management: A Proposal* by Sir Tim Berners-Lee
>
> (http://j.mp/html-proposal www.w3.org/History/1989/proposal.html)

This was in reference to the systems at CERN where Tim Berners-Lee worked, and the systems listed as examples (VM/CMS, Macintosh, VAX/VMS, UNIX) may not all be familiar. However, this ethos has become a fundamental underpinning of the Web and lives on in HTML's design principles as part of the core principle of universal access.

> *Features should, when possible, work across different platforms, devices, and media.*
>
> *-HTML Design Principles*, W3C
>
> (http://j.mp/html-principles-5-1 www.w3.org/TR/html-design-principles/#media-independence)

The best summation of this idea we've heard is from the irrepressibly passionate Molly Holschlag, who in 2009 at the Web Standards Project (WaSP) annual meeting at South by South West (SxSW) declared:

> *Anybody, anywhere, any user agent,* **one Web**.
>
> -Molly Holschlag, speaking at the WaSP Annual Meeting, SxSW 2009 [podcast; 1:03:30]
>
> (http://j.mp/wasp-2009 audio.sxsw.com/2009/podcasts/D4%20SXSW_PODCASTS/031609_PM2_HIL B_WASP_Annual_Meeting.mp3)

So why is this principle so important? It's because now, more than ever, the Web we use and build for is *a Web of many devices*. This trend is only accelerating, and it's up to us to adapt with new techniques to meet the challenge.

Evolution of monitor sizes

Back in the ancient mists of the 1990s anyone viewing the Internet was probably using an 800x600 px screen. As the average monitor size increased, web designers started to target 800x600 px monitors in

2000, then 1024x768 px monitors (with the 960 px width that many fixed-width CSS frameworks use today) in about 2007. (http://j.mp/960px-width)[1]

However, the arguments in 2006 over whether it was time to move on from 800x600 px pale in comparison to the turbulence of recent developments. Although mobile browsing has been around since 1998, it's only in the last few years that phones have actually been browsing the "one Web," rather than the sickly substitute of early WAP and cHTML attempts. The current explosion of so-called smartphones and tablets has brought true mobile browsing to the masses. While many smartphones have converged on the screen size of 320x480 px, there's lots of variety in both size and pixel density. Internationally, the most common mobile screen size at the time of writing is 240x320 px, generally at 152 ppi (pixels per inch), but there's a large (and growing) diversity in screen dimensions and resolutions.

At the other end of the spectrum, very large screens have recently become affordable, and high resolution displays are also appearing. In addition to phones, tablets and computers, we now also have TVs, game consoles, and even cars and fridges displaying web pages, all with wildly varying display sizes, browser capabilities, and bandwidth.

It's clear that our industry's previous standard of fixed-width layouts is not up to the challenge. In the face of this mass of devices and capabilities, what Scott Jenson calls "a zombie apocalypse of electronics" (http://j.mp/zombie-devices designmind.frogdesign.com/blog/the-coming-zombie-apocalypse-small-cheap-devices-will-disrupt-our-old-school-ux-assumptions.htm), what are we to do?

Separate sites optimized for each device? But that's crazy talk!

One approach is to create websites optimized for various classes of device. Currently, this generally means a standard site for desktop computers and a site optimized for smartphones. The arriving wave of tablets may add another category of devices to this list. By doing this, you can design an experience tailored to the strengths of each platform and ensure the design performs well.

In some regards this is a good solution. People often have very different content needs when accessing a website on the go than when they're at home or work. In addition, there are often different capabilities,

---

[1] Cameron Moll covers the development of the 960px grid in "Optimal width for 1024px resolution?" (www.cameronmoll.com/archives/001220.html)

such as the limitation of a much smaller screen or the ability to access geolocation data on a mobile device. (http://j.mp/mobile-web-friendly)[2]

However, soon even three versions may not be enough. This also means a large increase in complexity, as now you have multiple sites to test and maintain. While in an ideal world you'd have the resources to do justice to each site, unless you're very dedicated (and well funded) this often leads to one well-maintained site, with other versions falling into neglect.

Over the years folks have tried to address the problem of different device capabilities in various ways. In the bad old days, this generally meant *browser sniffing*, detecting a browser based on its user agent string, and then either sending customized content from the server, or customizing the site's display on the client. When implemented poorly, this approach was very fragile, often breaking when new browsers were released. The modern and more responsible equivalent is *feature sniffing* to detect a device's capabilities and customize content based on capability, using tools like Modernizr and YepNope. This is an extension of *progressive enhancement*, adding extra functionality for user agents that can support it. Internet Explorer's conditional comments have also played a part, for example together with the ever-popular IE6 universal stylesheet (http://j.mp/universal-ie6-css Universal Internet Explorer 6 stylesheet by Andy Clarke stuffandnonsense.co.uk/blog/about/universal_internet_explorer_6_css).

The ideal way would be to create a website that *adapts to the device used to view it*. While this may sound like something requiring black magic, in reality all we need to do is accept the innate characteristics of the medium, as **adaptability is what the web does by default**. John Allsopp sagely wrote about this more than ten years ago in what is perhaps the seminal article of our profession, "A Dao of Web Design."

> *It is the nature of the Web to be flexible, and it should be our role as designers and developers to embrace this flexibility, and produce pages which, by being flexible, are accessible to all.*

> -*A Dao of Web Design,* by John Allsopp, 2000

> (http://j.mp/dao-web www.alistapart.com/articles/dao/)

---

[2] Bruce Lawson covers becoming mobile friendly in Opera's "Mobile web optimization guide." (dev.opera.com/articles/view/the-mobile-web-optimization-guide)

While the Web may be flexible by default, pages with default styling are also less than compelling. It's not the perfect solution, but the easiest way to accommodate a web of many devices is to just code well and use a *flexible layout*. However, before we cover flexible layouts, let's quickly review the basics of how content is displayed in a browser.

The Visual Formatting Model of CSS—it's boxes all the way down!

The way elements are visually laid out in CSS can be complex, but at its heart is rather simple. Every element that is displayed is comprised of one or more boxes. These boxes can have different properties and can interact with each other in different ways, but the fundamental truth is everything's a box. Naturally, CSS has a model for that, too—the Box Model.

The Box Model: content, padding, border, margin

Thinking of boxes you might think of a beautifully gift-wrapped present (perhaps a cake!). The present is in a box, possibly surrounded by some protective space or padding. Unless it's touching other boxes, there's probably also some margin of space around the box. A CSS Box Model box is similar and is based on the element's content, plus its padding, border, and margin properties. You're already familiar with content from the first half of the book, so let's review padding, border, and margin, as these three properties affect how much space an element can take in the page.

- padding adds space to one or more sides of an element's content. It's transparent, so it reveals the element's background color and/or background image(s).

- border controls the appearance of the border on each side of the element, enclosing the content and padding. This is generally a colored or translucent line that the border property defines the width, style, and color of, but it can have rounded corners and perhaps even use a border image (see Chapter 11). The border is added between the element's padding and margin, and by default it overlays the element's background.

- margin also affects the space on one or more sides of an element and is transparent, but unlike padding it can also take negative values and the value auto. These let you move an element from its initial position or change how it interacts with surrounding elements. It can also be used as a part of CSS layouts, as you'll see in the "Changing column order with negative margins" section later in the chapter.

As you'll remember from Chapter 7's "CSS Shorthand" section, these three shorthand properties also come in per-side varieties (such as margin-top), and in the case of border, a slew of individual properties (such as border-bottom-color).

We should also mention outline here, which is like border but doesn't change the space a box takes. It's added outside the element's border, overlapping any margin, and stacked above the element's content. Unlike border, a single outline style is applied on all sides of the element's box. You'll mainly see outline in *browser default stylesheets* (the CSS rules that browsers apply to every page by default) for indicating :focus on links and form fields for accessibility. Generally, you'll want to leave outline alone and use the more flexible border instead.

The amount of space these properties take is defined in length units. These are:

- *%: A percentage of the containing block's width as a number followed by %, e.g. 33.3%*

Font-relative length units, such as:

- *em: The height of the font (well, the computed value of the element's font-size).*

- *ex: The font's x-height, which is generally the height of the character "x" (about 0.5em)*

- *ch: Character unit, which is defined as the advance width (a typography term) of the character "0". This is useful for specifying a value equivalent to number of characters in a monospace font, including Chinese, Japanese, and Korean fonts. (http://j.mp/defining-ch meyerweb.com/eric/thoughts/2012/05/15/defining-ch/)*

- *rem: The font-size of the root unit, <html>. This avoids inheritance issues with em.*

Viewport-relative length units such as:

- *vw: A percentage of the viewport's width. The viewport is the visible portion of the page, bound by the browser window. This differs from normal percentages in that it's a percentage of the initial containing block, which can be wider than an element's current containing block.*

- *vh: A percentage of the viewport's height.*

- *vm: The smaller value of vw and vh.*

Absolute length units, such as

- *px: CSS pixels; for the purpose of resolution 1px is equal to 1/96th of 1in, giving a fixed CSS resolution of 96dpi.*

- *cm:* Centimeters

- *mm:* Millimeters

- *in:* Inches

- *pt:* Points; 1pt is equal to 1/72 of 1 inch.

- *pc:* Picas; 1pc is equal to 12pt.

(Note that the unit is optional for relative and absolute units if the length is 0.)

Due to browser support, we're currently limited to %, em, and px for screen CSS, although with widespread browser support for rem in modern browsers, it's usable now with an em or px unit fallback (more details in Chapter 10). Absolute units (with the exception of px) should only be used in print stylesheets.

Pixels in CSS also deserve a little further explanation. These are potentially different than display pixels and are defined as a visual angle, so they appear about the same size regardless of distance. The relative size of a CSS pixel on a mobile phone and on a projector should appear the same to the viewer, despite the absolute sizes being very different. This also means a high resolution display might use more than one device pixel to display a CSS pixel, and a double-resolution display would use four device pixels per CSS pixel.

The order that non-zero-width padding, borders, margins, and/or an outline are displayed in starts with the element's margin and background color at the back, then background image(s), padding, the border, the actual content, and finally the outline on top. This is illustrated in Figure 9-1 in an exploded 3D diagram of the CSS Box Model for a block-level box.

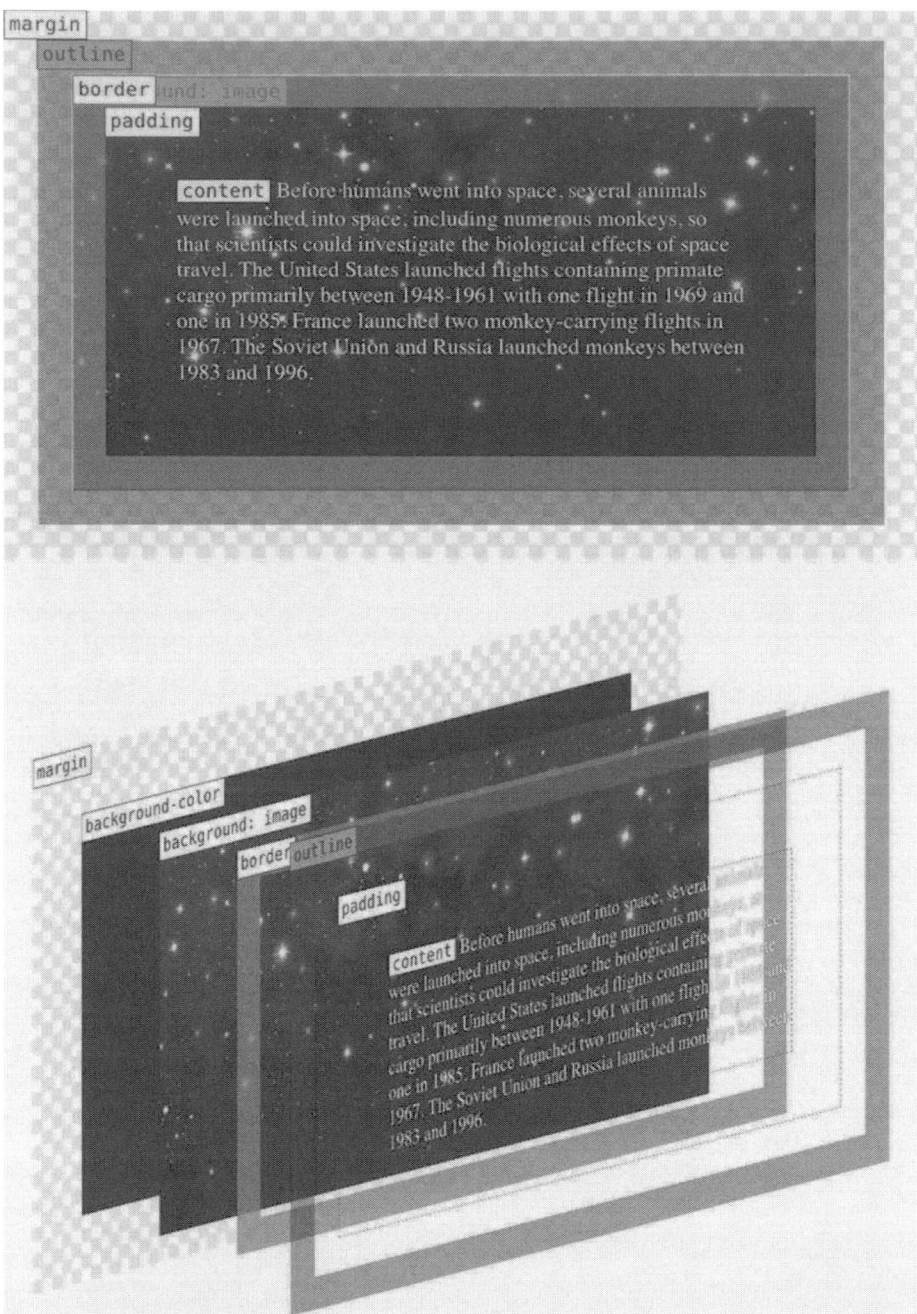

Figure 9-1. A CSS box (including outline), with an exploded view showing how the parts of a block-level box are stacked

This figure shows how the box model works for a block-level box, one that uses the style display: block;. The display property has a range of different values, but the two fundamental ones are block and inline. Generally, block-level boxes contain blocks of content, like the <p> element containing text, whereas inline boxes are added to the content, like the <strong> element around some of the text. They also work a little differently in the CSS Box Model, so let's look at them one at a time, starting with display: block;. But first, a brief digression on internationalization and positioning words.

> *One of the wonderful things about HTML and CSS is the huge amount of work that has gone into internationalization and accessibility. The "one Web" is international and multilingual, and it's important to keep this in mind during this chapter.*
>
> *While English and many European languages are written left-to-right and top-to-bottom, other languages are not, such as Arabic and Hebrew (right-to-left), and traditionally styled Chinese and Japanese (top-to-bottom, right-to-left). For simplicity, we will use English-based examples, in which text is left-to-right and content is read top-to-bottom. If you're using a language with different norms, keep this in mind.*

Block-level boxes with display: block

Block-level boxes are your structural building blocks. Elements with display: block; are by default as wide as their containing element and follow each other vertically down the page. The default height of a block-level box is the height required to contain the box's content. These are the element's *intrinsic dimensions*—the width and height it has before CSS is applied. While a paragraph's height can change if the text size or containing element's width changes, by default replaced content like an image will use its intrinsic width and height—even if it is cropped by the viewport. See Figure 9-2.

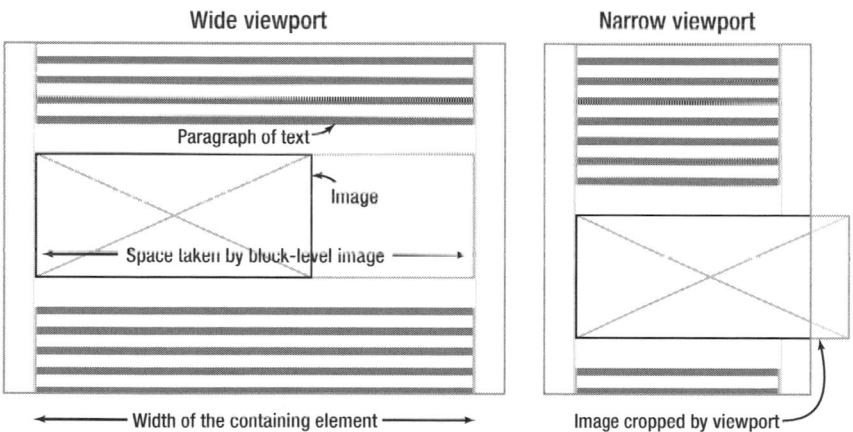

Figure 9-2. Block-level paragraphs and images. Note that the top paragraph's height adapts to contain the text when the viewport is narrow, but by default the image is cropped.

> The concept of containing elements is covered in detail in the "Block Formatting Context" section later in this chapter.

For block-level boxes you can change these intrinsic dimensions using the properties width and height. When using percentage values, these are based on the width and height of the containing element, respectively. Generally, hiding content is a bad idea, so we recommend against setting a height on an element that contains text or anything sized using font-relative units—it's asking for trouble. If the browser's font size is increased or the browser window is made smaller, you can easily end up with hidden content and scroll bars on the element. While you can control this behavior with the overflow property, it's far better to just not have content hidden at all. (If you can't avoid setting a height for a text block, use ems to adapt to text resizing, and test thoroughly.)

There are also the related properties of max-width and min-width, plus the less used max-height and min-height, which put upper and lower limits on an element's dimensions. These are very handy if you haven't specified a fixed width but don't want your line length to become overly long on a very wide browser window. They don't work in Internet Explorer 6, so it's best to add an IE 6-targetted fixed width for that browser.

The width and height calculation algorithm

By default the width and height of a CSS box is the size of its content—defined by the edge between content and padding. However, the space that a box takes is the content box **plus** any padding, borders, and margins. The default calculation is

- Total width = margin-left + border-left-width + padding-left + width + padding-right + border-right-width + margin-right

- Total height = margin-top + border-top-width + padding-top + height + padding-bottom + border-bottom-width + margin-bottom

Figure 9-3 shows an example div with a fixed width and height, plus margins, borders, and padding to demonstrate this.

```
.box {

  width: 240px;

  height: 160px;

  margin: 24px 48px; /* = 24px 48px 24px 48px */

  border: 1px solid #ddd;

  padding: 12px 18px 6px; /* = 12px 18px 6px 18px */
```

```
}
<div class="box">

  <h1>CSS.</h1>

  <p>It's boxes all the way down...</p>

</div>
```

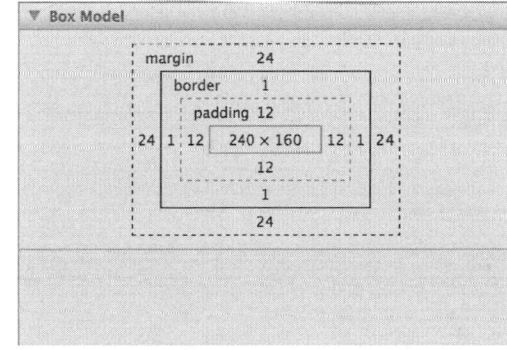

Figure 9-3. A box with padding, borders, and margins, and the same element in the Appearance tab of Safari's Web Inspector

You might initially expect the div to take up 240x160px, but by default it will take the following:

- Total width = 48px + 1px + 18px + 240px + 10px + 1px + 48px = 374px

- Total height = 24px + 1px + 12px + 160px + 6px + 1px + 24px = 228px

You normally first encounter this when trying to float two elements that are 50% wide side-by-side (we'll cover floats in just a moment). If you add *any* horizontal margin, border, or padding, the two boxes together become wider than 100%, and the second one will drop below. This also makes it difficult to use different units on margin, border, padding, and width, as the size of em and percentage units changes with the browser's font size and browser width respectively.

This probably contradicts your expectations, as when you're posting a present you pay for the size of the box *including* packaging, and not just the contents. Adding to the fun, Internet Explorer before version 6 misinterpreted the CSS Box Model, and *included* border and padding as part of width. If you forget to start your HTML with a doctype it still does, in what's called quirks mode. Don't forget the doctype!

The box-sizing property

However, everything old is new again, and using the box-sizing property you can now choose whether width and height refer to the default content-box or the more intuitive border-box (between margin and border, referred to as the *border edge*), which is easier for layout. Using border-box means that border and padding values will not add to the element's width and height, as they do with content-box.

- For content-box: width = content's width

- For border-box: width = border-left-width + padding-left + content's width + padding-right + border-right-width

Going back to the previous example in Figure 9-3, let's see how border-box has changed the math.

- Total width = margin-left + width + margin-right = 48px + 240px + 48px = 336px

- Total height = margin-top + height + margin-bottom = 24px + 160px + 24px = 208px

Figure 9-4 shows this difference clearly — the content-box content width is the same as the border-box border edge width.

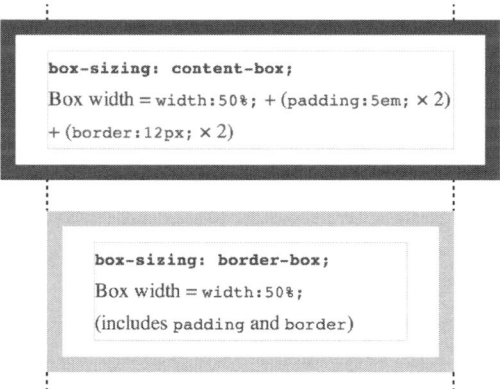

The difference between content-box and border-box

Figure 9-4. A comparison of the box-sizing property's content-box and border-box values

Note that by default an element's background is visible to the border edge, and the top-left corner of this is where a background image begins. If you change box-sizing, you'll probably want to change background-clip and/or background-origin, which we cover in Chapter 11. By default the dimensions shown in your browser's inspector tool when hovering over an element are to the border edge, so margin isn't included. You can check margins using the inspector tool's box model diagram we saw in Figure 9-3. (Opera's

Developer Tools and Firefox's Firebug also include other handy information there, including the element's box-sizing value.)

As you can see in Table 9-1, browser support for this is surprisingly good, although Firefox 13 and below can have problems when combining with min-/max-height, min-/max-width, SVG, and table cells.

Table 9-1. Browser Support for box-sizing (http://caniuse.com/#feat=css3-boxsizing)

IE	Mozilla	Safari	Chrome	Opera
8.0	2.0 -moz-	3.1 -webkit-	4 -webkit-	9.5
		5.1	10	

However, if your audience includes Internet Explorer 7 and below, using box-sizing will require custom workarounds for those browsers to avoid breaking your layout. While Modernizr can detect this and there are polyfills, unless you support a lot of legacy browsers, just adding IE-targeted styles is probably easiest.

There are many old versions of Internet Explorer still in use. Reasons include Windows XP (which doesn't run IE9 but is still widely used), corporate policy, and IE being the last major browser to move to auto-updating (beginning in 2012). We advocate testing occasionally in various versions of IE when creating a site, as you can normally avoid issues through good coding and progressive enhancement. However, while IE10 has finally joined the ranks of "modern browsers" sometimes you'll encounter a quirk or bug in earlier versions (more often in IE6-7) and need to give them a little nudge.

Historically this was done using CSS filters (http://j.mp/css-filter en.wikipedia.org/wiki/CSS_filter) (like the underscore and star hacks) or by loading IE-specific stylesheets using IE's conditional comments (http://j.mp/ies-cc dev.opera.com/articles/view/supporting-ie-with-conditional-comments/). Instead, we recommend using Paul Irish's conditional classes on <html> (http://j.mp/html-cc paulirish.com/2008/conditional-stylesheets-vs-css-hacks-answer-neither/):

```
<!--[if lt IE 7 ]>        <html class="ie6">        <![endif]-->
<!--[if IE 7 ]>           <html class="ie7">        <![endif]-->
<!--[if IE 8 ]>           <html class="ie8">        <![endif]-->
<!--[if IE 9 ]>           <html class="ie9">        <![endif]-->
<!--[if (gt IE 9)|!(IE)]><!--> <html> <!--<![endif]-->
```

You can then target any IE-specific styles by prefixing with the relevant class, like so:

```
img                       {max-width:                       100%;}
.ie6 img {width: 100%;}
```

Margins on block-level boxes

Positive margin values on block-level boxes will increase the space around the box. However, negative margin values work a little differently. For block-level elements, a negative top margin will move the element (and following elements) up, potentially overlapping earlier content, and a negative bottom margin will pull following content up to potentially overlap the element, as shown in Figure 9-5.

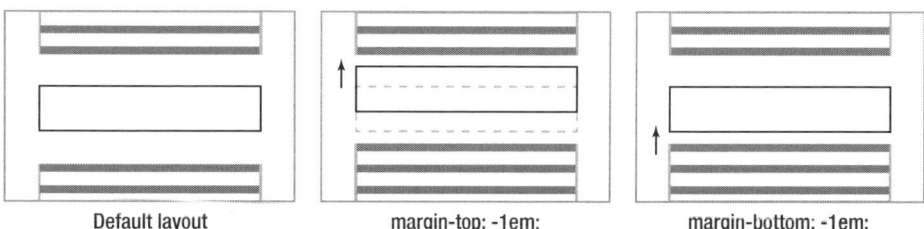

| Default layout | margin-top: -1em; | margin-bottom: -1em; |

Figure 9-5. Negative vertical margins applied to block-level boxes: the left example is for reference (no negative margins), the center example has a negative margin-top moving the element (and following content) up, and the right example shows a negative margin-bottom "pulling" following content up.

Negative left and right margins work differently depending on whether the width is auto or not. For block-level elements with a relevant width or height of auto, negative left or right margins will pull the edge of the box out, *widening* the element. For a block-level element with a set width (including replaced content like an image), a negative left margin will *move* the element to the left, and a negative right margin will pull in content to the element's right to potentially overlap the element (although you'll only see this when there's content beside the block, for example when applied to the first of two floats). This is shown in Figure 9-6.

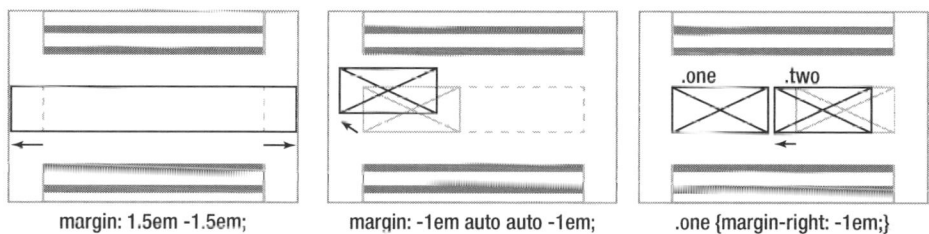

| margin: 1.5em -1.5em; | margin: -1em auto auto -1em; | .one {margin-right: -1em;} |

Figure 9-6. Negative horizontal margins applied to a block-level box with width: auto; on the left. The center example has a set width and negative left and top margins. The right example has a negative margin-right on image 1, which "pulls" in content to the right.

If the element's width isn't as wide as the parent element, using auto for left or right margins will absorb any unused space. As shown in Figure 9-7, by default an image will align with the left edge of its parent, but if the element has margin-left: auto; and margin-right: 0;, the element will touch the right side of the parent element. If both left and right margins are auto, the element will be centered in the parent element's width, as shown in the rightmost example.

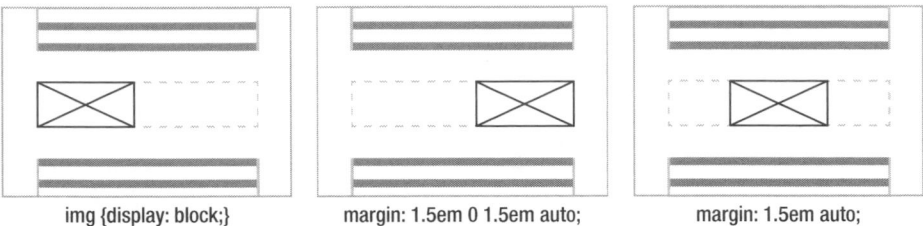

| img {display: block;} | margin: 1.5em 0 1.5em auto; | margin: 1.5em auto; |

Figure 9-7. For block-level boxes narrower than their parents, adding horizontal margins set to auto will absorb any extra space, allowing you to right-align or center elements within their parent.

Collapsing vertical margins

Another interesting aspect of the box model with block-level boxes is that *if two vertical margins touch, only the largest margin is used*. This sounds peculiar but is actually what you want to happen most of the time. For example, without collapsing margins the CSS p {margin: 1.5em 0;} means that the margin between paragraphs is *double* the top the first paragraph and the bottom of the last one, as you can see in the left of Figure 9-6. We could code for this, for example by only setting margin-top. However, with collapsing vertical margins we don't need to — the margins before and between paragraphs end up the same, as seen in the right example.

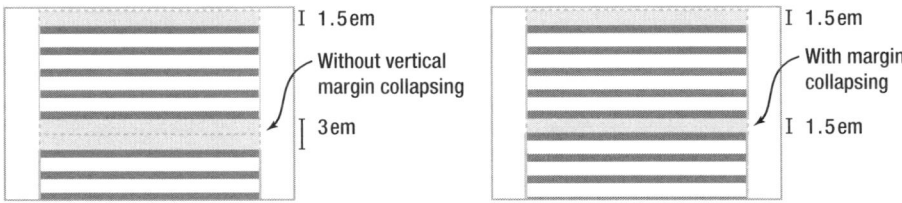

Figure 9-8. Two paragraphs, with p {margin: 1.5em 0;}. The left example demonstrates how cumulative vertical margins would work. The right example shows how collapsing vertical margins stop the space between paragraphs becoming much larger.

This seems like a minor issue, but becomes important when several nested elements all have touching top or bottom margins, such as a list (see Figure 9-9).

```
ul {margin: 1.5em 0 1.5em 1.5em;}
```

```
li {margin: 0.75em;}
```

```
<p>…</p>
```

```
<ul><li><p>…</p></li></ul>
```

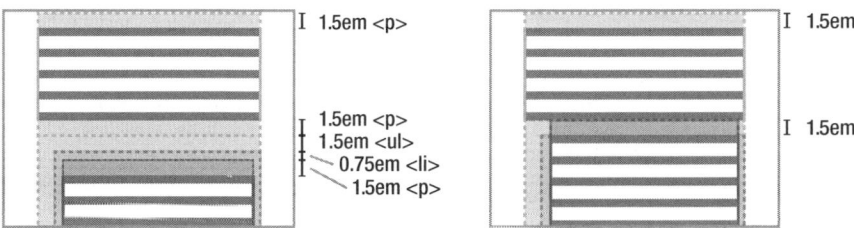

Figure 9-9. Multiple margins collapse to only the largest one if they're touching. Without margin collapsing the nesting of elements would lead to a 5.25em gap between these two paragraphs. With margin collapsing this becomes 1.5em, the largest single value.

The top and bottom margins of an element without borders, padding, content, or clearing to separate them are also touching, and also collapse together. This is why the intuitive but bad idea of adding empty paragraphs to add vertical space doesn't work. However, vertical margin collapsing is prevented as soon as margins are separated by padding, borders (even a transparent one), or content, as seen in Figure 9-10. The elements must also be *in-flow* (not floated etc), and in the same *block formatting context*, concepts we'll cover soon.

```
p {margin: 1.5em 0;}

<p>...</p>

<!-- two empty paragraphs -->

<p></p>

<p></p>

<p>...</p>
```

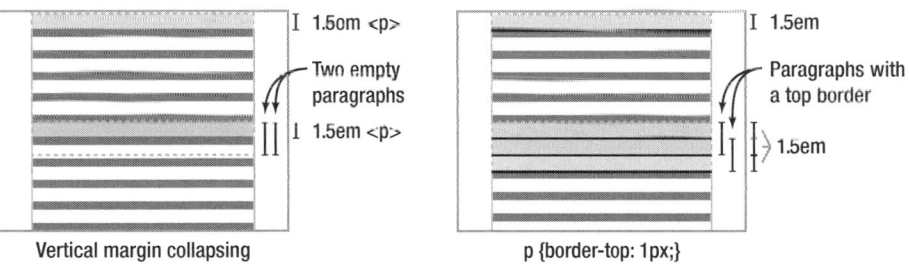

Figure 9-10. Between the bottom margin of the first paragraph and the top margin of the last paragraph, all vertical margins touch, and would be collapsed to a single 1.5em margin. However, adding p {border-top: 1px solid #000;} on the right means this border now prevents some margins from touching (and collapsing), and the empty paragraphs become visible.

Now that we've covered block-level boxes—elements with display: block;—let's meet inline boxes, the other common box type.

Inline boxes with display: inline

Inline box elements generally wrap words or phrases of text content, and HTML5's phrasing content elements are display: inline; by default. In contrast to block-level boxes, they are as long as their content, and rather than creating a rectangle, their boxes enclose the text *per line* (like a highlighter), wrapping over multiple lines if necessary, as seen in Figure 9-11. Inline boxes can't contain block-level boxes.

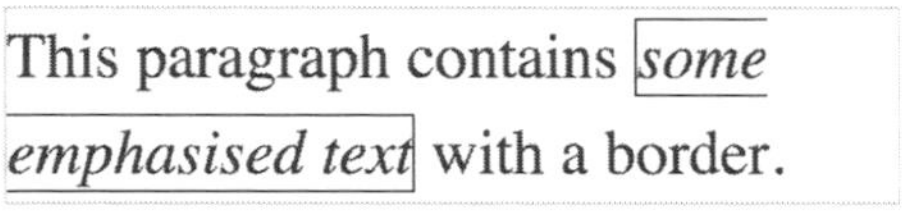

This paragraph contains *some emphasised text* with a border.

Figure 9-11. A prargraph containing an inline box with a border that wraps (is split) over two lines.

Replaced content includes elements that are linked to and embedded, such as images and video. Non-replaced content is everything else—content that is in the HTML file. Inline replaced and non-replaced content behave a little differently, so let's look at them one at a time.

Inline replaced content, such as an inline image, uses its intrinsic dimensions by default. It also uses the same box model as block-level content, with padding and margins affecting all sides of the element, as you can see in Figure 9-12.

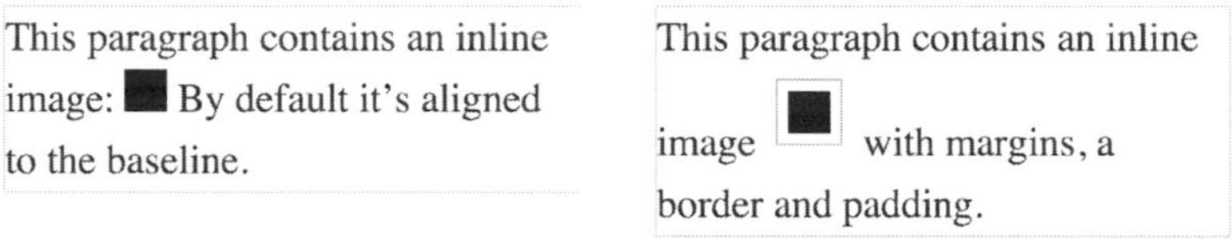

This paragraph contains an inline image: ■ By default it's aligned to the baseline.

This paragraph contains an inline image ■ with margins, a border and padding.

Figure 9-12. An example of inline replaced content. Padding, borders, and margins affect the space taken by this image in all directions.

Inline non-replaced content (which generally means text) gets its height from font-size and line-height. Unlike the inline image in Figure 9-12, padding and margins on inline non-replaced content are applied but only affect the element and surrounding content in the direction of text flow—in Figure 9-13 this is to the left and right. A negative left margin will move the element left, and a negative right margin will pull following content in, potentially overlapping the element.

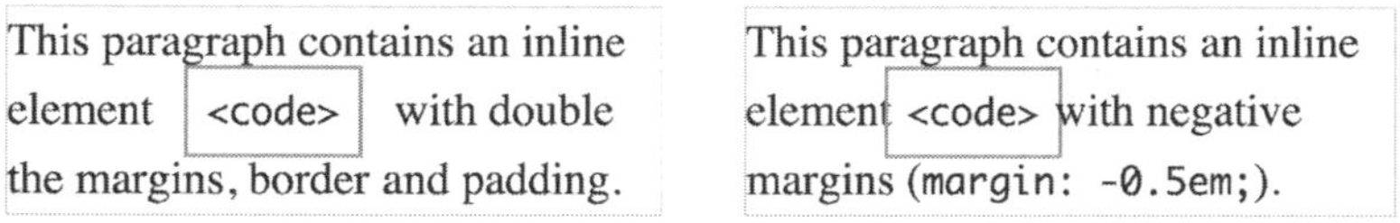

This paragraph contains an inline element `<code>` with double the margins, border and padding.

This paragraph contains an inline element `<code>` with negative margins (`margin: -0.5em;`).

Figure 9-13. Padding and margins on inline non-replaced content, including negative margins, only affect surrounding content in the direction of the text flow, in this case to the left and right.

Browsers display inline content (text and inline elements) one line at a time in *line boxes*. By default a line box is tall enough to contain the boxes of each inline element in the line. For replaced content (inline images) this comes from the content's dimensions plus vertical margins, borders and padding. This is why the image in the right example in Figure 9-12 increases the distance between lines. For non-replaced content (text) this is the content's line-height. Inline content is vertically aligned on the baseline by default, even if the font sizes are significantly different. This can be changed with the vertical-align property, which also affects the height of inline boxes. Figure 9-14 shows how adding line-height: 0; changes the inline boxes of large text and elements with a different vertical alignment, changing the height of the line box containing this content.

Image: large text and superscript text without and with line-height: 0;

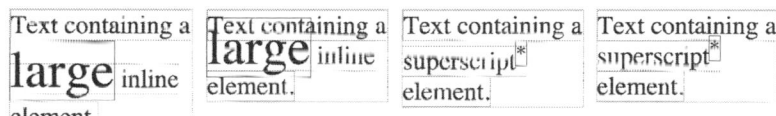

Figure 9-14. By default the line box will expand to include the inline boxes of its content. For non-replaced content you can prevent this using line-height: 0; on inline elements larger than the default line box.

> Refer to Eric Meyer's *Inline formatting model* article (published in 2000!) for exquisite detail on how inline boxes are laid out (*http://j.mp/inline-model meyerweb.com/eric/css/inline-format.html*).

Finally, if you're using images inline, vertical-align is something you'll want to experiment with (vertical-align: middle; is often what you're after). We cover the vertical-align property in more detail in Chapter 10.

Other values for display (notably inline-block and none)

While display: block; and display: inline; are the most common values, display also has a few others. The most useful of these is inline-block, which makes an element behave the same as inline replaced content, so it's "shrink-wrapped" to its content and treated as an inline box, but we can still use width, height, margin, and padding. However it behaves as a block-level container for any elements it contains, You can see a comparison between inline and inline-block in Figure 9-15.

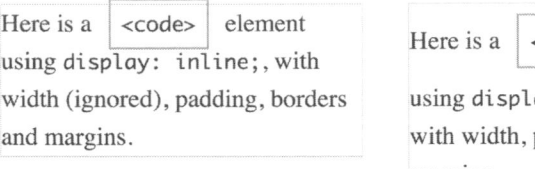

Figure 9-15. An element with width, padding, borders and margin as both display: inline; and display: inline-block;.For display: inline-block;, width (and height), and vertical padding and margin affect the element's box and surrounding elements, the same as for replaced inline content.

Note that IE 6-7 only accepts inline-block on elements that are display: inline; by default (http://j.mp/ppk-display www.quirksmode.org/css/display.html). You can trick them into faking it (http://j.mp/ie-inline-block www.mindfly.com/blog/2008/12/22/the-curious-case-of-inline-block/) by applying both display: inline; and zoom: 1; via styles targeted at IE6-7 only. Note that display: inline-block; can also be used for page layout, although with some caveats such as white space in your source code, and this is something we'll cover later in this chapter.

There's a large group of customized table-related ones, although you won't need to specify them for normal data tables as they're already in the browser's default stylesheet. However, you might use them if you use the CSS table model for layout on non-<table> elements, which we'll also cover later.

Then there's a few special-purpose ones that again you'll probably only see in a browser default stylesheet, such as list-item and ruby. Finally there's none, which prevents the element (and all children elements) from making a box at all.

Anonymous boxes

Block-level boxes can contain either block-level boxes or inline boxes. This might sound strange, as in the following code the <div> contains both text and a block-level element, and it's perfectly valid:

```
<!-- warning: this div contains inline and block-level content -->

<div>

  Some inline content

  <p>An <strong>important</strong> block-level paragraph</p>

</div>
```

In this situation, browsers add *anonymous boxes* (block-level or inline) to match the Visual Formatting Model's rules and make laying the content out easier. This also happens whenever an element's display property contradicts the visual formatting model. Figure 9-16 shows the boxes generated by elements on the left, and on the right is a representation of the anonymous boxes a browser would use.

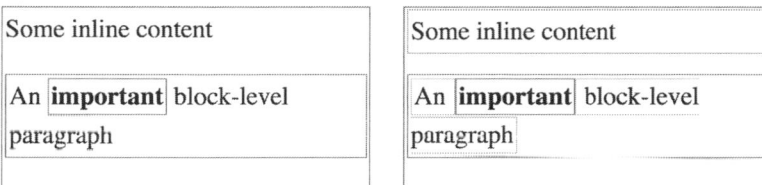

Figure 9-16. "Some inline content" would become a block-level anonymous box, because its sibling <p> is block-level. Inline content on either side of the <strong> element would become inline anonymous boxes.

It's important to note that you cannot style anonymous boxes *per se* using CSS—they get inheritable styles from their parent and take default values for everything else. However, it's good to know about anonymous boxes as sometimes this behavior can be the cause of unexpected rendering.

Not knowing the default display values for elements or their HTML5 content models can lead to unexpected rendering, so we recommend getting familiar with these so you know what can go where. It's knowledge you'll pick up over time, but when in doubt use a validator, and check with the specifications:

- *validator.nu (http://validator.nu/)*

- *HTML5 elements Index (http://j.mp/html5-elements-index www.whatwg.org/specs/web-apps/current-work/multipage/section-index.html#elements-1)*

- *HTML5 element content categories (http://j.mp/html5-element-categories www.whatwg.org/specs/web-apps/current-work/multipage/section-index.html#element-content-categories)*

- *CSS3 is a bit harder as it's modular, so try individual specifications or the CSS3 2010 properties index (http://j.mp/css-2010-properties dev.w3.org/csswg/css-2010/#properties)*

- *Finally, get to know your development browser's Inspector and work out how to check the computed value for display and other properties. This will tell you what the browser is actually using; if it's different from what you expect, something like this may be the cause.*

Positioning schemes and the position property

Earlier we learned that block-level boxes are as wide as their containing element and are added beneath the previous block-level element. This is called the *normal flow* (where boxes go by default) and is actually due to the default positioning scheme, position: static;. There are three other positioning schemes in CSS 2.1: relative, absolute, and fixed positioning. These three positioning schemes let you move an element from the scheme's default position using the properties top, right, bottom, and left, which take length values. If you set both top and bottom, or left and right, these will also set the element's height and width respectively,

- *Relative positioning*: A box with position: relative; takes the same space it would in normal flow (if it was position: static;). However you can move it *relative* to this position using top, right, bottom, and left. If the element is moved, the original space it took is preserved (content doesn't move up), and the moved element can overlap other content. position: relative; is also useful for establishing a *containing block* for an absolutely positioned element.

- *Absolute positioning*: An absolutely positioned element can also be moved (and sized) using top, right, bottom, and left. However, unlike a relatively positioned element, it "shrink-wraps" to the content's width if width isn't set, and it *doesn't* take any space in normal flow. An absolutely positioned element will initially appear in its static position, but if moved using top, right, bottom, or left it will be positioned relative to its containing block (which will be the nearest ancestor element that doesn't have position: static;), or the root element, <html>.

- *Fixed positioning*: This is a kind of absolute positioning. While an element with position: fixed; will also initially appear in its static position, top, right, bottom, or left will position it relative to the *viewport* (or each page for a print style sheet). Elements with position: fixed; do not move when the page is scrolled. Like absolutely positioned elements they can still overlap other content, and also "shrink-wrap" if no width is set.

You can compare these positioning schemes in Figure 9-17.

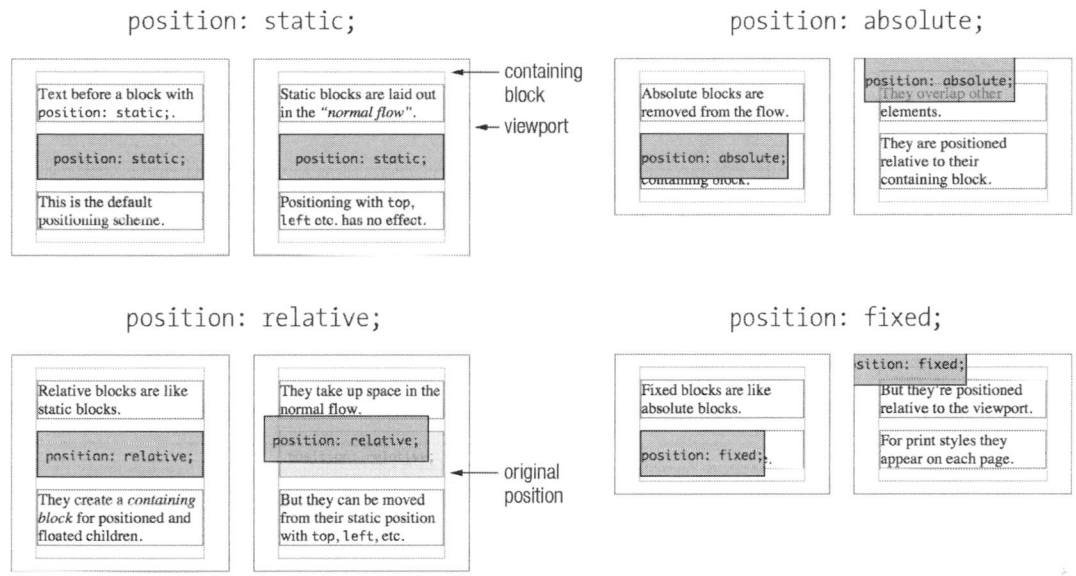

Figure 9-17. A comparison of the positioning property's four values. The positioned box in the right example in each pair also has the styles top: -1em, left. -1em;, and is slightly transparent to more easily see what't going on.

While positioning is a useful tool, positioned elements can easily overlap or hide content, making them unforgiving. Check that you've left space even when things like the font size and viewport width change.

Layers and the z-index property

When overlaps do occur, the default layering in CSS is that elements later in the HTML source will cover elements that are earlier. With the z-index property you can change this. It takes integer values, stacking elements in order from negative to positive, in addition to the default auto value. Positioned boxes (including position: relative;) with an integer value establish a *stacking context*, with children elements stacked based on their z-index value. Elements will need to have transparent or partially transparent backgrounds (such as opacity: 0.5;, HSLa or RGBa colors, or an image with opacity) to reveal elements they overlap.

Generally, overlapping or hidden content is not what you want, and you'll probably want to make space for a positioned element, for example by using a margin on another element, rather than using z-index. However, sometimes it's just the ticket. Finally, z-index integers are relative, so if you don't get the effect you want, using a huge z-index number won't help—look for the cause instead.

Introducing Floats

The float property was initially specified for allowing text to wrap around images. It takes the values left, right, none, and inherit. Applying float: left; to an image with the default width: auto; makes it a block-level box *with the dimensions of its content* ("shrink-wrapped"). Because of this, unless the content has an intrinsic width (like an image), you'll generally want to add a specific width too. float: left; moves the element left until it touches the edge of the containing box or another float, and float: right; does the same to the right. Floating an element also removes it from the document flow so it doesn't take up any space. This means subsequent block-level elements that aren't floated ignore the floated element and move up to fill the gap. However, inline elements and line boxes *do* still make space for the floated element. For example, see Figure 9-18.

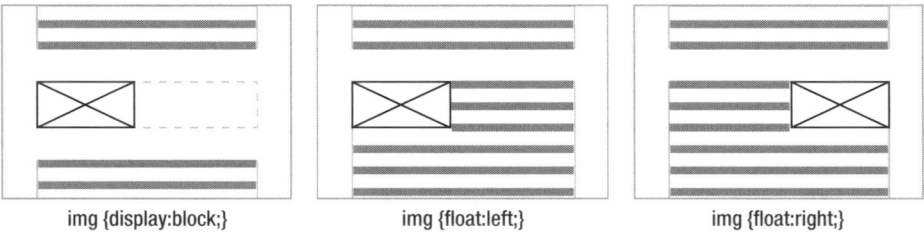

img {display:block;}   img {float:left;}   img {float:right;}

Figure 9-18. A block-level image followed by a paragraph. Applying float: left; or float: right; means the image no longer takes space in the normal flow (allowing the paragraph to move up), but the paragraph's line boxes *do* make space for the image.

If more than one consecutive element is floated, they will stack up beside each other as long as there's space. Elements with float: right; line up from right to left, as seen in the right image in Figure 9-19.

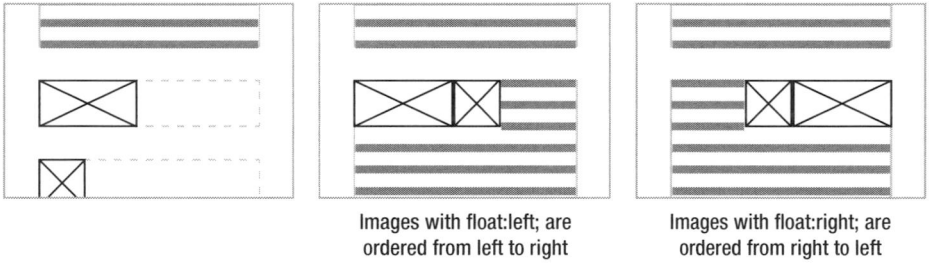

Images with float:left; are   Images with float:right; are
ordered from left to right   ordered from right to left

Figure 9-19. Floated elements will float beside each other if there's space. Elements with float:right; line up from right to left.

Once there isn't enough space, the float will "drop" beneath to the first available space. If the floats are of different heights (highly likely if text is involved) this may not be the space you hoped, as seen in Figure 9-20.

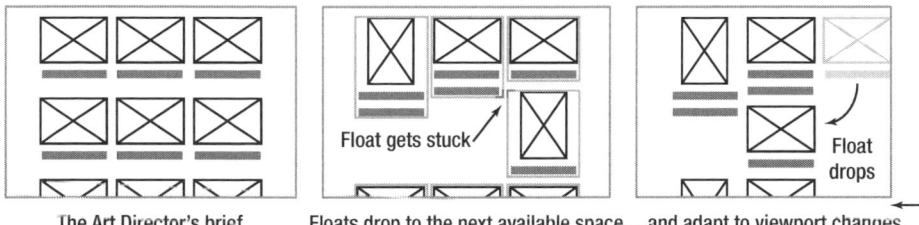

The Art Director's brief   Floats drop to the next available space ... and adapt to viewport changes

Figure 9-20. A dropped float will go to the first place with space. Unless every floated element is the same height, this won't be the place you want.

If your grid only contains images, you can control their size or use a wrapper element to make each image the same height to prevent this. While you *could* set a height in ems that's large enough to contain any content, if the objects in the Art Director's brief contain text it will probably be easier to use a different layout technique.

Clearing Floats

Because floated elements no longer take any space in normal flow, an element containing only a float will behave as if it has no content. This is no good if the float container is meant to provide a background to the float. Also, as a float that is taller than its container sticks out the bottom by default, it can interact with subsequent content. This is probably fine for text wrapping around an image, but not so good for the next section title. To control this you need to learn about *clearing floats*.

There are several ways to push an element below previous floated elements, or to make an element with a floated child expand to contain it. They each have their strengths and weaknesses, so let's look at them one at a time.

- *The* clear *property*: With the values left, right, or both, applying this property to an element prevents it appearing beside any previous elements with float: left;, float: right;, or either float value, respectively, moving it below the floated element instead. While you can add this to an element following one or more floats to "make space" for the floats, sometimes there isn't an element to add it to. Historically, people added <br style="clear:both;" /> after a floated element to make the float container expand to contain it, but there are better ways now.

- *The easy clearing method* (.clearfix): Originally developed by Tony Aslett, the clearfix method (http://j.mp/easy-clearing www.positioniseverything.net/easyclearing.html) gives the benefit of using clear: both; without adding an extra element, by using *generated content* with :after. While this is a popular technique, it actually has slightly different effects in IE<8, as Thierry Koblentz details in "Everything you Know about Clearfix is Wrong" (http://j.mp/clearfix-details www.tjkdesign.com/articles/clearfix_block-formatting-context_and_hasLayout.asp).

- *Floating the container*: A float automatically contains any floated elements inside it. Used alone, this has been termed the Floating Nearly Everything (FNE) method of clearing floats (http://j.mp/fne-method orderedlist.com/blog/articles/clearing-floats-the-fne-method/). In general, rather than floating things specifically for clearing with FNE, we recommend the following float clearing methods instead. However, knowing floats will contain floated children means you won't need to clear a float container that is itself floated.

- *The* overflow *property*: This controls what happens when a block-level element's content is too large for it, such as a long word or a <pre> block. By default, block-level elements will expand vertically, but if the element has a fixed height or width that's too small, it will show vertical or horizontal scrollbars to give access to the content. In general, anything apart from the browser's vertical page scroll bar should be avoided—people especially hate scrolling horizontally. Applying any value other than visible to an element will also "clear" floats beside or inside it. Adding overflow: auto; to a float-containing element is generally a good way to make it expand to contain a float, although you need to watch out for scroll bars for content that is wider or taller than the container. For images you can prevent this with max-width: 100%; height: auto; (CSS that we'll meet again when discussing Responsive Web Design), and for text you can use word-wrap, which we cover in Chapter 10. Note that overflow: hidden; can also be useful, although it should be used with great care. Finally, keep in mind that this does not work in IE6, where you'll need to use a different technique, such as the Micro Clearfix method or zoom: 1;.

- *The Micro Clearfix method:* Nicolas Gallagher extensively researched the problems with the traditional clearfix method and developed a new micro clearfix method (http://j.mp/micro-clearfix nicolasgallagher.com/micro-clearfix-hack/) that is both consistent across browsers and less code. When you need to clear floats and are not able to use overflow, we recommend using this.

```
/* For modern browsers */

.group:before,

.group:after {

    content: " ";

    display: table;

}

.group:after {

    clear: both;

}

/* For IE 6/7 (trigger hasLayout) */

.group {
```

```
*zoom: 1;
}
```

You can see the difference float clearing makes in Figure 9-21

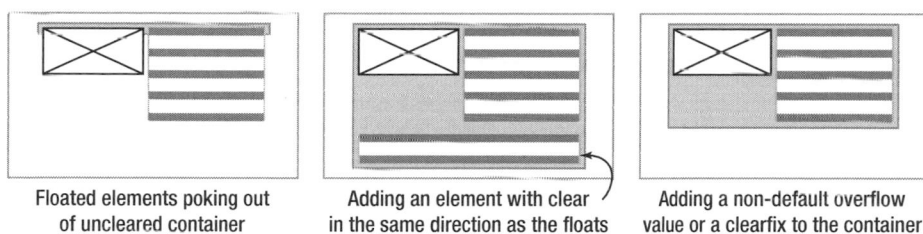

| Floated elements poking out of uncleared container | Adding an element with clear in the same direction as the floats | Adding a non-default overflow value or a clearfix to the container |

Figure 9-21. A non-floated container element won't expand to contain floated children. A later non-floated sibling element that's cleared, or applying a "clearfix" to the container (such as overflow: auto; or the Micro-clearfix), will expand the container to contain the floated children.

We find we generally use the micro clearfix and overflow methods, but only for elements that need it. However, the cross-browser problem with the easy clearing method gives us a good opportunity to examine *why* and mention one of the underpinnings of CSS layout along the way.

Block formatting context

You know that block-level boxes are laid out vertically, with their left edges touching the left edge of their containing block element (for left-to-right languages). But how does the browser know what the containing element is? An element that establishes a *block formatting context* becomes a containing element for its children. By default, this includes

- Floated elements

- Elements with any position value except static or relative (for example, absolute or fixed)

- Block containers that are not block-level boxes (display values of inline-block, table-cell, and table-caption)

- Block-level boxes with any value of overflow other than visible

Establishing a block formatting context can be very handy. For example, an unfloated element beside a float will make space for the float if it becomes a block formatting context, as demonstrated in Figure 9-22.

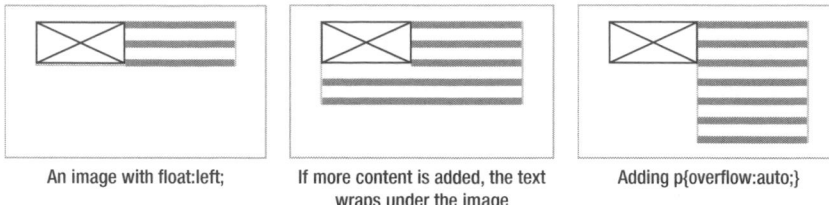

An image with float:left; If more content is added, the text wraps under the image Adding p{overflow:auto;}

Figure 9-22. Using overflow: auto; to establish a block formatting context on a paragraph

As you'll notice, this list includes several of the ways to clear floats we mentioned earlier—clearing floats is one of the properties of a block formatting context. In addition to clearing floats, keep in mind:

- A block formatting context acts as the container that absolutely positioned elements are positioned relative to.

- Margins don't stick out of a block formatting context.

- Only boxes in the same block formatting context experience vertical margin collapsing.

The block formatting context is an essential part of how browsers do layout, and taking the time to understand it gives you a lot more insight into how layout works. Here's some further reading on this advanced topic:

- "Overflow, a secret benefit" by Nicole Sullivan (http://j.mp/overflow-benefit www.stubbornella.org/content/2009/07/23/overflow-a-secret-benefit/)

- "CSS 101: Block Formatting Contexts" by Thierry Koblentz (http://j.mp/css-bfc www.yuiblog.com/blog/2010/05/19/css-101-block-formatting-contexts/)

> *Returning to the reason that the easy clearing method had slightly different results in IE 6-7, this is because these browsers don't support :after, and IE's proprietary zoom property was used to clear them instead. Note that zoom: 1; causes an element to be styled with IE's internal layout property, hasLayout: true;. Among other things, this causes the element to generate a new block formatting context and contain floats. However, the easy clearing, non-IE CSS rules don't do this, leading to potential display differences. The micro clearfix approach causes a new block formatting context in all browsers.*
>
> *As Internet Explorer 8 and higher support generated content and these versions do an increasingly good job of following the specs in general, knowing the peculiarities of hasLayout isn't as important as it used to be. However, it's still a good thing to know about when supporting IE6-7, so here's some background:*

"The Internet Explorer has Layout Property" by SitePoint (http://j.mp/ie-haslayout reference.sitepoint.com/css/haslayout)

"On having layout" by Holly Bergevin, Ingo Chao, Bruno Fassino, John Gallant, Georg Sørtun, and Philippe Wittenbergh (http://j.mp/having-layout www.satzansatz.de/cssd/onhavinglayout.html)

While we're on the topic of old IE quirks, if you encounter IE6's double margin bug (http://j.mp/doubled-margin www.positioniseverything.net/explorer/doubled-margin.html), you can fix it by applying display: inline; *for this browser. The computed style of floats is always* display: block; *so this doesn't have any negative consequences. Be aware that IE6 also expands floats if they contain content wider than the float's width, rather than letting the content stick out. You can use* overflow: hidden; *targeted at IE6 to prevent this leading to floats dropping if there's not as much space as expected.*

Floats for layout

Floated layouts just use the ability of floats to line up side-by-side with floated or unfloated content *without overlapping*, applying this to container elements for the parts of a layout. While they were not initially intended for layout, they have become the current layout workhorse, the best of CSS 2.1's not particularly good layout options.

So now that you know the basic floating and clearing floats, how do you actually use floats for laying out a web page? As content expands vertically, the common web design layout pattern is to have a full-width page header, followed by 1-3 columns for your content, and finally a full-width page footer appearing after the tallest column, as shown in Figure 9-23.

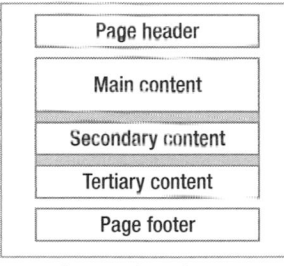
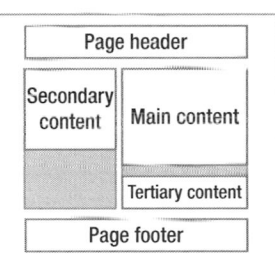
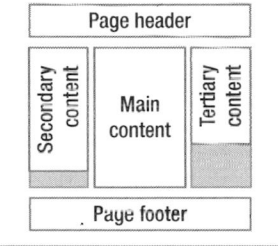

**A one-column layout
(also the default mobile layout)**   **A two-column layout**   **A three-column layout**

Figure 9-23. The common design pattern of header, footer and one to three columns of content in between. A one-column layout is the default for mobile phones in portrait mode. The gray background indicates the columns, but note that when using floats each float will only be as tall as its content.

A one-column layout is easy, as are a full-width header and footer—block-level elements are full-width by default. You can use floats to put block-level elements beside each other, such as two or more columns. However, you need to watch out for the total width of all the columns becoming larger than 100% of the containing element's width, as if there's not enough horizontal space the floats will adapt, meaning the last column will "drop" underneath. As mentioned earlier, mixing horizontal units (width in %, border in pixels, etc.) makes this likely unless you're using box-sizing: border-edge;. Our buggy friend IE 6 can increase element widths by a few pixels (in addition to not supporting box-sizing), so it's a good idea to have the columns' combined width be a little less than the containing element in order to prevent unexpected column dropping.

Let's have look at some options.

Two column layout methods

- *Float first column left into second column's large left margin*: Adding a left margin to one column gives you a place to float another column into.

- *Float first column right, second column has fixed width*: By narrowing one column you can create space on the right to float another column into.

- *Float both columns left*: While this works, any space left over appears to the right of the last float. If you have a visual right page edge, such as a border on the right float, its right edge won't be aligned with the container element.

- *Float first column left and second column right*: This makes sure the right column aligns with the right edge of the container element. Any space left over appears between the two columns—no margin required.

Layout methods for three or more columns

You can just use modified versions of the methods above to align more than two columns.

- *Central column unfloated with margins either side for floated columns*: By adding margins to both sides, you can create space for extra columns to float into.

- *Float columns left, except float the last column right*: Any space left over appears the left of the last column.

We recommend firing up your text browser (or using an online tool like Dabblet.com or CodePen.io), and recreating some of these layouts, assigning a different background color to each column element. By applying different CSS rules and seeing the results you'll start to get a feel for how to put together a simple layout using floats.

```
<style scoped>

  div {

    border: 1px solid #666;

    padding: 0.5em;

    background-color: #ddd;

}

.main {…}

.secondary {…}

.tertiary {…}

</style>

<div class="main">…</div>

<div class="secondary">…</div>

<div class="tertiary">…</div>
```

Remember to add some text to each div, or assign a width and height, so you can see them.

Faking full height column backgrounds

If you have background colors on your columns, you can see that the floated boxes only extend as far as their content. However, you'll probably want the column background color to extend to the footer, even for shorter columns. To get equal height columns, you can fake it using one of several techniques. Unfortunately, unless you're using pixel-based column widths (where Dan Cederholm's Faux Columns technique is perfect (http://j.mp/faux-columns www.alistapart.com/articles/fauxcolumns/)), there's no basic *and* widely supported method. However, Chris Coyier has compiled a list of the options on CSS Tricks to help you (http://j.mp/equal-height-cols css-tricks.com/fluid-width-equal-height-columns/), and by the time you've finished this book Nicholas Gallagher's clever pseudo-elements-based method should be no problem.

Changing column order with negative margins

In trying out some of these layout patterns, you will have noticed the HTML *source order* of the column elements dictates their placement. This is fine when that's the order you want, but sometimes it won't be. For example, it's ideal to have your content ordered by importance in your HTML (based on what the user would want to see first), so if your CSS doesn't load, the main content will be near the top. Ideally, you'll start with a simple, one-column, mobile-friendly layout (more on this when we cover Responsive Web Design later in the chapter) before adding the CSS for columns on wider displays towards the end of writing your CSS. If so, your content source ordering will probably already be by importance. Even if you're starting with a desktop layout, it's useful to think about this as a good source order helps when *linearizing* your design—removing floats on columns to make a one-column layout more suited to mobile devices.

While there's no property to change the order of sibling floats, when your columns use the same width units you can both keep your content in order of importance in the source, then rearrange your columns by using *negative margins*. For example, you can see the result of the following code in Figure 9-24.

```
<!-- note: using divs because we don't know the content -->

<div class="content">…</div>

<div class="nav">…</div>

<div class="sidebar">…</div>


div {

    float: left;

    /* box-sizing for easy testing */

    -webkit-box-sizing: border-box;

    -moz-box-sizing: border-box;

    box-sizing: border-box;

    border: 1px solid #666;

    padding: 0.5em;

    background-color: #ddd;

}

.content content {width: 50%;}

.nav secondary {width: 30%;}

.sidebar {width: 20%;}
```

```
/* nav - content - sidebar */

.content {margin-left: 30%;} /* space for nav */

.nav {margin-left: -80%;} /* 50% + 30% */


/* sidebar - content - nav */

.content {margin-left: 20%;} /* space for sidebar */

.sidebar {margin-left: -100%;} /* (50% + 20%) + 30% */


/* content - nav   sidebar */

/* This is easy as it's source order. Floating alone is enough! */


/* nav - sidebar - content

not necessarily a good layout, but to show how it's done */

.content {margin-left: 50%;} /* space for nav + sidebar */

.nav {margin-left: -100%;} /* (50% + 50%) */

.sidebar {margin-left: -70%;} /* 50% + 20% */
```

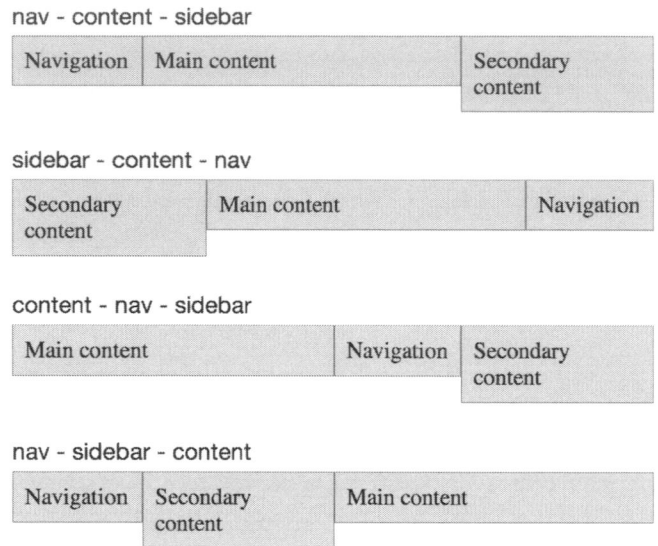

Figure 9-24. Rearranging floated elements using negative margins and math

To find out more about flexible layouts, we recommend Zoe Mickley Gillenwater's book *Flexible Web Design*. The following articles are also recommended:

- "In Search of the Holy Grail" by Matthew Levine (http://j.mp/ala-holy-grail www.alistapart.com/articles/holygrail)

- "Multi-Unit Any-Order Columns" by Eric Meyer (http://j.mp/meyerweb-columns meyerweb.com/eric/thoughts/2005/11/09/multi-unit-any-order-columns/)

The effects of different units for layouts

The three well-supported length units (pixels, percentages, and ems) have different properties when used for layout dimensions. Of course, you can use these layout techniques for parts of a page as well as page layouts. You can also mix various layouts techniques together as needed. Let's briefly look at each one in turn.

Pixel layouts

There's a long and glorious tradition of treating web design the same as print design, based on using inflexible pixel-based layouts. A pixel-based layout just uses pixel dimensions on container elements, such as <body> or <div class="wrapper">. Figure 9-25 shows an example of a pixel-based page layout.

> *Remember that setting a fixed height on anything containing text (or content sized using ems) is generally asking for trouble*

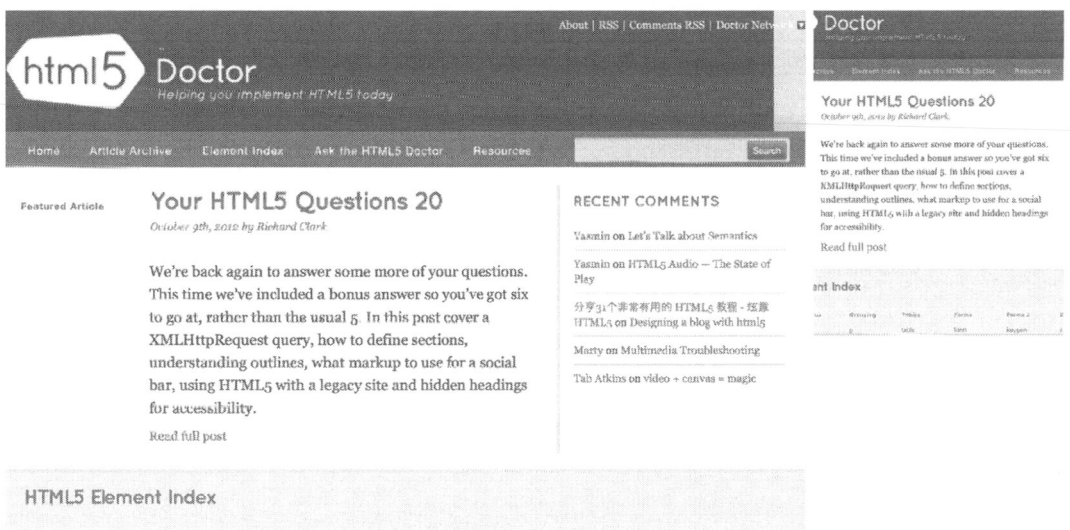

Homepage in a 1024px wide viewport   In a 320px mobile device

Figure 9-25. Pixel-based layouts work well at their intended viewport width, but without extra work will become far less usable at smaller sizes. Here we've zoomed in on the main content in the right image, so parts of the navigation are no longer visible. In a narrow viewport this would lead to horizontal scrolling. (http://html5doctor.com/)

Using pixel dimensions for layout can make sense when your content is mainly a fixed width, especially replaced content such as images or videos. It can also be useful in situations where every pixel is vital, such as a mobile site or a dense web application's interface. Another time to consider a pixel-based layout is when your design is dependent on the relation of text with background images (although we would caution against this kind of design), or when you need to incorporate large fixed-width banner advertising.

> *Aside: The viewport is the window through which the user sees the web page. If the web page is larger than the viewport, by default scroll bars appear.*

Pixel-based layouts do not adapt to changes in font size or viewport size. While this has been perceived as one of the strengths of pixel layouts, in truth this inflexibility makes them suitable only under ideal circumstances. Also, the window of usefulness on pixel-based layouts for mobile phones is limited, as mobile devices with screen sizes other than 320x480px explode. Because of this we find we don't use pixel-based layouts, except when testing or prototyping.

So what about content with a fixed width, such as images? Well, image width being *fixed* is all in your mind, as you'll soon see.

Flexible layouts

Flexible layouts are based on units that adapt the layout to the browser environment. While they can require a little more forethought (especially if you are used to pixel-based designs), they reward by being more bulletproof, or less likely to break under pressure.

Be like water with liquid layouts

Liquid layouts (also called *fluid layouts*) define horizontal measurements using percentages, adapting to the browser's width and helping prevent the dreaded horizontal scroll. The default style for block-level elements is equivalent to a full width, single column liquid layout. The main disadvantage of percentages is that without a little care it's easy to make unreasonably long line lengths on large displays, which hurt readability. Because of this, liquid layouts generally should be used with min-width and max-width values in ems or pixels. Figure 9-26 shows an example of a liquid page layout.

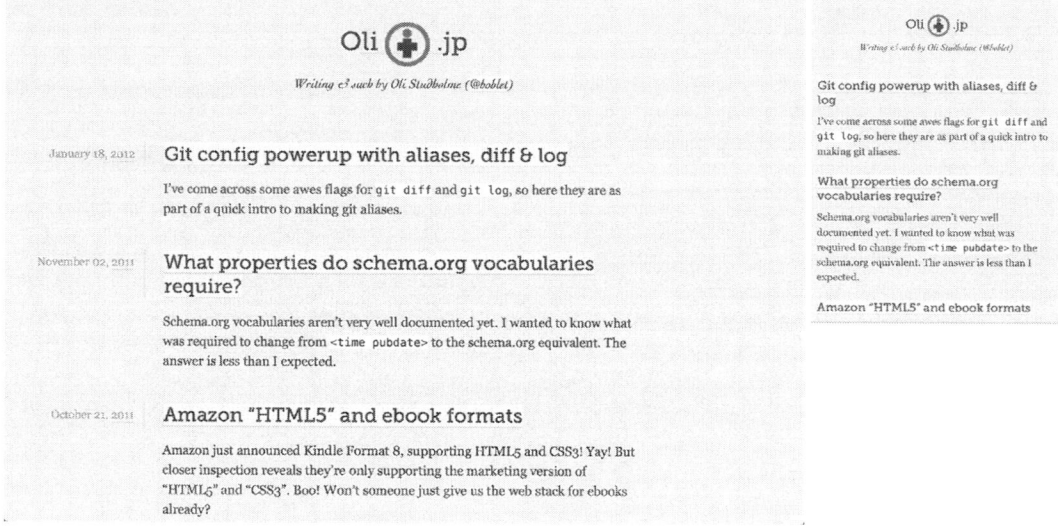

Longer line lengths in a wide viewport   Shorter line lengths

Figure 9-26. A liquid layout, where the width of elements changes to fit the space available. It uses max-width to prevent line lengths becoming unreadably long in wide viewports. (http://oli.jp/)

However, they work best with content that is also flexible. Wide or fixed-width content (such as images, tables, and blocks of code) require special care. One way to address this for replaced content like images is to use the max-width property.

```
<style>

img {

  max-width: 100%;

  height: auto; /* so images with a height attribute don't scale in one dimension */

}

</style>

<img src="img/earth.jpg" width="695" height="695" alt="The blue marble of earth, as seen from space">
```

By default the image will be the size of the width and height attributes (or the image's intrinsic width and height if these are not set), letting the browser assign space and preventing a reflow in desktop browsers. However, if the image's containing block becomes narrower than the image's width, the max-width and height properties will scale it. This prevents intrinsic image widths breaking a layout, and browsers generally do a reasonable job of scaling down images, too. Figure 9-27 shows the result.

Figure 9-27. A flexible image (with a max-width in relative uints) that is too large will be scaled by the browser. The image on the left has max-width: 100%;, and will be scaled when wider than the containing element or viewport. As seen on the right, a default image (using intrinsic dimensions) will not be scaled, and by default will trigger horizontal scroll bars.

When creating a liquid layout, you can get your width values in several ways. In addition to just using values based on a grid, or ones that seem appropriate (like 50%, 33%, 66% etc.), you can also create a pixel-based grid for a target screen width (perhaps based on a mockup), then convert using the formula of size ÷ context = result, treating the result to a percentage. For example, a 360 px wide column for a 960 px wide design would give 360 ÷ 960 = .375, which is 37.5%. Incidentally, this "desired size ÷ context = result" formula is also used to calculate typography in ems in Chapter 10. If doing this we recommend "showing your math" in a comment beside the value, for example:

```
.content {

  width: 37.7083333%; /* 362px/960px */

  …

}
```

While this might seem like a lot more work than just using pixels, the percentage-based layout will adapt gracefully to larger and smaller viewport sizes, a huge benefit. You will need some extra techniques to optimize your liquid layouts for very narrow and very wide screens, as it can only adapt so far. This is something we'll cover with media queries later in this chapter.

Liquid layout browser support issues

While we generally love liquid layouts, there's an important caveat to keep in mind. As with all length values specified in something other than pixels, the browser must convert percentage values to pixels for display. As John Resig documents in "Sub-Pixel Problems in CSS," (http://j.mp/css-sub-pixel ejohn.org/blog/sub-pixel-problems-in-css/) browsers have slightly different methods of doing this (see Table 9-2), which can result in small differences between browsers.

Table 9-2. Browser Sub-Pixel Rounding Methods

Rounding style	Browser
Round values down	WebKit (Safari, Chrome), Opera
Round values up	Internet Explorer 6 & 7
Round values up and down	Firefox, IE 8+

This can lead to issues such as an element being a few pixels too narrow when rounding down, occasional 1 px gaps between elements when rounding both up and down, and causing floated elements to drop below other content when rounding up. The first two are generally minor problems, but Internet Explorer's rounding up can break a layout based on floats. One way to avoid this is to make sure your width values total slightly less than 100%, giving a little wiggle room. Browsers are moving to using sub-pixel positioning (Firefox, IE 10, WebKit as of mid-2012…), so will more often do what you expect in the future.

Finally, there are some Internet Explorer issues to address. As mentioned, IE6 doesn't support min-width, max-width, min-height, or max-height. For content images, you can generally maintain fluidity by replacing max-width: 100%; with width: 100%; via styles targeted specifically at IE6. Note that max-width: 100%;

only affects images that would otherwise be wider than the containing block. Using width: 100%;, however, means the image will *always* be the width of the containing block. This is completely different and can lead to problems, so test thoroughly. There are also JavaScript-based polyfills such as Dean Edwards' IE7.js (http://j.mp/ie7-js code.google.com/p/ie7-js/) if absolutely necessary.

The other issue is that, unlike modern browsers, IE6 scales images very poorly. If this is a concern, you can address it with the CSS -ms-interpolation-mode: bicubic; or by using Microsoft's proprietary CSS filter AlphaImageLoader. For the details on the AlphaImageLoader technique and a handy script to automate the process, read Ethan Marcotte's "Fluid Images" (http://j.mp/fluid-images www.alistapart.com/articles/fluid-images/). This is a portion of Chapter 3 in his book *Responsive Web Design*, which we highly recommend reading.

Typographic focus with elastic layouts

An elastic layout uses ems for horizontal measurements, which is based on the browser's font size. By default 1em = 16px. This means if the user increases or decreases the font size, an em-based layout will adapt proportionally, maintaining line lengths. Figure 9-28 shows an example of an elastic page layout.

  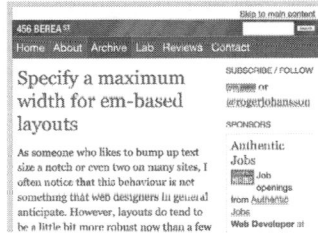

| Em based layout | Large font size with max-width disabled (horizontal scroll) | With max-width:100%; |

Figure 9-28. 456 Berea St. (http://www.456bereastreet.com/), the website of Roger Johansson, sporting an em-based layout. By turning off Roger's max-width declaration we can see horizontal scrolling in the second image, where the browser's font settings have been increased.

Historically, increasing or decreasing the size in browsers only changed the text size and didn't affect other content or the page's layout. By setting horizontal measurements in ems, you could make text size changes also scale the page layout, and even content like images (if they were sized in ems). Recent versions of all browsers now *zoom* the page by default, reducing the benefits of em-based layouts, but this is good to keep in mind for backwards compatibility.

Also, if the user sets a very large text size, this can seriously affect the layout, with horizontal scrollbars as the content becomes too wide for the viewport. As with liquid layouts, you should choose a range of text sizes to support, and use a max-width in a different unit (such as percentages or pixels) to prevent horizontal scrolling beyond this. While not commonplace, this is still a great technique to have in your toolbox, as you can combine layout techniques in a hybrid layout.

As flexible as you want with hybrid layouts

Hybrid layouts combine more than one layout method to create a layout. Generally, this is used to combine fixed-width content (a width declared in pixels) with fluid content. This can be a great choice when you have content which has a set width—such as advertising—in the sidebar, combined with a fluid main content column. Figure 9-29 shows a website using floats, elements with widths in ems, max-widths in pixels, plus some absolute positioning and use of display: inline-block; too.

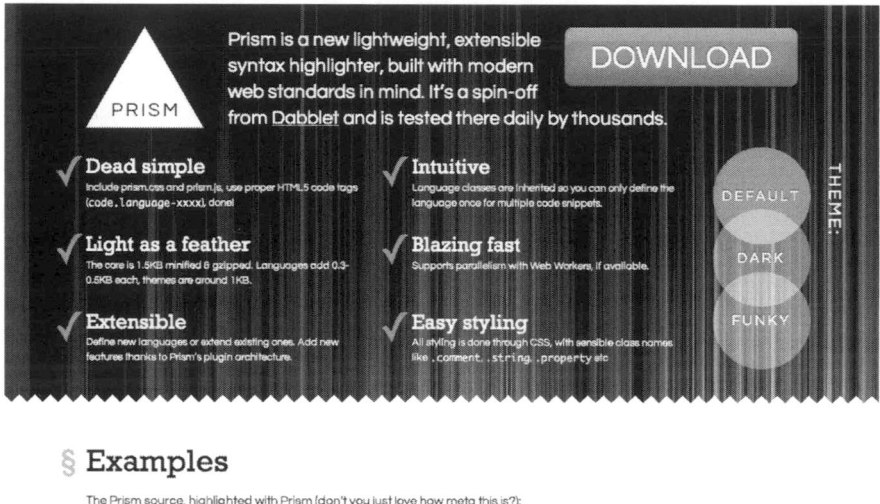

Figure 9-29. The website for Prism (http://prismjs.com/), a syntax highlighter by Lea Verou, is an example of a hybrid page layout, combining various layout methods.

One of the benefits of hybrid layouts is that you can mix your layout techniques to take advantage of the strengths of each. For example, you could set the width of a page in ems then the widths of columns in percentages to make an elastic design more bulletproof. However, recently we've found ourselves tending to just use page layouts with all columns in percentages plus min-width and max-width values in ems or pixels, instead of hybrid layouts with a pixel-based column.

To summarize, if you're beginning with CSS layouts, our best advice is to make some trial pages, view them using the browser's developer tools, and experiment. Try editing the CSS rules applied and see how this changes the element's position, computed layout styles, and interaction with other elements. After that, try seeing how different browsers display the same page, and you'll be well on the way to familiarity with both layout using CSS, browser differences, and browser-based tools.

Other CSS 2.1 layout methods

CSS layouts generally revolve around a full width page header and footer, with one or more columns in between. The most basic things you need for this are the following:

- Positioning columns beside each other

- The ability to set the columns' widths

It's also good if containing elements shrink-wrap their content so you don't need to explicitly set a width and/or height, and that columns adapt to their surroundings (in other words, they don't cover each other). While we've covered floats in detail, there are two other CSS 2.1-based methods that fulfill these requirements and that you can use for layout. Unfortunately both of them are ... challenging for Internet Explorer 6-7. Let's take a quick look.

Using display: inline-block; for layout

Elements with display: inline-block; line up beside each other, and also shrink-wrap their content. Even better, you can use properties like text-align: justify; to equally space children, text-align: center; to easily center elements, and vertical-align: top; to make a grid of boxes that will line up in rows. You can also use the negative margin technique, possibly combined with padding on a container element, to rearrange columns, just as you did with floats. Figure 9-30 shows the layouts of Figure 9-24 redone using display: inline-block;.

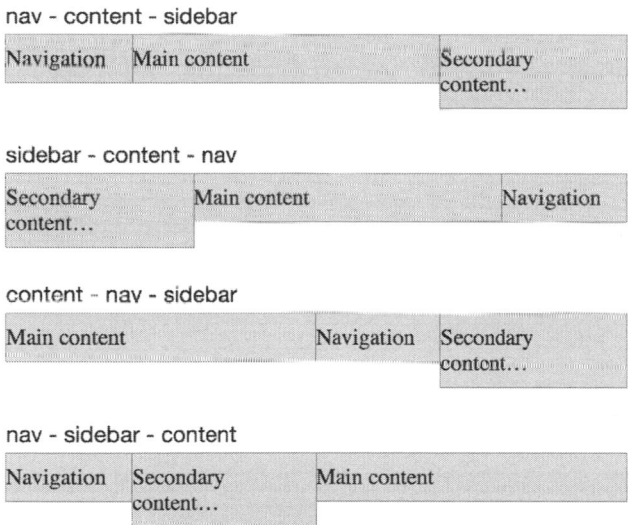

Figure 9-30. Using negative margins to reorder display: inline-block; columns. Compare this with Figure 9-24.

This seems great, but there are two browser support issues to solve. IE6 and 7 don't support inline-block, although as mentioned earlier, you can trick them into behaving by applying both display: inline; and zoom: 1;, using styles targeted at IE6-7 only.

The second problem is potentially more difficult—elements using inline-block naturally have a small space between them due to the way CSS collapses inter-element whitespace in HTML (the spaces, tabs, and line-breaks in your HTML code). This is about 4 px, but varies based on the container element's font and font-size, and the browser. As long as your design doesn't depend on aligning things precisely, or knowing the exact width taken by a row of inline-block elements, this isn't a problem. If your design *does* depend on this, such as navigation tabs that should touch, there are several ways to work around this. Unfortunately, none of them are ideal.

The easiest way is to remove whitespace between the elements in your HTML. You can do this by any of the following means:

- Putting everything on one line (possibly just by automatically minifying your HTML, which you might be doing anyway to improve performance).

- Putting the closing tag beside the next inline-block element's opening tag, with no space between.

- If you're using this technique for navigation, etc. where your inline-block elements are <li> elements, you can leave off the closing tag, as these elements are self-closing in HTML5. This won't work for elements such as <div>, <section>, etc. While we prefer explicit closing tags, this is perfectly valid HTML5.

- You could even wrap the line-break in an HTML comment.

See the following code samples for examples:

```
<!-- adjacent inline-block closing and opening tags together -->

<nav class="page-nav">

  …

</nav><article class="content">

  …

</article><aside class="sidebar">

  …

</aside>
```

```
<!-- no closing </li> tags  -->
<ul>

  <li>Home

  <li>Our Work

  <li>Articles

  <li>About Us

  <li>Contact

</ul>


<!-- wrapping line breaks in HTML comments -->
<nav class="page-nav">

   …

</nav><!--

--><article class="content">

   …

</article><!--

--><aside class="sidebar">

   …

</aside>
```

Other ways to address this are more fragile. You can try one of the following:

- Set font-size: 0; on the container element, then reset the font-size on the column elements. This stops font sizes inheriting, although you could reset it using rem in modern browsers or even use font-size: 1%; on the container element and font-size: 10000%; on the children.

- Use a right margin of about -0.3em. This can fail in IE6-7, and you'll need to adjust for the font you're using and test thoroughly. You could also set the font-family to Courier New, which should be exactly margin-right: -0.6em, although you'll then also have to reset the font-family on the column elements' children.

There's a way proposed in CSS4 to solve this using text-space-collapse: discard;, but, well, it's CSS4 and has zero support at the time of writing. None of these options are particularly good, but as long as your design doesn't depend on adjacent elements touching or knowing the exact width, this isn't a problem. This is demonstrated in the HTML5 Boilerplate website (http://html5boilerplate.com/) in Figure 9-31, which uses inline-block for laying out the navigation, buttons and content columns.

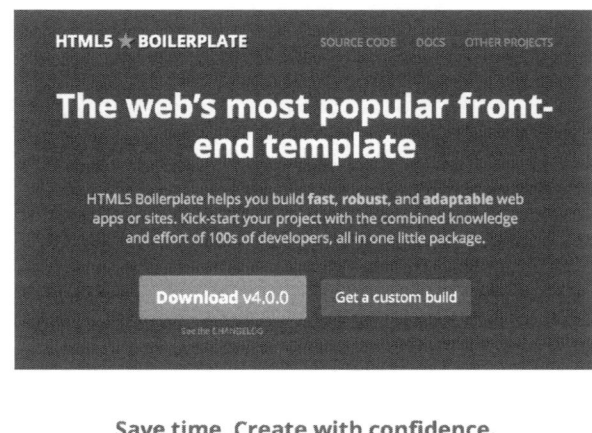

Figure 9-31. The HTML5 Boilerplate website using display: inline-block; extensively for layout.

If your design *does* depend on exact sizing, consider one of the "removing HTML whitespace" workarounds, or perhaps a different layout method.

Using display: table; for layout

After the web standards movement has spent the last 10 years fighting to stop the use of nested <table> elements for layout, it might seem strange to suggest tables for layout. However, the table-related display values are CSS-based presentation and are not an abuse of the semantics of the <table> element when applied to elements like <div> or <section>. By specifying display: table-cell; on the column elements, the columns will line up beside each other, and allow you to specify a width. Applying width values to both container and columns gives you a layout.

This also gives you the same benefits that made <table>-based layout so appealing. For example, border-collapse and border-spacing give you control over borders and spacing between cells, and cells on the same row will be the height of the tallest cell, so you don't need faux columns. You don't even need to assign display: table; or display: table-row; to container elements—for a single row the browser will add these as anonymous boxes to accommodate elements with display: table-cell;. You can also do fun things with some of the other table-related display values. For example, you can use display: table-caption; together with caption-side to rearrange the order of elements, as Jeremy Keith covers in "Re-tabulate" (http://j.mp/re-tabulate adactio.com/journal/4780/).

The bad news is that IE 6-7 don't support display: table; and there's no workaround other than creating a separate fallback layout for these browsers. There's also no CSS equivalent to the HTML attributes colspan and rowspan, and duplicating them generally requires complex nested elements with display: table; or display: table-row;. Keep in mind that table cells expand to contain their content, and with replaced content like images this can break a display: table;-based layout. You can add table-layout: fixed; to the element with display: table; to force cell widths to be respected. Finally, table layout comes with all the source order dependence that made table-based layout so fragile. At the time of writing, we think these are significant problems for anything other than progressive enhancement-style improvements.

Comparing inline-block and table layouts

The main differences between using display: inline-block; and display: table; are the following:

- If there's not enough width to contain all the columns, inline-block elements without a width will drop down to the next line (like floats), content in inline-block elements *with* a width will stick out, and display: table will trigger horizontal scrolling.

- The other properties you can use with each vary, such as text-align: center; for display: inline-block,, and border-collapse and border-spacing for display: table;, giving each technique a different set of strengths and weaknesses.

- The complete lack of IE 6-7 support for display: table;, requiring an alternative layout.

While display: inline-block; and display: table; are both potentially useful layout options, they both have potentially significant drawbacks. However, we think they're worth experimenting with and keeping in mind, as occasionally they'll be just what you're after.

In summary, these frankly inadequate CSS 2.1-based layout tools, plus spotty support in older browsers, have made complex layout a glaring pain point in CSS. Luckily for us, layout in CSS is finally getting some love and attention from both the World Wide Web Consortium (W3C) and from browser makers. However, before we have a look at what's coming, let's cover some related things that are usable (and essential) now: media queries, responsive web design, and techniques for dealing with high resolution displays.

Media queries and Responsive Web Design

We touched on responsive web design earlier while describing liquid or fluid layouts—layouts that use percentages for horizontal widths. In "On Being "Responsive" (http://j.mp/being-responsive

355

unstoppablerobotninja.com/entry/on-being-responsive/), Ethan Marcotte—who started that whole "responsive web design" thing—defines its three main requirements as:

- A flexible grid

- Flexible images (or images that work in a flexible grid)

- Using media queries to adjust these across different devices

Fundamentally, this is the elegant, modern successor of the ideas in John Allsopp's "The Dao of Web Design" article, a "letting go of control and becoming flexible." By designing with the fundamental philosophy of flexibility or adaptability, then using media queries to further adapt the design based on the device's properties, you *can* make a design that responds gracefully on a variety of devices. We've already covered flexible grids (percentage and em-based layouts) and images (max-width: 100%; height: auto;), so let's see how media queries can help us.

Introducing media queries

Media queries (http://j.mp/css3-mq dev.w3.org/csswg/css3-mediaqueries/) began as a way to provide different CSS depending on the media, such as a print stylesheet:

```
<link rel="stylesheet" media="screen" href="screen.css">
```

```
<link rel="stylesheet" media="print" href="print.css">
```

They also allow you to test against *media features* such as browser width, screen width, device resolution etc. This allows you to customize your CSS based on these features, for example:

```
@media screen and (min-width: 24em) {

  body {CSS for everything except small devices…}

  …

}

@media screen and (min-width: 42em) {

  body {CSS for tablets and larger screens…}

  …

}
```

In addition to including as an attribute on a stylesheet <link> element and as an @media block inside a stylesheet, you can also use media queries on an @import rule (in the same way as @media). However, for performance reasons we recommend against using @import because stylesheets included this way will only begin downloading after the first stylesheet is downloaded.

Media queries syntax

At the time of writing, media types include all (the default), braille, embossed, handheld, print, projection, screen, speech, tty, and tv. However, in most cases you'll only need all, screen, and print.

The list of media features is longer and is added to the media query in parentheses:

- width : The width of the browser's viewport, and the most commonly used query

- height: The height of the browser's viewport

- device-width: The width of the device's screen

- device-height: The height of the device's screen

- resolution: The density of pixels in the output device

- orientation: Either portrait or landscape

- aspect-ratio: The ratio of width to height (e.g. 16/9 for a widescreen TV aspect)

- device-aspect-ratio: The ratio of device-width to device-height

- color: The number of bits per color component of the output device

- color-index: The number of entries in the color lookup table of the output device

- monochrome: The number of bits per pixel in a monochrome frame buffer

- scan: The scanning process of TV output devices

- grid: To query whether the output device is grid or bitmap

Most of these also come in min- and max- variants, but the ones you'll generally use are the following:

- min-width or max-width

- min-height or max-height

- min-resolution (together with -wekbit-min-device-pixel-ratio)

The resolution properties are used to target devices with different pixel densities (for example Apple Retina displays) with custom CSS, and take values in dpi (dots per CSS inch), and the recently added dppx (dots per CSS pixel). However, WebKit implemented the related proprietary device-pixel-ratio property, which takes a number value. You've most likely seen this as -wekbit-min-device-pixel-ratio, with a normal display being 1, and a Retina display (with double the resolution) being 2. Other browsers also implemented this as -moz-min-device-pixel-ratio and -o-min-device-pixel-ratio (note the Opera variant takes a fractional value). However, these browsers also implemented resolution, and you can convert from device-pixel-ratio to dpi by multiplying by 96. This means at present to target double density displays (4 device pixels per CSS pixel), you'd use

- *@media screen and (-webkit-min-device-pixel-ratio:2), screen and (min-resolution: 192dpi) {...}*

- *In the future when dppx support becomes widespread, you will be able to use*

- *@media screen and (-webkit-min-device-pixel-ratio:2), screen and (min-resolution: 2dppx) {...}*

As you've just seen, you can combine media query selectors using the basic logical operators "and", or (as a comma), and "not." Here are some examples:

- screen and (min-width: 534px): Applies the following styles to all screen-based devices (e.g. not print) with a display that's 534 px or wider.

- screen and (max-width: 960px), screen and (max-height: 960px): Applies styles to a device with a width that's up to 960 px in either dimension.

- screen and (min-width: 20em) and (max-width: 32em): Applies the following styles to all devices with a display that's between 20em and 32em wide, based on the root font-size.

- screen and (max-width: 480px) and (-webkit-min-device-pixel-ratio: 2), screen and (max-width: 480px) and (min-resolution: 192dpi: Applies styles to a device that's up to 480 px wide with a double resolution display, such as a Retina display iPhone (either orientation).

Desktop-first, mobile-first, and content-first design

Websites built before the rise of mobile devices were built to a specific screen width. While this wasn't thought of as building a "desktop-first" site, in hindsight it's easy to see the bias. While it's still possible to design for a desktop browser first, then overwrite some of these styles in media queries for mobile phones, we find the workflow is easier (and the CSS is simpler) by initially designing for mobile browsers, then adding media queries with extra styles for larger screens. Another benefit is a mobile layout will at least be usable on any browser that doesn't support media queries, but a wide layout might not be on a small phone. Luke Wrobluski details the benefits of this approach in his presentation "Mobile First" (http://j.mp/mobile-first-preso www.lukew.com/presos/preso.asp?26).

However, philosophically we find *content-first design*, elucidated by Jeremy Keith in "Content First" (http://j.mp/content-first adactio.com/journal/4523/), is an even better fit. Before you begin thinking about a layout, you should be thinking about what content is appropriate and what the person viewing the page will want to achieve. Doing this prevents a common problem with the "desktop-first" approach: adding unnecessary content just because there's space. Starting with the content and functionality as the focus will help you with the site's (or app's) architecture, and make progressing into mobile then desktop designs easier. This also means you should have much of your content before beginning the design, and while this can be tricky with some clients, we find that when it's possible it makes a big difference to the final result by keeping your design grounded in reality.

While you can choose the widths to target with media queries by consulting browser screen size charts, we recommend taking a content-first approach here, too. Instead, stretch the content to see where it breaks (perhaps using Remy Sharp's useful Responsive px tool (http://responsivepx.com/), then set breakpoints based on this. There's also nothing requiring you to use pixels for your media query length units—checking for min-width etc. in ems also works well.

Finally, keep in mind you can make media queries *inclusive* by setting only one min- or max- feature per query, or *exclusive* by setting both. For example,

```
@media all and (min-width: 534px) {…}
```

```
@media all and (min-width: 961px) {…}
```

is very different from

```
@media all and (min-width: 534px) and (max-width: 960px) {…}
```

```
@media all and (min-width: 961px) {…}
```

This will affect what styles are applied and what styles may need overriding. This is one of the decisions you'll need to make at the start of each project. For more on your various media query-related choices and their consequences, we recommend reading Zoe Mickley Gillenwater's detailed article "Essential Considerations for Crafting Quality Media Queries" (http://j.mp/quality-mq zomigi.com/blog/essential-considerations-for-crafting-quality-media-queries/).

Browser support for media queries

There are several ways you can implement media queries. You could put all your CSS in a single stylesheet, using @media media query rules as appropriate. At the other extreme, you could split your CSS over several stylesheets, one per media query, and add them via <link>. Both of these techniques have pros and cons. For example, a single file is good because one 20KB download is faster than two 10KB downloads due to the overhead of beginning the download. Using <link> with per-query stylesheets is also good because older browsers that don't understand media queries will ignore those <link> elements, saving them from downloading unnecessary styles.

Unfortunately, there are bigger problems than this. As with many low-end phones, Internet Explorer version 8 and below support basic media queries (like screen and print), but *not* queries containing media features. Ouch. This means if you start with basic mobile styles and then use media queries to supplement and override these for desktop browsers, IE 6-8 will only apply the mobile styles. There are several ways to address this issue.

- *Do nothing*: If your layout is flexible, you could just let IE 6-8 get the default design. If this is the desktop layout, you're fine. However, if it's the mobile one, this is probably not an option, because while the content will still be usable, line lengths will become unreadable.

- *Minor IE-specific tweaks*: You could add specific styles targeted to IE8 and below, perhaps just supplementing basic mobile styles with a fixed width on <body> or wrapper elements (if the site is built with mobile styles as the default). Depending on how much you supplement, this can lead to "forking" your code and essentially maintaining two designs—something to avoid if possible.

- *Polyfilling with JavaScript*: There are a couple of options here, including Scott Jehl's excellent lightweight respond.js (http://j.mp/respond-js https://github.com/scottjehl/Respond) polyfill. However, this means if the script doesn't load or JavaScript is turned off, you're back to a "do nothing" approach.

- *Splitting your styles into multiple files for IE*: The most bulletproof approach is to make separate stylesheets for the classes of device you're going to support: perhaps base mobile styles for everything, intermediate styles, and desktop styles. Include the base styles for all browsers, then include other styles via media queries. Finally, include desktop styles without an advanced media query in an IE conditional comment. Jeremy Keith's article "Windows mobile media queries" (http://j.mp/windows-mq adactio.com/journal/4494/) details how, but here's the code:

```
<!-- assuming a mobile-first design: -->

<link href="/css/base.css" media="all"> <!-- mobile styles for everyone -->

<link href="/css/wide.css" media="all and (min-width: 30em)">

<!--[if (lt IE 9)&(!IEMobile 7)]>

  <link rel="stylesheet" href="wide.css" media="all">

<![endif]-->
```

The funky conditional comment here loads the wide.css stylesheet for versions of Internet Explorer less that IE9, but *not* for Internet Explorer Mobile 7, which can't parse feature-based media queries, but should get the mobile styles. If you're using a CSS pre-processor or similar, it should be no problem to arrange your CSS how you like—you could even create two versions of wide.css, one with customizations for intermediate devices in an @media block for modern browsers, and the other without this for older Internet Explorer. This is an issue you can avoid with a "desktop-first" approach, but if you do, you'll have the far harder challenge of dealing with mobile issues.

Viewport on mobile phones

Speaking of which, one way many smartphones deal with desktop-centric designs on a tiny screen is to pretend to be 960 px wide. You then zoom in and out to read and move the page in the viewport to navigate. However, you can tell mobile devices to use their actual CSS pixel width by adding this meta tag to the document's <head>:

```
<meta name="viewport" content="width=device-width, initial-scale=1.0">
```

Yes, width=device-width and initial-scale=1.0 are what you'd imagine: set the viewport's width to the device's width (in CSS pixels) and don't scale the display. There are other comma-separated values you can add to content, such as minimum-scale, maximum-scale, and user-scalable. Note that minimum-scale=1.0 may be useful, but applying maximum-scale=1.0 or user-scalable=no is generally user-hostile, and we recommend against it. Setting these things in CSS is also potentially coming via the CSS Device Adaptation specification's @viewport rule (http://j.mp/css-device-adapt   dev.w3.org/csswg/css-device-adapt/#the-viewport-rule), although at the time of writing this is only supported by Opera.

The trouble with images

You've seen how to make fluid images and how to use media queries to apply styles based on device resolution, but those pixel-based images are still a tricky problem in a responsive design. You want to send *appropriate* images to different devices—small, highly compressed images to devices with small screens, and larger ones to larger screens. High resolution displays make this even harder; double resolution images have *four* times the pixels, making them significantly larger. You definitely don't want to send large, high resolution images to someone out and about on their cell phone. Speaking of which, while there is a specification for bandwidth detection (the Network Information API spec http://j.mp/netinfo-api www.w3.org/TR/netinfo-api/), at the time of writing it's only supported by a tiny fraction of current mobile devices, so we're currently forced to guess bandwidth by correlating it with screen size, or even resorting to server-side browser sniffing. All of which makes high-resolution images a major problem.

The default behavior of browsers tends to be "DOWNLOAD ALL THE THINGS!" Browsers that understand advanced media queries will download all <link>ed stylesheets even if the media query doesn't apply. The latest browsers will not preload images that are in media queries that don't currently apply. However, they will begin pre-fetching all images on a page before CSS and JavaScript rules are applied. If an element has an image applied via background-image that's subsequently overridden in the cascade, older versions of Mobile WebKit in many Android and iOS mobile devices will download both images. All browsers will also download images that are in elements hidden with display: none;. At the time of writing, there's no official, implemented way to address this image problem (although it is being actively worked on). Collectively this means that currently there's no easy way to send appropriate images without some people having to download two versions of the same image.

Ignoring these issues for a moment, let's cover a basic way to add high resolution images to your page: use a suitably large image, then declare the desired dimensions using <img> element attributes or by using width and height in CSS. For example, if you want to add a double-resolution HiDPI image to be 320x240 CSS pixels and display at 640x480 device pixels on a double-resolution device, you'd create the image at 640x480 px, then use CSS or image element attributes to resize it to the desired size, like so:

- *<!-- resizing a 640x480px image using the HTML width and height attributes -->*
  <img src="miss-baker.jpg" width="320" height="240" alt="Monkey Baker with a model Jupiter vehicle (NIX collection, NASA)">
  / resizing a 640x480px image using the CSS width and height properties */*
  .hidpi{width:320px;height:240px;
  }
  <img class="hidpi" src="miss-baker.jpg" alt=" Monkey Baker with a model Jupiter vehicle (NIX collection, NASA)">

Alternatively, make the image fluid (max-width: 100%;) and place it in a container that won't grow bigger than the image's desired width. While you won't notice a difference on normal resolution devices, the difference will be clear on high resolution devices, as Figure 9-32 demonstrates:

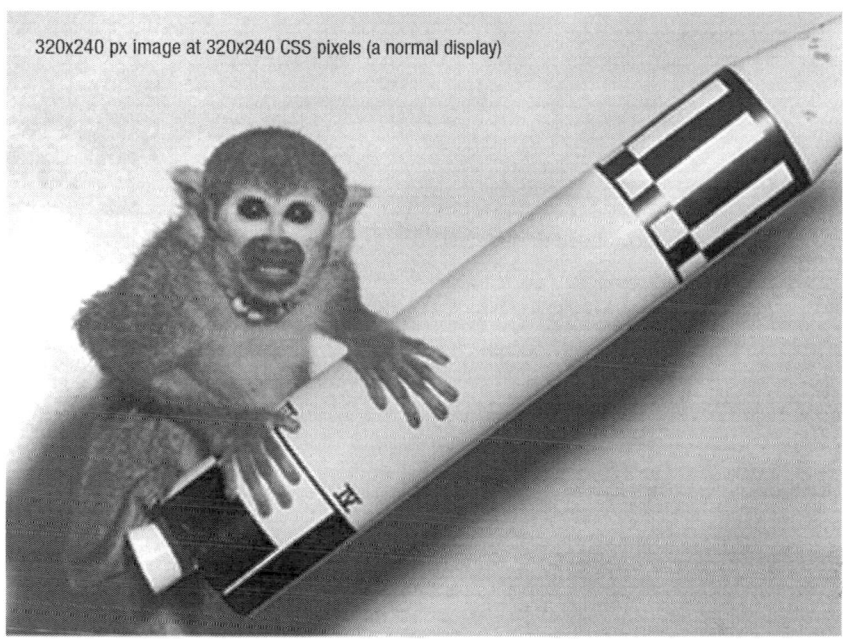

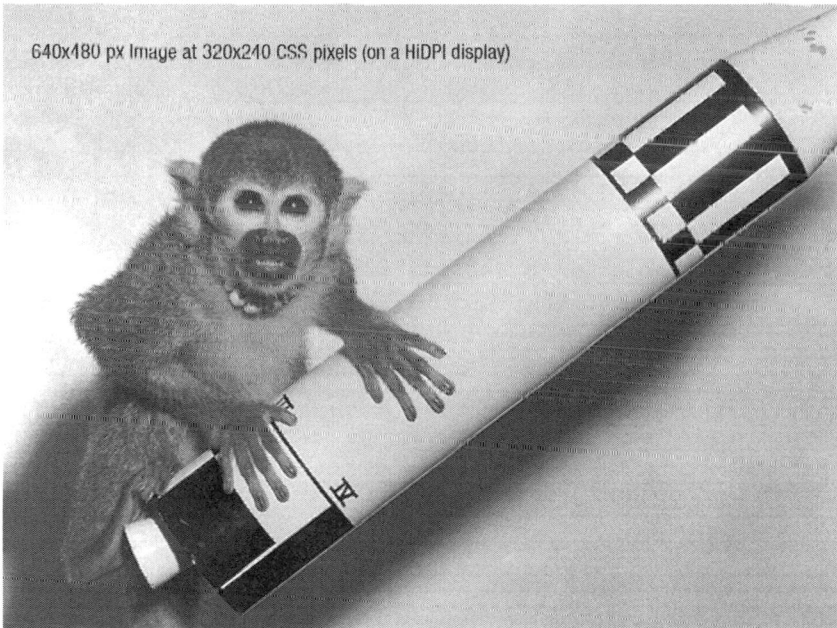

Figure 9-32. An image of space monkey Miss Baker at normal resolution, and at high resolution using one of the above techniques.

So, what to do? Luckily, creative people have been dreaming up ingenious ways to solve this. While none of them are perfect, at least there are some options. These include:

- Adaptive Images by Matt Wilcox, which relies on a server-side setup (PHP, .htaccess) and a little JavaScript, then tests a browser's viewport, and sets a cookie. Appropriate images are sent based on this cookie. It's the easiest way to make an established site HiDPI-friendly. (http://adaptive-images.com/)

- Riloadr by Tubal Martin is all client-side, using JavaScript, data-*, and a <noscript> fallback (for when JavaScript is disabled). It's very configurable and also optionally provides lazy loading and bandwidth testing. (http://j.mp/riloadr https://github.com/tubalmartin/riloadr)

Another option is to only create a HiDPI image, and compress it heavily with JPEG compression values around 30. This produces visible artifacts when viewed at normal size, but these artifacts are masked by browser resizing for normal resolution screens, and by the tiny pixels of HiDPI ones. The only drawback is you'll need to create the images on a HiDPI screen to get the best compression. This simplifies things wonderfully and doesn't require JavaScript, however it won't work for images that must use PNG or GIF, or where even after compression the images are still too large for mobile.

At the time of writing, this is an area of active development, so resources like Matt Wilcox's comprehensive overview "Responsive images: what's the problem, and how do we fix it?" (http://j.mp/responsive-img-problem dev.opera.com/articles/view/responsive-images-problem/) and Chris Coyier's "Which responsive images solution should you use?" (http://j.mp/responsive-img-solution css-tricks.com/which-responsive-images-solution-should-you-use/) may soon be out of date. A good place to keep up with the news is the Responsive Images Community Group (www.w3.org/community/respimg/), and This Is Responsive (http://j.mp/this-is-responsive bradfrost.github.com/this-is-responsive/), a collection of curated patterns, resources and news on responsive web design by Brad Frost.

In conclusion, while we can't make solid recommendations on adaptive and high resolution images at the time of writing, learning how to compress the heck out of images is something that never goes out of style.

- You can compress images before upload using the following programs:

  - The Mac OS X program ImageOptim by Kornel Lesiński (imageoptim.com)

  - Trimage for Linux by Kilian Valkhof and Paul Chaplin (trimage.org)

  - For Windows, Ardfry Imaging's PNGOUTWin (www.ardfry.com/pngoutwin/) or PNGGauntlet (www.pnggauntlet.com) by Benjamin Hollis

  - Or online with SmushIt (www.smushit.com), TinyPNG (tinypng.org), and JPEGMini (jpegmini.com).

- Convert PNG-24 images into PNG-8 with alpha transparency that works in IE6 using tools like Lesiński's ImageAlpha (pngmini.com) or Adobe Fireworks (www.adobe.com/products/fireworks.html).

- Learn how to better compress images, for example by blurring unnecessary detail in a JPEG, reducing the number of colors used in a PNG, and just making them physically smaller.

Another way of adding high resolution images to your designs is to use vector-based images, such as Scalable Vector Graphics (SVG) and icon fonts. These will scale smoothly and are much lighter than multiple images. "Towards A Retina Web" by Reda Lemeden gives a good overview of these and other HiDPI techniques (http://j.mp/sm-retina-web coding.smashingmagazine.com/2012/08/20/towards-retina-web/).

CSS3 layouts

It's fair to say that the CSS 2.1 tools we're using for layout were not intended for the layouts we're doing. Source order can constrain our layout options, horizontal alignment and vertical centering are difficult, and in general it's much harder than it should be to create robust layouts. However, we're hopeful this will change in the near future as several layout modules are currently under development, most with initial implementations in one or more browsers. Let's meet our future layout overlords:

- *CSS Positioned Layout Module Level 3*: Additional values for the position property, including long-sought-after easy vertical centering.

- *CSS Fragmentation Module Level 3*: This defines break-* and related properties, which are used by several layout specifications.

- *Multi-column Layout Module*: Adds newspaper-style columns to a block-level element and lets the content flow from one column to the next. This is more suitable for a part of a page than for page layout.

- *CSS Regions Module Level 3*: Creates a connected "region chain" of elements in any order, then pours content into it. Just like in desktop publishing software, the content will flow from one region to the next as necessary. You can also apply styles per region.

- *CSS Exclusions and Shapes Module Level 3*: Makes text flow inside or around non-rectangular shapes, making magazine techniques like text flowing around an image easy to achieve. You can also use different shapes on the inside and outside of the same element.

- *CSS Paged Media Module Level 3*: This describes the page model for content, which is presented in a "paged" format, such as when printing. It includes page-relevant styles, and when combined with the CSS Generated Content for Paged Media Module can also be used for a page-based interface, such as a slide deck or e-book.

- *CSS Generated Content for Paged Media Module*: Generated content useful for page-based layouts, including running headers and footers, leaders, cross-references, footnotes, page marks and bleed, and page-based navigation controls. Use together with the CSS Paged Media or Multi-column Layout modules.

- *The Flexible Box Layout Module*: A CSS box model optimized for laying out an interface. It allows you to arrange flex items horizontally or vertically, with deep control over how extra space is assigned, how boxes expand and contract when available space changes, and how boxes are aligned.

- *CSS Grid Layout Module*: Grid-based layout with no connection to source order. This allows us to place elements on a layout grid in a similar (but more powerful) way to table-based layout, perfect for web application layouts. It also allows aligning elements to horizontal and vertical guide lines (similar to guides found in popular graphics software), making it easy to implement traditional graphic design layouts.

We'll only cover most of these specifications briefly, but we hope you'll be excited by the potential and start thinking about how you could use them. OK, let's go!

CSS Positioned Layout Module Level 3

This specification covers positioning schemes based on your old friend, the position property. The CSS3 version introduces two new values: position: center; finally provides easy horizontal *and vertical* centering, with the properties top, right, bottom, and left acting as offsets from this, while position: page; creates an absolutely positioned box that's positioned relative to the initial containing block and can be paginated in paged media. There is also the offset group of properties, which act like the positioning properties top, right, etc., but language-dependently—useful for multilingual sites. Sadly, there's no browser support for these new features at the time of writing. See the CSS Positioned Layout Module Level 3 specification at http://j.mp/css3-positioning (dev.w3.org/csswg/css3-positioning).

CSS Fragmentation Module Level 3

This "helper" specification defines properties and rules for *breaking*, or how an element's content behaves when the element would be split in two due to a CSS layout. The properties are used to set or control breaks across columns in multi-column layout, regions in CSS regions, and flex containers in CSS Flexible Box Layout. They are closely related to page-break-* properties we'll mention presently as part of CSS Paged Media Module Level 3. The properties are as follows:

- break-before, break-after, and break-inside: Add and control column breaks in the following ways:

    - break-before and break-after: Values at the time of writing are auto, always, left, right, page, column, region, avoid, avoid-page, avoid-column, and avoid-region.

- break-inside: Values at the time of writing are auto, avoid, avoid-page, avoid-column, and avoid-region.

- orphans and widows: Control the minimum number of lines of the element's content that must appear after or before a break in the middle of an element respectively. The default is **2** lines.

Mainly you'll want to trigger a break before or after a block of content, or prevent a break inside an element, like so:

```
article {break-after: always;}

h3 {break-before: always;}

table {break-inside: avoid;}

p {

   widows: 4;

   orphans: 3;

}
```

At the time of writing browser support for break-* is tied to the layout modules that use it, and there are varying levels of support as part of multi-column layout, which we'll address next. widows and orphans are currently supported in IE 8+ and Opera 9.2+. See CSS Fragmentation Module Level 3 at http://j.mp/css3-break (dev.w3.org/csswg/css3-break/) for more information.

Multi-column Layout Module

The Multi-column Layout Module allows you to easily add newspaper-style columns to an element. The main properties of column-width and column-count (with the shorthand property columns) create equally sized column boxes for the content of the element to flow across. Because it's CSS, you can change the number of columns using media queries.

Here are the multi-column properties:

- column-width: The ideal width of each column. For example, {column-width: 15em;} adds as many 15em wide columns as the element's width (minus column-gap widths) allows, then increases the column widths equally to fill the element's width. Percentage values can't be used *(auto, length)*.

- column-count: The number of columns. For example, {column-width: 4;} creates four equally sized columns inside the element *(auto, integer)*.

- columns: Sets column-width and/or column-count. When both values are given, if the element's width is less than the width required the result will be as if column-width was used, and as if column-count was used if the width is greater.. If there's only one value the other is set to the default value of auto.

- column-gap: Controls the gap between columns. The same gap is applied between each column. The default normal is generally 1em *(**normal**, length)*.

- column-rule: Adds a line between columns, taking the same values as border and outline. You can also set the three values individually using the properties column-rule-width, column-rule-style, and column-rule-color. The rule width does not affect the width of column boxes.

- column-span: Allows a block-level element to span all columns with the value all, which also acts as a column break *(**none**, all)*.

- break-before, break-after, and break-inside: Add and control column breaks. While these properties are defined with the following values in the Multi-column Layout Module spec at the time of writing, we expect them to be superseded by the CSS Fragmentation Module definitions in the near future:

- break-before and break-after: Possible values are auto, always, avoid, left, right, page, column, avoid-page, and avoid-column.

- break-inside: Possible values are auto, avoid, avoid-page, and avoid-column.

- column-fill: Controls how content is spread across columns if height is greater than auto. The default balance tries to make all columns the same height, whereas auto completely fills each column one at a time *(**balance**, auto)*.

Multi-column basics

Here are some basic examples using multi-column layout. First up, column-width suggests the desired column width of each column. If there's enough room for one column, this acts as the minimum column width. The *number of columns* and the *column width* both change with the element's width to make sure the last column's edge touches the element's right edge. The width available for columns is the element's width minus the column-gap width(s).

For example, let's apply column-width: 10em; to a paragraph that's 42em wide, in Figure 9-33. While this is something we can happily leave to browsers, we can calculate the number of columns by using this pseudo-algorithm:

max(1, floor((available-width + column-gap) / (column-width + column-gap)))

With the default column-gap: 1em; that's max(1, floor((42em + 1em) / (10em + 1em))), which calculates to max(1, floor(3.90909)), or three columns. We can then work out the column widths using the pseudo-algorithm:

((available-width + column-gap) / number-of-columns) - column-gap

In this case it's ((42em + 1em) / 3) - 1em, which gives us three 13.333em wide columns.

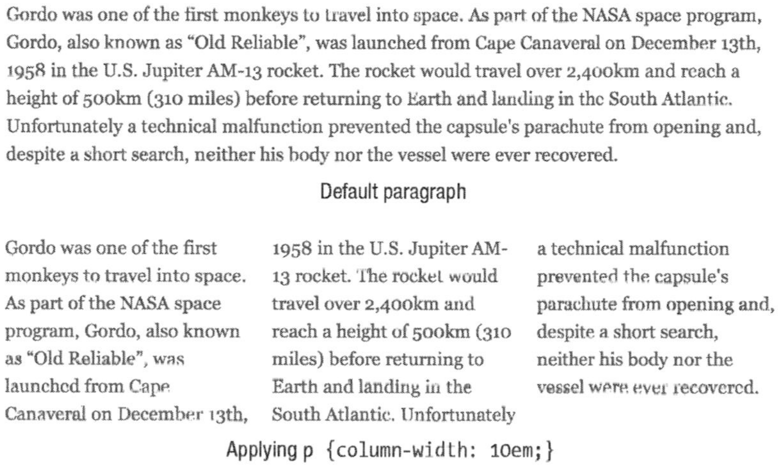

Gordo was one of the first monkeys to travel into space. As part of the NASA space program, Gordo, also known as "Old Reliable", was launched from Cape Canaveral on December 13th, 1958 in the U.S. Jupiter AM-13 rocket. The rocket would travel over 2,400km and reach a height of 500km (310 miles) before returning to Earth and landing in the South Atlantic. Unfortunately a technical malfunction prevented the capsule's parachute from opening and, despite a short search, neither his body nor the vessel were ever recovered.

Default paragraph

Gordo was one of the first monkeys to travel into space. As part of the NASA space program, Gordo, also known as "Old Reliable", was launched from Cape Canaveral on December 13th, 1958 in the U.S. Jupiter AM-13 rocket. The rocket would travel over 2,400km and reach a height of 500km (310 miles) before returning to Earth and landing in the South Atlantic. Unfortunately a technical malfunction prevented the capsule's parachute from opening and, despite a short search, neither his body nor the vessel were ever recovered.

Applying p {column-width: 10em;}

Figure 9-33 Applying column-width: 10em; to a 42em-wide paragraph, before and after. The columns end up being 13.333em wide to fill the width of the element.

Currently column-width (and column-gap) don't allow percentages. If you don't want to use a length unit with column-width, you can use column-count instead, as in Figure 9-34. This is the equivalent of percentages, as column-count gives us a fixed number of columns, and the *column width* changes with the element's width.

Gordo was one of the first monkeys to travel into space. As part of the NASA space program, Gordo, also known as "Old Reliable", was launched from Cape Canaveral on December 13th, 1958 in the U.S. Jupiter AM-13 rocket. The rocket would travel over 2,400km and reach a height of 500km (310 miles) before returning to Earth and landing in the South Atlantic. Unfortunately a technical malfunction prevented the capsule's parachute from opening and, despite a short search, neither his body nor the vessel were ever recovered.

Gordo was one of the first monkeys to travel into space. As part of the NASA space program, Gordo, also known as "Old Reliable", was launched from Cape Canaveral on December

13th, 1958 in the U.S. Jupiter AM-13 rocket. The rocket would travel over 2,400km and reach a height of 500km (310 miles) before returning to Earth and landing in the South Atlantic.

Unfortunately a technical malfunction prevented the capsule's parachute from opening and, despite a short search, neither his body nor the vessel were ever recovered.

```
width: 20em; column-width: 10em;          width: 20em; column-count: 3;
```

Figure 9-34. A comparison of column-width: 10em; and column-count: 3; when the element's width is only 20em (this is not quite wide enough for two 10em columns plus a column gap). While column-width adapts, column-count maintains the number of column boxes, even when they get unreadably narrow.

The shorthand property columns can set either or both the width and number of columns. When only one value is given, the other is the default auto. When both values are given, the result will be as if column-width was used if the element's width is less than the width required, and as if column-count was used if the width is greater. The order of the values isn't important. We tend to stick with column-width or column-count, and we find column-width is a little safer and more flexible.

Two other important properties are column-gap and column-rule, allowing you to specify a gap (or gutter) between columns, and a rule to be drawn in the center of this gap. While column-gap takes space, column-rule doesn't, and they apply to all columns, as demonstrated in Figure 9-35.

Gordo was one of the first monkeys to travel into space. As part of the NASA space program, Gordo, also known as "Old Reliable", was launched from Cape Canaveral on December 13th, 1958 in

the U.S. Jupiter AM-13 rocket. The rocket would travel over 2,400km and reach a height of 500km (310 miles) before returning to Earth and landing in the South Atlantic. Unfortunately a

technical malfunction prevented the capsule's parachute from opening and, despite a short search, neither his body nor the vessel were ever recovered.

```
column-width: 10em; column-gap: 4em; column-rule: 2px solid #bbb;
```

Figure 9-35. A multicolumn element with large column-gap and column-rule. Compare this to Figure 9-33, which is only seven lines tall due to the narrower column-gap.

Browser support for multi-column layout

Table 9-3 shows basic support for multi-column layout properties has been available in Mozilla, Safari and Chrome for a while now. More recently, full support has been added in Opera 11.10 and Internet Explorer 10.

Table 9-3. Browser Support for Multi-Column Layout Properties (http://caniuse.com/#feat=multicolumn)

Property	IE	Mozilla	Safari	Chrome	Opera
column-width	10.0	1.5 -moz-	3.0 -webkit-	5.0 -webkit-	11.10
column-count	10.0	1.5 -moz-	3.0 -webkit-	5.0 -webkit-	11.10
columns	10.0	9.0 -moz-	3.0 -webkit-	5.0 -webkit-	11.10[1]
column-gap	10.0	1.5 -moz-	3.0 -webkit-	5.0 -webkit-	11.10
column-rule	10.0	3.5 -moz-	3.0[2] -webkit-	5.0[2] -webkit-	11.10
column-span	10.0	-	5.0 -webkit-	8.0 -webkit-	11.10
break-before	10.0	-	5.1[3] -webkit-	8.0[3] -webkit-	11.10
break-after	10.0	-	5.1[3] -webkit-	8.0[9] -webkit-	11.10
break-inside	10.0	-	-	14.0[3] -webkit-	11.10
column-fill	10.0	-	-	-	11.10

[1] At the time of writing, Opera treats *columns* with both values the same as *column-width*.

[2] WebKit browsers (Safari and Chrome) and IE don't display a *column-rule* that's wider than *column-gap*. Firefox and Opera do display the rule, under the content.

[3] WebKit has preliminary support for *break-before*, *break-after*, and *break-inside*, with the proprietary properties *-webkit-column-break-before*, *-webkit-column-break-after*, and *-webkit-column-break-inside*. *-webkit-column-break-before* and *-webkit-column-break-after* support the values *always*, *left*, *right*, and

auto, and *-webkit-column-break-inside* supports the values *avoid* and *auto*. Unfortunately *-webkit-column-break-inside: avoid;* hasn't made it to Safari at the time of writing—a workaround is to use *display: inline-block;*.

In addition to the points noted above there are three other significant gotchas:

- When using multi-column layouts on lists in Opera and WebKit browsers, list item vertical padding can be split *across* column breaks, resulting in baselines being unaligned between columns. Avoid adding padding to elements in a multi-column layout.

- According to the specification, content with a fixed width that is wider than the column box should be cropped at boundary between column boxes (where a column-rule would be). However, Firefox *displays* this overflow content behind the next column's content. Avoid this by using fluid images (e.g. img {max-width: 100%;}). At the time of writing, Safari 6 crops at the edge of the column-gap instead (while we think this looks better, it's not per the spec).

- It's easy to end up with columns becoming taller than you expected (especially when using column-count) on a smaller screen. Having to scroll up to get to the top of the next column is almost as despised as horizontal scrolling to read each line. Be careful to test on mobile devices and avoid using multi-column layout on large blocks of content.

As you'd expect, for browsers that don't support these properties the element's content is displayed as normal—in a single column. While this may result in very long line lengths (careful!), the content is still readable and accessible, making multi-column layout potentially usable before more widespread browser support. If you already have wrappers around the content that will go in each column (such as three paragraphs you'd like to make into three columns), then it's really easy to add fallback styles with Modernizr's help using .csscolumns/.no-csscolumns. While spotty support for the more advanced properties mean it's not ready for layout heavy lifting yet, consider using multi-column layout for small progressive enhancement tasks—just remember to avoid vertical scrolling and test thoroughly!

One final warning—while we described multi-column layout as a way to "add newspaper-style columns," remember the web is *not* newsprint. Make sure your use is appropriate to your content—and is more than just aping a newspaper style.

Further reading

- CSS Multi-column Layout Module specification (http://dev.w3.org/csswg/css3-multicol/)

- "An Introduction To The CSS3 Multiple Column Layout Module," a good visual introduction by Aaron Lumsden (http://webdesign.tutsplus.com/tutorials/htmlcss-tutorials/an-introduction-to-the-css3-multiple-column-layout-module/)

- "Using CSS Multi-Column Layout," a detailed reference (https://developer.mozilla.org/en/CSS/Using_CSS_multi-column_layouts)

- "Deal-breaker Problems With CSS3 Multi-Columns," by Zoe Mickley Gillenwater. The "last column longer" WebKit bug has been fixed, but you may still encounter it in Mobile WebKit (http://zomigi.com/blog/deal-breaker-problems-with-css3-multi-columns/)

- "Hands-On Multi-Column," an interactive tool (http://ie.microsoft.com/testdrive/Graphics/hands-on-css3/hands-on_multi-column.htm)

CSS Regions Module Level 3

Most desktop publishing (DTP) programs allow you to link a series of text boxes together, so they act as a single box for their content. If there's too much content to display in the first box, the content will automatically overflow into subsequent boxes in order (see Figure 9-36).

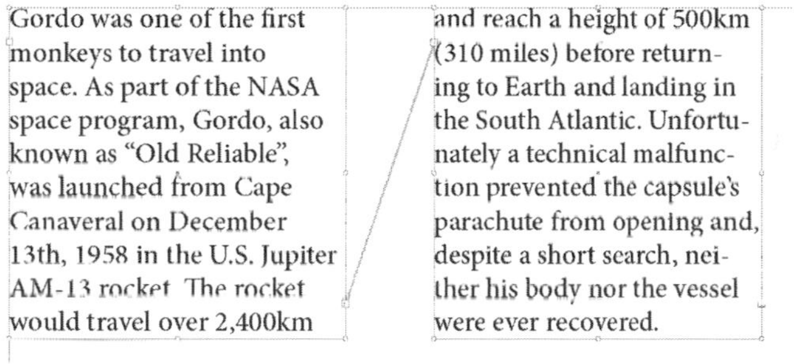

Gordo was one of the first monkeys to travel into space. As part of the NASA space program, Gordo, also known as "Old Reliable", was launched from Cape Canaveral on December 13th, 1958 in the U.S. Jupiter AM-13 rocket. The rocket would travel over 2,400km and reach a height of 500km (310 miles) before returning to Earth and landing in the South Atlantic. Unfortunately a technical malfunction prevented the capsule's parachute from opening and, despite a short search, neither his body nor the vessel were ever recovered.

Figure 9-36. Two text boxes linked with a connecting line in a desktop publishing program. The text flows from one box to the next.

CSS regions do the same thing—you assign an element to a *named flow* using the flow-into property. The content of this element will then be poured into a list of regions (a *region chain*) defined as selectors of a flow-from property with the same name, in the order the selectors are listed.

```
article {

  flow-into: article-chain;

}

/* IDs of regions in flow order: either existing elements or pseudo-elements to be created */

#lede, #part1, #part2, #part3 {

  flow-from: article-chain;
```

```
}

/* styles for positioning these elements */

...
```

CSS regions only defines how the named flow's content flows through the region chain. The regions can then be positioned using other layout modules, including as part of a multi-column layout, flexible box layout, or grid layout. The regions can be a scaffolding of empty elements, such as children of a grid layout, but don't have to be—pseudo-elements such as ::before and ::after or anything else that can be styled can become a region. The unofficial CSS Pagination Templates Module Level 3 specification proposes a way to define DTP-style "master templates" for page-based layout, and its @slot rules can also define regions without needing a framework of empty elements.

You can control the display of content in regions using the following properties:

- break-before, break-after, and break-inside: Set or avoid breaks between regions in the region chain, as defined in CSS Fragmentation Module Level 3.

- region-overflow: Together with the overflow property, this controls how overflow content in the last region is handled.

- @region rule: Applies box model, typographic, and color styles to the content in specific regions.

The pseudo-elements ::before and ::after can also be used on each region, and each region creates a new block formatting context and a new stacking context.

At the time of writing, there's partial, vendor prefixed support in Chrome 19+, Safari 5.2, and IE 10. WebKit uses -webkit-flow instead of flow-into, and -webkit-from-flow instead of flow-from, and at the time of writing Chrome needs to be launched with an enabling flag (or enable the "experimental WebKit features" flag in chrome://flags/ in Canary). CSS regions can also be detected by Modernizr 2.6+ (.css-regions). Finally, CSS Pagination Templates Module Level 3 also has initial, vendor prefixed support in WebKit nightlies.

Further reading

- CSS Regions Module Level 3 specification (http://dev.w3.org/csswg/css3-regions/)

- CSS Pagination Templates Module Level 3 specification, currently unofficial (http://dev.w3.org/csswg/css3-page-template/)

- When can I use… CSS Regions (http://caniuse.com/#feat=css-regions)

- CSS Regions information from Adobe (http://html.adobe.com/webstandards/cssregions/), including:

- CSS Regions example code (http://adobe.github.com/web-platform/samples/css-regions/)

- CSS Pagination Templates example code (http://adobe.github.com/web-platform/utilities/css-pagination-template/)

CSS Exclusions and Shapes Module Level 3

One of the interesting aspects of floats is the way non-floated block-level boxes ignore them, but those boxes' *line boxes* wrap around them. The CSS Exclusions part of this specification extends the ability to affect inline content to any element, using any positioning scheme. You can make text flow inside or around a shape (the CSS Shapes part), and use different shapes on the inside and outside of a single element. This makes magazine techniques like flowing text around images or inside shapes easy to achieve, as seen in Figure 9-37. Finally, freedom from the tyranny of the rectangle!

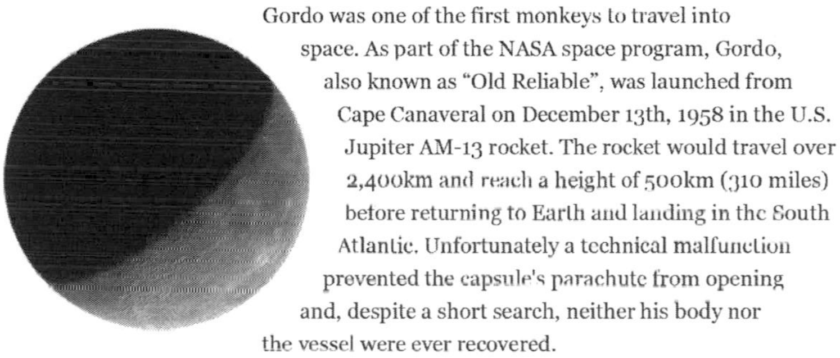

Gordo was one of the first monkeys to travel into space. As part of the NASA space program, Gordo, also known as "Old Reliable", was launched from Cape Canaveral on December 13th, 1958 in the U.S. Jupiter AM-13 rocket. The rocket would travel over 2,400km and reach a height of 500km (310 miles) before returning to Earth and landing in the South Atlantic. Unfortunately a technical malfunction prevented the capsule's parachute from opening and, despite a short search, neither his body nor the vessel were ever recovered.

Figure 9-37. Text flowing around an image on the left, and inside a matching half circle shape on the right.

You can control a block-level element's effect on inline content using the wrap-flow property. The values are auto (the default), both, start, end, minimum, maximum, and clear, providing a variety of wrapping effects. An element with a value other than auto affects inline content in the same containing block and establishes a new block formatting context. You can control the exclusion using the properties wrap-margin, wrap-padding, the shorthand wrap (covering the previous three properties), and wrap-through.

CSS Shapes are declared using shape-outside and shape-inside. While inside shapes can be applied to any block-level element, outside shapes only work when applied to an exclusion or a float. A shape can be defined by basic SVG syntax (rectangle(), circle(), ellipse(), and polygon()) directly in CSS, by referencing SVG shapes in an <svg> block, by an image with transparency (the path enclosing pixels with a greater opacity than the shape-image-threshold value, by default 0.5), or for shape-inside by using outside-shape—the same shape defined for shape-outside.

By combining exclusions and shapes, all sorts of exciting layout possibilities open up. However, if your print-inspired sensibilities get carried away, keep in mind magazine readers can't resize a magazine layout—make sure your use is "of the Web" and will adapt gracefully.

At the time of writing, there's initial, vendor prefixed support in IE 10 (who initially called it "Positioned floats"), preliminary support in WebKit (enable the "experimental WebKit features" flag in chrome://flags/ in Canary), and Adobe has also released a WebKit-based demo, although this uses an earlier syntax than the current spec. Modernizr can't detect Exclusions at the time of writing, due to some browsers returning false positives.

Further reading

- CSS Exclusions and Shapes Module Level 3 specification (http://dev.w3.org/csswg/css3-exclusions/)

- "CSS Exclusions," an introductory article by Robert Sedovšek (http://galjot.si/css-exclusions)

- CSS Exclusions and Shapes information from Adobe (http://html.adobe.com/webstandards/cssexclusions/), including:

    - CSS Exclusions prototype (http://adobe.github.com/web-platform/samples/css-exclusions/): The example images are informative, but at the time of writing the WebKit demo and code are obsolete

- CSS Exclusions documentation from Microsoft (http://msdn.microsoft.com/en-us/library/ie/hh673558(v=vs.85).aspx)

CSS Paged Media Module Level 3

This specification details the paged media formatting model, the one used when printing a web page, based on a *page box*. This can be styled using the @page rule (and related rules for areas surrounding the page, such as @top-center and @bottom-right-corner), and the :left, :right, and :first pseudo-classes. These can be used inside @media rules, and the spec also defines page-related properties, including:

- page-break-*: These are the precursors of the break-* properties in the CSS Fragmentation Module (as used by Multi-Column Layout, CSS Regions, CSS Flexbox, etc.), and work the same way.

- size: Specifies the page size (common paper sizes, or width then height), and if necessary orientation, such as size: A4 portrait; or size: 6in 4in;.

- page: Creates named @page rules you can then refer to using the page property to control what kind of page an element will ideally appear on.

For example, the following CSS specifies paper size and orientation, and page margins for left and right pages:

```css
@page {

  size: A5 portrait;

}

/* channeling Müller-Brockmann */

@page :left {

  margin: 15mm 10mm 30mm 20mm;

}

@page :right {

  margin: 15mm 20mm 30mm 10mm;

}
```

These can also be nested inside @media rules, for example:

```css
@media print and (width: 210mm) and (height: 297mm) {

  @page {

    /* rules for A4 paper */

  }

}

@media print and (width: 8.5in) and (height: 11in) {

  @page {

    /* rules for US Letter paper */

  }

}
```

orphans and widows from the CSS Fragmentation Module help control typographic stray lines if a page break occurs in the middle of an element with line boxes. Additionally, a couple of relevant properties in the CSS Image Values and Replaced Content Module Level 3 specification, object-fit and object-position, control how replaced content, such as in <img>, <video>, <object>, and <svg>, is displayed and positioned in its box:

- object-fit: This lets you resize the replaced content inside the element's box if its dimensions or aspect ratio differ. For example, this lets you choose to crop or letterbox a widescreen movie—great for templates that will handle a variety of content.

- object-position: This works the same as background-position, allowing you to offset the element's content in the frame of the element's box.

At the time of writing, browser support among these properties varies widely. For example, page-break-before is universally supported but page-break-inside isn't supported in Firefox, widows and orphans are supported in IE 8+ and Opera 9.2+, and only a custom build of Opera 12 supports object-fit and object-position.

Further reading

- CSS Paged Media Module Level 3 specification (http://dev.w3.org/csswg/css3-page/)

- CSS Image Values and Replaced Content Module Level 3 specification (http://dev.w3.org /csswg/css3-images/#sizing)

- When can I use… object-fit (http://caniuse.com/#feat=object-fit)

- "The CSS3 object-fit and object-position properties," by Chris Mills (http://dev.opera.com/ articles/view/css3-object-fit-object-position/)

CSS Generated Content for Paged Media Module

This specification provides styles for generated content like running headers, footnotes, and cross-references. It also includes four new values for the overflow-style property, paged-x, paged-y, paged-x-controls, and paged-y-controls. These give a page-based interface, with or without relevant navigation controls. These styles are perfect to pair with the CSS Paged Media and Multi-column Layout specifications.

If you wanted a chapter number and title-based running header, you could start by assigning the chapter's <h1> content to a *named string*, and tying it to a *counter*:

```
h1 {

  string-set: chapter-title content-element;

  counter-increment: chapter;

}
```

In this example we add the <h1>'s content-element content (the element's content, excluding any :before or :after content) to the string "chapter-title". We also increase a counter called "chapter" each time we encounter an <h1>. Using styles from the CSS Paged Media Module such as the @page rule, you can recall the named value you've set using string() and the current counter with counter(), display these using the content property, and position them appropriately for left and right pages using the :left and :right pseudo-classes. Continuing the above code:

```
title {

  string-set: book-title contents;

}

@page :left {

  @top-center {

    content: string(book-title);

  }

}

@page :right {

  @top-center {

    content: "Chapter " counter(chapter) ": " string(chapter-title);

  }

}
```

To use a paged user interface for an e-book, you could use the following CSS:

```
@media paged {

  html {

    height: 100%;

    overflow: paged-x-controls;

  }

}
```

The height: 100%; limits the height to the viewport, with extra content overflowing to the right, and accessible via default browser page navigation widgets. The spec also covers page-based navigation via @navigation, page- and line-based pseudo-elements, and e-book-style page turn transitions.

At the time of writing, there is a custom build of Opera 12 (http://j.mp/opera-gcpm people.opera.com/howcome/2011/reader/) with initial, vendor prefixed support.

Further reading

- CSS Generated Content for Paged Media Module specification (http://dev.w3.org/csswg/css3-gcpm/)

- Opera's guide to the CSS Generated Content for Paged Media Module (http://people.opera.com/howcome/2011/reader/), presented as a demonstration of the module's properties. It includes links to the custom build of Opera 12.

The Flexible Box Layout Module

The Flexible Box Model (or "Flexbox") began life as the way Firefox's user interface was laid out. An earlier version of this specification (using display: box;) achieved passable support on Firefox and WebKit browsers, but various issues led to it being "sent back to formula." After an awkward in-between stage (using display: flexbox;) it's re-emerged as the greatly improved *new* Flexbox (using display: flex;). The Flexbox spec defines "a CSS box model optimized for interface design," with properties for laying out and ordering boxes horizontally or vertically, plus deep control over how boxes are aligned and how they expand and contract ("flex") in relation to available space.

To use Flexbox, you first make an element into a *flex container* using display: flex; (or display: inline-flex; for the inline variation). The element then establishes a new *flex formatting context* (similar to a block formatting context but using flex layout), which forms a containing block, and prevents margin collapsing and overlapping by floated elements. Child elements of the flex container become *flex items*. A flex container can't use multi-column layout, and the properties float, clear, and vertical-align don't affect flex items.

Figure 9-38 shows example *single line* flexboxes for horizontal and vertical languages. Notice the terms for describing aspects of a flexbox are language-independent, and are appropriate to the language's writing mode.

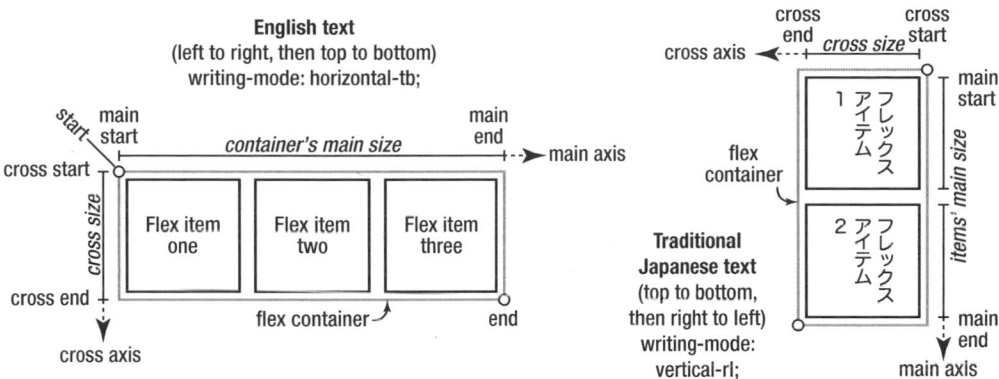

Figure 9-38. A single-line flex container with flex items, showing how the main axis and cross axis change for English and traditional Japanese, based on their different writing-mode values.

With Figure 9-38 as a guide, let's meet the properties applied to flex containers:

- flex-direction: This controls the direction in which flex items are laid out, and takes the values row (default), row-reverse, column, and column-reverse, with row meaning the main axis is the same direction as inline, and column in the same direction as block. These are based on the current language's writing direction, so the default row in English means from left to right, and in the traditional Japanese example in Figure 9-38 row is from top to bottom.

- flex-wrap: Flex containers can have a single line of flex items (the default nowrap), or contain multiple lines by using wrap or wrap-reverse. Multiple lines stack from start to end with wrap, or in the opposite direction for wrap-reverse.

- flex-flow shorthand property: This takes flex-direction and/or flex-wrap values, using the default value if one isn't declared.

- justify-content: This controls how flex items align in the *main axis direction* in a line. It might remind you of text-align for inline-block elements, which you'll meet in Chapter 10. The values are the default flex-start plus flex-end, center, space-between, and space-around.

- align-items: This controls how a flex items in a flex line align in the *cross axis direction*, and might remind you of the vertical-align property, also covered in Chapter 10. The values are flex-start, flex-end, center, baseline, and the default stretch, which makes all flex items the same height (for a row-based Flexbox).

- align-content: This controls the alignment of lines in a *multi-line* flex container in the cross-axis direction. The values are flex-start, flex-end, center, space-between, space-around, and the default stretch.

The properties applied to flex items are the following:

- order: This property allows you to reorder flex items and takes number values. Items are ordered from negative to positive, and items without an explicit order declaration use the default value of 0. Flex items with the same value appear in source order. This property should only be used for visual (not logical) reordering, and does not change order in speech readers.

- flex-grow and flex-shrink: These properties control if and how much a flex item is permitted to grow if there's extra space, or shrink if there's not enough space, respectively. Taken together for the flex items on the same flex line, they determine the *flex grow ratio* and *flex shrink ratio*, which determine proportionally how much each flex item grows or shrinks to fit. These properties take 0 and positive numbers, and the initial values are flex-grow: 1; and flex-shrink: 1;. This means flex items will default to being the same width (for a horizontal flow axis), and expanding or shrinking if there isn't enough space equally.

- flex-basis: This specifies the initial size of a flex item, before flex-grow or flex-shrink adjust its size to fit the container. It takes the same values as width (such as lengths and percentages), and the default is auto, which uses the item's width or height as appropriate (the dimension in the main axis direction). When used with flex this gives "relative flex". Values other than auto mean the item's width or height will be ignored. Setting flex-basis: 0%; or flex-basis: 0; sets the flex items' main axis dimension to 0, meaning its size will be dependent on flex-grow or flex-shrink, giving "absolute flex". Make sure you set a width or height as appropriate if using the value auto, or values close to (or equal to) 0.

- flex shorthand: This sets flex-grow, flex-shrink, and/or flex-basis. If no values are defined, its initial values are the individual property values. If you only set flex-grow and/or flex-shrink values, flex-basis will be 0, giving "absolute flex." If you only set flex-basis, you'll get "relative flex" instead, with flex-grow and flex-shrink using the default 1. Note that zero values for flex-basis in the flex property require a unit, for example 0px, to avoid confusing with the grow and shrink values. flex also has some useful shorthand values:

  - flex: initial; or flex: 0 auto;: The flex item will use its width and height properties and not expand, but will shrink if necessary. This is the same as the initial values of flex: 0 1 auto; and is useful when using Flexbox for its alignment properties, or in combination with auto margins.

  - flex: none;: Similar to initial, this stops flex items from flexing, even if their width or height cause them to overflow (equivalent to flex: 0 0 auto;).

  - flex: auto;: Starting from their declared dimensions (or content dimensions if using e.g. width: auto;), flex items will grow or shrink to fill the space. If all flex items in a flex line use auto, any extra space will be distributed evenly using "relative flex" (equivalent to flex: 1 1 auto;).

- flex: <positive-number> : This makes a flex item flexible and also sets the flex-basis to 0px (equal to flex: <positive-number> 1 0px;). This uses "absolute flex", so if all flex items in a line use this style of flex (or use flex-basis: 0%; or flex-basis: 0;). then their sizes will be proportional to their flex ratios, unaffected by their intrinsic dimensions.

- align-self: This aligns a flex item in the cross-axis direction and is the flex item equivalent of the flex container's align-items property. It takes the same values (flex-start, flex-end, center, baseline, and stretch) with the addition of the default auto, which inherits the align-items value.

To explain the difference between relative and absolute flex, let's compare the flex preset values by applying them to a simple navigation bar in Figure 9-39. We've left out flex: initial; as it appears the same as flex: none; when there's extra space.

```
<style>
.nav {

  display: flex; /* Establish a flex container */

  list-style-type: none;

}

/* First image: Flexbox with no flex */

.nav li {

  flex: none; /* equivalent to flex: 0 0 auto; */

}

/* Second image: Relative flex */

.nav li {

  flex: auto; /* equivalent to flex: 1 1 auto; */

}

/* Third image: Absolute flex */

.nav li {

  flex: 1; /* equivalent to flex: 1 1 0px; */

}
```

```
/* Fourth image: Differing flex values */

.nav li {

  flex: 1;

}

.nav li:nth-child(2) {

  flex: 2; /* equivalent to flex: 2 1 0px; */

}

/* Increase click target area */

.nav a {

  display: block;

  width: 100%;

  height: 100%;

}

</style>

…

<ul class="nav">

  <li><a href="/">Home</a></li>

  <li><a href="/articles">Space Monkey Articles</a></li>

  <li><a href="/dashboard">Log in</a></li>

</ul>
```

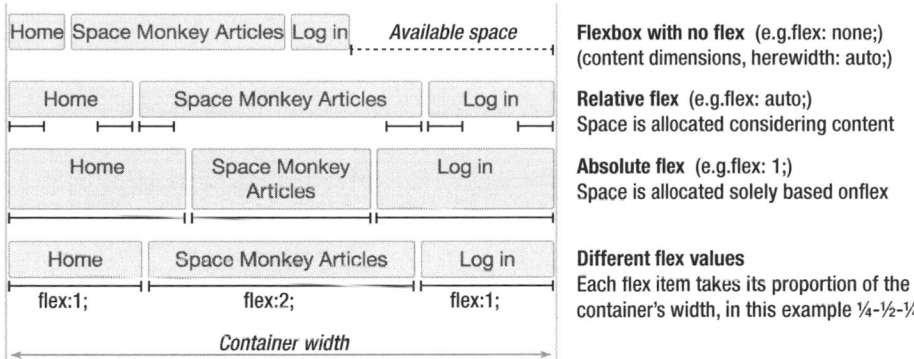

Figure 9-39. A simple navigation bar showing how extra space is distributed using relative flex (space is added to the content's width) and absolute flex (space is added ignoring the content's initial width).

If there isn't enough space, flex values (specifically flex-shrink) would control how (or if) each flex item shrinks to adapt. As you can see in the first image, just using Flexbox with no flex makes block-level elements stack beside each other, as if they were inline-block.

Perhaps Flexbox's best abilities are the deep control over alignment and ordering of flex items it gives us. To start, you can align flex items without flex (specifically those with flex-grow: 0;) if their container has extra space by using auto margins—any extra space will be equally distributed to margins in the axis direction that have the value auto. Note that this prevents alignment with the Flexbox property justify-content from working, because the auto margins absorb any free space after flex is calculated, but before Flexbox alignment occurs.

Let's use the same navigation buttons from the first image of Figure 9-39 (flex: none;) to demonstrate auto margin alignment, in Figure 9-40.

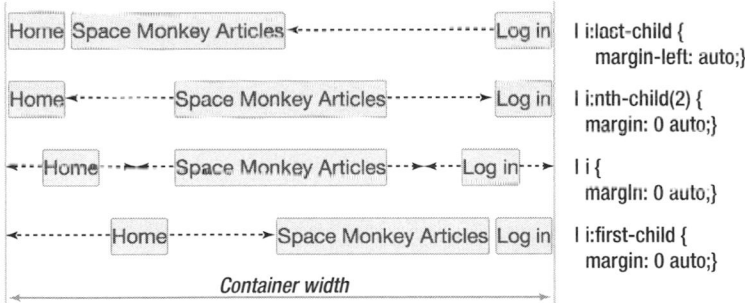

Figure 9-40. Any extra space is split equally between with any auto margins in the main axis direction on flex items.

Let's compare this to Flexbox's justify-content property, which allows us to quickly apply one of several common alignments, by applying each of its values to the same example navigation buttons in Figure 9-41.

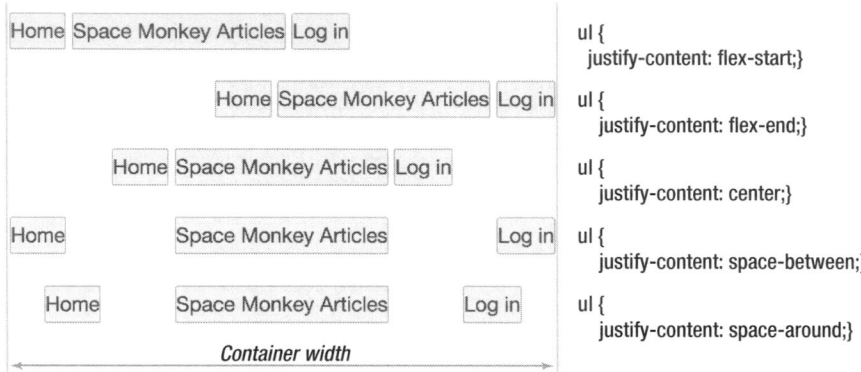

Figure 9-41. Applying justify-content values to the flex container.

In addition to aligning content in the main axis direction, Flexbox also gives us powerful tools for aligning in the cross axis direction too. The properties align-items and align-self take the same values, and allow us to align all flex items (by applying to the flex container) or individual flex items respectively. Let's compare the possible values of align-items in Figure 9-42.

Figure 9-42. Applying align-items values to the flex container. Note that for a horizontal row the default stretch automatically creates equal height flex items, center gives us easy vertical centering, and baseline aligns the first baseline of each flex item in the row.

Combined with align-content for aligning flex rows of a multi-line flexbox in the cross axis direction, Flexbox really has you covered for fine control over flex item alignment and distribution.

This all sounds perfect, but we advise caution when considering Flexbox for page layout. While you can reorder flex items in a line using the order property, a complex page layout would require extra wrapper elements, and layout rearrangement would often require HTML changes. Flexbox's strength is its amazing control for aligning and distributing *parts* of an interface or page, and it is not ideally suited to page layout *per se*. Unfortunately, while it is perfectly complemented by CSS Grid Layout, which is specifically intended for whole page layout, and what we'll cover next, we will probably have usable Flexbox support first, so you might find yourself grappling with Flexbox-based page layouts despite this.

At the time of writing Chrome 21 and Firefox 18 have initial, vendor prefixed support of the current Flexible Box Layout Module, and Opera 12.10 has unprefixed support. However, this specification is a candidate recommendation at the time of writing (W3C talk for "basically finished"), and all browsers have supported some version of Flexbox, so we expect support for new Flexbox, plus unprefixing, to happen comparatively rapidly. While Firefox and WebKit also support the first version of this spec (and IE the in-between second version), there are several significant gotchas in using these earlier specifications (ref: http://j.mp/old-flexbox oli.jp/2011/css3-flexbox/), and we recommend sticking with display: flex;. Modernizr detects both current (display: flex;) and original (display: box;) versions of Flexbox.

Further reading

- CSS Flexible Box Layout Module specification (http://dev.w3.org/csswg/css3-flexbox/)

- "Using CSS flexible boxes," a detailed article on the Mozilla Developer Network (https://developer.mozilla.org/en-US/docs/CSS/Using_CSS_flexible_boxes)

- "CSS Flexbox Please!" An interactive demo by Eiji Kitamura (http://demo.agektmr.com/flexbox/)

- When can I use... Flexbox (http://caniuse.com/#feat=flexbox)

The CSS Grid Layout Module

The grid layout is shaping up to be the "one true layout" method that we've been waiting for, the one worthy of *true love*. It's based on a grid (woo!), and has **no connection to source order**, allowing for layouts not possible with table layout or other CSS 2.1 layout schemes.

The grid is made up of horizontal and vertical *grid lines* which enclose *grid fields*. We can set up the grid by creating grid lines (which can be assigned roles), grid fields, or both, and any undefined but needed lines or fields will be added automatically. Block-level, replaced, and inline-block child elements of the grid are *grid boxes*, and can be positioned based on named grid fields, grid lines, or named grid line roles. You can span grid boxes across multiple lines, align the content to grid lines, overlap grid boxes or even assign them to the same location, and control their stacking order. These terms are shown in Figure 9-43.

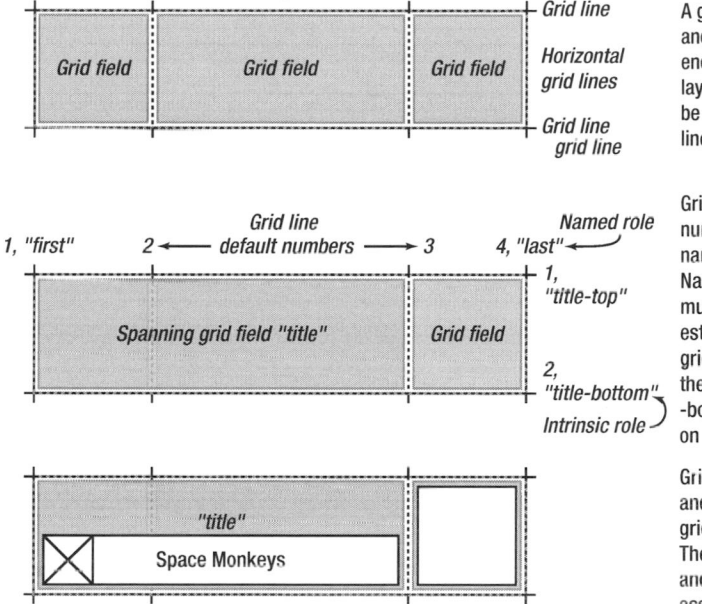

Grid Layout concepts
A grid elementcontains vertical and horizontal grid lines, enclosing grid fields. A grid layout (grid lines and fields) can be created by specifying grid lines, named grid fields, or both.

Grid lines have default numbers, and can also be named with one or more roles. Named grid fields can span multiple lines. They also establish an intrinsic role for the grid line on each edge, using the field name plus -top, -right, -bottom, and -left (shown here on horizontal grid lines).

Grid boxes can be positioned and aligned in the grid based on grid lines or named grid fields. They can overlap each other, and fill the field they're assigned to by default.

Figure 9-43. A diagram showing Grid Layout concepts at the time of writing.

You can define the grid in several ways:

- Using the grid-lines-horizontal and grid-lines-vertical properties

- Using the grid-fields property to make an ASCII-art representation

- A combination of both methods

The position of grid lines can be sized using

- Lengths

- A percentage of the grid element's size (width for rows, height for columns)

- A fraction of the remaining space (using the new fr unit)

- The size of the contents, which can be the maximum size (max-content) or minimum size (min-content) of the grid boxes contained by those two lines

- A size range, using a minmax function (minmax (*min*, *max*)), which can use any of the preceding value types for the minimum and maximum values

- The keyword auto, which is equivalent to minmax(min-content, max-content)

Note that if the "min-content" value of a minmax function uses fraction units, it is treated as 0 px.

> *Fractions (fr) are a new unit that represent a proportion of the space remaining after explicit lengths are subtracted from the container's width or height. Any extra space is then split between fields with fraction values in proportion to each fraction's value, similar to how flex-grow values control the relative proportioning of extra space in the Flexible Box Module. When the available space is undefined, the maximum content size of each field using with fractional units is calculated, and the largest one is used as the basis for 1fr, so relative proportions are maintained. Make sure to use a width (such as 100%) on grid elements to avoid horizontal scrolling*

After cautioning you about Flexbox for page layout, and extolling the page layout prowess of Grid Layouts, we regretfully have to return to reality. Based on feedback from an initial implementation in Internet Explorer 10, at the time of writing the Grid Layout specification is being overhauled to make it more suitable for graphic design-influenced layouts using grid lines. While Grid Layout is shaping up to be very flexible and powerful — perfect for creating an overall page layout then rearranging it with media queries — its current status at the time of writing means we won't get to use it for a couple of years yet either. On the bright side, this spec is a combination of the best ideas from several earlier layout specs, is being actively worked on, and all browsers are planning to implement it once it's stable.

We are eagerly awaiting the time when this specification (or a future variant) is finally widespread. We also expect to finally see decent GUI-based web design tools then too. In the meantime, CSS 2.1 layout techniques (with some Flexbox assistance for progressive enhancement until it's widespread enough to stand alone) will have to do.

Further reading

- CSS Grid Layout (http://dev.w3.org/csswg/css3-grid-layout/)

- When can I use… CSS Grids (http://caniuse.com/#feat=css-grid)

CSS3 layout modules in summary

Let us stress again that, with the exception of Multi-Column Layout, none of these specifications will have the browser support to be usable in production for a few years yet. In fact, many of them are still being edited. However, that means it's a great time to play with them and think how they might be useful in the future, and of course to provide feedback to the CSS Working Group.

Obviously, some of these specifications can't be used on the same element, for example Flexible Box layout and Grid Layout. However, you can turn a grid box into a flex container, and a flex item into a grid container.

Conclusion

We've covered a *lot* of ground in this chapter, starting with the basics of the box model and the various kinds of boxes, before progressing through the CSS 2.1-based layout possibilities of the position property, floats, display: inline;, display: inline-block;, and display: table; layout. We covered media queries and how to use them with adaptive layouts to achieve responsive web design, plus how to deal with high resolution displays. Finally, we touched on some of the coming CSS3 layout specifications, almost all of them frustratingly just out of reach at the time of writing, but holding the promise of *easy* CSS layouts.

The current state of things *is* frustrating—the CSS that actually has browser support is underpowered for page layout and often has major shortcomings. Specifications that offer real layout tools are still being written, meaning they're possibly several years from widespread browser support. Given how crucial layout is (it's not something we can easily add as progressive enhancement), widespread browser support is a prerequisite for use in all but exceptional circumstances. We may be lucky and get polyfills or other tools that make maintaining two layouts feasible, but in the near term it looks like we'll have to grin and bear the CSS 2.1 layout methods we have.

However there's a ray of sunshine in this: with Internet Explorer 10 in 2012, all major browsers now auto-update. This means rather than waiting the **10+ years** it has taken IE6 to fade, new specifications will see widespread auto-update-assisted adoption (and become *usable*) in a window of maybe 3-4 years from now on. It's not much of a consolation now, but it will be a game changer.

We'll close this chapter by returning to the underlying philosophy of designing for the web: *adapt*. Prepare for change, handle it gracefully, design to be bulletproof. By being future-friendly, your layout (and your site) will avoid being caught flat-footed by new devices and technology. Remember, the web is not print, and this is one of its strengths.

Further reading

- "Flexible Web Design," a book by Zoe Mickley Gillenwater (http://www.flexiblewebbook.com/)

- "Scalable and Modular Architecture for CSS," a book by Jonathan Snook (http://smacss.com/)

- "Responsive Web Design," a book by Ethan Marcotte (http://www.abookapart.com/products/responsive-web-design)

- "Retinafy your web sites & apps," a book by Thomas Fuchs (http://retinafy.me/)

- "Future Friendly," a manifesto to acknowledge and embrace unpredictability (http://futurefriend.ly/)

- "HTML5 Please" Advice on using "the new and shiny responsibly," covering HTML, CSS, JavaScript, and APIs. (http://html5please.com/)

- "* { box-sizing: border-box } FTW" by Paul Irish: check comments for browser issues. (http://paulirish.com/2012/box-sizing-border-box-ftw/)

- "CSS 101: Block Formatting Contexts" by Thierry Koblentz (www.yuiblog.com/blog/2010/05/19/css-101-block-formatting-contexts/)

- "Object-Oriented CSS (OOCSS)" by Nicole Sullivan: a methodology for writing high quality CSS, and a set of CSS stylesheets based on it (http://oocss.org/)

- "Give Floats the Flick in CSS Layouts" by Andrew Tetlaw: Discusses float layout problems, and covers inline-block and table-based alternatives. (www.sitepoint.com/give-floats-the-flick-in-css-layouts/)

- "Simple Stacks and Panels" by Jonathan T. Neal: Using display: inline-block; together with text-align: justify; to make a robust grid. (www.jonathanneal.com/blog/simple-stacks-and-panels/)

- "CSS Table Layout" by Rachel Andrew, an excerpt of Chapter 2 of the book *Everything You Know About CSS Is Wrong* (www.digital-web.com/articles/everything_you_know_about_CSS_Is_wrong/)

- "Examples of Flexible Layouts With CSS3 Media Queries" by Zoe Mickley Gillenwater (http://zomigi.com/blog/examples-of-flexible-layouts-with-css3-media-queries/)

- "Responsive Resources," a collection of resources about responsive web design by Brad Frost (http://bradfrost.github.com/this-is-responsive/resources.html)

- "Responsive IMGs Part 2: In-depth Look at Techniques" by Jason Grigsby (http://blog.cloudfour.com/responsive-imgs-part-2/)

- Responsive Images Chart, compiled by Christopher Schmitt and Chris Coyier (https://docs.google.com/spreadsheet/ccc?key=0Al0ll17fOl9DdDgxTFVoRzFpV3VCdHk2NTBmd VI2OXc#gid=0)

- "Love your devices: adaptive web design with media queries, viewport and more" by Chris Mills: A good overview of the responsive web design process. (http://dev.opera.com/articles/view/love-your-devices-adaptive-web-design-with-media-queries-viewport-and-more/)

- "Goldilocks and the Three Device Pixel Ratios" by Martin Sutherland: A well-illustrated article on the effects of pixel density on mobile devices, and the dangers of target-densitydpi. (http://sunpig.com/martin/archives/2012/03/18/goldilocks-and-the-three-device-pixel-ratios.html)

- "HTML5 Boilerplate," the world's most popular front-end template, and a great resource to learn the details of CSS from (http://html5boilerplate.com/)

Specifications

- CSS Values and Units Module Level 3: Information about CSS units, including the CSS reference pixel. (http://dev.w3.org/csswg/css3-values/, http://dev.w3.org/csswg/css3-values/#absolute-lengths)

- CSS Box model covers box dimensions, margins, padding, and borders. (www.w3.org/TR/CSS2/box.html) The updated version, CSS 3 basic box model is more detailed but still a work in progress at the time of writing. (http://dev.w3.org/csswg/css3-box/)

- CSS Basic User Interface Module Level 3 (CSS3 UI) covers outlines and box-sizing, plus user interface pseudo-classes and pseudo-elements, text overflow, and other UI-relevant features. (http://dev.w3.org/csswg/css3-ui/)

- CSS Positioned Layout Module Level 3: Updated specification for the position property, including helpful new values center and page, the offset group of properties, and detailed positioning algorithms. (http://dev.w3.org/csswg/css3-positioning)

- Media Queries: Detailed information on media features and useful examples of syntax. (http://dev.w3.org/csswg/css3-mediaqueries/)

- CSS 2.1: Tables: At the time of writing the CSS3 Tables specification is still fairly immature, so here's the CSS 2.1 version. (www.w3.org/TR/CSS2/tables.html)

- CSS Device Adaptation: Implementing the <meta viewport="..."> element in CSS as @viewport. (http://dev.w3.org/csswg/css-device-adapt/)

- CSS Fragmentation Module Level 3 (http://dev.w3.org/csswg/css3-break/)

- CSS Multi-column Layout Module (http://dev.w3.org/csswg/css3-multicol/)

- CSS Regions Module Level 3 (http://dev.w3.org/csswg/css3-regions/)

- CSS Pagination Templates Module Level 3: An unofficial proposal to bring DTP-style "master templates" to page-based layouts. (http://dev.w3.org/csswg/css3-page-template/)

- CSS Exclusions and Shapes Module Level 3 (http://dev.w3.org/csswg/css3-exclusions/)

- CSS Paged Media Module Level 3 (http://dev.w3.org/csswg/css3-page/)

- CSS Image Values and Replaced Content Module Level 3 (http://dev.w3.org/csswg/css3-images/)

- CSS Generated Content for Paged Media Module (http://dev.w3.org/csswg/css3-gcpm/)

- CSS Flexible Box Layout Module (http://dev.w3.org/csswg/css3-flexbox/)

- CSS Grid Layout (http://dev.w3.org/csswg/css3-grid-layout/)

Homework

We hope you've been experimenting with each new CSS 2.1 aspect of layout as they've been introduced, writing little tests, then checking the result in browser inspectors, and tweaking things to see what happens. With that under your belt, it's time to return to your homework page, and practice the *workflow* of making a layout. You already have your content, so now you can think how best to present it. Start with pencil and paper sketches of possible designs, beginning with a mobile version, then considering a desktop version. Build the mobile version first, then return to your sketches to work out how to convert this into a desktop version via a media query. For bonus marks test your breakpoints in several different devices, and add an additional intermediate media query or two to smooth over rough breakpoints if needed.

Chapter 10

Improving Web Typography

For a long time, web typography was a much-neglected field. While advances in type were piped back into editing software like Adobe Photoshop or InDesign, browsers had to deal with a very basic and limited suite of type technologies. However, all this is changing with CSS3. Before we dive into the new tools CSS3 provides to craft type, let's clarify what "type" means and the various terms that are used in web typography.

Typeface and fonts

Let's define the terms.

- *Typeface*: The term refers to type designs that are created by type designers. Georgia, Helvetica, and Futura are all typefaces. Typefaces can be created on paper and then tweaked in a type design application or created in software programs like Font Lab. Letters that form parts of a typeface have characteristics that can be tweaked with various settings.

- *Font*: Fonts enable the printing of a typeface. Fonts can be metal or, in the case of the Web, digital. We will only be dealing with digital fonts in this chapter.

> *Jon Tan writes about how a font is not a typeface and web designers shouldn't make that mistake.*

Anatomy of type

The anatomy of type is shown in Figure 10-1.

Figure 10-1. Anatomy of type

- *Baseline*: The line on which all characters "sit."

- *Mean line*: The line that determines where the non-ascending characters end in a typeface.

- *X-height*: The distance between the baseline and the mean line.

- *Ascender*: The part of a lower case character that extends above the mean line of a font. In Figure 10-1, it's the part of "h" that extends above all the other letters in that word.

- *Descender*: The portion of a lower case character that extends below the baseline of the font. In Figure 10-1, it's the part of the "p" that extends below all the other letters in that word.

- *Glyph*: A glyph refers to a unit of type. It could be an "ü" or a plain vanilla "a." These are glyphs that have unique styles depending on the typeface we use.

- *Ligature*: Two or more glyphs joined together to form a single glyph. It's not seen often in Latin scripts (popular Latin ligatures are ffl and ffi); it's much more commonly used in Indic and CJK scripts.

- *Leading*: This refers to the space between lines of text. We set this in our style sheet with the `line-height` property.

- *Letter spacing*: It refers to the amount of space between the letters in a word or a block of text. We can control this with `letter-spacing` property.

- *Kerning*: When we adjust the space between two specific characters, we *kern*. Monospace fonts by definition have fixed spaces between characters and can't be kerned. Most fonts have kerning definitions that are applied automatically by the typesetting engine. We will talk later about how to control the space between characters.

- *Generic font family*: This is a term exclusively used with web typography. When we set our type on the Web, it is possible that our desired type may not be available. In that case, we can specify which category of fonts we would like our page to be rendered with by declaring one of the generic font families. There are five generic font families: serif (e.g., Times), sans-serif (e.g., Helvetica), cursive (e.g., Zapf-Chancery), fantasy (e.g., Western), and monospace (e.g., Courier). Failure to set a generic font family results in the browser choosing its own default font (and this varies based on the browser and the user's customizations) to render our page.

- *Alignment*: The setting of the text relative to the page. Typical values include left, right, center, or justified. On the Web, justified text is prone to generate rivers of text. We will look at some solutions later.

- *Widows and orphans*: Short lines of text left dangling at the top or the bottom of a column. An orphan is left at the bottom and a widow is left at the top.

While there are various ways to tweak some of the characteristics of type, the ability to do so for web typefaces via CSS was introduced very recently. Here's a brief history of web type to help you understand how it all began and where we will be going next.

A brief history of web type

In the early days of the Web, stylesheets were not created by authors of sites, but only by users. As a user, you could specify a universal stylesheet with the kind of font you wanted to see, and all web sites you visited would be rendered with the styles you specified. This meant that you had full control of the fonts that were used to render the web pages.

This changed around October 1994 when stylesheets were proposed to be set, not by the user, but by those serving the HTML pages (quite a radical change!) This presented a problem. What if the users didn't have the font specified by the authors of the stylesheets? For example, if you as the designer specified the font-family of Helvetica Neue Light, how would the browser render the text if the font wasn't installed on the user's computer?

The original authors of CSS, Håkon Wium Lie and Bert Bos, considered this problem and came up with several options:

- *Serve the font from the server*: There was no commonly agreed-upon font format (in the early days, even TrueType or OpenType fonts did not exist), and with the bandwidth being so slow in the 90s (remember 96kbps modems?) it would have been impossible to download font files in time to render a page with it.

- Pass a few values and generate glyphs similar to the font requested on the fly: This was not optimal and sometimes led to ugly results.

- *The author sets a list of fonts in the order of preference in the hope that one of them is available*: The author could also set a default generic font that the browser would use to find a suitable font from the user's computer if none of the author-chosen fonts were available.

The last option might be familiar to you, as it became a standard in 1996.

Microsoft also created a freely distributable font stack that was legible on the screen and supported internationalization so that it could be used as a base for web typography. This led to the proliferation of Arial, Courier, and Comic Sans across various operating systems.

Unfortunately, there wasn't much more movement until 2008. Meanwhile, front-end designers tried to work around the desert of web typography creatively, through image replacement, sIFR, Cufon, or SVG fonts. Let's take a look at some of these options before we look into the modern miracle of web fonts.

> *The Web Typography page at Wikipedia covers a lot more ground on the history of various web typographic formats (http://en.wikipedia.org/wiki/ Web_typography).*

Text as image

The most common way to render a font that is not available on a user's machine is to serve it as a graphic. This technique came in countless variations, each eliminating or adding constraints to the manner in which these images could be used. Here are some of them.

Farhner Image Replacement (FIR)

Farhner Image Replacement is one of the earliest inventions to work around the typographic limitations within a stylesheet. Named after Todd Farhner, invented by C. Z. Roberton in 1999, and popularized by Doug Bowman and Jeffery Zeldman, FIR was the most popular way of replacing text with graphics using CSS. See Table 10-1 for information on browser support.

Table 10-1. Browser Support for Farhner Image Replacement

IE	Firefox	Safari	Chrome	Opera
5.0+	1.0+	1.0+	1.0+	5.0+

The debilitating disadvantages of this method was that it removed the text from being available to screen readers and rendered nothing to users who turned off images by default (which was a significant number given how constrained bandwidth was at that time).

> Go to *http://jsfiddle.net/nimbu/Q274j/* for the technique as represented in code.

Leahy/Langridge method

Seamus Leahy and Stuart Langridge independently discovered a solution that would help users with screen readers. By padding the text element, this method pushed the text beyond the viewable area of the element, making it still visible for screen readers but hiding it from desktop users. See Table 10-2 for information on browser support for this method.

Table 10-2. Browser Support for Seamus Leahy and Stuart Langdridge's Image Replacement Technique

IE	Firefox	Safari	Chrome	Opera
5.0+	1.0+	1.0+	1.0+	6.0+

Unfortunately, users who had images turned off were unable to see the text.

> Go to *http://jsfiddle.net/nimbu/pnRb8/* for the technique as represented in code.

Phark method

Meanwhile, Mike Rundle proposed a solution using `text-indent` to hide the text. This meant the text was still accessible to screen readers but users who had images turned off were unable to see text (Table 10-3).

Table 10-3. Browser Support for Phark Method

IE	Firefox	Safari	Chrome	Opera
5.5+	1.0+	1.0+	1.0+	6.0+

> Go to *http://jsfiddle.net/nimbu/8ZMmT/* to see the technique as represented in code.

Gilder/Levin method

Lovin Alexander, Petr Stanlcek (a.k.a. "Pixy"), and Tom Gilder invented a technique that worked for both with screen readers and users who disabled images. Basically, It made use of an ompty element to apply the background image to and was rendered on top of the text. It came with a big caveat: the image could not be transparent. See Table 10-4 for moro information

Table 10-4. Browser Support for Gilder/Levin Method

IE	Firefox	Safari	Chrome	Opera
5.+	1.2+	1.0+	1.0+	5.0+

> Go to *http://jsfiddle.net/nimbu/Ra6p5/* to see the technique as represented in code.

JavaScript Image Replacement (JIR)

Peter Paul Koch took a different approach by offering a JavaScript image replacement solution (`www.quirksmode.org/dom/fir.html`). This method first detected if images were disabled via JavaScript before doing image replacement, thereby solving the problems of text not being visible to screen readers or to users who disabled images. It was expanded upon by Stewart Rosenberger (`www.alistapart.com/articles/dynatext/`) to use PHP for automatically generating images on the server. See Table 10-5.

Table 10-5. Browser Support for JIR

IE	Firefox	Safari	Chrome	Opera
5.5+	1.0+	3.0+	1.0+	6.0+

Nonetheless, all these techniques suffered from the drawback of not scaling when font sizes were changed or when the width occupied by the text changed. They did not allow for any text to be fluid but only fit into predetermined boxes.

Enter sIFR

> Go to *http://jsfiddle.net/nimbu/Q6FBQ/* to see the technique as represented in code.
>
> A comprehensive list of image replacement solutions can be found on Mezzoblue (*www.mezzoblue.com/tests/revised-image-replacement/*).
>
> Nicholas Gallagher also wrote about the less-known Nash Image Replacement technique at *http://nicolasgallagher.com/css-image-replacement-with-pseudo-elements/*.

sIFR

Flash image replacement was first used in a big way by Mike Davidson on ESPN.com in 2001 to render custom type for headings using embedded Flash movies for those who had Flash installed and plain text for those who did not. In 2004, Shaun Inman invented a better technique (dubbed Shaun Inman Flash Replacement; see www.mikeindustries.com/blog/archive/2004/08/sifr) that worked on plain HTML and added a dynamically generated Flash movie via JavaScript to replace the plain text headings. By early 2000s, Flash was almost ubiquitous, which made this technique easy to get behind.

In late 2004, Mike Davidson and Shaun Inman combined forces to release a better version dubbed sIFR that handled multiple lines of text, did not need exact dimensions, and rendered the Flash movie to lay out the type to fit snugly within the dimensions occupied by plain text. The big drawbacks were that you had to use type that wasn't narrower than the font used to render the plain text type, and if you resized the text (say you clicked "text-size -> 200%") the text wouldn't resize. See Table 10-6.

Table 10-6. Browser Support for sIFR[1]

IE	Firefox	Safari	Chrome	Opera
5.0+	1.0+	1.0+	1.0+	7.0+

- These browsers need JavaScript enabled and have Flash 6 or greater installed.

Cufón

Cufón aimed to be a replacement for sIFR by using the new canvas element for modern browsers and VML for IE. Cufón required us to upload the fonts we wanted to use to their online generator, which converted them into a Cufón-understandable format. Then we needed to include the generated file with Cufón's JavaScript files to render the text in our custom font.

Cufón, like other image replacement solutions, now allows us to select the text that gets replaced. Like sIFR, the more text to be replaced, the longer it takes to be rendered.

> The Cufón Wiki at *https://github.com/sorccu/cufon/wiki/* has more details.

SVG fonts

In October 2001, the SVG 1.1 Working Draft was released with a font element that allowed users to specify glyphs in SVG syntax. The purpose of this element as outlined in the specification was

> *...to allow for delivery of glyph outlines in display-only environments. SVG fonts that accompany Web pages must be supported only in browsing and viewing situations...*
>
> *A key value of SVG fonts is guaranteed availability in SVG user agents. In some situations, it might be appropriate for an SVG font to be the first choice for rendering some text. In other situations, the SVG font might be an alternate, back-up font in case the first choice font (perhaps a hinted system font) is not available to a given user.*
>
> SVG 1.0 Specification, www.w3.org/TR/2001/REC-SVG-20010904/fonts.html

This is precisely the reason why SVG fonts have gained prominence recently. iOS devices do not support the ability to render Open Type font but Mobile Safari and Opera Mobile do render SVG fonts. Unfortunately, this means the fonts lose the hints and—depending on the font—look worse on small screens. We can include SVG fonts using the famous @font-face rule that we will look into shortly.

SVG fonts have some advantages. We can include several fonts within the same file. This saves on network requests, which are the main cause of slow page loads on mobile browsers.

Unfortunately, Firefox does not yet support SVG fonts, unlike the other major browsers today (https://bugzilla.mozilla.org/show_bug.cgi?id=119490). This makes SVG a peripheral player in the font formats war.

And now let's take a look at the remarkable phenomenon in recent history that has allowed us to smoothly transition to using web fonts for websites: the rise of @font-face.

@font-face

@font-face is a rule standardized in the CSS3 Fonts Module, which was first introduced as a Working Draft in 2002. @font-face allows us to declare where on the Internet fonts are located and their formats so they can be used later in our stylesheet as a value for the font-family property. The interesting thing is that @font-face has been in and out of the CSS specifications for a while without being implemented by most browsers. Let's look at its evolution.

Web fonts

We have come far without defining web fonts. *Web fonts* simply refer to all the fonts that are available to be used by declaring them in the @font-face rule. Typically all of these fonts have been optimized for web usage; thus they have small file sizes and are aliased to render correctly when used with smaller font sizes.

In the beginning

In 1996, when CSS Level 2 specifications were being worked on, Adobe, along with Bitstream, Microsoft, and others, put together the @font-face proposal that declared a @font-face rule like this:

```
@font-face {
font-family: 'Graublau Web';
src: url('GraublauWeb.ttf') format('ttf');
}
```

As there was no clear consensus on a font format for all platforms, the W3C did not recommend a font format. This rule was included as part of CSS 2.1.

This feature also did not account for any form of restrictions on downloading fonts, so font foundries became apprehensive that it would be exploited for font piracy.

Microsoft, in association with Monotype Imaging, came up with a garden-wall DRM solution that used a new font format (EOT) that couldn't be installed on any computers and could only be understood by browsers (in this case Internet Explorer) to render the font on the page. Unfortunately, other browser vendors did not want to adopt this technology. This meant almost no commercial font was available for use as a web font via the @font-face rule, so very few developers adopted this feature. This state of suspended animation continued until 2006.

@font-face strikes back

In 2006, CSS Working Group decided to take action to find a single format that would put an end to image replacement techniques. In October 2007, Webkit started supporting the @font-face rule to link to raw TrueType and OpenType fonts; Firefox followed in October 2008, and Opera in December 2008. None of them recognized the EOT format pioneered by Microsoft. A new font format was agreed upon, called WOFF (www.w3.org/TR/WOFF/). It provided lightweight compression of font data along with additional metadata for informing users of licensing information and more. See Table 10-7 for current support for the various formats.

Table 10-7. Browser Support for Various Formats via @font-face Rule

Browser	TTF	OTF	SVG	WOFF	EOT
IE	9+	9+	-	9+	5+
Firefox	3.5+	3.5+	-	3.6+	-
Safari	3.1+	3.1+	3.1+	5.1+	-
Chrome	4+	4+	0.3+	6+	-
Opera	10+	10+	9+	11+	-

Dissecting font face syntax: @font-face declaration

Let's take a minute to understand the @font-face rule. This is how the @font-face is declared in our stylesheet:

```
@font-face {
  font-family: bodytext;
  src: url(ideal-sans-serif.woff) format("woff"),
       url(basic-sans-serif.ttf) format("opentype");
}
```

In this rule, font-family declares the name we use to refer to this custom font when we actually use it. For example, the font specified in this rule can be used in the following manner:

```
p {
  font: 12px/1.5 bodytext, sans-serif;
}
```

This renders all text in p elements with the font we specified with the font family called "bodytext."

The second property src links to the actual URL for the font that we want to use.

The problem is that not all browsers understand all font formats (see Table 10-7), so we must specify one or more of these URLs along with the format function to indicate which format the URL references. This example first declares a URL for WOFF font format and then one for OpenType.

We can also use a local() function in the src to render a font if it is locally available. While this has good intentions, none of the text will be rendered if the local font is corrupt. This could be a critical issue that is beyond the control of web developers. For this reason, you should avoid using local fonts and only read from the font URL.

Within the font-face rule we can also use font descriptors like font-weight: bold or font-style: italic. These are indicators to browsers to not artificially generate bold or italic faces for these web fonts when necessary. When this font-face rule is applied to a heading, like so

```
H2 { font: 16px/1.5 bodytext, sans-serif; font-weight: bold; }
```

browsers are forced to artificially generate a bolder face of the font. To prevent this from occurring, we only need to describe our web font as a bold font so it can be used just as it is.

```
@font-face {
  font-family: bodytext;
  src: url(ideal-sans-serif.woff) format("woff"),
       url(basic-sans-serif.ttf) format("opentype");
  font-weight: bold;
}
```

This has no impact on our p selector but prevents our h2 headings from having a synthetic bold face (which looks much worse than including the font as-is).

Bulletproof syntax for @font-face

From the previous section you would think writing a @font-face rule that works across all browsers would not be much of a headache. Unfortunately, it is. We need to ensure browsers only download one of the several resources we specify so that our pages load quickly. Luckily there is a syntax that can do just that. Paul Irish came up with the first simple universal solution for it, which was then enhanced by Richard Fink and finally made most robust by Ethan Dunham.

```
@font-face {
font-family: 'MyFontFamily';
src: url('myfont-webfont.eot'); /* IE9 Compat Modes */
src: url('myfont-webfont.eot?iefix') format('eot'), /* IE6-IE8 */
url('myfont-webfont.woff') format('woff'), /* Modern Browsers */
url('myfont-webfont.ttf')  format('truetype'), /* Safari, Android, iOS */
url('myfont-webfont.svg#svgFontName') format('svg'); /* Legacy iOS */
}
```

If you are worried about generating fonts in each of these formats, fear not. FontSquirrel has a @font-face generator (at www.fontsquirrel.com/fontface/generator) that automatically converts your uploaded font into all the supported web font formats. Make sure you have permission to use your font as a web font first.

Downloading web fonts takes some time, which means that users need to wait to see the text with the font you specified. This creates an issue of a "flash of unstyled text," which you will learn about next.

> *Paul Irish's post on bulletproof syntax has a detailed explanation for each of these choices (http://paulirish.com/2009/bulletproof-font-face-implementation-syntax/).*

Avoiding the flash of unstyled text (FOUT)

Web fonts take a while to download and occasionally these requests time out (or the font assets might have moved, leading to a 404). During that time, a browser has to decide if it should wait for the font to download to render the text that requires it or render the text up front without waiting and then update the rendering once the font has finished downloading. Firefox (before 4) and Opera do the former, which has come to be known as a flash of unstyled text (FOUT). Sometimes the adjustments made on a page before and after downloading the web fonts are so drastic that it disrupts interactions with the page. Webkit-based browsers wait for about 3 seconds for the font to download and then render the text in fallback fonts if the font fails to download.

Paul Irish wrote an exhaustive post on how to defeat the flash of unstyled text; he outlines the techniques to do so at `http://paulirish.com/2009/fighting-the-font-face-fout/`. There are a few options.

- Google's WebFont Loader
- Using font.js

Google's WebFont Loader

Using Google's WebFont Loader we can hide the text entirely when JavaScript is enabled and only render it after the font is loaded by adding declarations based on the classes on the `html` element.

The WebFont Loader can automatically request from several font repositories that serve fonts upon request, such as Google, Ascender, Typekit, Monotype, and Fontdeck. In addition, we can use the custom configuration on fonts that we host on our server.

Note that if you use the WebFont Loader, you do not need to declare the @font-face rule. It will be taken care of by the WebFont Loader.

Once a request is made for a font, the WebFont Loader adds classes based on the state of the request of the asset. While the request is still being made, the WebFont Loader adds the class `wf-loading` to the HTML element. If the request fails, the WebFont Loader adds the class `wf-inactive`; if the font is downloaded successfully, `wf-active` is added to the HTML element.

We can use these classes to choose if we want to avoid the FOUT. For example, setting

```
.wf-loading h1 {
        visibility: hidden;
}
```

makes sure that h1s remain invisible while the request is being made.

Likewise, setting

```
.wf-inactive h1 {
        font-family: monospace;
}
```

ensures that a closely matching local font is used to render the h1s when the requested web font fails to download.

> See `http://jsfiddle.net/nimbu/HCgp8/` for how to use the WebFont Loader.

Using font.js

font.js (`http://pomax.nihongoresources.com/pages/Font.js/`) was created not as a solution to the problem of FOUT but as a way to represent fonts within the JavaScript Object Model. Nevertheless, it works well for loading fonts dynamically and renders content only when fonts are loaded.

To use font.js, include the `font.js` file in the page before the closing `</head>` tag.

```
<script type='text/javascript' src="Font.js"></script>
```

Then in the stylesheet, include web fonts using the bullet-proof @font-face rule discusse earlier.

On the appropriate selector, add these declarations:

```
#fontjs {
    visibility: hidden;
    font-family: 'Ultra', serif;
}
```

In this rule, 'Ultra' refers to the web font included using the bulletproof font-face syntax. Then we need to decide when to make the content in the selector visible. In this case, let's do so when the body element acquires a classname called `font-loaded` (you will see *how* it will acquire this shortly).

```
.font-loaded #fontjs {
    visibility: visible;
}
```

We also want the content to be visible if the web font fails to load and to provide an alternative generic font family when that happens. Let's do so when the body element acquires a classname called `font-error`.

```
.font-error #fontjs {
    visibility: visible;
    /* Our custom declarations to deal with the lack of web font availability */
    font-family: sans-serif;
    font-weight: bold;
}
```

Now, in JavaScript, we include the following snippet of code that will enable the addition of classnames `font-loaded` or `font-error` when the font loads successfully or not, respectively.

```
var font = new Font();

/* Font loads successfully */
font.onload = function() {
    document.body.className = 'font-loaded';
};

/* Font fails to load */
font.onerror = function(err) {
 document.body.className = 'font-error';
}

/* Kicks off the font loading */
```

```
font.fontFamily = 'Ultra';
font.src = font.fontFamily;
```

With font.js we have access to a bunch of font metrics like ascent and descent; we can even get the metrics for a specific string.

Unfortunately, font.js requires `canvas` support and it does not work in IE8 and below, which means Google WebFont Loader is the best choice to prevent FOUT.

> Go to *http://jsfiddle.net/nimbu/mRQpB/* to see how it looks when the font fails to load.
>
> You can also add fancy effects when the font is loaded at *http://jsfiddle.net/nimbu/LrqPb/*

Things to keep in mind while using web fonts

- Web fonts create a reflow of the whole page once the font loads. So keep the usage to the minimum.

- Firefox and IE9 will fetch web fonts from a server other than where your site is hosted, but only if the server explicitly allows it.

- Keep in mind the performance of the technique you use to load fonts. Some font hosting services offer better performance compared to serving it yourself (see www.artzstudio.com/2012/02/web-font-performance-weighing-fontface-options-and-alternatives/).

- IE9 does not recognize OpenType fonts if the embedding bit is not set to *installable*. This is most likely the case for the majority of the OpenType web fonts available, so make sure you use the bulletproof syntax so IE9 can use WOFF or EOT if it is unable to use the OpenType format.

- If a user has enabled high security settings on IE6, a security box will pop up when a page uses a web font. There is no way around this, other than to exclude serving web fonts to IE6.

- IE6-8 will try to download the font specified in a @font-face rule as soon as it encounters it, which might slow down the download of other assets from the same server (this can be mitigated somewhat by serving fonts from another server).

- If you are using a bold typeface for headings, make sure you set `font-weight` correctly. If you would like to use a bold face of a font, make sure you set `font-weight` to bold within the @font-face rule if you want to use it in selectors that have `font-weight` set to bold (http://jsfiddle.net/nimbu/wcBmD/). Otherwise, browsers will synthetically make your bold font face bolder, leading to unappealing results (see Figure 10-2).

Figure 10-2. Synthetic bold appear much thicker than the naturally bold bold.This is how it appears in Firefox.

Finding web fonts

There are a plethora of fonts to choose from, ranging from free to very expensive. Before we look at the options, note that it's important to make sure any font you intend to use as a web font has the appropriate license for it. The license will usually state if it is allowed to be "embeddable" or be used as a web font. If a font's license does not state it, make sure you clarify the terms from the font provider.

Free web fonts

There are many sites that offer free fonts. However, not all of them are worth using as web fonts (some may have glyphs missing or may simply be too big to qualify as a web font). These sites offer the best web fonts possible:

- Font Squirrel (www.fontsquirrel.com/) has the largest database of free web fonts with handy @font-face kits for each. It lists some fonts that are available for use as web fonts.

- The League of Movable Type (www.theleagueofmoveabletype.com/) offers beautiful open-source fonts we can use and not just as web fonts.

- Google Web Fonts (www.google.com/webfonts) does not directly let us download font files but they are available with Open Source licenses but are hosted by Google and served via its web fonts API.

- Kernest (http://kernest.com/) also hosts a number of free fonts that we can either download or serve from Kernest servers.

Commercial web fonts

Ralf Herrmann has a list of commercial foundries that offer web fonts for purchase at http://webfonts.info/wiki/index.php?title=Commercial_foundries_which_allow_%40font-face_embedding.

FontFont Library (www.fontfont.com/) also opened up its catalogue for use as web fonts. Fonts are downloadable and available for use after paying a one-time license fee.

Lost Type (`http://losttype.com/`) offers web fonts that are available for a price that we name.

Font as a service

There are now many sites that offer web fonts as a service. All we need to do is to link to their stylesheet or a script file and then use the font in our stylesheet. Costs vary across the services and are accurate at the time of writing. Table 10-8 lists a few of the popular ones.

Table 10-8. Web Font Services

Service	Subscription	Minimum Cost	JS/CSS	Notes
Typekit, `https://typekit.com/`	Yearly and bandwidth-limited	Free (Typekit badge required)	JS	Typekit has a huge collection of fonts from various foundries including Adobe.
Font Deck, `http://fontdeck.com/`	Yearly per website	USD2.5/year/font	CSS	There are no other pricing plans and their plan offers 1 million page views per month and unlimited bandwidth per font per website.
WebINK, `www.webink.com`	Monthly per four domains and restricted by bandwidth	USD0.99 for 1GB bandwidth limit per month	CSS	Features Adobe and Mark Simonson's Studio along with a few other foundries not found elsewhere.
Typotheque, `www.typotheque.com/`	One time license fee covers 500MB of monthly bandwidth. €5 for every GB extra.	30-day free trial and price varies per font.	CSS	Has a good collection of multi-lingual web fonts including Latin, Greek, Cyrillic, Armenian, Arabic, and Devanagari fonts.
Web Fonts by Monotype Imaging, `http://webfonts.fonts.com/en-US`	Monthly in slots of 250,000 page views.	Free (badge required and limited to 25,000 page views)	JS	Monotype has a huge library of fonts including Cyrillic, Greek, Hebrew, Indic, Japanese, Korean, Simplified Chinese, Thai, and Traditional Chinese.

Service	Subscription	Minimum Cost	JS/CSS	Notes
Webtype, `www.webtype.com/`	Yearly or downloadable	30-day free trial and price varies per font.	CSS	Fonts optimized for being readable on websites by celebrated typographic foundries like The Font Bureau and Monotype Imaging.
Kernest, `http://kernest.com/`	Per website and/or downloadable	Most are free.	CSS	A lot of the fonts are free and the rest are charged per website use. Kernest also sells paired font stacks for use on your site.

Designing with web fonts

The biggest drawback of web fonts that are offered as a service is that we can't easily use them in Photoshop comps. However, there is an Adobe Photoshop CS5 plugin (`http://www.webink.com/webfontplugin`) that offers fonts from several foundries for use in our comps.

Typecast (`http://beta.typecastapp.com/`) claims to let us quickly create prototypes from our browser using fonts from several foundries. However, this service was not yet launched at the time of writing.

> *Chris Coyier has a demo at `http://css-tricks.com/examples/IconFont/` that outlines why web fonts are great for icons.*

Using web fonts as icons

A new trend has been to use fonts as icons. Simurai has a great tutorial on how to use them (http://lab.simurai.com/buttons/). Note that it would be best to map these icons to their nearest Unicode mappings as screen readers are prone to read them out as letters.

Web fonts in summary

We looked at how web fonts came to be and the best syntax for declaring web fonts. We also looked at some techniques for loading fonts to avoid a flash of unstyled text. We then looked at some resources for web fonts and how web fonts have been repurposed to render icons.

Now that you have seen how to use custom fonts on the Web, you are undoubtedly curious about how to manipulate type. Read on!

Baselines

Make sure to use the right defaults when using web type in order to provide the best possible experience for all browsers. Here is the first thing to do:

```
html { font-size: 100%; }
```

This will make sure the fonts all start with a standard default on all browsers. On the desktop, this is 16px. On mobile devices, the rendering of fonts depends on the resolution and device pixel ratio.

You can choose to either reset all possible browser default font choices with Eric Meyer's reset.css or make sure you provide the same consistent default browser experience across all browsers.

We highly recommend the second choice, and Nicolas Gallagher and Jonathan Neal's normalize.css (http://necolas.github.com/normalize.css/) provides the best defaults out of the box. Even if you are using normalize.css, do make sure to set the font properties correctly when you override them later in your stylesheet.

Setting font-family

When we specify a font family, we want to ensure the text renders in a readable format when our choice of font is unavailable. We can do that by setting the fallback generic font. Code Style has a great list of good font stacks (www.codestyle.org/). CSS Font Stack (http://cssfontstack.com/) is another resource for aesthetic font stacks.

```
body {
font-family: 'Helvetica Neue', Helvetica, Arial, sans-serif;
}
```

The two most often used generic font families are sans-serif and serif. Make sure you remember them (especially the hyphen between *sans* and *serif*)! Also remember to put font names that have spaces within them in quotes, like 'Helvetica Neue'.

> An interesting idea explored by iotic.com is to create a font that is an average of all system fonts found on his machine. It is a very interesting read; find it at *http://iotic.com/averia/*.
>
> Mathias has written in greate detail on which font-family names can be unquoted; find it at *http://mathiasbynens.be/notes/unquoted-font-family*

Setting vertical spacing

When setting the type, be sure to set the line-height property. Line heights can take unitless values; this mean any selector and the elements that inherit a style from that selector have their line heights calculated as a product of that unitless value and their current font size. It's a good practice to set a unitless value for line-height that is greater than 1 to ensure your text is always readable.

Setting font sizes

Use the em unit to set font sizes. When we specify `font-size` in ems, the resulting font size is a product of the em value and the inherited font size. For example,

```
body { font-size: 100%; }
h2 { font-size: 2em; }
```

results in the computed font size of the h2 element to be about 32px. This is an easy way to set type sizes to be relative to the base font-size. If we increase the base font-size, every other element automatically adjusts itself.

The most popular means of setting font-sizes is by using pixels. It is very easy to do, but when the client demands larger text sizes, it's pretty painful to adjust all of them. However, it's trivial if we use ems. But then again, using ems can easily become a maintenance nightmare if three are several levels of nesting and element styles being overridden accidentally by a selector of higher specificity. Luckily there's a better solution: the *rem* unit.

The rem unit

The rem unit allows us to set the font size relative to that of the root element (in typical use, the `html` element). By using rem instead of em, we avoid the specificity headaches of ems and simply change the font size of the root element to make the text larger or smaller in unison; see Table 10-9.

Table 10-9. Browser Support for font-weight

IE	Firefox	Safari	Chrome	Opera
9+	3.6+	5+	5+	11.6+

We highly recommend setting fonts with the rem unit with a fallback to the em unit.

Next, let's look at how to render text that is pleasing to read. We do this by setting type to a vertical rhythm.

> *Jonathan Snook has a great article on using rem unit with a good fallback; see* `http://snook.ca/archives/html_and_css/font-size-with-rem.`

Designing with a grid

In a seminal article, Richard Rutter laid out the secrets to establishing a typographic vertical rhythm. He explains:

The basic unit of vertical space is line height. Establishing a suitable line height that can be applied to all text on the page, be it heading, body copy or sidenote, is the key to a solid dependable vertical rhythm, which will engage and guide the reader down the page.

There are two ways to do this, one by using *em* units and the other (far easier) way of using pixel units. Here is the markup we will be using vertical rhythm on:

```
<p>There were four of us—George, and William Samuel Harris, and myself, and Montmorency.
We were sitting in my room, smoking, and talking about how bad we were—bad from a medical
point of view I mean, of course.</p>
<p>We were all feeling seedy, and we were getting quite nervous about it.  Harris said
he felt such extraordinary fits of giddiness come over him at times, that he hardly knew what
he was doing; and then George said that he had fits of giddiness too, and hardly knew what he
was doing.  With me, it was my liver that was out of order.</p>
<p class="aside">I knew it was my liver that was out of order, because I had just been
reading a patent liver-pill circular, in which were detailed the various symptoms by which a
man could tell when his liver was out of order.  I had them all.</p>
```

Before we go any further, we need to decide the base unit of our rhythm. Then we can proceed to implement multiples of this base unit (to create a *rhythm*) in either pixel units or em units. For readability, in our case, we want our base unit to be 1.5 times that of the default font size. This turns out to be 1.5em or 24px depending on which unit we use in our implementation. Let's look at both methods.

With pixels

```
body {
  /* font size is 16px */
  font-size: 100%;

  /* Yay, base unit */
  line-height: 24px;
}

p {
/* total space vertically above and below each paragraph equals to one base unit: 24px  */
  margin: 12px 0;
}
```

In this code, we have established the baseline font spacing. Now let's start with the first paragraph. We want it to be bigger than any other paragraph but still maintain the vertical rhythm.

```
p:first-child {
  font-size: 24px;
}
```

Every time you declare margins, paddings, borders, make sure the sum of the top and bottom values is a multiple of the base unit. Especially note that margin collapsing can disrupt your vertical rhythms, so you need to compose your margins carefully based on the margins applied to the previous element.

Go to `http://jsfiddle.net/nimbu/CV2Kt/7/` to see how this markup looks with this style applied. As you can see, each line fits perfectly into the vertical grids.

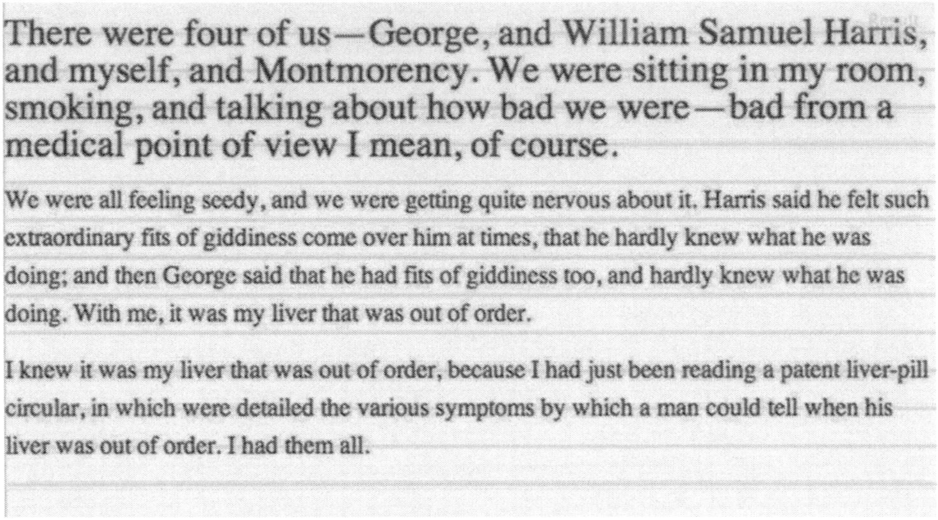

There were four of us—George, and William Samuel Harris, and myself, and Montmorency. We were sitting in my room, smoking, and talking about how bad we were—bad from a medical point of view I mean, of course.

We were all feeling seedy, and we were getting quite nervous about it. Harris said he felt such extraordinary fits of giddiness come over him at times, that he hardly knew what he was doing; and then George said that he had fits of giddiness too, and hardly knew what he was doing. With me, it was my liver that was out of order.

I knew it was my liver that was out of order, because I had just been reading a patent liver-pill circular, in which were detailed the various symptoms by which a man could tell when his liver was out of order. I had them all.

Figure 10-3 Text fitting the grid using vertica rhythm with pixels

Let's set the last paragraph to have a border and a smaller font size.

```
p:last-child {
  font-size: 12px;

  /* margin-top is already margin-collapsed to be 12px, we now need to allocate rest of the
margin to the bottom margin so in total with border-width it would be a multiple of the base
unit */
  margin: 12px 0;

/* Padding top and bottom is 12px each, total = 24px */
  padding: 12px 0;
}
```

Here is how it looks like:

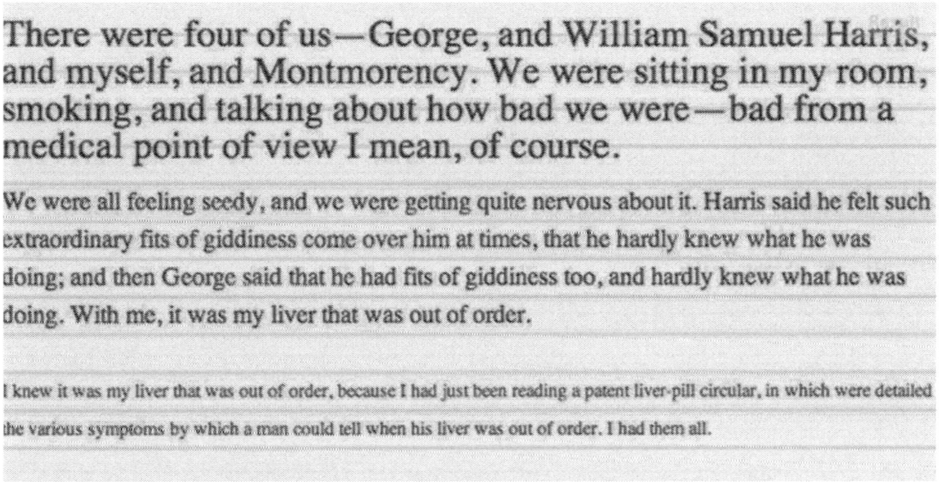

There were four of us—George, and William Samuel Harris, and myself, and Montmorency. We were sitting in my room, smoking, and talking about how bad we were—bad from a medical point of view I mean, of course.

We were all feeling seedy, and we were getting quite nervous about it. Harris said he felt such extraordinary fits of giddiness come over him at times, that he hardly knew what he was doing; and then George said that he had fits of giddiness too, and hardly knew what he was doing. With me, it was my liver that was out of order.

I knew it was my liver that was out of order, because I had just been reading a patent liver-pill circular, in which were detailed the various symptoms by which a man could tell when his liver was out of order. I had them all.

Figure 10-4. Last paragraph is smaller but still fits into the grid.

Calculating in pixels is a lot easier to do. Here is how to do so with *ems*.

With ems

```
/* gives us a base font-size of 16px, base line height of 24px on desktop browsers */
body { font-size: 100%; line-height: 1.5em; }

p {
/* vertical space above and below each paragraph totals to one line: 24px (0.75em = 12px)  */
   margin: 0.75em 0;
}

p:first-child {
   /* font-size is now 24px, line-height if not redeclared will be now 36px */
   font-size: 1.5em;

   /* line height is redeclared, now same as font size! 24px */
   line-height: 1em;

   /* vertical space above and below each paragraph totals to one line: 24px  */
   margin: 1em 0;
}

p:last-child {
   /* font size is now 12px, line height is redeclared and will be 2*12px = 24px  */
   font-size: 0.75em;
   line-height: 2em;
```

```
/* previous paragraph has margin bottom set to 12px, hence margin collapsing means we cannot
set a smaller margin-top  for this selector.  We now need to allocate rest of the margin to
```

```
the bottom margin (12px/7.2px = 1.667em) so in total with border-width it would be a multiple
of the base unit */
  margin: 1em 0;

/* Padding top and bottom is 12px each, total = 24px */
  padding: 1em 0;
}
```

Here's how the markup looks with this style applied (http://jsfiddle.net/nimbu/eg8D6/15).

If you override the font size of any of these elements elsewhere, the grid will go haywire. In case of vertical rhythm with pixels, unaccounted-for elements (such as images with sizes that are not a multiple of the base unit, ads, browser chrome that shows up in form elements, or dynamically loaded text like Twitter widgets) will cause the same problem.

Setting the grid

Setting the baseline grid manually is not a trivial task. We need to account for the interactions of not just the current element but also the previous elements to which it has been applied. After several layers of nesting, this becomes a very hairy prospect. We also need to account for margin collapsing especially if the larger margin is not a whole multiple of the vertical rhythm unit.

This process of defining a baseline grid is much easier if we set a grid image as a background for immediate visual verification. There are many ways to do this, but in all of them we need to provide the size of the base unit.

- *With a plugin*: Gridbuilder (http://gridbuilder.kilianvalkhof.com/) generates an image based on the options we provide, which we can then set as a background image.

- *With a CSS gradient*: We can use repeating gradients in this manner to set up a grid background image (http://jsfiddle.net/nimbu/BUvMw/). Chapter 11 goes more in depth about gradients.

- *Using a bookmarklet*: Andrée Hansson has a bookmarklet that renders the grid for us on the page we use it on (http://peol.github.com/960gridder/).

Automating vertical rhythms

There are not many tools out there that create automatic vertical rhythms, but the following are useful:

- Iain Lamb's Typographic tool (http://lamb.cc/typograph/) is a good way to understand how to apply vertical rhythm.

- Andrew has a tool (http://drewish.com/tools/vertical-rhythm) to compute CSS for vertical rhythm if we input the target font sizes. This should be sufficient for most basic cases.

- Smashing Magazine has a roundup of Photoshop tools for working with grids (www.smashingmagazine.com/2011/11/09/establishing-your-grid-in-photoshop/).

- Compass (the CSS framework on top of Sass preprocessor) provides handy vertical rhythm mixins that makes composing to a vertical rhythm trivial (http://compass-style.org/reference/compass/typography/vertical_rhythm/).

Baseline grid in summary

Setting baseline rhythm is not an easy task, but grid tools make this process easier and ultimately fruitful for an elegant presentation of content. Next, we will look at different ways to adjust type with CSS3. There are many more options now than before!

Fun with web type

Remember the anatomy of type lesson? This section shows some real-world application of those terms. CSS3 offers a lot of support for adjusting type. Here are some of the ways to work with type in CSS3.

Choose the weight of glyphs

Using the `font-weight` property we can set text to render darker and heavier. It can have the following values:

- `100 to 900`: These values form an ordered sequence, where each number indicates a weight that is at least as dark as its predecessor.

- `normal`: The font renders as though a weight of 400 has been specified.

- `bold`: The font renders as though a weight of 700 has been specified.

- bolder: Uses a weight that is bolder than the inherited value. For example,

```
body { font-weight: normal; }
p { font-weight: bolder; }
```

sets the text of all paragraph elements to be of weight larger than 400.

- lighter: Uses a weight that is lighter than the inherited value. For example,

```
body { font-weight: normal; }
p { font-weight: lighter; }
```

sets the text of all paragraph elements to be of a weight smaller than 400.

The exact mappings for the bolder and lighter keywords are in Table 10-10.

Table 10-10. List of Font Weights and Their Respective Bolder and Lighter Values

Inherited Value	Bolder	Lighter
100	400	100
200	400	100
300	400	100
400	700	100
500	700	100
600	900	400
700	900	400
800	900	700
900	900	700

The interesting feature (and one that causes the most heartburn for typographers) is that the browser generates bold/light font faces for fonts that have no defined settings for bold or light values. For example, if we use Helvetica Neue Light and set the font weight to be 800, because there is no bolder font of Helvetica Neue Light available by default on a user's computer, the browser will generate a bolder version to render the text on screen (see Figure 10-3). Table 10-11 lists the browser support for font-weight.

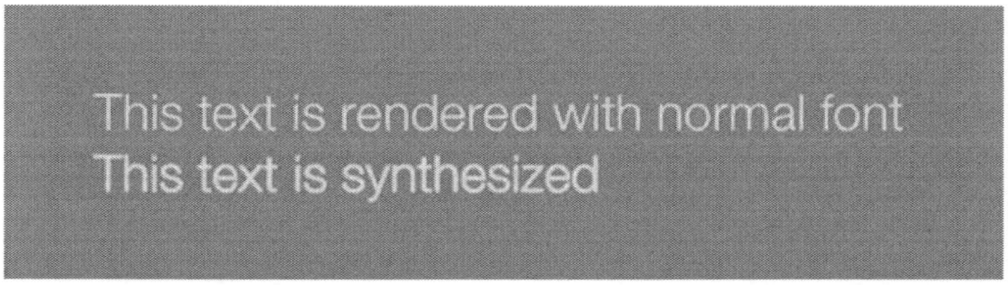

Figure 10-3. Synthesized text

Table 10-11. Browser Support for font-weight

IE	Firefox	Safari	Chrome	Opera
5.5+	1+	1.3+	2+	9.2+

Choosing the right font width

With font-stretch we can select a normal, condensed, or expanded typeface from a font family. Support is limited to IE9+ and Firefox 9+ (see Table 10-12).

Table 10-12. Browser Support for font-stretch

IE	Firefox	Safari	Chrome	Opera
9	9	-	-	-

Control text overflow

When the text overflows its block container (which has overflow set to anything but visible), we can control how to clip the overflowing text. This property gets triggered when

- The white-space property of the block element is set to nowrap

  or

- A word is longer than the width of the block container (in case of text written in horizontal text like English).

We can set the text to either clip or render an ellipsis (…) after the first few visible characters. Figure 10-4 shows an example of how it renders. See Table 10-13 for browser support.

Figure 10-4. text-overflow: ellipsis in action

Table 10-13. Browser Support for text-overflow

IE	Firefox	Safari	Chrome	Opera
6, 7, 9[1]	7+	1.3+	1.0+	9+[2], 11.0+

[1] *IE 9 requires -ms- prefix.*
[2] *Opera 9-10 require -o- prefix.*

Align text vertically from baseline

The vertical-align property allows us to set the position of an inline element with respect to its parent. Note that it refers to *inline* element. By default, inline elements (like b, i, em, img, strong, etc.) are aligned to the baseline of the parent element. But we can tweak the placement of the inline element to match several of these options: baseline (default), sub, super, top, text-top, middle, bottom, text-bottom, inherit. We can also set them with length units and percentages, like so:

```
sup { vertical-align: 30%; }
```

Figure 10-5 shows an example. See Table 10-14 for browser support.

Figure 10-5. The character 1 is placed above the baseline with vertical-align set to 30% of line height

This code raises the position of the sup from the baseline by a percentage of the line-height value. If we want to raise/lower the position from the baseline by a fixed value, we can use length units.

```
sup { vertical-align: 20px; }
```

Table 10-14. Browser Support for vertical-align

IE	Firefox	Safari	Chrome	Opera
5.5+	1.0+	1.3+	2.0+	9.2+

> *CSS3 redefines the values allowed in vertical-align radically to take into account languages other than English (www.w3.org/TR/css3-linebox/#vertical-align-prop).*

Control the white space between letters of a word

Letter Spacing lets us set the space between two characters in the text. A negative value indicates that the space between the two characters will contract. See Figure 10-6 for an example and Table 10-15 for browser support.

```
p { letter-spacing: 5px; }
```

Figure 10-6. letter-spacing: 5px in action

In CSS, we can only set a uniform letter spacing that will add the same spacing between two sets of characters in text. To customize this (to tweak the spacing between different set of characters), we can use lettering.js (http://letteringjs.com/), a jQuery plugin that wraps each character in a span element with a classname, which we can then use to tweak the setting for each character. Figure 10-7 shows an example of it in action.

Figure 10-7. Lettering.js used to good effect on Trent Walton's blog post trentwalton.com/2011/11/18workspace/

Table 10-15. Browser Support for letter-spacing

IE	Firefox	Safari	Chrome	Opera
5.5+	1+	1.3+	2.0+	9.2+

In CSS3, this has been updated to take 1 to 3 values each of which specify the optimum spacing, minimum spacing, and maximum spacing respectively. No browser has implemented this new syntax yet.

Adjust spacing between words

`word-spacing` specifies the behavior of the space between two words. A negative value indicates contraction of space between words.

`h2 { word-spacing: 2px; }`

We can also use this creatively on inline block elements to prevent white space from affecting their placement in this manner (`http://jsfiddle.net/nimbu/UrLBk/`).

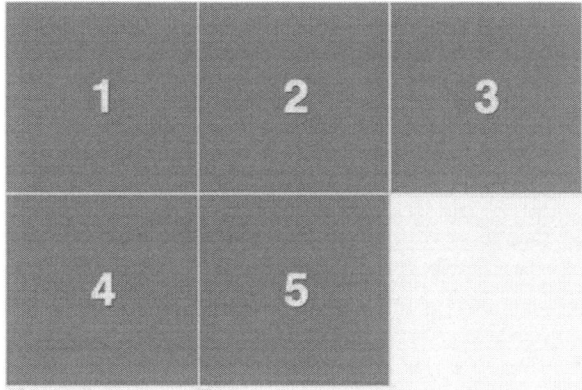

Figure 10-8 shows another example. See Table 10-16 for browser support.

Figure 10-8. word-spacing: 20px in action

Table 10-16. Browser Support for word-spacing

IE	Firefox	Safari	Chrome	Opera
6+	1+	1.3+	2.0+	9.2+

> *In CSS3, this has been updated to take 1 to 3 values each of which specify the optimum spacing, minimum spacing, and maximum spacing respectively. No browser has implemented this new syntax yet.*

Break Long Words

If a sentence contains an unbreakable word (like "antidisestablishmentarianism"), browsers usually render it in the same line even if it overflows the width of the container. We can use word-wrap: break-word to tell browsers to break the word if it is too long to fit the width of its container. Figure 10-9 shows and example and Table 10-17 lists browser support.

```
h2 { word-wrap: break-word; }
```

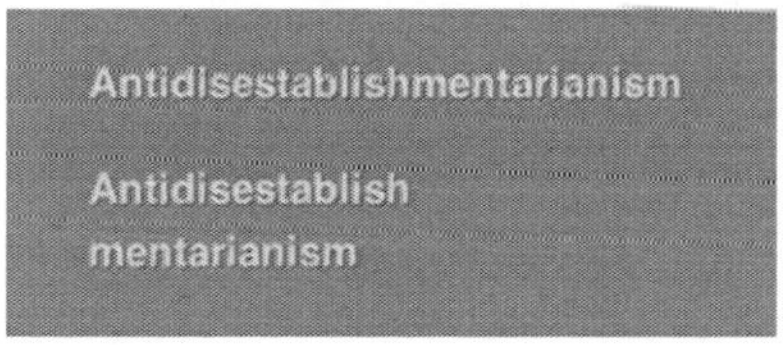

Figure 10-9. word-wrap: break-word in action. The first word expands beyond the width of the container as it is wider, but by using word-wrap: break-word, the second word breaks to fit into the width of the container.

Table 10-17. Browser Support for word-wrap

IE	Firefox	Safari	Chrome	Opera	
5 5+	3.5+	1.0+	1.0+	10.5+	

Control white space and line breaks

The white-space property simply selects one of the following options for handling of white spaces in text for the selected element:

- normal: Collapses white space and breaks lines as necessary to fill the dimensions (and not when newlines are present).

- nowrap: White spaces are collapsed, but lines are not broken.

- pre: White spaces are not collapsed, and lines are broken only if there is a newline In the text or, in the case of generated content, "\A".

- pre-wrap: Behaves like pre but lines are broken as necessary to fill the dimensions or if newline is present.

- pre-line: Behaves like pre-wrap except it also collapses spaces and tabs.

Figure 10-10 shows an example and Table 10-18 lists browser support.

425

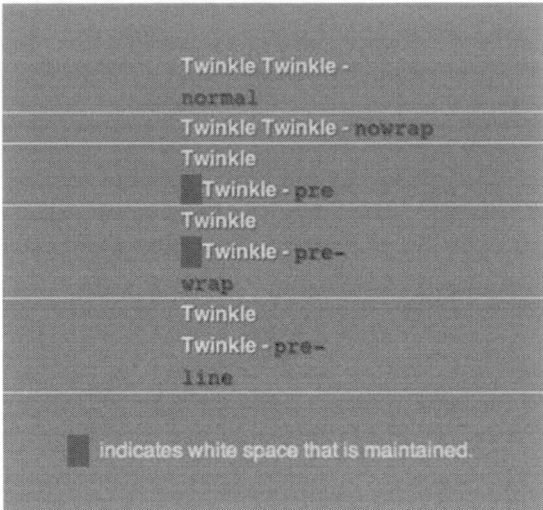

Figure 10-10. white-space property with all the available keyword values in action

Table 10-18. Browser Support for white-space

IE	Firefox	Safari	Chrome	Opera
8+	3.5+	1.3+	2.0+	9.2+

Print hyphens

For years, web designers have attempted to find a solution that would allow them to justify text beautifully—with hyphens. Fortunately, a lot of work has recently been done to get some control over the hyphens in CSS.

hyphens

With the hyphens property, we can control the display of hyphens. It takes one of the following values:

- none: Words are not broken into separate lines.

- manual: Words are broken into separate lines if there are line-breaking characters within them like a soft hyphen (­) or a hyphen character (-).

- auto: Words are broken at appropriate hyphenation points. Note that a browser requires the knowledge of the language used for the text that gets hyphenated, so this only works on text that has an appropriate language declared (via the lang attribute on a parent element, which could be html or body) and for which the browser has the right hyphenation resource.

```
h2 { hyphens: auto; }
```

See Figure 10-11 for an example and Table 10-19 for browser support.

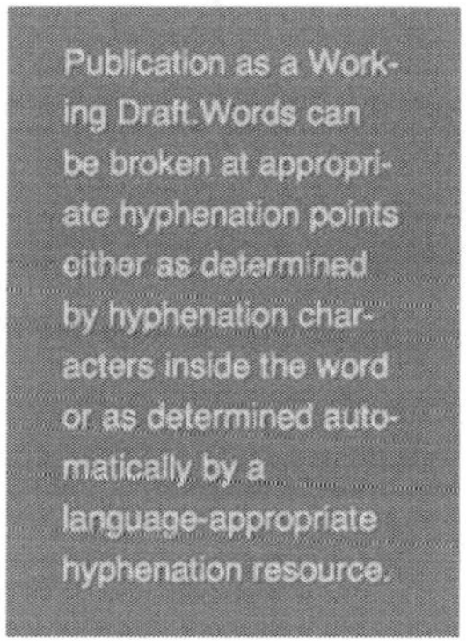

Figure 10-11. hyphens: auto in action

Note that the initial value for hyphens is manual. For words to be hyphenated automatically, this property should be set to auto.

Table 10-19. Browser Support for hyphens

IE	Firefox	Safari	Chrome	Opera
10+[1]	6+[2]	5.1+[3]	-	-

[1] *Needs a –ms-preflx.*
[2] *Needs a -moz- prefix.*
[3] *Needs a –webklt- prefix.*

Go to *http://jsfiddle.net/nimbu/Rv6vV/* for a demo of hyphens.

Soft Hyphens

A soft hyphen (represented in HTML entity as ­) is used to indicate to a browser where the word can be hyphenated. This is not a CSS property but it's currently the only way to implement hyphens that work across all browsers. Here is a paragraph with the soft hyphens in use:

A slightly longer but less commonly accepted variant of the word can be found in the Duke Ellington song "You're Just an Old Antidisestablish­mentarianismist"[3] although the correct construction of that word would be "antidisestablish­mentarianist" (without the "ism").

This paragraph renders identical to one without soft hyphens in situations where soft hyphens are not necessary, as you can see in Figure 10-12.

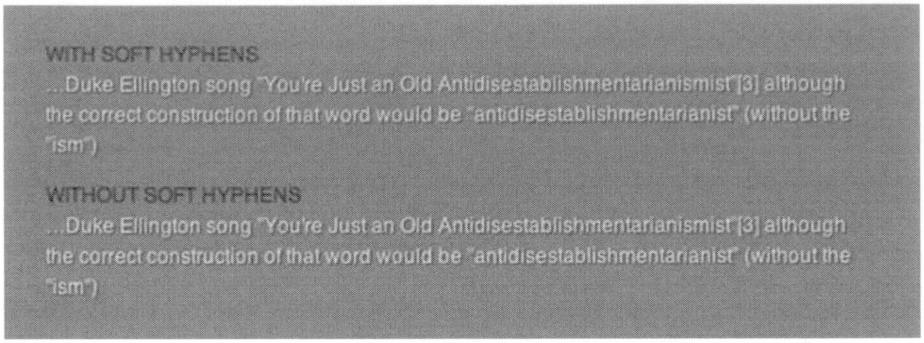

Figure 10-12. Soft hyphens do not render when they are not needed (here both sections look identical).

But once the words start breaking, the words with soft hyphens start to look different, as you can see in Figure 10-13.

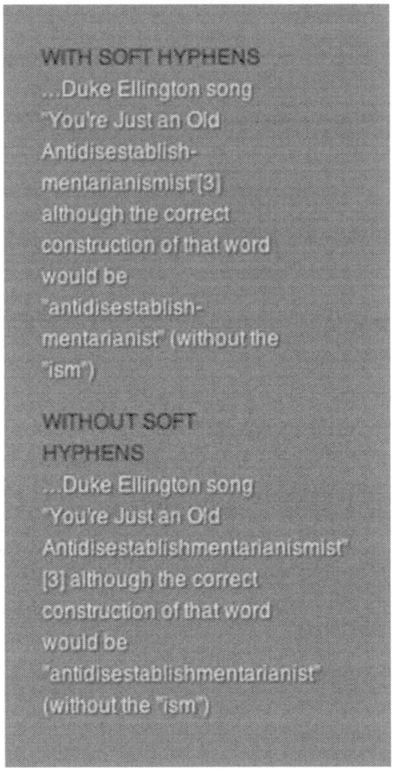

Figure 10-13. Soft hyphens render when the words need to be broken as they meet line breaks.

It is hard to remember to add soft hyphens in the text. Fortunately, there are some tools we can use. Ideally we shouldn't be doing this client-side, but if it's necessary, we can use the no-longer-updated

Sweet Justice (http://carlos.bueno.org/2010/04/sweet-justice.html) or Soft Hyphenator (http://www.softhyphen.com/). Table 10-20 lists browser support for soft hyphens.

Table 10-20. Browser Support for Soft Hyphens

IE	Firefox	Safari	Chrome	Opera
5.5+	3.0+	3.0+	1.0+	9.6+

Control the quote glyphs

With the quotes property we can set the glyph that will be used for opening and closing quotes for each level of quotes (outermost to innermost). Then, by using the content property with open-quote or close-quote keywords, we can set the quotes for each selector.

Markup:

```
<blockquote><p>Imagine a puddle waking up one morning and thinking, <q>This is an interesting world I find myself in — an interesting hole I find myself in — fits me rather neatly, doesn't it?</q></p></blockquote>
```

Style:

```
blockquote { quotes:  "+" ";" "<" ">"; }

blockquote::before,
q::before { content: open-quote; }

blockquote::after,
q::after { content: close-quote; }
```

Figure 10-14 shows the resulting text (the quote glyphs are indicated in black). Table 10-21 lists browser support.

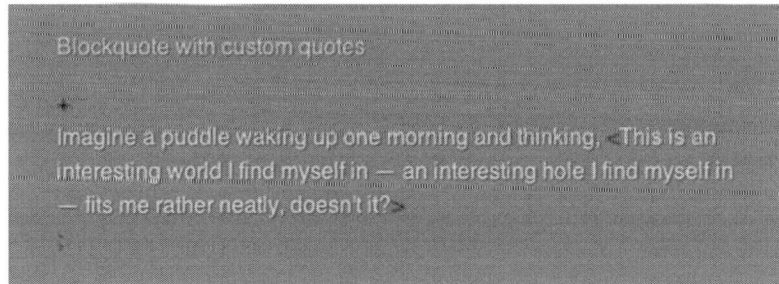

Figure 10-14. Custom quote glyphs in action

Table 10-21. Browser Support for Quotes

IE	Firefox	Safari	Chrome	Opera
8+	1.0+	-	12.0+	9.2+

Hanging Punctuation

In document layout tools, we can typically set punctuation marks such that they do not disrupt the flow of text. However, this was not possible in the browser. With CSS3, we can now do this! It can take on the following values:

- none: No characters can hang.

- first: An opening bracket or quote at the start of the first formatted line of an element hangs. See Figure 10-15 for an example.

Figure 10-15. hanging-punctuation: first in action

- last: A closing bracket or quote at the end of the last formatted line of an element hangs.

- force-end: A stop or comma at the end of a line hangs. See Figure 10-16 for an example.

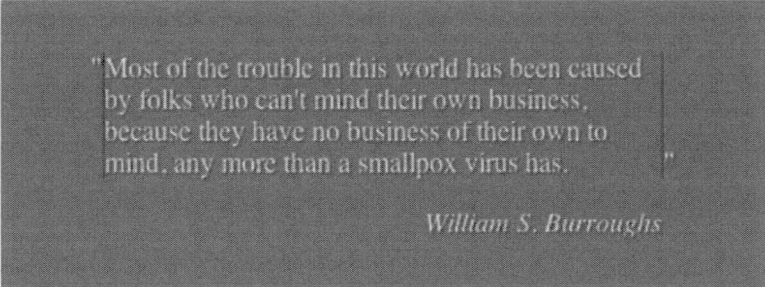

Figure 10-16. hanging-punctuation: force-end in action

- allow-end: A stop or comma at the end of a line hangs if it does not otherwise fit prior to justification.

We can use it in this manner:

```
p {
    hanging-punctuation: allow-end;
}
```

- hanging-punctuation, when set, is not considered when measuring the line's content for fit, alignment, or justification. This property has no support in any browser at the time of writing but holds great promise!

Control the rendering of non-latin web type

CSS3 introduces many new properties that allow for greater flexibility and styling of non-latin type. Here are a few such features.

word-break

This sets how we want words to be broken (if at all) while distributing words across lines. Here are the options:

- normal: Lines are created as per usual rules.

- break-all: Lines break at every word that "overflows" the width of the container. This is only useful if we use CJK (short term for Chinese, Japanese, Korean scripts) characters predominantly and would like the text to be distributed more evenly across lines.

- keep-all: CJK characters have implied break points that are no longer be applied when this value is used. This value means words will not be broken (which is equivalent to normal for other scripts).

text-emphasis

In CJK scripts, emphasis is represented by small symbols next to the emphasised characters. There are four properties that we can use to style and render these symbols:

- text-emphasis-style: This property allows us to set the kind of symbol we would like to use for emphasis. We can choose from the available keywords or set our own character to be used as the symbol.

```
h2 em { text-emphasis-style: double-circle; }
```

- text-emphasis-color: We can make these emphasis marks be of a different color than the body text.

```
h2 em { text-emphasis-color: red; }
```

- text-emphasis-position: This property lets us specify where we want the emphasis marks to be.

```
h2 em { text-emphasis-position: above right; }
```

- text-emphasis: This shortcut property allows us to set `text-emphasis-style` and `text-emphasis-color` together. However `text-emphasis-position` depends on the language of the text and is inherited (as it needs to be set only once). Here is a demo of text-emphasis (view it in Chrome or Safari 5.1).

```
h2 em { text-emphasis: double-circle indianred; }
```

Currently only Chrome and Safari 5.1+ support `text-emphasis` with the –webkit- prefix.

Use ligatures and additional OpenType font features

OpenType format provides a lot of additional font features that are usually only available for use through applications such as Adobe InDesign. Within CSS3 Fonts Module, these features are now exposed for web developers to use. When this is implemented, we can use ligatures, swashes, small caps, and tabular figures in our text. The syntax is as follows:

```
h2.fancy {
  /* enable small caps and use second swash alternate */
  font-feature-settings: "smcp", "swsh" 2;
}
```

`smcp` and `swsh` are case-sensitive OpenType feature tags. The full list of tags can be found on the OpenType specification at `www.microsoft.com/typography/otspec/featurelist.htm`. The value 2 next to `swsh` indicates the index of the glyph to be selected.

Firefox 4 has an implementation of the `font-feature-settings` that is slightly different.

```
h2.fancy {
  -moz-font-feature-settings: "smcp=1,swsh=2";
}
```

Table 10-22 lists browser support.

Table 10-22. Browser Support for Font Features

IE	Firefox	Safari	Chrome	Opera
10+	4.0+	-	16.0+	-

> Read John Daggett's post describing CSS3 font-features at *http://jsfiddle.net/nimbu/Rv6vV/* and Fontdeck's blog post on font features (*http://blog.fontdeck.com/post/15777165734/opentype-1*) and Internet Explorer's demonstration (*http://ie.microsoft.com/testdrive/Graphics/opentype/opentype-fontbureau/index.html*).

Summary

We showed the history of web typography from the dark ages to the present with its plethora of features for controlling type. We showed how @font-face has evolved and the different ways to adjust type on a page. In this chapter, you also learned to set type according to a rhythm both in relative and absolute units. We also looked briefly at some of the properties for controlling non-latin type.

Further Reading

- CSS Text Module (`http://dev.w3.org/csswg/css3-text/`): Some of the features in this chapter are outlined in greater detail here.

- CSS Generated Content Module (`http://dev.w3.org/csswg/css3-content/`): More information on the quotes property can be found in this module.

- CSS Fonts Module (`http://dev.w3.org/csswg/css3-fonts/`): This module explains @font-face rule in depth and the font feature settings that are available for OpenType formats

- CSS Line Layout Module (`http://dev.w3.org/csswg/css3-linebox/`): Vertical alignment as it is proposed in CSS3 is discussed in great detail here.

- "Compose to a Vertical Rhythm" (`http://24ways.org/2006/compose-to-a-vertical-rhythm`): Ground-breaking article explaining vertical rhythms.

- "Bulletproof @font-face syntax" (`http://paulirish.com/2009/bulletproof-font-face-implementation-syntax/`): Documents the evolution of a font-face rule that works across all browsers over a year.

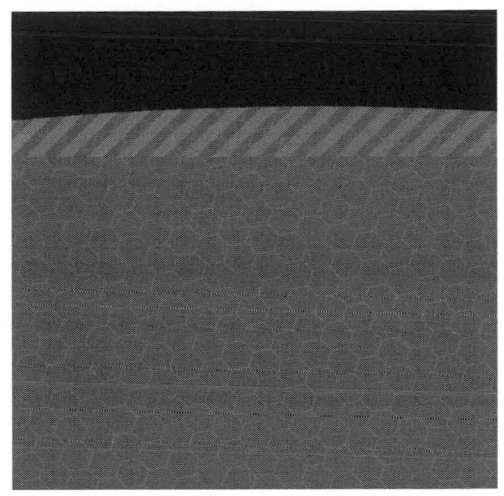

Chapter 11

Putting CSS3 Properties to Work

So far in the second half of this book you've had a refresher on CSS basics; learned about new selectors; created beautiful, flexible layouts; and wandered through the wild world of web typography. Now it's time to put some more CSS3 properties to work and add those subtle sprinkles to your site.

In this chapter we'll look at new color models, transparency, and background properties; we'll also show how to apply multiple backgrounds, borders, shadows, and gradients. So whether you want to create a visually stunning, cutting edge design or a crazy, loud, over-the-top Web 2.0 monstrosity, we've got your back.

Color and transparency

We're used to expressing color values with either their keyword (red, blue) or hexadecimal (hex) values (#fff or #ffffff) in our style sheets. The CSS3 color module (http://j.mp/css3color[1]) introduces two new ways to write color values: RGBa and HSLa. Before deciding which method to use, we need to understand the difference between RGB and HSL.

---

[1] www.w3.org/TR/css3-color

RGB

No doubt you've heard of RGB before. To clarify, it represents the red, green, and blue color model in which you create a color using three numerical values for each color. Thinking back to art school, RGB is an *additive* color model whereby a color is created by adding the three primary colors together. This works in the same way as a hexadecimal calculation by multiplying the three values together, the difference being that the values are represented in different ways. RGB uses a number between 0-255. Figure 11-1 shows RGB values specified in Photoshop's color picker.

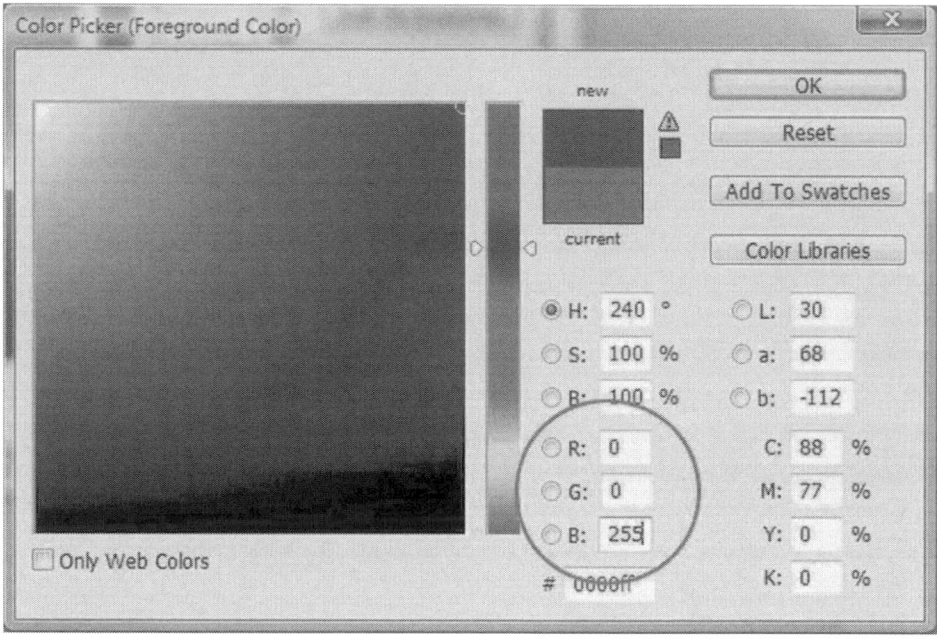

Figure 11-1. Color picker in Photoshop

We're used to describing color, such as pure blue for example, with CSS in one of three different ways: the name, shorthand hex code, and full hex code.

```
color: blue;
color: #00f;
color: #0000ff;
```

To implement color using RGB, you use the `rgb` keyword followed by the RGB values in brackets. To describe pure blue using RGB, we can use numerical or percentage values for red, green, and blue. The RGB value is actually part of CSS 2.1 but hasn't been commonly used until recently. Here are both the numerical and percentage values (note that the rest of the examples will use the numerical value).

```
color: rgb(0,0,255);
color: rgb(0,0,100%);
/* color: rgb(red, green, blue); */
```

> Note: Don't forget that *rgb* doesn't just have to be used with the *color* property; you can use it in your CSS anywhere that you declare a color value, such as *background* and *border-color*.

You can start using RGB values in your work right away. It's supported in all browsers from IE6, Safari 3, Firefox 3, Chrome, and Opera 10 upwards.

RGBa transparency

By adding a fourth value to your property, you can control the transparency. The fourth value, the "a" in RGBa, stands for alpha. Its function is exactly the same as changing the alpha channel in Photoshop.

To implement RGBa, you need to change your rgb keyword to rgba; this allows us to set the transparency. The 'a' (alpha) value is set by adding a number between 0 and 1 (where 0 is fully transparent and 1 is fully opaque). The value 0.6 is equivalent to setting the transparency at 60%.

```
color: rgba(0,0,255,0.6);
/* color: rgba(red, green, blue, alpha); */
```

Figure 11-2 shows varying values of alpha transparency from fully opaque (1) to fully transparent (0).

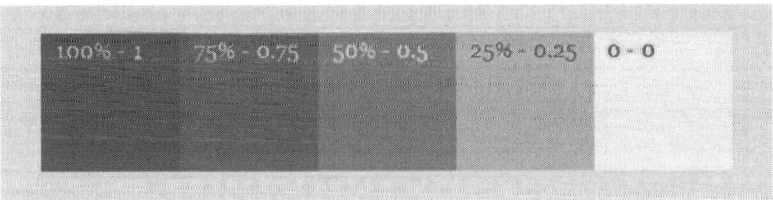

Figure 11-2. RGBa transparency in action

A number of high profile sites have started using RGBa. One of the best examples is 24 Ways (http://j.mp/24ways.org[2]) designed by Tim Van Damme (http://j.mp/timvd[3]) (Figure 11-3).

---

[2] http://24ways.org
[3] http://maxvoltar.com

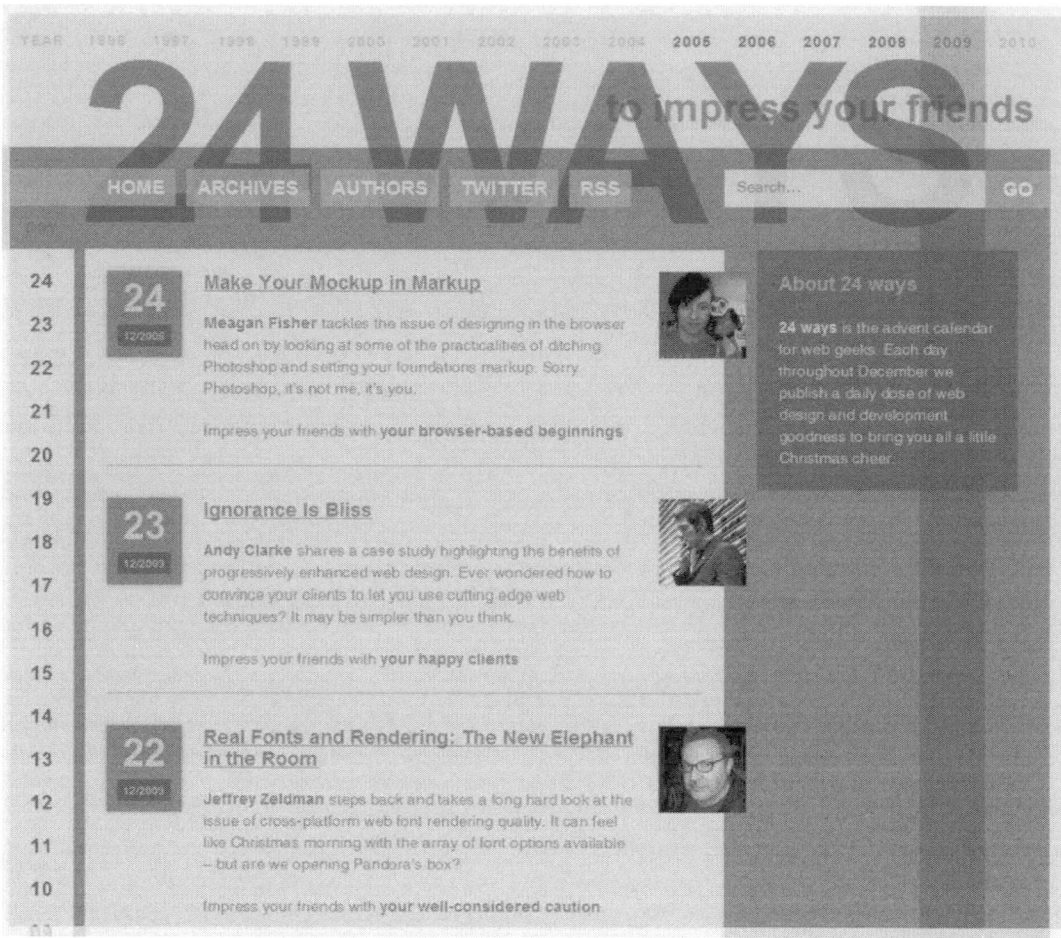

Figure 11-3. The 24 Ways site is built with heavy use of RGBa.

Browser support for RGBa isn't as far ranging as it is for RGB. It is supported in all the browsers stated earlier, with the exception of IE 6-8. It *is* supported in IE9, however. To cater for those less capable browsers, add a solid color fallback into your style rule.

```
a {
  color:rgb(0,0,255); /* Fallback for less capable browsers */
  color:rgba(0,0,255,0.6);
}
```

Browsers apply the last property they understand, so adding the RGBa keyword last ensures that more capable browsers will apply the transparency. Those that don't understand RGBa will simply ignore it and implement the property they do understand (the first color value). In cases where you can't make do with a solid color, you can add a fallback PNG in just the same way.

```
article {
  background:url(white50.png); /* Fallback for less capable browsers */
  background:rgba(255,255,255,0.6);
}
```

Having the ability to edit alpha transparency without the use of images means we can apply it to borders and outlines as well. Plus, editing only your CSS when changes are required is easier and quicker than returning to Photoshop to update multiple images. Finally, as a fortunate side effect, the number of server requests is reduced (because you're not loading images), which will make your site faster.

HSLa

An alternative method for adding color using CSS3 is to use HSLa (hue, saturation, lightness, and alpha). HSL is more intuitive than RGB. You can make an informed guess at the initial color by thinking about a color wheel and then adjusting the saturation and lightness values until we find the exact shade we're after.

The hue value is represented by a value of 0-360 degrees. Looking at the color wheel in Figure 11-4 we can see that red is represented by 0 and 360 degrees with the other two primary colors at 120 degree intervals (green = 120 and blue = 240).

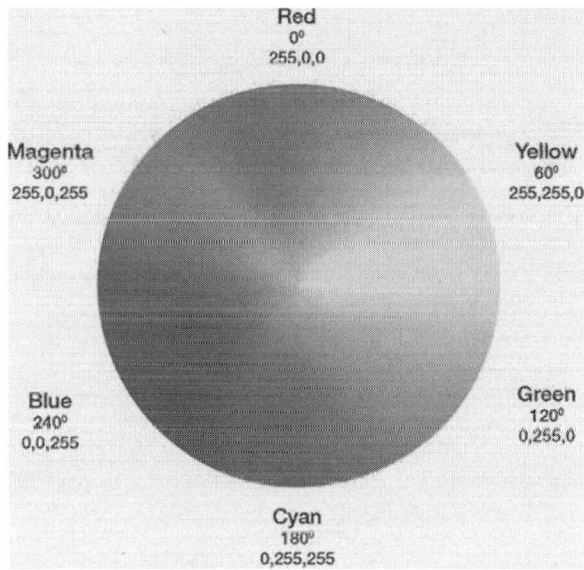

Figure 11-4. HSLa color wheel from blulob.com

The second value in the HSL notation is for saturation, or the intensity of a particular color. It is a percentage value described as the colorfulness compared to grey where 0 is grayscale and 100% is full color saturation. The third value represents lightness and is specified as a percentage with 0 being dark or black, 50% as normal lightness, and 100% as white.

To achieve pure red using HSLa, we need to combine the three values for hue (0 or 360 degrees), saturation (100%, full saturation), and lightness (50%, normal lightness). In addition, the alpha channel should be set to 1 to ensure the color is fully opaque.

```
hsla(0,100%,50%,1)
/* hsla (hue, saturation, lightness, alpha) */
```

> Note: HSLa color values are a mix of degrees and percentages plus an alpha channel.

Figure 11-5 shows a number of variations of the pure red example created by editing the respective values for hue, saturation, lightness, and alpha. It's worth trying this out for yourself to get the idea; a black and white book doesn't always convey the full effect.

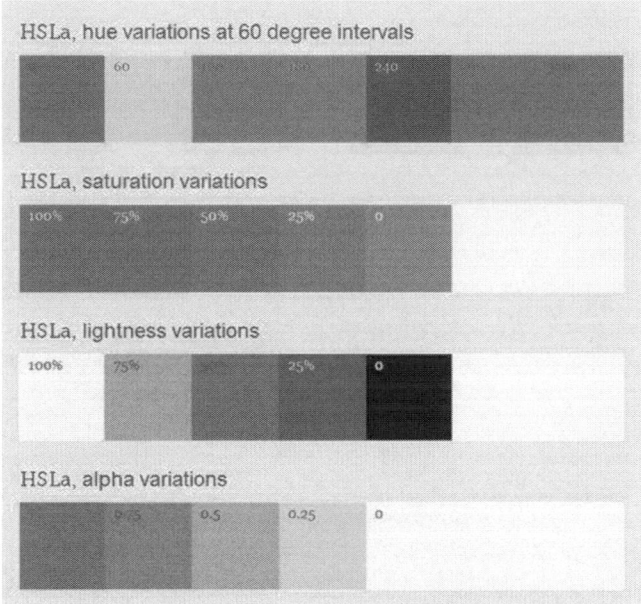

Figure 11-5. Demonstration of how to achieve color variations using HSLa

As with RGBa, HSLa is supported by most major browsers (including IE 9) with the exception of IE 6-8.

Calculating RGB values can be difficult for a designer working only with CSS. In contrast, HSL allows us to choose one color for the hue (a value between 0-360) and then refine it using the saturation and lightness values. This is all with a minimum of fuss and saves having to keep skipping back into Photoshop to check that the color values are correct.

Note: The HSL Color Picker (`http://hslpicker.com/`) by Brandon Mathis is exactly that—a handy little tool for picking a hue and adjusting the saturation and lightness. It also provides the hex and rgb equivalents of the color you choose.

Opacity

Alpha transparency is not the only way of creating see-through elements; an alternative approach is to use the opacity property. It works in a similar way to the alpha channel in RGBa or HSLa by taking a value between 0 and 1—the difference being that it is the only value specified for the property. This means you still need to declare the color using another property such as background-color or color. To set an article's background to be 50% opaque, we would use:

```
article {
  background-color:#fff;
  opacity:0.5;
}
```

The problem, as you can see in Figure 11-6, is that when opacity is set, it affects the transparency of *all* child elements contained within the parent. RGBa and HSLa, in contrast, only affect the element and property to which it is applied.

Figure 11-6. The left shows the article without opacity and the right with 50% opacity applied.

Given the choice, on most occasions you'll want to use RGBa or HSLa for adding transparency. Opacity can be useful when you want an element to fade into the background until it's interacted with (ads or forms for example).

Using and changing opacity values in conjunction with pseudo classes such as :hover or :focus can be effective. You can also use it for visited links and fade them into the background once visited. The same effect could be achieved using RGBa or HSLa but if links are in multiple colors on your site, using opacity will target them all without you needing to write rules for each color instance.

```
a:visited {
  opacity:0.5;
}
```

Figure 11-7 shows this in action.

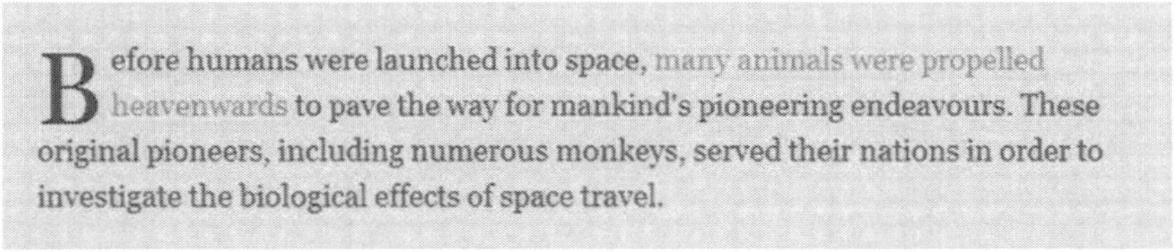

> **B**efore humans were launched into space, many animals were propelled heavenwards to pave the way for mankind's pioneering endeavours. These original pioneers, including numerous monkeys, served their nations in order to investigate the biological effects of space travel.

Figure 11-7. An example of opacity at 50% for visited links (in this instance "many animals were propelled heavenwards")

Note that opacity works in all browsers except for IE 6-8. There are specific filters available to get opacity working in IE but, as highlighted in Chapter 7, we would only use them as a last resort.

As we've seen, CSS3 provides new ways of adding and adjusting color in our designs. You've seen how to implement opacity, the RGB and HSL color models, and how to add alpha transparency. When and where you use RGBa, HSLa, and opacity is up to you but without a doubt all three have their place in our bag of CSS goodies.

Backgrounds

One of the most interesting CSS3 modules with a wide range of implementations is the Background and Borders module (http://j.mp/css3background[4]), currently a Candidate recommendation. We'll come back to borders later in the chapter but in the meantime, let's discuss background clipping, multiple backgrounds, and the option to set background size.

---

[4] www.w3.org/TR/css3-background

background-clip

We're used to seeing backgrounds extending into their borders (Figure 11-8). Introduced in the Background and Borders module is the background-clip property, which allows us to specify whether the background extends into the border or not.

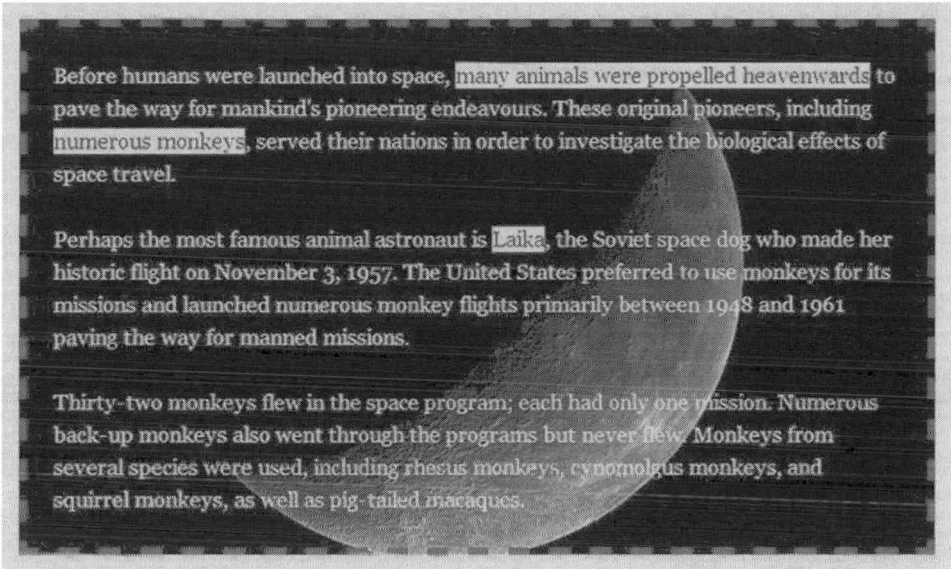

Figure 11-8. Background image extending into the border of an element

background-clip can take the following three values:

- border-box
- padding-box
- content-box

The border-box value is the default should background-clip not be declared (Figure 11-8).

Adding the padding-box value to the property clips the background to render inside the border.

```
#introduction {
  border:5px dashed rgb(255,0,0);
  background:rgba(255,255,255,0.7) url(img/bg-moon.jpg) 50% 50%;
  padding:0 20px;
  color:rgb(255,255,255);
  -moz-background-clip:padding;
  background-clip:padding-box;
}
```

Figure 11-9 shows the background rendered inside the border. Opera 10.5+, IE 9+, Safari 5+, Firefox 4+, and Chrome 5+ all implement the `background-clip` property without a vendor prefix.

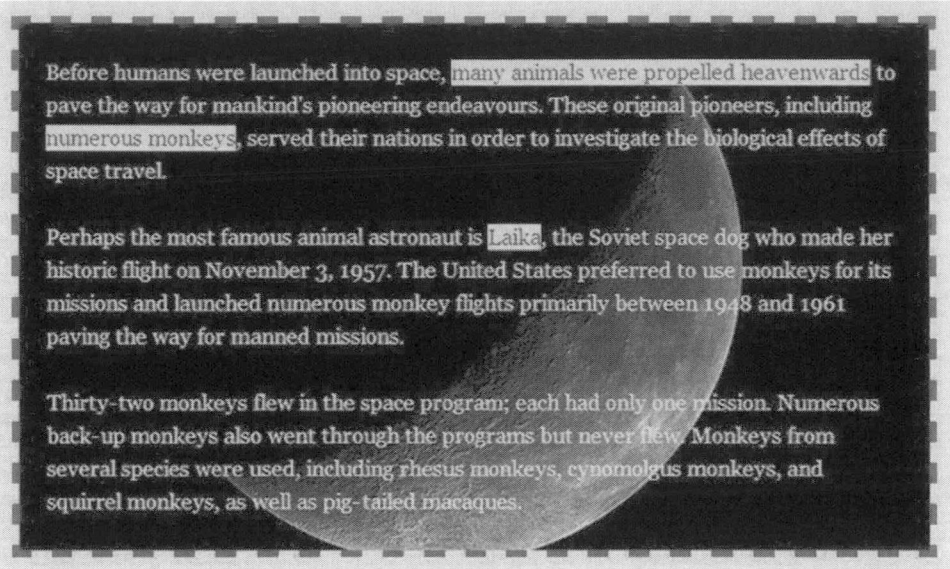

Figure 11-9. CSS3 background-clip property with the padding-box value applied

The third value, `content-box,` clips the background to the box's content area (Figure 11-10), which is the area inside the padding.

```
#introduction {
  border:5px dashed rgb(255,0,0);
  background:url(img/bg-moon.jpg) 50% 50%;
  padding:0 20px;
  color:rgb(255,255,255);
  background-clip:content-box;
}
```

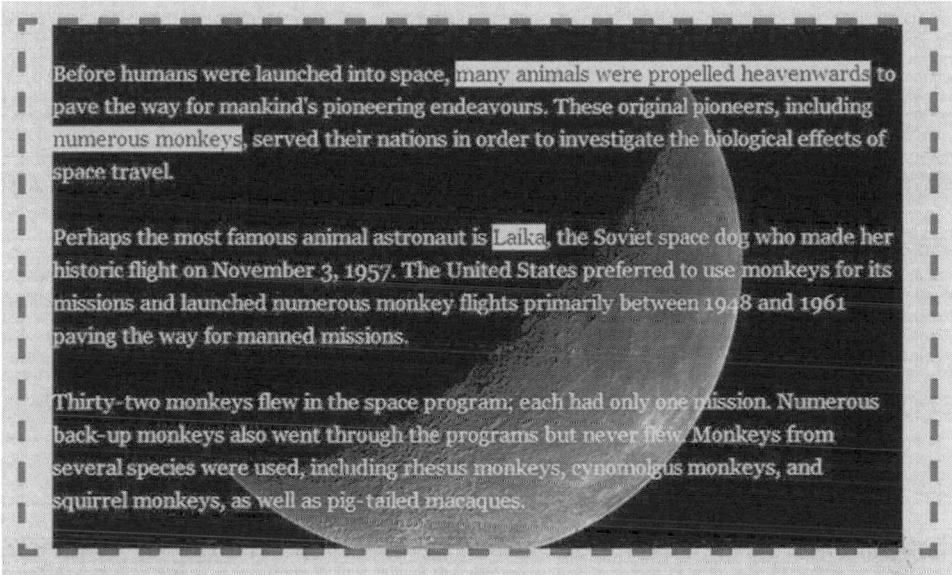

Figure 11-10. CSS3 background-clip property with the content-box value applied

background-origin

background-origin allows us to specify the starting point for the background position of a given element. It can take the same values as background-clip. For example, if your background is positioned top left (0,0), the default padding-box (Figure 11-11) value positions the background to the outer edge of the padding (also the inner edge of the border).

```
#introduction {
  border:5px dashed rgb(255,0,0);
  background:url(img/bg-moon.jpg) 0 0;
  padding:0 20px;
  color:#fff;
  background-clip:border-box;
  background-origin:padding-box;
}
```

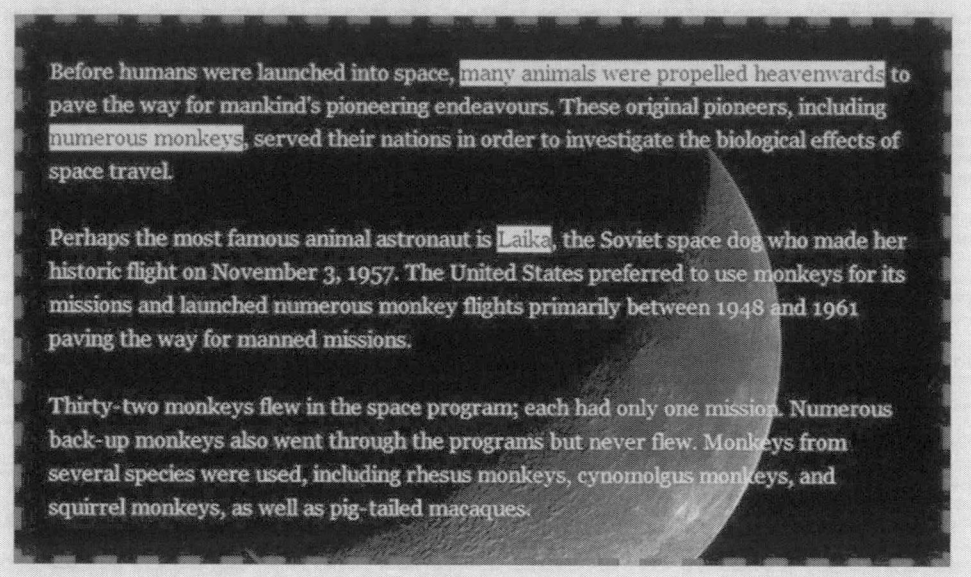

Figure 11-11. CSS3 background-origin property with the padding-box value applied

As with background-clip, background-origin is supported natively in Opera, Safari, Firefox, Chrome, and IE 9.

> *Note: The values for background-clip and background-origin don't have to be the same.*

The border-box value positions the background to the outer edge of the border (Figure 11-12). Depending on the width of your border, this change can be very subtle.

```
#introduction {
  border:5px dashed rgb(255,0,0);
  background:url(img/bg-moon.jpg) 0 0;
  padding:0 20px;
  color:#fff;
  background-clip:border-box;
  background-origin:border-box;
}
```

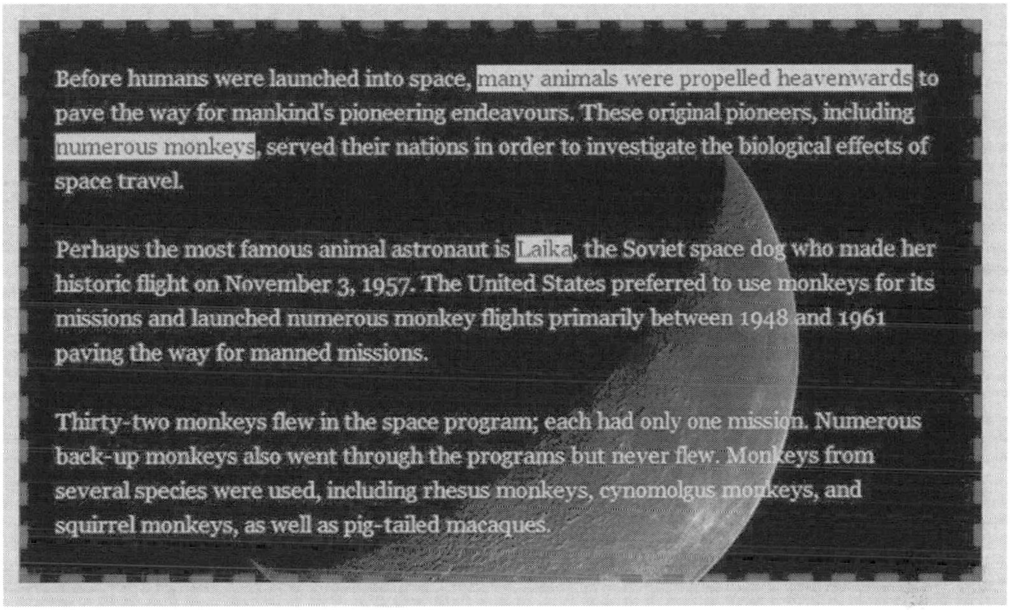

Figure 11-12. CSS3 background-origin property with the border-box value applied

The final value that `background-origin` can take is content-box, which sets the background starting point to the edge of the content, or the inner edge of the padding (Figure 11-13).

```
#introduction {
  border:5px dashed rgb(255,0,0);
  background:url(img/bg-moon.jpg) 0 0;
  padding:0 20px;
  color:#fff;
  background-clip:border-box;
  background-origin:content-box;
}
```

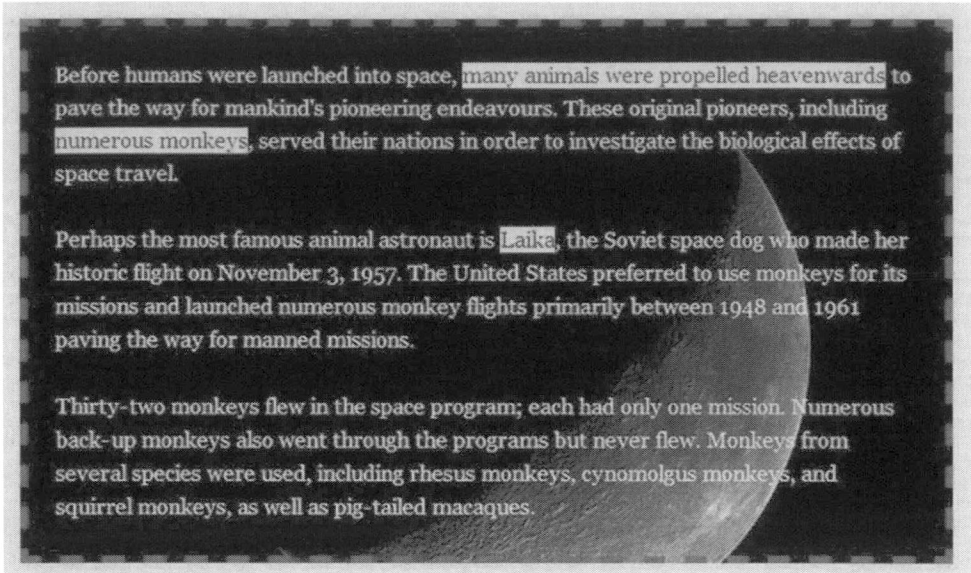

Figure 11-13. CSS3 background-origin property with the content-box value applied

Although sometimes barely noticeable, you may find background-origin to be a worthwhile alternative to using pixel positioning for your background images, depending on the effect you want to achieve.

background-size

The background-size property can be used to simplify one of those issues that web designers have been wrestling with since time (OK, maybe just the Internet) began. The problem: the need for full size background images, regardless of browser window size or screen resolution, without having to rely on Flash or JavaScript. The solution: the background-size property.

As the name suggests, it allows you to specify the size of the background image across a container in both the X (horizontal) and Y (vertical) axis. This means that if you are building a fluid design, you can use background-size to make sure that any background images you are using scale according to the size of the viewport or width of the browser.

It can take two values for width and height as well the keywords auto, contain, and cover. Width and height values can be expressed as pixels or percentages. The first value is the width, the second the height. Setting background-size to 85% gives us the effect shown in Figure 11-14.

```
html {
  background-image:url(img/earth1.jpg);
  background-position:50% 50%;
  background-repeat:no-repeat;
  background-attachment:fixed;
  background-size:85% 85%;
```

```
/background-size: width height */
}
```

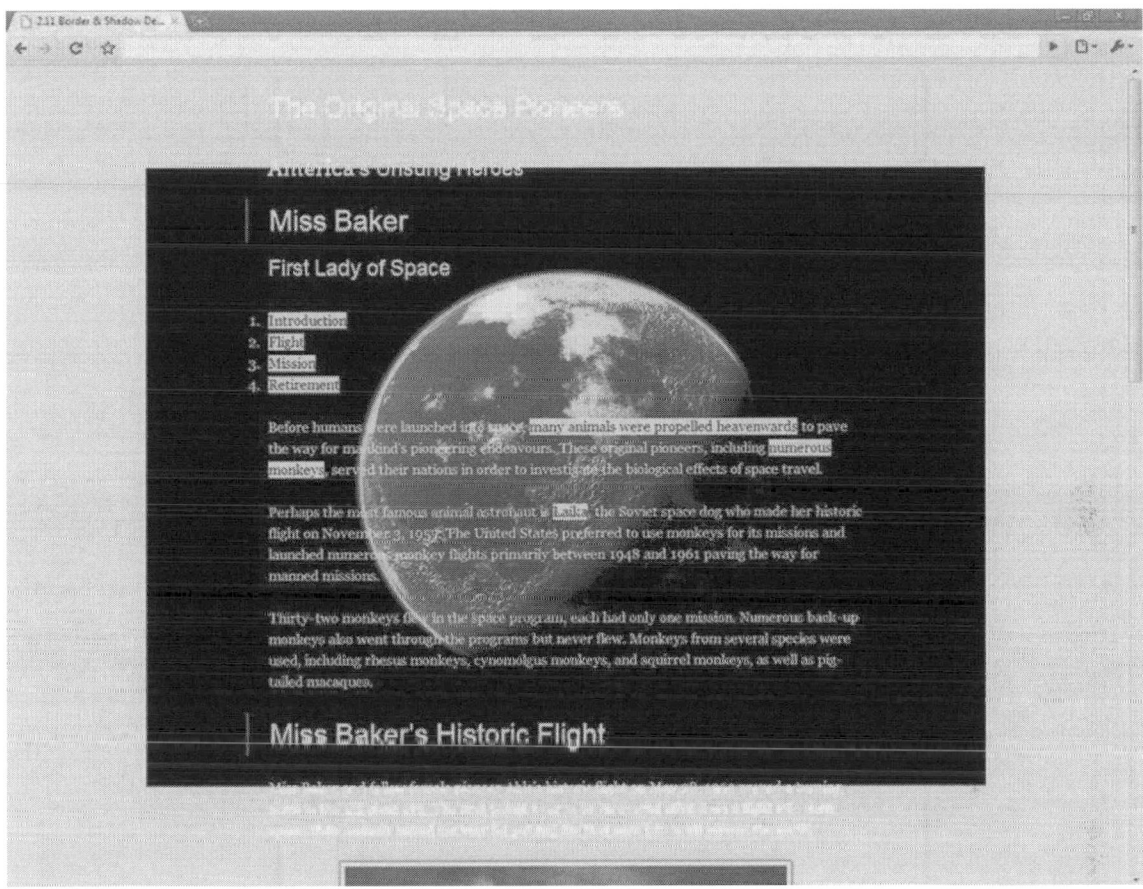

Figure 11-14. CSS3 background-size property with the width and height at 85%

You don't have to set a height value; in fact, if no height is set, the default value is auto. In this case, this has a minimal effect.

Similar to the aforementioned background properties, Opera, Safari, Firefox, Chrome, and IE 9 all support background-size.

The contain keyword scales the background and preserves its aspect ratio. The background will take the largest size in which its width *and* height can fit inside the element to which it is applied (in our case the html element). This ensures that no part of the image is clipped when using contain. If your container is too large for the image, you must make sure that your image fades to a flat color that you can use as your background default (Figure 11-15). You can "contain" either the X or the Y axis using comma-separated values (e.g. contain, 250px) or both using the contain keyword on its own.

In addition, if no width and height values are set, they are both assumed to be auto and the backgrounds size takes the same effect as using contain.

```
html {
  background-image:url(img/earth1.jpg);
  background-position:50% 50%;
  background-repeat:no-repeat;
  background-attachment:fixed;
  background-size:contain;
}
```

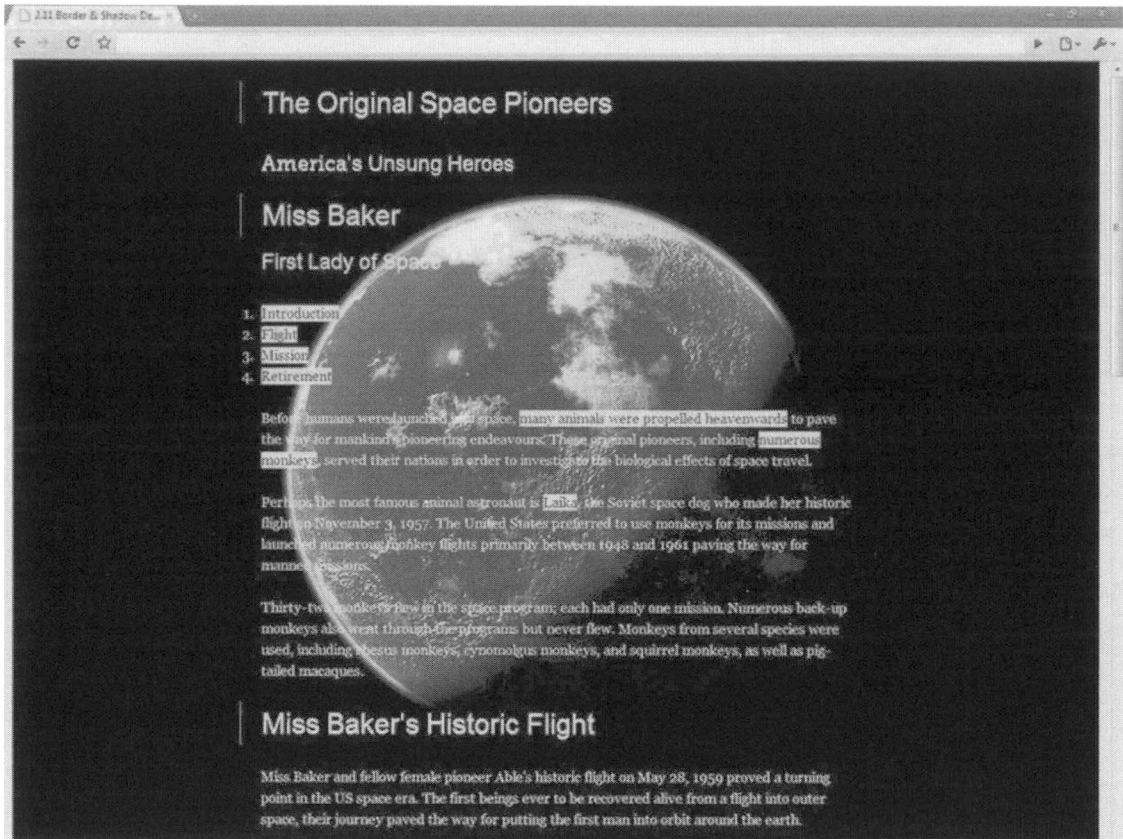

Figure 11-15. CSS3 background-size property with the contain value applied

The cover keyword, on the other hand, *always* takes over the whole background of the element. It will resize as the browser window changes size and shape but may clip a few edges of the image (Figure 11-16).

```
html {
  background-image:url(img/earth1.jpg);
  background-position:50% 50%;
  background-repeat:no-repeat;
  background-attachment:fixed;
  background-size:cover;
}
```

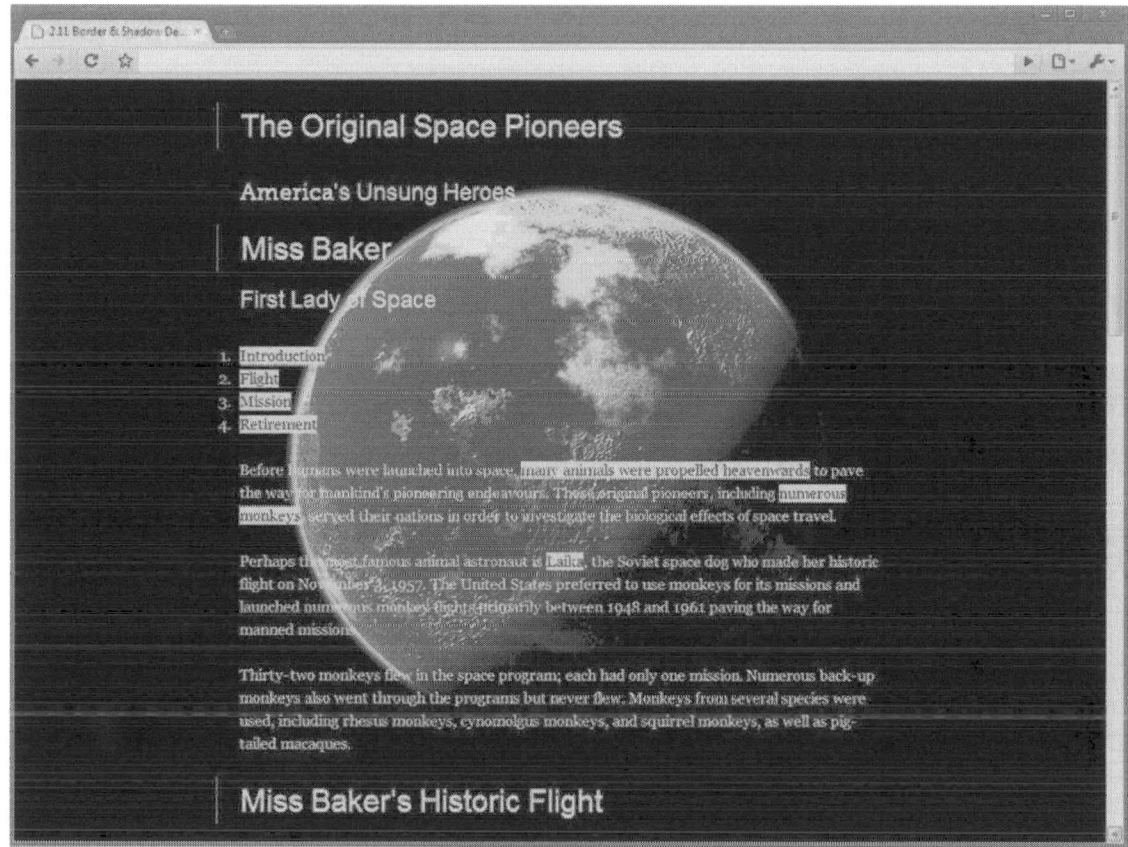

Figure 11-16. CSS3 background-size property with the cover value applied

Stephanie Rewis takes an in-depth look at background-size in an article in *.net* magazine
(http://j.mp/bgsize[5]) and links to a helpful tool created by her husband Greg for testing the cover and
contain keywords (http://j.mp/bgsizetool[6]). Using this quickly illustrates how the different keywords
create different effects.

---

[5] www.netmagazine.com/tutorials/take-advantage-css-background-size-property
[6] http://assortedgarbage.com/presario/background-size.html

In addition, in an article for A List Apart (`http://j.mp/supersizebg`[7]), Bobby van der Sluis explains how you can combine `background-size` and media queries (see Chapter 9) to ensure that your background doesn't scale down too small at lower screen resolutions. Be sure to try check out the article and implement some of Bobby's techniques.

Finally, a useful reference for all background properties, values, browser support, and more is Estelle Weyl's in-depth guide to "Everything you could possibly want to know about CSS Background Properties: Interpreting the w3c specifications with browser support and links to examples and test cases" (`http://j.mp/estellebg`[8]). Well, perhaps it's not quite everything as it doesn't cover multiple backgrounds that we'll look at next.

Multiple backgrounds

No doubt you've seen sites such as Clearleft's Silverback App (`http://j.mp/gorillaux`[9]) holding page (Figure 11-17). Created by Paul Annett (`http://j.mp/nicepaul`[10]) the site layers a few `div`s positioned using percentages with differing PNG transparent backgrounds to create the illusion of depth. When the browser window is resized, the user sees a parallax (`http://j.mp/whatisparallax`[11]) effect as the background images move to retain their proportion inside the browser.

Effects such as this tend to create a lot of unnecessary markup that doesn't have any *meaning* (due to being held in `div`s). What if we could do away with that extraneous markup? Well, guess what? With CSS3 multiple backgrounds, we can.

---

[7] www.alistapart.com/articles/supersize-that-background-please
[8] www.standardista.com/css3/css3-background-properties
[9] http://silverbackapp.com
[10] http://nicepaul.com
[11] http://en.wikipedia.org/wiki/Parallax

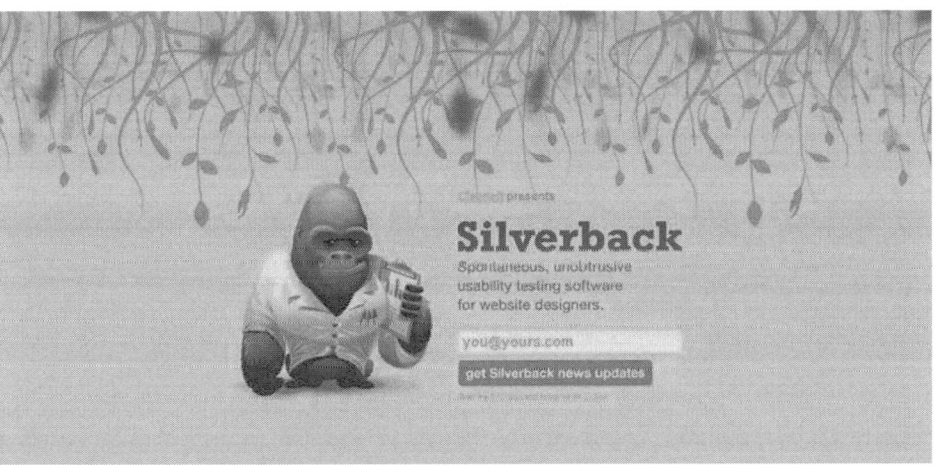

Figure 11-17. The original holding page for Clearleft's Silverback app

Specified in the CSS3 backgrounds and borders module is the ability to add multiple backgrounds to a single element. The number of comma-separated values for the background-image or shorthand background property defines the amount of backgrounds applied. We'll show you examples using both background-image and background, so don't worry about getting confused between the two. For these examples, we're going to use three images (Figure 11-18) and layer them atop each other in front of a full page background.

Figure 11-18. The three individual images

Firstly, let's look at our CSS so far. We've set a background image on the html element and set its background-size property to cover the entire browser window (Figure 11-19).

```
html {
  height:100%;
  background-image:url(img/bg-cosmos.jpg);
  background-repeat:no-repeat;
  background-attachment:fixed;
  background-size:cover;
}
```

Figure 11-19. Your starting point: the background applied to the html element.

Now we're going to add the multiple backgrounds to the body element. We could add them to the html element as well but using another element provides easier maintenance and a better fallback for less capable browsers.

To add our first background image, we'll use the standard notation that you're used to seeing in CSS 2.1. The body's height is set to 100% to ensure it is tall enough for our image to fit.

```
body {
  height:100%;
  background-image:url(img/planet1.png);
  background-repeat:no-repeat;
  background-position:50% 30%;
}
```

Figure 11-20 shows this first background image in position.

Figure 11-20. One background image applied to the body element

To add our second background to the body element, we add an additional value for each background property separated from the first by a comma. We then repeat the steps for the background-repeat and background-position properties.

```
body {
  height:100%;
  background-image:url(img/planet1.png), url(img/planet2.png);
  background-repeat:no-repeat, no-repeat;
  background-position:50% 30%, 15% 90%;
}
```

Notice how the second image has appeared underneath the first (Figure 11-21). This is defined in the specification:

> *The first image in the list is the layer closest to the user; the next is painted behind the first, and so on. The background color, if present, is painted below all of the other layers.*

www.w3.org/TR/css3-background/#layering

455

Figure 11-21. Two background images applied to the body element.

As you've seen, when declaring multiple values, each value within each property is separated with a comma. We can, however, simplify our example slightly by removing one of the no-repeat values for background-repeat. This is because if no multiple (second in this case) value is applied, the browser is told to repeat the first value.

```
body {
  height:100%;
  background-image:url(img/planet1.png), url(img/planet2.png);
  background-repeat:no-repeat;
  background-position:50% 30%, 15% 90%;
}
```

To contrast that, if we accidentally forgot to add our second background-image value but did include two background-position values, the browser will render another instance of our first background image repeated in both positions (Figure 11-22). This is because the browser is repeating the first value of the background-image property.

```
body {
  height:100%;
  background-image:url(img/planet1.png); /* Oops we've forgotten to add our second image! */
  background-repeat:no-repeat;
  background-position:50% 30%, 15% 90%;
}
```

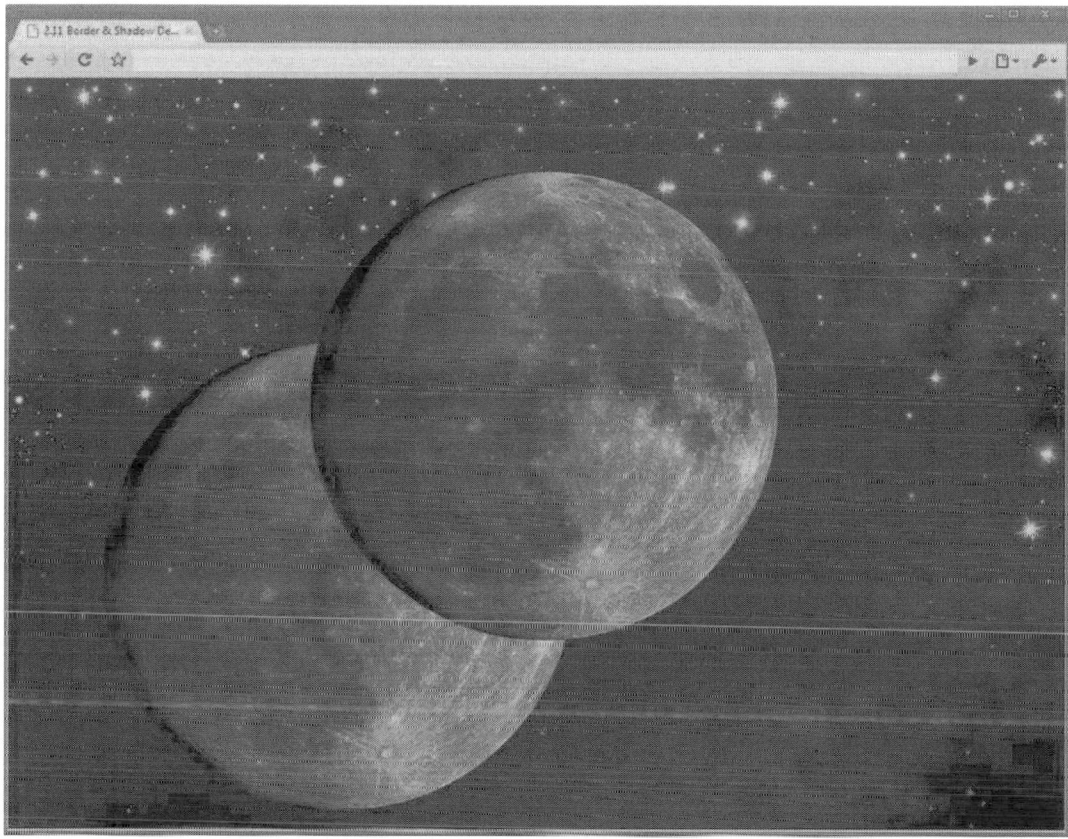

Figure 11-22. Two instances of one background image

Not wanting to make that mistake again, let's make sure that we add all our background values when adding the third image. This time we're going to use shorthand CSS notation using the background property. It works in exactly the same way; you just separate each set of values with a comma.

```
body {
  height:100%;
  background:url(img/planet1.png) 50% 30% no-repeat, url(img/planet2.png) 15% 90% no-repeat,
url(img/planet3.png) 75% 20% no-repeat;
}
```

Figure 11-23. Three background images applied to the body element.

There you have it: three background images applied to a single element (Figure 11-23). The beauty of using percentage values is that when you resize the browser, the images will start to move around and hide behind each other (Figure 11-24), just like the parallax effect in the Silverback site.

Figure 11-24. Multiple backgrounds in a small browser window

Browser support for multiple backgrounds is wide ranging. It works natively in Safari 5, Chrome 5, Opera 10.5, Internet Explorer 9, and Firefox 3.6. There is a gotcha, though (isn't there always?). If a browser doesn't support multiple backgrounds, it won't render any of them. For this reason (and dependant on your design) you may want to declare the most important background image on its own line to ensure at least one of your backgrounds is rendered.

```
body {
  height:100%;
  background:url(img/planet1.png) 50% 30% no-repeat;
  background: url(img/planet1.png) 50% 30% no-repeat , url(img/planet2.png) 15% 90% no-repeat,
url(img/planet3.png) 75% 20% no-repeat;
}
```

It's a relatively straightforward technique you can start using today. Remember that you don't have to just use multiple background images on html or body; they can be applied to any element. Patrick Lauke has created an example of how to recreate the sliding doors effect using CSS3's multiple backgrounds (http://j.mp/laukedoors[12]) (Figure 11-25). Rather than using different background images on different parts of the markup, like Douglas Bowmans 2003 original (http://j.mp/aladoors[13]), Patrick simply uses multiple backgrounds on the element for the left, right, and central background images.

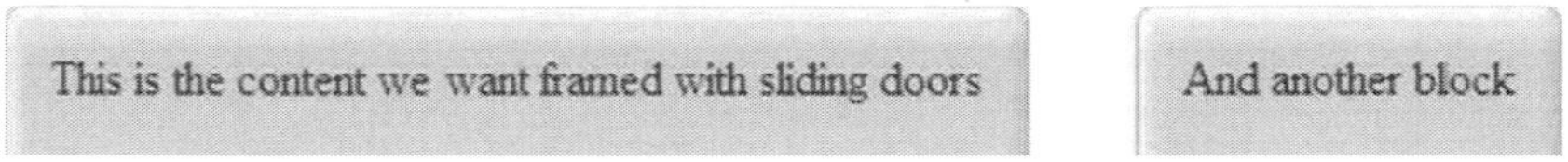

Figure 11-25. Patrick Lauke's multiple background sliding doors example

Of course Patrick's example could be created a lot more easily if only we had a way to easily make round cornered boxes ... oh, how convenient! The next section covers the other half of the Background and Borders module: borders.

Borders

The call of web designers around the world has been heard. No longer shall we have to battle through the monotony of adding extraneous markup or slicing extra images simply to create those little details such as a rounded corner to make our design that bit more persuasive. Behold border-radius, for it provides us with the ability to add native round corners using only the power of CSS.

The Backgrounds and Borders module simply can't stop giving, don't you think? It also gives us the ability to add images to our borders, as we'll see later. First, let's look at implementing border-radius.

border-radius

Adding rounded corners to any element can now be achieved by simply writing a few short lines of CSS. No longer do we have to add extra spans to our markup or use JavaScript to recreate what should be a quite straightforward task. The shorthand border-radius property is here, along with properties for individual corners such as border-top-left-radius.

Digging deep to remember that a radius is half the diameter of a circle (Figure 11-26), we can achieve equal round corners on an element by specifying a single value for each corner.

```
#introduction {
  border-top-left-radius: 20px;
  border-top-right-radius: 20px;
  border-bottom-right-radius: 20px;
  border-bottom-left-radius:20px;
}
```

---

[12] http://people.opera.com/patrickl/experiments/css3/sliding-doors
[13] www.alistapart.com/articles/slidingdoors

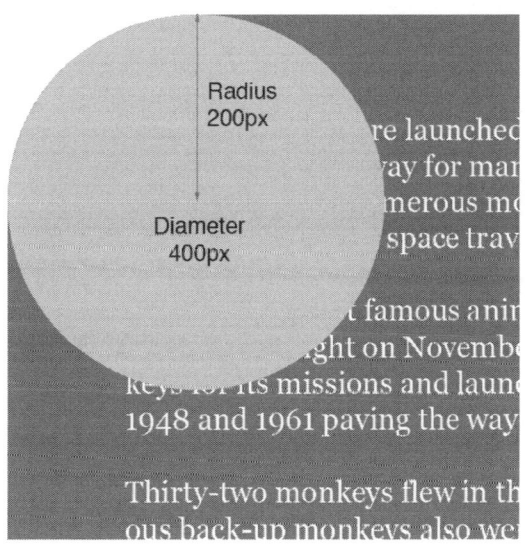

Figure 11-26. Radius is half the diameter of the circle.

This markup works without a vendor prefix in Chrome 5, Safari 5, Firefox 4, Internet Explorer 9, and Opera 10.5.

> *Note: If you don't fancy writing those long-hand values for all browsers yourself, you can always automate the process using a tool like* http://border-radius.com. *Input your corner values and it will create the CSS for you.*

Rather than always writing out four properties for each individual corner, we can use the shorthand border-radius property just like we can with margin and padding. Our simplified markup looks like this:

```
#introduction {
  border-radius:20px 20px 20px 20px;
}
```

You've probably now guessed that just like margin and padding can use one, two, three, or four values when writing the shorthand CSS (see Chapter 7). They affect the corners like so:

- One value: All four corners have the same radius.

- Two values: The first value is top left and bottom right, the second value is the top right and bottom left.

- Three values: The first value is top left, the second value is the top right and bottom left, and the third value is the bottom right.

- Four values: In the order of top left, top right, bottom right, bottom left.

Because the border radius for all corners in our example is the same, we can reduce our rule to the following:

```
#introduction {
  border-radius:20px;
}
```

The previous three examples all achieve the same result (Figure 11-27), we've just simplified the code using the shorthand property and values.

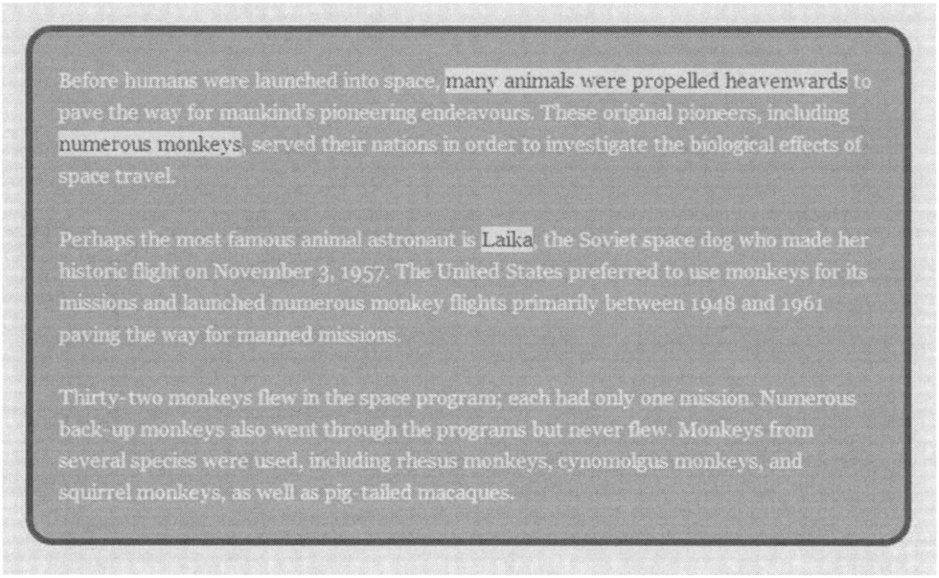

Figure 11-27. Box with equal border-radius

The `border-radius` values can be applied as ems, pixels, and percentages. It can also be applied with a background image present (Figure 11-28).

```
#introduction {
  background:rgba(0,0,0,0.3) url(img/bg-moon.jpg) 50% 50% ➥
no-repeat;
  border-radius:2em;
}
```

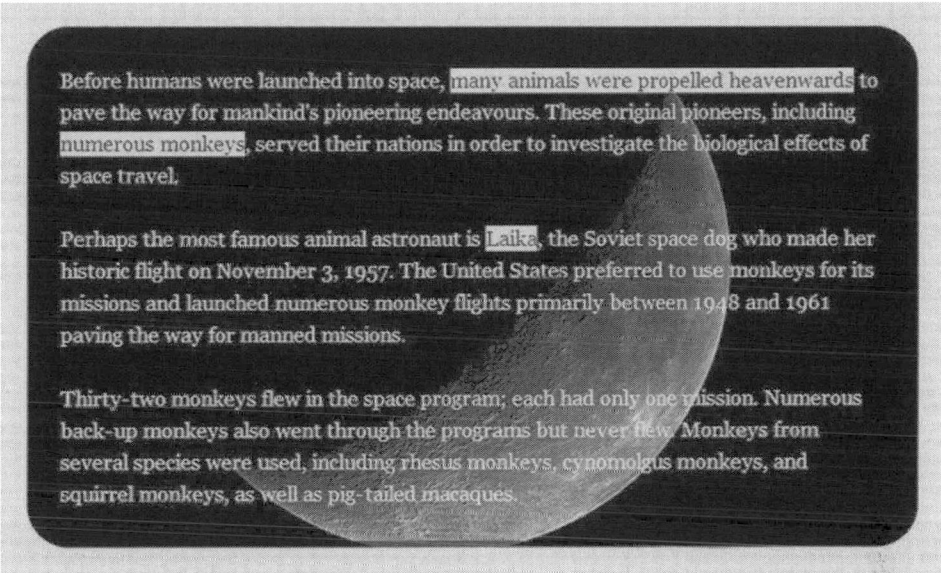

Figure 11-28. Box with border-radius and background image

To complicate matters (but also to make the property more flexible and useful), a border radius can have two length values: one for the X axis (horizontal) and one for the Y axis (vertical). This allows us to create elliptical shapes. The horizontal and vertical values are separated by a forward slash (/) placed between them. The value(s) before the slash are for the horizontal radius and the values after the slash are for the vertical radius. Figure 11-29 shows the results.

```
#introduction {
  background:rgba(0,0,0,0.3) url(img/bg-moon.jpg) 50% 50% ↵
no-repeat;
  border-radius:2em / 6em;
}
```

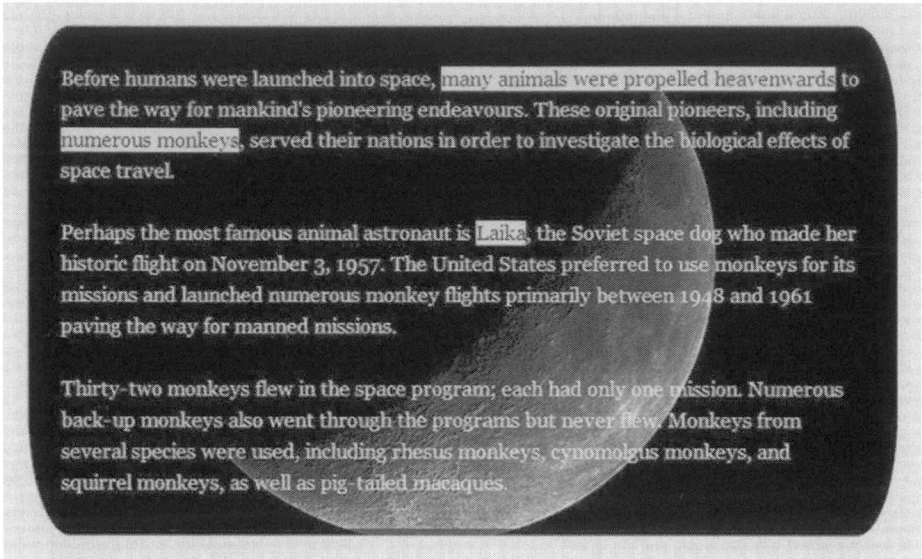

Figure 11-29. Box with border-radius and different values for horizontal and vertical radius

You can have different radii for each corner in the horizontal and vertical if you wish. This can be written using the shorthand border-radius and declaring eight values (four and four separated by a slash) or using the individual corner properties (border-top-left-radius) with two values space separated *without* a slash. These two examples have the exact same effect on the div (Figure 11-30).

Shorthand:

```
#introduction {
    background:rgba(0,0,0,0.3) url(img/bg-moon.jpg) 50% 50% ↪
no-repeat;
    border-radius:2em 4em 6em 8em / 9em 7em 5em 3em;
}
```

Individual corner properties:

```
#introduction {
    background:rgba(0,0,0,0.3) url(img/bg-moon.jpg) 50% 50% ↪
no-repeat;
    border-top-left-radius: 2em 9em;
    border-top-right-radius: 4em 7em;
    border-bottom-right-radius: 6em 5em;
    border-bottom-left-radius: 8em 3em;
}
```

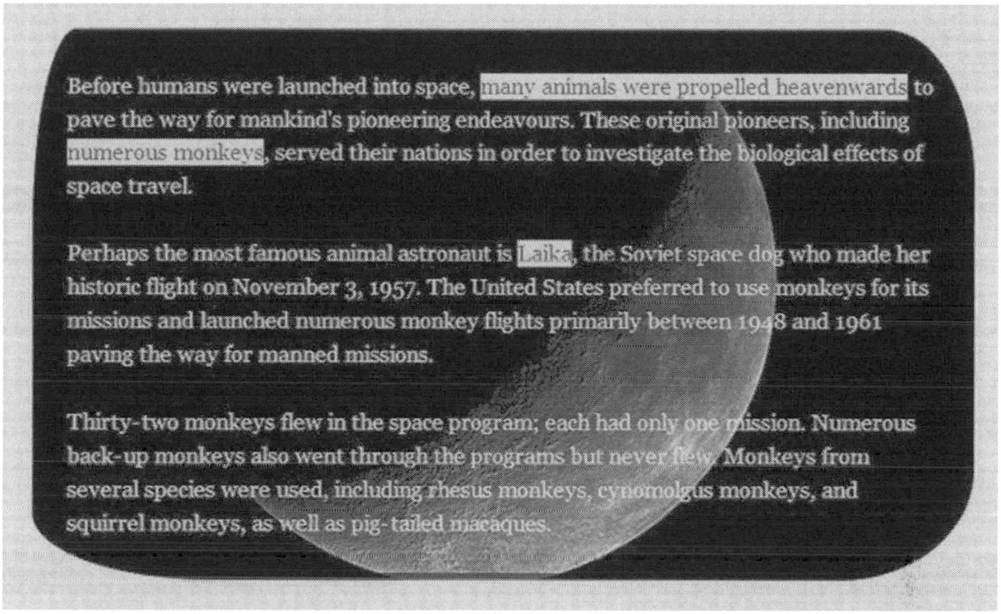

Figure 11-30. Box with different border-radius values for horizontal and vertical radius on each corner

APPLYING BORDER-RADIUS DIRECTLY TO THE IMG ELEMENT

A word of caution if you want to apply `border-radius` directly to the `img` or `video` elements: the border radius doesn't clip the image correctly (Figure 11-31) in any browser. The best solution is to work around it by applying the styles to the outer `figure` or `div` instead.

Figure 11-31. border-radius directly on an img element

Remember that you don't have to just style `div`s, `article`s, or `section`s with `border-radius`; it can also be applied to anchors, inputs, or even tables. If you're really feeling the `border-radius` love, there's nothing stopping you from going whole hog and creating circles, ellipses, or more to really spice up your designs.

border-image

Border image, as you might expect, allows you to specify an image to act as an elements border. We're going to explain the shorthand version of border-image but if you want to use the specific properties on their own, detail is provided in the Background and Borders module (http://j.mp/css3background[14]).

Border images are created using a single image that is then sliced and repeated or stretched along various axis with the border around the element. In other words, the image is divided (or sliced) into nine slices using four lines, just as if you were creating a naughts and crosses board, as in Figure 11-32.

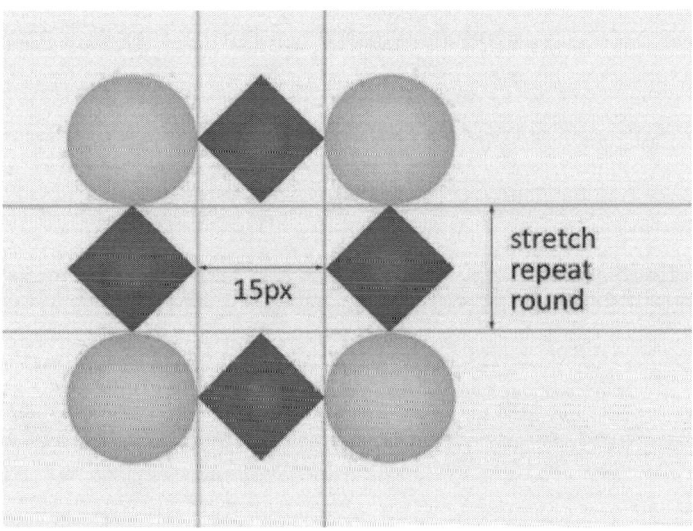

Figure 11-32. Border image with nine slices overlaid

The four corner slices are then used to create the four corners of the elements border. The four remaining edge slices are used by border-image to fill in the four sides of the elements border. You then specify the width of the slice and whether you want them to repeat or stretch to span the entire length of the element's side. The central slice, if not blank, will fill the background of the element to which the border-image is applied.

The basic border-image property syntax is

border-image: <image> <slice> <repeat>

where

- image is the URL of the image to be used a border.

---

[14] www.w3.org/TR/css3-background/#border-images

- slice is up to four values in either percentages or numbers for the size of a slice.

- repeat is the way in which the border should be treated in order to repeat. This can take two values from round, stretch, space, and repeat.

> Note: The slices don't have to be equal and the sizes are entirely up to the author. For further detail consult the border image section of the spec (http://j.mp/borderimage[15]).

In Figure 11-32, each tile is 15px wide. This is the slice value that we'll use with the border-image property. Because of this, we'll also declare the border-width property to 15px. We want the edge tiles to repeat so we'll use the repeat keyword.

Taking all of the above into consideration, to apply the border image shown in Figure 11-33, use the following code:

```
#introduction {
  border-width:15px;
  border-image:url(img/border1.png) 15 15 15 15 repeat;
}
```

The result is shown in Figure 11-33.

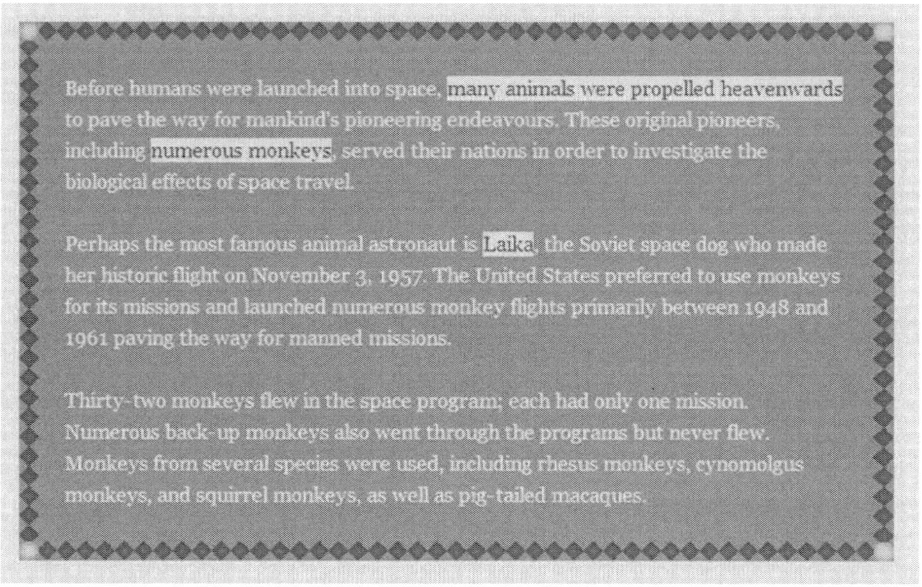

Figure 11-33. Border image applied in Opera

---

[15] www.w3.org/TR/css3-background/#border-images

Because of the size of our div, using repeat isn't very effective and some of the pattern disappears behind the corner images. However, as previously mentioned, there are four stretch options available to us

- round: The image repeats to fill the area. If a whole number of tiles doesn't fit, the image is scaled accordingly.

- stretch: The image is stretched to fill the area.

- repeat: The image repeats to fill the area.

- space: The image repeats to fill the area. If a whole number of tiles doesn't fit, the images are spaced to fill the area.

We can add up to two values for the repeat: the first for the horizontal borders and the second for the vertical borders. We're now going to apply the stretch and round values to our example. Because our slices are equal, we can also reduce the number of slice values from four to one.

```
#introduction {
  border-width:15px;
  -moz-border-image:url(img/border1.png) 15 stretch round;
  -webkit-border-image:url(img/border1.png) 15 stretch round;
  border-image:url(img/border1.png) 15 stretch round;
}
```

Figure 11-34 shows how the stretch and round values have been applied to our div.

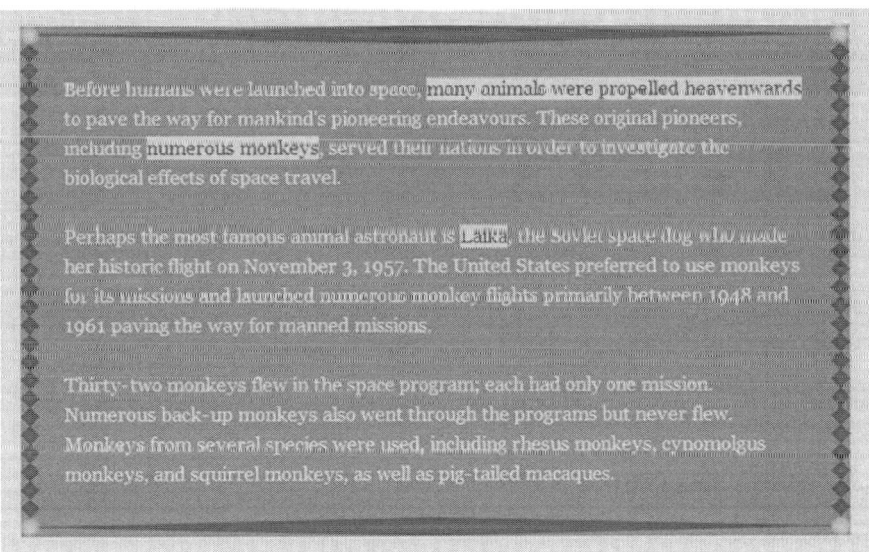

Figure 11-34. Border image applied with stretch and round keywords in Opera.

Opera, Chrome, Safari, and Firefox support the border-image property. Internet Explorer currently doesn't support border-image and as yet support isn't included in any of the IE 10 platform previews.

Note: Eric Meyer, a man who knows a thing or two about CSS, wrote a post in January, 2011 entitled "Border Imaging" in which he set a challenge to readers to create a border using a single 5px by 5px image. What's interesting is that with the spec as it stands, this isn't possible, but it is entirely plausible to think it should be. Just remember how Microsoft Publisher allowed you to add borders. Reading the comments, it doesn't seem like the spec is going to change. However, the blog post, comments, and mailing list entry all make for interesting reading (http://j.mp/meyerborder[16]).

Being thoughtful, diligent craftsmen, you are no doubt wondering what happens when you combine border-image with border-radius. Well, as you can see in Figure 11-35, the border image remains in place while the radius is applied to the background. To get around this issue should your design require it, simply re-create the round corners in the four corner slices of your border image graphic.

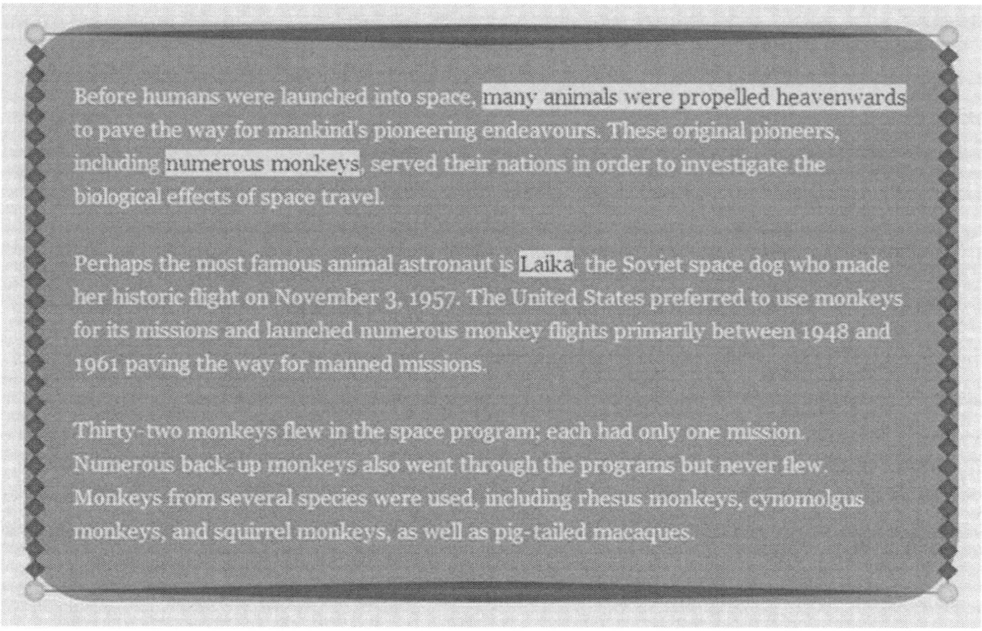

Figure 11-35. border-image applied with border-radius

While there's much fun to be had creating crazy border images, be sure that you don't step back into a parallel universe made up of geocities-style designs built with CSS3.

---

[16] http://meyerweb.com/eric/thoughts/2011/01/24/border-imaging

Drop shadows

Ah, drop shadows. Every designer's "must have" when dreaming up their creative concepts. Here's a pro tip for you about shadows: if and when a designer uses default drop shadows in their Photoshop comps, get a new designer.

Once, along with rounded corners and gradients, adding shadows to boxes was a nightmare. With the box-shadow property in CSS3's backgrounds and borders module, this is no longer the case.

box-shadow

Adding box-shadow to an element is quite simple. It can take up to six values: a horizontal offset (X), a vertical offset (Y), a blur, a spread distance, a color, and an optional inset keyword to turn the shadow from an outer one to an inner one.

```
box-shadow:inset [offsetX offsetY <blur> <spread> <color>];
```

This sounds complicated so let's ease into it by looking at the minimum requirements for box-shadow, which are the two offset values. If you wish, you can use negative offset values. Positive values draw the shadow to the right and down, respectively, while negative values go up and to the left. The combination you choose is up to you (and where your fake light source is coming from!).

```
#introduction {
  border:5px solid rgba(0,0,0,0.7);
  background:rgba(255,255,255,0.7);
  padding:0 20px;
  border-radius:20px;
  box-shadow:15px 15px;
}
```

By not including a color value, box-shadow will adopt a color specified by the browser, so let's add a color to the example by using rgba.

```
#introduction {
  border:5px solid rgba(0,0,0,0.7);
  background:rgba(255,255,255,0.7);
  padding:0 20px;
  border-radius:20px;
  box-shadow:15px 15px rgba(0,0,0,0.4);
}
```

Without specifying a blur radius value, the shadow will not blur so the edge will be sharp. The blur radius is the third value in our notation (in this instance 10px). You can't use negative values for the blur radius.

```
#introduction {
  border:5px solid rgba(0,0,0,0.7);
  background:rgba(255,255,255,0.7);
  padding:0 20px;
  border-radius:20px;
  box-shadow:15px 15px 10px rgba(0,0,0,0.4);
}
```

> *Note: If you're interested in learning more about blur radius, how it works, and what it means, David Baron of Mozilla has a detailed write-up on his blog at* `http://j.mp/blurradius`[17].

The next value you'll add is the spread radius, and the bigger the value, the more the shadow expands. Unlike the blur radius, you can use negative spread values. If no spread value is included, the shadow will not spread. We've set our spread radius value to 5px (Figure 11-36).

```
#introduction {
  border:5px solid rgba(0,0,0,0.7);
  background:rgba(255,255,255,0.7);
  padding:0 20px;
  border-radius:20px;
  box-shadow:15px 15px 10px 5px rgba(0,0,0,0.4);
}
```

Values can be pixels or ems for the offset, blur, and spread. Opera, Safari, Chrome, Firefox, and Internet Explorer 9 all support box-shadow.

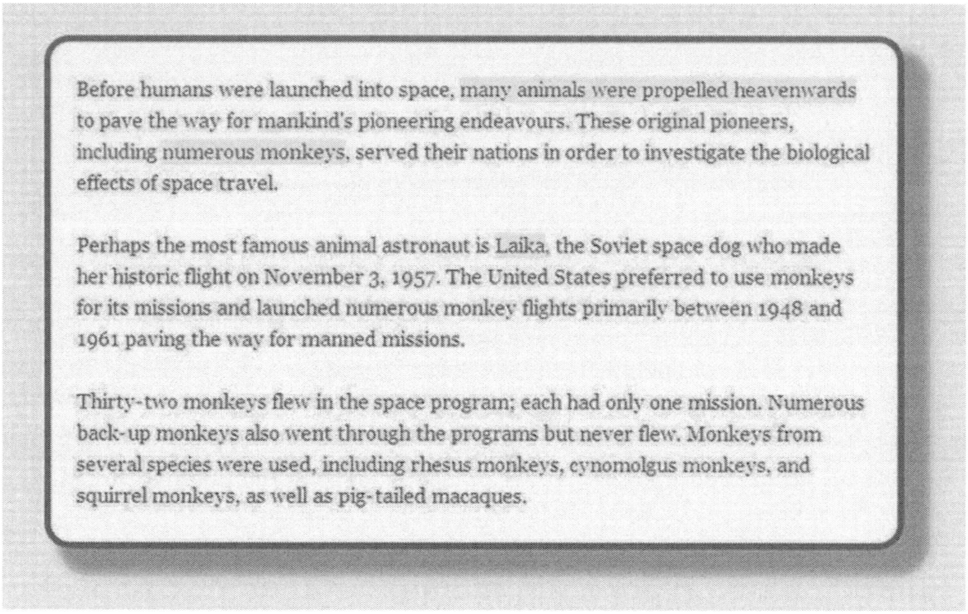

Figure 11-36. box-shadow working without a vendor prefix in Opera 10.6.

---

[17] http://dbaron.org/log/20110225-blur-radius

The final value to look at is the inset keyword, which places the shadow inside of the element. You can see this in action in Figure 11-37: as the shadow is now inside the element, we've reduced its size.

```
#introduction {
  border:5px solid rgba(0,0,0,0.7);
  background:rgba(255,255,255,0.7);
  padding:0 20px;
  border-radius:20px;
  box-shadow:3px 3px 3px 2px rgba(0,0,0,0.4) inset;
}
```

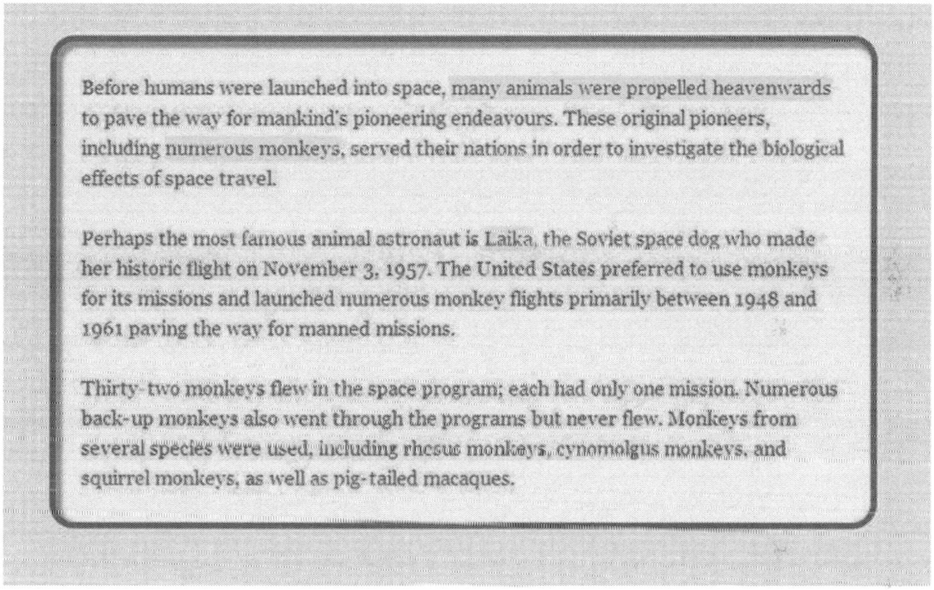

Figure 11-37. An internal box-shadow using the inset keyword in Opera 10.6.

There is a handy app (*http://j.mp/thany*[18]) created by Thany that allows you to view the differences in renderings of box shadows in different browsers. You simply check the browsers you wish to see and view the examples. Currently you can view Firefox 3.6 and 4, Internet Explorer 9, Chrome 10, Safari 5, Opera 11.10, Android 2.2, iOS 4.2, and Opera Mobile 11.

The fun with shadows doesn't stop here. You can have multiple shadows by simply separating each shadow with a comma (see Figure 11-38).

[18] http://thany.nl/apps/boxshadows

```
div#introduction {
  border:5px solid rgba(0,0,0,0.7);
  background:rgba(255,255,255,0.7);
  padding:0 20px;
  border-radius:20px;
  box-shadow:3px 3px 3px 2px rgba(0,0,0,0.4) inset, 15px 15px 10px 5px rgba(0,0,0,0.4);
}
```

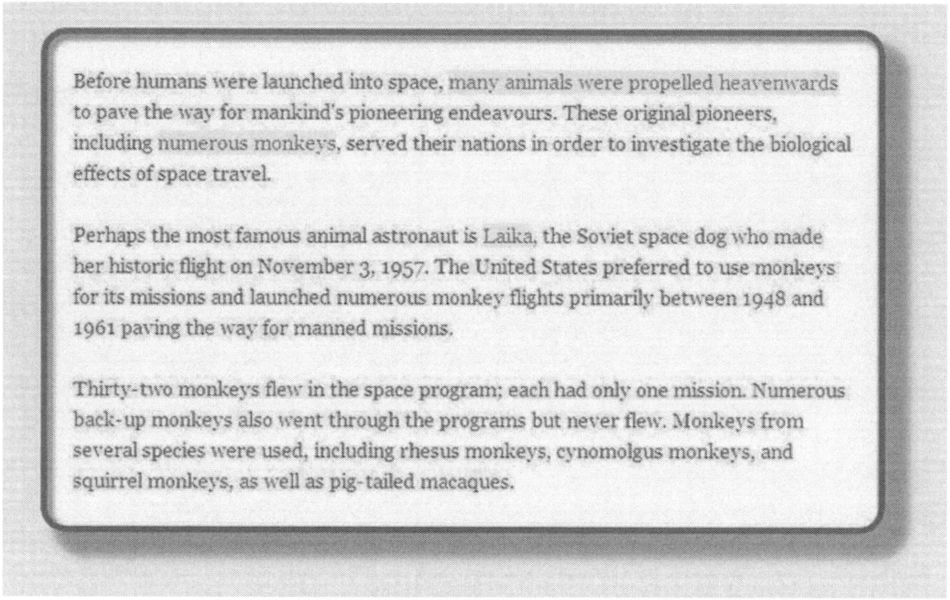

Figure 11-38. Multiple box-shadows in Opera 10.6

Note: Using too many shadows can affect site performance. The issue is seen when a user scrolls: the scrolling lags. Grant Lucas has written up his findings on his blog (`http://j.mp/grantlucas`[19]). This issue seems to have been resolved in newer versions of browsers but you should test thoroughly in a range of browsers for similar types of issues. This is what Andy Edinborough found when testing a site, although this time `border-radius` was the culprit. To that end, Andy created a CSS Stress Test bookmarklet which allows you to identify the cause of performance issues. You can read more about CSS Stress Test on Andy's blog (`http://j.mp/cssstresstest`[20]).

---

[19] www.grantlucas.com/archive/august/2010/performance-hit-when-using-css-box-shadow-text-boxes
[20] http://andy.edinborough.org/CSS-Stress-Testing-and-Performance-Profiling

Finally, as mentioned, you can also use negative offset values and invert the shadow, giving the effect of a light source coming from a different direction (Figure 11-39).

```
div#introduction {
    border:5px solid rgba(0,0,0,0.7);
    background:rgba(255,255,255,0.7);
    padding:0 20px;
    border-radius:20px;
    box-shadow:-3px -3px 3px 2px rgba(0,0,0,0.4) inset, -15px -15px 10px 5px rgba(0,0,0,0.4);
}
```

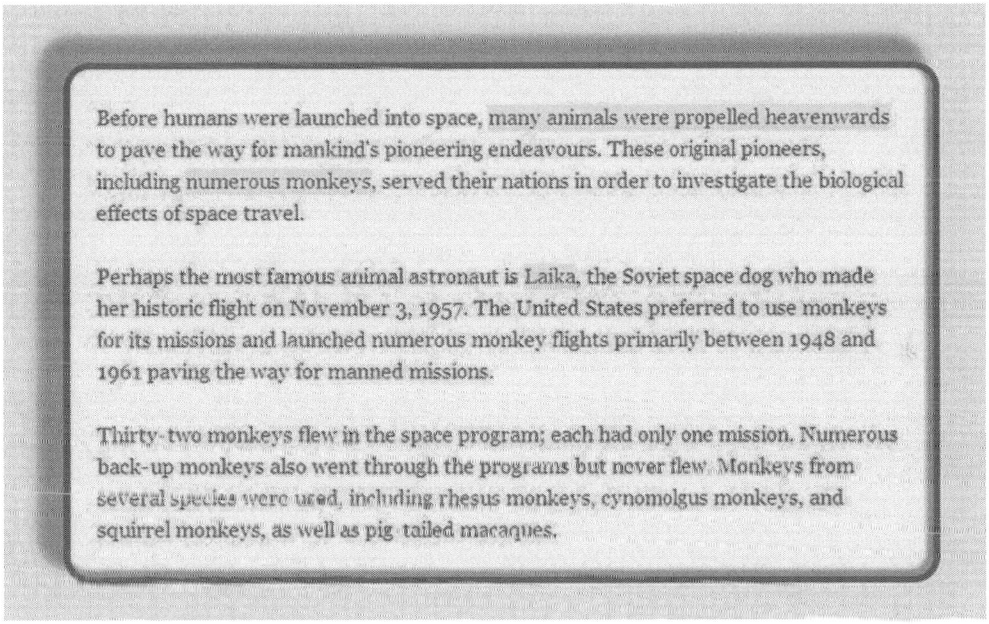

Figure 11-39. Negative box-shadows in Opera 10.6

There are myriad opportunities with CSS3's box-shadow property. In fact, the team at Viget wrote an article entitled "39 Ridiculous things to do with CSS3 Box Shadows" (http://j.mp/39shadows[21]) in which they demo 39 box shadow variations, each with a unique name. Our favorites are the "Soft Focus" and naturally, the "Batman." Nicolas Gallagher, with inspiration from author Divya Manian and Matt Hamm, looks at creating page curl effects and more in his article "CSS drop-shadows without images" (http://shadowmagic[22]) in which he uses the :before and :after pseudo-elements to position the shadows. Clever indeed.

---

[21] www.viget.com/inspire/39-ridiculous-things-to-do-with-css3-box-shadows
[22] http://nicolasgallagher.com/css-drop-shadows-without-images

Ultimately, although there is some fun to be had, the key with box-shadow is not to abuse it, to use it subtly, and certainly don't make it look like Photoshop's default drop shadow.

text-shadow

We've already seen the box-shadow property; unsurprisingly text-shadow is spookily similar. It's part of CSS 2.1; however, it appears to have attracted more attention with the rise of CSS3. You can apply one or several shadows to text using the same notation as box-shadow, namely horizontal offset, vertical axis offset, blur, and color. Note that there is no spread value or inset keyword for text-shadow.

```
h1 {
  color:#777;
  text-shadow: 5px 5px 10px rgba(0,0,0,0.5);
  /* text-shadow: x offset y offset blur color; */
}
```

You can see the example code applied in Figure 11-40.

Figure 11-40. text-shadow in Chrome

As with box-shadow, you can apply multiple shadows to your elements. There is no inset keyword to help us create internal shadows. By thinking around the problem and using multiple text-shadows, some with negative values, we can achieve the look of letterpress (or inset) typography (Figure 11-41).

```
h1 {
  text-shadow: -1px 0 0 rgba(0,0,0,0.5), 0 -1px 0 rgba(0,0,0,0.3), 0 1px 0
rgba(255,255,255,0.5), -1px -2px 0 rgba(0,0,0,0.3);
}
```

Figure 11-41. Letterpress typography created using text-shadow

Although text-shadow was introduced in CSS 2.1, Internet Explorer doesn't support it natively just yet but it will be in IE 10. If you *really have to have* text shadows in IE, you can render them using proprietary Microsoft filters. More often than not, it's likely you can live without IE users seeing a shadow or two in the name of progressive enhancement. Opera, Safari, Chrome, and Firefox all support text-shadow.

Before we finish with text-shadow, we'll leave you with a little something to get you thinking. Why not use text-shadow to create some faux anaglyphs and make your site really "pop" in 3D (Figure 11-42. Download the example files to see this in glorious technicolor!)?

```
.anaglyph {
  color:rgba(0,0,0,0.8);
  text-shadow: 0.1em 0 0 rgba(0,245,244,0.5), -0.05em 0 0 rgba(244,0,0,0.9);
}
```

Figure 11-42. Faux 3D anaglyph using CSS3 text-shadow

The anaglyph is nice but who wears 3D glasses to view web sites? What we need is real 3D, and that's just what Mark Otto, has done (Figure 11-43). Mark's demo uses a total of 12 shadows on the text so it may have some performance issues in some browsers, but it does look great. Mark has written up the experiment on his blog (http://j.mp/3dshadow[23]), which we suggest you delve into.

Figure 11-43. 3D text by Mark Otto using CSS3 text-shadow

For our final trick with text-shadow, we'll use it to create an outline around the text. The trick is to apply a shadow to each side of the text. In order for the effect to work, we have to declare a color value for the text that matches the background color to create the transparent effect (Figure 11-44).

```
.title {
  color:#ccc;
  text-shadow: -1px 0 rgba(0,0,0,0.5), 0 1px rgba(0,0,0,0.5), 1px 0 rgba(0,0,0,0.5), 0 -1px
rgba(0,0,0,0.5);
}.
```

Figure 11-44. WebKit browser using multiple text shadows to create an outline effect

---

[23] www.markdotto.com/2011/01/05/3d-text-using-just-css

> *If your target audience is using only WebKit browsers (which it shouldn't be), there is a proprietary* -webkit-text-stroke *property that will achieve the same effect as shown in Figure 11-44. Unlike* text-shadow, *there is no blur value. It works as follows but isn't in any specification yet (there has been debate over whether the property should be named be* text-outline *or* text-stroke*):*

```
h1 {
  color:transparent;
  -webkit-text-stroke:rgba(0,0,0,0.5);
}
```

Gradients

Here we are at the business end of the build it with CSS3 phenomenon: gradients. No longer will you be creating reams of single pixel-wide images to repeat through your designs. Perhaps more importantly, we won't have to keep diving back into Photoshop or Fireworks to edit those graphics when we want to change the color or length of a gradient. We'll simply be able to edit our CSS.

CSS Gradients reside in the CSS Image Values and Replaced Content module (http://j.mp/css3images[24]), which is currently in Working draft. This means that it's another case of chicken and egg, or rather specification vs. implementation. Still, as we've shown so far in this book, implementation is generally the top trump, so let's get stuck in.

Gradients

CSS-based gradients are currently supported by Firefox, Safari, Chrome, and Opera browsers and will be included in Internet Explorer 10. They can be achieved in older versions of Internet Explorer through the use of filters but, as you've heard from us before, this approach isn't recommended. For browsers that don't support CSS gradients, make sure that you specify a background color as a backup.

Gradients are available in two flavors: linear and radial. We'll show you how to use both.

Linear gradients

We'll start by introducing linear gradients. The linear-gradient value effectively generates an image that can be used in the same places as an image in CSS, such as background-image, border-image, or list-style-image properties. It was designed this way because people are familiar with using images for gradients; therefore a gradient *can't* be used as a color value. The basic notation looks like this:

```
linear-gradient([ [ <angle> | to <side-or-corner> ] ,]?
        <color-stop>[, <color-stop>]+  )
```

---

[24] www.w3.org/TR/css3-images

The values are as follows:

- angle: The angle for the direction of the gradient (e.g., 90deg). You can use negative values or values greater than 360 degrees.

- side-or-corner: Defines the starting point of the gradient (if an angle isn't used) and is specified by up to two keyword from the four available (top, bottom, left, right). The default value is top left and if only one value is declared the second value defaults to "center."

- color-stop: In its simplest form, a color value. Optional stop position(s) along the gradient can be added as a percentage of value between 0% and 100%. The color value can be a keyword, hex code, or rgba or hsla notation

If you think of a gradient being applied in Photoshop, CSS gradients work in just the same way with color stops being added along the gradient at varying positions from start (0%) to end (100%), as shown in Figure 11-45.

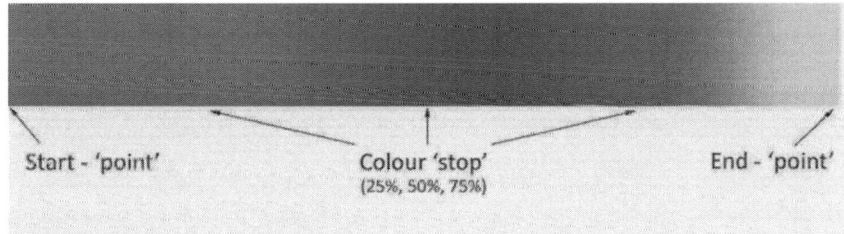

Figure 11-45. Example of color stops

To create a vertical gradient from grey to black, you would use:

```
#introduction {
    background:#000; /* fallback for browsers that don't support gradients */
    background:linear-gradient(to bottom, #ccc, #000);
}
```

or:

```
#introduction {
    background:#000; /* fallback for browsers that don't support gradients */
    background:linear-gradient(90deg, #ccc, #000);
}
```

which is the same as writing

```
#introduction {
    background:#000; /* fallback for browsers that don't support gradients */
    background:linear-gradient(#ccc, #000);
}
```

This is because there is no need to declare an angle, side, or corner; the gradient will be vertical by default. All you need are two color values.

We must now confess that we did lie a little about it being the only markup we need to create the gradient, the reason being that none of the browsers mentioned earlier support gradients without a vendor prefix. So to create our gradient shown in Figure 11-46, we'll add in the vendor prefixes.

```
#introduction {
  background:#000; /* fallback for browsers that don't support gradients */
  background:-ms-linear-gradient(#ccc, #000);
  background:-moz-linear-gradient(#ccc, #000);
  background:-o-linear-gradient(#ccc, #000);
  background:-webkit-linear-gradient(#ccc, #000);
  background:linear-gradient(#ccc, #000);
}
```

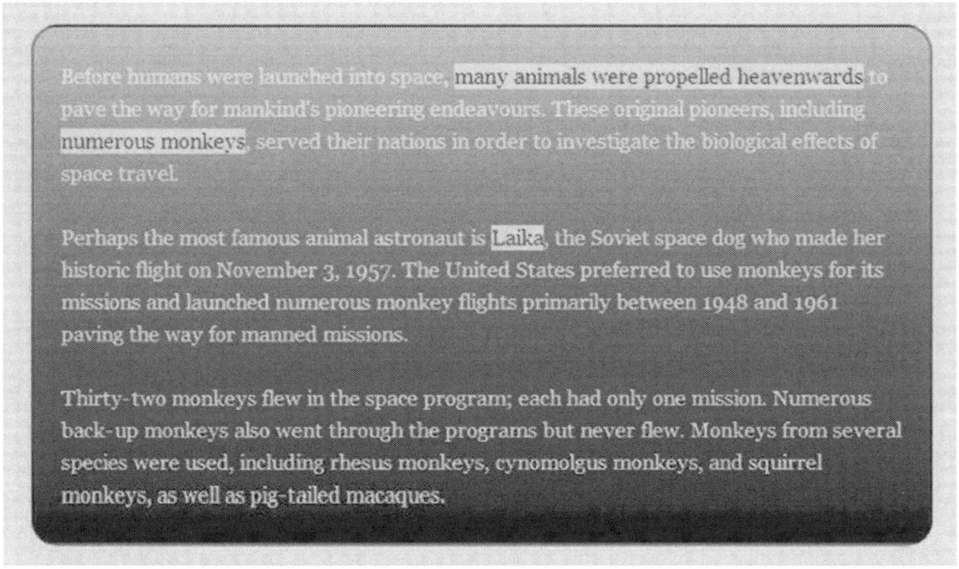

Figure 11-46. Vertical linear gradient in Firefox

You saw previously how a 90deg angle argument meant that the gradient was drawn from top to bottom. The angle value sets the angle of the gradient starting from the left where

- 0deg = left
- 90deg = bottom
- 180deg = right
- 270deg = top
- 360deg = left again, having completed a full circle

You can also use negative values for the gradient but they'll be equivalent to a positive counterpart travelling counter clockwise (e.g., -90deg = 270deg). To create a gradient going from the bottom left to top right (as in Figure 11-47),we'll use a 45 degree angle.

```
#introduction {
  background:#000;
  background:-ms-linear-gradient(45deg, #ccc, #000);
  background:-moz-linear-gradient(45deg,#ccc, #000);
  background:-o-linear-gradient(45deg, #ccc, #000);
  background:-webkit-linear-gradient(45deg, #ccc, #000);
  background:linear-gradient(45deg, #ccc, #000);
}
```

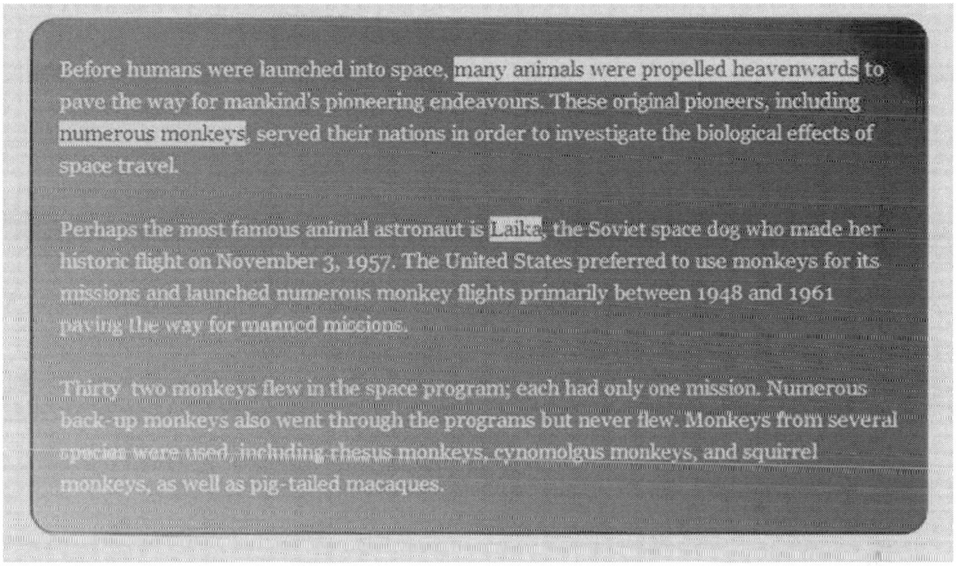

Figure 11-47. Diagonallinear gradient in Firefox

Color stops are added by simply adding another color value to the argument. Gradients are rendered evenly unless you specify a value to accompany the color stop. Figure 11-48 shows a color stop at 50% but you can also use pixels or ems to specify where the stop should appear.

```
#introduction {
  background:#000;
  background:-ms-linear-gradient(45deg, #ccc, #c8c8c8 50%, #000);
  background:-moz-linear-gradient(45deg, #ccc, #c8c8c8 50%, #000);
  background:-o-linear-gradient(45deg, #ccc, #c8c8c8 50%, #000);
  background:-webkit-linear-gradient(45deg, #ccc, #c8c8c8 50%, #000);
  background:linear-gradient(45deg, #ccc, #c8c8c8 50%, #000);
}
```

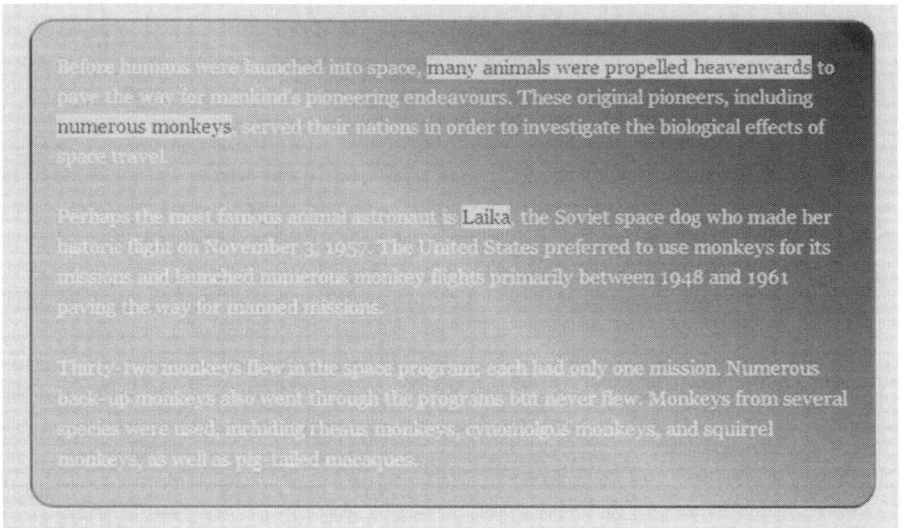

Figure 11-48. Diagonal linear gradient with color stop in Firefox

It's worth spending some time creating test cases for gradients to see what affect changing the various values has in the browser.

> *Note: Safari 4 and Chrome from versions 3-9 used a different syntax for CSS gradients that only specified a single* -webkit-gradient *property. The type of gradient (linear or radial) then follows in the first parameter. The syntax is based on the* canvas *elements APIs notation. You can learn about this legacy syntax on the WebKit blog (*http://j.mp/oldwebkitgrads[25]*). If you have to support gradients in these older browsers, add the* -webkit-gradient *value before the now standardized* linear-gradient *values to ensure that newer WebKit browsers use the newer syntax, as shown below this note.*

```
#introduction {
  background:#000;
  background:-webkit-gradient(linear, 0% 100%, 100% 0%, from(#ccc), to(#000), color-stop(0.5,
#c8c8c8));
  background:-ms-linear-gradient(45deg, #ccc, #c8c8c8 50%, #000);
  background:-moz-linear-gradient(45deg, #ccc, #c8c8c8 50%, #000);
  background:-o-linear-gradient(45deg, #ccc, #c8c8c8 50%, #000);
  background:-webkit-linear-gradient(45deg, #ccc, #c8c8c8 50%, #000);
  background:linear-gradient(45deg, #ccc, #c8c8c8 50%, #000);
}
```

---

[25] www.webkit.org/blog/175/introducing-css-gradients

To stir your imagination about gradients and what's possible, we suggest you investigate the highly creative CSS3 Patterns gallery created and curated by Lea Verou (http://j.mp/veroupatterns[26]). Lea also explains how to create patterns using gradients in an excellent article for 24 Ways (http://j.mp/veroupatterns2[27]). You can also combine gradients with the multiple backgrounds that you looked at earlier in the chapter. You'll be amazed at what you can achieve using CSS3 gradients.

Radial gradients

The syntax for radial gradients is ever so slightly more complicated than for linear gradients. Here is the standard notation:

```
radial-gradient(
  [ [ <shape> || <size> ] [ at <position> ]? , |
    at <position>,
  ]?
  <color-stop> [ , <color-stop> ]+
)
```

where:

- position is the starting point of the gradient, which can be specified in units (px, em, or percentages) or keyword (left, bottom, etc). Using a keyword works in the same way as background-position and the default value is "center."

- shape specifies the gradient's shape. It can be circle (constant-radius ellipse) or ellipse (axis-aligned ellipse). The default value is ellipse. If no shape is declared, the end shape is inferred from the length units. If one length, the shape defaults to a circle; if two, an ellipse.

- size is the size of the gradient's ending shape. If not included, the default is farthest-side. Size can be set using units or keywords.

  - closest-side positions the gradient so it touches the side or sides of the element nearest its center. If the shape is an ellipse, it meets the side in the horizontal and vertical.

  - farthest-side is the same as closest-side but the ending shape is based on the farthest side.

  - closest-corner positions the gradient so it touches the corner or corners of the element nearest its centre. If the shape is an ellipse, it meets the corner in the horizontal and vertical.

  - farthest-corner is the same as closest-corner but the ending shape is based on the farthest side.

  - contain is the same effect as closest-side.

  - cover is the same effect as farthest-corner.

---

[26] http://lea.verou.me/css3patterns
[27] http://24ways.org/2011/css3-patterns-explained

- color-stop is in its simplest form a color value. Optional stop position(s) along the gradient can be added as a percentage of value between 0 %& 100%.

This all sounds quite confusing so let's get down to business and create some gradients. Just like with the linear gradients, you'll need to include all your vendor prefixes.

To draw a simple circular radial gradient that stretches to the edge of your container (Figure 11-49), all you need to declare is:

```
#introduction {
  background:#000;
  background: -moz-radial-gradient(circle closest-side, #ccc, #000);
  background: -ms-radial-gradient(circle closest-side, #ccc, #000);
  background: -o-radial-gradient(circle closest-side, #ccc, #000);
  background: -webkit-radial-gradient(circle closest-side, #ccc, #000);
  background: radial-gradient(circle closest-side, #ccc, #000);
}
```

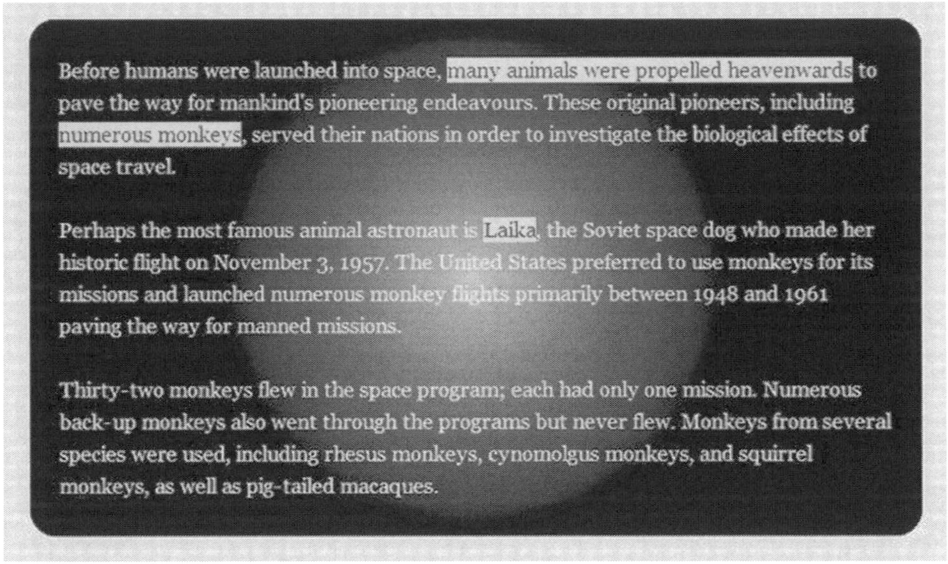

Figure 11-49. Circular radial gradient in Firefox

Try changing the shape and size values to ellipse and farthest-side to see what effect this has.

```
#introduction {
  background:#000;
  background: -moz-radial-gradient(ellipse farthest-side, #ccc, #000);
  background: -ms-radial-gradient(ellipse farthest-side, #ccc, #000);
  background: -o-radial-gradient(ellipse farthest-side, #ccc, #000);
  background: -webkit-radial-gradient(ellipse farthest-side, #ccc, #000);
  background: radial-gradient(ellipse farthest-side, #ccc, #000);
```

```
}
```

You can see this has squashed your circle into an ellipse with more reach (Figure 11-50).

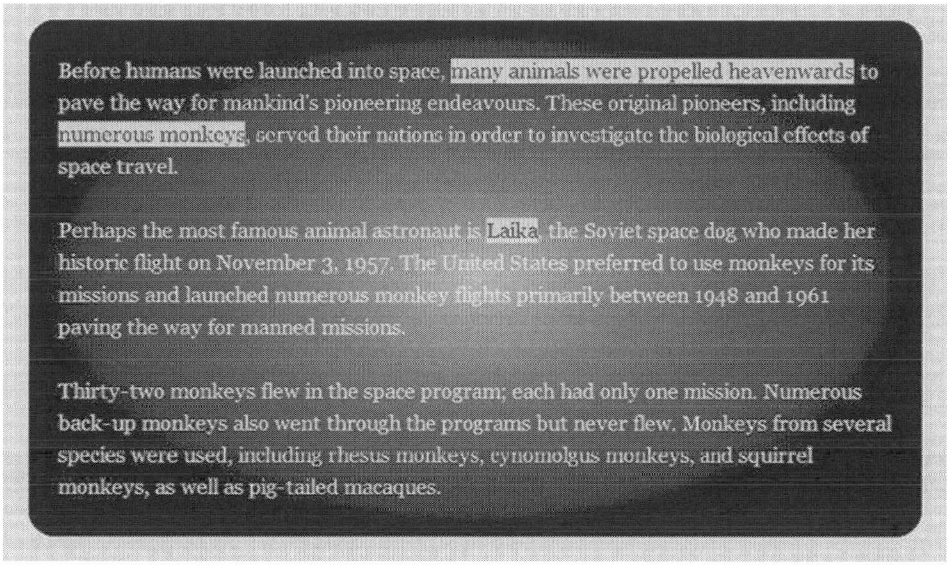

Figure 11-50. Elliptical radial gradient in Firefox

By adding position values we can move the gradient off center (left top). We'll also add an additional color stop at 200px (Figure 11-51).

```
#introduction {
  background:#000;
  background: -moz-radial-gradient(left top, ellipse farthest-side, #ccc, #75aadb 200px,
#000);
  background: -ms-radial-gradient(left top, ellipse farthest-side, #ccc, #75aadb 200px, #000);
  background: -o-radial-gradient(left top, ellipse farthest-side, #ccc, #75aadb 200px, #000);
  background: -webkit-radial-gradient(left top, ellipse farthest-side, #ccc, #75aadb 200px,
#000);
  background: radial-gradient(left top, ellipse farthest-side, #ccc, #75aadb 200px, #000);
}
```

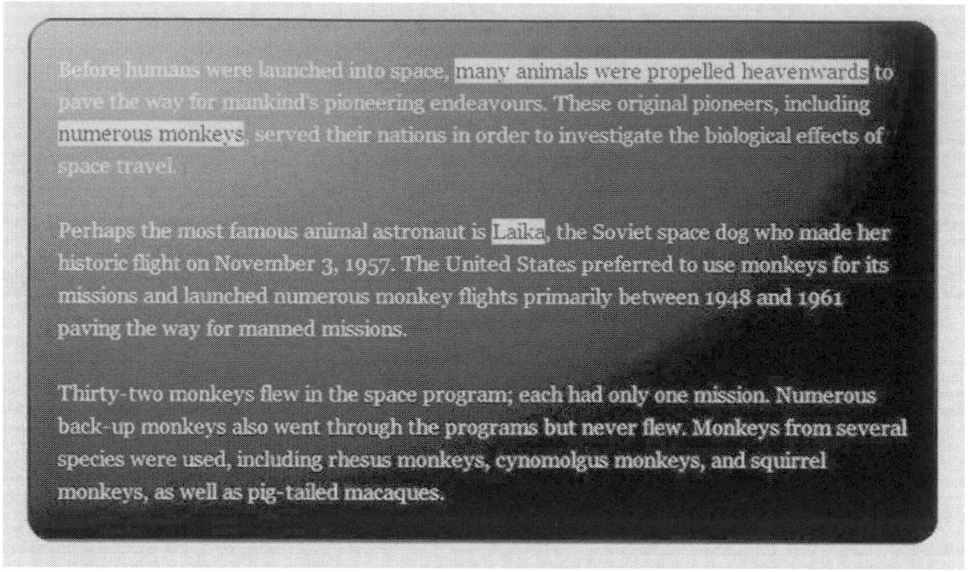

Figure 11-51. Elliptical radial gradient in Firefox starting top left

As with linear gradients, the best way to get to a grip on the syntax is to try it. Set yourself some challenges to recreate various effects using gradients; you'll be surprised at what you can achieve with a few lines of CSS3. However, if you'd like to get under the skin a little more, John Allsopp has written a fabulous article on radial gradients (http://j.mp/allsoppgrads[28]) as has the technical reviewer of this book, Chris Mills (http://j.mp/millsgrads[29]). We suggest you add these to your ever-increasing reading list.

> Note: We include the legacy WebKit syntax for the best amount of support available but remember your Good CSS Developers Pledge[TM] to keep your vendor-prefixed properties up to date. Once you decide to drop support for this older browser, you'll no longer need to include this code. Note we've placed the legacy WebKit syntax as the second declaration, just like we did earlier, so it gets overwritten by the up-to-date versions that support the standard syntax.

---

[28] www.webdirections.org/blog/css3-radial-gradients
[29] http://dev.opera.com/articles/view/css3-radial-gradients

```
#introduction {
  background:#000;
  background: -webkit-gradient(radial, 0 0, 20, 0 0, 450, from(#ccc), to(#000), color-
stop(50%, #75aadb));
  background: -moz-radial-gradient(left top, ellipse farthest-side, #ccc, #75aadb 200px,
#000);
  background: -ms-radial-gradient(left top, ellipse farthest-side, #ccc, #75aadb 200px, #000);
  background: -o-radial-gradient(left top, ellipse farthest-side, #ccc, #75aadb 200px, #000);
  background: -webkit-radial-gradient(left top, ellipse farthest-side, #ccc, #75aadb 200px,
#000);
  background: radial-gradient(left top, ellipse farthest-side, #ccc, #75aadb 200px, #000);
}
```

In summary, by altering values and adding additional color stops, you can create cones, light rays, and more. There are a number of tools available to help you when creating gradients (and save you from having to write out multiple lines of CSS each time). The best we've found is the Ultimate CSS Generator from ColorZilla (Figure 11-52) (http://j.mp/zillagrads[30]). Unlike other generators that list the declarations in the incorrect order or haven't been updated to reflect WebKit's syntax change, the Ultimate CSS Generator has everything you need in an easy-to-use interface. Go play.

---

[30] www.colorzilla.com/gradient-editor

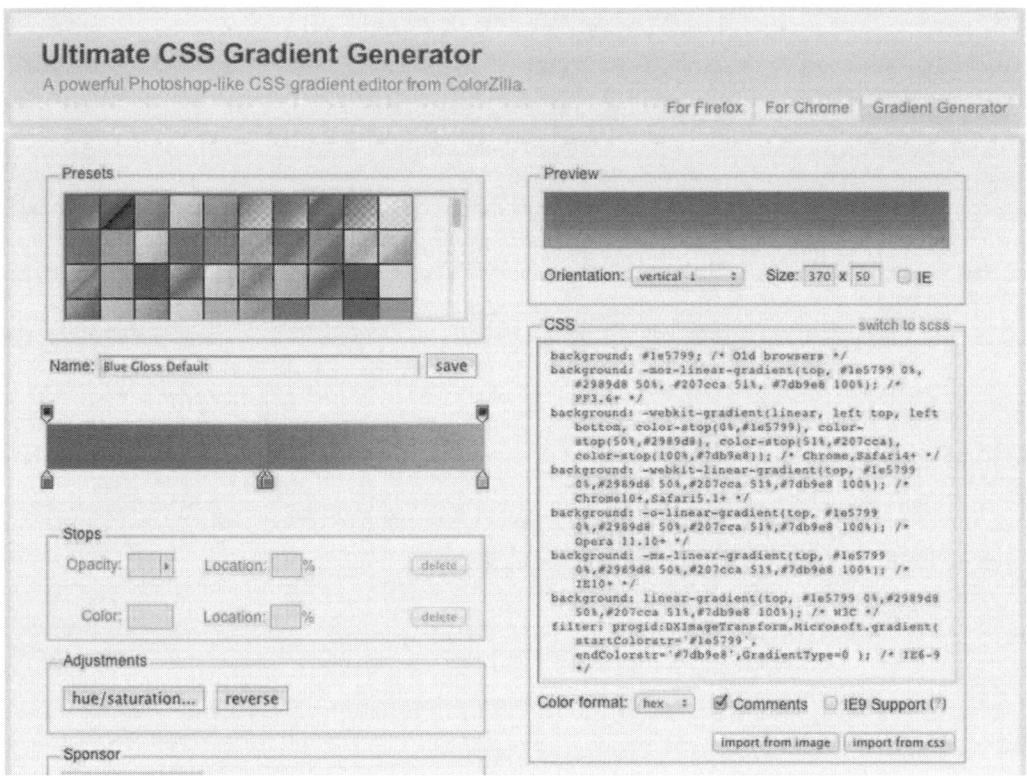

Figure 11-52. ColorZilla Ultimate CSS Generator

Repeating gradients

If you fancy getting a bit more creative, you can also use repeating-linear-gradient or repeating-radial-gradient, which allow us to create repeating gradients. The repeating patterns (Figure 11-53) are created using multiples in the difference between the first and second color stops values. As with the earlier gradients, you'll need to use a vendor prefix to ensure you get good support in modern browsers.

```
div#introduction {
  background:#000;
  background: -ms-repeating-linear-gradient(#333, #ccc 60px, #333 55px, #ccc 30px);
  background: -moz-repeating-linear-gradient(#333, #ccc 60px, #333 55px, #ccc 30px);
  background: -o-repeating-linear-gradient(#333, #ccc 60px, #333 55px, #ccc 30px);
  background: -webkit-repeating-linear-gradient(#333, #ccc 60px, #333 55px, #ccc 30px);
  background: repeating-linear-gradient(#333, #ccc 60px, #333 55px, #ccc 30px);
}
```

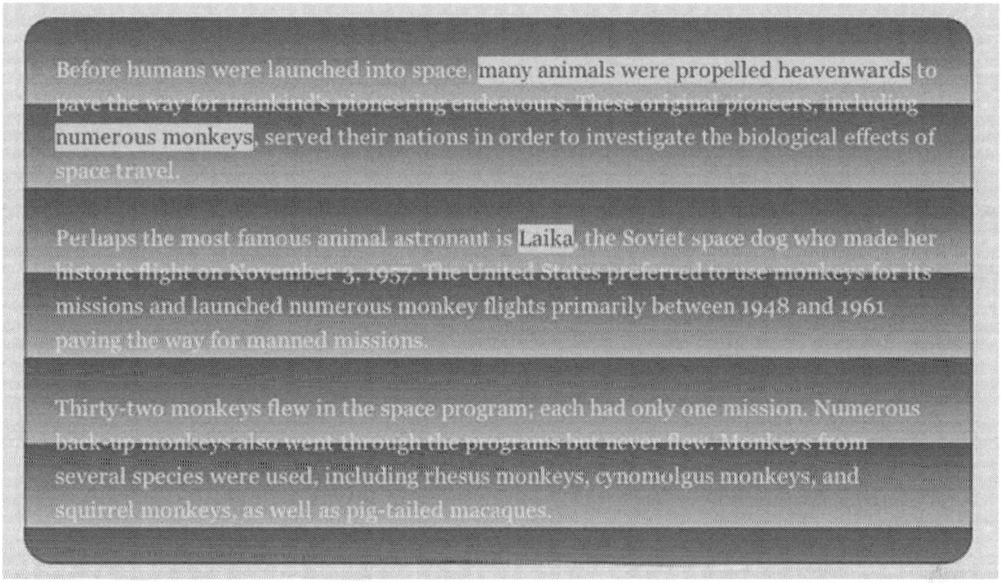

Figure 11-53. Diagonal repeating linear gradient in Chrome

And for radial gradients we would use the following code (see Figure 11-54 for the results):

```
#introduction {
background:#000;
background: -ms-repeating-radial-gradient(center, 30px 30px, #ccc, #333 50%, #999);
background: -moz-repeating-radial-gradient(center, 30px 30px, #ccc, #333 50%, #999);
background: -o-repeating-radial-gradient(center, 30px 30px, #ccc, #333 50%, #999);
background: -webkit-repeating-radial-gradient(center, 30px 30px, #ccc, #333 50%, #999);
background: repeating-radial-gradient(center, 30px 30px, #ccc, #333 50%, #999);
}
```

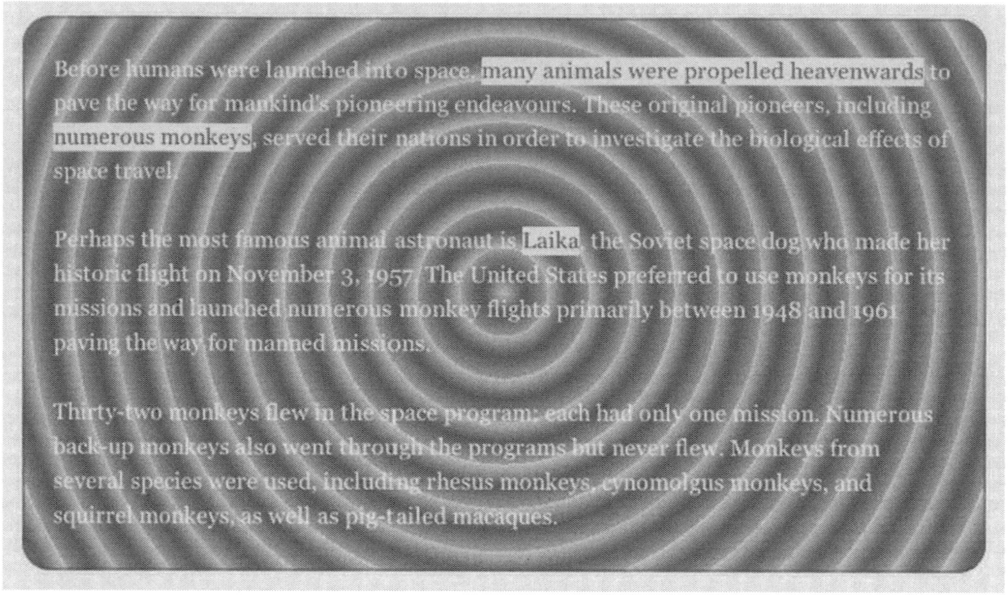

Figure 11-54. Radial repeating linear gradient in Chrome

Repeating gradients in the garish examples shown here perhaps aren't the prettiest but they do have their uses.

Detecting support and helping other browsers

Throughout the chapter, we've touched on browser support and what is or isn't supported. Generally speaking, Safari, Chrome, Firefox, Opera, and Internet Explorer 9 and 10 have good, wide ranging support for these properties while Internet Explorer 6-8 don't. So what to do about those browsers? In essence there are three main options.

- Add fallbacks to your CSS to ensure that less capable browsers receive an appropriate experience.

- Run a detection script such as Modernizr (see Chapter 7) and organize your style sheets accordingly.

- Plug the gaps with a JavaScript library such as CSS3 Pie introduced in Chapter 7.

The first option is what we've been doing throughout this chapter. We're now going to briefly explain options two and three.

Using Modernizr

We briefly touched upon Modernizr (http://j.mp/modernizr[31]) earlier in the book; now we're going to look at it in relation to the CSS3 properties we've seen in this chapter.

When a user visits your site, Modernizr runs and detects support for CSS3 and HTML5 features within a user's browser and adds a series of classes to the html element. For example, Modernizr will add a class of no-cssgradients to Internet Explorer. This is very useful as it means you can have two rules within a single style sheet to cater for both browsers. Let's say you have a design that requires a gradient background and it *has* to be there—you can't fall back to a solid color. For Safari, Chrome, Opera, and Firefox, you would style

```
.cssgradients {
  background:-moz-linear-gradient( center bottom,rgb(240,120,14) 50%,rgb(250,151,3) 90%);
  background:-webkit-linear-gradient( linear, left bottom, left top, color-stop(0.5,
rgb(240,120,14)), color-stop(0.9, rgb(250,151,3)));
background: -o-linear-gradient( linear, left bottom, left top, color-stop(0.5,
rgb(240,120,14)), color-stop(0.9, rgb(250,151,3)));
background: -ms-linear-gradient( linear, left bottom, left top, color-stop(0.5,
rgb(240,120,14)), color-stop(0.9, rgb(250,151,3)));
background:linear-gradient( linear, left bottom, left top, color-stop(0.5, rgb(240,120,14)),
color-stop(0.9, rgb(250,151,3)));
}
```

For older versions of Internet Explorer, you could create the gradient using an image and add the property to the no-cssgradients class.

```
.no-cssgradients {
  background:#ccc url(img/bg-rpt.png) 0 0 repeat-x;
}
```

Not only does using this method mean that those browsers with excellent CSS3 support get the best experience, but those that have less support can still receive a very good experience.

CSS3 Pie

You saw CSS3 Pie (http://j.mp/css3pie[32]) in Chapter 7; let's use it here to apply some border radius to IE 6, 7, and 8. Here's our rule with no pie:

```
#introduction {
  background:#ccc;
  padding:20px;
  -moz-border-radius:20px;
  border-radius:20px;
}
```

---

[31] www.modernizr.com
[32] http://css3pie.com

To add support for IE6, 7, and 8, you simply add the pie `behavior: url(js/PIE.htc);` line to your rule and ta-da, you get rounded corners in Internet Explorer.

```
#introduction {
  ...
  behavior: url(js/PIE.htc);
}
```

CSS3 Pie covers a large percentage of what we've learned in this chapter, so if you really can't bear for there not to be rounded corners in Internet Explorer and can afford the performance hit, or you can't get away with using progressive enhancement, then CSS3 PIE might just be for you.

Combining CSS3 effects

You've learned many new properties that are available in CSS3 but so far they've all been shown in isolation. Now it's time to put them all together. We're going to style a lovely-looking submit button using a whole host of the properties we've discovered in this chapter. Our button's basic styles (Figure 11-55) are as follows:

```
input[type="submit"] {
  font-size:18px;
  width:auto;
  padding:0.5em 2em;
  color:#fff;
  background:orange;
}
```

Figure 11-55. Basic button styling

First, convert that background color to use `rgb` values of R = 240, G = 120, and B = 14. And remove that ugly border by using `hsla` for the border color (Figure 11-56).

```
input[type="submit"] {
  font-size:18px;
  width:auto;
  padding:0.5em 2em;
  color:#fff;
  background:rgb(240,120,14);
  border:1px solid hsla(30,100%,50%,0.8);
}
```

Figure 11-56. Button styled with rgb and hsla

Next, round off those sharp square corners by adding some border-radius.

```
input[type="submit"] {
  font-size:18px;
  width:auto;
  padding:0.5em 2em;
  color:#fff;
  background:rgb(240,120,14);
  border:1px solid hsla(20,100%,50%,0.7);
  border-radius:5px;
}
```

A small shadow around the button will help lift the button slightly and make it more noticeable (Figure 11-57).

```
input[type="submit"] {
  font-size:18px;
  width:auto;
  padding:0.5em 2em;
  color:#fff;
  background:rgb(240,120,14);
  border:1px solid hsla(20,100%,50%,0.7);
  border-radius:5px;
  box-shadow:1px 2px 3px rgba(0,0,0,0.5);
}
```

Figure 11-57. Button with rounded corners and outer shadow

Now, apply the inset text we created using text-shadow earlier in the chapter to make the text look as though it's recessed into the button. For this, we add four shadows to the text, each separated by a comma.

```
input[type="submit"] {
  font-size:18px;
  width:auto;
  padding:0.5em 2em;
```

```
  color:#fff;
  background:rgb(240,120,14);
  border:1px solid hsla(20,100%,50%,0.7);
  border-radius:5px;
  box-shadow:1px 2px 3px rgba(0,0,0,0.5);
  text-shadow: -1px 0 0 rgba(0,0,0,0.3), 0 -1px 0 rgba(0,0,0,0.3), 0 1px 0
rgba(255,255,255,0.5), -1px -1px 0 rgba(250,151,3,0.5);
}
```

To soften the button slightly, we'll use a CSS-generated gradient for the background (Figure 11-58). Remember these will only work in Firefox, Safari, Opera, and Chrome, so we'll leave our existing background property as a fallback. There we have it: our complete CSS3-styled button! A thing of beauty!

```
input[type="submit"] {
  font-size:18px;
  width:auto;
  padding:0.5em 2em;
  color:#fff;
  background:rgb(240,120,14);
  border:1px solid hsla(20,100%,50%,0.7);
  border-radius:5px;
  box-shadow:1px 2px 3px rgba(0,0,0,0.5);
  text-shadow: -1px 0 0 rgba(0,0,0,0.3), 0 -1px 0 rgba(0,0,0,0.3), 0 1px 0
rgba(255,255,255,0.5), -1px -1px 0 rgba(250,151,3,0.5);
  background:-moz-linear-gradient( center bottom,rgb(240,120,14) 50%,rgb(250,151,3) 90%);
  background:-webkit-linear-gradient( linear, left bottom, left top, color-stop(0.5,
rgb(240,120,14)), color-stop(0.9, rgb(250,151,3)));
  background:-o-linear-gradient( linear, left bottom, left top, color-stop(0.5,
rgb(240,120,14)), color-stop(0.9, rgb(250,151,3)));
  background:-ms-linear-gradient( linear, left bottom, left top, color-stop(0.5,
rgb(240,120,14)), color-stop(0.9, rgb(250,151,3)));
  background:linear-gradient( linear, left bottom, left top, color-stop(0.5, rgb(240,120,14)),
color-stop(0.9, rgb(250,151,3)));
}
```

Figure 11-58. Button with text-shadow and CSS gradient backgrounds

Don't stop there! Add some styles for the :hover and :focus states. Using position:relative combined with top:1px; gives the effect of a button being pressed on hover. In addition, we've reversed the background gradient, lessened the box shadow, and moved the text shadow to achieve the desired contrast between the two states (Figure 11-59).

```
input[type="submit"]:hover, input[type="submit"]:focus {
  position:relative;
  top:1px;
```

```
    cursor:pointer;
    box-shadow:1px 1px 2px rgba(0,0,0,0.5);
    text-shadow: -1px 0 0 rgba(0,0,0,0.3), 0 1px 0 rgba(0,0,0,0.3), 0 0 0 rgba(255,255,255,0.5),
-1px 1px 0 rgba(250,151,3,0.5);
    background:rgb(250,151,3);
    background:-moz-linear-gradient(center bottom, rgb(250,151,3) 50%, rgb(240,120,14) 90%,);
    background:-webkit-linear-gradient( linear, left bottom, left top, color-stop(0.5,
rgb(250,151,3)), color-stop(0.9, rgb(240,120,14)));
    background:-o-linear-gradient( linear, left bottom, left top, color-stop(0.5,
rgb(250,151,3)), color-stop(0.9, rgb(240,120,14)));
    background:-ms-linear-gradient( linear, left bottom, left top, color-stop(0.5,
rgb(250,151,3)), color-stop(0.9, rgb(240,120,14)));
    background:linear-gradient( linear, left bottom, left top, color-stop(0.5, rgb(250,151,3)),
color-stop(0.9, rgb(240,120,14)));
}
```

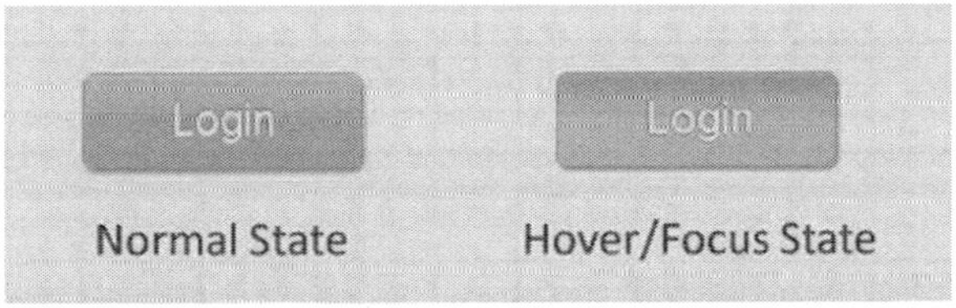

Figure 11-59. Button in normal and :hover states

The complete style rules may look in-depth but the effect is simple to achieve. When broken down into bite sized chunks and combined, you can create beautifully styled elements using CSS3 properties.

> Note: If you can't remember the syntax for a particular property or can't remember which needs prefixes or not, there are sites to help. One such site is CSS3 Please (http://css3please.com/) by Paul Irish and Jonathan Neal. The site allows you to edit rules on the fly and automagically updates the prefixed properties for you. It's a real time-saver that you'll find yourself using over and over.

Hold the cheese

Here's the thing: you're now armed with all this new knowledge of CSS3 properties. The question is where and how are you going to apply them? The answer is up to you but the key is subtlety. We'll say it again to make sure you remember: the key is *subtlety*. Nothing says lazy like a 100% black shadow or a round corner in the wrong proportions.

Unfortunately we won't be there to guide you every time you want to add a gradient background or border image. Instead, every time you're going to add a cool CSS3 effect, stop and ask yourself these questions:

- What purpose does this serve?

- What does it add to my design?

- Will it provide my users with a better experience?

495

If you're not sure or the answer to any of the questions is no, leave it out.

Figure 11-60. colly.com, the celebrated new miscellany of Mr Simon Collison

If you're not convinced by us, try listening to Simon Collison (who knows a thing or two about designing for the Web). He says this about using CSS3 when designing his site (Figure 11-60).

> *I had to be bold and do away with some of the coolest stuff I've done with CSS in years, but I don't regret it really. The gimmicks were potentially cheapening the idea anyway. Use with caution, I say.*

> Redesigning the Undesigned, Simon Collison

To reaffirm, in case it hasn't sunk in yet, the two main takeaways regarding CSS3 properties are

- Subtlety is the key.
- Use with caution.

Summary

Take a look around the Web and you'll find examples of people using these techniques to create numerous icons, shapes, buttons, backgrounds, and logos using only CSS. Some use semantic HTML (Figure 11-73), others use numerous additional divs or spans to achieve something that should, in essence, be an image. If you're reading this book, you know better. You know to only use CSS3 properties subtly and only when it's appropriate.

Moving away from how to implement CSS3 properties or what they can achieve, it's time we started thinking about *how* using them might improve our workflow or our testing practices.

- Do we as web designers need to sell this progressive enhancement to our customers?

- By using it, are we reducing the time spent worrying about cross-browser compatibility?

- Are we spending more time designing in the browser rather than creating endless Photoshop comps?

- Does this mean we're giving our clients better value for their money?

We don't have all the answers, but it's time we wised up and learned how using CSS3 properties like those in this chapter might help us in more ways than we might think. We *can* use these techniques today and progressively enhance our work while ensuring that less capable browsers receive an acceptable experience. Our message to you is simple: go play with CSS3 properties, but remember the key is to use them subtly and appropriately.

Homework

For your homework, go through the pages you've been working on throughout the book and add CSS3 properties where you can. Be careful not to overdo it. Remember that most touches should barely be noticeable. You should find backgrounds that could do with some added depth, buttons that need greater affordance, sections of content that could use graphical borders, text that requires some carefully crafted shadows, and much, much more.

Chapter 12

Transforms, Transitions, and Animation

Back in the early days of the web things weren't really much different to now—web designers (and clients) loved shiny new things. While the goals may not have changed, we've come a long way from when "Make it pop!" equalled <blink>, <marquee>, or the classic "flaming logo" animated .gif.

The mid-90s saw the introduction of two new tools for adding some sizzle—Flash and JavaScript. By the dot-com boom they were both popular ways of achieving things that weren't possible with HTML and CSS alone, such as button rollovers, the beginnings of streaming video, and those googly eyes that followed your mouse cursor around (http://j.mp/googly-eyes, http://arc.id.au/XEyes.html).

However, with abuses like distracting animating ads, pages that were unusable without JavaScript (and barely usable with it), and the infamous "Skip Intro" Flash movie, both technologies ended up with something of a bad name. JavaScript has recovered, thanks to solid coding best practices (like Hijax, (http://j.mp/js-hijax, http://domscripting.com/blog/display/41)) and a mass of libraries. Flash also went on to be used for great things, but with the <video>, <audio> and <canvas> elements in HTML5, its star is waning.

Animation and user interface effects have long been a big part of Flash's appeal. CSS3 makes many of these abilities native in the CSS Transformations, Transitions, and Animations specifications. We'll look at how to use these CSS3 specifications to easily add Flash-like effects in the browser. With the addition of hardware acceleration (especially in mobile devices), CSS3 is a viable option for adding some "wow!" where it wasn't possible before. Chapter 13 rounds out this book with a look at some exciting things coming to CSS in the near future.

Now, those of you who remember the web trifle may be saying, "Hold on. This is behavior not presentation!" While this is true to a point, this ship already sailed with the :hover pseudo-class. Adding movement to CSS3 makes these popular features far more accessible than they have been in JavaScript. You may still choose JavaScript (or Canvas or SVG with SMIL or even Flash) for advanced animations, but for the basics you've now got some wonderfully accessible tools.

Before we delve into the delicious CSS3, let's start with two warnings.

> *The browser support for the CSS in this chapter ranges from pretty good to bleeding edge. Because of this (and as usual), it's essential to remember that some users won't see these effects—consider the experience of people with browsers that lack support. As Lea Verou eloquently stated:*
>
> *If you design a page with graceful degradation in mind, it should work and look fine even without any CSS3. If you don't, you'll have bigger problems than that.*
>
> *— Five questions with Lea Verou, CSS Tricks (http://j.mp/lea-verou-5q, http://css-tricks.com/five-questions-with-lea-verou/)*
>
> *The bookmarklets "deCSS3" (http://j.mp/decss3-bm, http://davatron5000 .github.com/deCSS3/) by Dave Rupert, Alex Sexton, Paul Irish and François Robichet, "CSS3-Striptease" (http://j.mp/css3striptease, http://css-tricks.com/examples/CSS3StripTease/) by Chris Coyier, and "ToggleCSS3" (http://j.mp/togglecss3, http://intridea.com/2010/4/12/toggle-css3-bookmarklet) by Michael Bleigh can help, but ideally you're building from the content out (or "mobile first") anyway, and leaving adding CSS3 until the end.*
>
> *Also, these specifications are all useful for adding movement. Whether it was skip intro movies or animating ads, we've all been annoyed by too much movement so remember that feeling when adding it yourself. Make sure it assists (rather than annoys) your users in completing their goals. Just a dash is often all you need.*

So without further ado, let's have a look at moving things with CSS3 Transforms.

Translate, rotate, scale, skew, transform: 2D and 3D CSS transforms

Transforms give us the ability to perform basic manipulations on elements in space. We can translate (move), rotate, scale and skew elements, as demonstrated in Figure 12-1. A transformed element doesn't affect other elements and can overlap them, just like with position:absolute, but still takes space in its default (un-transformed) location. This is generally a big advantage over varying an element's width/height/margins etc., as your layout won't change with transforms. They're specified in two separate specifications: CSS 2D Transforms Module Level 3 (http://j.mp/2d-transforms, http://dev.w3.org/csswg/css3-2d-transforms/) and CSS 3D Transforms Module Level 3 (http://j.mp/3d-transforms, http://dev.w3.org/csswg/css3-3d-transforms/). Combined with transitions and animations (which you'll meet later this chapter) this provides some powerful tools for good ... and (of course) evil!

```
.translate {transform: translate(-24px, -24px);}
```

```
.rotate {transform: rotate(-205deg);}
```

```
.scale {transform: scale(.75);}
```

```
.skew {transform: skewX(-18deg);}
```

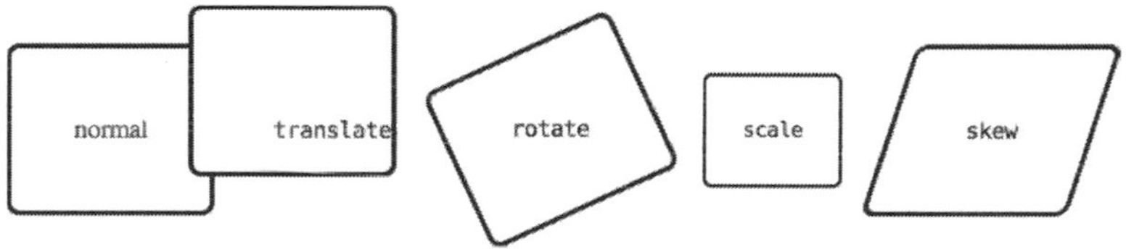

Figure 12-1. Examples of the 2D transforms translate(24px, 24px), rotate(-205deg), scale(.75) and skew(-18deg). The label for each box is transformed an equal and opposite amount.

Assuming you're on the side of good, here's a handy overview/cheatsheet of the transform properties and functions. Before that, however, we need to briefly touch on CSS values and units.

CSS VALUES AND UNITS

The overview contains shorthand for allowed values and units, based on CSS Values and Units Module Level 3 (http://j.mp/css3-values, http://dev.w3.org/csswg/css3-values/).

Table 12-1. CSS Values and Units[1]

Integer	Whole numbers preceded by an optional + or - sign, such as -1.
Number	Numbers including decimals, preceded by an optional + or - sign, such as .95.
Percentage	A number followed by %, such as 33.3%.
lengths	A unit of length followed by a unit (optional if the length is 0), such as 24px. Length units include the following: Relative units: **em**, ex, ch, rem, vw, vh, vm Absolute units: cm, mm, in, **px**, pt, pc
angles	A number followed by an angle unit, such as 18deg. Angle units include **deg**, grad, rad, and turn.
times	A number followed by a time unit, such as 400ms. Time units include **ms** and **s.**

---

[1] Check browser support carefully if you're considering using one of the uncommon units.

- transform: This property takes one or more space-separated *transform functions* (listed below) to apply to an element, for example transform: translate(3em, -24px) scale(.8);. Transform functions can take negative values, and the default is none. The transform functions include the following:

    - translate(): Moves the element from its transform-origin along the X, Y, and/or Z-axes. This can be written as translate(tX), translate(tX, tY), and translate3D(tX, tY, tZ) (percentage except tZ, lengths). There's also the 2D translateX(tX) and translateY(tY), and the 3D translateZ(tZ).[2]

    - rotate(): Rotates the element around its transform-origin in two-dimensional space, with 0 being the top of the element, and positive rotation being clockwise (angles). There are also the rotateX(rX), rotateY(rY), and rotateZ(rZ)[3] transformation properties to rotate around an individual axis. Finally, there's rotate3D(vX, vY, vZ, angle) to rotate an element in three-dimensional space around the direction vector of vX, vY, and vZ (unitless numbers) by angle (angles).

    - scale(): Changes the size of the element, with scale(1) being the default. It can be written as scale(s), scale(sX, sY), and scale3D(sX, sY, sZ) (unitless numbers). There's also the 2D transforms scaleX(sX) and scaleY(sY), and the 3D transform scaleZ(sZ).[4]

    - skew(): Skews the element along the X (and, if two numbers are specified, Y) axis. It can be written as skew(tX) and skew(tX, tY) *(angles). There's* also skewX() and skewY().[5]

    - matrix(): This transform property takes a transformation matrix that you know all about if you have some algebra chops. matrix() takes the form of matrix(a, b, c, d, e, f) (unitless numbers). matrix3D() takes a 4×4 transformation matrix in column-major order. The 2D transform matrix()

---

[2] translate(0, 50px) is the same as translateY(50px).

[3] rotate(45deg) is the same as rotateZ(45deg).

[4] scale(1,2.5) is the same as scaleY(2.5).

[5] skew(45deg) is the same as skewX(45deg).

maps to matrix3D(a, b, 0, 0, c, d, 0, 0, 0, 0, 1, 0, e, f, 0, 1) (unitless numbers). If you have the required giant brain, this lets you do (pretty much) all other 2D and 3D transforms at once.

- perspective(): Provides perspective to 3D transforms and controls the amount of foreshadowing *(lengths)*—think *fish*-eye lenses in photography. The value must be greater than zero, with about 2000px appearing normal, 1000px being moderately distorted, and 500px being heavily distorted. The difference with the perspective property is that the transform function affects the element itself, whereas the perspective property affects the element's children. Note that perspective() only affects transform functions *after* it in the transform rule

- perspective: This works the same as the perspective transform function, giving 3D transformed elements a feeling of depth. It affects the element's children, keeping them in the same 3D space.

- perspective-origin: This sets the origin for perspective like transform-origin does for transform. It takes the same values and keywords as transform-origin: keywords, lengths, and percentages. By default this is perspective-origin: 50% 50%;. It affects the children of the element it's applied to, and the default is none.

- transform-origin: Sets the point on the X, Y, and/or Z-axes around which the transform(s) will be performed. This can be written transform-origin: X;, transform-origin: X Y;, and transform-origin: X Y Z;. We can use the keywords left, center, and right for the X-axis, and top, center, and bottom for the Y-axis. We can also use lengths and percentages for X and Y, but only lengths for Z. Finally, for a 2D transform-origin you can use offsets by listing three or four values, which take the form of two pairs of a keyword followed by a percentage or length. For three values a missing percentage or length is treated as 0. By default transform-origin is the center of the element, which is transform-origin: 50% 50%; for a 2D transform and transform-origin: 50% 50% 0; for a 3D transform.[6]

- transform-style: For 3D transforms this can be flat (the default) or preserve-3d. flat keeps all children of the transformed element in 2D—in the same plane. preserve-3d child elements transform in 3D, with the distance in front of or behind the parent element controlled by the Z-axis.

---

[6] transform-origin: 0; is equal to transform-origin: 0 50% ; and transform-origin: left center;.

- backface-visibility: For 3D transforms this controls whether the back side of an element is visible (the default) or hidden.

While we've used upper-case X, Y, Z, and 3D in individual function names like scaleY(), this is only to make them easier to discern. Lower-case, as in scaley(), is also fine and much more fun to write for ophiophiliacs.

> Note: We can use multiple space-separated transform functions in transform, but we can't apply different values of other transform properties (like transform-origin) to each one. Apply each group of properties to a wrapper element instead.
>
> If you're using any 3D transforms, you'll need to apply perspective to the transformed element for them to appear 3D. You'll want to use the perspective property on an ancestor element if you're transforming more than one element to keep them in the same 3D space. You'll probably also want to use transform-style: preserve-3d;.

> Warning: Transforms apply to "block-level and atomic inline-level elements" (http://j.mp/2d-transforms, http://dev.w3.org/csswg/css3-2d-transforms/#transform-property), but these aren't necessarily elements with display: inline;. If you want to apply transforms to inline elements, try using display: inline-block;.

Let's see each property in action!

Using transform and the transform functions

The transform property is the basis of these transformations, and it can have one *or more* 2D/3D transform functions separated by spaces. If there's more than one transform function, they are applied in order. The transform functions range from easy to mind-bending. They are based on algebraic transformation matrices, and the CSS definitions are based on the Coordinate Systems, Transformations, and Units chapter of the SVG specification (http://j.mp/svg-matrix, www.w3.org/TR/SVG/coords.html#TransformMatrixDefined).

Moving elements with transform: translate(); and transform: translate3d();

transform: translate(); is perhaps the easiest place to start, allowing us to move an element and its children along the X, Y, and/or Z-axes. It takes lengths (px, em, rem, etc) and percentages, with the default value 0.

- transform: translate(tX)

- transform: translate(tX, tY)

- transform: translateX(tX)

- transform: translateY(tY)

- transform: translateZ(tZ)

- transform: translate3D(tX, tY, tZ)

The transform: translate(); example in Figure 12-2 contains both one and two value translations, including negative values.

```
div {width: 25%; height: 100px; /* by default translate: transform(0); */}

span {display: inline-block; width: 50%; height: 50px; transform: translate(-3px,47px);}

div, span {border-width: 3px; transition: all 1s; /* ease by default */}

figure:hover div {transform: translate(280%); /* same as translateX(280%); */}

figure:hover span {transform: translate(90%,-3px);}
```

Note that we've made the inner box cover the outer box's border so we can demonstrate a `translate` with a negative value.

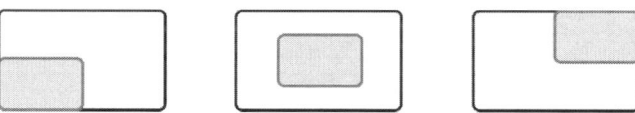

Figure 12-2. A box that animates on hover, showing transform: translate() with one value (the outer box moves from left to right) and two values (the inner box moves horizontally and vertically)

transform: translate3d(); ends up being very similar to a 2D translation. If you also use transform-style: preserve-3d; it's like a 2D translation that also allows you to change z-index. However, once you add perspective, the Z-axis works like a 2D scale transformation, as demonstrated in Figure 12-3.

```
.outer-box {

  perspective: 800px;

  transform-style: preserve-3d;

}

.inner-box {transform: translate3d(-3px,47px,-50px);} /* 50px behind the div */
```

```
.outer-box, .inner-box {transition: all 1s;}

.container:hover .outer-box {transform: translate3d(280%,0,0);} /* the same as translate(280%)
*/

.container:hover .inner-box {transform: translate3d(90%,-3px,200px);} /* 200px in front of the
div */
```

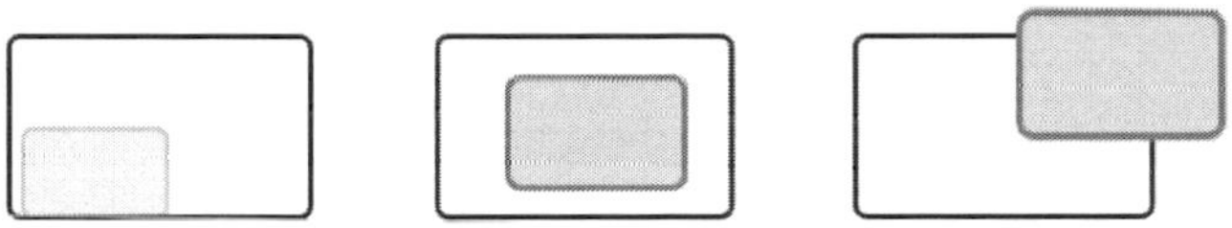

Figure 12-3. The same box, but with transform: translate3d() on the inner box, starting with a negative value (further away from the viewer and behind the container box), and transitioning to a positive value (closer to the viewer) by the end of the animation.

The rotate() transform function takes angle values (deg, rad, grad, and turn), including negative values and values greater than one rotation, as demonstrated in Figure 12-4. For positive values, the rotation direction is clockwise; for example, transform: rotate(360deg); is one full rotation clockwise.

- transform: rotate(angle)

- transform: rotateX(rX)

- transform: rotateY(rY)

- transform: rotateZ(rZ)

- transform: rotate3D(vX, vY, vZ, angle)

```
div {width: 100px; height: 100px;}

span {display: inline-block; width: 50px; height: 50px;}

div, span {transition: all 1s;}

figure:hover div {transform: rotate(180deg);

figure:hover span {transform: rotate(-450deg);}
```

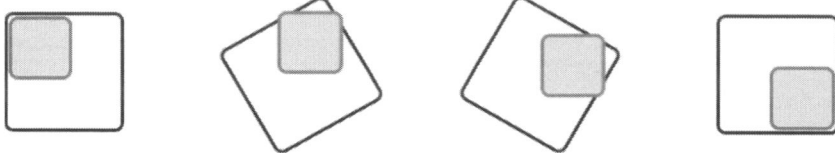

Figure 12-4. A box that rotates on hover, showing transform: rotate() with a positive (clockwise) value on the outer box, and a negative (counter-clockwise) value on the inner box.

A 3D rotation allows us to rotate around the direction vector (http://j.mp/direction-vector, http://en.wikipedia.org/wiki/Direction_vector) specified by the first three values, by the angle specified in the fourth value. The direction vector values are unitless numbers, but what's important is their ratio: rotate3d(2,1,0,90deg) is equivalent to rotate3d(10,5,0,90deg). The 2D transform: rotate(); is equivalent to rotating around the Z-axis with transform: rotate3d(0,0,1,angle);, but note that rotate3d() angle values greater than 180° behave differently to transform: rotate();. We compare rotating one axis at a time with rotate() and rotate3D() in Figure 12-5.

div {transition: all 1s;}

figure:hover .rotate3d-x {transform: rotate3d(1,0,0,180deg);}

figure:hover .rotate3d-y {transform: rotate3d(0,1,0,180deg);}

figure:hover .rotate3d-z {transform: rotate3d(0,0,1,180deg);}

figure:hover .rotatex {transform: rotateX(180deg);}

figure:hover .rotatey {transform: rotateY(180deg);}

figure:hover .rotatez {transform: rotateZ(180deg);}

figure:hover .rotate {transform: rotate(180deg);} /* for comparison */

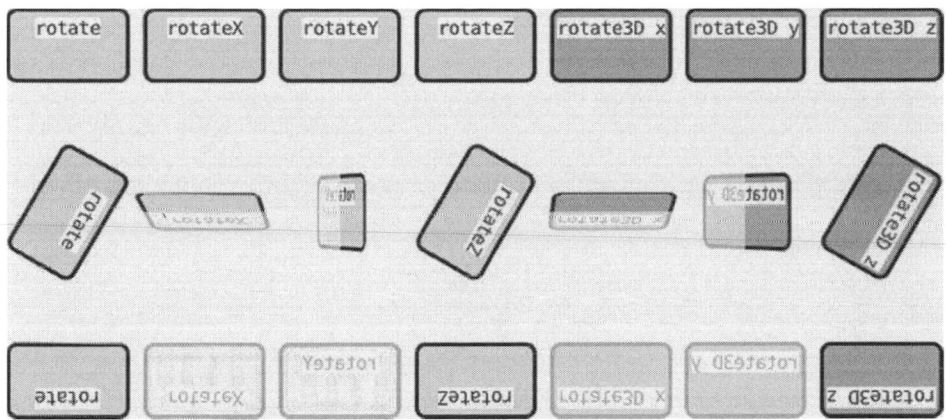

Figure 12-5. A series of boxes showing the different 3D rotations. The first box is standard rotate(). The next three boxes use the 2D individual axis properties to rotate 180° around the X, Y, and Z-axes, respectively. The last three boxes use transform: rotate3d() to do the same. Note that rotating around the Z-axis via rotateZ(180deg) or rotate3D(0,0,1,180deg) is effectively the same as rotate(180deg). The containing element is slightly opaque, visible in X and Y-axis rotations.

Scaling elements with transform: scale(); and transform: scale3d();

The scale() transform function resizes elements, with scale(1) being the default size, taking unitless numbers as values. Smaller values make the element smaller, so scale(.5) is half size; likewise, bigger values make the element larger, so scale(2) is twice the size.

- transform: scale(s)

- transform: scale(sX, sY)

- transform: scaleX(sX)

- transform: scaleY(sY)

- transform: scaleZ(sZ)

- transform: scale3D(sX, sY, sZ)

As shown in Figure 12-6, we can use two values to scale horizontal and vertical dimensions separately, and even negative values to invert an element (notice the inner box's borders). The individual scaleX() and scaleY() functions are the equivalent of setting two values for scale() where one value is 1, thus scaleX(2) is the same as scale(2,1).

.one {transform: scale(.5);} /* the same as scale(.5,.5) */

.one span {transform: scale(-3);}

.two {transform: scale(.75,1);} /* the same as scaleX(.75) */

.two span {transform: scale(-3,-1.5);}

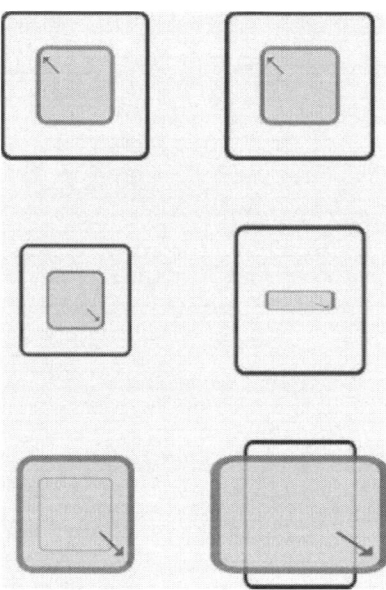

Figure 12-6. The first box uses a single value (uniform scaling) and the second uses two values, scaling the X and Y-axes separately. When these values differ the object is distorted. The inner boxes have a negative scale(), shrinking *past* zero and inverting.

When it comes to scale3d() and scaleZ(), we run into the problem that elements don't have any depth. Because of this, in most cases scaling an element along the Z-axis doesn't really change anything. Generally you'll want to translate along the Z-axis instead with transform: translateZ();.

Skewing elements with transform: skew(); and friends

The skew() transform with one value skews the element horizontally (on the X-axis), and if there's a second value it controls vertical skew. It takes angle units (deg, grad, rad, and turn) like rotate().

- transform: skew(sX)

- transform: skew(sX, sY)

- transform: skewX(sX)

- transform: skewY(sY)

Figure 12-7 shows examples of each of these.

```
.one {transform: skew(10deg);} /* the same as skewX(10deg) */

.one span {transform: skew(-20deg);}

.two {transform: skew(0,10deg);} /* the same as skewY(10deg) */

.two span {transform: skew(0,-20deg);}

.three {transform: skew(10deg,10deg);}

.three span {transform: skew(-20deg,-20deg);}

/* CAUTION! large values animate unpredictably */

.four {transform: skewX(180);} /* the same as skew(0) */

.four span {transform: skewY(-180deg);} /* the same as skew(0,0) */
```

Figure 12-7. Examples of skew() with one value (equivalent to skewX()), two values with the first one 0 (equivalent to skewY()), and two identical values (skewing both X and Y-axes). At 180deg (or -180deg) the skewed element appears the same as skew(0), and at 90deg (or -90deg) the skewed element becomes infinitely long and invisible (so it looks a little crazy when animated), as demonstrated in the +-180deg example. (Screenshots at 0deg, 120deg and 180deg).

While skew() can take negative and large values, skew(90deg) makes an element vanish as its two parallel edges touch and it becomes infinitely long. Values greater than 90deg (or -90deg) appears as a mirror image up to 180deg (or -180deg), where they appear the same as 0. This means skew(10deg) will appear the same as skew(190deg), but if animated it looks a bit crazy as it passes through 90deg. Generally you'll only need values between 45deg and -45deg. There is no 3D version of skew().

skew() is not something you'll use a lot, but it's there if you need it. It has its uses, as Russ Maschmeyer proves in his "Foldup" demo (http://strangenative.com/foldup/) in Figure 12-8.

Figure 12-8. Using skew() for typographic effect, via Dave Rupert's Lettering.js

The phenomenal cosmic power of transform: matrix(); and transform3d: matrix();

We do not pretend to deeply comprehend matrix transformations. However, math geeks will be right at home with the six-value transform: matrix(); that can perform all of the 2D transformations *at once* (with caveats). Here is the helpful definition of transform: matrix();.

> *Matrix specifies a 2D transformation in the form of a transformation matrix of six values. matrix(a,b,c,d,e,f) is equivalent to applying the transformation matrix [a b c d e f].*
>
> CSS 2D Transforms Module Level 3 (*http://j.mp/2d-transforms, http://dev.w3.org/csswg/css3-2d-transforms/#transform-functions*)

If you're wondering what in the world that means, the answer is algebra—the values *a* to *f* define a 3*3 transformation matrix (http://j.mp/svg-matrix, www.w3.org/TR/SVG/coords.html#TransformMatrixDefined) (using the SVG specification's definitions), as in Figure 12-9.

$$\begin{vmatrix} a & c & e \\ b & d & f \\ 0 & 0 & 1 \end{vmatrix}$$

Figure 12-0. Representing the definition of transform: matrix();—as a matrix. The third row ("0, 0, 1") is the same for each transformation. It's necessary for multiplying matrices, but we'll leave it out below.

Let's see how each of the 2D transformation functions can be represented using transform: matrix();.

- translate(tX, tY) = transform: matrix(1, 0, 0, 1, tX, tY);, where tX and tY are the horizontal and vertical translations.

- rotate(a) = transform: matrix(cos(a), sin(a), -sin(a), cos(a), 0, 0);, where a is the value in deg. Swap the sin(a) and -sin(a) values to reverse the rotation. Note that the maximum rotation you can represent is 360°.

- scale(sX, sY) = transform: matrix(sX, 0, 0, sY, 0 ,0);, where sX and sY are the horizontal and vertical scaling values.

- skew(aX, aY) = transform: matrix(1, tan(aY), tan(aX), 1, 0 ,0);, where aX and aY are the horizontal and vertical values in deg.

When doing more than one transformation at once, it's best to just use non-matrix transformations and list them in order, as in Figure 12-10.

```
div {transform: translate(50px, -24px) rotate(180deg) scale(.5) skew(0, 22.5deg);}
```

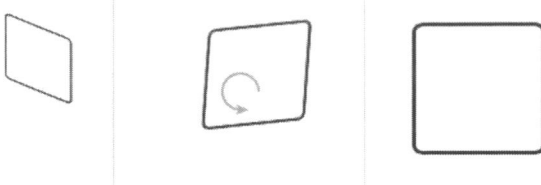

Figure 12-10. Applying multiple transforms. If animated, the rotation between rotate(0) and rotate(180deg) is clockwise.

However, if you're familiar with multiplying matrices together, or use a conversion tool like Eric Meyer and Aaron Gustafson's The Matrix Resolutions (http://j.mp/matrix-tool, http://meyerweb.com/eric/tools/matrix/), you could use transform: matrix(); to write that shorthand, as in Figure 12-11. Note that we've included vendor-prefixed CSS to show px units on translations for Firefox.

```
div {

  -webkit-transform: matrix(-.5,-.207,0,-.5,50,-24);

    -moz-transform: matrix(-.5,-.207,0,-.5,50px,-24px);

    -ms-transform: matrix(-.5,-.207,0,-.5,50,-24);

     -o-transform: matrix(-.5,-.207,0,-.5,50,-24);

        transform: matrix(-.5,-.207,0,-.5,50,-24);

}
```

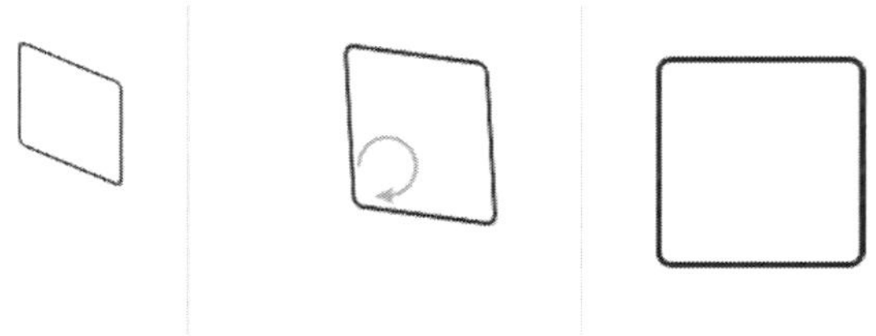

Figure 12-11. Applying the same transformations via matrix(). The rotation is now anti-clockwise if animated.

The default value is matrix(1,0,0,1,tX,tY), using numbers. Currently translations in a matrix (tX and tY) only accept pixel values (with no units) in Opera, Internet Explorer, and WebKit. However, Firefox 3.5+ accepts length values but requires units, and also accepts unitless numbers from version 10. When animating rotation-based matrix transformations, transitioning from 0deg to 180deg will only rotate counter-clockwise. While transform: matrix(); is more concise for multiple transforms and is how browsers perform transforms internally, it's generally not the best choice. It's a lot more complex so it's harder to grasp what will actually happen.

3D transform matrices are even more exciting, making up a "4x4 homogeneous matrix of 16 values in column-major order." As an example of how exciting, here's what rotate3d() looks like as a 3D matrix:

```
transform: matrix3d(1 + (1-cos(angle))*(x*x-1), -z*sin(angle)+(1-

cos(angle))*x*y, y*sin(angle)+(1-cos(angle))*x*z, 0, z*sin(angle)+(1-

cos(angle))*x*y, 1 + (1-cos(angle))*(y*y-1), -x*sin(angle)+(1-

cos(angle))*y*z, 0, -y*sin(angle)+(1-cos(angle))*x*z, x*sin(angle)+(1-

cos(angle))*y*z, 1 + (1-cos(angle))*(z*z-1), 0, 0, 0, 0, 1);
```

Unless you're an algebra fan, we recommend using the other transformation functions.

Rather than getting further into the excitement of the matrix, we refer you to Zoltan "Du Lac" Hawryluk's The CSS3 matrix() Transform for the Mathematically Challenged article (http://j.mp/css3-matrix, www.useragentman.com/blog/2011/01/07/css3-matrix-transform-for-the-mathematically-challenged/) and Wikipedia's article on transformation matrices (http://j.mp/wikipedia-matrix, http://en.wikipedia.org/wiki/Transformation_matrix#Examples_in_2D_graphics). You can also use Peter Nederlof's Playing with matrices tool (http://j.mp/play-matrix, http://peterned.home.xs4all.nl/matrices/) to manipulate a box and see the matrix output. Anyone wanting to use matrix3d() will no doubt need no assistance. ;)

There's one more transform function, transform: perspective();. It controls the perspective and foreshadowing of 3D transforms. As there's also a transform property perspective for the same purpose, let's compare and contrast them.

Putting 3D things into perspective with perspective and transform:perspective()

By default, transforms happen on a flat plane. We can give an illusion of depth to 3D-transformed elements by adding the property perspective, or the transform function transform: perspective();.These work by specifying a perspective projection matrix (http://j.mp/3d-projection, http://en.wikipedia.org/wiki/3D_projection).

> Note that while "transform" uses a three-dimensional coordinate system, the elements themselves are not three-dimensional objects. Instead, they exist on a two-dimensional plane (a flat surface) and have no depth.
>
> — CSS 3D Transforms specification (http://j.mp/3d-transforms, http://dev.w3.org/csswg/css3-3d-transforms/#introduction)

515

If you think of perspective being a pyramid, with the scene on the base and the viewer at the apex, the perspective value is the distance between the viewer and the scene. The shorter the pyramid, the more fish-eye lens-style distortion. In both properties a length value controls this foreshortening. For example, 2000px is very subtle, 800px gives obvious foreshortening, and 250px is very distorted. The value needs to be greater than zero, and unitless values are treated as pixels. Applying perspective also makes elements with larger Z-axis values appear larger.

Note: Using *perspective()* only affects transform functions that follow it. For example, *transform: perspective(800px) rotateY(-45deg);* has perspective, but *transform: rotateY(-45deg) perspective(800px);* doesn't.

```
.box {

  transform-origin: left center;

  transition: all 1s;

}

/* using the perspective() transform function */

.one .box {transform: perspective(2000px) rotateY(-45deg);} /* slight perspective */

.two .box {transform: perspective(800px) rotateY(-45deg);} /* perspective */

.three .box {transform: perspective(250px) rotateY(-45deg);} /* fish-eye */

/* alternatively, using the perspective property

.four {perspective: 2000px;}

.five {perspective: 800px;}

.six {perspective: 250px;}

.four .box, .five .box, .six .box {transform: rotateY(-45deg);}

*/

.container:hover .box {transform: rotateY(-180deg);}
```

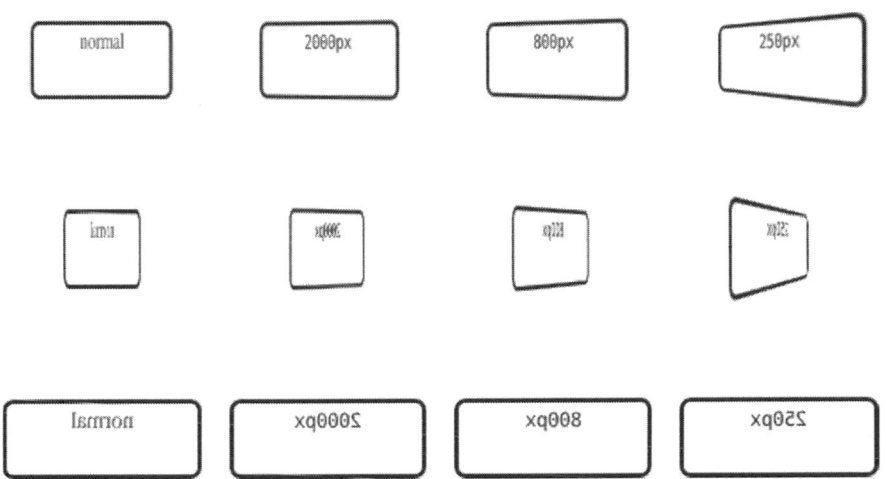

Figure 12-12. A rotated element with varying perspective() transform function values at rotateY(-45deg), rotateY(-112.5deg), and rotateY(-180deg). We can also achieve this by applying the perspective property to a container element.

The difference between the two methods is that the transform function transform: perspective(); applies perspective directly to the element, whereas the perspective property applies perspective to the element's children If you're applying a 3D transform to more than one element you want perspective on a wrapper element, as then all the child elements will be in the same 3D space. The size of an element with perspective affects the amount of foreshadowing for child elements, as does using a non-default transform-origin.

Changing the origin of perspective with the perspective-origin property

This sets the origin point for perspective, which by default is the center of the element (perspective-origin: 50% 50%;). It takes lengths, percentages, and keywords (like X and Y values for transform-origin). When using two keywords, or a keyword other than center and a value, the browser can work out which value is X (= left or right) and which is Y (= top or bottom). Otherwise, the first value will be on the X-axis and the second value (if present) will be on the Y-axis. We recommend you stick with the default perspective-origin: pX pY; order even when using keywords. Returning to our pyramid, changing the perspective-origin is like moving the apex (the viewer's location) away from the center of the scene.

- perspective-origin: pX;

- perspective-origin: pY; /* if top or bottom */

- perspective-origin: pX pY;

Changing transforms via transform-origin

transform-origin allows us to set the center of a transform's movement, which can really alter the resulting transformation. It can take one to four values:

- If there are one or two values, these can be keywords, lengths, and/or percentages. Lengths and percentages are calculated from the top left (0,0).

- A 3D transform can take three values, where the first two can be keywords, lengths, and/or percentages, but the third value must be a length.

- A 2D transform can also take three or four values, which represent offsets and must be written as two pairs of a keyword followed by a length or percentage, for example transform-origin: top 12px right 0;. If there are only three values, the missing offset is assumed to be zero, for example transform-origin: top 12px right;. (Note that support for this is nascent, and current browsers only use the first two values.)

By default tX and tY are 50% and _tZ_ is 0, so the default value is transform-origin: 50% 50%; for a 2D transform, and transform-origin: 50% 50% 0; for a 3D transform.

As with perspective-origin, when using keywords only we recommend you stick with the orthodox ordering: pX (pY (pZ)).

- transform-origin: tX;

- transform-origin: tY; /* if top or bottom */

- transform-origin: tX tY;

- transform-origin: tX tY tZ; /* for a 3D transform */

Returning to our earlier transform: rotate(); example in Figure 12-4, let's see the difference that transform-origin can make. The previous example didn't specify a transform-origin, so it used the default value of the elements' centers. In Figure 12-13 the outer boxes still do; however, the inner boxes all use a different corner via transform-origin. The origin point is indicated with a square corner.

```
/* Figure 12-4 code, plus… */

.top-left {

  border-top-left-radius: 0;

  transform-origin: left top; /* the same as 0 0 */

}
```

```
.bottom-left {

  border-bottom-left-radius: 0;

  transform-origin: left bottom; /* the same as 0 100% */

}

.top-right {

  border-top-right-radius: 0;

  transform-origin: right top; /* the same as 100% 0 */

}

.bottom-right {

  border-bottom-right-radius: 0;

  transform-origin: right bottom; /* the same as 100% 100% */

}
```

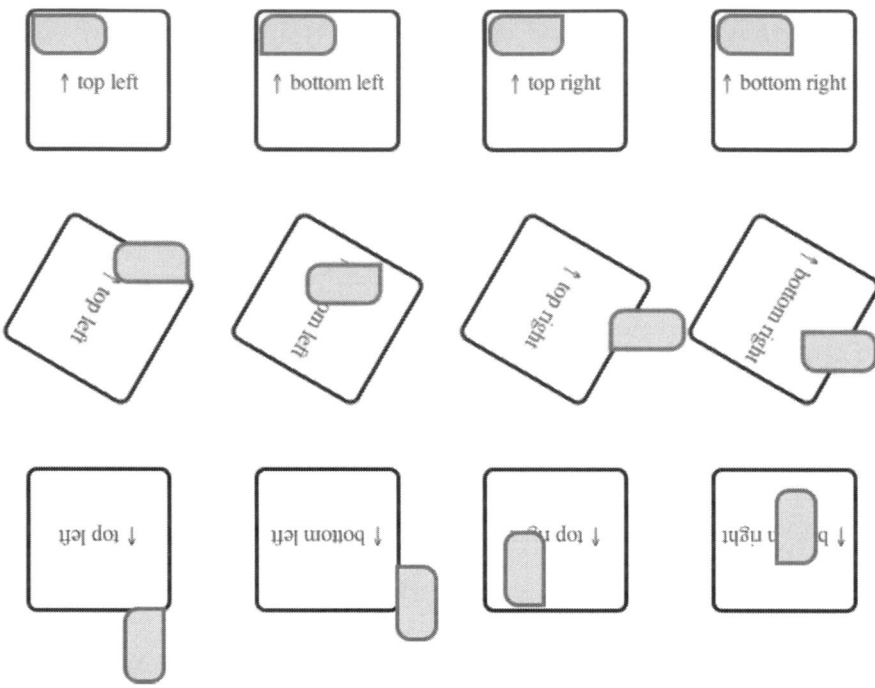

Figure 12-13. Examples of the difference transform-origin makes to transform: rotate() with a positive (clockwise) value on the outer box, and a negative (counter-clockwise) value on the inner box. (Screenshots at rotate(0deg), rotate(120deg), and rotate(180deg) for the outer box.)

While this completely changes the transforms, specifying a point further away from the element has an even greater effect.

Specifying a 3D transform-origin is just the 2D transform-origin we've met plus a length value for the Z-axis. Again, a larger value gives a greater effect, as shown in Figure 12-14.

```
.container {perspective: 800px;}

.container:hover span {transform: rotate3d(1,1,0,180deg); /* inner box */}

.top-left {transform-origin: left top 20px;}

.bottom-left {transform-origin: left bottom 40px;}

.top-right {transform-origin: right top 80px;}

.bottom-right {transform-origin: right bottom 160px;}
```

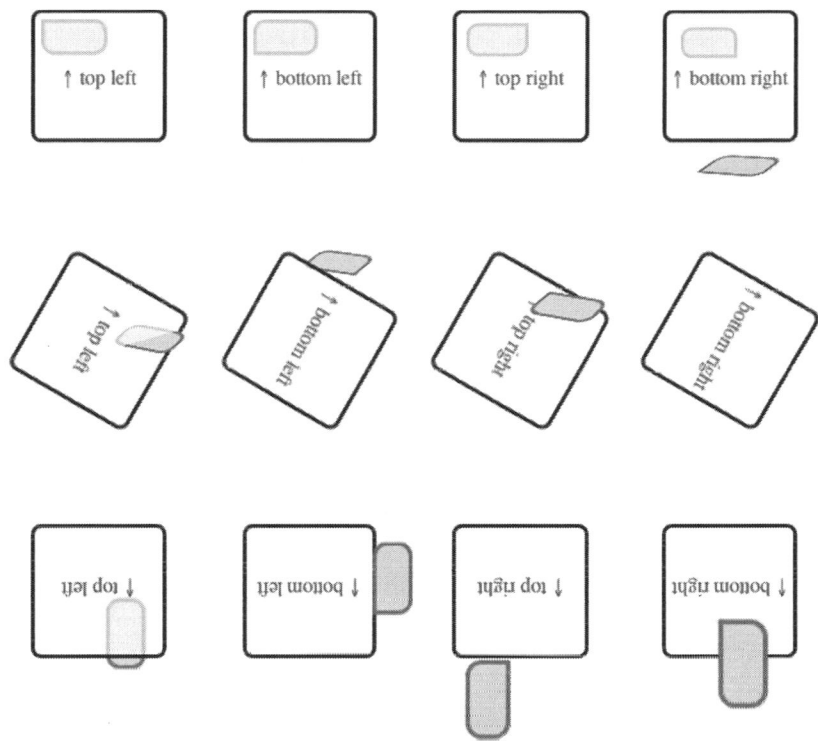

Figure 13-14. Examples of the difference a 3D transform-origin with successively larger Z values makes to transform: rotate(). We've also added perspective and transform-style: preserve-3d; to give the illusion of 3D. (Screenshots at rotate(0deg), rotate(120deg), and rotate(180deg) for the outer box.)

3D or flat transforms with transform-style

By default, elements appear in the same plane as their parent, with the stacking order dictated by the HTML source. We can change the stacking order using z-index, but we're still dealing with a two-dimensional plane. 3D transforms give us a Z-axis, but the default transform-style is flat—again, still on the same plane. To fully see the effects of Z-axis transforms we need to use transform-style: preserve-3d;, which applies to the element's children.

For 3D transforms you'll probably want to use transform-style: preserve-3d; together with perspective or perspective().3D transforms can lead to elements being transformed *behind* others, so you might need to explicitly use transform-style: flat; on an element to override an ancestor's preserve-3d.

521

Hiding and showing the back of a transformed element with backface-visibility

When an element is rotated 180° or more in 3D around the X or Y-axes, by default the element's back side is visible. This property allows us to hide it, which for example can be useful in making a double-sided playing card from two elements aligned back-to-back. It also comes in handy when making 3D boxes or spaces. As Figure 12-15 demonstrates, without it the illusion of the card flip, transition is broken.

```css
.card {

  transform-style: preserve-3d;

  perspective: 1000px;

}

.back, .front {

  position: absolute;

  width: 169px;

  height: 245px;

  -webkit-transition: .8s all;

}

.front {transform: rotate3d(0,1,0,180deg);}

.card:hover .back {transform: rotate3d(0,1,0,180deg);}

.card:hover .front {transform: rotate3d(0,1,0,0deg);}

.backface .back, .backface .front {backface-visibility: hidden;}
```

```html
<div class="card">

  <div class="back">Back</div>

  <div class="front">Front</div>

</div>
```

```
<div class="card backface">

  <div class="back">Back</div>

  <div class="front">Front</div>

</div>
```

Figure 12-15. A card-flip transition, with the left card using the default backface-visibility: visible; (with the initial state showing flicker between the sides as the animation begins), and the right card using backface-visibility: hidden;. Note that without a background the "Front" and "Back" text in the left card are visible at the same time.

Browser support for CSS transforms

CSS transforms tend to involve substantial changes and can look broken without a fallback in non-supporting browsers. While 2D transforms are fairly well supported in modern browsers, the lack of support in earlier versions of Internet Explorer may give you pause in using them. The scale() transform function can easily be duplicated via Internet Explorer's CSS zoom property, and other 2D transforms can be duplicated in IE (with a certain amount of suffering) via the MS Matrix filter.

For 3D transforms, the situation is bleaker. Limited browser support and no polyfills severely restrict where we can use them, and the performance isn't quite up to games programming yet, either.

We generally stick with using CSS transforms for *progressive enhancement only*, such as nonessential styling that only supporting browsers get. For anything that isn't just progressive enhancement you'll need to carefully consider your audience and use fallbacks or alternative methods of achieving your goals.

Browser support for 2D transforms

Modern browsers *including* Internet Explorer 9 support 2D transforms, and even better recent versions of Internet Explorer, Firefox and Opera support them without vendor prefixes, as you can see in Table 12-2.

Table 12-2. Browser Support for 2D Transforms (http://j.mp/c-transforms2d, http://caniuse.com/#feat=transforms2d)

Property	IE	Firefox	Safari	Chrome	Opera
Transform	9 -ms-	3.5 -moz-	3.1 -webkit-	1 -webkit-	10.5 -o-
	10	16			12.5
transform:translate()	9 -ms-	3.5 -moz-	3.1 -webkit-	1 -webkit-	10.5 -o-
	10	16			12.5
transform:rotate()	9 -ms-	3.5 -moz-	3.1 -webkit-	1 -webkit-	10.5 -o-
	10	16			12.5

Property	IE	Firefox	Safari	Chrome	Opera
transform:scale()	9 -ms- 10	3.5 -moz- 16	3.1 -webkit-	1 -webkit-	10.5 -o- 12.5
transform:skew()	9 -ms- 10	3.5 -moz- 16	3.1 -webkit-	1 -webkit-	10.5 -o- 12.5
transform:matrix()	9 -ms- 10	3.5 -moz-[1] 10 -moz- 16	3.1 -webkit-	1 -webkit-	10.5 -o- 12.5
transform-origin	9 -ms- 10	3.5 -moz- 16	3.1 -webkit-	1 -webkit-	10.5 -o- 12.5

[1]Firefox 3.5-9 accepts lengths not numbers for tX and tY values in transform: matrix();. It also accepts unitless numbers from version 10.

Browser support for 3D transforms

Browser support for 3D transforms doesn't extend back nearly as far, as demonstrated in Table 12-3.

Table 12-3. Browser Support for 3D Transforms (http://j.mp/c-transforms3d, http://caniuse.com/#feat=transforms3d)

Property	IE	Firefox	Safari	Chrome	Opera[1]
transform (3D transforms)	10 -ms-	10 -moz-	4.0.5 -webkit-	12 -webkit-	-
transform:translate3d()	10 -ms-	10 -moz-	4.0.5 -webkit-	12 -webkit-	-

Property	IE	Firefox	Safari	Chrome	Opera[1]
transform:rotate3d()	10 -ms-	10 -moz-	4.0.5 -webkit-	12 -webkit-	-
transform:scale3d()	10 -ms-	10 -moz-	4.0.5 -webkit-	12 -webkit-	-
transform:matrix3d()	10 -ms-	10 -moz-	5 -webkit-	12 -webkit-	-
transform:perspective()	10 -ms-	10 -moz-	4.0.5 -webkit-	12 -webkit-	-
Perspective	10 -ms-	10 -moz-	4.0.5 -webkit-	12 -webkit-	-
perspective-origin	10 -ms-	10 -moz-	4.0.5 -webkit-	12 -webkit-	-
transform-origin: *X Y Z*	10 -ms-	10 -moz-	4.0.5 -webkit-	12 -webkit-	-
transform-style	10 -ms-	10 -moz-	4.0.5 -webkit-	12 -webkit-	-
backface-visibility	10 -ms-	10 -moz-	4.0.5 -webkit-	12 -webkit-	-

[1] *3D transitions are being worked on for Opera, but they're not in Opera Next at the time of writing*

Polyfills, fallbacks, and Internet Explorer's filter property

If you choose to, you can extend the browser support of CSS 2D transforms. One option is to use Internet Explorer's proprietary CSS filter property, basically an ugly precursor to translate: matrix(), allowing you to support Internet Explorer 6-8.[7] Enter your prefix-less transforms CSS into the Transforms Translator (http://j.mp/ie-transforms, www.useragentman.com/IETransformsTranslator/) by Zoltan Hawryluk and Zoe

---

[7] Note that IE's filters animate … poorly — test thoroughly if you use them.

Mickley Gillenwater, and it will output the equivalent IE filter-based transform, along with vendor prefixed transforms for other browsers. You can then add the filter CSS to an IE-only stylesheet and include via an IE conditional comment.

If you choose to go the polyfill[8] route, here are two JavaScript polyfills that convert 2D transforms CSS to Internet Explorer filter properties on the fly. Of course, if the user has JavaScript disabled nothing happens—*caveat emptor*.

- Transformie (http://transformie.com/) is a jQuery plug-in by Paul Bakaus that adds basic transform support to IE6-8.

- cssSandpaper (http://j.mp/csssandpaper, www.useragentman.com/blog/2010/03/09/cross-browser-css-transforms-even-in-ie/) by Zoltan "Du Lac" Hawryluk adds support for IE6-8 and Opera 10.0+, plus box-shadow, linear gradients, and radial gradients.

Finally, transforms (and transition animations) can also be done via JavaScript, for example using jQuery's effects (http://j.mp/jq-effects, http://api.jquery.com/category/effects/). CSS 2D and 3D transforms are detected by Modernizr, so you can set up fallback content—either extending behaviors to non-supporting browsers via a polyfill for 2D transforms or using a suitable non-transforming alternative, such as an image. At the time of writing, there are no polyfills for 3D transforms.

CSS transforms gotchas

As CSS 2D and 3D transforms have only recently been implemented, there are still quirks and bugs. Here are some tricks and tips for common issues

- WebKit browsers don't transform display: inline; elements. Opera 11+ and Firefox 4+ work as expected. The workaround is to use display; inline-block;.

- When using transform: rotate(); in iOS, the straight edge of a rotated image can appear aliased. Thierry Koblentz found that using background-clip: padding-box; solves this.

- As already mentioned, in Firefox 3.5-9 the translate values in transform: matrix(); were implemented as lengths, not the spec's numbers. You'll need to add px for Firefox only. From Firefox 10 both types of values are supported. See transform: matrix(); for more information.

- Transformed text is not anti-aliased in Opera 11.60

---

[8] As mentioned in Chapters 2 and 7, a polyfill adds support for something to a browser that doesn't support it natively, typically using JavaScript.

- 3D transforms disable sub-pixel anti-aliasing in WebKit browsers for performance reasons. In Safari, the rendering is still ok, but it can be noticeable in Chrome. Also in Chrome, this can disable it on elements that aren't themselves 3D transformed, and these will have rougher anti-aliasing than those that are. Dave DeSandro found that adding a background color to affected elements re-enables sub-pixel anti-aliasing in Chrome 16.

- There are some issues when transitioning or animating transforms, such as browser bugs when transitioning between transform states with different units. We'll address these issues in the upcoming sections.

CSS transforms in summary

While the transformations and associated properties can seem overly simple on the surface, combining them together allows us to do some impressive manipulations. For example, Dirk Weber's CSS Warp (http://j.mp/csswarp, http://csswarp.eleqtriq.com/) in Figure 12-16 is a "text to path" tool *made with CSS transforms*.

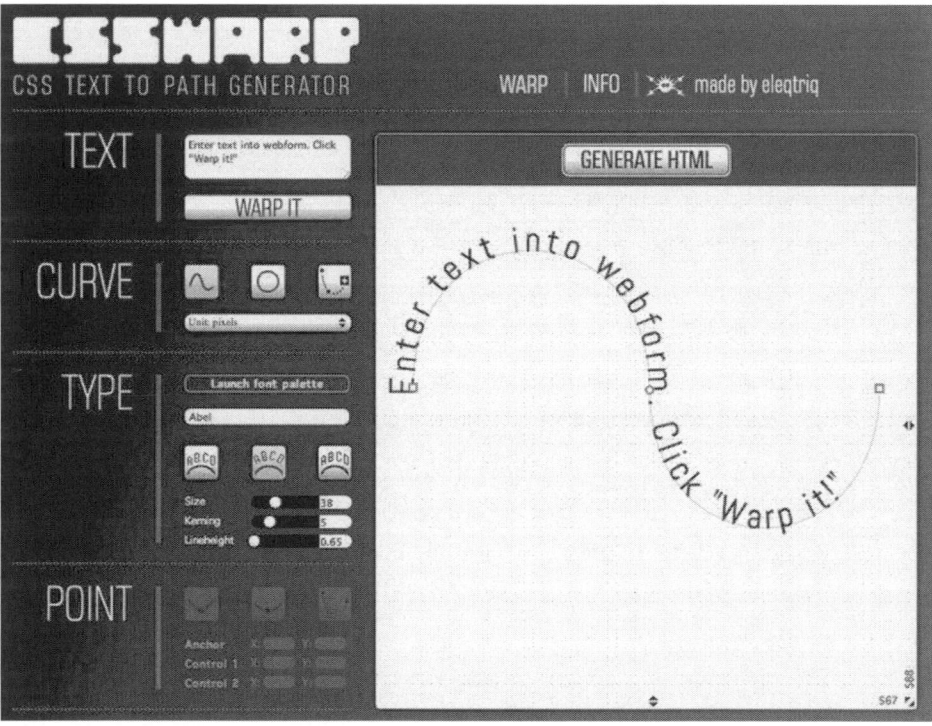

Figure 12-16. CSSWarp, which uses CSS transforms to place text on a path.

However, the magic really starts when using transformations together with transitions, animation, and JavaScript. Hakim El Hattab's 3D carousel slideshow (http://j.mp/3d-slideshow, http://hakim.se/inc/components/slideshow/) is a beautiful example of 3D transformations and transitions with a little JavaScript. It even works on the iPhone and iPad, which have 3D transform support.

Although they are still comparatively new, we think it's time to start using 2D transforms today—*where appropriate*—for subtle improvements to user experience. The use of 2D transforms for more than progressive enhancement, or *any* use of 3D transforms, is probably premature unless you have a suitable audience. Make sure to test thoroughly, as support is relatively recent. Despite this (and the occasional browser bug), CSS transforms are great for adding some subtle flavor, and if your user stats support, it can play a more central role, for example on sites for iOS devices. If nothing else, they're a taste of the not-yet-widely-distributed future and lots of fun to play with!

Moving right along, let's see how we can change elements (including CSS transformed ones) *over time* with CSS transitions and CSS animations.

CSS transitions and CSS animations: compare and contrast

These specifications both allow us to "interpolate CSS property values" or animate the changing of an element's property's value over time. We'll cover both in detail, but to understand the differences, let's start with a quick comparison. The following is what the CSS3 Animations specification says:

> CSS Transitions provide a way to interpolate CSS property values when they change as a result of underlying property changes. This provides an easy way to do simple animation, but the start and end states of the animation are controlled by the existing property values, and transitions provide little control to the author on how the animation progresses.
>
> [CSS Animations] introduces defined animations, in which the author can specify the changes in CSS properties over time as a set of keyframes. Animations are similar to transitions in that they change the presentational value of CSS properties over time.
>
> — CSS Animations specification (http://j.mp/css3-animations, http://dev.w3.org/csswg/css3-animations/#introduction)

While there are a lot of similarities—for example, both operate on the same "animatable" properties and use the same timing functions—for us these are the major differences:

- CSS transitions can be triggered by a CSS *change in state* and JavaScript. CSS animations *play by default* once declared, although you can also trigger them by a CSS change in state[9] and JavaScript.

- CSS transitions apply a transition to an *existing* instant change. CSS animations *add* styles to an element and animate using them.

- CSS transitions occur between two *intrinsic styles*,[10] the element's intrinsic style before and after the transition is triggered (such as non-:hover and :hover values). CSS animations animate from the element's *intrinsic state* and between (multiple) keyframes. By default, the element will return to its intrinsic state when the animation ends.

- CSS transitions are simple, with wider browser support. CSS animations are more powerful and complex, with less browser support.

For future reference, Table 12-4 summarizes the differences.

Table 12-4. A Comparison of CSS Transitions and CSS Animations

	CSS Transitions	CSS Animations
Properties	One, many (same properties)	
Enumerating properties	Individually, all	Individually when declaring values in keyframes
Timing functions	Yes (same functions)	
Delay	Yes (positive/negative)	
CSS to animate	Element's styles pre- & post-change of state (2 states)	Element's intrinsic state, rules in keyframes (2 or more states)

---

[9] An example of a change of state is mousing over an element with :hover.

[10] An element's intrinsic style is the CSS styles it has before a transition or animation is applied.

	CSS Transitions	CSS Animations
Applied by	CSS change in state, JavaScript	Being declared, CSS change in state, JavaScript
Fallback	Change of state is instant	Nothing happens
Repeatable	No	Yes

CSS transitions are great for a simple enhancement when you need to animate between two states. CSS animations can do everything CSS transitions do plus more, but with their power comes a little more complexity and CSS to write. Let's examine both in detail. First up, CSS transitions.

CSS transitions: bling in 4D!

We're sure you're all familiar with link rollovers, the basic interactivity provided by our friends the :link, :visited, :hover, :focus, and :active pseudo-classes. These changes are useful, but instant.

The CSS Transitions Module (http://j.mp/css3transitions, http://dev.w3.org/csswg/css3-transitions/) takes things up a notch, giving us the simple ability to control the change of an existing CSS property from one value to another *over time*. This fourth dimension opens up a world of possibilities, and we can easily apply these transitions via a *CSS change in state*. This includes the following pseudo-classes (see Chapter 8 for more information). It also includes using @media queries (see Chapter 9), and using JavaScript by adding a class to an element, for example.

- :link
- :visited
- :hover
- :focus

- :active
- :disabled
- :enabled
- :checked

For more on triggering transitions, refer to Louis Lazarus' articles "CSS3 Transitions Without Using :hover" (http://j.mp/transitions-pseudo, www.impressivewebs.com/css3-transitions-without-hover) and "Triggering CSS3 Transitions With JavaScript" (http://j.mp/transitions-js, www.impressivewebs.com/css3-transitions-javascript).

We control a transition using the following properties:

- transition-property: A list of transitionable properties to apply the transition to. By default, this is transition-property: all; and there's a table of transitionable properties coming right up.

- transition-duration: The length of the transition in units of time, such as seconds (.4s) or milliseconds (400ms). By default, this is the instant transition-duration: 0s; so it's the same as not using a transition.

- transition-timing-function: Controls the *relative* speed of the transition over the transition-duration to make the transition start slowly and end quickly, for example. Values include linear, ease (the default), ease-in, ease-out, ease-in-out, cubic-bezier(), step-start, step-end, and steps().

- transition-delay: A delay before the transition starts (times), with the default of transition-delay: 0s;. This can also take a negative value, making it appear to start already part-way through the transition.

- transition: A shorthand property that takes transition-property, transition-duration, transition-timing-function, and transition-delay, in that order. Missing properties use default values, giving a default of transition: all 0s ease 0s;.

Setting what to transition with transition-property

transition-property allows us to specify one or more comma-separated animatable CSS properties to transition, with a default value of all. Note that properties with vendor prefixes need to be written with the vendor prefix in transition-property, too. For example, here's vendor-prefixed code to transition the transform property (aligned for column selection):

```
.postcard {

  -webkit-transition-property: -webkit-transform;

    -moz-transition-property:    -moz-transform;

     -ms-transition-property:     -ms-transform;

      -o-transition-property:      -o-transform;

         transition-property:         transform;

}

...
```

See Multiple Transition Values, and the transition shorthand property below for more on multiple values.

Animatable properties for CSS transitions and CSS animations

You can apply CSS transitions to many but not all CSS properties, as you can see in Table 12-5 (based on the table in the CSS3 Transitions specification[11]). These properties are also the ones we can animate with CSS animations, which are covered later in this chapter.

Table 12-5. Animatable CSS Properties (for CSS Transitions and CSS Animations)

Property Type	Property Name	Transitionable Values
Catch-all	All	(all transitionable properties)
Text properties	color	color
	font-size	length, percentage
	font-weight	number, keywords (excluding bolder, lighter)
	letter-spacing	length
	line-height	number, length, percentage
	text-indent	length, percentage
	text-shadow	shadow
	vertical-align	keywords, length, percentage

[11] In newer CSS specifications, animatable properties are indicated in the summary of the property's definition.

Property Type	Property Name	Transitionable Values
	word-spacing	length, percentage
Box properties	background[1]	*color (currently)*
	background-color	color
	background-image[2]	*images, gradients*
	background-position	percentage, length
	border-left-color etc[3]	color
Box properties	border-spacing	length
	border-left-width etc[3]	length
	border-top-left-radius etc[3]	percentage, length
	box-shadow	shadow
	clip	rectangle
	crop	rectangle
	height, min-height, max-height	length, percentage
	margin-left etc[3]	length

Property Type	Property Name	Transitionable Values
	opacity	number
	outline-width	length
	outline-offset	integer
	outline-color	color
	padding-left etc3	length
	width, min-width, max-width	length, percentage
Positioning properties	bottom	length, percentage
	top	length, percentage
	grid-*4	various
Positioning properties	left	length, percentage
	right	length, percentage
	visibility	visibility
	z-index	integer
	zoom	number

Property Type	Property Name	Transitionable Values
SVG properties	fill	paint server
(http://j.mp/svg-props, www.w3.org/TR/SVG/ propidx.html)	fill-opacity	float
	flood-color	color, keywords
	lighting-color	color, keywords
	marker-offset	length
	stop-color	color
	stop-opacity	float
	stroke	paint server
	stroke-dasharray	list of numbers
	stroke-dashoffset	number
	stroke-miterlimit	number
	stroke-opacity	float
SVG properties	stroke-width	float
	viewport-fill	color

Property Type	Property Name	Transitionable Values
	viewport-fill-opacity	color

1. While the shorthand background isn't actually in the spec, it works (at least for background-color and background-position values).

2. This is a little up in the air, with background-image in CSS Backgrounds and Borders Module Level 3 changing from "only gradients" to "Animatable: no" as the spec became a candidate recommendation. However, support has appeared in Chrome 19 Canary, and this is something that designers want. Until widespread support arrives, simple transitioning gradients can be faked with a transition on background-color plus an overlaying gradient and background image transitions via image sprites and background-position or opacity.

3. Currently the spec only defines individual properties containing -top-, -bottom-, -left- and -right- for border-width, border-color, margin, and padding. WebKit browsers, Firefox and Opera 12 can also animate the shorthand properties.

4. grid-* are properties of the Grid Positioning module, covered in Chapter 9.

5. Finally, note that transitioning colors occur in RGBa color space, and transitions involving transparent or colors with alpha channel may not occur as you expect. See the "Transition gotchas" section later in this chapter for more details.

More properties will become animatable in the future, so keep this in mind when choosing whether to use all or only specific properties. While all is convenient, it's safer to be explicit when using only one property. For example, when using JavaScript to transition elements, transition: all; will fire the transitionEnd event every time a transition ends *for each property changed*. Also, currently Firefox supports the following additional properties (with the -moz- prefix), which will also be transitioned with transition-property: all;. All but the three properties with asterisks will probably be added to the transitions specification in the future, and many are also supported in WebKit browsers.

- -moz-background-size
- -moz-border-radius
- -moz-box-flex*
- -moz-box-shadow
- -moz-column-count
- -moz-column-gap
- -moz-column-rule-color
- -moz-column-rule-width
- -moz-column-width

- -moz-font-size-adjust
- -moz-font-stretch
- -moz-image-region*
- -moz-marker-offset
- -moz-outline-radius*
- -moz-text-decoration-color
- -moz-transform
- -moz-transform-origin

There are some properties not in the spec that you'll want to transition. These only have partial support at the time of writing; they work in Firefox, WebKit and Opera browsers.

- border-radius
- box-shadow

There are also several properties or values you'll want to transition, but they are both unspecced and unsupported at the time of writing.

- background-image, including gradients

- float

- height or width using the value auto (currently both values must be a *length* or *percentage*)

    The same applies to top, right, bottom, and left, but despite the spec (and probably due to a bug) WebKit browsers *can* animate these using auto.

- display between none and anything else

- position between static and absolute

The CSS Working Group is aware of these issues and some of them will be addressed (for example, the transitioning background-image is being worked on and transitioning auto is expected in CSS4 transitions) so this list will decrease in the future.

Faking auto on width and height with max-width and max-height

Animating between auto and 0 would be really useful for things like a "sliding drawer" effect for dialogs, as demonstrated by jQuery's slideToggle effect (http://j.mp/jq-slidetoggle, http://api.jquery.com/slideToggle/). We can give the *appearance* of animating width and height to/from auto by substituting a value on max-width or max-height, respectively, that's larger than the content it contains (http://j.mp/faking-auto, http://dabblet.com/gist/1676548), as shown in Figure 12-17.

```
.box {

    max-height: 5em; /* larger than your content: 200px would also work here */

    overflow: hidden; /* otherwise the text will be visible */

    padding: .5em .25em;

    transition: all 0.5s;

}
.wrapper:hover .box {

    max-height: 0;

    opacity: 0;

    padding: 0 .25em;

}
```

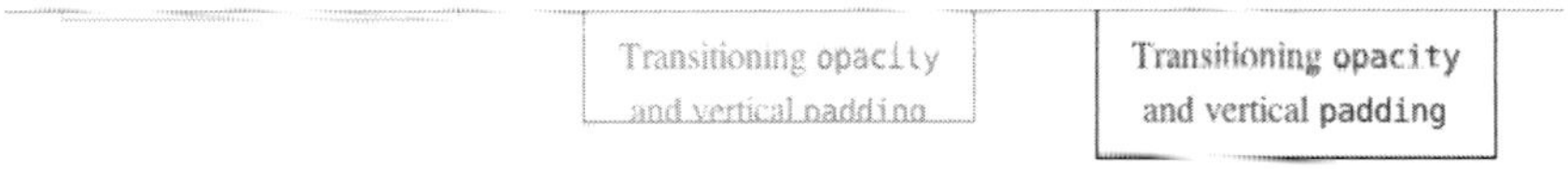

Figure 12-17. Faking transitioning from height: auto; to height: 0; via max-height, plus opacity and padding. For a short transition this is passable.

This really helps for faking animating height because actually using a fixed height (in px) is asking for trouble (people do resize!). However, a very large value introduces a delay, so we think using a value in ems for max-height is safer. In the previous example, the boxes are about 5em high, so we used max-height: 8em;.

Controlling the duration of a transition with transition-duration

The transition-duration property sets the duration of a transition and takes time values in seconds (s) or milliseconds (ms), with three durations shown in Figure 12-18.

```
.one {transition-duration: .2s;}

.two {transition-duration: .4s;}

.three {transition-duration: 1s;}
```

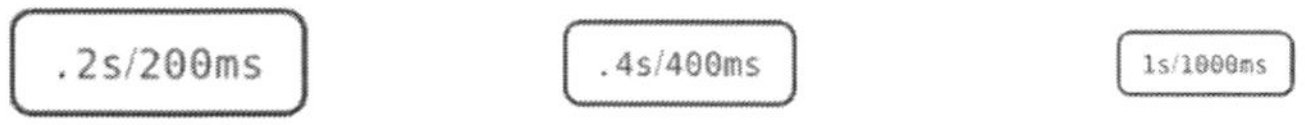

```
.2s/200ms          .4s/400ms          1s/1000ms
```

Figure 12-18. A comparison of three transition durations — the first one has already finished in this screenshot.

How a transition's duration appears will be affected by how noticeable the change in state is. For obviously different states of a link's :hover state, a transition as fast as transition-duration: .2s; (or transition-duration: 200ms;) can be used to smooth a quick change, but anything faster than this becomes indistinguishable from no transition. We find a value of .4s (or 400ms) tends to works well for a subtle transition. However, if you're moving an element any distance, .4s could be way too short. Longer transitions tend to draw more attention to themselves, but when used sparingly can be useful for a specific effect, especially when combined with the transition-timing-function property, which is coming up next.

transition-timing-function, cubic Bézier curves, and steps()

The transition-timing-function property is the hardest part of transitions to get your head around. Luckily, it's all pretty simple once you've seen some examples. The property has functions based on Bézier curves[12] (moving on an arc) and steps (stop-start movement). Cubic Bézier curves have four points: the start and end locations are diagonally opposite each other in the corners of a square (0,0 and 1,1), and the other two points are the control handles that define the curve, as seen in Figure 12-19. In contrast, the stepping functions (steps(), etc.) divide the transition into equally sized intervals, dependent on the number of steps.

---

[12] Bézier curves (http://j.mp/bezier-curves, http://en.wikipedia.org/wiki/Bézier_curve) are just the curved paths with handles you'll be familiar with from vector graphics like SVG and software like Adobe Illustrator and Inkscape.

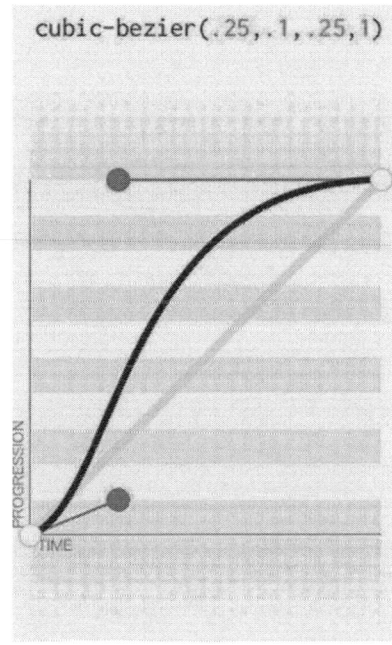

cubic-bezier(.25,.1,.25,1)

Figure 12-19. The cubic-bezier equivalent to transition-timing-function: ease;, from Lea Verou's excellent cubic Bézier visualiser http://cubic-bezier.com.

transition-timing-function values include cubic-bezier() and steps(), plus several common presets.

- cubic-bezier()

- This allows you to make a custom cubic Bézier curve by setting the X,Y handle locations for the start and end points in the pattern cubic-bezier(X1, Y1, X2, Y2). There are also several common preset values.

  - linear: The transition has a constant speed. Equivalent to cubic-bezier(0, 0, 1.0, 1.0).

  - ease: The default transition, it starts quickly then tapers out, like a faster, smoother version of ease-out. Equivalent to cubic-bezier(0.25, 0.1, 0.25, 1.0) (default).

  - ease-in: The transition starts slow and accelerates to the end. Equivalent to cubic-bezier(0.42, 0, 1.0, 1.0).

  - ease-out: The transition starts fast then slows down. Equivalent to cubic-bezier(0, 0, 0.58, 1.0).

541

- ease-in-out: The transition starts and ends slowly, but transitions quickly in the middle. Equivalent to cubic-bezier(0.42, 0, 0.58, 1.0).

- steps(): The transition jumps from one step to another, rather than transitioning smoothly like Bézier-based transitions. It has a value with the number of steps and can also take a second value—either start or end—that controls how the transition proceeds.[13]

    - step-start: The transition is instant and happens immediately when triggered. This is equivalent to steps(1,start).

    - step-end: The transition is instant but happens at the end of the transition-duration. This is equivalent to steps(1,end).

Figure 12-20 shows a demonstration of the preset values (we're reordered them to make the differences more obvious).

---

[13] Peter Beverloo has made a nice demonstration of steps() transitions (plus cubic-bezier presets) (http://j.mp/css3-ttf / http://peter.sh/experiments/css3-transition-timing-functions).

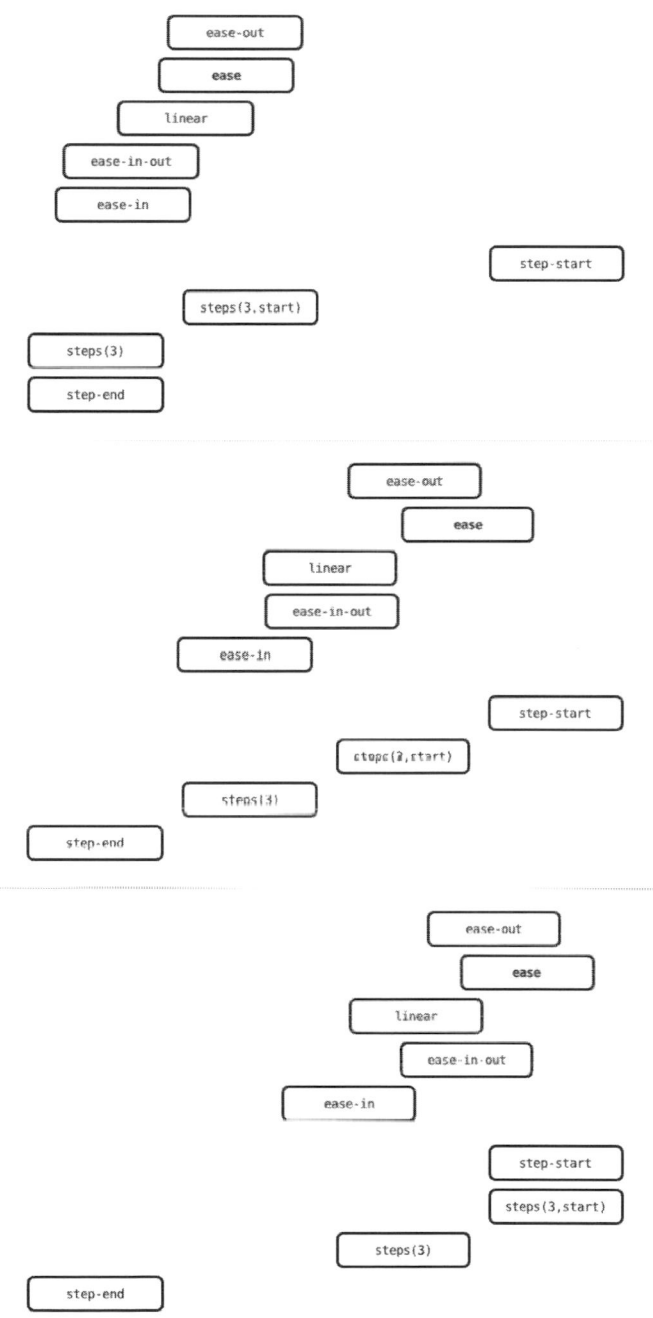

Figure 12-20. A comparison of the preset values of transition-timing-function over time, including some example steps() functions. (Screenshots approximately ¼, ½, and ¾ through the transition.)

The default ease is a good all-round choice, although linear animates more smoothly for transitions with a small movement. While the presets are generally enough, for a specific effect in a long transition you can make your own Bézier timing function using cubic-bezier(X1, Y1, X2, Y2).

Y values can exceed 0-1.0, causing the transition to "bounce," as demonstrated in Figure 12-21.

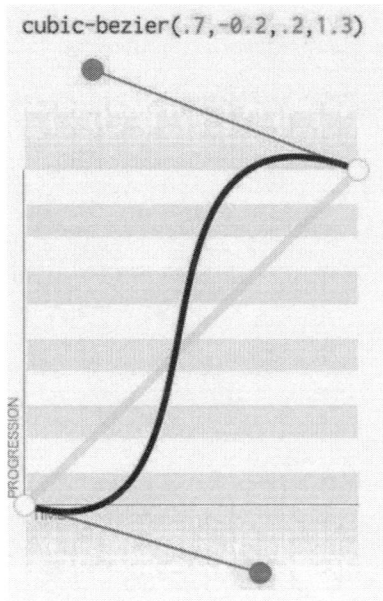

Figure 12-21. A cubic-bezier value with "bounce" (Y values less than 0 or greater than 1)

You can progressively add a cubic-bezier timing function with Y values less than 0 or greater than 1 by using a "clamped" fallback first (one with values between 0 and 1), as demonstrated in Figure 12-22. This will be closer to the timing function you want than the default ease.

```
.ease {transition-timing-function: cubic-bezier(.25,.1,.25,1);} /* = ease */

.clamped {transition-timing-function: cubic-bezier(.7,0,.2,1);} /* Y=0~1 */

.bounce {transition-timing-function: cubic-bezier(.7,-.2,.2,1.3);}


/* our recommended way to include a cubic-bezier with bounce: */

.bulletproof { /* including vendor prefixes to show WebKit fallback */

  -webkit-transition-timing-function: cubic-bezier(.7,0,.2,1); /* fallback */
```

```
-webkit-transition-timing-function: cubic-bezier(.7,-.2,.2,1.3);

 -moz-transition-timing-function: cubic-bezier(.7,-.2,.2,1.3);

  -ms-transition-timing-function: cubic-bezier(.7,-.2,.2,1.3);

   -o-transition-timing-function: cubic-bezier(.7,-.2,.2,1.3);

      transition-timing-function: cubic-bezier(.7,-.2,.2,1.3);
```

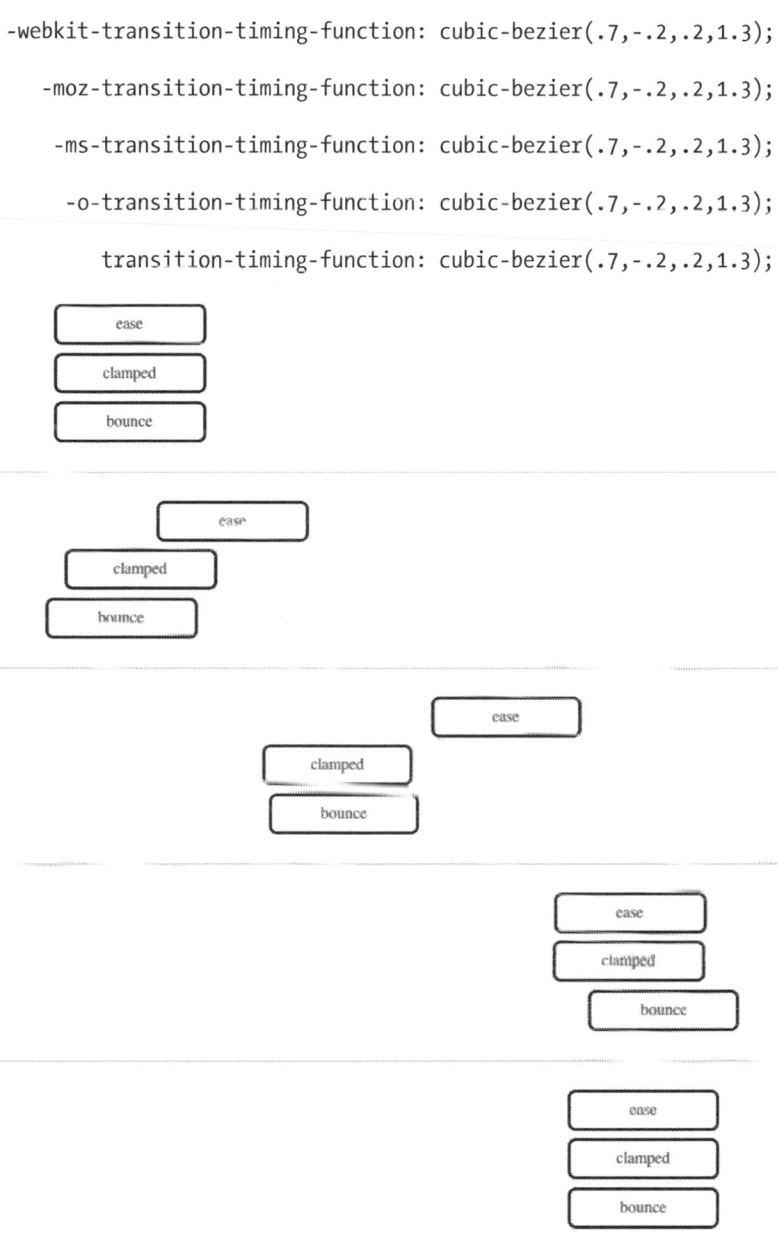

```
}
```

Figure 12-22. In browsers that don't support Y values outside 0-1, the default ease timing function will be used instead. By adding a "clamped" cubic-bezier fallback before one with bounce, you can get a closer approximation in these browsers.

The steps() timing functions can be used to make things happen at the start or end of a transition. They can be used for frame-based animation, as demonstrated by Lea Verou in "Pure CSS3 typing animation with steps()" (http://j.mp/typing-steps, http://lea.verou.me/2011/09/pure-css3-typing-animation-with-steps/) and "Simurai in Sprite Sheet animation" (http://j.mp/sprite-steps, http://jsfiddle.net/simurai/CGmCe/).

Finally, while these cubic Bézier and step-based timing functions are great, they don't cover the full scope of potential timing functions. Some of the timing functions that Scripty2 has would require something else, like CSS Animations or JavaScript, for example (http://j.mp/scripty2-ttf, http://scripty2.com/doc/scripty2%20fx/s2/fx/transitions.html).

Delaying the start of a transition with transition-delay

As you might expect, transition-delay allows us to delay the start of a transition after it has been triggered. Just like transition-duration, it takes time values in seconds or milliseconds. When the value is positive, the transition is delayed by the value's amount. When the value is negative, the animation is *jump-started* by the transition-delay's value, beginning as if that time had already elapsed. Compare these to the default transition-delay: 0 in Figure 12-23.

```
hover .box {transition-duration: 3s;}

:hover .positive-delay {transition-delay: 1s;} /* "delay 1s" box */

/* transition-delay is 0 by default (the "no delay" box) */

:hover .negative-delay {transition-delay: -1s;} /* "delay -1s" box */
```

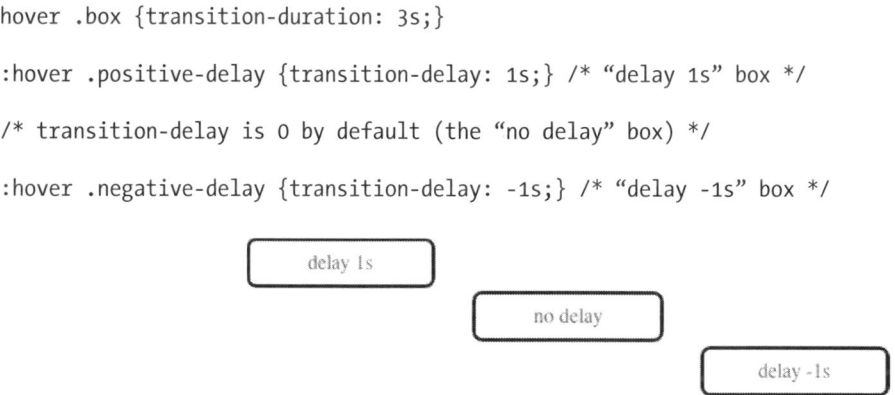

Figure 12-23. We can delay or jump-start the start of a transition using transition-delay. This figure shows 1s into a 3s linear animation.

When a transition is triggered but the trigger is removed before it completes (for example, a mouseover then mouseout of a transition triggered by :hover), the transition will then play in reverse from its current state to its initial state. If there's a transition-delay, this will also occur when the transition reverses—for a positive delay the element will freeze, and for a negative delay the element will jump, before continuing.

5466

Multiple transition values and the transition shorthand property

All of these properties can take more than one value, separated by commas, allowing us to transition more than one property at once with different settings. When using multiple values for each transition-* property, the order of the values is important, as the values of each property are grouped together based on this order. For example, this code block

```
.warning {

  transition-property:  left, opacity, color;

  transition-duration: 600ms,    300ms, 400ms;

    transition-delay:    0s,      0s, 300ms;

} /* values aligned to make their groupings clear */
```

is equivalent to these three comma-separated transitions

```
.warning {transition: left 600ms, opacity 300ms, color 400ms 300ms;}
```

transition shorthand property order

When using the transition property, it's important to stick to this order for the values (or for each comma-separated group of values for multiple transitions):

1. transition-property

2. transition-duration

3. transition-timing-function

4. transition-delay

Any values we don't declare will use the default value. We don't declare transition-timing-function in the first example above, so the transition will use the default ease. In addition, while we do need to declare 0s values for transition-delay in the first example so that the last value is applied to color, we don't when using transition in the second example, as 0s is the default.

Browser support for CSS transitions

Modern browsers, with the sad exception of Internet Explorer 9, support transitions pretty well, as you can see in Table 12-6.

547

Table 12-6. Browser Support for CSS Transitions (http://j.mp/c-transitions, http://caniuse.com/#feat=css-transitions)

Property	IE	Firefox	Safari	Chrome	Opera
transition-property	10	4 -moz- 16	3.2 -webkit-	1-webkit-	10.5 -o- 12.5
transition-duration	10	4 -moz- 16	3.2 -webkit-	1 -webkit-	10.5 -o- 12.5
transition-timing-function[1]	10	4 -moz- 16	3.2 -webkit-	1 -webkit-	10.5 -o- 12.5
:steps()[2]	10	5 -moz- 16	5 -webkit-	8 -webkit-	12 -o- 12.5
"bounce"[2]	10	4 -moz- 16	6 -webkit-[3]	16 -webkit-[3]	10.5 -o- 12.5
transition-delay	10	4 -moz- 16	3.2 -webkit-	1 -webkit-	10.5 -o- 12.5
transition	10	4 -moz- 16	3.2 -webkit-	1 -webkit-	10.5 -o- 12.5

1. This covers support for basic cubic bézier-based timing functions.

2. steps() (plus the presets step-start and step-end) and Y values outside 0-1 for cubic-bezier values ("bounce") are comparatively recent additions to the spec.

3. See the previous section on transition-timing-function for a WebKit fallback.

Apart from older versions of Internet Explorer, browser support for transitions is good. Luckily this isn't really a problem—transitions as typically used aren't essential to functionality. While they will improve the user experience when used intelligently, the lack of them just means an instant change in state, which is a perfectly acceptable fallback. Because of this you should use them whenever they're appropriate.

CSS transitions gotchas

As usual, there are some things that can catch you out, plus a few browser quirks to keep you on your toes. Here are some we've come across:

- When using transitions with link states like :hover, you probably want to apply them to the default state, so that all link state changes transition. If you add the transition to the :hover state instead, the transition will occur on mouseover, not on mouseout.

- Colors are transitioned in RGBa color-space, which may give you unexpected results if you're using e.g. HSLa.

- Browsers that use non-premultiplied color interpolation transition colors with an alpha channel unintuitively, such as RGBa and the color transparent. During the transition other colors may be visible; for example, transparent to red would show some black because transparent is treated as rgba(0,0,0,0). Using premultiplied colors avoids this by applying the alpha value to each channel. At the time of writing, Opera is using non-premultiplied colors, Chrome and Safari changed to using premultiplied colors in 2010 (so it affects Safari 4.0.5), and Firefox has always used promultiplied colors.[14] You can generally avoid problems by converting transparent (and HSLa etc) into suitable rgba() values. This avoids the dark shade mid-transition and also uses the cascade to support IE6-8.

```
.box {

  background-color: transparent; /* IE6-8 */

  background-color: rgba(255,0,0,0); /* modern browsers (transparent red) */

}
```

---

[14] Note that the specification is still undecided regarding premultiplied or non-premultiplied color, so both ways are currently valid.

```
.box:hover {

  background-color: #f00; /* IE6-8 (or #ff0000 or red) */

  background-color: rgba(255,0,0,1); /* modern browsers */

}
```

- For performance reasons, for transitioning or animating text browsers turn off sub-pixel anti-aliasing (WebKit) or don't anti-alias at all (Opera), making this text look lighter. Opera 11.60 also doesn't anti-alias *transitioned* @font-face text (fixed in Opera 12).

- You can't apply a transition by changing property values using JavaScript without triggering a reflow or using a delay before setting the second style. For more see Divya Manian's presentation "Taking Presentation out of JavaScript One Setinterval at a Time" (http'//nimbu.in/txjs/).

Gotchas with transitioning transforms (and animations)

Combining transitions with CSS transforms is an obvious step, but again there are some browser quirks waiting for you.

- Avoid transitioning between different units, such as from left: 12px; to left: 50%;. Opera and Chrome transition instantly, and Safari is buggy if the transition is interrupted. Firefox works as expected.

- Opera up to 11 doesn't transition translate() on click via a JavaScript addEventListener *unless* you force a reflow. This is fixed in recent versions.

Fuzzy transforms, z-index, and hardware acceleration

If we apply a transition to a 2D transform, the elements become fuzzy in WebKit browsers during the transition. However, a sneaky trick via Thomas Fuchs gets around this: adding a 3D transform (even one that does nothing) makes the transform use hardware acceleration, avoiding flicker and keeping things smooth and fast (http://j.mp/hw-accel, http://mir.aculo.us/2010/08/05/html5-buzzwords-in-action/). This also works for opacity. For example, you could add the following:

```
-webkit-transform: translateZ(0);
```

You may also need to apply -webkit-transform: translateZ(0); (or some other 3D transformation) to other non-transformed elements to bring them in front of 3D-transformed ones, as Estelle Weyl notes. 3D transforms effectively have a z-index of infinity.

> Note: While using hardware acceleration can improve performance, this comes at the expense of memory, as Ariya Hidayat explains in "Understanding Hardware Acceleration on Mobile Browsers" (http://j.mp/mobile-hw, www.sencha.com/blog/understanding-hardware-acceleration-on-mobile-browsers/).

Stopping transforms from flickering when transitioning (and animating)

Transitioning or animating transforms (especially 3D transforms) can be very demanding, especially on iOS and Android where the mobile's relatively puny hardware adds to our problems. First, avoid transitioning or animating elements larger than the viewport. If you can't, or still encounter flickering or stuttery animation, Wes Baker suggests try using backface-visibility: hidden; on animated elements (http://j.mp/anim-flicker, http://stackoverflow.com/questions/2946748/iphone-webkit-css-animations-cause-flicker), possibly in conjunction with perspective and/or a 3D transform, as mentioned previously.

```
-webkit-backface-visibility: hidden;

backface-visibility: hidden;

/* possibly combined with… */

-webkit-transform: translateZ(0); /* …or any 3D transformation */

-webkit-perspective: 1000;

perspective: 1000;
```

Of course, if your animation is complex or you're animating nested elements, consider if it's possible to simplify the animation first. As the 3D transform is just a default value and for performance on mobile devices only, it's fine to not add an unprefixed property. As always, test thoroughly. Finally, as transitions are demanding, consider restricting them to capable devices only. For more detail, refer to Matt Seeley's "WebKit in your living room" speech (http://j.mp/anim-perf http://www.youtube.com/watch?v=xuMWhto62Eo).

CSS transitions in summary

CSS transitions allow us to control a CSS change in state over time, so without them the change will just occur instantly. In pretty much all cases this means they're fine to use to enhance the user's experience, and we feel it's not worth polyfilling them for non-supporting browsers using JavaScript. Keep the the following things in mind:

- Make sure the properties you transition behave the same in different browsers.

- Check especially carefully when the transitioned property is also fairly new, such as with transform.

- Overusing transitions may have performance implications, especially in mobile browsers.

- :hover transitions won't work on touch-based mobile devices.

As with everything in this chapter, err on the side of snappy and subtle. Large amounts of movement and slow, showy interactions may seem impressive when used the first time, but both will make your site feel overblown after a few uses.

CSS transitions provide an easy-to-use tool to spice up UI interactions, but they have their limits. Sometimes you want more *control* over the animation, for example the ability to loop. Next up we'll look at CSS animations, a more powerful and involved alternative.

Keyframin' with CSS animations

CSS animation is like elaborate icing on top of an expensive cake at a birthday party. While it may only be a very small part of the party, it has the potential to steal the show, as Figure 12-24 attests.

Figure 12-24. Mmmm, everyone loves cake…

You've seen how to do basic movement via CSS transitions. The CSS animations specification (http://j.mp/css3-animations, http://dev.w3.org/csswg/css3-animations/) takes things a step further with *keyframe*-based animations. The idea of keyframes will be familiar to anyone who's done animation with programs like Flash or Director. We set up how we'd like things to be at certain points during the animation, then the browser handles the *tweening* (the in-between animation) to smoothly get us from one keyframe state to the next. There are some examples of animatable properties in Lea Verou's Animatable (http://j.mp/css3-animatable, http://leaverou.github.com/animatable/), and how to use keyframe animations in the real world on Dan Eden's Animate.css (http://j.mp/animate-css, http://daneden.me/animate/).

Unlike CSS transitions, properties animate from and to the element's intrinsic style—the *computed values*[15] the browser uses to display the element with no animation applied. This means that if the from (or to) keyframe is different to the element's intrinsic style, when the animation starts (or ends) this change occurs instantly for a default animation.

CSS animations are added in two parts, as shown in the following code.

1. A @keyframes block containing individual keyframes defining and naming an animation.16

2. animation-* properties to add a named @keyframes animation to an element and to control the animation's behavior.

```
@keyframes popup { /* ← define the animation "popup" */

  from {…} /* CSS for any differences between the element's initial state and the animation's initial state */

  to {…} /* CSS for the animation's final state */

}

.popup {animation: popup 1s;} /* ← apply the animation "popup" */
```

[15] *Computed values* are the styles the browser uses to display the element, based on the CSS cascade of all applicable styles. When the animation is applied the computed values are a combination of intrinsic style and the animation's styles.

[16] There's no need for a @keyframes block to be before a declaration applying it in the CSS file. We generally add them to a section towards the end of our CSS based on the principle of *general to specific*.

Each keyframe rule starts with a percentage or the keywords from (the same as 0%) or to (the same as 100%) acting like a selector and specifying where in the animation the keyframe occurs. Percentages represent a percentage of the animation-duration, so a 50% keyframe in a 2s animation would be 1s into an animation. The following code shows an @keyframes declaration with several keyframe rules:

```
@keyframes popup {

  0% {…} /* the start of the animation (the same as "from") */

  25% {…} /* a keyframe one quarter through the animation */

  66.6667% {…} /* a keyframe two thirds through the animation */

  …

  to {…} /* the end of the animation (the same as "100%") */

}
```

Add the properties you want to animate to a keyframe. The browser will only use animatable properties, with the addition of the animation-timing-function property that overrides the animation's timing function for that keyframe only. Refer to Table 12-5 for a list of these. Non-animatable properties (apart from animation-timing-function) will be ignored.

> Note: Property values in each keyframe rule are only animated when tweening from and to a different value. They don't cascade and are not inherited by later keyframes. This might mean you have to add a declaration to more than one keyframe.

After naming and defining an animation, we can apply it to an element and control how the animation occurs using the animation-* properties. These can take multiple values in a comma-separated list to define multiple animations (we'll cover this in a later section).

- animation-name: The name (or comma-separated names) of @keyframes-defined animations to apply. By default this is none.

- animation-duration: The time for the animation to occur once, in seconds (s) or milliseconds (ms). By default this is 0s or the same as no animation.

- animation-timing-function: The timing function (just like in CSS transitions) to use for the animation. Values include linear, ease (the default), ease-in, ease-out, ease-in-out, cubic-bezier(), step-start, step-end, and steps().This can also be added to the @keyframes declaration to override the animation's animation-timing-function per -keyframe.

- animation-delay: A delay before the animation starts, in seconds (s) or milliseconds (ms). The default is 0s and this can also take a negative value, appearing to start already part-way through the animation.

- animation-iteration-count: The number of times the animation repeats. Acceptable values are 0 (no animation), positive numbers (including non-integers), and infinite. The default count is 1.

- animation-direction: This takes the values normal (the default) and alternate, and only has an effect when the animation-iteration-count is greater than 1. normal causes the animation to play forward (from start to end) each time, where as alternate causes the animation to play forward then reverse.

- animation-fill-mode: This controls if the from keyframe affects the animation during an animation-delay and/or if the ending state is kept when an animation ends, via the following values:

  - animation-fill-mode: none;: Applies from keyframe values only when a positive animation-delay ends and uses the element's intrinsic style when the animation ends. This is the default state.

  - animation-fill-mode: forwards;: This causes the element(s) to retain the properties defined by the final keyframe (usually the 100% or to keyframe) after the animation finishes. The forwards value (or both) makes an animation's end state behave the same as CSS tTransitions.

  - animation-fill-mode: backwards;: This causes the element(s) to have any properties defined by the first keyframe (0% or from) during an animation-delay with a positive value.

  - animation-fill-mode: both;: This is the same as both forwards and backwards

- animation-play-state: By default this value is running, but when this is changed to paused the animation pauses. The animation can be resumed from the same place by changing back to running. This gives us an easy way to pause animations using JavaScript.

- animation: The animation shorthand property takes a space-separated list of these animation properties (all the above except animation-play state). Multiple animations are separated by commas.

> *The CSS animations specification is still being actively developed and is expected to change.[17] Because of this we recommend leaving out un-prefixed animation-* and @keyframes declarations for now. However, for simplicity most of our example code will show the un-prefixed syntax.*

A simple animation example with animation-name and animation-duration

Let's see how much code a simple animation requires — *including* vendor prefixes — in Figure 12-25.

```
.box {position: absolute;}

:hover .box {

  -webkit-animation-name: moveit;

    -moz-animation-name: moveit;

     -ms-animation-name: moveit;

      -o-animation-name: moveit;

  -webkit-animation-duration: 1s;

    -moz-animation-duration: 1s;

     -ms-animation-duration: 1s;

      -o-animation-duration: 1s;

}

@-webkit-keyframes moveit {to {left: 100%;}}
```

---

[17] This is because the CSS Working Group plans to move Animations (http://j.mp/web-anim, www.w3.org/2012/01/13-svg-minutes.html#action02) to a combined, generalised "effects" specification, that will also be used for SVG animation.

```
@-moz-keyframes moveit {to {left: 100%;}}

@-ms-keyframes moveit {to {left: 100%;}}

@-o-keyframes moveit {to {left: 100%;}}
```

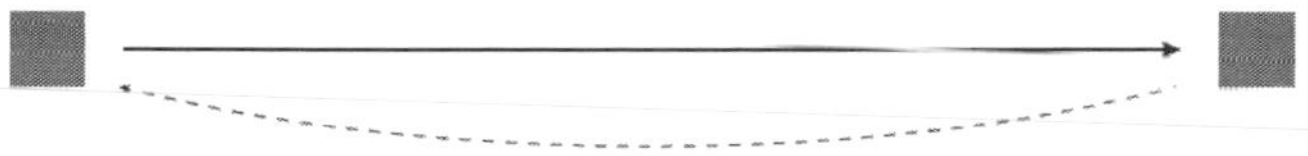

Figure 12-25. Even a simple animation currently requires a lot of vendor-specific CSS. But hey, keyframed animations in CSS!

That seems like a lot because we're writing declarations to define the animation (the @keyframes block) *and* to call it (the animation-* properties), plus we're writing everything four times due to browser prefixes, but really it's unusually *little*. Did we really just get animation in CSS with only this?[18]

```
:hover .box {

  animation-name: moveit;

  animation-duration: 1s;

}

@keyframes moveit {to {left: 100%;}}
```

But how? As usual, we are helped by defaults. Every animation *needs* an animation-name, and we suspect you'll want an animation-duration greater than the default 0s. However, all the other animation * properties are optional, as their default values don't prevent an animation from happening. We, of course, need a @keyframes declaration with at least one keyframe, in this case to {left: 100%;}, the state we'd like to animate to. The animated element itself provides the animation's starting state—for our animated property left it's 0. While we can style the start of the animation explicitly using from {} or 0% {}, in this example there's no need.

> *Note: Not all properties and not all values of animatable properties can be animated. Refer to Table 12-5 earlier in this chapter for details.*

---

[18] Please note, this code is only for example — don't use unprefixed animation-* and @keyframes declarations for now.

There's not much else to tell about animation-name and animation-duration. If you've read the earlier section on CSS transitions, you'll already know animation-duration accepts values in milliseconds (ms) and seconds (s), just like transition-duration. To be safe, we recommend you avoid using other property values as an animation-name to avoid potential browser bugs when using the animation shorthand.

- alternate
- backwards
- both
- ease
- ease-in
- ease-in-out
- ease-out
- forwards
- infinite

- linear
- none
- normal
- paused
- running
- step-end
- step-start
- steps

Controlling an animation using @keyframes

The example is simple; we could just as easily have used a transition because it's only animating between the initial and final states. Let's add some keyframes in Figure 12-26.

```
.box {position: absolute;}

:hover .box {

  animation-name: shakeit;

  animation-duration: .5s;

}

@keyframes shakeit {

  10%, 37.5%, 75% {left: -10%;}

  22.5%, 52.5% {left: 10%;}

  75% {left: -7%;}
```

```
}


/* This @keyframes declaration could also be written:

@keyframes shakeit {

    10% {left: -10%;}

    22.5% {left: 10%;}

    37.5% {left: -10%;}

    52.5% {left: 10%;}

    75% {left: -7%;}

} */
```

Figure 12-26 @keyframes allow us to do complex animations not possible using transition. Imagine the box shaking back and forth here.

We can use commas between keyframes properties when they share the same value, and percentage keyframe properties can contain decimal places. We made a mistake in this example by defining the value for 75% twice. If a property is defined for the same keyframe percentage selector in two different keyframes, the later value (in this case left: -7%;) will be used.

Timing functions with animation-timing-function

As long as you've already read the section "transition-timing-function, cubic Bézier curves, and steps()" earlier in this chapter, this property is a piece of cake. You'll be happy to hear that animation-timing-function works exactly the same as transition-timing-function, and takes all the same values.

- cubic-bezier()
- linear
- ease

- ease-in

- ease-out

- ease-in-out

- steps()

- step-start

- step-end

Figure 12-20 demonstrated these values using transitions and transition-timing-function, but we can achieve the same result using animation, as demonstrated in Figure 12-27. In addition we can use different timing functions for different parts of the animation.

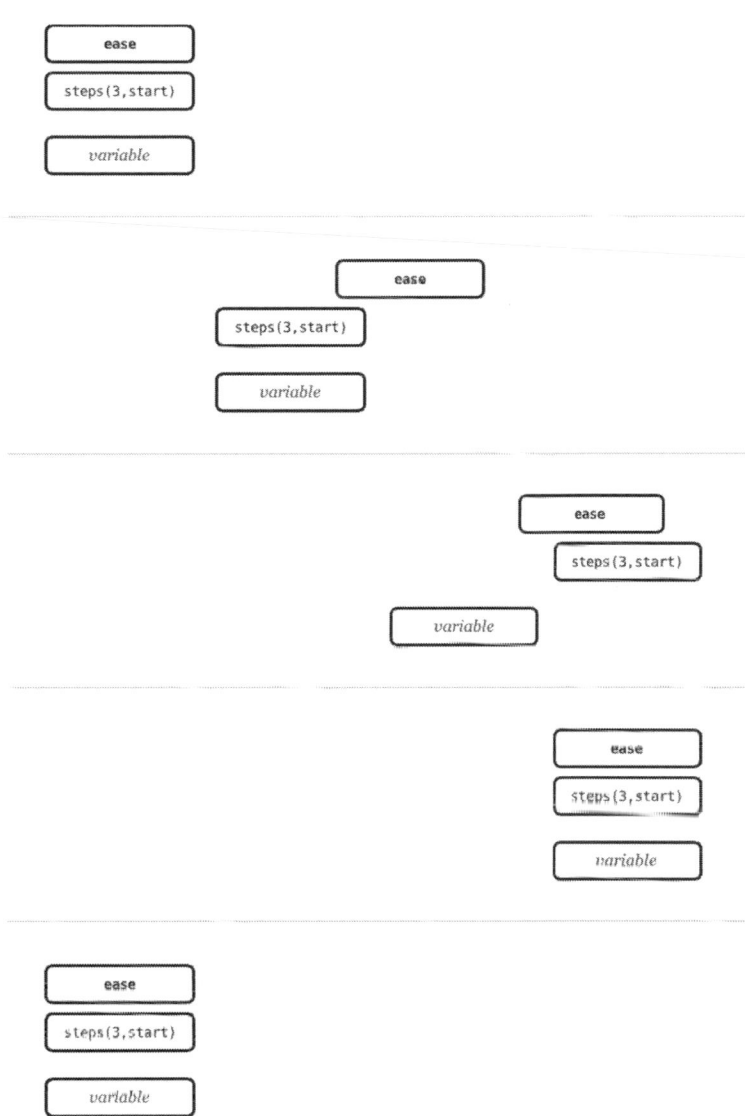

Figure 12-27. A demonstration of some timing function values in an animation using animation-timing-function, with the first two working the same as they would in a transition. The "variable" box uses ease, step-start, and then ease-out.

Unlike CSS transitions, an animation can have more than one timing function, as you can change the timing function *per keyframe* by adding animation-timing-function to the keyframe's ruleset. This will override the animation's timing function for that keyframe only. We did this for the "variable" box in Figure 12-27 using the following code:

```
@keyframes presets {

  33% {

    transform: translate(113%,0);

    animation-timing-function: step-start;

    }

  67% {

    transform: translate(227%,0);

    animation-timing-function: ease-out;

    }

  to {transform: translate(340%,0);}

}
```

This uses three timing values.

- 0%-33% uses ease (the default).

- 33%-67% uses step-start, defined in the 33% keyframe ruleset.

- 67%-100% uses ease-out, defined in the 67% keyframe ruleset.

As mentioned in the section "transition-timing-function, cubic Bézier curves, and steps()", these timing functions don't cover all the timing functions you might want. As Thomas Fuchs points out in "CSS animation transition-timing-functions and why they are not enough," you may have to emulate the timing function you want using multiple keyframes (or JavaScript).

Changing how an animation starts using animation-delay

As you'd expect, animation-delay takes a time value and changes the start time of the animation. It's also conveniently just like transition-delay. When the value is positive, the start is delayed by the value's amount. When the value is *negative*, the animation is *jump-started* by the animation-delay's value, beginning as if that time had already elapsed. Let's see how animation-delay affects things in Figure 12-28.

```
:hover .box {animation-duration: 3s;}

:hover .positive-delay {animation-delay: 1s;} /* "delay 1s" box */
```

```
/* animation-delay is 0 by default (the "no delay" box) */

:hover .negative-delay {animation-delay: -1s;} /* "delay -1s" box */
```

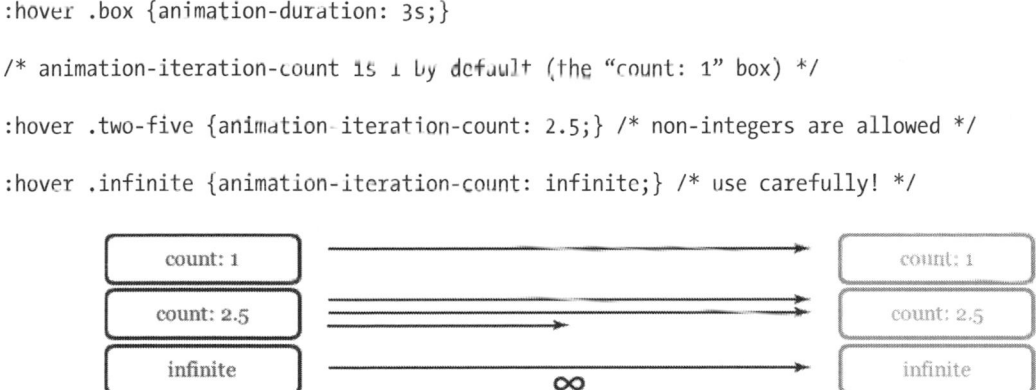

Figure 12-28. We can delay or jump-start the start of an animation using animation-delay.

In this example, the default animation doesn't declare animation-delay, so it has the default value 0s and the animation takes three seconds. Adding animation-delay: 1s; means the animation starts after a one second delay and takes *four* seconds to end. Adding animation-delay: -1s; means the animation starts immediately from where it'd be if one second had already elapsed, and the animation ends in only *two* seconds.

How many times? *animation-iteration-count* will tell you!

When an animation is triggered, by default it will play once then reset to its initial state (more on that in a moment). Using animation-iteration-count we can play the animation more than once or with the value infinite until the browser window is closed. Figure 12-29 shows this in action.

```
:hover .box {animation-duration: 3s;}

/* animation-iteration-count is 1 by default (the "count: 1" box) */

:hover .two-five {animation-iteration-count: 2.5;} /* non-integers are allowed */

:hover .infinite {animation-iteration-count: infinite;} /* use carefully! */
```

Figure 12-29. animation-iteration-count controls how many times an animation will play

Using a non-integer value like 2.5 will make the animation play two and a half times before ending in supporting browsers. Negative values are treated the same as 0. As animations are generally very distracting (as Flash ad makers know so well) and can be a performance hog[19], so use the infinite value responsibly!

Mixing it up with animation-direction

You've seen how to increase the number of times an animation plays with animation-iteration-count. If the number is greater than 1, we can use animation-direction to control whether subsequent even-numbered animations also go from start to end (the value normal), or in reverse with the value alternate. As animation-direction: normal; is the default, let's apply animation-direction: alternate; to our previous example, in Figure 12-30.

```
:hover .box {

    …

    animation-direction: alternate;

}
```

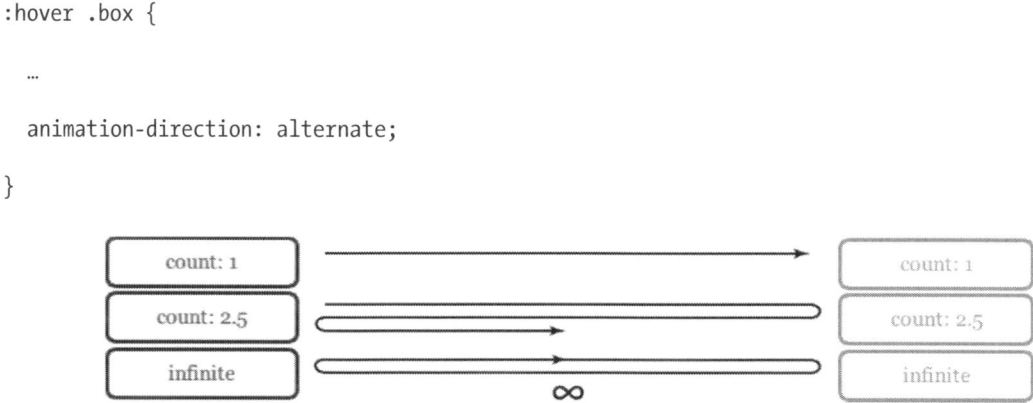

Figure 12-30. animation-direction: alternate; changes animations with an animation-iteration-count greater than 2 to reverse their direction on even counts.

Although a simple property, you'll find animation-direction invaluable if you ever need to make a Cylon eye using CSS.

Control how elements behave before and after an animation with animation-fill-mode

As you've no doubt noticed in the examples so far, unless an animation is playing it has no effect. This includes during a positive animation-delay—any from keyframe values are only applied after the delay ends. This also means that, unlike CSS transforms, animated elements will return to their intrinsic style by

---

[19] Although animations will pause at the next keyframe when the browser tab (or browser) is not active.

default when an animation ends, even if the animation trigger still applies. This is due to the animation-fill-mode property's default value none, but the values forwards, backwards, and both let us control these things.

- animation-fill-mode: forwards;: Animated elements will keep the animation's ending keyframe's properties. Normally this is the 100% or to keyframe, but not always given animation-iteration-count and animation-direction.

- animation-fill-mode: backwards;: Animated elements will be styled by the animation from or 0% keyframe during a positive animation-delay.

- animation-fill-mode: both;: This is a combination of forwards and backwards behavior.

Let's see examples of each animation-fill-mode in action, including the default value of none, in Figure 12-31.

```
:hover .box {

  animation-duration: 3s;

  animation-delay: 1s;

}

@keyframes pushit {

  0% {background-color: #bfbfbf;} /* start gray */

  to {left: 100%;} /* end on the right */

}

/* animation-fill-mode is none by default */

  /* forwards: keep the animation's final state when it ends */

:hover .fill-forwards {animation-fill-mode: forwards;}

  /* backwards: use the from/0% keyframe styles during animation-delay */

:hover .fill-backwards {animation-fill-mode: backwards;}

  /* both: the same as forwards and backwards */

:hover .fill-both {animation-fill-mode: both;}
```

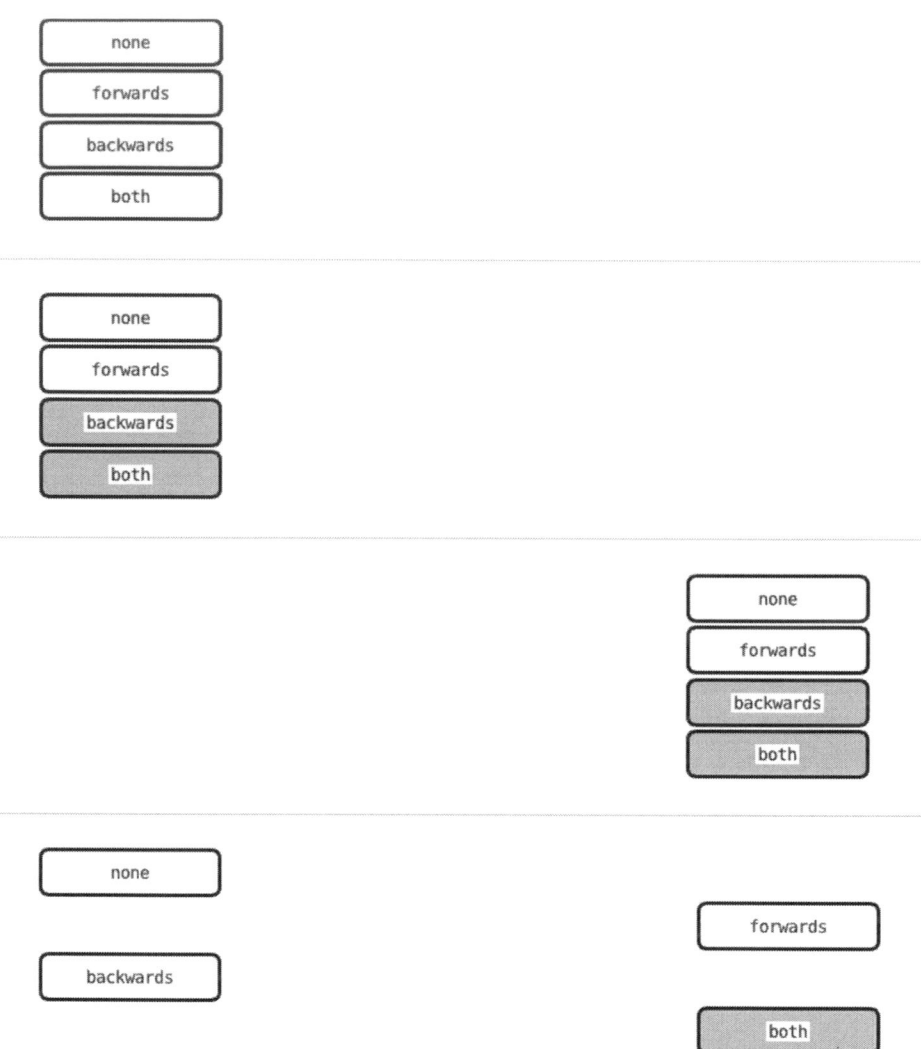

Figure 12-31. Examples of the four animation-fill-mode values: none, forwards, backwards, and both.

The initial keyframe has a gray background-color, but the animation also has a one second delay. The backwards and both values apply the 0% keyframe's style during the animation-delay. The forwards and both values keep the last keyframe's styles, rather than reverting to the element's intrinsic style. This animation is triggered on :hover, so in this example keeping the last keyframe's styles (via forwards or both) will only apply while mousing over the element.

Pausing an animation using animation-play-state

This simple property has the value running by default. Changing this to paused will pause the animation, as shown in Figure 12-32. If the value is then changed to running, the animation will resume from where it left off.

```
:hover .box {

  animation-name: runner;

  animation-duration: 3s;

  animation-timing-function: ease-in-out;

  animation-iteration-count: infinite;

  animation-direction: alternate;

}

.box:hover {animation-play-state: paused;}
```

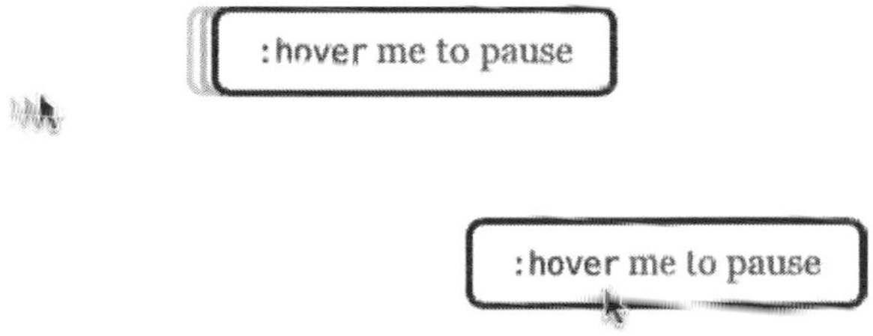

Figure 12-32. The animation will start when you hover over this figure, but if you hover over the box it will be paused.

While you can stop an element animating via JavaScript by just removing the class that applies it, this will instantly change the animated element(s) to their pre-animation state. Being able to pause the animation (with or without JavaScript), and then pick up from where we left off, opens up some nice new interactivity options.

> Note: You can't restart an animation by removing and adding the animation class using JavaScript. Chris Coyier's article "Restart CSS Animation" (http://j.mp/restart-anim, http://css-tricks.com/restart-css-animation/) covers ways that do work (removing the element and re-adding it, or controlling animation-play-state via JavaScript), but a simple yet kludgy non-JavaScript way is to define an identical @keyframes animation with a different name.

The animation shorthand property and comma-separated animation-* values

We've looked at each of the animation-* properties in turn and, as with transition, we can specify several values together using the animation shorthand property. This takes the values of each of the animation-* properties (except animation-play-state).

ANIMATION SHORTHAND PROPERTY ORDER

The spec says order is important, but only mentions putting animation-duration before animation-delay. We recommend using the following order to avoid potential browser bugs:

1. animation-name

2. animation-duration

3. animation-timing-function

4. animation-delay

5. animation-iteration-count

6. animation-direction

7. animation-fill-mode

For example, WebKit browsers need animation-name before animation-iteration-count and animation-direction.

Our last animation used individual animation-* properties.

```
:hover .box {

  animation-name: runner;

  animation-duration: 3s;
```

```
animation-timing-function: ease-in-out;

animation-iteration-count: infinite;

animation-direction: alternate;

}
```

It's equivalent to this (much shorter) animation property – remember that we don't have to include any properties with a default value, in this case animation-delay and animation-fill-mode.:

```
:hover .box {animation: runner 3s ease-in-out infinite alternate;}
```

We can also specify more than one animation, using commas to separate values, for both individual animation-* properties and for the shorthand animation property. Both ways are demonstrated in Figure 12-33.

```
/* Using individual properties for multiple animations: */

:hover .box {

            animation-name: moveit,      colorstep, fade;

        animation-duration:      3s;                        /* one value? */

    animation-timing-function: linear, steps(2,start);      /* two values? */

} /* values aligned to make their groupings clear */

/* The same styles using the animation shorthand property:

:hover .box {

    animation: moveit 3s linear, colorstep 3s steps(2,start), fade 3s linear;

} */
```

Figure 12-33. Using two animations so we can use different timing functions for each one—linear for movement, and steps(2) for background color. The individual properties and shorthand declarations are equivalent.

> *Note: In the individual properties form the first value of each property will be associated with the first animation-name value. If there aren't enough values for the number of animation names, the values that are present are repeated, as is the case in Figure 12-33 with animation-duration and animation-timing-function. By repeating the value(s), these will be treated as animation-duration: 3s, 3s 3s; and animation-timing-function: linear, steps(2,steps), linear;.*

Browser support for CSS animations

As another Apple baby, CSS animations have been supported in WebKit browsers Safari and Chrome for quite a while, as Table 12-7 shows. Firefox and most recently Internet Explorer have added support, and Opera will join the party soon. *However*, despite three implementations, the CSS animations specification is changing, so it's *not* stable enough to add an unprefixed version at the time of writing.

Table 12-7. Browser Support for CSS Animation (http://j.mp/c-animation, http://caniuse.com/#feat=css-animation)

Property	IE	Firefox	Safari	Chrome	Opera
Animation-name	10	5 -moz- 16	4 -webkit-	1 -webkit-	12 -o- 12.5
Animation-duration	10	5 -moz- 16	4 -webkit-	1 -webkit-	12 -o- 12.5
Animation-timing-function[1]	10	5 -moz- 16	4 -webkit-	1 -webkit-	12 -o- 12.5
:steps()[2]	10	5 -moz- 16	5 -webkit-	8 -webkit-	12 -o- 12.5

Property	IE	Firefox	Safari	Chrome	Opera
"bounce"[2]	10	5 -moz- 16	- [3]	16 -webkit-[3]	12 -o- 12.5
Animation-delay	10	5 -moz- 16	4 -webkit-	1 -webkit-	12 -o- 12.5
Animation-iteration-count	10	5 -moz- 16	4 -webkit-	1 -webkit-	12 -o- 12.5
Animation-direction	10	5 -moz- 16	4 -webkit-	1 -webkit-	12 -o- 12.5
Animation-fill-mode	10	5 -moz- 16	4 -webkit-	1 -webkit-	12 -o- 12.5
Animation-play-state	10	5 -moz- 16	4 -webkit-	1 -webkit-	12 -o- 12.5
Animation	10	5 -moz- 16	4 -webkit-	1 -webkit-	12 -o- 12.5
@keyframes	10	5 -moz- 16	4 -webkit-	1 -webkit-	12 -o- 12.5

1. This covers support for basic cubic Bézier-based timing functions.

2. steps() (plus the presets step-start and step-end), and Y values outside 0-1 for cubic-bezier values ("bounce"), are comparatively recent additions to the spec.

3. In Chrome cubic-bezier timing functions with "bounce" work when animating between the same units. They don't work in Safari 5.1.2.

4. WebKit browsers only support integer values and infinite for animation-iteration-count; non-integer number values are treated as 1.

5. WebKit browsers can sometimes show a flash of default-styled content when a paused animation resumes, although this appears to be fixed in recent versions.

6. While it claims to support animations, Android 2.13-3 can only animate a single property. Android 4+ works as expected.

As we need to use browser prefixes for both animation-* properties *and* @keyframes blocks, with three rendering engines plus the unprefixed version this quickly becomes a lot of code. However, remember your Good CSS Developer pledge! If you use prefixed properties, *when* another browser adds prefixed support you'll need to add it in. And if the spec changes you'll need to update your code.

A little animation-related JavaScript detour

As with transforms, adding animations means we have to decide what to do about non-supporting browsers. For small animations that merely add visual flair, we think that *no* fallback is perfectly acceptable. However, if you're making animations a central part of your experience, you'll have to make some decisions. This includes what technology you want to use, as in addition to CSS animations, JavaScript, Canvas, SMIL plus SVG, and even Adobe Flash are all capable, each with their own pros and cons.

The easiest way (after reading this chapter) will probably be to use CSS animations where supported, with a JavaScript equivalent fallback. Happily, there are a lot of frameworks you can use, including

- jQuery's native Effects (http://j.mp/jq-effects, http://api.jquery.com/category/effects/) (basic) or jQuery UI (http://jqueryui.com/)

- jQuery plugins like jquery.transition.js* by Louis-Rémi Babé (http://j.mp/jq-transition, https://github.com/louisremi/jquery.transition.js/) or jQuery.animate-enhanced.js* by Ben Barnett (http://j.mp/jq-animate, https://github.com/benbarnett/jQuery-Animate-Enhanced)

- YUI Transition library* (http://j.mp/yui-transition, https://yuilibrary.com/yui/docs/transition/)

- $fx() (http://fx.inetcat.com/)

- scripty2 (http://scripty2.com/) and script.aculo.us (http://script.aculo.us/) (both based on Prototype)

Some of these (indicated with an asterisk) are polyfills and automatically convert your animation CSS to a JavaScript equivalent if the browser doesn't support it natively. Others will require a little simple scripting, plus Modernizr to detect browser support. For more on doing this, Addy Osami has written the informative article "CSS3 Transition Animations With jQuery Fallbacks" (http://j.mp/jq-fallback, http://addyosmani.com/blog/css3transitions-jquery/).

For anything more than basic CSS3 animations, a little JavaScript generally helps; the more advanced you want to get, the more you'll probably need. Combining CSS animations with JavaScript also broadens your horizons, allowing you to

- Expand on CSS3 Animation's native abilities, for example Isotope by David DeSandro (http://j.mp/jq-isotope, http://isotope.metafizzy.co/) or the iDangero.us jQuery Chop Sliders (http://j.mp/jq-cs, www.idangero.us/cs/).

- Receive events for each keyframe, such as using Joe Lambert's CSS3 Animation Keyframe Events JavaScript library (http://j.mp/cssa-events, www.joelambert.co.uk/cssa/).

- Create, access, and modify animations (http://j.mp/anim-store, http://blog.joelambert.co.uk/2011/09/07/accessing-modifying-css3-animations-with-javascript/) using Joe Lambert's CSS Animation Store.

Another article worth your time is Dan Mall's "Real Animation Using JavaScript, CSS3, and HTML5 Video from 2010's 24 Ways" (http://j.mp/24-anim, http://24ways.org/2010/real-animation-using-javascript-css3-and-html5-video). This article and "The Guide To CSS Animation: Principles and Examples" by Tom Waterhouse (http://j.mp/anim-principles, http://coding.smashingmagazine.com/2011/09/14/the-guide-to-css-animation-principles-and-examples/) cover how to make your animations feel more natural—useful advice even if you're doing pure CSS animations.

Animation gotchas

Here are some assorted things to watch out for when using CSS animations.

- Check you're trying to animate properties that can be animated, and check these properties can be animated *on the element you're targeting*. For example, as with CSS transforms, WebKit browsers can't animate an element with display: inline;, although Firefox can. In this case, the workarounds are to use display: inline-block; or see if it's possible to achieve the same result with CSS transitions, which *do* work on inline elements.

- At the time of writing only Firefox 4 and above can transition and animate CSS generated content, such as the CSS in below:

```
div:before {

  content: "";

  position: absolute;

  left: 0;

  width: 44px;

  height: 44px;

  -webkit-animation: moveit 3s ease-in-out infinite alternate;

    -moz-animation: moveit 3s ease-in-out infinite alternate;

    -ms-animation: moveit 3s ease-in-out infinite alternate;

}
```

- If your animation isn't working and doesn't have a from {...}/0% {...} or to {...}/100% {...} keyframe, try adding one, making sure the values are different to the element's default styles.

- You can't apply an animation to the same element twice, such as on load and via the :hover states. The workaround is to duplicate the animation's @keyframes declaration with a different name.

- More generally, while animation is new and exciting, it's new enough that there are still a lot of browser bugs being found, and performance may not be what you hope. If your animation is performing badly, try dialing it back a bit and making it simpler. If it doesn't work at all, check that your syntax is valid using the browser's inspector or try making a simpler version to test. If you suspect a bug, search the browser bug trackers, especially if you are trying something out of the ordinary. If you *find* a bug, make sure to do your bit and report it (http://j.mp/report-bugs, http://coding.smashingmagazine.com/2011/09/07/help-the-community-report-browser-bugs/)!

CSS animations in summary

We have to admit it, CSS animations are the CSS equivalent of your favourite overly rich dessert—they're just irresistibly delicious! For example, Cameron Adams' use of CSS animations (together with transforms and transitions) as part of his amazing title sequences for the Web Directions South 2010 (http://j.mp/wds-2010, http://themaninblue.com/writing/perspective/2010/10/18/) and 2011 conferences (http://j.mp/wds2011, http://themaninblue.com/writing/perspective/2011/10/27/) (Figure 12-35) was just spell-binding—cinematic experiences done entirely using the web stack to demonstrate what browsers can now do.

Figure 12-35. Web Directions South 2011 title sequence, done by the Man in Blue using CSS3, HTML5, and JavaScript, and projected using two computers synced using WebSockets.

However, after mentioning Cameron's mind-blowing work, we'd be remiss not to talk about using the right tool for the job. CSS3 animations are good for *enhancing* content. For making *animated content* you're probably better off looking at canvas, SMIL+SVG, WebGL, or Flash.

As far as using CSS animations now, as the browser support table indicates it's premature to rely on them *unless* you've also got fallback strategies in place for other browsers. As usual, Modernizr can help you with this. However, when used like transitions as progressive enhancement to smooth the user experience and add visual flourishes, we say they're fine to use *right now*.

You may be tempted to overdose on these sugary treats, but we advise restraint. Movement is very noticeable and should be used cautiously and with restraint. As with transforms and transitions, animation can be a performance hog, even in a modern browser. Our advice is *you only need a sprinkle*, and too much will leave your users queasy.

Putting it all together

We'll leave you with a few amazing sites that really make use of these specs. They're a bit intimidating to "View source…" on, but a great example of what's possible.

Steven Wittens' website Acko.net (Figure 12-36) uses 3D transforms plus JavaScript to animate the page in 3D as you scroll down. The 3D transforms are controlled using Mr.doob's Three.js JavaScript library (http://j.mp/three-js, http://mrdoob.github.com/three.js/). As support for 3D transforms is limited, there's a static image fallback for non-supporting browsers. The implementation writeup is also excellent.

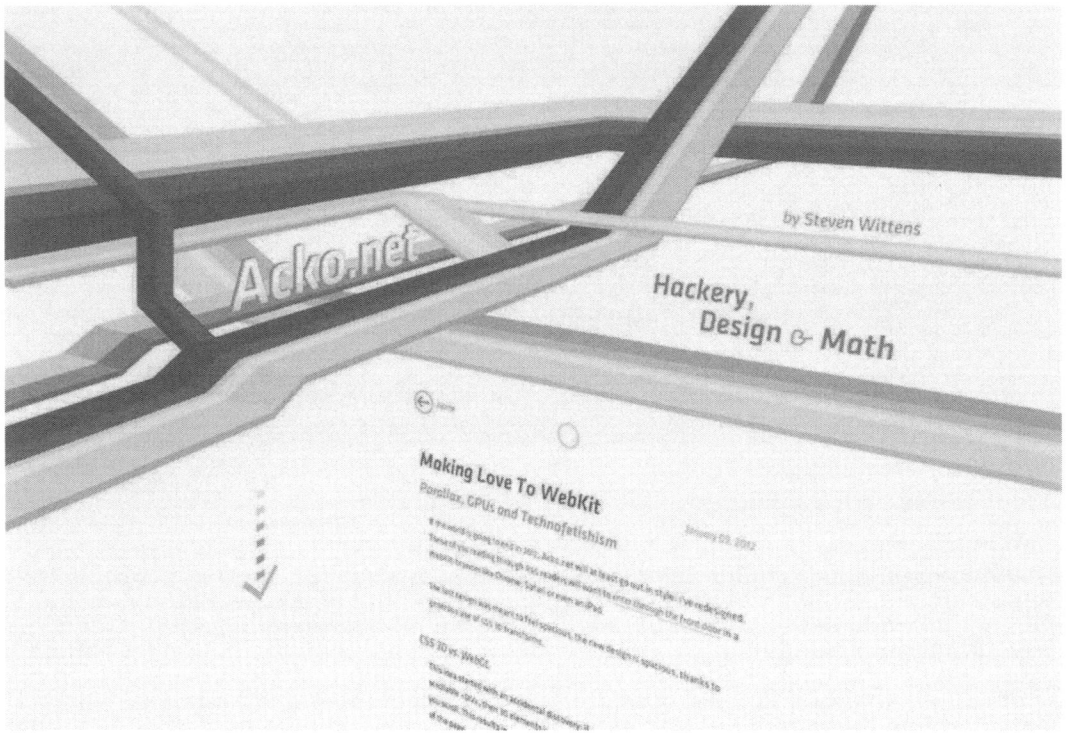

Figure 12-36. 3D Transformed Acko.net on load by Steven Wittens (http://j.mp/3d-acko, http://acko.net/blog/making-love-to-webkit/)

When Apple introduced the iPhone 4S (Figure 12-37) the web page was beautifully executed, with the images and text for the six marketing points gracefully sliding on and off the screen. It worked by positioning all the elements in a <div> stage much larger than the screen (3200px × 3900px), of which we see only a fraction. Individual elements plus the stage are then moved with 2D transforms plus transitions, using the Script.aculo.us JavaScript library to control everything by adding inline styles. It also degrades nicely with a slideshow-style fade for non-supporting browsers.

Figure 12-37. Apple Inc.'s expertly produced "hero" animation for the IPhone 4S

Anthony Calzadilla explains this in "CSS3 Animation Explained: Apple's iPhone 4S Feature Page" (http://j.mp/iphone-expl, www.anthonycalzadilla.com/2011/10/css3-animation-explained-apples-iphone-4s-feature-page/), but It's John Hall's explanation animation (http://j.mp/iphone-anim, http://johnbhall.com/iphone-4s/) showing the stage and frame that really reveals the animation's secrets. While this looks like CSS animation, we suspect transitions were used for their wider browser support.

Further Reading

Transforms, transitions, and animations can be complex, so here are some links for further reading.

- "2D Transforms in CSS3" by John Allsopp (http://j.mp/wxmbT2, www.webdirections.org/blog/2d-transforms-in-css3/)

- Understanding CSS3 2D Transforms by Klemen Slavič (http://j.mp/x7QcUR, http://msdn.microsoft.com/en-us/scriptjunkie/gg709742)

Chapter 12

- Using 2D and 3D Transforms, in Apple's Safari Developer Library (http://j.mp/xNNVgK, http://developer.apple.com/library/safari/#documentation/InternetWeb/Conceptual/SafariVisualEff ectsProgGuide/Using2Dand3DTransforms/Using2Dand3DTransforms.html#//apple_ref/doc/uid/T P40008032-CH15-SW16)

- "Intro to CSS 3D transforms" by David DeSandro (http://j.mp/zcuGcr, http://desandro.github.com/3dtransforms/)

- Understanding CSS 3D Transforms series by Dirk Weber, including parts 2 (3D matrix) and 3 (natural rotation with JavaScript) (http://j.mp/AvL3Of, www.eleqtriq.com/2010/05/ understanding-css-3d-transforms/)

- "Understanding CSS3 Transitions" by Dan Cederholm (http://j.mp/AwWDCP, www.alistapart.com/articles/understanding-css3-transitions/)

- "Let the Web move you — CSS3 Animations and Transitions" by John Allsopp (http://j.mp/AncW08, www.webdirections.org/blog/let-the-web-move-you-css3-animations-and-transitions/)

- "Using CSS3 Transitions, Transforms and Animation" by Rich Bradshaw (http://j.mp/wrpwop, http://css3.bradshawenterprises.com/)

- "CSS3 Transition Animations With jQuery Fallbacks" by Addy Osmani (http://addyosmani.com/blog/css3transitions-jquery/)

- "A masterclass in CSS animations" by Estelle Weyl (http://j.mp/y1iWsB, www.netmagazine.com/tutorials/masterclass-css-animations)

- Animating With Keyframes, in Apple's Safari Developer Library (http://j.mp/xEl6On, http://developer.apple.com/library/safari/#documentation/InternetWeb/Conceptual/SafariVisualEff ectsProgGuide/AnimatingWithKeyframes/AnimatingWithKeyframes.html#//apple_ref/doc/uid/TP40 008032-CH14-SW5)

- Replacing Subtle Flash Animations with CSS3 by Louis Lazaris (http://j.mp/zFYPEh, www.impressivewebs.com/replace-flash-with-css3-animation)

- "JavaScript: Controlling CSS Animations" by Duncan Crombie (http://j.mp/wNXyJU, www.the-art-of-web.com/javascript/css-animation/)

- Adding Interactive Control to Visual Effects, in Apple's Safari Developer Library (covers making Transforms and Transitions usable on touch devices) (http://j.mp/ygau6U, http://developer.apple.com/library/safari/#documentation/InternetWeb/Conceptual/SafariVisualEff ectsProgGuide/InteractiveControl/InteractiveControl.html#//apple_ref/doc/uid/TP40008032-CH16-SW7)

- Taking Presentation out of JavaScript One Setinterval at a Time, a presentation by Divya Manian (slides: http://nimbu.in/txjs/, video: http://vimeo.com/26844734).

Here are some tools that make understanding CSS transforms, transitions, and animations easier, and that help you generate the code required.

- 2D Transforms tool by John Allsopp (http://j.mp/wvUNey, http://westciv.com/tools/transforms/)

- 3D Transforms tool by John Allsopp (http://j.mp/zless7, http://westciv.com/tools/3Dtransforms/)

- Animations tool by John Allsopp (http://j.mp/wi3lcQ,http://westciv.com/tools/animations/)

- CSS 3D Transforms Explorer by Dirk Weber (linked from Understanding CSS 3D Transforms) (http://j.mp/ydQy2f,www.eleqtriq.com/wp-content/static/demos/2010/css3d/css3dexplorer.html)

- Matrix 2D Explorer by Dirk Weber (linked from The Matrix Revolutions) (http://j.mp/xxZSDR, www.eleqtriq.com/wp-content/static/demos/2010/css3d/matrix2dExplorer.html)

- Matrix 3D Explorer by Dirk Weber (linked from The Matrix Revolutions) (http://j.mp/yDSc7q, www.eleqtriq.com/wp-content/static/demos/2010/css3d/matrix3dexplorer.html)

Chapter 13

The Future of CSS

or, Awesome Stuff That's Coming

So where does CSS go from here? You'll be happy to know that work has already started on *CSS4*, with some initial work already done on the specifications including:

- CSS Backgrounds and Borders Module Level 4
- CSS Image Values and Replaced Content Module Level 4
- CSS Pseudo-elements Module Level 4
- Media Queries Level 4
- CSS Selectors Level 4
- CSS Text Level 4

While there's a lot left to do before browsers implement CSS3 fully, it's nice to know that all browser makers are actively participating in the CSS Working Group, and that competition is fierce to both implement quickly *and* according to the specifications. As mentioned in Chapter 9, we see layout as the major area in need of improvement. Happily, given that browser release cycles are getting shorter and that as of Internet Explorer 10 all browsers now auto-update, you should be able to use the new hotness currently being implemented in only 2-3 years rather than 6-10, as has been the case.

Let's wrap up this book with a brief look at what you'll be getting excited about in the next year or two.

Hardware acceleration and CSS performance

We imagine you're *already* pretty excited by hardware acceleration for 3D transforms, and on the HTML5 side Canvas and even WebGL (for some browsers). We covered using a 3D transform to enable hardware acceleration for transitions and animations in Chapter 12. By offloading CPU-intensive processes to the device's GPU, the browser can get a significant performance boost. There's support (to varying degrees) in Firefox 3.7+, Internet Explorer 9+, Chrome 7+, Safari 5+, and Opera 12+. The real excitement is that, in search of even better performance, browser makers will use hardware acceleration even more heavily in the future, including for things like SVG and general layout.

CSS performance in general is also getting attention. Selector performance is improving, and we finally have developer tools to measure it. This is part of the recent general focus on performance, kicked off with the amazing improvements of browser JavaScript engines. This means faster performance in more browsers, plus the ability to try things that just haven't been possible until recently. Expect this battle to continue, with all of us being the winners!

However, these improvements don't mean we can stop worrying about performance. Mobile browsing is overtaking desktop, and speed will always be essential for happy users. You can learn more about performance in Paul Irish's presentations "DOM, HTML5, & CSS3 Performance" (video and slides) (http://j.mp/pi-perf[1]) and "CSS Performance" (http://j.mp/css-perf[2]), and Matt Seeley's "WebKit in your living room" speech (http://j.mp.anim-perf http://www.youtube.com/watch?v=xuMWhto62E0).

Internationalization

Well, maybe you won't be *excited* per se, but if you're a web developer in a non-western country, this is good news. CSS 2.1 specifications didn't address many aspects of typography, and sometimes didn't fully consider right-to-left (RTL) and bidirectional (Bidi) text. Browsers have also traditionally been slow at implementing support for internationalization features, but both specifications and implementations are finally catching up. One example of how this makes things better for everyone is the counters in the CSS Counter Styles Level 3 module, used for the counters in lists (http://j.mp/css-counter-styles http://dev.w3.org/csswg/css-counter-styles/[3]).

Define your own list counters with the CSS Counter Styles Module

In CSS 2, the allowed values for list-style-type are:

---

[1] http://paulirish.com/2011/dom-html5-css3-performance
[2] http://dl.dropbox.com/u/39519/talks/cssperf/index.html
[3] http://dev.w3.org/csswg/css3-lists

- disc
- circle
- square
- decimal
- decimal-leading-zero
- lower-roman
- upper-roman
- lower-greek
- lower-latin
- upper-latin
- armenian
- georgian
- lower-alpha
- upper-alpha
- none
- inherit
- hebrew*
- cjk-ideographic*
- hiragana*
- katakana*
- hiragana-iroha*
- katakana-iroha*

(Types with asterisks were dropped in CSS 2.1 but are supported in everything except Internet Explorer.) While this is a lot, it still doesn't cover all of the list types that are needed by the world's languages. For example, Firefox also implements an additional *31* vendor-prefixed values, from arabic-indic to urdu.

Luckily, CSS3 has taken a different tack, with the CSS Counter Styles module defining counters based on seven algorithms.

- repeating
- numeric
- alphabetic
- symbolic
- non-repeating
- additive
- override

Using these in a new @counter-style declaration, you can replicate all of the CSS 2 list-item-type values, plus Firefox's extra values. In addition, this allows you to *define your own list counters*, like:

```
@counter-style dice {
  type: additive;
  additive-symbols: 6 '⚅' , 5 '⚄' , 4 '⚃' , 3 '⚂' , 2 '⚁' , 1 '⚀' ;
  suffix: ' ';
}
```
⚀ One

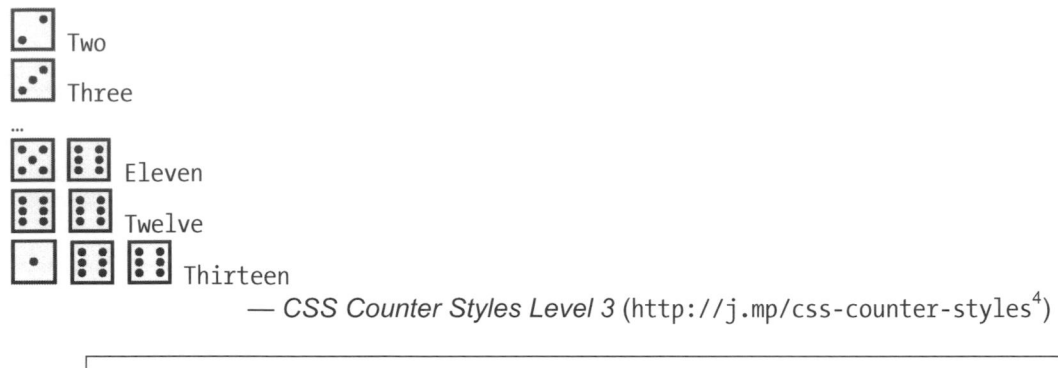

— *CSS Counter Styles Level 3* (http://j.mp/css-counter-styles[4])

> *The spec also defines **all** the preset CSS 2 list-item-type values, although the ones not in CSS 2.1 are currently "at risk."*

The calc() and attr() functions

These two functions in the CSS Values and Units Module Level 3 specification (http://j.mp/css3-values[5]) are baby steps toward CSS as a programming language.

The calc() function allows you to use mathematical expressions as values, and it can be used in place of *length*, *frequency*, *angle*, *time*, or *number* values. We can use +, -, *, and /, and standard mathematical operator precedence rules apply.

Liquid layouts are a good example. When using CSS floats with the default box model, padding and border are added to the box width, making it easy for a floated element to drop underneath rather than line up horizontally. One workaround is to use box-sizing: border-box; (covered in Chapter 9), which will include padding and border in the element's width and is supported on all current browsers except IE 6-7 (http://j.mp/c-boxsizing[6]).

With calc() you could instead subtract horizontal margin, border, and padding values from the width.

```
.content, .sidebar {
  float: left;
  padding: 1em;
}
.content {width: calc(100% / 3 * 2 - 1em * 2);} /* spaces for * and / */
.sidebar {
  margin-left: 1em;
  border-left: 2px solid #999;
  width: calc(100%/3 - 1em - 2px - 1em*2); /* no spaces for * and / */
}
```

---

[4] http://dev.w3.org/csswg/css3-lists
[5] http://dev.w3.org/csswg/css3-values
[6] http://caniuse.com/#feat=css3-boxsizing

This would give a layout with the content being 2/3 of the page width minus padding and a sidebar that's 1/3 of the page width minus margin, border, and padding.

> *Note: When using the + and – operators, make sure they have a space on either side, as otherwise they'll indicate if the following number is positive or negative. Spaces are optional for * and /.*

Unlike CSS Counter Styles, calc() is actually supported in Firefox (4+ with the vendor prefix -moz- and 16+, unprefixed) Internet Explorer 9+ (no prefix), and WebKit (Chrome 19+ and Safari 6+ with –webkit-) at the time of writing (http://j.mp/c-calc[7]). This means it's useful now in cascade, for example: WebKit is also implementing calc(), so it's not too far off being useful in the cascade, for example:

```
.sidebar {
  width: 30%; /* bodge for non-supporting browsers */
  -webkit-calc(100%/3 - 1em - 2px - 1em*2);/* For Chrome 19+, Safari 6+ */
  width: -moz-calc(100%/3 - 1em - 2px - 1em*2); /* for Firefox 4+ */
  width: calc(100%/3 - 1em - 2px - 1em*2; /* for IE 9+, Firefox 16+ */
}
```

The attr() function (or "attribute reference") allows you to use the value of an element's attribute as a value in a CSS property. In CSS 2.1 this could only be used in the content property, but in CSS3 it can be used in almost any property. While the browser will presume units based on the property's defaults, we can also set the units with a second attr() value, and even include a valid fallback as a third value

```
.box:after {content: attr(attribute);} /* CSS 2.1 */
.box {width: attr(attribute);} /* CSS3 ... */
.box {width: attr(attribute, unit);}
.box {width: attr(attribute, unit, fallback);}
```

Back in Chapter 4 we discussed HTML5's new data-* attributes. Combined with attr(), these seem a great fit for things like bar graphs in CSS, rather than the current options of inline styles or classes.

```
.bar {width: attr(data-width);}
.bar {width: attr(data-width, %);}
.bar {width: attr(data-width, %, 100px);} /* fallback can be auto, use different units etc */
<div class="bar" data-width="10">Widget sales</div>
```

Very handy for when you need to style several similar things individually. Sadly, while basic support for attr() in the content property is good (modern browsers plus IE8+), there's no support for attr()'s CSS3 features yet (http://j.mp/mdn-attr[8]).

Looking even further into the future, combining calc() with attr() has the potential to make these functions even more tasty.

---

[7] http://caniuse.com/#feat=calc
[8] https://developer.mozilla.org/en/CSS/attr

Variables, mixins, and nesting

Recently, CSS preprocessors such as Sass (http://sass-lang.com) and Less (http://lesscss.org) have become popular, and they allow the use of calculations like the calc() function. They also provide three useful programming concepts: variables, mixins, and nesting. These help simplify CSS coding in the following ways:

- *Variables*: You assign a commonly used value (such as a color) to a variable in one place, then use the variable in your CSS in place of the value. If you need to change the value, you only need to change the variable definition.

- *Mixins*: These let you combine (mix in) snippets of CSS. They can also accept values when called. This allows you to make a snippet library but still make changes when you use the snippet, again reducing CSS duplication.

- *Nesting*: By indenting a declaration inside another declaration, the nested selector inherits its ancestor selectors, saving you from needing to type them.

While the inclusion of these in CSS is still contentious, there is a CSS Variables Module Level 1 editor's draft (http://j.mp/css-variables[9]) and a growing interest in this functionality. The nice thing about the current options such as Less and Sass is they generate straight CSS, and a CSS specification syntax for these could also be pre-processed to produce fallback CSS. This means if you want to use these features now, *you can* as part of your workflow, and then use the generated CSS.

While these functions are great, it's also easy to generate a lot more CSS than you would by hand-coding, and to make overly qualified declarations (declarations with more selectors than needed). Be sure to check the quality of the CSS produced.

Turning the "OMG!" up to 11 with CSS shaders

Based on SVG filter effects, the CSS shaders proposal from Adobe (http://j.mp/css-shaders[10]) will allow these to be applied to CSS and HTML, too. These are added using a filter property, which includes the following defaults:

- blur
- drop-shadow
- hue-rotate
- saturate
- invert
- grayscale
- opacity
- gamma
- sepia

---

[9] http://dev.w3.org/csswg/css-variables
[10] https://dvcs.w3.org/hg/FXTF/raw-file/tip/custom/index.html

However, `filter` is also extensible, meaning that with a little math you'll be able to *make your own*. If you remember the first time you discovered Adobe Photoshop's Filters menu, prepare for the same giddy excitement all over again… but *in your browser* this time. If you thought the great "Wet Floor effect" pandemic of '06 was bad, you ain't seen nothin' yet!

As the true power of CSS shaders is something you need to *experience* for yourself, we'll give up trying to describe them and instead point you at "Introducing CSS shaders: Cinematic effects for the web" by Vincent Hardy (`http://j.mp/shaders-intro`[11]).

Go forth and make awesome

Our whistle-stop tour through the highlights of HTML5 and CSS3 has come to an end. We hope you've enjoyed the ride and have learned a lot along the way. While leaving you able to build your own delectable web treats has been our main goal, it's actually been *a ruse to cover our nefarious plot*. We want you to…

Figure 13-1. Get Excited and Make Things by Matt Jones[12]

take the skills you've learned, combine them with your enthusiasm, and do the best you can do to make this web—*our web*—the best it can be (see Figure 13-1). If you need some suggestions on where to direct the laser focus of your skills+enthusiasm, we encourage you to visit Move The Web Forward (`http://movethewebforward.org`), a "guide to getting involved with standards and browser

---

[11] www.adobe.com/devnet/html5/articles/css-shaders.html
[12] CC By NC SA, used with permission

development" by Mat Marquis, Aaron Forsander, Connor Montgomery, Paul Irish, Divya Manian, Nicolas Gallagher, Addy Osmani, and friends.

Now go forth and **make awesome!**

Appendix: essential links

To help you on your way, here are our essential links.

- HTML5 specifications (for more info, see `http://j.mp/html5-specs`[13])

  - HTML, The Living Standard by WHATWG: The full specification (`http://whatwg.org/C`)

  - HTML5, A technical specification for Web developers: The specification minus implementer details (`http://developers.whatwg.org`)

  - HTML, The Markup Language: A quick reference guide (`http://dev.w3.org/html5/markup`)

- HTML5 information

  - HTML5 Doctor: In-depth articles plus quick reference info (`http://html5doctor.com`)

  - Mozilla Developer Network, HTML5 and HTML5 Elements: Comprehensive wiki-based coverage (`http://j.mp/mdn-html`[14])

  - HTML5 Rocks: HTML5-related presentations, tutorials, and code (`www.html5rocks.com`)

  - HTML5 Demos and Examples: API demos by Remy Sharp (`http://html5demos.com`)

  - Planet HTML5: An HTML5 news and views aggregator (`www.w3.org/html/planet`) (also see Paul Irish's Web browser, frontend, and standards feeds to follow) (`http://j.mp/html5-feeds`[15])

- HTML5 books online

  - *HTML5 For Web Designers* by Jeremy Keith: An excellent overview (`http://html5forwebdesigners.com`)

  - *Dive Into HTML5* by Mark Pilgrim: Detailed information (`http://diveintohtml5.info`)

- Tools for using HTML5

  - HTML5 Please: Recommendations on what HTML5 features to use (and not to use) (`http://html5please.us`)

  - When can I use… for HTML5 by Alexis Deveria: Detailed browser support information (`http://j.mp/c-html5`[16])

---

[13] `http://html5doctor.com/html5-for-web-developers/#what-to-use`
[14] `https://developer.mozilla.org/en/HTML/Element`
[15] `http://paulirish.com/2011/web-browser-frontend-and-standards-feeds-to-follow`

- HTML5 Boilerplate by Paul Irish, Divya Manian, Shichuan, Mathias Bynens, Nicolas Gallagher, and friends: Knowledge bomb on HTML5 and CSS3 best practices (http://html5boilerplate.com)

    - Validator.nu by Henri Sivonen: Check your code (http://validator.nu)

- CSS3 specifications

    - A list of CSS3 specifications sorted by stability from w3.org: Use the links in the "Upcoming" column (http://j.mp/css-roadmap[17])

- CSS3 information

    - CSS Tricks by Chris Coyier: All things CSS (http://css-tricks.com)

    - Mozilla Developer Network, CSS: Comprehensive wiki-based coverage (http://j.mp/mdn-css[18])

    - *Smashing Magazine* CSS articles: A wide-ranging collection of articles (http://j.mp/smag-css[19])

    - CSS3.info: Includes occasional posts by CSS Working Group members (www.css3.info)

- Tools for using CSS3

    - HTML5 Please: Recommendations on what CSS3 features to use (and not to use) (http://html5please.us)

    - When can I use... for CSS by Alexis Doveria: Detailed browser support information (http://j.mp/c-css[20])

    - HTML5 Boilerplate by Paul Irish, Divya Manian, Shichuan, Mathias Bynens, Nicolas Gallagher and friends: Knowledge bomb on HTML5 and CSS3 best practices (http://html5boilerplate.com)

    - W3C CSS Validation Service (change the options to check CSS3, etc.): Unfortunately this doesn't fully support the latest specifications and can show a lot of false errors (http://jigsaw.w3.org/css-validator)

    - CSS Lint by Nicholas Zakas and Nicole Sullivan: While not a validator and fairly opinionated, it does help catch actual errors that may be missed in the W3's CSS Validator. Again, change the options. (http://csslint.net)

- Online code sandboxes

    - Dabblet: An interactive playground for quickly testing snippets of CSS and HTML code by Lea Verou (http://dabblet.com)

---

[16] http://caniuse.com/#cats=HTML5
[17] www.w3.org/Style/CSS/current-work#roadmap
[18] https://developer.mozilla.org/en/CSS
[19] http://coding.smashingmagazine.com/tag/CSS
[20] http://caniuse.com/#cats=CSS

- JS Bin: Collaborative JavaScript debugging by Remy Sharp (`http://jsbin.com`)
- jsFiddle: Online editor for the Web (`http://jsfiddle.net`)
- jsdo.it: Share JavaScript, HTML5, and CSS (`http://jsdo.it`)

Index

X, Y, Z

Made in the USA
San Bernardino, CA
23 June 2013